BLOOMSBURY

DICTIONARY

OF IDIOMS

SECOND EDITION

Gordon Jarvie

A & C Black • London

First published as *Idioms* in 1996
This revised paperback edition first published in Great Britain 2009

A & C Black Publishers Ltd
36 Soho Square, London W1D 3QY
www.acblack.com

A CIP record for this book is available from the British Library.

ISBN: 9–781–4081–1406–3

This book is produced using paper that is made from wood grown in managed, sustainable forests. It is natural, renewable and recyclable. The logging and manufacturing processes conform to the environmental regulations of the country of origin.

Design by Fiona Pike, Pike Design, Winchester
Typeset by Saxon Graphics, Derby

Printed in the United Kingdom by the MPG Books Group

For Frances, Sally, Andrew and the late Daisy Jarvie, for whom idioms were never quite the same again. They cheerfully got into the spirit of the project, fed it lots of useful suggestions and steadfastly refused to let it *drive them up the wall* (qv within).

The author and publishers are grateful to R R Jordan and to Modern English Publications for permission to quote the poem 'The Idiomatic English Teacher', by R R Jordan, in the Introduction to this book. It first appeared in the journal *MET*, vol 4, no 3, 1995.

Books by the same author

ON LANGUAGE
Scottish Names, 1992
Good Punctuation Guide, 1992
Bloomsbury Grammar Guide, 1993

POETRY
Ayrshire Recessional, 1998
Time's Traverse: Poems 1991–2001, 2002
Room for a Rhyme from Time to Time, 2004
Another Working Monday, 2005
The Tale of the Crail Whale, 2006
Climber's Calendar, 2007
Poems Mainly from the East Neuk, Fife, 2007
Watching the Sun, 2008
La Baudunais and Other Poems of Brittany, 2009

FOR YOUNG READERS
Edinburgh: A Capital Story (with Frances Jarvie), 1991
Scottish Castles, 1995
The Clans, 1995
Scotland's Vikings (with Frances Jarvie), 1997
Flight in Scotland (with Frances Jarvie), 2009
Robert Burns in Time and Place (with Frances Jarvie), 2009

AS EDITOR
The Wild Ride and Other Scottish Stories, 1986
The Genius and Other Irish Stories, 1988
Scottish Folk and Fairy Tales, 1992
Irish Folk and Fairy Tales, 1992
Scottish Short Stories, 1992
A Friend of Humanity: Selected Stories of George Friel, 1992
The Scottish Reciter, 1993
Great Golf Stories, 1993
A Nest of Singing Birds: Nine Fettes Poets, 1995
Writing from Scotland, 1997
Crème de la Crème (with Cameron Wyllie), 2001
100 Favourite Scottish Poems to Read Out Loud, 2007

CONTENTS

How to use this dictionary

You are urged as far as possible, when using this book, to 'think idioms'. All idioms are listed alphabetically according to their first word, so you'll find the entry for **above board** under the headword **ABOVE**, while **across the board** is under **ACROSS**. And so on. If you forget to think idioms, and decide for example to 'think nouns', you may want to look up these entries under the word **board**. You won't find them under **board** in the main dictionary.

If you fail to locate the idiom you're looking for in the main dictionary, you should consult the 'Index of Additional Keywords' at the back of the book (from page 297). If you look there at **board**, you'll find all the various idioms in the dictionary which contain the keyword 'board' listed alphabetically under that keyword. Thus, by cross-referring, the Index gives you another way in which you'll be able to locate **above board** and **across the board**, even if you start from a word within the idiom. All the key words in each idiom are listed in the Index.

The 4,500 entries in the dictionary are alphabetically arranged, but certain lexical items are discounted from the alphabetical order. All bracketed items are discounted, as are the words 'someone', 'something' and 'one' (when used as a possessive pronoun, not as a numeral). Thus, in **pull someone's leg**, the word 'someone' doesn't count for purposes of alphabetisation, so this idiom precedes **pull out all the stops** – because 'leg' precedes 'out'. Similarly, in **take something in good part** and **take it into one's head**, words like 'something' and 'one's' do not affect the alphabetical order.

Alphabetisation is also by whole word, not part word. Thus, under the headword **TAKE**, entries are listed in the following way (the bold type draws your attention to how the alphabetisation operates):

take **a** raincheck
take **a** rise out of
take **a** running jump
take **a** shine to
take **account** of
take **an** oath
take someone **as** one finds her/him
take someone **at** his/her word
take someone's **breath** away
take **by** storm
take **by** surprise

There is one other component of the book to which the reader's attention should be drawn here. This is the series of boxed articles on topics like simile, cliché, dyad, phrasal verb, etc. These are terms that feature from time to time throughout the dictionary, sometimes quite frequently. So it seemed like a good idea to explain exactly what the terms mean. The titles of these articles are listed on page xi of the Introduction, and the boxes themselves are located as near as possible to their alphabetical location in the main dictionary.

There are five components in the organisation of the main dictionary, each drawing on a specific typographical style:

1. The headword, or first word of the idiom, is in **BOLD CAPITAL LETTERS**;
2. The idiom itself comes next, in lower case, but also in **bold type**;
3. A definition or gloss of the meaning of the idiom follows in ordinary type;

4. One or sometimes two example sentences, in light type, show the context in which the expression is used; and

5. Lastly, in ordinary type, there is an etymology or anecdote about the history of the expression, if there is anything interesting to report about it.

Introduction

Idioms are everywhere in English today. You cannot utter two or three sentences without recourse to them. You cannot open a newspaper without being beaten about the head by them. One of the main problems with idioms in the modern world, apart from their ubiquity, is that they are commonly, and deliberately, mixed up if not made up. Without hunting them out, I read the following references in my daily newspaper: someone is 'seriously out to lunch' (meaning – I take it, from the article's context – mad, or extremely eccentric); a project is bedevilled by 'too many cooks and not enough Indians'; and someone 'stoops to the heights of absurdity'. The authors, or perpetrators, of these creations are professional journalists, presumably with a feeling for language. They are not splicing or garbling their idioms in the heat of animated conversation (which one hears happening often enough). One has to conclude that there is today a widespread tendency for people to take the view that an expression says what I want it to say, not what the dictionary says it says; that idioms are perhaps *old hat*, and therefore *fair game* for tweaking or bludgeoning into amusing new shapes and forms. But the three examples cited don't work very well, for my money. One wants to ask the writer, What exactly did you mean? To which s/he would probably have had to reply, I'm not sure, but it sounded witty at the time.

Of course, it is possible to play around with idioms in an amusing and effective way, just as it is with words. We all enjoy the pun and anticlimax and sheer style and acerbity of the following, which contains at least three nicely qualified idiomatic expressions (the italics are mine): 'Experts nest in TV studios, where they are treated as *big guns* (of small calibre and immense bore). They regard free speech not as a right but as a continuous obligation and, *generally speaking*, they are generally speaking. Experts bore to death millions of innocent men, women and children but TV and radio must have them and Britain is rich in experts *letting off self-esteem*.' The writer (Dorothy-Grace Elder, in *Scotland on Sunday*, October 1994) says exactly what she means. Unfortunately, this is exceptional.

Idioms may have always been around. They have not always been acceptable – far less fashionable – for writers of English. In the 18th century, writers avoided using idioms believing them to be vulgar, impure and barbarous. Dr Samuel Johnson claimed in *The Rambler* (no 208, 14 March 1752) to have 'laboured to refine our language to grammatical purity, and to clear from it colloquial barbarisms, *licentious idioms*, and irregular combinations' (my italics) – pretty strong stuff, but representative of the age. Nowadays, we do not pejoratively label idioms as being (necessarily) bad or even slang or colloquial, and we do not dismiss them in the way authoritarian teachers of formal English used to. Today, we enjoy idioms for their incisiveness, their frequent wit, their polish, their savour. But we have as much of a duty as past generations to be clear about what we mean when we use them as we are wont to, so blithely, so unthinkingly and – often – so inaccurately.

It seems to me that idioms today are fashionable, on the one hand, and therefore perhaps over-used, especially among the chattering, scribbling classes. On the other hand, it has often been their fate to be badly mangled because of the contemporary sloppy-creative approach to language. Idioms have to have generally agreed meanings if they are to work properly, and writers should try not to forget this when the creative urge is hot upon them.

What is an idiom?

The emphasis in this dictionary is on expressions whose meanings cannot be worked out from the words they contain. When we *separate the sheep from the goats*, when *we pour oil on troubled waters*, when we *come out of the closet* and *kick the bucket*, we are using indubitable idioms (and incidentally confusing many foreign learners of English). Making distinctions between good and less good students, workers, etc. has nothing to do with sheep or goats; pacifying belligerents has nothing to do with the literal pouring of oil; declaring one's homosexuality or some other secret hasn't too much to do with closets; and on the face of it, bucket-kicking seems to have very little to do with death.

One clear aim of this book therefore is to *throw some light* on some of these colourful expressions, and to *let the cat out of the bag* for those readers who may be unsure of their exact meanings.

Most idioms are metaphors. As Dr Johnson and Eric Partridge and many others have observed, just about every transferred sense is – originally – a metaphor. If you say that the price of shares *fell through the floor*, or that the inflationary pay settlement for MPs *opened the floodgates*; that better times are *on the horizon*; or that the government is *on its knees* or perhaps merely *on the slippery slope*; there is no doubt that you are using metaphors. But are you using idioms? Opinions will differ on this, as on most aspects of language, but it seems to me that idioms are not much more than metaphors which have acquired agreed meanings and are in general use.

Under the capacious umbrella of metaphor, some of the figures of speech that seem to have most productively affected our idiomatic creativity are separately glossed in boxed entries within the main dictionary. These include the following:

catch-phrase	38
cliché	43
dyad	68
euphemism	72
exclamation	74
filler	78
hyperbole	117
simile	238

There are also boxed entries for:

one-word idiom	183
phrasal verb	195
proverbs and sayings	205

All these terms are used in the main dictionary, some of them frequently. It is therefore worth defining them or at least explaining and amplifying them in this way.

Readers may occasionally read an entry and think, 'Is that a genuine idiom, or is it just a catch phrase?' I have not tried with any rigour to demarcate boundaries in this particular minefield, and readers interested in studying categories in greater depth are referred to the masterly Introduction to Betty Kirkpatrick's *Dictionary of Clichés* (1996). Other areas of idiom in which this book for reasons of space makes no attempt to be inclusive are: one-word idioms; obsolete or old-fashioned expressions; transparent idioms, i.e. those whose meanings are comparatively obvious; and phrasal verbs, which are so numerous they need a book to themselves.

Modernity

It used to be the case that successful idioms did not seem to become established and to spread through the language all that fast. It took about 20 years (1969–89) for the expression *ballpark figure* to cross the Atlantic and become acceptable currency among British speakers of English who knew nothing about baseball, and cared less. Few of us will have seen or studied the plays of Samuel Beckett, though most of us 50-something years on from the play will have an idea of what the term *Waiting for Godot* means. The computer has given us a more recent crop of terms, and although it is to be hoped that colourful items like *mouse potato* will catch on, it seems to me they are not yet general even though there are lots of us about.

This dictionary tries to include as many modern idioms as possible, but it makes no attempt to maintain a stop-press listing. There are plenty of annual publications of new words and expressions, and a high percentage of the latter turn out to be as ephemeral and briefly shining as fireflies in the night.

Etymologies

It can be interesting to learn where an idiom like *kick the bucket* or *nine days' wonder* probably came from. Often we cannot be completely sure of the etymology of idioms. They were in the spoken language long before they were written down, in most cases, unless they are based on a literary quotation. Sometimes, too, there are plausible alternative 'explanations', often no more than amusing anecdotes. But if there is something interesting to tell about the history of an idiom, especially if it helps us to a precise or a more accurate use of the expression, I have tried to list it. I believe that true idioms of the opaque, *raining-cats-and-dogs* variety are best understood and remembered through their histories. They are literally senseless otherwise: remember that idioms were once also called idiotisms!

Conclusion

I revert to my earlier assertion that today idioms are everywhere. For back-up to this statement, I offer readers the following amusing and delightful poem from the pages of *MET* (*Modern English Teacher*), a professional journal for teachers of English as a foreign language. One conclusion that I hope you will share with me from a reading of R R Jordan's poem is that native speakers of English can communicate pretty well by using nothing but idioms – in this case, 38 of them, by my calculation. But what is the poor learner of English to make of this?

The Idiomatic English Teacher
(or Keeping Body and Soul Together)

by R R Jordan

To you who…
Often do not turn a hair
When replying off the top of your head,
Which should be screwed on the right way.

Often you are up to your eyes in work,
And need eyes in the back of your head.
You also need to keep your nose clean,
As well as keeping it to the grindstone.

Your ears are often burning,
Having kept one of them to the ground.
You often play it by ear,
And have to turn the other cheek.
(That was said with tongue in cheek!)

You often live from hand to mouth,
And need to keep your chin up.
Sometimes you have to stick your neck out,
And may even become a pain in the neck!
You should not get a chip on your shoulder,
But must keep abreast of the times.

Usually your heart is in the right place,
And you have no stomach for infighting.
Sometimes you have to chance your arm –
More power to your elbow!

Frequently you have your hands full,
And may become all fingers and thumbs,
But somehow you keep your finger on the pulse.
At bottom you are dedicated,
And are often on your last legs.
Revive! Students think you are the bee's knees!

Fortunately, you have your feet firmly on the ground.
Occasionally you must dig your heels in,
And even put your foot down.
A pity you sometimes put your foot in it!

At times you have to toe the line,
Even though you may tread on someone's toes.
All in all, you are a teacher, from top to toe.

I hope readers will accept the bouquet of idioms culled in the pages of this book in the seriously light-hearted spirit in which they are offered. Some of them – the more recent ones – are freshly picked and still smelling quite sweet. Some – perhaps especially some of those that are foreign to us personally – may smell a little exotic, and need to be tried out for size. The vast majority however are probably old friends, and sadly, like old friends, they are too often taken for granted. But we should not use them unthinkingly, and we should remember that they can be bludgeoned to death. Our language articulations may improve from a renewed awareness of their precise communicative functions.

Acknowledgements

The author wishes here to record his sincere thanks to Vivienne McDonald, without whose invaluable electronic assistance he would never have nailed this project down. The book's long-term debt is to the inspirational Tom McArthur, author of the *Dictionary of English Phrasal Verbs and their Idioms* (1974) and countless language texts.

Some further reading

There are occasional references to some of the following authors or titles in this dictionary, all of which I have found useful and enjoyable.

American Heritage Dictionary, 1969
Ayto, John: *Euphemisms*, 1993

Blevins, Winfred: *Dictionary of the American West*, 1993. Good on 'cowboy' language and expressions of Spanish origin.

Brewer's Dictionary of Phrase and Fable, 15th edition, 1996

Bryson, Bill: *Mother Tongue*, 1990

Bryson, Bill: *Made in America*, 1994. Interesting on American origins.

Burchfield, R W: *Fowler's Modern English Usage*, 3rd edition, 1996

Cowie, A P, and R Mackin: *Oxford Dictionary of Current Idiomatic English*.

    1975, vol 1, *Verbs with Prepositions and Particles*

    1983, vol 2 (with I R McCaig), *English Idioms*

Fowler, H W: *Dictionary of Modern English Usage*, 1926

Gowers, Sir Ernest: *The Complete Plain Words*, 1954

Grant, W and Murison, D D: *The Scottish National Dictionary*, vols 1–10, 1931–76

Grose, Francis: *A Classical Dictionary of the Vulgar Tongue*, 1963

Holy Bible, King James version, 1611. The wording of this edition has had the biggest impact on our language and usage.

Howard, Philip: *The State of the Language*, 1984

McArthur, Tom (ed): *Oxford Companion to the English Language*, 1992

Kirkpatrick, Betty: *Dictionary of Clichés*, 1996

Partridge, Eric: *Dictionary of Clichés*, 5th edition, 1978

Partridge, Eric: *Dictionary of Catch Phrases*, 2nd edition, 1985

Rees, Nigel: *Phrases and Sayings*, 1995

Shorter Oxford English Dictionary, 1944

Thorne, Tony: *Dictionary of Contemporary Slang*, 1990

Waterhouse, Keith: *Waterhouse on Newspaper Style*, 1989

Webster's Ninth New Collegiate Dictionary, 1990

Wood, Frederick T: *Current English Usage*, 1981

A

A. A1 in good order; of high quality. He had no difficulty selling his vintage car, since everything about it was A1. A1 is the highest grading category used by Lloyds Register to describe the condition of a ship and its cargo for insurance purposes.

ABC the elementary or first elements; the simplest knowledge. He's bought himself a sort of ABC of how to build your own house. The first three letters of the alphabet were once used as the generic name for a spelling book for infants, or school primer.

A–OK fine; good; in perfect working order. Everything was A–OK last night when we inspected the premises. An abbreviation meaning 'all (systems) OK', popularised by US astronauts in the 1960s. Compare **all systems go**.

(from) A to Z thoroughly, including anything one might need to know. Everything from A to Z is spelt out for you in the instructions.

ABOVE. above board open; straight; legitimate; without concealment. No tricks, please, I want everything open and above board. Originally from gambling: dishonest card-players, by putting their hands below the board, or table, could take the opportunity to cheat their opponents by changing cards, etc. Compare **on the up and up**.

above someone's head too hard for someone to fully understand. I think they were talking about buying and selling shares, but it was all a bit above my head.

above oneself conceited. He seems to have got a bit above himself since he went to work in London.

ACCORDING. according to Cocker/Hoyle/Gunter according to the accepted arbiter on a subject; in the prescribed or fair way. Let's stop mucking about and do the job properly, according to Hoyle. Edward Cocker's *Arithmetick* (1664) was for many years the bestseller of its day, going into more than a hundred editions, and much referred to for rulings on subjects under dispute; Edmund Hoyle (1671–1769) was an authority on card games; Edmund Gunter (1581–1626) was another famous English mathematician who devised navigational aids and a modern method of land surveying. The expression 'according to Cocker' in its present sense was introduced by an otherwise forgotten contemporary Irish playwright called Arthur Murphy. 'According to Gunter' is mainly used in America.

ACE. ace in the hole hidden advantage. The general warned his enemies not to tempt him to use his ace in the hole, or they'd get a nasty surprise. An Americanism popularised by the title of a Cole Porter song (1941), the reference is from the game of stud poker. The 'hole' card is one that is not shown. This is worth a lot if it is an ace. The British equivalent is 'ace up one's sleeve', the reference being to a cardplayer who has concealed an ace card in his clothing.

ACHILLES'. Achilles' heel vulnerable spot; weak point in something that is otherwise strong. A successful career politician cannot afford to have an Achilles' heel. From the Greek myth of Achilles, whose mother took him as a baby and dipped him in the River Styx to render him invulnerable. As a warrior, his one vulnerable spot was the heel by which his mother had held him; eventually Paris, Prince of Troy, fired an arrow at this spot and killed him. Compare **feet of clay**.

ACID. acid test method of proving the worth, truth, etc. of something. Joining the Eurocurrency is seen by many as the acid test of the European Union. From chemistry. The original acid test was the testing of gold with nitric acid. If it was genuine and pure, it was unaffected; if false or mixed with other metals, these would corrode.

acid trip period spent under the influence of 'acid', or the drug LSD, which sometimes causes hallucinations. He tried to speak to her, but she was acting as if she was miles away; clearly she was on another of her rather sad acid trips. The so-called drug culture spawned many 'acid' compounds, including 'acid house' (electronic dance music), 'acid flash' (recurrence of the effects of LSD), 'acid freak' (user of LSD), 'acid rock' (electric guitar music of the 1960s and 70s), etc.

ACROSS. across the board applicable without exception and in all cases. The union negotiated an across-the-board reduction in working hours for its members. Originally an American expression from betting: an across-the-board bet backed the same horse to win, or to be placed second, third or fourth.

ACT. act one's age try to behave in an adult way. He can be extremely childish sometimes, and I wish he'd act his age. Often applied to young people. Also used in conjunction with **grow up**.

act of God catastrophe; unforeseen action of a natural force (such as an earthquake, hurricane, lightning strike, etc.) in causing an accident. I'm sorry, but your policy does not insure you against acts of God. A legal term, mainly used to describe events against which one cannot claim insurance compensation.

act the (giddy) goat behave in a deliberately foolish manner. He can't seem to behave seriously, but always has to be acting the goat. Compare **play the fool**.

ACTION. action stations a state of readiness for some action is achieved. Right, let's go! Let the cameras roll – action stations! Originally a naval command clearing a ship for battle action: each member of the crew was to go to his battle station and await further orders. Compare **panic stations**.

AD. ad hoc makeshift; unplanned. The group have formed themselves into an ad hoc committee to look at problems as and when they arise. The Latin means 'for this', in other words for the specific purpose mentioned and not having any wider application. Compare **play something by ear**.

ADAM'S. Adam's ale water. If he's all that thirsty, let him take a glass of Adam's ale from the tap. Old fashioned. Sometimes and more crudely, 'Adam's piss'.

Adam's apple lump visible in the front of a person's neck, formed by the thyroid cartilage. The victim's neck was swollen and there was considerable bruising around the Adam's apple. Originally believed to have been formed by a piece of the apple from the tree of knowledge that stuck in Adam's throat when he tasted the forbidden fruit, in the biblical story of the Creation.

ADD. add fuel to the flames/fire make a bad situation worse. It was a minor squabble till Lizzie added fuel to the flames by accusing us all of disloyalty to her. Also 'fan the flames'.

add insult to injury upset or insult someone twice over, thereby compounding the original remark or action. First of all he 'borrowed' my car without permission, then he added insult to injury by crashing it. This expression has Latin origins. Compare **to cap it all**.

AFTER. after a fashion not very well; not entirely true, accurate, etc. He speaks English after a fashion, but he's not easy to understand.

AGAINST. against the clock with limited time in which to achieve/complete something. The doctors fought against the clock to save the boy. Also 'against time' (same meaning).

against the grain against one's inclinations, instincts, etc. It is still very much against the grain for some people to work on a Sunday. From carpentry, and working against the grain of the wood.

AGONY. agony aunt female confidant. Tell Mrs Stein if you've got any work-related problems – she's the agony aunt in this office. The original agony aunts wrote 'agony columns' in women's magazines answering readers' letters about their problems or worries, mainly of a romantic nature.

AHEAD. ahead of the game in a situation where one is ahead of industrial or technological developments, schedules, etc. Agencies work extremely hard to keep ahead of the game in advertising, because it's such a competitive industry.

AIRS. airs and graces socially pretentious mannerisms. He may have all the airs and graces, but he's got very few basic manners. An invariably derogatory dyad, the implication is of affectation in a person who lacks sincerity.

AIRY. airy fairy impractical. He's full of airy-fairy schemes for saving humanity. A reduplication, the opposite of **down to earth**.

ALIVE. alive and kicking very lively and alert. She hadn't seen her friend for years, and was delighted to see him alive and kicking at a concert last weekend. A common dyad. Various origins are proposed for this expression, including a description of fresh fish flopping on the fishmonger's slab, or the late stage of a woman's pregnancy when she is able to feel her baby's kicking movements.

ALL. all and sundry people in general; everybody, without discrimination. Nobody calls her Mrs Mackintosh; she is known to all and sundry as Jessie. A dyad. The opposite of **those and such as those**.

all chiefs and no Indians all bosses and no workers. It's one of those inefficient organisations that's all chiefs and no Indians. Originally American, from cowboy and Indian movie culture. Also 'too many chiefs and not enough Indians'.

all ears agog to hear something. You only have to mention food to a teenage boy and he's all ears.

all hands on deck everyone lend a hand and get down to work. We couldn't get the barbecue fire to go sooner because of the rain, so the meal is late – but it's all hands on deck now, and we'll soon be ready to give you some dinner. A nautical

exhortation, now usually found in the context of a domestic emergency.

all hell's let loose pandemonium, confusion, uproar ensues. Don't let that dog into the house or anywhere near my cats – or all hell will be let loose. Also 'all hell breaks loose/out'.

all in 1. exhausted. After a day's Christmas shopping, she was all in and had to go to bed for a rest. 2. with all costs included. Is that price all in, or are there extras? Short for 'all inclusive'.

all in a day's work all part of one's normal routine or job or range of experience. Yesterday they rescued six drowning men from a capsized fishing boat, but that's all in a day's work for the lifeboatmen.

all in all everything considered. He may not be brilliant, but all in all I think he did quite well in his exams.

all my eye (and Betty Martin) all nonsense; utter rubbish. He spun her some sob-story about being a homeless orphan, which was all my eye – I know his parents very well. The exclamation 'My eye!' was once synonymous with the more current 'My foot!' There are several variations of the longer version, none of which are now commonly heard. Partridge (in *Catch Phrases*) hypothesises that Betty Martin was a larger-than-life London 'character' of the 1770s who may have been given to exclaiming 'My eye!' That is roughly when the longer expression was first recorded.

all out with all one's effort; singlemindedly. This term he has to go all out for a place in the team.

all over bar the shouting almost finished, and with the outcome entirely predictable. We didn't watch the end of the competition – having heard Katy's wonderful performance, we knew it was all over bar the shouting. The 'shouting' is the applause, etc. at the end of a game or other performance.

all over someone behaving in an overaffectionate or sycophantic fashion towards someone. He was all over Angela when he discovered her brother was a film director who could get him a job.

all singing, all dancing the latest or smartest or 'mostest' version of something. He's just spent a small fortune installing the most amazing, state-of-the-art, all-singing, all-dancing desktop computer system. Originally a metaphor from the world of entertainment.

all square 1. even; with all obligations cleared. I've just returned his loan of £100, so now we're all square. 2. **having equal scores.** The score was all square at the final whistle with one goal each. The expression is from the early 19th century, and was applied to golf and other sports by the 1880s.

all systems go everything is in a state of readiness. Tonight is the final dress rehearsal for the concert, and we're nowhere near all systems go. Nowadays often humorous, the late 1960s origins of the expression are in the US space exploration programme and referred to the state of readiness on the launchpad prior to the countdown for a rocket's takeoff. Compare **A–OK**.

all that jazz/crap etc. all that sort of thing. He told me to work hard and play hard and all that jazz. Americanisms, similar to **and so on/forth**.

all the rage highly fashionable. She was wearing one of those ghastly ra-ra skirts that were all the rage in the 1980s.

all the world and his wife everybody. It was a huge party, and all the world and his wife were there. Similar to **all and sundry**, although sometimes there is an implication of 'everybody who is anybody', i.e. anybody of importance.

all there sane. Some of the things she says are so stupid you wonder if she's all there.

all things to all men 1. description, often critical, of an ingratiating person who tries to please everybody. One has to question the sincerity of people who are all things to all men. May be influenced by the old proverbs, 'All men cannot do all things' and 'All things fit not all men.' 2. indispensable person. The army made genuine efforts to appeal to both sides of the divided community, trying its hardest to be all things to all men and defuse potentially explosive issues in an even-handed way. From the New Testament book of 1 Corinthians ix. 22: 'To the weak became I as weak, that I might gain the weak; I am made all things to all men, that I might by all means save some.' Thus the original sense of this expression was probably less cynical than the more current sense 1.

all one's worldly goods one's property and movable belongings. In 1939 many Jews escaped from Germany with nothing, leaving all their worldly goods behind. From the marriage service in the Book of Common Prayer and other services: 'With all my worldly goods I thee endow.' Compare **goods and chattels**.

all up with someone no hope is left for someone. It must be all up now with finding any survivors – they couldn't have survived long in this cold.

ALMIGHTY. almighty dollar wealth and its power. It's frightening to see what people are prepared to do in the name of the almighty dollar. Washington Irving used the expression in 'The Creole Village' (1836): 'The almighty dollar, that great object of universal devotion.'

ALONG. along/on the right lines in the correct way and in a generally appropriate direction. The project appeared to be developing more or less along the right lines. Also 'on the right tracks'.

ALPHA. alpha and omega the first and the last, beginning and end. The battle against inflation is the alpha and omega of the government's economic policy. Alpha and omega are the first and last letters of the Greek alphabet. Used in the King James Bible, in Revelation i.8 and 11: 'I am Alpha and Omega, the beginning and the ending, saith the Lord' and 'I am Alpha and

Omega, the first and the last.'

ALSO. also-ran not very successful person. We didn't bother interviewing John for the post, considering him a bit of an also-ran. Usually derogatory. A racing term to describe a horse which finishes the race without being placed.

ANCHOR. anchor-man/woman key person in an enterprise, on whom its success mainly depends. Like all the very popular TV chat programmes, the show depended very heavily on its anchor-woman. From tug-of-war competitions: the anchor-man was traditionally the biggest, heaviest and most powerful member of the team, and was expected to hold his ground.

AND. and a half very big, special, important, etc. Those were onions and a half – I've never seen such huge ones!; He must be a lawyer and a half if he got you off all the charges. Usually an expression of admiration.

and how conversational gambit signalling emphatic agreement. 'He's quite an important man in the city, they say.' 'And how – he's the governor of the Bank of England!' Compare **you can say that again**.

and I don't think ironic conversation marker, which often indicates an opposite viewpoint to that spoken. He's a very generous fellow, and I don't think – he wouldn't lend you a half-smoked cigarette! Also 'And I must say!' (similar sense). 'And the band played (on)!' also has a similar drift. The implication here is of a listener doubting the claims of a speaker and interrupting him with this put-down comment. 'I've got plans to make my first million before I'm 30.' 'Oh yes, and the band played.' Compare **pigs might fly; pull the other one; Queen Anne's dead**.

and so on/forth and other things of that sort; etc. He goes to lots of social events like parties and gallery openings and so forth. Used as a shorthand way of skipping long lists of details. Similar to **all that jazz**.

and then some and more as well. Shakespeare is generally agreed to be the greatest English dramatist, and then some. An informal way of emphasising the drift of what one is saying.

ANGEL. angel of mercy person who brings help, food, etc. at an appropriate moment, i.e. when it is particularly needed. Fortunately an angel of mercy appeared on the scene in the unlikely shape of Mrs Brown, and she was able to drag the drowning child from the river. A hyperbolic cliché.

ANY. any day under any circumstances. I'd prefer a Mercedes to a Mini any day!

any old how carelessly; untidily. He takes very little care about his appearance, and tends to dress any old how.

any number a large number. There were any number of applications for the job.

any port in a storm any respite, hospitality, etc. available. He seems to have gone for lunch with Mrs Appleton which sounds like a serious case of any port in a storm, i.e. he must have been desperate for food or company. A proverbial observation, from sailing.

ANYTHING. anything but the reverse of; not at all. I'm afraid he's anything but well just now; in fact, he's just had a heart attack. A litotes.

APOLOGY. apology for something a very poor specimen of something. I want to complain to the head waiter about the apology for a meal to which we have been subjected.

APPLE. apple of discord something which gives a pretext for strife or dissension. The media has to be the villain of the piece, busy dropping apples of discord here there and everywhere – and all for a good story. Now rather old fashioned and literary. In Greek myth, Eris – personification of discord – tossed a golden apple into the assembly of gods, and it was fought over by Venus, Minerva and Juno.

apple of one's eye person on whom one dotes;

person of whom one is extremely fond; favourite. *She has five children, but John is the apple of her eye.* Literally, as precious and cherished to the speaker as his eyes are. Long ago, the apple of the eye was another name for the pupil, when it was believed to be a solid entity. The idiom had acquired its present meaning by 1600, and the King James Bible uses the expression several times, as in the description of the Lord keeping Jacob 'as the apple of his eye', in Deuteronomy xxxii.10; and 'Keep my commandments, and live; and my law as the apple of thine eye', in Proverbs vii.2. Scholars have pointed out that 'apple' may be a misnomer or mistranslation of the original Hebrew word, and that we probably ought to be talking about the apricot or the quince of one's eye! Compare **(be someone's) pride and joy**.

apple-pie order all neat and tidy. *I expect this house to be in apple-pie order when I get home – just as I left it.* Various plausible, mainly French, explanations of the origins of 'apple-pie' are proposed including Sir Walter Scott's *nappe pliée* (= neatly folded table linen), and *cap à pied* (= head to foot). The expression also occurs in **apple-pie bed**, which is based on a childish joke, in which the bed only appears to be neat and tidy; when the victim of the joke tries to get into the bed, he finds that it is made up with a single sheet folded in such a way as to deliberately prevent entry. Compare **spick and span**.

ARGUE. argue the toss dispute a decision. *He's a very difficult client, always arguing the toss.* From tossing a coin and shouting 'Heads!' or 'Tails!' as an agreed means to settle a dispute. The loser by this process then unsportingly declines to abide by the decision.

ARMED. armed to the teeth fully equipped (with weapons, arguments, etc.). *The defendant was ready for all their questions, and armed to the teeth with proof of his innocence.* From medieval idioms in which teeth and nails were weapons

of defence, such as **fight tooth and nail**, etc.

ARSE. arse about face back to front; in a disorderly way. *Never trust John to do a practical job; he does everything arse about face and you end up with a worse mess than you started with.* With the same gist, but by humorous or mock-erudite analogy with 'vice versa', one also hears the reduplicative and punning 'arsy-versy'.

arse-licker sycophant; flatterer. *It would make you sick to watch all those corporate arse-lickers toadying to the managing director as if their lives depended on it.*

ART. art and part implicated in something both by art (or contrivance) and part (or active participation). *The police know perfectly well that he's involved art and part in many of the recent break-ins.* A dyad from Scots law, perhaps derived from Latin *tam arte quam parte*. Compare **part and parcel**.

ARTY. arty farty culturally pretentious. *He didn't much care for Stephanie, describing her as a typical arty-farty type.* A reduplication.

AS. as...as A standard simile pattern. See under the appropriate adjective, and also the Simile article on page 238.

as a last resort in the end; having no other option. *As a last resort, he had to smash the window before he could get into the house.* Literally, as a final expedient. From French *en dernier ressort*.

as a rule normally; usually. *As a rule, I eat my meal of the day in the evening.*

as broad as it's long the same, whatever way you look at it. *To go to Madrid for the weekend, or stay at home and splash out on dinner and two tickets for the opera – they couldn't decide which to do, and certainly Jane thought the choice was just about as broad as it was long.* Compare **six of one and half a dozen of the other**.

as good as almost. *The man as good as backed*

his car straight over that poor dog – he certainly knocked it down.

as regards (something) as far as (something) is concerned. Let's forget Item 1 for a minute; but as regards Item 2, I need your honest opinion right away.

as the crow flies in a straight line; without making any detours. It's only two miles to Onich as the crow flies, but it's all of 12 miles if the bridge is closed and you have to drive round the top of Loch Leven. Used as a measure of distance when not following the meanderings of roads, railways, etc. Compare **bee line**.

as we speak right now. They're working on your car as we speak and it'll be ready for you at 2pm.

as yet so far; at the present time. There is no word as yet about how successful the operation was.

as you were conversational way of saying, 'Sorry, my mistake.' Let's meet at noon at King's Cross, as you were, at St Pancras Station. Originally a military way of correcting oneself. Sounds pompous nowadays.

ASKING. asking for it/trouble behave in a way that is almost bound to provoke trouble. To insult a thug like that is just asking for it.

AT. at a loose end with nothing special to do. John offered to take the dog for a walk because he was at a bit of a loose end and needed the exercise, he said. From the days of sailing ships: when sailors hadn't much else to do, the captain of the ship often ordered them to make a thorough check for loose riggings, and bind these up to prevent them further unravelling.

at a loss not sure what to do or say. The police are at a loss to know how to stop these random attacks.

at a low ebb depressed; unsuccessful. He was at a very low ebb for several months after Rose's death. A tidal metaphor.

at a pinch if strictly necessary. You could always see if you could borrow £10 from next door at a pinch, and promise to pay them back tomorrow.

at a premium very valuable, because hard to get. Tickets for the men's and women's finals at Wimbledon are always at a premium. A financial term which means sold at or worth more than something's nominal value, the opposite of 'at a discount'.

at a price at a high price. You'll get a room at the Hilton – at a price. An understatement, or ironic phrase.

at a rate of knots at great speed. Did I see you running up the High Street at a rate of knots this morning? 'Knots' are a nautical measure of speed, so the expression only becomes idiomatic when applied to overland movement, as in the example sentence.

at a stretch 1. with difficulty. We can get one more person into the car at a stretch, but no more than that. 2. continuously; without interruption. He thinks nothing of sleeping for 12 hours at a stretch.

at any rate at least; that is to say. He looks quite well – a bit better than last time at any rate. A conversational marker.

at bay at a distance. There was a serious flu epidemic, but luckily I was able to keep it at bay. From stag-hunting. Also 'at arm's length'.

at daggers drawn mutually hostile; at the point of quarrelling seriously. You can't invite both of them to supper together – they've been at daggers drawn for years. From the days when daggers resolved many arguments and ~~temper~~ tantrums. The medieval version was ~~drawing'.

at death's door at the point (~ It is always distressing to see ~ door. From the Book of C~ 107.18: 'Their soul abh~ and they were even ~

at one's fingertips within one's capabilities. He's supposed to have about five languages at his fingertips.

at first glance/sight on an initial, perhaps cursory inspection; one's first impression. It looks like a chaotic mess at first sight, but they tell me it's a work of artistic genius.

at heart basically; according to one's deepest feelings or beliefs. A lot of people find him gruff and grumpy, but at heart he's a very good and generous man.

at it cheating; stealing. It's about time he got the sack – he's been at it for years. Colloquial; compare **on the fiddle**.

at large 1. at liberty. A tiger escaped from the zoo last week, and it's still at large. 2. including a variety of topics, people, etc. in general. He'll happily waffle on at large about the problems of the planet. The world at large knows all about her medical problems.

at loggerheads in serious dispute; at odds; with serious differences of opinion. The two governments were at loggerheads over deep-sea fishing rights in that part of the ocean. A loggerhead was once another name for a blockhead, or 'thick' person. The original image was therefore of two such wooden-tops in direct confrontation, and failing to knock much sense into one another, as invariably happens.

at odds in dispute. The pair of them were at odds over where to go for their holiday.

at pains taking great care. He seemed at such pains to say how happy he was that I began to suspect he wasn't enjoying himself at all. Also 'take pains'.

at sea at a loss; perplexed and uncertain what to do. When it came to teaching grammar, most teachers were completely at sea, and didn't know where to start. Also 'all at sea'.

and sevens in disarray; in a state of confusion or neglect; higgledy piggledy. We're all at sixes and sevens just now, because of the various sales conferences and planning meetings we're having. The term comes from playing with dice, and originally signified carelessness in the hazarding of one's whole fortune – and the ensuing disarray.

at the cutting/leading edge at the forefront. You could hardly say that his poetry is at the cutting edge of modern literature. A vogue expression of the 1990s, originally from technology, once much overused. Opposite of **behind the times**. Compare **in advance**; **lose one's (competitive) edge**; **sharp end of something**.

at/on the double very fast. She phoned 999 and asked for an ambulance, and it was there at the double. From the army parade-ground command for double-quick marching. Americans prefer 'on the double'.

at the drop of a hat at the slightest signal; immediately. You only had to raise an eyebrow, and at the drop of a hat a waiter was beside you ready to take your order. With a nod in the direction of new technology, the idiom 'at the touch of a button' has a similar meaning.

at/near the end of one's tether at/near the limit of one's patience, mental resources, etc. He had a lot of debts, and he once told me he was near the end of his financial tether. From the farmer's practice of tethering a beast, the metaphor catches the frustration of an animal which may wish to graze further afield.

at the end of the day in the final analysis. Peace cannot be imposed: at the end of the day, it is the community which must choose it and defend it.

at this point in time now. The prime minister said there would be no further statements at this point in time. A circumlocution.

at this/that rate if this/that is the case. He claims to know nothing about the problem, but at that rate why did he phone the police?

at one's wits' end completely bereft of the ability to make decisions. It's a serious problem, and she's at her wits' end to know how she can resolve it. The gist of this expression suggests increasing desperation.

AUGUR. augur well/badly is a good/bad omen, prognostication, etc. The by-election result augurs badly for the government. Augury was the Roman practice of divination, and the augurs were religious officials who interpreted the omens for the future.

AULD. auld lang syne old bygone days (of 'long since'). Before he left the house, his hosts drank a toast with him to auld lang syne. A Scots idiom quoted in a traditional song adapted by the poet Robert Burns (1788), and now a popular anthem across the English-speaking world.

AUNT. Aunt Sally scapegoat; target for ridicule, blame, criticism, etc. The boss treated him very unfairly as a sort of convenient Aunt Sally, realising that he could thus divert attention from his own rather painful shortcomings. From the popular name of a fairground dummy, a target at which people bowled or pitched missiles.

AVOID. avoid something/someone like the plague deliberately distance oneself from something/someone, usually because one dislikes it/them. He claims not to like garlic in his food, and normally he avoids it like the plague.

AXE. axe to grind private or ulterior motive to further, often a selfish one. He's not a very impartial chairman of the committee, having too many axes of his own to grind. American in origin, Benjamin Franklin uses the expression in the late 18th century in a story describing how a clever man had asked him to demonstrate how his grindstone worked, and then produced an axe which needed sharpening.

AYE. aye right! a laconic way of expressing disbelief, originally Scottish. He told us the forecast for the whole of April was for unseasonably warm and dry weather, and I thought 'Aye right!' A foreshortened version of 'aye, that'll be right!', which may be compared with **that'll be the day!** or the more colourful **tell that to the marines**. Like American 'yeah right!', this is an idiom of the 21st century.

B

BACK. back a winner/loser undertake a successful/unsuccessful enterprise, assignment, etc. It is more than a product developer's job is worth to back too many losers. From betting, and backing horses to win a race.

back in harness back at work after illness, holiday, etc. He's a complete workaholic, and after a fortnight's holiday he can't wait to get back in harness. The metaphoric reference being to men and women as workhorses. Also equestrian in origin, with a similar meaning: 'back in the saddle'.

back number person who has ceased to be influential, up-to-date in outlook, etc. After he lost his position on the main board of the company, he became a bit of a back number in the business. Literally, an issue of a magazine, newspaper, etc. earlier than the current one.

back of beyond some far-distant and inaccessible place. It is well known that for Londoners anywhere north of Barnet is the back of beyond. Originally Scottish, there is perhaps an echo here from George MacDonald's classic Victorian fairy story called *At the Back of the North Wind* (1871). Compare **off the beaten track**.

back off invitation or challenge to someone to get out of one's private space. Sorry, but if you don't back off right now I may have to thump you. A phrasal verb from animal behaviour: compare **show one's teeth**.

back the wrong horse support the losing cause, wrong person, etc. He declined to give me his vote, saying that he wouldn't back the wrong horse twice. From betting.

back to square one return to where one started from. Jenny spent weeks building the most wonderful Lego house, but this morning her little brother knocked it down, so she's had to go back to square one and start all over again. In the days of radio, football commentators divided the football pitch into numbered squares, for the benefit of listeners, and the *Radio Times* in the 1930s regularly printed a map showing their position on the pitch. Earlier board games, such as Snakes and Ladders, also used numbered squares, and these are probably the origin of this expression.

back to the drawing board back to the planning stage. The client rejected all the architect's original proposals, so he had to take the project back to the drawing board several times. Literally, to the design stage which is usually sketched out on a drawing board, and where many projects thus start life. The origins of this idiom go back to a cartoon caption showing a bemused pioneer aircraft designer whose prototype aircraft has just crashed.

back(s) to the wall 1. situation from which it is hopeless to think of escaping. With her back to the wall she was a desperate woman, and she fought her assailant accordingly. 2. **making a spirited defence in a generally difficult situation.** There was not much point in the employees organising a backs-to-the-wall standoff with the liquidators of their erstwhile employer. Often used adjectivally. The most popular quotation to make use of this idiom is probably Earl Haig's order made 12 April 1918 to the troops on the Western Front – to stand firm and resist Germany's last great offensive of the war. 'With our backs to the wall, and believing in the justice of our cause, each one of us must fight on to the end.' Compare **up against it** and **drive something/someone to the wall**.

BACKHANDED. backhanded compliment ambiguous statement – one that can be taken as a compliment, but which might also be construed as an insult. She told me I was looking much better than I usually did, which was a bit of a backhanded compliment. Also **left-handed compliment**.

BACKROOM. backroom boys scientific

researchers whose work is frequently crucial to an organisation's viability, but who are not generally known to the public. The police have very little in the way of hard evidence, but the backroom boys and girls from forensic are sifting through everything very thoroughly, and it's amazing what they can come up with. Invariably plural, the term was coined in the Second World War after a speech by Lord Beaverbrook, referring to people whose war work was secret: 'Now who is responsible for this work of development on which so much depends? To whom must the praise be given? To the boys in the back rooms. They do not sit in the limelight. But they are the men who do the work.' *The Listener,* 27 March, 1941. Another nickname for these people is 'boffins'.

BACK-SEAT. back-seat driver 1. literally, passenger in car who keeps telling the driver what to do. My aunt Bessie used to be a dreadful back-seat driver. **2. idiomatically, anyone who interferes in another's business.** Please stop telling me what to do: I'll let you know if I need a back-seat driver.

BACKWARD. backward at coming forward shy; modest. He's one of those people who like to hear the sound of their own voice, and he's not normally backward at coming forward. Often used with a negative.

BAD. bad blood ill feeling, resentment. Ever since the massacre of Glencoe in 1692 there's been bad blood between the MacDonalds and the Campbells.

bad egg scoundrel; rogue. Her eldest son seems to have been a bit of a bad egg, and ended up in jail for assault. The expression now sounds old fashioned, and tends to betray the slightly Victorian resonance of its origins; it is of course balanced by its opposite – 'good egg'. An alternative with the same meaning is 'bad hat'. Compare **black sheep (of the family)**.

bad hair day a day when things don't work out

well, when one has lots of set-backs, accidents, etc. To put it mildly, he had a bad hair day at the office yesterday.

bad language swearing or blasphemy. He was always careful in his speech, and I never heard him use bad language.

bad lot dishonest and untrustworthy person. The membership refused unanimously to allow a bad lot like Jimmy Dobson to join their club. Someone who is not a complete reprobate may be described as 'a bit of a bad lot'.

bad news unpopular or unwelcome person. People like John and Betty are bad news, so we didn't invite them to the party. An Americanism of the 1960s.

BAG. bag and baggage (with) all one's belongings. His landlady has had enough of his antisocial behaviour, and she has finally thrown him out bag and baggage. Originally military (meaning civilian bags and military baggage), now a common dyad. Compare **goods and chattels**.

bag of bones thin and emaciated person. She was never plump, but she's been a bag of bones since her last illness. An alliterative word-picture. Also 'bundle of bones' (same meaning).

bag of nerves very jumpy and nervous person. He's been a bag of nerves since the crash, and he completely refuses even to go near a car.

bag of tricks gear, equipment, etc. needed to perform a particular job. The electrician has a wonderful bag of tricks, with all sorts of tools of his trade in it.

BAKER'S. baker's dozen 13. It was a very large nest, with a clutch of about a baker's dozen of eggs in it. In medieval England the baker was an unpopular figure, selling at high prices and trying to cheat customers by giving short weight. Strict penalties were introduced in 13th-century legislation, and in order to avoid these (and to make themselves more popular) bakers started to introduce an extra loaf, called a 'vantage loaf', with every 12-loaf order. A 'devil's dozen' is also 13, and was a reference to the number of witches who were said to congregate at a summons from the devil.

BALANCING. balancing act attempt to please two (or more) parties in a dispute, etc. simultaneously. The United Nations had to perform a difficult balancing act in the Bosnian situation during the 1990s.

BALD. bald as a coot completely bald. He came back from the barber's with all his hair cut off, and looking (as) bald as a coot. The standard simile. The coot is a black-feathered pond bird of the rail family with a white patch of hard skin on the forehead; this gives it its impression of slightly comic baldness.

BALL. the ball is in your/her, etc, court the initiative for taking action lies with you/her, etc. Everybody has told him what he ought to do; but the ball's firmly in his court and no one can do the job for him. From tennis.

ball of fire keen and energetic person. He turned out to be a real ball of fire, and he soon got the firm going again. Sometimes called a 'whizz kid'.

BALLOON. the balloon's gone up the alarm's gone off; the excitement has begun. The balloon went up as soon as the press got wind of the scandal of MPs taking bribes for asking questions in the House of Commons. From the activities of barrage balloons during the First World War. Their function was to protect the targets of enemy air raids, and it was a sign of impending action when people saw them 'go up'. Now a journalistic cliché, frequently followed by 'all hell's let loose'.

ballpark figure more or less accurate costing; approximate or estimated price. He's got to come up with some ballpark figures for the sales conference. An Americanism from the baseball field, where 'in the ball park' means within certain limits. The expression is now an overflogged cliché favoured by sections of the business community on both sides of the Atlantic, and in this context definitely sounds best when uttered with a nasal delivery. Compare **different ball park/ball game**.

BANANA. banana republic third-world country, usually located in the tropics, usually with an economy dependent on the export of one cash crop, usually ruled by a military junta. It's all very well to write these places off as a scatter of diminutive banana republics… The expression is a derogatory attempt at journalistic stereotyping, with the adjective 'tinpot' often thrown in for good measure. As Gustave Flaubert would have said in his *Dictionary of Received Ideas*: 'Tonner contre' (or thunder against), nowadays perhaps with the enthusiastic support of Little Englander stereotypes such as 'Colonel Apoplexy of Eastbourne'.

banana skin trap for the unwary to slip on and cause them embarrassment or humiliation, etc. The interviewer was extremely wily, and gave the foreign secretary several banana skins at least two of which the latter contrived to slip on. Cartoonists tend to draw in a real banana skin.

BANDY. bandy something about spread unfounded rumours. He's been bandying stories about that his main competitor's business is close to collapse. 'Bandy' was originally a game like hockey in which players 'bandied' a puck to and fro.

bandy words with someone argue; discuss. I can't be bothered bandying words with someone whose opinions I despise. The impression is of fencing, even of hair splitting, rather than serious debate.

BANG. bang goes something jocular expression indicating that one has parted unwillingly with something, frequently a sum of money, thus hinting at possible meanness. We went to a show last night – it was pretty poor, but anyway, bang went 30 quid. From a bursting balloon. The expression 'bang went saxpence' was popularised by Sir Harry Lauder, that stereotype stage Scotsman of Edwardian Britain. The term was soon broadened to indicate the likely loss or failure of anything. The President's Middle Eastern policy was perceived as being very hard on the Israelis, so bang went his Jewish vote in the elections.

bang one's head against a brick wall try to achieve something without success. I tried to get some compensation from the bank for their incompetence, but that was like banging my head against a brick wall. 'Bang' is usually found with -ing ending in this expression, and in the form of a simile. Compare **waste one's breath**.

bang in the middle of exactly or right in the middle of. He lives bang in the middle of Paris. An adverbial intensifier, used to emphasise something; thus also 'bang on target', 'bang up-to-date'.

(caught) bang to rights red-handed, or in an indefensible position; rightfully. He had no choice but to admit his guilt, having been caught more or less bang to rights. Now old-fashioned, this was a popular Cockney expression up till the 1930s. The American version is 'dead to rights'.

BANK. bank on something/someone rely or count on something/someone. I know she is banking on my visit, so I mustn't let her down. I'm afraid you mustn't bank on her support. Meaning, 'her support is not so definite or guaranteed that you could exchange it for cash in the bank.'

BAPTISM. baptism of fire unpleasant introduction to something, but one which may subsequently provide valuable experience; harsh initiation. He had a real baptism of fire as a public speaker last night: he had to make an impromptu and off-the-cuff speech at the dinner when the guest speaker failed to arrive. Originally theological: in the early church, 'baptism of blood' meant martyrdom, and this term was adapted in 16th-century Europe when so many

religious martyrs were burnt at the stake for their beliefs.

BARE. bare bones basic or essential facts. I haven't time to listen to all the details – just give me the bare bones of the problem. Literally, the skeleton. The metaphor is often amplified with an invitation to 'flesh out' the details at a later time.

BARK. one's bark is worse than one's bite one sounds a lot more dangerous, etc. than one actually is. He's always shouting at his staff, but they assure me that he's a good boss and his bark is much worse than his bite. From dog behaviour.

bark up the wrong tree pursue a false track; focus one's efforts in the wrong direction; have a mistaken notion about something. It was a very difficult case, and not helped by the fact that for fully six months the police were barking up the wrong tree. Usually found with -ing, i.e. in the present or past continuous. Originally an American frontier term referring to raccoon hunting, and used by Davy Crockett in his memoirs, *Sketches and Eccentricities*, 1833. Raccoon hunting took place at night, and hunted raccoons tended to climb into trees. The coon dogs hunting them often got the wrong tree. Compare **jump to conclusions, up a gum tree**.

BASKET. basket case mad person. He's a complete basket case, and particularly dangerous behind the wheel of a car. Also 'head case', 'nut case', 'fruit and nut case'.

BAT. (not) bat an eyelid (not) show emotion. When the judge pronounced the prisoner guilty of murder, the man just stood there without batting an eyelid. Almost invariably negative. The idea is of betraying signs of emotion by blinking, etc. 'Bat' was originally 'bate', meaning 'flutter'.

BATED. (with) bated breath agog with excitement, worry, etc. to the point that one's breath has stopped (abated). He stood there behind the curtain with bated breath, too frightened to move an inch.

BATS. (have) bats in the belfry or **be bats/ batty** be crazy, or at least not quite sane. Miss Jarvie was our art teacher – she was great fun because she had a few harmless bats in the belfry. That was rather a batty idea! Also **batty brilliant** exceedingly clever. This is my cousin John; he's the batty brilliant member of the family. A popular facetious expression, indicating a widespread awareness that genius and madness are often not far apart. Similar to 'absent-minded professor'.

BATTEN. batten down the hatches make oneself as secure as possible, frequently in a financial context. The businesses which survived the recession best were those which had managed to batten down the hatches at the first signs of the economic downturn. A metaphor of nautical origin; ships secured all hatches and coverings when a storm threatened.

BATTLE. battle axe harridan; fierce or belligerent female. When you first meet the ward sister, you think she's a dreadful old battle axe, and it's not till you know her better that you realise what a kindly person she really is.

battle royal hard-fought contest, often a free-for-all. The last election was a battle royal and resulted in a hung parliament. The original expression was used in cockfighting in the 17th century; it described a bout where several birds fought it out until there was only one survivor.

BE. be a devil usually a humorous exhortation to someone to act boldly and forget about the consequences. I know your mother doesn't let you go in pubs, but come on – be a devil and come with me for a beer.

be-all and end-all thing of overriding importance; objective to which everything is subordinate. Remember that money is not the be-all and end-all, even if it's nice to have a little. Frequently used in the negative. Shakespeare's Macbeth (1606) uses the expression when he kills Duncan: '…if the assassination…might be the be-all and the end-all here.' Act i.7.

be an angel please help me. Would you be an angel and drive old Mr Ogilvie home? A clichéd hyperbole.

be in good hands be well looked after. She lives in a residential care home, where she knows she is in good hands.

be in the same boat be in identical circumstances. When he lost his job, he quipped that it was nice to know he was in the same boat as about three million other people in Britain.

be that as it may nevertheless. It's been a very interesting day – but be that as it may, it's also been a long one and I now have to go home. A conversational marker phrase, indicating a desire to change the subject or bring the conversation to a close without either agreeing or disagreeing with what has just been said.

BEAN. bean counter person who counts money and does nothing much else; bureaucrat. Is it wise to have the Education Service and the National Health Service in this country run entirely by bean counters? Usually a term of disparagement, similar to 'pen pushers', although the former tends to imply people with no vision while the latter merely suggests people in menial positions.

bean feast party; binge. Our neighbours are most hospitable, and every so often they throw a party for half the street – and a real bean feast it usually is too! Originally an annual dinner given by employers to their workforce in the early 19th century, at which beans were often a prominent feature of the menu.

BEAR. bear fruit produce good results. Their careful investments over the years are now beginning to bear fruit. Biblical and literary in origin.

bear garden rowdy place. This classroom is an utter bear garden, and I don't want to hear another word from anybody. From the Elizabethan pleasure gardens at Vauxhall and elsewhere, which had caged bears to draw and entertain the populace. If one 'talked bear garden' in the 17th century, one was using bad language.

bear in mind remember. Bear in mind that there are no second chances in the university of life.

bear something out confirm, corroborate. The collapse of the business amply bears out your earlier suspicions.

bear the brunt of something take the main force, often of a criticism or unpleasant event. When the postal workers went on strike, they forgot they'd have to bear the brunt of public anger when they finally went back to work. 'Brunt' is probably an echoic word from Scots 'dunt' (= a blow).

bear with a sore head bad-tempered or viciously angry person. She daren't tell her boss, because he's been like a bear with a sore head all day. A standard simile, from animal behaviour. Compare **get up on the wrong side of the bed**.

bear with someone be patient with someone. I can explain everything if you'll just bear with me for five minutes.

bear witness/testimony/record confirm. He worked very hard for the exams, as you can bear witness. Rather formal sounding, originally from legal English.

BEARD. beard the lion in his den confront the issue, protagonist, etc. He knows he has to see the headmaster at four o'clock, but he's not looking forward to bearding the lion in his den. The allusion is biblical, to Daniel in the lion's den.

BEAT. beat a (hasty) retreat run away; abandon something (speedily). The milkman beat a hasty retreat as soon as he heard the dog's furious barking from the back of the house. Originally military: drummers once beat retreat on the battlefield to signal an organised withdrawal, as they also still do at night in more ceremonial fashion for soldiers in barracks.

beat about the bush avoid getting to the point of a conversation; try to express oneself over-cautiously or in roundabout ways. Why don't you spit it out and say exactly what you want – you won't get anywhere if you keep beating about the bush. From hunting, where beating about the bush was a preliminary to making the kill. Compare **hum and haw; come/get to the point; short and sweet; straight from the shoulder**.

beat someone at his own game do something better than an acknowledged expert does it. If we want justice, we've got to try to beat the bureaucrats at their own game.

beat someone at the post defeat someone narrowly, and/or at the very last moment. It was a surprise result, and Mr Brown was beaten at the post – by a single vote. A metaphor from horse racing, and almost winning a race at the finishing post. If the defeat was a particularly narrow one, you might also say the horse (or the vanquished person) was 'beaten by a short head'. Compare **narrow squeak; pipped at the post**.

beat hollow utterly and thoroughly defeat. We had hoped to win the game, but I'm afraid we were beaten hollow. From a now-obsolete colloquial meaning of 'hollow' (meaning 'wholly') in the 18th century. See also **win hands down**.

beat/hop it! go away! They told me to beat it for 10 minutes – I guess they must have something private to discuss.

beat someone to it do something before someone else gets a chance to do it. Scott wanted to be the first person to reach the South Pole, and it must have been a very big disappointment to him when he learnt that Amundsen had beaten him to it. Also with this meaning 'beat someone to the draw': originally an Americanism, popular in cowboy culture. Compare **steal someone's thunder**.

BEAUTY. beauty sleep sleep that restores one to one's best condition, appearance, etc. I think it's bedtime for those of us who need our beauty sleep.

beauty spot 1. mark of beauty on a woman's face. In the past, women sometimes painted a beauty spot on their face. 2. **place of great beauty.** They took me to Friar's Crag, a local beauty spot with fine views of lake and mountain.

BED. bed of roses easy option. It can't be much of a bed of roses being head teacher in such a tough school. A rather clichéd metaphor, usually deployed in the negative.

BEDROOM. bedroom eyes romantic look. She was making very obvious bedroom eyes at her new friend, so I decided to leave them alone. A euphemism, the implication is of a look inviting sexual relations. Also referred to as a 'come-on' or a 'come-hither expression'. Also 'come-to-bed eyes/heels/shoes'.

BEE. bee in one's bonnet obsession. Whatever you do, don't mention horoscopes – she's got a bee in her bonnet about the signs of the zodiac. A metaphor comparing the incessant cerebral buzzing of a personal obsession with that of an alarming or too-close-for-comfort bee in one's headgear. Often used to imply that someone is being a crank about something. Compare **have a thing about**.

bee line shortest and fastest route between two places. As soon as he gets in from school, he makes a bee line for the fridge. Compare the more languorous **as the crow flies**.

bee's knees someone/something very special and superior; the very best around. A witty reduplication, originally American, dating from the 1920s. Being the only girl in a family with six boys, her father has always regarded her as the bee's knees, if not the cat's whiskers. Compare **cat's pyjamas/whiskers** and also **top drawer**. Other supposedly humorous combinations devised to indicate the same idea of superiority include 'the cat's adenoids', 'the clam's garter' and 'the flea's eyebrows'.

BEEN. been and gone and done it something clumsy, foolish, dangerous, etc. has been done. 'Now you've been and gone and done it!' I said when I heard the sound of breaking glass from the neighbours' garden. Usually humorous, to indicate a blunder on someone's part. Compare **that's torn it**.

been there, done that(, bought the T-shirt) an irritating, ungracious contemporary refrain of the world-weary and blasé achiever. Asked if they'd like to visit the Tower of London, one of them shook his head and muttered, 'Been there, done that.' Along the same lines as the tourist boast, 'If this is Paris, it must be Tuesday' (or vice versa).

BEER. (all) beer and skittles fun and amusement. If he thinks life here's all beer and skittles, he's got another think coming to him. A dyad of pubs and fairgrounds, frequently deployed in a negative form.

BEFORE. before one can say Jack Robinson as quickly as can be; straight away. The service in that restaurant is excellent: you make your order, and before you can say Jack Robinson your meal is served. In use throughout the 18th century, the original identity of this eponym is lost in the mists of time, although there is speculation that Sir John Robinson, Guardian of the Tower of London between 1660–79 might have been the reference. The king's man at the Restoration of the monarchy, he was no slouch at beheading former enemies of the crown.

before one is/has finished eventually; sooner or later. They've been told not to play near the cliffs or someone's going to have an accident before they're finished. Often used as a form of warning to children.

before one knows where one is too quickly; very soon. It was a wonderful holiday, but before we knew where we were it was time to go back to work again.

BEG. beg the question fail to properly address the issue under discussion. Asked about the government's view on a single European currency, the prime minister contrived to talk for 10 minutes and still beg the question however one examined his response. From Latin *petitio principii*, the name for this reprehensible tactic in the medieval logic of Duns Scotus.

beg to differ politely register one's formal disagreement. Your party may wish to abolish the monarchy, but mine begs to differ. A frozen expression from politer times.

BEGGAR. beggar description be beyond the powers of description. You should have seen the mess – it beggared description. Shakespeare used the expression to describe by how far Cleopatra's beauty 'outdid nature': 'For her own person, it beggared all description.' *Antony and Cleopatra*, ii.2.

BEGGARS. beggars can't be choosers people who receive charitable gifts are not in a position to be too fussy about what they are offered. I know his car is just an old banger, but it was generous of him to lend it to me while mine was being repaired, and – as you know – beggars can't be choosers, can they? A proverbial observation.

BEHIND. behind someone's back without someone's agreement or permission; surreptitiously, and often treacherously. Her parents were shocked to learn that their daughter had been smoking behind their backs for years.

behind the scenes privately; outside the glare of publicity. The French government seems very effective behind the scenes at getting its nationals released by terrorists. The original, 18th-century reference was to the stage.

behind the times not up-to-date or modern. Forgive me if you find my outlook a bit behind the times. The opposite of being **at the cutting edge**.

BELIEVE. believe it or not whether you believe it, or whether you don't. I've got some good news for you – believe it or not, you've won the lottery!

BELL. (by) bell, book and candle (by) all that is holy. He swore by bell, book and candle never to rest until he had captured the murderer. These three items are used in the celebration of the Roman Catholic mass, and a form of medieval excommunication was to curse a person 'by bell, by book and by candle'. According to the symbolism of the ceremony, the bell was rung, the book closed and the candle quenched; this consigned the cursed person to spiritual darkness by depriving him/her of the church's holy sacraments.

bell the cat undertake a dangerous assignment. Everyone wanted Bloggs expelled from the club, but no one would agree to bell the cat and expose his dishonesty to the police. An old idiom from the fable of the mice and the cat. The mice realised that if they could hang a bell around the cat's neck, they would forever after be warned of his approach. The expression was in use in 15th-century Scotland, and was used in the notorious assassination of Robert Cochrane, favourite of King James III in 1482. Threatened and outraged by this relationship, the Scottish nobility wanted rid of Cochrane, and one of them is said to have asked, 'Who will bell the cat?' Archibald Douglas, Earl of Angus, volunteered to strike the blow, and was thereafter known in Scottish history as Archibald Bell-the-Cat.

BELOW. below par not up to standard. He went home at lunchtime, because he was feeling a bit below par this morning. From golf: see also **on a par with; par for the course**. 2. not up to the face value. These shares aren't worth holding on to; they've performed consistently below par for almost two years. With specific reference to the stock market.

below the belt unfair; not within the rules of engagement. My colleague's reference to my marital problems was a bit below the belt, since that had nothing to do with the matter under discussion. From boxing, where the Queensberry Rules forbid a punch below the level of the belt.

BEND. bend someone's ear talk continually to someone about something, sometimes to the point of irritation; nag someone. His mother's been bending his ear yet again about finding himself a job.

bend over backwards do all in one's power (usually to achieve something or accommodate someone). We bent over backwards to make them feel at home, but they showed no hint of appreciation.

bend the elbow be fond of drinking alcohol. For the last six months he's been tending to bend the elbow a little too enthusiastically. A coy euphemism.

bend the rules almost cheat; interpret the rules to suit one's purposes. I don't know how little Tommy got a place at that school: they probably had to bend the rules a bit.

BESIDE. beside oneself in a state of emotional hypertension, fury, distress, etc. He was beside himself with grief at the news of the accident.

beside the point not relevant. She stole the car; whether or not it's a good car is completely beside the point. Compare **wide of the mark**.

BEST. best bib and tucker best clothes. He looked as if he was going to a funeral or an interview – all dressed up in his best bib and tucker, and looking smarter than I've seen him for years. A dyad which may originally have referred to items worn by ladies to protect their best clothes from spills, rather than to the outfits themselves. Now slightly old fashioned. Compare **Sunday best**.

best man bridegroom's main supporter or attendant at his wedding. The best man made a very witty speech and flirted with all the bridesmaids. Originally Scottish, this term replaced the older 'groomsman' in the early 19th century.

best of both worlds two sets of advantages not normally available to the same person. They have a town house for the working year and a country cottage for the holidays, which is really getting the best of both worlds.

best/greatest thing since sliced bread the most wonderful innovation to occur for some time. All the youngsters seem to think the new album is the best thing since sliced bread. An emphatic way of emphasising how good you think something is. The hugely successful commercial marketing of sliced bread in America was the great bakery innovation of the 1920s, and spawned this US advertising slogan of the 1940s and 50s.

BET. bet one's bottom/last dollar wager everything. I have a funny feeling there's going to be an election, though I wouldn't bet my bottom dollar on it. Often an expression of the speaker's certainty about something. Also 'bet one's shirt' (same meaning).

BÊTE. bête noire pet hate; bugbear. One of his bêtes noires used to be a certain sports commentator, and he would switch off the TV whenever her face darkened his screen. The French expression (literally, 'black beast') means the same as the English.

BETTER. better/other half one's wife. We've been invited to a concert on Friday, but I'm afraid we can't go, as my better half has another engagement. Sir Philip Sidney and the 17th-century English Metaphysical poets were fond of the conceit that two true lovers became as one being, with the spouse often referred to as the better half. Nowadays mainly used humorously. More polite than the disparaging 'her upstairs/indoors' or 'she who must be obeyed'.

better the devil one knows (than the devil one doesn't) expression meaning that people prefer to deal with people known to them (rather than with strangers). None of them was very fond of the boss, but they supported him as the devil they knew against all these unknown incomers. The complete sentence is an old proverb.

BETWEEN. between shows temporarily

unemployed. He's been at home for a few months, probably between shows and applying for lots of jobs. Like its famous cousin 'resting', this is a euphemism from the acting profession which is now more generally used. Compare **garden leave**.

between/betwixt the devil and the deep blue sea in difficulty, and without a satisfactory alternative. He'll be shot if he goes back to Africa, and if he stays here he'll be jailed as an illegal immigrant; so you could say he's between the devil and the deep blue sea. Also conveying a similar sense of unresolvable dilemma: 'between a rock and a hard place' or 'between the hammer and the anvil'. Compare **horns of a dilemma** and see also **devil to pay**.

between you and me (and the bedpost/ gatepost) in confidence. The prizewinner will not be announced till after Christmas, but between you and me and the bedpost I don't think you'll be disappointed in the result. The longer version is an elaboration, to emphasise the aspect of confidentiality.

BEYOND. beyond a joke not funny. Sometimes he can be magnificent, but last night's performance was beyond a joke – it was dire. Compare **no laughing matter**.

beyond a shadow of doubt without any doubt; indubitably. His innocence is now proved beyond a shadow of doubt. Sometimes also heard: 'beyond a peradventure', which is so old fashioned as to occasionally sound humorous.

beyond the pale uncivilised; beyond the bounds of decency; unacceptable to polite or civilised people. The behaviour of some of these football hooligans nowadays is quite beyond the pale. In the 15th and 16th centuries, the English Pale was the nickname of two areas enclosed within a fence or paling. These were two early efforts at colonisation by England, and were the immediate hinterland of the towns of Calais in France (1494) and – especially – Dublin in Ireland (from 1547). Viewed from Dublin Castle,

the rest of Ireland was literally 'beyond the Pale'. And because it was not governed by the English crown, it was controlled by 'the king's Irish enemies' perceived by the English garrison as being barbaric, lawless and dangerous. The typical colonising mindset thus has a long pedigree, although the idiomatic use of the expression in its current sense only dates from about 1800.

BIBLE. bible thumper aggressively religious or evangelical person. Ironically, it is the bible thumpers who tend to put people off the Christian religion.

BIG. big brother (is watching you) the authorities (have you under surveillance, or are spying on you). I don't think big brother would approve of that sort of thing. A slogan from the novel *Nineteen Eighty-Four* (1954), by George Orwell, based on the state propaganda put out by various British ministries during the two 20th-century world wars (such as 'Your country needs you').

big cheese important person. Who's the big cheese in this office? American 1920s. Also with this meaning, by analogy: 'big (white) chief', from the Indian title; and the more ironic and deflationary 1970s 'big enchilada', which is a Mexican pancake. See also **big noise, big shot, big wig**.

big deal matter of importance. So he's won the class prize again, but it's no big deal. Originally American, mainly used in the negative. Sometimes still used as an ironic exclamation. Big deal! She's asked me to stay with her in the holidays and cook her meals.

big fish in a small pond person who is important or influential only within the confines of a small community. He seemed a bit pompous to my London friends, as big fish from small ponds sometimes do. She's head of a two-teacher school in the Hebrides, and I think she quite enjoys being a big fish in a small pond. Opposite of the less common **little fish in a big pond**.

big head conceited person. He became an intolerable big head after getting into Parliament.

big idea/picture vision. The party seems to have lots of grotty little policies but absolutely no big idea. Don't give me the details – just the big picture. A vogue term in the unvisionary 1990s. Compare **joined-up thinking**.

big noise boss, important person. Some big noise from Brussels was visiting the office yesterday. See also **big cheese**.

(be) big of someone (be) generous of someone. I must say it was very big of him to lend me his French road atlas – he's obviously forgotten that I gave it to him as a gift! Frequently ironical.

big shot famous person. I forget his name – he's just another small-town big shot. Usually facetious. Similar to **fat cat**. See also **big cheese**.

big time success and fame. He writes articles for the local press, but one day he says he's going to make the big time. Originally an American reference to the bright lights of movie stardom. Sometimes 'big league' (same meaning), from baseball. Compare **small time**, its opposite.

big top circus; big tent. The elephants were quite accustomed to performing in/under the big top.

big wig important person. Some big wig from the gas board wrote me a letter of apology. From the 17th and 18th century, when all gentlemen wore a wig. The biggest wigs were worn by the most important members of society, such as the judges, bishops and nobility. The American **big noise** has the same meaning. See also **big cheese**.

BIRD. bird in the hand something in one's possession, often modest but better than nothing. It may not be the best of jobs, but it's a bird in the hand and I'm not giving it up till I can find a much better one. From the proverb, 'A bird in the hand is worth two in the bush.'

BIRD'S. bird's-eye view aerial view, or panoramic view from a good vantage point. He took the funicular to the top of the mountain and got an amazing bird's-eye view of the entire city. Literally, the view that a bird would get.

BIRDS. birds and bees knowledge about sexual reproduction in humans. Fourth-year girls are to get a talk about the birds and the bees from Mrs Jones. A common euphemism, like the **facts of life**, devised to divert reference to the mechanics of sex from the human to certain non-human species, which many people find less embarrassing to discuss.

birds of a feather people with similar tastes and interests. They're all birds of a feather, and they tend to congregate at John's house on a Friday night. From the saying, 'Birds of a feather flock together.' Compare **of that ilk; of the same kidney; of the same stripe; two of a kind**.

BIRTHDAY. birthday suit stark naked. He was standing there in his birthday suit looking rather silly. An 18th-century euphemism which is thought to derive ingeniously from the folktale of the emperor's new clothes. All the courtiers were commanded by the intellectually challenged emperor to admire his wonderful new birthday suit and – fearing for their necks more than for his excellency's sanity – they dutifully did so, even though his excellency was actually standing there naked. The best-known version of this story is probably that of Hans Christian Andersen (1835).

BIT. bit by bit gradually; by stages. In the pitch dark, he could only feel his way bit by bit along the passageway.

bit of all-right understatement for a very good-looking person. Isn't he a bit of all-right? A general statement of approval. Compare **get a load of that/this**. Expressions of this sort are disparaged by people who try to be politically correct.

bit of fluff frivolous female, or one so regarded. Who was the blonde bit of fluff I saw you with last night then? Exclusively and still widely used by male speakers, this sexist expression is not politically correct. Similar is the unisex **bit of all-right**.

bit of rough aggressive and sometimes physically brutal lover. She had one of those slightly pathetic stage roles of the not-so-demure but sexually frustrated madam looking for a bit of rough. This term, like the expression 'rough trade', is often found in a homosexual context.

bit thick hard to accept or tolerate. John does no training and yet he expects to be selected to play for the team – that's just a bit thick, it seems to me.

BITE. bite/snap someone's head off speak sharply and angrily to someone, often for no good reason. I only asked a civil question, so there's no need to bite my head off.

bite off more than one can chew try to do something that is too difficult/expensive, etc. for one, or that one cannot manage or complete in the limited time available. She has decided not to try and bite off more than she can chew, so she'll not try to move house for another year or so. Said to have originated in 19th-century America, from the practice of chewing tobacco.

bite the bullet confront a difficult issue courageously; face up to something difficult or unpleasant. It took me a long time to bite the bullet and accept that I would have to give up my job. Wounded soldiers on the battlefield in the days before chloroform and later painkillers were given a bullet to bite to prevent them crying out in agony as they submitted to the surgeon's knife. Compare **grasp the nettle**.

bite the dust die; disintegrate. Her old television bit the dust this morning, so she had to go and buy a new one. The expression goes back to Latin, and originally meant 'to die in battle'; it became popular in the days of the action-packed cowboy-and-Indian silent movies, with their racially stereotyped and politically incorrect captions like 'Another treacherous Indian bites the dust'.

bite the hand that feeds one be ungrateful enough to act/speak cruelly or in hostile manner towards one's benefactor. He failed to realise that only a fool will bite the hand that feeds him. From animal behaviour.

bite/hold one's tongue refrain from saying something one wants to say, because the moment is inappropriate. She has a very quick temper and doesn't always manage to bite her tongue in an argument.

BITS. bits and bobs/pieces 1. miscellaneous, mainly small objects. There were bits and pieces of wreckage all over the field, which we put in black bin bags. 2. belongings; possessions. He's left a few of his bits and bobs in the garage. A common dyad. Compare **odds and bobs/sods**.

BITTER. (to) the bitter end (to) the last. He disliked school, and even at the bitter end he'd think up all sorts of excuses to be absent. Perhaps influenced by the Bible: 'But her end is bitter as wormwood, sharp as a two-edged sword.' Proverbs v.4.

bitter pill hard thing to accept. The loss of his job was a very bitter pill to swallow.

BLACK. black affronted deeply and utterly ashamed and embarrassed. His behaviour was appalling, and his family were black affronted with him. A Scots idiom, 'black' here functioning as an intensifier.

black and blue bruised and discoloured. There was a huge black and blue mark on his chin, but he insisted that nobody had hit him.

(in) black and white 1. (in) simple terms. He's one of those simple souls who like to see everything set out in black and white for him. An idiom which means less and less in times of affluence and huge non-print based visual sophistication. 2. (in) terms of wrong and right. It was a difficult situation, and there was no point reducing it to black and white issues – there was far too much grey in the overall picture.

black as one is painted bad as people say one is. Like many war criminals, he wasn't quite as black as he was painted by the propaganda machine of the victors.

black ball veto. The majority of the club's membership black balled his application to join them. The black ball was originally a club's method of controlling its membership by secret ballot. By extension, it came to mean ostracising someone from social participation in something.

black dog fit of depression. She suffered for weeks on end with fits of the black dog, during which she saw no one. The expression is old, but was used most notably by Winston Churchill to describe the lower reaches of his own mood swings. The dog in question was another name for the devil. Also found as a black poodle in Goethe's *Faust*.

black economy that informal – and illegal – part of a country's economy where money is earned but where no taxes are paid. There is a thriving black economy of market traders in the back streets of most big cities. A euphemism. The notion of 'black' being illegal comes probably by extension from **black market**.

black hole place into which things/people seem to disappear. I don't know how she can find anything in such a black hole of an office, and I wouldn't dare give her one of my manuscripts. In science, this is an astronomical term for the field of a former star which has collapsed.

blacklist ostracise; list of people/organisations, etc. which have in some way contravened a code, etc. Firms which took government contracts were often blacklisted during the Troubles. Various historical figures including Queen Elizabeth I and King Charles II are supposed to have kept black lists of their enemies – to be appropriately punished as opportunities presented themselves; nowadays we might talk of a **hit list** rather than a black list. The term may be used as a verb or a noun; it is sometimes written as

two separate words, more commonly as a single word, and is sometimes hyphenated. Compare **in the black books**.

black maria police or prison van. The trial lasted three months, and every night the accused returned from the high court to her prison cell in a large black maria. Originally American, the eponym is said to derive from Maria Lee, a large and very strong black woman who in the 1840s owned a sailors' lodging house in Boston, Massachusetts, adjacent to the police station. She often assisted the police in the apprehension of criminals, and sometimes when the officers needed help they sent out the SOS, 'Send for Black Maria.'

black market system of trading that omits to keep business accounts in accordance with the laws governing a country's trade. He was arrested in Frankfurt for trying to sell guns on the black market. Compare **black economy**.

black sheep (of the family) reprobate; person who does not conform; worthless member (of the family). My Uncle Tom was the black sheep of our family. The black sheep in a flock used to be unpopular with shepherds, because their wool could not be dyed as effectively as white wool. Perhaps there is also a faint echo of the old proverb, 'A black sheep is a biting beast.' Compare **bad egg**.

black spot place that is notorious for something. Drive carefully – accident black spot.

BLACKBOARD. blackboard jungle the urban school system, particularly those parts of it where pupils are violent or uncontrollable. He taught for 20 years and then suddenly decided he'd seen enough of the blackboard jungle. From the title of an American novel by Evan Hunter (1954) and a successful film (1955) about the discipline problems in US high schools. The drift of the metaphor was that the law of the jungle applied in this, as in various other aspects of urban life. Hence also 'asphalt jungle' or **concrete jungle**.

BLANK. blank cheque complete authority or unrestricted freedom of action. He was given a blank cheque as far as the redesigning of the garden was concerned. Literally, a signed cheque which does not specify the amount of money to be paid: the sum is to be filled out by the recipient. Thus the expression originally meant permission to spend an unlimited sum of money. Compare **free hand/rein**.

BLAZE. blaze a trail pursue a line of research that points the way to great discoveries. These inventions in microelectronics have blazed a trail to today's computer highway. Compare **leading edge**.

BLEED. bleed someone dry/white seriously weaken someone by using up all their financial resources. Taxation is still very high in this country, and some people claim that it is bleeding us dry.

BLESSING. blessing in disguise misfortune which turns out to have advantages; good outcome from evil situation, etc. The war in that country may have been a blessing in disguise, because now they are getting a lot of foreign aid to rebuild their shattered society. Compare **every cloud has a silver lining**.

BLIGHTY. (dear old) Blighty England. He enjoyed the job in Saudi Arabia, but it was always nice to get back to Blighty for a bit of home leave. Army slang from the First World War, this is an adaptation of the Hindi word *bilayati* (= foreign), in turn taken from Arabic *welayet* (= district) and Turkish *vilayet* (= name given in the 19th century to a province of the Turkish Empire ruled by a *vali*). In the 1930s and 40s, it was an affectionately nostalgic term for 'home' among English colonial officials of the former British Empire. The expression has resurfaced sporadically among British military personnel involved in overseas duties.

BLIND. blind as a bat very blind. Take away his spectacles and he's (as) blind as a bat. From a standard simile.

blind drunk totally and uncontrollably drunk. He used to come home blind drunk and knock the place about, so his landlady chucked him out. 'Blind' here is an intensifier, although it also nicely conveys the idea of the drunk knocking into things like a blind person. Drunkenness has of course spawned a whole gamut of idiomatic expressions: see also **feel no pain; halfseas over; high as a kite; in one's cups; pickled/ pissed as a newt; stewed to the gills; tired and emotional; under the influence**.

blind impulse sudden and unaccountable desire to do something. Acting on what appeared to be a blind impulse, he bought an airline ticket to Mexico.

blind leading the blind expression which means that a person who is advising others knows as little as they do. I agreed to help her with her maths homework, although I told her it would be a case of the blind leading the blind. An expression often used to describe weak or ineffectual leadership. In the Bible, Jesus said this to his disciples about the Pharisees: 'Let them alone: they be blind leaders of the blind. And if the blind lead the blind, both shall fall into the ditch.' Matthew xv.14.

blind spot any subject/person that one cannot objectively or rationally discuss, etc. Like most people, he has a blind spot about his family – they can do no wrong! In ophthalmology, the reference is to the sole location on the retina of the eye from which visual cells are absent. Compare **pet aversion/hate**.

blind someone with science use technical or scientific arguments to confuse one's listener. I told her to stop blinding me with science from the further reaches of her macroeconomic theories. Also 'talk gobbledy-gook'. Compare **(play) the numbers game**.

BLOT. blot one's copybook damage one's good reputation. He failed to recognise his boss yesterday – that's the sort of thing that really blots your copybook in this office. **In the days when people took pride in their fine handwriting,** one's copybook was where one kept examples of all one's best work, and it was always kept scrupulously free of ink blots. Compare **take a leaf out of someone's book**.

blot on the landscape something that spoils the view or outlook. It was a lovely summer, and the only blot on the landscape was the prospect of his impending operation.

blot on one's escutcheon something that discredits one. Bankruptcy used to be something of a blot on a person's escutcheon, but not nowadays apparently. From heraldry, where an escutcheon is a family's shield and, more symbolically, its honour. Now rather a formal usage, as in: 'Dirt is only matter out of place; and what is a blot on the escutcheon of the Common Law may be a jewel in the crown of the Social Republic.' John Chipman Gray, in *Restraints on the Alienation of Property*, 1895.

BLOW. blow a fuse/gasket become very angry. He blew a gasket when he saw the mess. From electrical engineering and motor mechanics.

blow by blow very detailed, especially if the details are gory. Tell me the gist of what happened, but do please spare me the blow-by-blow account.

blow hot and cold be undecided about something, sometimes appearing in favour of it, at other times hostile to it; fluctuate between moods of enthusiasm and apathy. We invited her for Christmas lunch, but she blew hot and cold about it for so long that we gave up trying to persuade her. Recorded in Plautus; also in the Aesop Fable of the malcontent who blew on his hands to keep them warm, and then blew on the soup he was given in order to cool it. The soup's donor exclaimed that he wanted no more to do with a man who blew hot and cold from the same mouth. Compare **shilly-shally**.

blow it spoil one's chance of something; handle

a situation poorly. He had the chance of an excellent job, but he blew it by that last remark.

blow one's mind daze one; overwhelm one with awe, admiration, etc. The performance was wonderful – it just blew my mind. **Originally this term was used by the drug culture of the 1960s.** The wider thrust of the expression today is that one is transported into a euphoric state by someone, or by some event or happening, not necessarily drug-related.

blow one's own trumpet brag; boast about one's achievements or skills. I'm not one to blow my own trumpet, but I negotiate most of the important jobs in this office. **If one 'trumpets' something, one is stating it publicly and noisily because one wants other people to know about it, admire one for it, etc.**

blow the gaff/gab reveal a secret or a plot, sometimes unintentionally; blab. There's no point in pretending you're innocent – half your mates have blown the gaff on you and told us you were present on the raid. The 'gab' or 'gaff' was verbal gabble, or news. Compare **give the game away; let the cat out of the bag; shoot one's mouth off**.

blow the whistle on something call a halt to something by exposing it, in the same way as a football referee does when he sees foul play. The press has blown the whistle on that little racket, and quite right too. **From the 1930s.**

BLUE. blue blooded royal; genuine. He's a real blue-blooded member of the Swedish royal family. From the Spanish *sangre azul* (= azure blood) which implied purity from Moorish or Jewish racial admixture, probably because of the blue-looking veins of fair-skinned native Castilian people.

blue-chip financially secure; sound and profitable. Although not really a gambler on the stock market, he has always had a few blue-chip investments. **In the 19th century, chips were another name for wooden counters in games of chance; blue chips had the highest value, hence**

they became a slang name for sovereign coins.

blue-eyed boy favourite. He gets to go to all the horrible places for the firm, but not to New York – that trip is kept for the blue-eyed boy. There are overtones of nepotism in this expression. Blue eyes and fair hair were of course the hallmark of the stereotypical Anglo-Saxon hero, just as black hair and a moustache tended to trick out the typecast villain of the piece. Compare **bee's knees**.

blue fit attack of mental distress or shock. She had a blue fit when she saw the state of her precious grand piano.

blue funk panic. The news of his arrest put him into a complete blue funk. From the long-gone connection between the colour blue with omens of death, ghosts, or the devil. Compare **scream/ yell blue murder**.

blue ribbon/riband top prize; badge of the highest honour. His last novel won him the Man Booker Prize, which is regarded as the blue ribbon by most people in the publishing industry. From the blue ribbon of the Most Noble Order of the Garter (founded 1348), the highest accolade of British chivalry in the gift of the sovereign. The French equivalent expression is *cordon bleu* (now applied in English only to cooking of the highest standard). There are various extensions of the English idiom, such as 'blue ribbon of the turf', which is the Derby, and 'blue ribbon of the Atlantic', which is awarded to the ship which makes the quickest crossing.

blue-sky thinking brainstorming; de-cluttering and opening your mind wide. On Friday afternoons we try to do some blue-sky thinking about future projects. A piece of management-speak, not unlike **push the envelope**.

blue stocking woman with artistic or literary inclinations or pretensions. She was a typical blue stocking, with no interest in her appearance or dress, but with lively views about the most arcane developments in abstract painting. The expression

is usually contemptuous or depreciative. In the 17th and 18th centuries, there were various political and social coteries whose frequenters – generally male – bore this epithet. The expression became exclusive to literary ladies in the 19th century, and has recently widened out to embrace the arts in general.

BOB. bob or two some money. He worked for five years in the Middle East, and I gather he's now worth a bob or two. Often an understatement, meaning in this case 'a lot of money'. A 'bob' in pre-decimal British currency was a shilling. You can also say 'a few bob' (same sense). She may look a bit of a tramp but I'm told she's worth a few bob.

Bob's your uncle(, Fanny's your aunt)! exclamatory phrase, meaning 'There you are!' or 'That was easy, wasn't it!' Just put the container in the microwave for five minutes, and – Bob's your uncle – supper's ready! The longer version is not often heard, but is perhaps meant for extra emphasis. Compare **hey presto!** The phrase is thought to have originated in 1886 when the prime minister, Robert Cecil (Uncle Bob), appointed his nephew to a high office of state.

BODY. body and soul with all one's effort and ability. He is committed body and soul to making that business work.

body blow serious setback. One more increase in the mortgage rate was a body blow to many investors. A journalistic cliché.

BOLT. bolt from the blue unexpected happening; complete surprise. The prime minister's sudden resignation was a complete bolt from the blue, especially for the political pundits – not one of whom had forecast it. The 'blue' of the idiom is of course the sky, whence thunderbolts sometimes drop without warning. Compare **manna from heaven; out of the blue**.

bolt upright absolutely erect. I sat bolt upright when I heard the knock at the door. Literally, as straight as a bolt (= arrow) in the quiver.

BONE. bone idle utterly lazy. That boy will get nowhere in life, and you know why – because he's bone idle. Literally, idle right to the bones of one's body. Compare **to the marrow/core**.

bone of contention subject of argument or disagreement. A serious bone of contention between the warring factions was the repatriation of refugees. A metaphor from canine strife or aggressive behaviour over meat bones. See also **make no bones about something**.

bone to pick with someone topic on which to express disagreement. I've got a bone to pick with you, and I think you know why. Another canine idiom. Two dogs will not normally pick at the same bone in peaceable fashion.

BOOT. boot is on the other foot expression which means that someone now has power over a person who used to be more powerful than they were. Miss Young was his teacher in primary school, and he used to be terrified of her; but now he looks after her in the care home where he works – so the boot's on the other foot, as you might say. Until the end of the 17th century, boots were not made specifically for left and right feet. When they hurt, as they often did, the wearer tried wearing them on opposite feet.

BORED. bored to tears/death utterly bored. His endless talk about local politics bored most of his listeners to death. Common hyperboles.

BORN. born on the wrong side of the blanket illegitimate. More than half the kids in this school don't know their father because they were born on the wrong side of the blanket. Nowadays facetious, this is an old-fashioned euphemism dating from the 18th century, when illegitimacy carried a serious stigma in polite society. The implication is of an impregnation which occurred outside the marriage bed.

born to the purple born into the aristocracy or some other privileged background. With a la-di-da voice like that you'd think she'd been born to the purple. From the Roman purple toga, worn by all the chief members of the state. This also gave 'raised to the purple', or 'resign the purple'.

born with a silver spoon in one's mouth being from an affluent background. He left school at 14 and went to work in the mines, so you couldn't exactly say he'd been born with a silver spoon in his mouth. See also **hand someone something on a plate**. Compare **(born/cradled in) the lap of luxury**.

born yesterday naive, inexperienced. He seems to think he can trick me, but he'll soon discover I wasn't born yesterday. If you were a baby born yesterday, you hadn't had time to learn many of life's tricks. Similar to Scots 'I didn't come up the Clyde in a banana boat'.

BOSOM. bosom friends close friends who share confidences. Throughout their youth John and his cousin James were bosom friends. Biblical: Saul and Jonathan were the friends of King David's bosom.

BOTTLE. bottle out run away (from something). A standard phrasal verb. The opposite of a person who 'has a lot of bottle' (i.e. who is very courageous). Please stick with the project and don't bottle out at this late stage. See also **lose one's bottle**.

BOTTOM. bottom drawer linen and other soft furnishings for the house, especially of a newly wed woman. Her grandparents presented her with a magnificent dinner set for her bottom drawer. Old fashioned, another term for a dowry.

bottom line 1. a business's profitability. It's a huge company that has grown too fast for the stockmarket's liking, for the simple reason that it hasn't had a very impressive bottom line for several years. From accountancy: the bottom line of a set of accounts indicates the profits or losses of an enterprise. 2. in the final analysis. The bottom line is that you were speeding, and there's no getting round a police fine and penalty points on your driving licence. This is an inelegant but widespread extension of the first sense: it is a form of jargon.

BOWL. bowl someone over overwhelm someone with generosity, joy, shock, horror, etc. The television pictures of the disaster completely bowled us over.

BOX. box clever behave cunningly and carefully in order to gain advantage over an adversary. It was fascinating watching the accused man in the dock – he was boxing very clever, and the prosecution couldn't catch him out at all. A metaphor from boxing with one's brain – by feint and ploy – and not just with one's fists and brawn.

BRAIN. brain drain geographical flow of talent, skill, etc. usually from poorer to wealthier countries. There has always been a brain drain in skilled medical personnel from Britain to America.

BRAND. brand new completely new and unused. This year he bought his first brand-new car; in the past, he always bought second-hand ones. From the 16th century, meaning that the brand mark on a newly made item fresh from the foundry was still entirely visible and undamaged.

BRASS. brass hat important person in an organisation, etc. Some brass hat from the local water board was on television last night. The phrase was originally military, used to describe a high-ranking officer. This context also gives the collective term 'top brass'. There is an office car park, but only for the top brass.

brass monkeys very cold. I couldn't stand for long at the bus stop: it was positively brass monkeys in that east wind. Slang: from the humorous observation, in Arctic weather conditions, that, 'It's cold enough to freeze the balls off a brass monkey.'

brass neck insolence; brazen effrontery. She had the brass neck to ask me to lend her £1,000. An earlier version was 'brazen face' (16th century), and we can still talk of a brazen hussy or minx. 'Brass' means boldness and also coin, in addition to being the name of a metal, hence the standard simile 'bold as brass'. 'Neck' was a dialect word for 'cheek' or 'gall', as in **stick**

one's neck out. Compare also **have the cheek to; have a nerve; what a nerve/cheek**.

BRAT. brat pack youthfully precocious clique of would-be trendsetters; younger generation of personnel in an organisation, etc. It was a difficult assignment, but one of our brat pack was happy to tackle it. A slightly worldweary back formation from 'rat pack'. The 'Brat Pack' was the nickname of a group of Hollywood filmstars in the 1980s, just as the 'Rat Pack' had been a similar grouping in the 1950s. Compare **eager beaver**.

BREAD. one's bread and butter one's livelihood. He's a professional golfer, so I guess you could say that playing golf is his bread and butter.

BREAK. break cover come out into the open from a place of concealment. The fox went to ground for some weeks, but last night it broke cover briefly when John spotted it in the long meadow. From game hunting.

break even make neither profit nor loss, because earnings and outgoings balance. The company hasn't had a very good year, but they're hoping to just about break even. From book-keeping.

break one's heart be deeply upset or saddened. His wayward behaviour broke his mother's heart. A standard cliché-cum-hyperbole.

break (something) in 1. tame and train something (such as a horse). His grandfather was a drover and a cowboy, and he could break in the meanest horse. A standard phrasal verb. 2. rob or commit robbery. There was a break-in at the bank last night.

break one's neck be in a great hurry to get somewhere. I wish I'd known the meeting was cancelled – I nearly broke my neck trying to get here in time.

break someone's neck verbally threaten someone with violence. Tell him I'll break his neck if he doesn't switch off that radio. Hopefully a hyperbolic term.

break new ground do something innovative. It's a very interesting discovery which definitely breaks new ground in the country's energy programme. An agricultural metaphor of the Wild West frontier.

break ranks cease to present a united front with one's friends, allies, etc. Working as a research team they had major influence, but after they broke ranks and split up they were of no importance. Originally military, referring to soldiers leaving their position in a line.

break the back of something complete the hardest part of an assignment, etc. He had broken the back of the project by September, even though it was Christmas before he got it completed.

break/bust the bank leave oneself short of money. The flight to Australia wasn't cheap – in fact it almost broke the bank for me to get there. In gambling, the bank is broken/bust when there is no money left in the casino's payout pot for the payment of winnings.

break the ice overcome initial conversational stiffness between strangers. She soon broke the ice by telling me all about her life in Egypt, since I too had spent some time in that country. Also **ice-breaker** an act or comment that breaks the ice. The speaker started off with a couple of excellent jokes: that was a good ice-breaker. Compare **set/ start the ball rolling**.

break the mould start something absolutely new and fresh. One of the declared aims of the Social Democratic party in the 1980s was to break the mould of British politics. Literally, destroy or throw away the old moulds used for casting metal, etc. Compare **change the face of something**.

break the news communicate bad news. It was a terrible accident and I'm glad I didn't have the job of breaking the news to the next of kin.

break wind burp; relieve flatulence. There was a loud sound of someone breaking wind in the kitchen. A euphemism tailored for societies in which burping and belching are considered impolite.

break one's word fail to keep one's promise. Don't break your word to her if you promised to help her. From the old notion that one's word is one's bond, something to be honoured and not broken. Opposite of **keep one's word**.

BREATHE. breathe down someone's neck 1. be very close behind someone in a competition, race, etc. Chelsea are top of the Premier League, with Arsenal breathing down their neck one point behind. 2. supervise someone too closely and deprive them of space; covet someone's job and try to bypass them in the promotion stakes. Let me get on with the job: stop breathing down my neck! The original image is from racing, conveying the idea of a competitor so close behind that one can hear or feel his breath on the back of one's own neck.

breathe freely/easily de-stress; relax. It was many months after the robbery before I could breathe freely again.

BRIGHT. bright as a button very lively, perky, keen, etc. She's a nice kid, and bright as a button. The standard simile, from days when buttons were showier things than they are nowadays, the expression is easiest applied to children or people whom the speaker regards with affection. It would, for example, be hard to so describe the Lord Chancellor or the Archbishop of Canterbury, even if it were true. Similar, and with similar qualifications, is 'bright-eyed and bushy-tailed'. This idiom compares the person described with a cat, squirrel, etc. in healthy physical condition.

bright spark intelligent and lively person. Some bright spark at my bank has accidentally closed my account. Often used ironically.

BRING. bring home the bacon 1. earn enough money to feed one's family. Most wage slaves are only in work in order to bring home the bacon. The literal meaning is probably from the days of man the hunter. Later, a popular entertainment at country fairs was a competition to catch a greased pig; if you won, you brought home the bacon. Compare **earn one's keep**. 2. win the prize; get good results; complete something successfully. I'm not at all keen on your methods, but I have to admit that they bring home the bacon.

bring home to make a person realise and fully appreciate something. Her illness brought home to him, once again, just how much he depended on his wife.

bring someone in from the cold rehabilitate someone who has been out of favour, whose views have been proscribed, etc. Most mafia organisations seem to have one or two semi-respectable members, and they look to these people to bring them in from the cold when the time is right.

bring/get/keep (people) onside ensure that people support something, or at least refrain from opposing it. I'm so glad you've managed to bring Stella onside: she'll be a very useful ally. Initially from the football field.

bring someone round 1. restore someone to consciousness; resuscitate someone. Paramedics were at the scene, trying to bring a couple of the worst cases round. 2. persuade someone to the speaker's point of view; win over. I've done my utmost to bring her round to my point of view, but without success. A phrasal verb.

bring someone to book make someone account for his conduct. It was one of the most frustrating cases, because no one was ever brought to book for the crime. The metaphor is from the sort of imaginary judgment book or law book in which our wrongdoings are listed, and which indicates the punishments to be meted out.

bring someone to his/her knees humble or weaken someone. The collapse of the Communist economies brought the countries of eastern Europe to their knees for several years. Compare **on/to one's knees**.

bring to light reveal. The accountant brought to light some financial irregularities.

bring to mind serve as a reminder. His use of colour brings to mind the paintings of some of the French Impressionists. 'Mind' used to mean 'memory'.

bring up the rear occupy a position at the end of a line of people, items, etc. It was a long procession, and a first-aid unit brought up the rear. 'Rear' is formed by clipping from 'arrear' (French *arrière* = last, behind). From the field of battle.

BROAD. broad brush in general outline terms, and without details. The accountants are looking for a broad-brush indication of your division's trading profile over the next three years. From painting.

broad church organisation, etc. which tries to embrace a wide spectrum of opinions, styles, etc. The election campaign is a very broad-church coalition of views. This expression is from a Victorian designation of the Church of England, which tried to be comprehensive in its appeal. 'Broad church' was the term used by supporters of this comprehensiveness; its enemies called it 'Latitudinarian' and accused it of trying to be 'all things to all men'. Nowadays we might use the term 'rainbow alliance'. Compare **united front**.

broad daylight full light of day. You're not telling me they robbed the house in broad daylight, are you?

broad in the beam large around the hips. He's always been very broad in the beam, a waddler rather than a walker. From shipping, meaning a vessel that is wide in proportion to its length.

BROKEN. broken reed undependable person. The situation was very tense and Mary couldn't cope with it – so she was something of a broken reed until things sorted themselves out. From the biblical metaphor of man the reed shaken by the wind in Matthew xi.7, via the Pascalian concept of man the thinking reed, and Edward Young's 'Lean not on Earth…A broken reed at best', in *Night Thoughts* (1742–5).

BROWN. brown as a berry deeply sunburnt or tanned. The weather had been very sunny, and they were all brown as berries. A standard simile.

brown study state of deep preoccupation or mental abstraction. Something is clearly bothering him – he's been in a brown study all day, and hasn't said a word to anyone. Originally, simply 'in a study'. The adjective 'brown' once had the figurative sense of 'serious', or 'gloomy', so the Elizabethans could have said they felt brown in the way we now say we feel blue. This was later phrased as 'browned off' or fed up. He told me he was completely browned off with the job. Compare **penny for them/penny for your thoughts**.

BROWNIE. brownie points good marks for credit. You're not going to earn many brownie points for an incompetent job like that. Originally American, the expression has at least two suggested origins. It may derive from credits gained by Brownies (junior Girl Guides) for doing a good deed; or its origins may be in the sycophantic action of 'brown-nosing' or ingratiating oneself with superiors, etc. by metaphorically kissing their backsides.

BRUSH. brush up on something refresh or improve one's knowledge of a topic. She is going to have to brush up on her French before the exam. Literally, make one's knowledge shine.

brush up well appear smarter/younger/more beautiful than usual. 'I almost didn't recognise you in that flash designer suit!' 'Yes, don't I brush up well!'

BULL. bull in a china shop extremely awkward, clumsy person. We were having a very useful meeting until Jones came roaring in like a bull in a china shop. A clichéd proverbial stigma, the image is of a wild animal loose among precious and breakable trinkets.

bull session conversation, usually between males. They train every Friday at the gym, and then usually have a bit of a bull session at the pub to discuss the week's events. Originally American, bulls have also given rise to 'talking a lot of bull', and 'bullshitting' (= talking rubbish, in both cases).

BULLY. bully for you/her, etc. how nice for you/her, etc. He tells me he's been made a company director – bully for him, I'm sure! Often facetious.

BUM. bum note discordant or dissonant sound in a piece of music, or in a conversation. His joke about the royal family struck a bum note; he later discovered that his hostess was a cousin of the Queen.

bum steer useless information. Ridley's tip for the Derby this year was a bum steer as usual. Originally American, where the literal meaning of the term was a worthless bullock. If you say you need a 'steer' on something, you mean you'd welcome some advice or direction.

BUM'S. bum's rush enforced ejection; instant refusal. He's the author of several successful novels, but when his last manuscript got the bum's rush from all the publishers he decided to publish it himself. Originally American, where bums are tramps and often ejected rapidly and without ceremony from bars, etc. Similar to **one-two**.

BUMP. bump someone off kill someone. It's a real Elizabethan tragedy, with someone getting bumped off in just about every scene. A phrasal verb, originally American. Compare **put (someone) out of the way**.

BUN. (have a) bun in the oven (be) pregnant. Oh no, don't tell me she's got another bun in the oven! An old and semi-euphemistic usage.

BUNCH. bunch of fives fist; punch. He came to my door and threatened me with a bunch of fives for parking outside his house. A 19th-century slang term which originally referred to a hand of cards.

BUNDLE. bundle of nerves person who is very unrelaxed, full of apprehensions, etc. After I heard the shooting, I have to admit I was a bundle of nerves. Various other 'bundles' have evolved semi-analogously: **bundle of energy** keen or energetic person. She's a bundle of energy, and I just don't know where her enthusiasm comes from.

bundle of fun entertaining or amusing person. She wasn't exactly a bundle of fun at the party last night. Often negative and ironic.

BURDEN. burden of proof obligation to show evidence supporting one's point of view, etc. The burden of proof rests with your accuser – there is no need for you to prove anything. From the legal tag *onus probandi* (= burden of proving).

burden of (the) years old age. She has a very keen mind despite the burden of years. Biblical.

BURN. burn a hole in one's pocket spending money begging to be spent. As soon as she has a few pounds, it's burning a hole in her pocket until she can fritter it away on something. Compare **money to burn**.

burn one's boats/bridges destroy one's possibility of retreat; act decisively and in such a way that one cannot change one's mind later. For a week he hesitated; then, yesterday at lunchtime, he burnt his boats and posted his letter of resignation. The Romans sometimes traditionally and ceremonially burnt their boats/bridges behind them after invading a territory from the sea or across a river. This brought home to every Roman soldier the basic message of do or die, all or nothing: they had to win whatever battles were ahead of them or perish, because there was no option of retreat.

burn one's fingers suffer for something one has done, often as a result of a speculative venture. He burnt his fingers quite badly when he bought that mansion. Also 'get one's fingers burnt'.

burn rubber drive hard. Having burnt rubber for almost a week, he came home exhausted. An Americanism, implying that the driver is heavy on tyres, brakepads, etc. Also 'burn up the road'. A hard-riding cowboy was similarly said to 'pound leather'.

burn the candle at both ends overdo it. She's terribly busy, and doesn't look too good; I expect she's been burning the candle at both ends and probably needs a good holiday. The expression is immortalised in Edna St Vincent Millay's poem: 'My candle burns at both ends;/It will not last the night./But ah, my foes, and oh, my friends –/It gives a lovely light.' From 'First Fig', in *A Few Figs from Thistles*, 1920.

burn the midnight oil work long hours and hard. It was a very tough assignment, and we had to burn the midnight oil to get it completed on time. The literal sense meant 'to work through the hours of darkness'. As the poet Francis Quarles has it: 'We spend our midday sweat, our midnight oil;/ We tire the night in thought, the day in toil.' In *Emblems*, 1635, Bk 2, number 2. Compare **worth the candle**.

BURNING. burning issue/question matter of overriding interest, concern, etc. beside which no other issue is of any importance. The burning question had to be, 'Did he jump or was he pushed?'

BURST. burst at the seams be full to capacity. The school is bursting at the seams, and they cannot find room to enrol any more pupils.

BURY. bury the hatchet make peace; end a quarrel. They'd been nagging and bickering for so long, that no one believed they'd ever bring themselves to shake hands and bury the hatchet. From the American Indian custom of burying tomahawks to symbolise a cessation of hostilities. This act was often followed by the equally ceremonial smoking of the pipe of peace. Compare **clean slate; let bygones be bygones**.

BUSH. bush telegraph network for gathering gossip or transmitting information. There is an excellent bush telegraph in our office, so it wasn't long before everyone knew what had happened. The expression originated in the Australian bush or outback in the 1930s, where the telegraph was the only form of communication between isolated communities. See also **on the grapevine**.

BUSMAN'S. busman's holiday time off work spent doing very much as one would have been doing at work. Her school break last Easter was something of a busman's holiday: she took her class of children to France. The innovation of holiday travel for the working classes more or less coincided with the arrival of mass transportation. Driving a vehicle was deemed to be no holiday for a working bus driver, though it was often expected of him in the days when not many people could drive.

BUSTED. busted flush something that's gone seriously awry. When we learnt that the receivers had been called in, it was clear that his business plan was a busted flush. Originally a worthless hand of cards, because short of a flush by one maverick card. American.

BUSY. busy as a bee very busy, in a purposeful and pleasurable way. He's been busy as a bee all weekend. A standard simile.

BUTTER. butter someone up flatter someone, usually because you want something from them. The unions have been very actively buttering the management up, because they want a good pay rise for their employees. A phrasal verb idiom. Compare **soft soap**.

butter wouldn't melt in her/his mouth she/he looks incorruptibly virtuous – and isn't. I was amazed at the tissue of lies she'd told me, all the while looking as if butter wouldn't melt in her dainty mouth. In use in early 16th-century England.

BUTTERFLIES. butterflies in one's stomach sensation of nervous anticipation or apprehension. He tends to get butterflies in his stomach before making an important speech.

BUY. buy someone off bribe someone. The police warned him to stay quiet and hinted at some deal for him, but he told them they couldn't buy him off. A phrasal verb idiom.

BY. by a long chalk easily; by far. She was the cleverest girl in the school by a long chalk. From the days of chalk-marking, which preceded the invention/use of pencils. Also 'by a long shot'.

by and by later; in due course; before long. The train meandered in and out of tunnels and over viaducts, and by and by they came to a big town. Rather old-fashioned phrase much favoured by 18th- and 19th-century picaresque novelists.

by and large for the most part; generally speaking. She manages on her own quite well, by and large; though occasionally she gets a bit lonely. Originally from sailing.

by fits and starts fitfully; with much stopping and starting. He's been writing that book for 30 years by fits and starts. A dyad.

by hook or by crook by one means or another; by fair means or foul. He decided that he'd attend the meeting by hook or by crook. In use by Sir Edmund Spenser in *The Faerie Queene*, Book iii, canto 1, 1596. The exact origins of the phrase are obscure. But in certain parts of medieval England, herdsmen were once permitted to take for firewood those branches of trees which they could pull down with their billhooks or shepherds' crooks. It may have been that an element of desperation crept into their foraging during particularly cold winters. Compare **one way or another**.

by jove! a euphemistic exclamation, nowadays quite mild and innocuous, used as a substitute for the blasphemous 'By God!' Also 'By George!' and 'By Gum' are found as alternative euphemisms. By jove, doesn't she make good pancakes! In use from the Middle Ages, Jove was of course the planet and Roman god Jupiter. (Many Victorians avoided the expression, erroneously thinking that Jove meant Jehovah.) Compare **good gracious!**

by leaps and bounds fast. His new book is progressing by leaps and bounds. A dyad.

by the by/way incidentally. What's for supper? I'm frightfully hungry, by the by.

by the short hairs firmly in one's power. At last the police have found some good evidence, and I think you'll now discover they've got the accused by the short hairs. The reference is to pubic or genital hairs. Also 'by the short and curlies'.

by the skin of one's teeth just and no more; with little margin for manoeuvre. The train had actually started to move off, so I only caught it by the skin of my teeth. The source of the idiom may be biblical: 'My bone cleaveth to my skin and to my flesh, and I am escaped with the skin of my teeth.' This sentence from Job xix.20 means that Job escaped with only the skin of his teeth, and none of his possessions. The modern idiom has exchanged the preposition 'with' for 'by'.

C

CA'. ca' canny go carefully, gently, shrewdly, etc. Tell John to ca' canny with the whisky next time – that was a huge tumblerful! The tenors were a bit too loud just now, so can they ca' canny on the night please? A common Scots idiom which gave rise to the rural philosophy of Ca'cannyism, or moderation (*ca'* = call, go).

CALL. call a spade a spade speak plainly and directly, without euphemism or circumlocution, and without attempting to soften any criticism, etc. I never know what she's talking about – I wish she'd just get on with it and call a spade a spade. From Aristophanes and Plutarch. As Partridge has ruefully commented, most people nowadays call it 'a bloody shovel' if not worse, i.e. they have no problem speaking plainly. There is a memorable Victorian exchange, in Oscar Wilde's *The Importance of Being Ernest* (1895), which nicely sends up a dilemma for a polite society which is now obsolete:

> *Cecily*: When I see a spade I call it a spade.
> *Gwendoline*: I am glad to say that I have never seen a spade.

Compare **straight answer**.

call someone's bluff challenge someone's threats to see if they will really carry them out. Certain MPs kept threatening to resign, and eventually the prime minister decided it was time to call their bluff. From the card table, where players try to bluff their opponents into believing they have a better hand than they really have. When a player's bluff is called, he must show his hand and – often – expose the hollowness of his pretence.

call it a day decide that one has done enough; adjourn a meeting; stop working. After his second heart attack, he decided it would be best to follow his doctor's advice and call it a day. A euphemism for taking retirement, and sometimes for dying. Compare **hang up one's boots**.

call it quits agree that neither party in an enterprise owes the other party anything, both having invested equally in it. He bought two rounds of drinks and I only bought one; so I'll get the next one and then we can call it quits. Compare **quits with**.

call names say uncomplimentary or offensive things about someone. They called him all sorts of silly names.

call of nature need for urination, defecation, etc. We'll break for 15 minutes and everyone can have a cup of coffee, attend to calls of nature, check for incoming messages, etc. A standard euphemism which dates from the 18th century, and politely alludes to man's animal origins and needs.

(not) call one's soul one's own (not) be in control of the circumstances controlling one's life. You can't call your soul your own after you walk in that door – it's 'do this, do that' till the minute you leave at night. Usually negative.

call the shots be in charge of what is happening. The government give the impression of being out of control, and it seems to be the opposition that are calling all the shots these days. From target practice; the person who calls the shots tells the shooters where to fire.

call the tune give the orders. You'll be very surprised to learn that it is our little old white-haired grandmother who calls the tune in this household. From the saying, 'He who pays the piper calls the tune', meaning that the person who picks up the bill has the right to dictate how the money is spent. See also **pay the piper**.

CAMP. camp follower associate; supporter. The trouble with having a pop star for a brother is all the camp followers and fan clubs and so on that are forever trying to invade your privacy. Medieval armies had camp followers to look after their tents and animals and supply their various logistic needs.

camp it up act in a posturing or exaggeratedly effeminate way. It was one of those serial comedies about a department store, full of male shop assistants in pin-striped suits camping it up in the most ridiculous fashion. An idiomatic verb phrase from the slang adjective 'camp' (= affected, effeminate).

CAN. can a duck swim? Jocular put-down expression for 'Don't ask obvious questions.' Alternatives are mostly non-PC and include 'Can a Welshman sing?' or 'Can a black man dance?' or even 'Is the Pope a Catholic?'

can of worms complex and usually disagreeable state of affairs. No one wanted to work on that project, knowing that it was a particularly nasty can of worms. A picturesque metaphor. Compare **open a Pandora's box**.

can you beat it/that? isn't that hard to believe? Can you beat it – that ghastly novel has just won the Man Booker Prize!

CAN'T. can't make head nor tail of something can't understand something. It was a weird painting, and even after studying it for half an hour I still couldn't make head nor tail of it.

can't see the wood for the trees unable to distinguish between unimportant details and the important general picture. Many commentators believe the government has lost its way, and can no longer see the wood for the trees. Always negative. Compare **see no further than one's nose**.

can't take it with one be unable to use one's wealth, possessions, etc. after one is dead. I think she's quite right at 90 to take as many holidays as she can afford – after all, she can't take it with her. Invariably negative. From the saying, 'You can't take it with you when you go.'

CAP. cap in hand humbly and contritely. He stormed out of the house a week ago, but today he returned penniless and cap in hand, to say he was sorry and could he have a meal. From one of the expected stances of a beggar.

CARBON. carbon footprint total of greenhouse gas (GHG) emissions caused by people, organisations or events. The company has worked hard to reduce its carbon footprint and its GHG emissions. The concept features in the ecological debate: it is dictated by how much gas your car guzzles, how effectively you heat your house, how many air miles you notch up per year, etc. 'Carbon offsets' are ways of mitigating these. Solar, tidal or wind energy are also ways of managing a community's carbon footprint. Many individuals and almost all countries now accept the need to cut their carbon footprint, and to become 'carbon neutral'.

CARD. card short of a deck mentally deficient in a minor way. He's got a funny way of looking at you, and his speech is slurred, so most villagers assume that he's a card short of a deck. A common euphemism implying the absence of a small but finite portion of a person's intelligence, similar to 'tuppence off the full shilling' or 'a brick short of a load'. See also **one sandwich short of a picnic; not the sharpest tool in the box**.

CARDS. on the cards likely to happen. It is quite on the cards that such a catastrophe will happen in the next few months. From the use of playing cards in fortune telling, especially Tarot cards.

CARROT. carrot and stick mixture of rewards and punishments. Promise him a nice present if he passes the exam, and stop giving him any pocket money if he fails; sometimes a bit of carrot and stick works well with a youngster. The original strategy was, of course, devised as a policy for motivating and training horses.

CARRY. carry a big stick wield a lot of influence and power. Some of the multinational oil companies carry a bigger economic stick than the entire national economies of the states whose reserves they are developing or exploiting. Also **carry clout**. From the old adage, 'Speak softly and carry a big stick: you will go far.' This was most memorably quoted in a 1903 speech by US President Theodore Roosevelt.

carry all before one 1. overcome all resistance. It was a heated argument, and there was a lot of opposition from his fellow directors, but John prevailed in the end and succeeded in carrying all before him. **2. win all the prizes.** Last season was our team's most successful ever, and they carried all before them.

carry clout wield influence. I don't think she carries much clout in the organisation nowadays. A 'clout' is a knock or blow, so the idiom is similar to **pack a punch**.

carry coals to Newcastle do something completely unnecessary, especially to take something to a place which already has lots of that commodity. They've opened yet another video shop on our main street – talk about carrying coals to Newcastle! From the 16th century, when the port of Newcastle upon Tyne supplied all England's coal needs.

carry something off succeed in some venture. It's a risky plan, and I don't know if we can carry it off – but we'll try. A phrasal verb.

carry the can bear responsibility; accept blame. Everyone says it was a tragic accident, but no one is willing to carry the can for it. Naval in origin, the can in question is thought to have been a tin filled with explosives used for blasting your enemy out of the water, which would certainly explain the sense of reluctance in the carrier.

carry weight have influence. She may have been prime minister once, but her influence doesn't carry much weight nowadays. From boxing and riding.

CASCADE. cascade down disseminate via a top-down method of communication. Group leaders are expected to cascade this project down to their membership next month. A phrasal verb of the 21st century, compare **roll (something) out**.

CASE. case in point relevant example. I was telling you about my absentmindedness, and now I can't remember where I put my glasses – which is a good case in point.

CASH. cash one's chips 1. terminate a business transaction in order to realise one's cash profits. He seems to have decided to cash his chips rather than

to bale the company out once again. **2. die.** Like so many workaholics forced into sudden retirement, Mr Jones seemed to lose interest in life – he had cashed his chips within the year.

cash cow something that provides a regular and accruing profit or income long after it was created. Royalties from the book and its film rights have been a useful cash cow for the author's widow. Formerly a 'milch cow', which was milked for profits.

cash in on something take unfair advantage of something. When a business goes into receivership, it usually emerges that a lot of asset strippers and other sharks are just waiting to cash in on its problems.

CAST. cast an eye on/at something look critically at something. He writes a weekly newspaper column in which he often casts a critical eye on the local political scene. Often 'cast a cold eye', which is the wording in 'Under Ben Bulbin' (1939), the poem and epitaph of W B Yeats.

cast aspersions try to defame someone or disparage their integrity. She was always trying to cast aspersions at his professionalism. A rather formal idiom, sometimes mocked by the malapropism of 'cast nasturtiums'.

cast one's bread upon the waters act generously, without looking for immediate reward. She does a lot of work for charity, saying that she was brought up to cast her bread on the waters. From biblical advice not to be a hoarder, in Ecclesiastes xi.1: 'Cast thy bread upon the waters: for thou shalt find it after many days.'

cast one's mind back try to recollect a past event, occasion, etc. Try to cast your mind back to that fateful party, and tell us all you can remember about it. From psychoanalysis.

cast pearls before swine waste good or precious things on unappreciative people. He wanted to take his class to a Mahler concert, but a colleague laughed at him and asked why he was so keen on casting pearls before swine. **From a biblical admonition: 'Give not that which is holy unto the dogs, neither cast ye your pearls before swine.' Matthew vii.6.**

cast the first stone be the first person to make criticisms or accusations. Casting the first stone, she called him an incompetent layabout. **A misquotation from the Bible story of Jesus and the woman taken in adultery, whom the Pharisees wanted to stone to death as a sinner: 'He that is without sin among you, let him first cast a stone at her.' John viii.7.**

CASTLES. castles in Spain/the air fantasies. He talks all the time about his big-time ambitions, but it's all castles in Spain stuff. **The French have** *châteaux en Espagne* **with the same sense. Perhaps the Spanish allusion is to Don Quixote, the classic daydreamer.**

CAT. cat-and-dog life life of constant bickering **and quarrelling.** They have led each other a cat-and-dog life since they were married 20 years ago.

cat and mouse process of attempted deceit **and confusion between two or more unequal parties, in order for one to defeat the other by outwitting him/her/them.** Much international politics is a cat-and-mouse power game, with UN funds at stake for the victors. **Sometimes the animals are called 'Tom and Jerry', being the names of the participants in the best-known cat-and-mouse Walt Disney cartoon.**

cat got one's tongue expression used to **express surprise at someone's unaccustomed silence.** What can be bothering him today – has the cat got his tongue? **Usually a question.**

CATCH. catch a cold 1. suffer a financial loss. Like most people who play the stock market, he catches a cold from time to time. **Business jargon, the reference is generally to a temporary affliction.** 2. catch a venereal disease. He seems to have caught a cold somewhere and is attending the hospital for treatment. **A euphemism from the 1940s.**

(not) catch someone dead (not) do something **which one would thoroughly dislike doing.** They went to the Palais de Dance, but you wouldn't catch me dead in a dreadful dump like that. **Almost invariably negative.**

catch someone's eye be noticed by someone. I was looking out of the window when a puff of smoke from the garden caught my eye.

catch it receive a punishment. You'll catch it if I ever see you breaking a window again. **Commonly used to threaten youngsters, the unspecified 'it' is supposed to strike terror into the hearts of a young age group.**

catch someone napping surprise someone **who should be prepared, or paying attention, etc.** Try as they might, the prosecuting lawyers couldn't catch the witness napping; she was ready for all their tricks. **The expression 'as Moss caught his mare napping' dates to the 16th century, and the original image was of a rustic or yokel farmer having difficulty saddling an elusive and un-cooperative mare. The only way he could catch her was to wait till she lay down to take a nap. Compare catch someone on the hop.**

catch someone on the hop catch someone **unprepared.** The sudden change in the weather caught us all on the hop – who would have expected snow? **Also 'catch someone napping': literally, when they're half-asleep; or 'catch someone with his pants down': literally, at an embarrassing moment. Compare see which way the cat jumps.**

catch someone out force someone to admit **an error, mistake, etc.** I'm not trying to catch you out, but we need to ask you a few questions. **From the game of cricket.**

catch someone redhanded find someone in **the very act of wrongdoing.** The police had caught him redhanded, which meant that he was unable convincingly to deny involvement in the affair. **From the idea of catching the murderer with the blood of his victim on his hands. Also 'catch**

someone in the act'. The Latin version 'in flagrante delicto' (literally, while the crime is blazing) is also often used in English. Compare **nail someone**.

Catch-22 situation situation in which one cannot win. *I can't get the job without any experience, and I can't get any experience till somebody gives me a job – it's a real Catch-22 situation.* From the title of a novel by Joseph Heller (1961). Compare **chicken and egg situation; vicious circle**.

CATCH-PHRASE

A catch-phrase tends to have a more ephemeral resonance than an idiom. It is a fixed phrase which has gained media popularity and thus spreads into the wider culture. It is often based on a memorable jingle, slogan, stock response or quotation from an advertiser, a politician or an entertainer. Sometimes a catch-phrase is a complete sentence. Often it attains a range of resonances far beyond the intentions of its originator. Included in this book is a selection of only those catch-phrases which seemed to double well as idiomatic expressions. Examples of catch-phrases which tend in this direction are:

From politics

John Major's *Back to basics* (1993) and Margaret Thatcher's *You turn if you want to: The lady's not for turning* (1980) may not have the stuff of enduring quotations, but both still have a certain resonance many years on. Winston Churchill has left many catch-phrases echoing in the language cupboard, including frequent references to the *broad sunlit uplands*, probably his equivalent of the pot of gold at the end of the rainbow; as well as the rousing *blood, sweat and tears* and *not the beginning of the end but the end of the*

beginning. Whether we use the entire sentence or only the first half, George Bush Senior's *Read my lips, no new taxes* (1988) is still good for the odd, hollow-ish laugh, and we still use *The buck stops here* (Harry S Truman, died 1972), *Speak softly and carry a big stick* (Theodore Roosevelt, died 1919) and *The last, best hope on earth* (Abraham Lincoln, died 1865).

From the Bible, proverbs, literature and films

Biblical echoes permeate the language, from *A land of milk and honey* (Exodus iii.8) to *The poor are always with us* (Matthew xxvi.11). Book and film titles are fertile sources of catch-phrases, from *Life is just a bowl of cherries* (song, 1931), *Life begins at forty* (book, 1932) and *Miss Lonelyhearts* (book, 1933) to *All quiet on the western front* (film and book, 1930), *A walk on the wild side* (film, 1962), *Diamonds are forever* (film and book, 1956) and *The silence of the lambs* (book 1988, film 1991). Certain fictional expressions have also caught on in the wider language, from Conan Doyle's *Elementary, my dear Watson* (1894) and Dickens's *Never say die* (1833) to Raymond Chandler's *Down these mean streets (a man must go)* (1950) and George Orwell's *Big Brother (is watching you)* (1948).

From advertising slogans and mottoes

From *The mint with the hole* (Polo) to *Beanz meanz Heinz*, from *Put a tiger in your tank* (Esso), *Gotta lotta bottle* (Milk Marketing), and *The beer that made Milwaukee famous* (Schlitz), right back to *Every picture tells a story* (Sloan's Backache and Kidney Pills) and *The customer is always right* (Selfridges), these expressions tend to stick in our minds, just as the advertisers intended; and to be used in our speech, sometimes in emended form. They need not necessarily be commercial in origin, as

Be prepared (Boy Scouts' motto), *Better red than dead* (nuclear disarmament), *Black is beautiful* (US Black civil rights) and *Flower power* (hippy slogan) – among many – remind us.

From radio and TV

Kenneth Horne's *Read any good books lately?* (Much Binding in the Marsh, 1940s) and *I don't mind if I do* (Tommy Handley, ITMA, 1940s) have had a good innings, as have *Beautiful downtown Burbank, Look that up in your Funk and Wagnalls, What you see is what you get* and *You bet your sweet bippy* (all Rowan & Martin's Laugh-In, 1967–73); *Know what I mean? Say no more! And now for something completely different* (Monty Python's Flying Circus, 1969–74); and *What do you think of it so far? There's no answer to that* and *Short, fat hairy legs* (Morecambe and Wise Show, 1970s).

Some catch-phrases end up as clichés, which may mean they have come to the end of their productive existence, and are ready for replacement by something more vital and up to the minute. It's happening *even as we speak* (catch-phrase for 'right now'). *Watch this space*, as the phrase-collectors might say.

CAT'S. cat's paw accomplice. The police always seem to manage to catch the cat's paw, but the brains behind the operation always escape. The expression derives from the fable in which a cat is persuaded by a clever monkey to pick roasted chestnuts off a hot stove. The cat is thus being used as a tool in the monkey's plan. Around 1600, the idiom was 'the cat's foot', and 'paw' wasn't substituted for another hundred years. A famous painting by Landseer (1824) illustrates this story.

cat's pyjamas/whiskers paragon of charm, virtue, attractiveness, etc. Of course his mother

thinks he's the cat's pyjamas – that's a mother's prerogative. Compare **bee's knees**; **blue-eyed boy**.

CENTRE. centre stage the most important or significant place, or person occupying that place. It takes an ex-prime minister a while to get used to the idea that he no longer occupies centre stage. Compare **in the limelight**.

CERTAIN. (in a) certain condition pregnant. I saw at a glance that she was in a certain condition. A euphemism, from the days when a lady's shape was not referred to. Nowadays used humorously, if at all.

(of a) certain age no longer young. The door was opened by an attractive woman of a certain age. A euphemism, from the days when a lady's age was not discussed.

CHALLENGED. intellectually challenged (= stupid), **vertically challenged** (= small), **chronologically challenged** (= old), **aesthetically challenged** (= ugly), etc. A productive idiomatic construction of the late 1980s for the formation of politically correct euphemisms. Rather over-used, and therefore rapidly becoming clichéd.

CHAMPING. Champing/chafing at the bit waiting impatiently to do something. It was a hot day and the children were champing at the bit to go swimming. From racehorses, eager for exercise or the start of the race.

CHANCE. chance one's arm take a risk in the hope of achieving something. I don't want to chance my arm on something as dubious as that. Compare **push one's luck**.

CHANCES. chances are that it is likely that. You could always phone him at the office, but chances are that he's already left.

CHANGE. change hands pass into new ownership. It was a very well-thumbed dictionary, and looked as if it had changed hands many times.

change horses (in midstream) alter course,

one's intentions, etc. in the middle of an assignment. The project has suffered from frequent changes of senior personnel, even though everyone realised it was a bad idea to change horses in midstream. An expression thought to be influenced by Abraham Lincoln's observation, 'It is not best to swap horses when crossing streams' (1864).

change of life menopause; cessation of menstruation. She was one of those lucky women who appeared untroubled by the common traumas of the change of life. A standard euphemism, now old fashioned.

change the face of something alter something in a major and fundamental way. Darwin's discoveries changed the face of evolutionary science. Compare **break the mould**.

change one's tune adopt a different attitude. He started out being pretty nasty to us, but when he discovered who we were he soon changed his tune. Compare **laugh on the wrong/other side of one's face/mouth**.

CHAPTER. chapter and verse verbatim; word-for-word details. I was asked if I could give a chapter-and-verse account of what had been said. He was able to quote chapter and verse from the company's health-and-safety handbook. From the Victorian rote method of learning the biblical catechisms, leaving nothing out.

chapter of accidents series of mishaps or unlucky events. The holiday was disastrous – a chapter of accidents from start to finish.

CHARITY. charity begins at home one has to make adequate provision for one's family before one makes provision for needy strangers. They want me to help fund an appeal for battered wives, but charity begins at home and I'm afraid I can't afford the time or the money right now. A saying.

CHASE. chase the dragon smoke opium or heroin. He's not a well man since he started chasing the dragon. The expression is supposed to describe the shape of the smoke curling in dragon shapes across the smoker's line of heightened vision.

chase a/the rainbow pursue an ideal, illusion, etc. He seems to have spent most of his lifetime chasing the rainbow of critical approval. From the Irish fairy tale of the crock of gold at the end of the rainbow: it kept moving further away when you thought you were getting closer to it.

CHEEK. cheek by jowl inconveniently close together. During the three years of our imprisonment, we lived cheek by jowl together. 'Jowl' is another word for cheek. A dyad.

CHEESED. cheesed off annoyed or fed up. I was thoroughly cheesed off at their decision. Alternative expressions with the same meaning include 'browned off' and 'pissed off'.

CHEW. chew the rag/fat converse idly. They sat around the campfire chewing the rag until the sun set. Originally American.

CHICKEN. chicken and egg situation situation in which it is impossible to say which of two things was original or caused the other. Should I muddle along in the job until I earn a bit of money and then buy the equipment, or should I borrow some money to buy the equipment and then start the job? It's a bit of a chicken and egg situation. From the old riddle, 'Which came first, the chicken or the egg?' Compare **Catch-22 situation**.

chicken-feed insignificant amount of money. He offered a reward of £5,000 for the lost painting, which is a lot of money for you or me, but it's chicken-feed for a painting valued at £10 million.

chicken out of something lose one's nerve and try to avoid doing something. As soon as I saw the door open for the parachute drop, I knew I couldn't face it and that I'd have to chicken out of the jump. 'Chicken' has meant scared or cowardly from about the 1930s.

CHICKENS. chickens come home to roost past errors or omissions return to worry one, or to have an adverse effect on one's current circumstances. For years they starved their company of development funds, and now their chickens – or lack of them – are coming home to roost: they have no new products to sell.

CHIEF. chief cook and bottlewasher general factotum; person in charge. I've got a complaint about the service in this shop, and I want to speak to the chief cook and bottlewasher. A slightly disparaging designation.

CHILD'S. child's play very easy work. He was extremely fit and healthy, and made running the marathon look like child's play.

CHINLESS. chinless wonder gormless aristocrat. The manager was one of those old-school chinless wonders with a good Oxbridge accent and a pinstriped suit. From the popular notion of aristocratic inbreeding producing chinless offspring of limited intelligence. A similarly disparaging term is 'upper-class twit'.

CHIP. chip off the old block very like one of one's parents in character, behaviour or appearance. His father captained the school at cricket before playing for Yorkshire, and young Jones's batting suggests he may well turn out to be a chip off the old block. The concept is classical, and the reference is to a chip of wood gouged from the block. It usually refers approvingly to a son's resemblance to his father.

chip on one's shoulder feelings of imagined inferiority or grievance often leading to aggressive or antisocial behaviour. She's had a bit of a chip on her shoulder since the divorce, and I can hardly blame her. Originally American, apparently from the frontier practice of young men balancing a chip of wood on their shoulder as an open challenge to their macho fellows to knock it off.

CHIPS. chips are down moment of crisis, when people's true worth becomes apparent.

It's hard to know just how well he's going to cope until the chips are down. From gambling: the chips are down and further betting is forbidden when the game, race, etc. is under way and the result of the fixture is about to be decided.

CHOC. choc-a-bloc/chockablock packed or crammed full. The train was choc-a-bloc, so we decided to wait for a later one. From a nautical expression meaning two blocks of tackle rammed together.

CHOP. chop and change repeatedly change. One minute he's going to be a policeman, the next he wants to study medicine – he'll have to stop chopping and changing and make his mind up. Compare with the similar dyad **hum and haw**.

CHRONOLOGICALLY. chronologically chall- enged/gifted old. There's a large home for the chronologically gifted in the village square. Two recent euphemisms or circumlocutions, the second in particular redolent of political correctitude. Often meant to be humorous, but see also **challenged**.

CHUCK. chuck wagon canteen, usually of the mobile variety. They were lucky enough to find an all-night chuck wagon and bought some coffee and grub to keep themselves awake. This was the name of the cook-house in the American West, later used by the military. 'Chuck' was what cowboys called food, originally a cut of beef as in 'chuck-steak'.

CINCH. it's a cinch it's very easy. Beating Arsenal last week was a cinch. Same meaning: 'it's a dawdle', 'it's a walkover'. 'Cinch' is American English for a saddle girth, from Spanish cincha (= a belt). It later came to mean a firm grip, and then 'a dead certainty'.

CIRCUMFERENTIALLY. circumferentially challenged fat. It's a special shop for the circumferentially challenged. A humorous euphe- mism, but see also **challenged**. Also 'horizontally challenged' (= short), 'follically challenged' (= bald).

CIVIL. civil liberties people's basic rights in a free society, to say, think and do as they please, so long as they respect and do not infringe the rights of others. The civil liberties of this country have been under sustained attack for many years. Also 'civil partnership', a same-sex relationship recognised by law in the United Kingdom.

CLAM. clam up on someone refuse to continue talking to someone. Don't let her think you're prying, or she'll just clam up on you. From the notion of a clam closing its shell tight. In the 19th century, the Americans had the simile 'as close/tight as a clam' as a term of contempt for a tight-mouthed person.

CLAP. clap eyes on see. No, I don't know him – I've never clapped eyes on him in my life.

CLAPPED. clapped out knackered; exhausted; worn out. He still drives the same clapped-out old Rover. 'Clapped' probably originally meant 'diseased', as in 'the clap', a colloquial name for gonorrhoea since the 16th century. .

CLASS. class act high-class performance or display; also the person performing. Millions of people watched Roger Federer in the tennis final, and they knew a class act when they saw one.

CLEAN. clean as a whistle totally clean and uncorrupt. Try Maclean if you need a good, honest lawyer – I can guarantee he's clean as a whistle. A standard simile for moral rectitude. Compare **smelling of roses**.

clean bill of health declaration of fitness and good health. Young Chalmers took a bad knock at last Saturday's training session, but the fans are hoping he'll have a clean bill of health for tomorrow's big game. A journalistic cliché nowadays, the term dates from the days when a ship was not allowed to berth passengers until they were all certified free of infectious diseases.

clean round the bend/twist completely mad. He started yelling and screaming and acting like someone who'd gone clean round the twist. 'Round

the bend' was a slang term for 'mad', common among seafarers. In the 1930s, Harpic was the lavatory cleaner with the slogan that it 'cleans round the bend'. This usage was a pun on the earlier meaning. A similar expression: 'stark staring bonkers/mad'.

clean slate fresh start. They've decided to forget about their past arguments, and start off again with a clean slate. From the Victorian use of slates in schools, for writing on. If the pupil made a mess, the slate could be easily cleaned and he could start again. Also 'wipe the slate clean'. Compare **bury the hatchet; let bygones be bygones**.

clean sweep fresh start. A new management often makes a clean sweep of factory rules and regulations.

clean up one's act improve one's conduct; stop behaving badly, irresponsibly, etc. If the British press doesn't clean up its act, it will rightly face tough legislation to make it do so.

CLEANSE. cleanse the Augean stable purge a situation, etc. of corruption, immorality, etc. Tax legislation is a complete mess, and one day someone is going to have to cleanse that particular Augean stable – not a job many governments will relish. From one of the legendary labours of Hercules who had to clean out the filthy stables of King Augeas.

CLEAR. clear as a bell very clear. I thought I heard a shot – there's another one, clear as a bell. A standard simile, as is **clear as mud** not at all clear; obscure. She asked if we'd understood her lecture and if everything was now clear, and someone muttered, 'Yes, clear as mud!' A jocular catch phrase, the opposite of **clear as crystal/ daylight**. It was as clear as daylight to me that our visit was unwelcome. The last two indicate visible clarity.

clear blue water the advantage of space. In one week, Barack Obama had established clear blue water between his administration and that of his discredited predecessor. Originally the term was from competitive rowing: it referred to the space between the leading boat and those behind it. In the 1990s, the term was transposed to party politics and was used to describe the distance between the views of opposing political parties.

clear one's name prove one's innocence. I demanded a public printed apology from the press in order to clear my name of all the malicious gossip that the papers had been printing about me. The notion of clearing one's name of a slur or imputation is found in several places in Shakespeare.

clear of the field ahead of the competition. As dictionary publishers, Oxford were once well clear of the field. From horse racing.

clear the air clarify or get rid of a difficult or complex problem. The government's attitude has been ambivalent for some years, so today's statement clears the air considerably.

clear the decks prepare for action. The reception is on Saturday, so we'd better start clearing the decks right away. From the navy, where a ship's decks were cleared to prepare for battle or a storm.

CLICHÉ

A cliché is defined as a stereotyped, or hackneyed, or trite phrase or expression. Many idioms and other phrases become clichés through over-use, and others have derived from once-fresh and striking literary quotations (and just as often from misquotations).

Eric Partridge (1940) describes the main criterion of a cliché as 'its commonplaceness, its too-frequent employment, rather than its phrase-nature…The excessive use, not the phrasal quality, determines the cliché.' Sir Ernest Gowers (1954) defines it as 'a phrase whose aptness in a particular context when it was first invented has won it such popularity that it has become

hackneyed, and is used without thought in contexts where it is no longer apt.' He adds that 'it is by definition a bad thing, not to be employed by self-respecting writers.'

Following Partridge and Philip Howard (1984) and other experts, there are four main categories of cliché:

1. over-used idioms;
2. non-idiomatic, hackneyed catch-phrases;
3. over-used quotations and catch-phrases from foreign languages;
4. over-used quotations from English literature.

Partridge claims that at least 80 per cent of the cliché 'corpus' comes under headings 1 and 2. A few examples of each must suffice, although category 1 is of greatest relevance in the context of this book.

1. Over-used idioms

In his listing of over-used idioms, Partridge lists expressions like *at daggers drawn, behind the scenes, bolt from the blue, darken the door of, lead a dog's life, leave the sinking ship, know the ropes, set one's hand to the plough, stick to one's last, stick to one's guns, take pot-luck*, etc. Betty Kirkpatrick (1996) lists similar phrases, among them *acid test, add fuel to the fire/ flames, armed to the teeth, be all ears, any port in a storm, tied to the apron strings, cost an arm and a leg, head and shoulders above, hive of industry, horns of a dilemma, jockey for position*, etc. Now-rare and old-fashioned expressions such as *set one's hand to the plough* and *stick to one's last* remind us that, in cliché, we are dealing with style, an area where there are no absolutes. Just as some expressions are said to become clichéd, they can and do also move out of cliché status.

At most, with over-used idioms such as

these, it is probably good to be aware that some people regard them as clichés, and therefore to use them deliberately – whether for allusion, or for humorous or other effects. A few idioms are marked as 'usually or often clichés' in the main dictionary.

2. Hackneyed catch-phrases

The line between an idiom and a catch-phrase is a fine one, on which experts disagree. Partridge lists items such as *add insult to injury, armed to the teeth, any port in a storm, blissful ignorance, call of the wild, cheer to the echo, dim and distant past, fate worse than death, nip something in the bud, salt of the earth, second to none*, etc. Kirkpatrick gives similar expressions like *beyond the pale, in cold blood, do someone proud, Dutch courage, jam tomorrow, jobs for the boys, point of no return, plot thickens, that would be telling, there are ways and means, without more ado, word to the wise*, etc.

3. Over-used quotations and catch-phrases from foreign languages

Although Latin still supplies the biggest stock of clichéd idioms in English, it is arguable that their number is now dropping away from cliché status as a result of the rapid decline of Latin in our education system. French is the other main source. Here are a few:

LATIN: *ab origine, deo volente, deus ex machina, genius loci, in flagrante delicto, mutatis mutandis, nil desperandum, persona non grata, pro bono publico, saeva indignatio, sic transit gloria mundi, status quo, sub rosa, terra firma, arma virumque cano, et tu, Brute?*

FRENCH: *bête noire, bon mot, carte blanche, cause célèbre, coup de grâce, cri de coeur,* *entente cordiale, fait accompli, faute de mieux, mot juste, pièce de résistance, plus ça change plus c'est la même chose.*

ITALIAN: *basso profundo, la dolce vita, lingua franca, prima donna.*

GERMAN: *Schadenfreude, Sturm und Drang, Weltgeist, Weltanschauung.*

4. Over-used quotations from literature in English

It is perhaps wise to be a little more precise and refine this heading to say that it embraces over-used snippets, allusions, part-quotations and misquotations. These include, pre-eminently, the Bible, especially the King James Version, whose cadences have put down very deep roots in English. The following selection of idiomatic cliché-quotations is the merest smattering, from six random sources.

THE BIBLE: *Strain at a gnat, Swallow a camel, Render unto Caesar, Beware of false prophets, No room in the inn, Fishers of men, The woodworm and the gall, All is vanity, The righteous shall flourish.*

WILLIAM BLAKE: *Ah, sunflower weary of time, Everything that lives is holy, Tiger, tiger burning bright,/In the forests of the night, England's green and pleasant land.*

ROBERT BURNS: *Man's inhumanity to man, A man's a man for a' that, The best-laid schemes (o' mice and men), Great chieftain o' the puddin-race, Facts are chiels (that winna ding), We'll tak a cup o' kindness yet,/For auld lang syne.*

H W LONGFELLOW: *Footprints on the sands of time, I stood on the bridge at midnight, Life is but an empty dream, Sail on, o ship of state, A hurry of hoofs in a village street, Ships that pass in the night, Under a spreading chestnut tree.*

WILLIAM SHAKESPEARE: *Murder, most foul, My salad days when I was green in judgment, A horse, a horse, my kingdom for a horse, O thereby hangs a tale, Thy wish was father, Harry, to that thought, But answer made it none, I am…doomed for a certain term to walk the night, O pardon me thou bleeding piece of earth.*

W B YEATS: *I will arise and go now, I hear lake water lapping (with low sounds by the shore), Too long a sacrifice (can make a stone of heart), Cast a cold eye (on life on death), In dreams begins responsibility.*

Although nearly all commentators are disparaging in their remarks about clichés, they also tend to agree that clichés can be useful, that they do sometimes express ideas that would be hard to express otherwise (especially with a measure of succinctness), that they are not *invariably* trite, and that sometimes they are the best way of saying what you want to say. In which case, it seems to me, use them. They are part of the vast cupboard of the English language, and to lock that door and throw away the key would be cutting off your nose to spite your face (cliché?! – touché!). As Fowler says, 'The hardest-worked cliché is better than the phrase that fails…Journalese results from the efforts of the non-literary mind to discover alternatives for the obvious where none are necessary…'

To describe an expression as a cliché is to make an accusation, which is no real part of lexicography. Before levelling the accusation, it is important to look at the context in which the expression is used and who is using it. Mature and gifted authors at the height of their creative powers tend not to trade much in clichés, certainly not of the throwaway variety. But

when 10-year-old children write that 'smacking children makes them put up their defence barriers', or that someone is 'as old as the hills', or somesuch, they are checking out their command of English by exploring its many nooks and crannies. That has to be encouraged without qualification, and without reference to red herrings like clichés.

Like nostalgia, clichés are not what they were. We may still tend to avoid them in our creative writing classes, but they are perfectly acceptable currency in everyday speech and functional writing. Language nowadays is changing so rapidly that clichés hardly have time to get properly established, and one man's cliché is often another's 'bon mot'. 'Flavour of the month' no sooner approaches cliché-hood than it is spurned as a fuddy-duddy term. Part of our frenetic urge to be up to date seems to ensure that yesterday's lingo now gets scrapped very quickly indeed.

CLIFF. cliff-hanger situation of prolonged and mounting tension. Each episode ended with a real cliff-hanger, which made viewers desperate to know what was going to happen in the next installment.

CLIP. clip someone's wings restrict someone's ability to do something. Losing his job has financially clipped his wings. From the practice of clipping the wings of domestic fowls to prevent them flying away.

CLOAK. cloak-and-dagger melodramatic; involving much clandestine scheming and plotting. I believe he's involved in some sort of mysterious, cloak-and-dagger scheme to persuade the government to sell arms to the rebels. From the appearance and conduct of the stock villains of 17th- and 18th-century comic melodramas.

CLOSE. close ranks act in unison, often defensively. The company's workforce have closed ranks and refuse to speak to the press about the matter. Originally a military description, of soldiers regrouping and moving closer together for mutual protection.

close shave narrow escape. He managed to jump from the sinking vehicle just as it hit the water, but it was a pretty close shave. Also a 'close thing', 'close call' or 'close-run thing' (same meanings). Compare **narrow squeak; near thing**.

close to home rather personal; something about which one is sensitive. Films about the war are too close to home for me – too many members of my family were killed in the war. Compare **near the knuckle/bone**.

CLOSED. closed book 1. mystery; something you know nothing about. All my life, algebra and geometry have been a closed book to me. 2. subject that is closed, and not to be reopened. Don't talk to me about my ex-wife – that is a closed book, as far as I am concerned. Usually used in the context of an argument, quarrel, etc.

CLOUD. cloud cuckoo land fanciful region of unreality unlinked to real life. Don't expect much useful advice from him – he's been living in cloud cuckoo land for years. From an imaginary mid-air city in the ancient Greek comedy of *The Birds*, by Aristophanes (414 BC). Compare **flight(s) of fancy**.

cloud nine place of intense happiness. He's been on cloud nine since he heard the news of his promotion. A US expression dating from the 1950s. Perhaps from the ninth heaven of Dante's Paradise, whose inhabitants were the nearest to God and therefore the most blissfully happy. Compare **seventh heaven**.

CLUED. clued up on something knowledgeable about something. Ask Andrew anything about cars; he's completely clued up on new and second-hand prices, depreciation and so forth.

CLUTCH. clutch at straws be prepared to do anything to get out of a dangerous or desperate

situation. It was clear that he was clutching at straws when he asked to speak to another specialist about his wife's condition. From the proverb, 'A drowning man will clutch at a straw.'

COAST. coast is clear the danger has passed; the way ahead is now open. The company is in financial difficulties, no one is interested in buying it, so the coast is clear for competitors to woo its customers. The original context was military, and referred to coastal defences.

COCK. cock-a-hoop elated; jubilant. Everyone is cock-a-hoop at the news of the cease-fire. Origins uncertain, but probably from 'to set the cock a-whooping.'

cock a leg urinate. Please excuse me for a minute, I need to cock a leg. A euphemism. From the behaviour of a male dog.

cock a snook express derision, contempt or defiance. Now that he's left school, he thinks he can go around cocking a snook at his former teachers. In the 18th century, the expression involved making a rude gesture by putting one's thumb to one's nose and extending the fingers. Compare **thumb one's nose at**.

cock and bull story complicated, ridiculous, or unbelievable story. He started to tell some cock and bull story about finding a bag containing £50,000 in his car. The origins of this expression are unknown, although by the 17th century 'a tale of cock and bull' was the name given to any long, rambling and less-than-credible story.

cock of the walk top man in the pecking order. He may be cock of the walk just now, but there's an election next year and I'm sure he'll lose his seat in Parliament. From the behaviour of farmyard fowls, the 'walk' being the name of the chicken run. By analogy, in North-East Scotland, the Duke of Gordon's nickname was 'Cock o' the North'.

cock something up mismanage something. The marketing department completely forgot to advertise the new product, and hence cocked up the launch.

CODSWALLOP. load of (old) codswallop lot of rubbish or nonsense. I couldn't sit there any longer listening to such a load of old codswallop. The word codswallop is said to be made from 'Mr Codd's wallop', Mr Codd being an enterprising Victorian businessman who made an inferior form of 'wallop', a slang term for beer. See also **mumbo jumbo**.

COIN. coin it make lots of money. It's a very good little neighbourhood business, and it's on an ideal site, so for seven days a week the shopkeeper is coining it.

COLD. cold comfort no comfort at all. So John and Susan also failed the exams, just like me: that's cold comfort, I suppose. A sort of oxymoron, favoured by Shakespeare, as in 'He receives comfort like cold porridge', *The Tempest* ii.1; 'I beg cold comfort', *King John* v.7.

(have/get/take) cold feet (have/get) misgivings; not want to do something one originally agreed to do. The rehearsals went very well indeed, but the leading actor suddenly got cold feet on the first night of the show and for a couple of hours he couldn't be found anywhere. Fear of failing is the usual cause of this condition. In the 16th century, people with cold feet were poor people with no shoes, or no decent ones.

cold fish unemotional and unsympathetic person. He shows no interest in people, and most of the neighbours regard him as a bit of a cold fish.

cold shoulder someone ignore or snub someone. After his offensive behaviour, we just cold shouldered him. Also **give the cold shoulder to someone**. The unexpected guest at a feast might receive some leftovers of cold meat rather than a hot meal.

COLLATERAL. collateral damage unintentional or accidental killing or infrastructure damage that occurs in war. Sadly, the collateral damage in Iraq runs into hundreds of thousands of civilian fatalities in that particular 'war on terror'. Originally a US military euphemism first used in the Vietnam War. Compare **friendly fire**.

COLOUR. colour of someone's money someone's willingness/ability to pay for something. We've stopped supplying that customer's account, because he owes us thousands and we need to see the colour of his money before we supply him with any more goods. It was once common practice to check a coin's colour to see if it was counterfeit.

COME. come a cropper suffer a failure or a serious reverse. He seemed to come a cropper shortly after his promotion to the top job. From horse riding, a 'cropper' was a heavy fall. If you fell 'neck and crop', you fell bodily and heavily.

come again? please repeat that; I beg your pardon? Come again, I didn't quite catch what you said.

come and get it come and eat. Come and get it, she shouted from the kitchen. Originally the basic military version of 'Dinner is served'.

come apart at the seams be in a dilapidated state, on the point of failure, collapse, etc. Sadly, the education system in this country seems to be coming apart at the seams.

come clean admit to or tell the truth about something; make a full confession. After long interrogation, the prisoner finally decided to come clean and explain exactly what had happened.

come down hard on be very strict with. Loutish behaviour by pupils has always been discouraged, and the headmaster comes down very hard on it. The standard simile is 'to come down like a ton of bricks'.

come down in buckets rain torrentially. Don't go out in that rain or you'll get soaked – it's coming down in buckets. Literally, by the bucket-load.

come down in the world live in reduced circumstances, through poverty, etc. They came down in the world quite a lot after the stockmarket crash and the credit crunch.

come down on someone like a ton of bricks punish someone severely; be furious with someone, and turn one's full anger on them. The headmaster came down on them like a ton of bricks when he found them smoking behind the bike sheds. The standard simile.

come down to earth (with a bump/bang/ thud) return to mundane everyday realities after a period of high excitement. She had a wonderful trip to Brazil, so she came down to earth with a bit of a thud when she got home and walked back through her office door. Compare **airy fairy; flight(s) of fancy**.

come/turn full circle return to an earlier fashion, position, etc. Educational fashions, like everything else, come full circle and one day soon we'll have a chance again to see some good class teaching of children sitting in rows at desks and paying attention to what the teacher is saying. From the medieval wheel of fortune, and the view that people's fate rose and fell with it.

come hell or high water come what may; whatever the difficulties. She's decided she's going to write her life-story, come hell or high water. An alliterative dyad.

come in for attract or receive. It was one of the prime minister's worst speeches, and it came in for much critical press comment. A phrasal verb.

come into one's own be able to use one's skills, knowledge, etc. to good advantage. When the conversation turned to Mozart, John got quite animated and came into his own – it turned out that he'd just performed at the Mozart Festival. A metaphor from coming into one's inheritance on the death of parents or at the age of 21.

come into the body of the kirk come forward and join the conversation or the main group of people. He was sitting on his own by the door looking lonely, so we asked him if he'd not rather come into the body of the kirk. Usually an invitation to someone sitting apart. A Scots idiom.

come it be cheeky. The bus driver told the kids that if they tried to come it with him, he'd radio at once for the police. Also exclamatory 'Don't come it!'; 'Don't come the daft lad with me!' or 'Don't come the giddy idiot!'

come off it don't be silly. He told me he never wanted to see his family again, but I told him to come off it and stop exaggerating. Expression used to indicate that one considers a remark stupid, unbelievable, etc. Also exclamatory 'Come off it!'

come on (too) strong/hard overstate one's case. John apologised if he'd got a bit carried away and had come on a bit strong. See also **in your face**.

come out (of the closet) 1. publicly state that one is homosexual. He changed his lifestyle quite a lot after he came out. The closet was where one used to be supposed to keep one's dark secrets. 2. go public on something; admit to a secret interest in something. It took her a long time to come out of the closet as a fan of the royal family. Compare **nail one's colours/flag to the mast**.

come the raw prawn try to fool someone. Don't try to come the raw prawn with me, young man! From the Australian use of 'raw prawn' to mean an act of deception, literally something 'difficult to swallow', from the 1940s.

come to grief fail. It would be a great pity to see all that effort and hard work come to grief. When something fails, it often causes grief.

come to light become known. It was a silly mistake, but it didn't come to light until long after the book was printed.

come to pass happen. The islanders have been petitioning for a bridge for many years, but I don't think it will ever come to pass. A common biblical expression in the Authorised Version: 'And it came to pass, as Jesus sat at meat in the house, behold, many publicans and sinners came and sat down with him and his disciples', in Matthew ix.10; 'All these things must come to pass, but the end is not yet', in Matthew xxiv.6.

come/get to the point reach the nub of the matter. She's one of those annoying people who seem unable to come to the point until they're about to leave you. Opposite of **beat about the bush**, with which this idiom is often bracketed, as in 'Stop beating about the bush, and come to the point.' Compare **point blank**.

come to think of it commonly interjected clause when one has just remembered something. I haven't seen John for ages, and come to think of it, he wasn't at the football match on Saturday. Literally, 'that reminds me'.

come unstuck fail to work out; go wrong. Like so many complicated plans, it came unstuck at an early stage.

come what may no matter what may happen. We're taking a foreign holiday this year, come what may.

come/go with the patch/territory responsibility/ duty that has to be anticipated in the context of a particular assignment, etc. If you marry a film star or into the royal family, you must expect lots of media attention – that's just one of those things that comes with the patch.

COMFORT. comfort zone (one's) sphere of competence. She was invited to talk about the latest developments in nanotechnology, but she declined, saying that was outside her comfort zone.

COMMON. common ground area on which people agree. The best way to settle an argument is to find the common ground between the parties, and then try to build out from that.

common or garden ordinary; not special. It was one of the great French vintages, none of your common-or-garden table wines. From gardening,

where a 'common or garden' variety of plant is the opposite of the exotic cultivar.

common touch ability to get on well with ordinary people. He may be the prime minister but he's never lost the common touch.

COMPARE. compare notes exchange views. While waiting for that day's discussion to begin, John and I compared notes on the events of the previous day.

COMPLIMENTS. compliments of the season usually, Christmas greetings or best wishes, although sometimes another season is implied. He sent me a beautiful bunch of freshly picked Victoria plums from his garden, with the compliments of the harvest season.

CONCRETE. concrete jungle community of inner-city deprivation, usually featuring soulless, high-rise concrete blocks of flats and urban motorways and flyovers. They grew up in the concrete jungle of the east end of London. Not so long ago, we used to think that savages lived in the tropical jungle; but nowadays we know that we in the so-called developed world may be the real savages, as this expression implies. Compare **blackboard jungle**.

CONTRADICTION. contradiction in terms statement containing a contradiction. He told me that, in his view, military intelligence was a contradiction in terms. When this is a deliberate attempt at making a special poetic or humorous impact, it is called an oxymoron, as in expressions like 'cruel kindness', 'reckless caution', 'deafening silence' or 'sublimely bad'.

CONVERSATION. conversation piece item which usually stimulates conversation between strangers. The painting above the fireplace is a large and very striking 18th-century seascape, and an invariable conversation piece at parties. A Victorian term.

COOK. cook someone's goose spoil someone's plans; ruin something for someone. I think the bankruptcy of their main supplier is going to very effectively cook their goose for some time. **If you say, 'His goose is well and truly cooked,' you mean 'He is well and truly in difficulties/trouble, etc.'**

cook the books concoct false financial accounts or records, especially in order to conceal fiscal irregularities. After he was sacked, it was discovered that he'd been cooking the firm's books for some time. Compare **creative accounting**.

COOL. cool as a cucumber extremely calm; unruffled; laid back. There she stood, cool as a cucumber and totally oblivious to the mayhem that was going on all about her. **The standard 'coolness' simile, often a cliché.**

cool, calm and collected audacious, but very relaxed and composed. Considering the nature of his crimes, the prisoner was very cool, calm and collected in his account of what had happened. **An alliterative triad.**

cool one's heels be detained or obliged to wait, especially as a deliberate form of punishment. The police officer decided to leave the two young thugs to cool their heels in the police station overnight.

cool it calm down; relax. Could we please stop shouting and try to cool it for five minutes? **An idiomatic appeal to defuse an explosive situation.**

CORRIDORS. corridors of power higher echelons of government. I told my MP about the problem; he was a government minister and therefore knew his way around the corridors of power. **Now almost a cliché, the phrase is a quotation from C P Snow's political novel** *Homecomings* **(1956, chapter 22): 'The official world, the corridors of power…'**

COST. cost a bomb cost a lot of money. Wait till you see his new car – it must have cost him a bomb. Also 'cost an arm and a leg' (same meaning).

COTTON. cotton on to something realise or understand something. He couldn't quite cotton on to the fact that she didn't want to see him any more. **Probably a variation of the metaphor of 'catching the thread' of something.**

COUCH. couch potato inactive person who spends a lot of time watching television. Most Fridays we're so exhausted that we're happy to spend the evening at home in front of the TV, just like a couple of lazy couch potatoes. **An American idiom of the TV age, usually deployed to convey disapproval of the undiscriminating and vegetable passivity, the inertia and dull slobbishness of the person described, slumped on his couch in front of the box. Compare lounge lizard; mouse potato. Sometimes, a 'sofa loafer'.**

COUNT. count one's chickens (before they're hatched) plan something which unwisely anticipates an event, development, etc. which may not happen. The doctors have told me she should get home from hospital by Christmas, and when she's strong enough I'd like to take her for a holiday – but I shouldn't be counting my chickens too far in advance. **From the popular warning, 'Don't count your chickens before they're hatched.'**

COURAGE. courage of one's convictions moral convictions which are strong enough to motivate one to act on them. He's always telling me about his socialist views on this and that, but there's very little evidence in the way he conducts his life to suggest that he's got the courage of his convictions.

COVER. cover one's back/rear be able to protect oneself against criticism. I always keep the most scrupulous records of business expenditure, knowing how important it is to cover one's back. **Probably influenced by other metaphoric expressions like stab in the back.**

CRACK. crack a joke make a witty remark. The children enjoy the company of their Aunt Eliza, because she's forever cracking jokes and teasing them. The expression reminds us that you do not just 'say' a joke, which would be far too tame in a matter where delivery is all: you deliver it with such zest and sparkle that it 'cracks'.

crack down on someone/something act forcefully against someone/something. The coastguards have cracked down heavily on smugglers over the last few months.

crack of dawn very early in the morning. The raid began at the crack of dawn, to benefit from the element of surprise. If you say of someone that he gets up every morning 'at the crack of noon', you are drawing attention to his laziness, etc. because 'crack' and 'noon', unlike 'crack' and 'dawn', do not normally collocate in this way.

crack of doom eternity. I hope I won't be doing a boring job like this till the crack of doom. The image is of an apocalyptic day of judgment, with lightning cracking and storms raging. Shakespeare used the term, in *Macbeth* iv.1: 'What, will the line stretch out to the crack of doom?' Also 'edge of doom', with the same meaning.

CRACKED. (not all/what it's) cracked up to be (not as wonderful as it's) supposed to be. According to the travel brochure, it was a magnificent hotel, but I can assure you that it was nothing like it was cracked up to be. Often negative.

CRAMP. cramp one's style inhibit one's success, enjoyment, etc. He's very sensitive, and nothing cramps his style so much as a personal criticism – he simply can't bear it.

CRASHING. crashing bore thoroughly boring person. I fell asleep at dinner last night because I was sitting beside a crashing bore. Perhaps the image is of the poor listener's head crashing on a table after falling asleep.

CREAKING. creaking gate/door term used to describe the oxymoron of a healthy invalid. Don't worry about old John – he's been a creaking gate for years and years. Used as a paradoxical criticism based on the proverbial, 'They say a creaking gate hangs long on its hinges.' There

is a hint of moaning minnies behind this expression which is used of invalids who outlive the quieter and apparently healthy folk looking after them.

CREATIVE. creative accounting a euphemism for massaging figures, whether with the aim of making a company's results look better than they are, or to persuade investors to put their money into a business. Earlier euphemisms for this practice were 'cooking the books', or 'pulling the wool over someone's eyes'. The bank took the line that its problems were best glossed over by a spot of creative accounting.

CREATURE. creature comforts any material thing (good food, drink, shelter, warmth, smart clothes, etc.) that contributes towards a person's sense of physical well being. As soon as you entered the flat, it was obvious that here lived a person who valued his creature comforts – and could afford to indulge them to the point of luxury.

CREDIT. credit crunch reduction in availability of loans. Sometimes a verb. Despite the economic downturn the shops have had a good season, and most have been less credit-crunched than expected. The credit crunch of 2008 came about when a number of banks failed or found themselves short of funds because of their own 'toxic debt'.

credit to someone someone or something that brings a person honour or respect. Your thoroughness and tenacity are a credit to you. Also **do someone credit.** Your children do you great credit.

CROCODILE. crocodile tears pretence of tearfulness, grief or sorrow. Her performance was masterly, especially the show of crocodile tears when she referred to the tragic death of her late husband. Everyone knew she really hated his guts. Probably so called because of the alleged deceitfulness of the crocodile, reported by early explorers and travel writers like Mandeville and Haklyut, who claimed that the animal shed tears as it devoured its prey – a story which persisted literally until the 16th century. The key point about crocodile tears is that they are hypocritical and insincere, and therefore not to be trusted.

CROSS. cross a bridge when one comes to it Also plural: cross one's bridges...resolve a problem when it occurs, rather than try to solve it in advance. Let's cross that bridge if and when we come to it.

cross one's fingers hope for good luck. Well – cross your fingers – I think I've managed to fix the car. From the old Christian belief that making the sign of the cross was a protection from harm.

cross one's heart promise. 'I don't believe a word of it.' 'But it's true, cross my heart and hope to die! I swear it's true!' A schoolchild's protestation of truthfulness, based on old Christian practice.

cross one's mind occur to one. She looked so well it never crossed my mind that she was ill.

cross someone's path 1. meet someone casually. I don't think she's crossed my path since we left school 20 years ago. 2. threaten someone who opposes one. I warned him not to cross my path again or I'd thump him. Usually found in the negative.

(at) cross purposes misunderstanding. He's rather deaf and we often find ourselves at cross purposes. Usually refers to two (or more) people.

cross swords quarrel; have a disagreement. I don't like to cross swords with my wife in public. From fencing: combatants crossed swords before the actual engagement.

cross the line offend; behave in an unacceptable or antisocial way. Some of the jokes were pretty crude, and for one or two people in the audience they obviously crossed the line.

cross the Rubicon take a decisive, irrevocable and usually fateful step. After a sleepless night of much agonising, he posted his letter of resignation – and thus crossed the Rubicon. The River Rubicon was the frontier between Italy and Cisalpine Gaul, and Roman generals were forbidden by the Roman Senate to cross the Rubicon into Italy proper. When Julius Caesar crossed it with his army in 49AD therefore, he knew he was directly challenging the authority and the military might of Rome's central government. Compare **the die is cast**.

CRY. cry one's eyes out weep inconsolably. He was crying his eyes out because he'd just seen his dog run over. The idea behind this expression is that one could run out of tears.

cry over spilt milk vainly regret something that has happened and cannot now be rectified. I'm sorry about your car being damaged, but I wouldn't cry over spilt milk if I were you. From the commonsense and semi-proverbial wisdom that spilt milk cannot be put back in the bottle. Often, 'There's no use crying over spilt milk.'

cry wolf give a false warning of danger, etc. by crying unnecessarily for help. He has cried wolf so often that no one pays any attention to him nowadays. From Aesop's fable of the shepherd boy who amused himself by crying 'Wolf!' and frightening the villagers, when no wolf was there. When a real wolf duly appeared, and the boy genuinely needed help, the villagers ignored his cries and all his sheep were killed.

CRYING. crying need urgent need. Many schools are in crying need of repair, textbooks, smaller classes, etc. Literally, crying out for attention, resources, etc.

crying shame great shame. It's a crying shame that the government cannot fund a better education service. Literally, shameful enough to make you want to weep.

CRYSTAL. crystal ball something to help one see into the future and forecast what is going to happen. I regret that I'm not one of those people who can just peer into his crystal ball and tell you whether or not it's going to be a wet day tomorrow. From the glass ball used by fortune-tellers to predict future events.

CULTURE. culture shock feelings of disorientation or anxiety sometimes experienced by people from one society when they enter a very different one. I've been to Nigeria many times, but arriving at Ikeja Airport is always a real culture shock for me. A frequent condition for travellers in the global village.

culture vulture person with an avid interest in the arts. She's always been a bit of a culture vulture.

CUP. one's cup of tea to one's liking, taste, etc. I decided not to go to the concert with them, because pop music isn't my cup of tea. Britons, being very fond of tea since the 17th century, convey genuine disapproval by saying something is not their cup of tea.

CUPBOARD. cupboard love friendly or loving behaviour manifested towards a person who is in a position to supply food, shelter, etc. Our cat always comes purring round my feet and licking me with cupboard love when it's hungry.

CURATE'S. curate's egg something that is good in some ways but not in others. I didn't much enjoy the concert – it was a bit of a curate's egg. Often found in the expression 'like the curate's egg – good in parts.' This derives from a famous cartoon in *Punch* in 1895 showing a curate (a junior priest in the Anglican church) being entertained to high tea by his bishop. Being served a bad egg, and not wishing to appear critical of his host, the curate diplomatically declares that the egg is good in parts.

CURRY. curry favour seek to gain advantage by flattery. He's a perfect example of the totally sycophantic employee, always currying favour with the management. Originally, in popular medieval allegories, from currying (dressing down or grooming) the mythical horse Favel. There were many stories about the currying of Favel, and smoothing him down and flattering him, and by the 16th century the expression had changed to its present form.

CURTAINS. curtains for someone the end of life for someone. It would have been curtains for him if he hadn't just left the room five minutes before the terrorists arrived. From the theatre curtain coming down at the end of the play.

CUSHY. cushy number easy job. He has a nice little cushy number in the civil service. 'Cushy' is from a Hindi word meaning easy, and dates in British army slang from about 1915. It also sounds like 'cushioned', a suitable comparison. Compare **piece of cake**.

CUT. cut above better than. This session there are some really good actors in 5th and 6th year – so the school play is a cut above most of the previous ones I can remember. Also **have an edge on**.

cut and dried prepared or resolved to the smallest detail; clear and definite. He tried to tell me that the plans were all cut and dried, but I told him that I needed to revise several of them. This dyad was originally from a reference to dried herbs.

cut and run make a quick exit; depart at speed. When the police surrounded the building, there wasn't even time to cut and run. Originally nautical, from warships threatened by sudden enemy attack. If there wasn't time to haul in the anchor, the hempen anchor cables were cut, so that the sailing ship could make a run for the open sea.

cut and thrust fierce competition, debate, etc. He decided in the end that he wasn't suited to the frantic cut and thrust of modern advertising. From fencing.

cut both ways have advantages and disadvantages; offer advantages to both parties in an argument, etc. It's a very effective drug for hay fever, but it also tends to make you sleepy – so I'm afraid its effects cut both ways.

cut one's coat to suit one's cloth or **according to one's cloth** make sure one's plans are appropriate to one's resources; adapt to one's circumstances. Life can be quite tough if you suddenly get made redundant, but you just have to try to cut your coat according to your cloth. **A proverbial saying from less socially fluid times, which in the 16th century meant that one should try to live within one's rank and station in life.**

cut corners economise on time, money, materials or effort, perhaps unwisely. It is not a good idea to cut corners with national security.

cut someone dead ignore an acquaintance, or fail to acknowledge that one has seen him, as a sign of one's disapproval, etc. I've cut him dead ever since he insulted my wife.

cut someone down to size make a pompous or self-important person aware of his insignificance in the larger scheme of things; humble someone. If someone doesn't cut the prime minister down to size, he's going to believe he's indispensable.

cut it fine leave a very small amount of time; be almost too late (for something). We've got 10 minutes to check in, so we're cutting it rather fine to catch that plane.

cut it out stop it. They were fooling about and making too much noise, so I told them to cut it out. **Also a simple imperative.** Cut it out! I'm fed up with your fooling about!

cut no ice make no impression; fail to impress. It was a lot of clever talk, but it cut no ice with me I'm afraid. **From American ice-skating. A skater with sharp blades on his skates moves around the ice fast and decisively. A skater with blunt blades makes no impression on the ice, and so makes little progress.**

cut of someone's jib a person's general characteristics and style, and how s/he performs. He's working for us for a trial period of six months; if we like the cut of his jib we'll offer him a permanent post. **The original nautical reference was to how a ship's sails were arranged.**

cut off one's nose to spite one's face harm one's own interests in order to ensure that somebody else gets punished or hurt, usually out of spite, hurt pride, etc. He was so fed up with his boss that he resigned; but with no other job to go to, that seemed a bit like cutting off his nose to spite his face.

cut out for temperamentally, physically etc. suited for. I don't think you're cut out for this kind of work, do you? **Frequently negative. A phrasal verb.**

cut one's teeth on learn and use a basic skill at an early stage of one's development. He enjoys playing the bagpipes now, but first of all he had to spend a few years cutting his teeth on learning to play the chanter. **When one cuts one's eye-teeth, or baby teeth, they emerge through the gums; one is thus emerging from babyhood and (figuratively) becoming more knowledgeable.**

cut the cackle stop the superfluous talk, often implying 'and get to the point'. The teacher told them to cut the cackle and get on with their essays. **An alliterative phrase.**

cut the ground from under someone/ something cause plans to become ineffective or inoperable; sabotage the basis of someone's plans, often unwittingly. We planned to fly up to Glasgow on Tuesday, but the airline strike rather cut the ground from under that idea. **Compare pull the rug from under someone**.

cut the mustard perform very well. He looks quite smart and I'm told he really cuts the mustard on the football pitch, but what else is he good at? **An Americanism, probably linked to keenness, as in keen as mustard. Also 'cut it'.** We gave him a job for six months but he didn't quite cut it, so we fired him.

cut to the chase come/get to the point. There was a bit of humming and hawing before they cut to the chase and told him he wasn't up to the job. **From the hunting field.**

cut to the quick deeply offended. His remarks were very cruel, and cut her to the quick. **The 'quick' is the sensitive skin under the fingernail and is**

very easily hurt. More generally 'quick' used to mean 'living', as in the Bible passages referring to 'the quick and the dead'.

cut up distressed. She was terribly cut up at the news of the tragedy. **A phrasal verb.**

cut up rough get angry and aggressive. When the customer started to cut up rough, the shopkeeper became alarmed and phoned for the police.

CUTTING. **cutting edge** 1. ahead in researching something new. Our parish priest is a darling but he's not exactly at the cutting edge of theological debate. The hospital is right at the cutting edge of stem-cell research. **2. advantage over a competitor, opponent, etc.** His experience of the US market gave him a cutting edge that was lacked by the other candidates for the job.

D

D-day date on which something is scheduled to happen. The scheduled D-days for the opening of the new motorway have twice come and gone, but still we have no motorway. From the so-named secret Allied plan for the invasion of Normandy (6 June 1944), in which 'D' was merely a coded reference. The immediate run-up to the invasion was referred to in terms of 'D-day plus four', etc.

DAB. dab hand at expert or adept at; one skilful at. Try a slice of John's excellent fruit loaf, and I think you'll agree he is a dab hand at baking. In the 17th century, it was enough to say someone was 'a dab at something'. As the word dropped from circulation it lost its independent noun status and became a qualifier, stranded in this fixed phrase.

DADDY. daddy of (them) all ultimate or extreme exemplar of. He woke up yesterday morning with the daddy of all hangovers. I thought I'd seen a few big crocodiles in my time, but that one was the daddy of them all. Compare the slightly more formal **father and mother of all**.

DAFT. daft as a brush very stupid; bereft of intelligence. Anyone who tries to swim across that torrent has to be either desperate or daft as a brush. Originally 'daft as a brush without bristles' (1920s). A standard colloquial simile. Compare **mad as a hatter**.

DAILY. daily dozen workout; series of a dozen physical keep-fit exercises performed daily. Every day, at lunchtime, he goes to a gym and performs his daily dozen.

DAMAGE. damage limitation propagandist effort to gloss a piece of damaging information in the most positive way, preferably without resorting to outright lying. The word of the resignation is out, and the government has to do a bit of nimble damage limitation to ensure that tomorrow's newspapers carry a reasonably appropriate headline.

A contemporary euphemism for giving a favourable slant to a piece of bad news, a job nowadays given to that pundit of political media-speak, the **spin doctor**.

DAMN. damn all nothing at all. She's bone idle, and does damn all around the house even when there's lots to be done.

damn with faint praise compliment something/ someone in such a grudging or ambiguous way that, by implication, one communicates one's dislike of it/them. The critics mostly commented politely that they found her work very interesting, and then quickly changed the subject, which was an effective method of damning her with faint praise. The effect of this sort of comment is deliberately underwhelming. This is an epigrammatic and paradoxical idiom based on a quotation from Alexander Pope's 'Epistle to Dr Arbuthnot' (1735): 'Damn with faint praise, assent with civil leer,/And without sneering teach the rest to sneer…' This in turn may be a reworking of lines from the Prologue to William Wycherley's play *The Plain Dealer* (1677): 'You who scribble, yet hate all who write…And with faint praises one another damn.'

DAMP. damp squib joke or anecdote that peters out or fails to draw a positive response; unlively sort of person. He's a sort of failed comedian who specialises in telling damp squibs about topical events. Don't invite Peter to the party, he's such a damp squib. From damp fireworks that fail to ignite properly, going off 'not with a bang but a whimper' (to paraphrase T S Eliot), and therefore disappoint the children watching them. Also **go off like a damp squib** go badly. Very few people turned up at the reception, which went off like a damp squib. Compare **party pooper**.

DANCE. dance attendance on someone wait on someone in an obsequious or over-solicitous manner. I wish she'd stop dancing attendance on that spoilt child of hers. Usually critical.

DARBY. Darby and Joan elderly and devoted couple. Everybody in the village loved Mr and Mrs Cripps – they were a real Darby and Joan pair, weren't they? It is not known who the eponymous pair were, but the term was in use by the 18th century to describe a couple of humble, contented rustics, as well as a well-matched pair of china figures for the mantelpiece.

DARE. (I) dare say (I) suppose or imagine. He seemed dreadfully upset, so I dare say he may have problems at home. A vestige from the days of more formal speech.

DARK. dark horse mysterious person, about whom little is known; person whose abilities are untested. Members of the party are whispering about Mr X as a dark horse in the leadership stakes. Originally from horse racing, referring to a horse whose form was unknown, the expression was popularised by Benjamin Disraeli. Not to be confused with a **stalking horse**, nor a **horse of a different colour**, nor yet a **black sheep**. Compare **wild card**.

DARKEN. darken someone's door. Never darken my door again: you're not welcome here. Usually found in the negative sense of 'cast a shadow'.

DAVY. Davy Jones's locker a watery grave; the bottom of the sea. It was a dreadful hurricane and sank many boats, mercilessly consigning hundreds of people to Davy Jones's locker. Sometimes simply 'Davy's locker'. In nautical slang, Davy Jones was the devil of the sea and a fearsome piratical personification. It is not known whether there was an eponymous historical figure bearing this name, which is recorded from the mid-18th century.

DAY. day in, day out every day, without respite. He works away on his laptop, day in, day out. The main implication is of monotonous regularity. Similar to **year in, year out**.

some day on some unspecified future occasion. I'd love to visit the Pyramids some day.

DAYLIGHT. daylight robbery gross and blatant overpricing of something. They're asking £5,000 for the painting, which I'd say was nothing but daylight robbery.

DAYS. someone's days are numbered someone is unlikely to survive or succeed for very much longer. If that mine closes as they are threatening, this whole community's days are numbered.

DEAD. dead ahead straight ahead. You can't miss it – first right at the church, then about 400 metres dead ahead you'll see the theatre. 'Dead' here means precisely or exactly. Compare **dead heat**.

dead as a dodo truly dead. Last year's fashions are dead as a dodo today. The dodo was a large, clumsy, flightless bird, once native to the islands of Mauritius and Réunion. It was hunted to extinction by European settlers before the end of the 17th century, so there is no chance of it making a comeback. Hence the finality of this alliterative simile.

dead as a doornail utterly lifeless. I'm afraid there's a body in the garage – and it's as dead as a doornail. A doornail was a large flat-headed nail of a sort once used to stud doors. The simile is long established, having been used in *Piers Plowman* (1362) and by Shakespeare. It probably came about through alliteration rather than through some unspecified link between death and doornails, since 'deaf', 'dumb' and 'dour as a doornail' were also formerly popular idioms. Another standard simile of lifelessness is 'dead as mutton'.

dead beat 1. exhausted. He told the nurse he was dead beat, and needed to lie down for a while. Meaning completely beaten, or tired. 2. useless and sponging idler. He's a complete dead beat, and has never done a day's work in his life. Originally American.

dead cert/certainty utterly predictable outcome. The signs seem to suggest that an autumn election is more or less a dead cert. From gambling on sport.

dead duck someone or something that is unlikely to survive; victim. *He's been told to forget the plan – it's a dead duck now that the funds aren't available. You're a dead duck if you step on one of those mines.* Compare **come a cropper** and **dead letter**.

dead end 1. cul-de-sac. *He lives in a nice, quiet dead-end street with very little traffic.* 2. situation, job, etc. with no prospects of improvement. *She had climbed the career ladder by her early 30s, and spent the rest of her working life in a bit of a dead-end job.*

dead eye good marksman. *I asked for a kilo of tomatoes, and when the assistant weighed them out on her scales they weighed exactly that amount. 'Dead eye!' she said, with a smile.* **'Dead' here means exact, or unerring.**

dead from the neck up dull; bereft of wit or intelligence. *Why send him to college if the child's dead from the neck up?*

dead heat race in which two or more competitors cross the finishing line simultaneously. *It was an exciting race right to the finish, with Jones and Christie declared the joint winners in a dead heat even after the judges replayed the film of the race several times.*

dead letter something that has lost its urgency or authority, without being formally abandoned or abolished. *There's no point discussing that notion any further – it's a dead letter now because there aren't any funds to implement it.* Compare **dead duck**.

dead loss completely useless or hopeless person or thing. *That goalie was a dead loss – he let 10 goals into the net.*

dead man empty wine, beer or spirit bottle. *There were several bottles lying about the room, but unfortunately they were all dead men.* **The expression does not apply to lemonade or milk or vinegar, etc. bottles. Only alcoholic drink tends to be favoured with humanising metaphors of this**

sort, as in 'A pint of plain is your only man' (Flann O'Brien).

dead of night middle of the night, when it is darkest. *At dead of night they crept up to the house and surrounded it.* **An atmospheric idiom, scary and spooky.**

dead ringer (for) close or exact likeness (to). *Standing in that light, she's a dead ringer for her mother 20 years ago.* **Originally from the idea of something that 'rings' false. A 'ringer' was a fake or imposter, and once referred to a horse deceptively substituted for another in a race. 'Dead' is a colloquial intensifier.**

dead set 1. very keen. *She's dead set on becoming a violinist.* 2. determined attempt to gain a friend, lover, etc. *It was clear he was completely in love with her, for he was making a dead set at her.*

dead to the world fast asleep; unconscious; oblivious to what's going on around one. *He was lying on the sofa in front of the TV, dead to the world and snoring loudly.*

DEAR. dear knows nobody knows, including the speaker. *Dear knows what she wants to complain about now.* **Originally 'dear God knows' or 'dear goodness knows'.**

DEATH. (catch/get one's) death of cold (get) a very bad cold. *Don't go out in weather like this without a coat or you'll catch your death (of cold).*

death trap dangerous building, piece of road, etc. that is potentially very dangerous to life. *I hate that A77 road – it's a real death trap.*

death's door close to death. *Knowing she was at death's door, she asked to see a priest.* **From the English Prayer Book.**

DEEP. (in) deep water (in) difficult circumstances, or a situation which one cannot easily get out of. *He got into very deep water when he tried to criticise the way they ran their business.* **Also 'in deep shit/doodoo'. Compare up to one's neck.**

DEFICIT. deficit spending the spending of money raised by borrowing rather than by taxation. The only way the chancellor could come up with the funds was by inaugurating a form of deficit spending. A euphemistic oxymoron for government incompetence, many would say, and now a generally discredited kind of economics.

DELIVER. deliver the goods achieve what one undertakes to achieve; fulfil one's promises. They're bright folk with bright ideas, but can they deliver the goods? American in origin; compare **do the business**.

DEMOB. demob happy looking forward to a holiday or break. The kids couldn't settle properly to their classwork today, being excited and demob happy in anticipation of their mid-term break. 'Demob' is short for 'demobilisation' or disbandment of military personnel, and the expression was widely known after both world wars among uniformed men and women about to return to 'Civvy Street', i.e. civilian life.

DEO. Deo volente/d.v. God willing. I'll see you next week d.v. A straight translation from Latin, which was the language of the Roman Catholic church. Still widely heard in predominantly Catholic countries such as the Irish Republic. Sometimes written with capital letters. Similar to **fingers crossed**.

DESIGNER. designer stubble makings of a beard, rather than a properly grown one. He was a familiar figure on our TV screens, with his trendy clothes and good-looking designer stubble. This look has been fashionable among young designers and arty men since the 1980s. Compare **five o'clock shadow**. There is a sporadic and rather snobbish media tendency to use 'designer' as an adjective adhering to the least likely nouns. It started in the fashion industry of the 1980s and soon spread from 'designer clothes' to 'designer water', 'designer living', 'designer socialism', etc.

DEVIL. devil may care reckless or carefree. I'm not at all surprised that he's crashed the car again – he is a real devil-may-care driver.

devil take the hindmost don't waste time worrying about the stragglers. Never mind about anyone else's right to the job – just apply for the promotion yourself and devil take the hindmost. A phrase from the saying 'Every man for himself and the devil take the hindmost.' Another version of that classic of selfish advice, '**look after number one**'.

devil to pay dire consequences are likely. There will be the devil to pay if you lose that necklace. The idiom is medieval, and the reference is to the Faustian bargains made by wizards and magicians selling their immortal souls to Satan for worldly advantage, and to the ultimate and inevitable price paid in the end – the loss of their souls, the direst thing that could befall a medieval Christian. See also **between the devil and the deep blue sea**.

DEVIL'S. devil's advocate person presenting the opposing or less-accepted point of view, especially for the sake of argument. His role in the business was essentially negative – he was nothing more than a sort of devil's advocate to the creative ideas of the editorial department. Originally a Papal appointment, the 'advocatus diaboli' or devil's advocate had the job in the Roman Catholic church of critically examining and formally opposing candidates for canonisation or beatification by putting across the devil's point of view.

DICE. dice with death risk death or serious repercussions. Don't even look at my girlfriend unless you like to dice with death – for I'm a very jealous person. Often used hyperbolically or humorously nowadays. From playing a game of dice with death, which of course humans cannot win. Compare **die is cast**.

no dice no success or luck. I asked for a bank loan, but no dice – they said I was too big a risk.

DICKENS. dickens of a very serious. I'm afraid the business is in a dickens of a mess. 'Dickens' is a corruption of the word 'devilkin', or little devil, and has nothing to do with Charles Dickens. See also **what the dickens**.

DIE. die for something want something very much indeed. He's been dying to see you all week. Hence the more recent version of this hyperbole, the idea of something 'to die for', or something wanted to the point of total and life-denying desire. You should have seen their chocolate gateaux – they were to die for! Compare **give one's right arm for something**.

die hard struggle hard to survive; disappear reluctantly and very slowly. These old country traditions die hard.

the die is cast an unalterable decision has been reached, or step taken. She agonised about the decision for several days, but eventually she posted the fateful letter with a sigh, saying, 'Now the die is cast!' A translation of an ancient Greek proverb, meaning that once the dice were thrown players had to abide by the results, however uncomfortable; they could not be unthrown. 'Die' is the old singular of 'dice', the latter being originally and exclusively a plural noun. Julius Caesar knew this proverb, and quoted it when in 49BC he disobeyed the Roman senate and crossed the Rubicon with an army and uttered his famous words 'Alea iacta est'. Compare **cross the Rubicon** and **dice with death**.

DIFFERENT. different as chalk from cheese extremely unalike. Nobody guessed they were sisters – in appearance as well as temperament they were as different as chalk from cheese. A standard comparison, of two alliterative substances of very different consistency.

different ball game/ball park another subject; entirely different matter. First he wanted a new car, but now he's also asking for a pay rise, and that – as you know – is a different ball park. Common in business-speak. See also **ballpark figure; something else (again)**.

different strokes for different folks different people have different requirements. OK, so the guy's gay. What of it – different strokes for different folks! There was a sexual overtone to the original expression, a Black US idiom which became the title of a TV series in the late 1970s, and really means 'each to his own tastes'. Compare **live and let live**.

DIG. dig in one's heels refuse to agree to something; decline to authorise something, etc. I'm afraid I just had to dig in my heels and say there would be no party that year.

dig the dirt try to find stories, etc. that will embarrass a person or damage their reputation. There's nothing the British tabloid press like better than digging the dirt on some hapless MP. Also 'dig for dirt' or 'dig up dirt'. Having found something suitably titillating or salacious, investigative journalists then like to **dish the dirt**, an activity which provides them with huge job satisfaction.

DILLY. dilly-dally take one's time over something that could be done quickly. She's a terrible dilly-dally, so don't expect her to get the job done quickly. A reduplication which can be used as verb or noun, probably by analogy with another 18th-century formation, **shilly-shally**.

DIRE. dire straits difficult financial conditions or circumstances. The family have been in dire straits since the father's death. 'Straits' are distressed or constricted circumstances. 'Dire' is an intensifier, meaning 'extreme' or 'terrible'.

DIRT. dirt cheap very cheap. It's quite a famous painting, but luckily enough I was able to buy it dirt cheap in a junk shop. Literally, as cheap as dirt.

DIRTY. dirty linen private information publicly exposed, often resulting in distress or embarrassment. Can we talk about this later, please – I don't think the assembled gathering is all that interested in our dirty linen.

dirty look unfriendly expression in one's face. I got a dirty look when I asked how they expected to fund their project. Also 'a black look'.

dirty money money which may be stolen or dishonestly acquired. The organisation is rumoured to be funded by dirty money from the mafia and other racketeers. The expression led in due course to the concept of 'money laundering'.

dirty old man lecherous male, displaying aspirations/actions appropriate to younger men. Watch him – he's nothing but a dirty old man. Sometimes abbreviated to 'DOM'.

dirty word objectionable term. Profit is said to be a dirty word among old-fashioned socialists. Originally, the reference was to oaths and swear words, but nowadays the context usually indicates one form or other of social or political prejudice.

dirty work 1. uncongenial work. It's not fair; why should I do all the dirty work, but he gets to take the clients out to lunch? 2. **dirty/funny work (at the crossroads)** dubious behaviour. I'm not sure how he got the job, but most people suspect there was a bit of dirty work at the crossroads. The innuendo is that there is more to something than meets the eye, even perhaps a hint of foul play. The crossroads reference brings in the dilemma: which way to look? Compare the more neutral **behind the scenes**; see also **the plot thickens**.

DISAPPEAR. disappear into thin air vanish completely and without trace. I put four cakes on that table two minutes ago, and now they've disappeared into thin air.

DISCRETION. discretion is the better part of valour wise people avoid taking unnecessary risks. When the students started throwing rotten eggs at him, the speaker decided that discretion was the better part of valour and left the building by a side door. A saying from popular wisdom. In his *Lytton Strachey* (1967), the phrase spawned Michael Holroyd's now-famous epigram, 'Discretion is not the better part of biography.'

DISH. dish the dirt spread scandal or malicious gossip. C'mon, dish the latest dirt on Mr X for us, will you? American, with 'dish' meaning to serve up some gossip to an expectant audience.

DO. do a double take take a second look at something surprising, interesting, etc.; often a delayed reaction after an initial failure to perceive anything out of the ordinary. I had to carry a very real-looking rubber skeleton down the street in the rush hour, and several people stopped and did a quick double take. From film making, a 'take' being a scene shot without interruption.

do a runner escape or disappear. A couple of kids did a runner from the camp, because they were homesick. Literally, run away from something without paying, without permission, etc. Also 'do a moonlight'; see **moonlight flit**.

do away with someone/something 1. get rid of or abolish something. Countries within the European Union have now done away with physical customs barriers between member states. 2. **kill someone secretly**. It is now widely known that King Richard III did away with the Princes in the Tower. A euphemism.

do one's bit assist. In a small firm like this, everyone has to do his bit.

do someone down denigrate someone; cheat someone. She obviously hates that man, and cannot miss an opportunity to do him down.

do someone in kill someone. Burke and Hare were two famous body-snatchers who made their living by doing old folk in and then selling their corpses for medical research.

do one's nut become infuriated, and lose one's composure. He can't stand cheeky kids and with that class of troublemakers he soon did his nut.

do or die win or die in the attempt; make one's final or greatest effort. The medieval knights thought it was a glorious thing to do or die for their king on the battlefield.

do someone out of something unfairly prevent someone from acquiring something. At the eleventh hour, someone persuaded him to change his will and do his children out of their inheritance.

do someone over physically beat someone up. A bunch of hooligans attacked him in the street for no reason, and proceeded to do him over.

do one's own thing follow one's own inclinations. They keep trying to organise me to go on trips with them, when all I want is to be left alone to do my own thing. A once-cool hippy expression of the 1960s. Compare **paddle one's own canoe**.

do someone proud/handsome entertain someone lavishly. They often entertained us to dinner, and they always did us proud.

do the business do what is expected of one, or what has to be done. Come on then, let's try and do the business before lunch time. American. Compare **deliver the goods**.

do the dirty on someone play a dirty, or unfair, trick on someone. Churchill may have won the war for Britain, but afterwards the electorate did the dirty on him and voted him out of government.

do the honours fulfil the role of host/ess. John, would you be good enough to do the honours and pour everyone a glass of sherry, please.

do the trick successfully achieve a result. If you want to stop a bout of hiccups, try to hold your breath for as long as possible – sometimes that does the trick.

do something to death repeat something too often with the result that it becomes boring. He may love listening to the 'Hallelujah Chorus', but there's such a thing as doing it to death – couldn't he listen to something else once in a while, just for a change?

do something up redecorate or improve something, i.e. a house, room, car, etc. They bought an old tumbledown cottage in the country, and are planning to do it up.

DODGY. dodgy dossier a suspicious official file or document, often with contents protected by the Official Secrets Act. The original dodgy dossier was transformed in the week before it was published to make it more persuasive of public opinion. It dated from 2003 and the wholly invented Iraqi 'weapons of mass destruction'. This alliteration is a gift of the Blair government to the English language; see also **sex (something) up** and **spin doctor**.

DOG. dog collar clerical collar worn by many Christian ministers of religion. I didn't realise he was a priest, because he wasn't wearing a dog collar. So called from its similar appearance to the collar worn by dogs.

dog days hottest period of the summer. With no air conditioning, it is quite hard to work through the dog days of summer in New York. The name is Roman, from *dies caniculares*, which was the hot and humid period in July and August when wealthy Romans left the city for the Trasimene lake and other cooler resorts. During this period, the constellation of the dog-star Sirius was prominent in the night sky.

dog eat dog expression which usually describes a ruthlessly competitive business environment. You have to be pretty sharp to survive in the dog-eat-dog world of the media and advertising. From the doctrine of the survival of the fittest.

dog in a/the manger spiteful killjoy; person witholding from others something useless to himself. Having had the book for years and never read it, as soon as I asked to borrow it he decided in a rather dog-in-the-manger fashion that he'd like to read it himself. From Aesop's fable of the spoilsport hungry dog. It could find nothing to eat, so it decided to prevent the hungry ox from enjoying its meal of hay and sat in the ox's stall snapping at it whenever it attempted to eat.

dog watch on the lookout during the early morning hours of sleep, when the human metabolism is at its least dynamic. It wasn't till his turn came to keep awake during the dog watch that he had time to sit there and contemplate the awfulness of their predicament. **Nautical, specifically refers to the two half-watches between the hours of 4 and 6 a.m. and 6 and 8 a.m. Most people, during this period, are of course drowsy, and very often 'dog tired'.**

DOG'S. dog's breakfast/dinner mess. You should see their filing system – I'd call it a complete dog's breakfast!

dog's chance very poor chance. He applied for the job, although he knew he probably hadn't a dog's chance of getting it.

dog's life miserable existence. It was a very unhappy marriage, and they led each other a dog's life.

DOLCE. (la) dolce vita life of luxury and self-indulgence. She doesn't live here any more – she's gone to Hollywood looking for the dolce vita. **An Italian expression, meaning 'the sweet life' of high society, it was the title of a famous film by Federico Fellini (1960).**

dolce far niente life of delightful idleness. He still dreams from time to time of retiring to a desert island and a life of dolce far niente. **An Italian expression popular in English in the 19th century, it literally means 'doing sweet nothing.' It sounds a bit precious nowadays.**

DOMINO. domino theory theory of the cumulative or knock-on effect, when one event initiates a sequence of similar events. The domino theory tells me that if we lose client X, client Y will not be far behind. **A metaphor from the game played with 28 rectangular pieces which can be so arranged that by knocking one down, they all fall down. The term was often used by American politicians during the Cold War to describe the spread of communism, i.e. if South Vietnam fell to communism, Cambodia would be the next to go, etc. Also 'domino effect'.**

DONE. done for likely to die or fail; in serious

trouble. Anyone trying to sail a boat in a gale like that is done for, I'm afraid.

done thing acceptable social behaviour; good form. It isn't really the done thing for a young person to speak like that to a distinguished elder statesman.

done to death used or repeated too many times. I don't think I could bear to hear his jokes again – he's done them to death long since.

DONKEY. donkey work hard, physical work; drudgery. She loves pottering in the garden, but she has a man in to attend to the donkey work like digging and rolling the lawn. **From the donkey's role as a domestic beast of burden.**

DONKEY'S. donkey's years a very long time. I hadn't seen him in donkey's years, and we had a lot to talk about. **Donkeys are not particularly noted for longevity, and the original expression was thought to have been 'not for as long as a donkey's ears', and of course donkeys are noted for big ears.**

DON'T. don't (even) go there or **let's not go there** don't (even) consider doing something. 'Do you realise we could be put in jail for this?' 'Oh, let's not even go there!' **An apostrophic figure of speech, a recent variant of perish the thought. Compare moving swiftly on.**

don't knock it don't criticise it. Don't knock it if you haven't tried it. **1930s American in origin.**

don't mention it formal British English expression used to acknowledge thanks. 'Many thanks for all your help.' 'Oh, don't mention it.' **Also 'you're welcome.'**

don't put all your eggs in one basket spread one's risks, efforts, etc. rather than concentrate everything on a single venture. She's applying for several jobs, knowing not to put all her eggs in one basket. **A proverb.**

don't shoot the messenger don't blame the bearer of bad news for the information itself. The civil servant who spoke to the press was sacked, but the government minister who caused the scandal got off scot-free: it was the usual case of shooting the messenger.

DOSE. dose of one's own medicine receive the same unpleasant treatment one gives to others. I'm told he's lost his job – which is a dose of his own medicine for someone who's made so many people redundant in the past.

DOT. dot the i's and cross the t's be meticulous and precisely accurate; take care over the details of something. He chucked me a first draft of the report, telling me he wanted someone to flesh it out a bit, then dot the i's and cross the t's and give him a final version for a press release by 6 o'clock that evening.

DOUBLE. double-barrelled name two surnames usually hyphenated. A lot of British aristocrats have double-barrelled names, such as Armstrong-Jones, Douglas-Home and Bowes-Lyon. A metaphor from the double-barrelled firearm (late 17th century), which had double impact because it could fire twice.

double bind dilemma; quandary. He was in a real double bind – whether to attempt to rescue his colleague, and probably kill himself in the process; or leave him and run for help, and probably get lost. A technical term from modern psychology, meaning conflicting advice to a child or dependant from a parent, teacher, etc.

double dutch anything incomprehensible; gibberish. Somebody said they were talking Gaelic, but it sounded like a lot of double dutch to me. Another piece of English chauvinism against their one-time Dutch rivals which is now embedded in the language. Compare **dutch auction; dutch courage**, etc. and **(it's all) Greek to me**.

double quick very quickly. The roof looked as if it would collapse any minute, so we all left the building double quick. From the military parade ground, where 'double-quick march' is a comically fast marching time.

double talk stating one thing but implying something else. I'm fed up with her double talk, and I wish she'd get to the point. Compare **speak with forked tongue; two-faced**.

double time period when an hourly paid worker is paid double the hourly rate for the job. We were paid double time for working over the weekend and getting the shop ready for opening on Monday.

DOUBTING. doubting Thomas habitually doubtful person, i.e. one who doubts everything until he sees the hard evidence in front of him. He'll have a hard time convincing all those doubting Thomases that he can do the job. From the Bible: Thomas was the apostle who doubted the resurrection of Jesus until he had touched the nail-marks in his hands.

DOWN. down and out homeless or penniless person. London seemed to be full of dossers and down and outs during the early 1990s. A dyad from the boxing ring, referring to a fighter who has been knocked down by his opponent and counted out by the referee. Nowadays there is also an echo of the title of George Orwell's autobiographical *Down and Out in Paris and London* (1933), describing the author's impoverished young manhood.

down at heel shabby; unkempt. They live in a flat in a rather down-at-heel Victorian mansion which has seen better days. From the literal meaning, of shoes that need mending and which, by implication, the wearer is too poor to repair.

down in the dumps unhappy; in low spirits; in melancholy mood. Mary has been very down in the dumps this week, and nobody can cheer her up.

down in the mouth miserable looking; discouraged. The kids looked very down in the mouth this morning when I told them we'd have to postpone our holiday.

down payment part payment, made or put 'down' at the time of purchase, with the balance to be paid later. He made a down payment of

£5,000 on the car, and will pay the remainder by Christmas.

down the hatch humorous exclamation or toast, an alternative to 'Cheers!' or 'Bottoms up!' and generally spoken with a glass raised. The 'hatch' is the mouth down which the libation is tipped.

down the line in the future. Who knows what they'll be doing or where they'll be two or three years down the line. A spatio-temporal railway metaphor of life's journey.

down the tube/pan/drain/plughole lost; abandoned; completely spoiled or wasted. When he started to take drugs, we could only stand by in dismay and watch a brilliant career go down the tube.

down to earth practical and straightforward; realistic. His advice is worth seeking out, as it is bound to be down to earth. Opposite of **airy fairy**.

down tools cease working. At 2.30 precisely, the entire school downed tools and went home to have a siesta.

Down Under Australia and New Zealand. TV soaps from Down Under were once very popular in Britain. A British colloquialism arising from the idea that these countries are straight through the globe of the earth, literally down under Britain.

DOWNWARD. downward adjustment downward revision of an estimate. Their budgeted profit of £10 million is not now achievable, and there has had to be a substantial downward adjustment in their forecast. A euphemism for a poorer than anticipated performance.

DRAG. drag one's feet act reluctantly or without enthusiasm. He's supposed to be making a business trip to Egypt but for some reason his manager is dragging his feet about letting him go.

drag someone's name in/through the mud by bad behaviour, etc. bring disgrace to someone's reputation. By their appalling conduct, the rampaging football hooligans have once more dragged their club's name in the mud. Compare **(one's) name is mud**.

DRAW. draw a blank fail to remember or find something/someone. I've tried all the Mitchells in the telephone directory, but I've still drawn a blank. From 'blank' lottery or raffle tickets which, unlike numbered ones, win no prizes.

draw a parallel make an analogy or comparison. I don't think you can draw a parallel between these two events – they have nothing in common.

draw a veil (over) keep discreetly private; refrain from discussing. Some very cruel things were said in the heat of the moment, but we'll draw a veil over all that.

draw blood cause deep offence. Judging from the fury of her reaction to your comments, some of what you said has drawn blood.

draw/pull in one's horns economise; act in a less assertive way. Last winter we had to draw in our horns a bit to manage within our reduced income. Probably from the behaviour of some snails, which draw in their horns when threatened.

draw the/a line at refuse to authorise/do. I offered to help, but I drew the line at letting them come and stay with me for a month.

draw the short straw back a losing option; choose a loser. He drew the short straw and got the hard job of breaking the dreadful news. From the old chance game, of choosing straws from a clenched hand; after the choice was made and the fist was unclenched, the result was known – the loser being the person with the shortest straw.

DRESSED. dressed to kill dressed to attract attention. She arrived at the studio dressed to kill. Literally, so well decked out that one kills the chance of any sartorial competition.

dressed (up) to the nines very formally dressed in one's best clothes; over-dressed. Some people still get all dressed up to the nines when they go to the opera, in order to show themselves off in their finery during the interval. Perhaps from the idea that 10 equalled perfection, so nine was pretty high in the ratings. This expression may be a corruption of 'dressed up to the eyes', which had a similar meaning.

DRESSING. dressing down scolding. He received a severe dressing down for his drunken and loutish behaviour, and quite right too. Originally equestrian: horses are brushed or 'dressed down' after exercise. Compare **tear strips off someone**.

DRIBS. in dribs and drabs in small amounts and at irregular intervals. The client was unable to give me the whole job to work on at once, but wanted to hand it over in dribs and drabs. Perhaps an attempt at a more assonant variation of 'in drips and drops'.

DRINK. drink in the last-chance saloon have one's final opportunity to succeed at something. The prime minister fails to realise that one more ministerial resignation will see him drinking in the last-chance saloon. From US cowboy movies, and the penultimate scene before the shoot-out.

drink like a fish drink very substantial amounts of alcohol. A lot of these workmen drink like a fish as soon as they receive their pay packet, so they are not very reliable wage earners. A standard simile for someone who habitually drinks too much alcoholic liquor.

drink (to) someone's health wish good health to someone by raising one's glass and drinking a toast to them. After the speeches, the diners all raised a glass and drank the president's health.

drink someone under the table be able to drink large amounts of alcohol and remain conscious when similar amounts would render another person unconscious. He has a prodigious capacity for whisky and could drink any of us under the table. When a medieval big shot threw a feast and his guests failed to drink themselves under the table, he was probably deemed to have been less than hospitable.

DRIPPING. dripping roast something which provides income long after the work which made it profitable has been completed. The book was a bestseller, and the royalties from it have been a dripping roast to its author for many years. From cooking, and the idea that a really succulent and well-cooked roast should continue to drip for some time after it has been cooked.

DRIVE. drive a coach and horses through something clearly demonstrate the inadequacy of something. If the secretary of state allows the building of a new hospital on that prime agricultural site, he is driving a coach and horses through government's green-belt policy. The expression is attributed to Sir Stephen Rice of the Irish Exchequer, a Roman Catholic, who in 1670 opposed the Act of Settlement (of Protestants) in that country, and threatened to breach it in this colourful way.

drive a nail in the/someone's coffin hasten the end or failure of something; destroy something. All these wars drive more nails in the coffin of world peace.

drive something home make something thoroughly understood. For years, the government has been trying to drive home the need for us all to curb inflation.

drive someone round the bend/twist annoy or exasperate someone beyond toleration. I can't stand that programme; it drives me right round the twist. Also 'drive someone nuts/loopy/mad/up the wall/to distraction', similar meanings.

drive/force something/someone to the wall force something/someone out of business or into a hopeless situation, such as bankruptcy. It is one of the myths of capitalism that inefficient businesses are usually driven to the wall. The metaphor is of a cornered individual with nowhere to run to. Also used of a failed venture: 'go to the wall'. Compare **back(s) to the wall**. Compare **(something) nips your head**.

DROIT. droit de seigneur lordly privilege. The new boss is a lecherous type who thinks he has some sort of droit de seigneur over all the secretaries in the typing pool. From French, and the supposed legal or customary right ('droit') – some say it was a male fantasy – of the 'seigneur' or feudal lord to have sexual intercourse with a female peasant on her wedding night, if he chose to exercise that right. This was called the law of the first night, or 'ius primae noctis'.

DROP. drop a bombshell make an unexpected, startling or disturbing announcement. She couldn't have dropped a bigger bombshell if she'd told me she wanted to marry my brother.

drop a brick/clanger say something tactless, inappropriate and often hurtful. I dropped a bit of a clanger when I asked how her husband was – he had died the previous week. The noise of a clanger is presumably harsh, echoic and painful on the ear – not something that can be easily ignored, muffled or brushed aside without proper response.

drop a hint suggest, without making an open statement. There was an article in yesterday's paper which I now realise dropped a hint that the factory might be in difficulty.

drop a line send a brief letter. I promised to drop her a line to let her know I'd arrived home safely.

drop dead 1. expression of anger asking someone to go away, stop bothering one, etc. Most of the businesses he approached for funds didn't just say no, they more or less told him to drop dead. Similar to **take a running jump**. 2. a flavour-of-the-month adjective from the 1990s, used as an intensifier. Wait till you see his sister – she's drop-dead gorgeous.

drop in the bucket/ocean insignificant amount. He gives a proportion of his monthly income to that charity, but he knows it's only a drop in the ocean for them. Biblical, from Isaiah xl.15: 'Behold, the nations are as a drop in a bucket, and are counted as the small dust of the balance; behold, he taketh up the isles as a very little thing.'

drop the pilot dismiss the political leader (who has been piloting the ship of state). Things may be pretty desperate, but I don't think this is a very good time to drop the pilot. From J Tenniel's famous captioned cartoon of Kaiser Wilhelm II's dismissal of Bismark in a sea pilot's uniform (*Punch*, March 29, 1890), titled 'Dropping the pilot'.

DROWN. drown one's sorrows drink alcoholic beverage with the aim of deadening the pain of some disappointment, setback, etc. Their team lost the match and all keen supporters afterwards went to the pub to drown their sorrows. From the popular fallacy that 'Malt does more than Milton can to justify God's ways to man' (A E Housman, *A Shropshire Lad*, 1896).

DRUGSTORE. drugstore cowboy good-for-nothing person. There she was – married to a no-good drugstore cowboy. An American expression from the drugstore culture of the 1920s, originally referring to a young man who dressed up as something he wasn't.

DRUNK. drunk as a lord/coot/skunk very drunk. By bedtime most nights he was as drunk as a skunk. Standard similes of inebriation.

DRY. dry as a bone very dry. After the drought, half the reservoirs were as dry as a bone. A standard simile, giving the compound adjective 'bone-dry'.

dry someone out cure someone of alcoholism. He's been sent on a residential course for people with drink problems in an attempt to dry him out.

dry run rehearsal; trial or practice exercise. The city chambers are closed today because they're having a dry run in preparation for next week's royal visit. Originally American military, referring to the firing of weapons without live ammunition. Similar to **dummy run**.

DULL. dull as ditchwater deadly, crashingly boring; skull-numbingly tedious. He gave a long rambling speech in a voice which was as dull as ditchwater. **A standard simile.**

DUMMY. dummy run practice or trial rehearsal, made to check if something works. It isn't the sort of job where you can set up a dummy run, so we'll just have to wait and see if the contraption works or not after it's unveiled. **Similar to dry run.**

DUTCH. dutch auction public sale at which items are offered at a high price, the price being slowly lowered until somebody buys them. She had few belongings, and they were quickly disposed of by a sort of dutch auction among her erstwhile neighbours. **According to English custom, where items were sold to the highest bidder, this was the wrong way around and therefore a procedure only worthy of their once-hated rivals, the Dutch.**

dutch courage artificially induced feelings of bravery, acquired through the consumption of alcohol. Knowing how nervous he could get, he had a large whisky before the wedding in order to try to acquire a bit of dutch courage. **The original implication was of basic cowardice, and the expression dates to the 17th century when the English had nothing nice to say about their mercantile rivals the Dutch.**

dutch treat outing at which one pays or provides food for oneself. It was a nice party, but it was something of a dutch treat since we all had to bring our own food. **Originally a disparaging reference to supposed Dutch meanness from the days of the 17th century, when England felt threatened by that country. See also go dutch.**

dutch uncle person who gives advice in a kindly but pedantic and long-winded manner. He's really a very sincere person though he sometimes talks to young people like a dutch uncle. **Dating from the 17th century, when Englishmen could apparently only refer to the Dutch in terms of contempt or derision.**

DUTY. duty bound obliged by one's duty (to do something). Do you not realise that I am duty bound to report any breaches of security to the guards?

DYED. dyed in the wool inveterate and uncompromising; unshakably fixed in one's views. As a dyed-in-the-wool socialist he tends to get a bit worked up about topics like the national health service and private education. **From the idea that the colours hold fast in a well-dyed fabric; so too a person's fixed opinions are not easily shifted.**

DYAD

Dyads, or doublets, are pairs of words that commonly collocate. The word dyad is from Greek *dyo* (= two). Fowler called dyads Siamese Twins. They are plentiful in but not peculiar to English. Examples are:

aid and abet, alarums and excursions, alive and kicking, best bib and tucker, (every) nook and cranny, footloose and fancy free, hearts and minds, hue and cry, high and dry, might and main, movers and shakers, null and void, pick and choose, rack and ruin, rank and file, rock and roll, sackcloth and ashes, scot and lot, spick and span, tooth and nail, well and truly.

One suggestion for their frequency in English is that dyads became popular during the Norman period, being often made up of one Anglo-Saxon and one Norman French component, as in *goods and chattels, full and plenty, might and main*. This was one sure way of ensuring understanding in a bilingual society. Certainly we find dyads aplenty in Chaucer and Caxton. And certainly the 'crafted' prose style which popularised much Middle English in the 14th to 16th centuries had many characteristics which have been retained by the dyad; these include alliteration, assonance, rhyme and balanced constructions and patterns. Alliterative dyads include *bag and baggage, brightest and best, chop and change, dribs and drabs, rack and ruin, safe and sound, slow but sure, warp and woof.* Assonance or rhyme gives *fair and square, happy clappy, high and dry, naming and shaming, wear and tear,* etc. All these features were once meant to ensure a convention of stylised linguistic elegance. And they remain the blood and bone of English.

Recent dyads are, for the most part, slightly underwhelming: *shock and awe* (from the US bombing of Baghdad), *suited and booted* (= dressed up), *rights and responsibilities* (a political cliché?), *down and dirty* (coarse and unscrupulous), *no pain no gain* (well known in Puritan philosophy).

Dyads may be adjectives, adverbs, nouns or verbs. Because of their age, many dyads retain lexical components which are otherwise obsolete in English; see the individual entries for *best bib and tucker, goods and chattels, meet and right, might and main, spick and span.* It is partly this etymological opacity which today makes dyads indubitably idiomatic.

By extension, there are also a few triads, or triplets, in English: see for example the entries for *bell, book and candle; hook, line and sinker* and *lock, stock and barrel.*

E

EAGER. eager beaver enthusiastic or industrious person; over-eager or -zealous person. He's a real eager beaver, always first into the office and last to leave. American, from the observation that beavers are very industrious animals. Hence also the simile 'work like a beaver', and the phrasal verb 'beaver away'. The connotation is sometimes of a person who tries too hard to please. Compare **brat pack**.

EAGLE. eagle eye keen or sharp surveillance. The police have been keeping an eagle eye on all airports for the last 48 hours. Most birds of prey have phenomenally keen vision.

EARLY. early bird person who is up and working at an early hour – sometimes 'up with the lark'. Don't phone him before 11.30 in the morning – he's not exactly an early bird, you know. From the proverb, 'The early bird catches the worm.' Opposite of **night owl/bird**.

early days too soon to know for certain. The operation seems to have gone as well as can be expected, but it's early days for the doctors to commit themselves to the prospects for the patient's permanent recovery.

EARN. earn one's keep earn the money to buy food, shelter, clothing and other basics necessary to keep one alive. He earns his keep as a press photographer. Also 'earn one's living/ crust/daily bread'.

EARS. (someone's) ears are burning comment made by or about someone who thinks s/he is being talked about. Here comes Mrs Bloggs to join the gossip – I'm sure her ears are burning. From the old notion, going back at least as far as the Roman writer Pliny, that a sensation of burning in the ear is an indication that people are talking about you behind your back. Compare **take one's name in vain**.

EASIER. easier said than done it is easier to tell someone how to do a thing than to actually do it. He's decided he wants to enter the House of Commons, but he may find that's easier said than done. A common saying.

EASY. easy as pie very easy indeed. They told me it was quite a difficult test, but I thought it was as easy as pie. There is doubt about whether the original reference was to 'eating pie' or a more ironical allusion to the Greek letter π used in mathematical formulae which are usually anything but easy. Other standard similes are 'easy as falling off a log' and 'easy as ABC'.

easy come, easy go observation, often uttered wistfully, that one has to be relaxed about one's material possessions. So he lost a fortune at gambling – if he hadn't already won one at the gambling tables, he'd have had nothing to lose; easy come, easy go, as they say! May also be used of a person with a knack of getting through a lot of friends, etc. She's going about with yet another easy-come-easy-go boyfriend of hers.

easy does it relax; a statement meaning that our object is best achieved by easy, or gentle, stages. Don't get worked up and rush your fences – easy does it!

easy on the eye gorgeous, good to look at. She's a very competent managing director, and she also happens to be rather easy on the eye. Originally American.

EAT. eat from/out of someone's hand be willing to do anything for a person. She was very dubious about the new boss for a while, but now she seems to be eating out of his hand. The image is of a wild animal prepared to trust a human being.

eat humble pie admit one is at fault; abase oneself. I've been rather silly about Elizabeth, and I don't mind eating humble pie on that subject. A deer's innards (kidneys, liver, etc.) used to be called its 'umbles'. An umble pie was made from these parts rather than from its venison. It was more usually served to the lower orders than at the top table, and thus did 'umble' become 'humble'. The more abject and crudely direct 'eat dirt/shit' are Americanisms. So too is 'eat crow', which means accepting something one has fought against. Oh well, I guess I was wrong and I'll just have to eat crow.

(I will) eat my hat (I will) be very surprised. I'll eat my hat if my ticket wins the lottery. Expression indicating that something is very unlikely to happen, in the speaker's opinion. Thus it is a fairly safe bet to offer to eat one's hat. Similar to **eat one's words**.

eat (someone) out of house and home said of a visitor whose huge appetite strains the hospitality of his host. He stayed for a week and ate us out of house and home – we'd forgotten how much a 15-year-old boy can eat!

eat your heart out a sort of refrain, meaning: This is something for you to be jealous of! Compete with that if you can! Suffer that silently! It's probably the best whodunnit detective novel ever written – eat your heart out, Agatha Christie! Probably Jewish American in origin, now widespread.

eat one's words contradict one's earlier statement. I told her she'd never pass her driving test, and she's just passed it – so I've been forced to eat my words. A step short of **eat my hat**, but similar.

ECONOMICAL. economical with the truth less than honest. I didn't tell a lie, I was simply economical with the truth. Like Winston Churchill's 'terminological inexactitude', this is a euphemistic expression for lying. It became notorious most recently in 1986, when the British Cabinet Secretary admitted in these words (not his coinage) to being less than frank in an Australian court of law. When this expression in turn became too clear in its meaning, one was treated to 'economical with the vérité' (as if it sounded any better with a French word dropped in).

EGG. egg someone on urge a person to do something, often against their better judgment.

John is the ringleader, and it was he who egged the younger kids on. A phrasal verb from an old Norse word that has nothing to do with eggs.

(have/get) egg on one's face (have) an appearance of foolishness, or of having made a wrong choice; (look) embarrassed. We thought we were helping a genuine charity; to learn that they were actually a bunch of crooks leaves us all with egg on our faces. An expression thought to derive from the protesters' habit of throwing eggs at political opponents, and hence of making them look foolish.

ELBOW. elbow grease effort; hard work. You'll not get a job like that done without using a bit of elbow grease. Similar to **put one's back into something**. Compare also **spit and polish**.

elbow room space in which to manoeuvre. Stop crowding her and give her a bit of elbow room – then she'll get the job done. Literally, enough space to move one's elbows without knocking them against obstacles.

ELEPHANT. elephant in the room the big issue that must not be ignored. Financing schools has become a problem about equal to having an elephant in the living room: it's so big you just can't ignore it. (In *New York Times*, 20 June, 1959.) Most often the reference is to a taboo subject that people try to ignore or sweep under the carpet.

ELEVENTH. (at the) eleventh hour (at the) last possible moment. Right up to the eleventh hour, we were hoping for a reprieve. Given the 12-hour day, the eleventh hour is late in the sequence, by any criterion. In Christ's parable of the labourers (and of the makings of an early industrial dispute), the men hired at the eleventh hour received the same payment as those who had worked all day. 'So the last shall be first, and the first last…' In Matthew xx.1–16.

END. end of story that is emphatically the end of that topic of conversation. Your mother is not coming to stay with us, and that's that – end of story. Similar to 'that's flat!'

end of one's tether limit of one's patience, endurance, etc. I think you'd better stop teasing John, who looks as if he's fast approaching the end of his tether. From a tethered animal, which can only graze as far as its rope will permit it to wander and becomes frustrated when it can go no further.

end of the line/road juncture beyond which one cannot proceed. The factory had a workforce of 2,000 when it closed down – and with so little alternative employment in the town, it was the end of the road for many workers.

ENEMY. enemy within traitorous person from within one's own ranks (rather than an outsider). Far more dangerous than the enemy without is the enemy within the gates. Expression favoured by Margaret Thatcher, British prime minister 1979–90.

ENFANT. enfant terrible prodigy, often brilliant but wayward. One of the problems with the so-called Bloomsbury set was that everybody wanted to be its enfant terrible when most of them were just spoilt brats. The French expression simply refers to a child who embarrasses his elders by his comments. In English, the term is more literary, and refers to an unorthodox, innovative and avant-garde person whose unconventionality causes anger, social outrage or controversy among colleagues.

ENOUGH. enough is enough warning that one has had enough, and is prepared to tolerate no more. Suddenly the host started shouting, 'Enough is enough – get out of my house, the lot of you!' Compare **straw which breaks the camel's back**.

ETHNIC. ethnic cleansing purgation of a population, to remove minorities or other unwanted people, often achieved by mass executions, population movements, etc. From the beginning of the crisis, the Serbs pursued a policy of deliberate ethnic cleansing in territories they regarded as theirs. A translation from Serbo-Croat,

a reference to the atrocities committed in former Yugoslavia in the 1990s, now a notorious euphemism.

EUPHEMISM

A euphemism is a circumlocution: a word or phrase which we sometimes use to refer to a topic which is surrounded by taboos, such as death, God, sex and madness, as well as things of which we are ashamed. In these contexts, some words are regarded as too explicit or offensive or unpleasant, and we feel the need to use something milder or vaguer. The substitute expressions tend to be highly idiomatic, but some are listed in the dictionary. Here is a smattering.

Jesus!: *Gee whiz!, Jeez!, Jeepers Creepers!*

By God!: *By gosh!, By gum!, By golly!, By jove!, By George!*

Lord!: *Losh!*

Prostitute: *erring sister, fallen woman, scarlet woman, woman of easy virtue, nymph of darkness, masseuse, sing-song girl, lady of trade, lady of the night, street walker, demi-mondaine, fille de joie, sex care provider.*

Lavatory: *WC, toilet, washroom, rest room, powder room, personal hygiene station, comfort station, the facilities, the plumbing, the whatsit, men's/ladies' room, little boys'/girls' room, the smallest room in the house, the thunderbox, loo, john, crapper.*

Old: *senior, elderly, mature, distinguished, seasoned, getting on, of a certain age, not as young as one was, not in the first flush, chronologically gifted, experientially enhanced, grey panther.*

Dead/death: *at rest, at peace, asleep (in Jesus/the Lord), in happy release, gone across, passed over, not lost but gone before, terminally inconvenienced, depart this life, push up the daisies, kick the bucket, bite the dust, settle one's account, resign one's spirit, with Jesus, in Abraham's bosom, in a better place, go to one's reward, summoned, sent for, gone to glory, no longer with us, deceased, written out of the script, fallen off one's perch.*

Some euphemisms have been created by politicians and others to deliberately confuse/disguise contentious issues: *extraordinary rendition* and *collateral damage* are two of the more recent and memorable (see entries).

A sub-category of euphemism is the **minced oath**, also sometimes called an expletive-deletive or a pseudo-profanity. A person who uses these is a bit like a horse refusing to jump a fence: they have arrived at the offending word but cannot bring themselves to utter it. There are many such terms dating back to Elizabethan and Jacobean English and beyond: *Sblood* (by God's blood), *Zounds* (by God's words), *Gadzooks* (by God's hooks – the nails on the Cross), *Egad* (O God), *Odds bodkins* (by God's little body) are old examples.

EVER. ever so very. *She's ever so generous to her friends.* Adjective intensifier. Similar to **ever such a (something)** a real (something). *He can be ever such a nuisance when one is trying to finish a job against a deadline.*

EVERY. every cloud has a silver lining there is no such thing as a scenario of unmitigated gloom; even the darkest hour is followed by the dawn. *He was very upset about being made redundant, but every cloud has a silver lining – he's just been appointed to a much better position.* An optimistic piece of folk-wisdom. Compare **blessing in disguise**.

every dog has its day we all have our moment of glory. *It's nice to see him enjoying some success at last; every dog has its day, as they say.* A saying.

every man jack every one; all. *I want you all out of this house in two minutes, every man jack of you.* Also 'every last one' (same sense).

every other each alternate; every second. *She comes in to help us with housework every other day.*

every so often occasionally; from time to time. *Most Sundays he visits his mother, and every so often she comes to visit him.*

every Tom, Dick and Harry everybody; all and sundry (without discrimination). *Remember that this is my home, and I don't want to have every Tom, Dick and Harry wandering around in my kitchen.* Being among the most frequently used male forenames, Tom, Dick and Harry convey a good impression of 'the man in the street'. To have used another trio of forenames, as in 'every Lionel, Jocelyn and Julian', would not have communicated a very democratic resonance. Compare **rag-tag and bobtail**.

EXPLETIVE. expletive deleted journalistic way of indicating that a taboo word has been omitted from a text, especially a spoken transcript. *He was told to go and – – – – (expletives deleted).* The print equivalent is a series of asterisks or dashes. The Watergate tape transcripts, published in 1974, were adorned with many of these.

EXTRAORDINARY. extraordinary rendition the once-covert practice of transporting foreigners suspected of crimes into third countries for indefinite detention and interrogation. *A victim of extraordinary rendition, he was 'rendered' into Morocco where he was tortured for many months.* This euphemistic mouthful describes a US government practice articulated in the late 1990s, but developed on a large scale after 11 September 2001. Someone said it sounds like a phrase from Gilbert and Sullivan, but it is much more serious than that.

EYE. an eye for an eye (and a tooth for a tooth) the punishment is the same as the crime. When one reads about some of the horrendous terrorist atrocities committed nowadays, one naturally tends to think in terms of an eye for an eye. From the Old Testament laws of summary justice, in Exodus xxi.23–4.

eye candy (usually) a beautiful person. He was strutting up the street with this incredible piece of eye candy on his arm, the show-off! Originally American. See also **get a load of that/this!**

eye-opener something that enlightens one. His graphic account of the recent events in Rwanda was a complete eye-opener to me.

eye to eye in agreement. We've never quite seen eye to eye on the subject of the British constitution.

eye to the main chance alertness to the possibilities of profiting from any opportunities or other openings in an enterprise, assignment, etc. He accepted the invitation to the party with an eye to the main chance, knowing that his boss would also be present, i.e. he hoped to profit by social contact with his boss.

EYEBALL. eyeball to eyeball in confrontational mode. The two armies are facing each other eyeball to eyeball along the truce line. Originally American, the term received widespread use during the Cuban missile crisis (1962). If you 'eyeball' someone nowadays, you confront them.

EXCLAMATION

To the limited range of standard exclamatory idioms, such as *Wow! Unbelievable! How exciting! What a fool! What rotten luck! I say! I mean – really! My word! My goodness! Hard lines/luck! Happy days! Cheers! Ouch! Crickey! Many happy returns!* have to be added a set of catch-phrases such as *On your bike! Big deal! My foot! No way! Not (bloody/bleeding) likely! Get stuffed/knotted! Give over! Down the hatch! Pull your finger/digit out! Push off!* There is additionally a sizeable range of more taboo amplifications or inelegant variations of most of these, often of a contemporary and occasionally of a local nature.

Recent exclamations include *As if! Bless! Deal with it! Doh! Enjoy! Go for it! Mega! O. My. God!* (Note the full stops, which are important pauses.) *Too much information! Way to go! What are you like?* Most of these phrases double as clichés.

Exclamation is not to be confused with its less idiomatic and more poetic sister, apostrophe. **Apostrophe** is a kind of rhetorical address or speech to the audience of a play or to an absent listener, as in:

Blow winds and crack your cheeks! (Shakespeare, *King Lear*)

What in me is dark illumine, what is low raise and support! (Milton, *Paradise Lost*, Book 1)

Milton! Thou shouldst be living at this hour: England hath need of thee! (Wordsworth)

Come away, O human child, to the waters and the wild! (Yeats)

No answer is expected in apostrophe.

F

(sweet) FA/Fanny Adams nothing at all. He knows sweet FA about the whole matter. A euphemistic abbreviation for the more taboo **fuck-all**. The original Fanny Adams was a 19th-century murder victim, and a rather tasteless synonym or nickname in the British Navy for tinned meat.

FACE. (someone's) face fell (someone) looks suddenly disappointed or distressed. His face fell the moment he heard the news.

face like fizz/thunder a very angry look or expression. She had a face like thunder when he accidentally smashed one of her crystal whisky glasses. The standard similes.

face the music be prepared to confront the enemy, or to accept whatever punishment may be coming to one. You can't run away for ever – one day you'll have to go back and face the music. From the theatre: the singer has to face the musicians of the orchestra pit as well as the audience when performing.

face to face facing one another, i.e. with the people concerned present at a meeting. It was 30 years since he'd last seen her, and yesterday they met once again face to face.

face up to (something/someone) accept, meet, confront (something/someone) with courage. It took her many years to face up to the fact that her son was an evil scoundrel. A phrasal verb.

face value having the value that something appears to have. He is always hinting at this and that, and I never know whether to take his remarks at face value. Literally, having the value printed upon something, such as a currency note, cheque, etc.

FACTS. facts of life knowledge about human procreation. When they were about 10, their mother briefly explained the facts of life to them. Like the

birds and the bees, this was a popular Victorian euphemism.

FAIR. fair and square fairly and conclusively; without cheating or lying. The visitors won the match fair and square. Also 'fair play'. The opposite of **foul play**.

fair game legitimate or justifiable target for attack, pursuit or ridicule. As far as press scrutiny of their financial dealings and sex lives are concerned, politicians are generally considered fair game. From the easing of the country's draconian Game Laws in the 19th century, and legislation stating which birds and animals might be fairly or lawfully hunted. As late as 1816, you could still be transported to Australia for seven years for poaching a rabbit.

fair sex women in general. After the cigars, the gentlemen rejoined the fair sex in the salon. Old fashioned and nowadays politically incorrect.

fair-weather friend person who is only friendly so long as s/he sees some personal advantage accruing from the friendship. After the scandal broke, all our fair-weather friends disappeared without trace.

FALL. fall between two stools fit into neither of two main categories, with the result that the thing so described occupies an awkward in-between position. It's a work that falls between two stools, being neither an opera in the traditional sense nor a modern musical. Another way of saying this would be to say something was 'betwixt and between', or **neither fish nor fowl**.

fall by the wayside falter; fail to live up to certain standards. He's supposed to be working hard for his exams, but every so often he falls by the wayside and goes off on a binge. Biblical, from the parable of the sower and the seed in Matthew xiii.4.

fall guy dupe; sucker; scapegoat. It was you who caused the problem, so why should I be the fall guy? Originally American, from the US idiom 'take a fall' (meaning to be caught, or arrested, whether rightly or wrongly). Compare **whipping boy**.

fall/land on one's feet be successful or have good luck. Don't worry about John – he always manages to fall on his feet. From animal behaviour, with particular reference to cats, which are rarely wrong-footed.

fall short be not good enough or adequate enough for a given purpose; fail to measure up. I'm afraid the candidates all fall far short of what we are looking for, so the position will have to be re-advertised.

fall through fail; come to nothing. They had various plans for developing a leisure centre, but they all seem to have fallen through. A phrasal verb.

FALLEN. fallen woman prostitute; promiscuous woman. Mr Gladstone was one prime minister who took a keen interest in the welfare of fallen women. No longer used seriously, this was a popular Victorian euphemism and referred to the woman's fall from grace.

FAMOUS. famous last words comment made after someone has made a rash – or fatuous – statement. 'I'll soon have your car fixed,' said the mechanic. Famous last words – he's had it for a week now, and the damn thing still won't start. Often jocular, or jeering: the reference being not to a dying person's final utterance (a different kind of 'famous last words' often solemnly collected in anthologies) but merely to a foolish mortal's rash undertaking.

FANCY. fancy man/woman/piece lover. We saw Amanda at the party last night with her current fancy man. In the 18th century, the reference was simply to a sweetheart, or a 'man who is fancied'. By about 1820, it had the meaning of 'a pimp'. Nowadays, the reference is still disparaging, and really refers to the lover as a sex object. Compare **toy boy**.

fancy meeting you (here) exclamation, meaning 'What a surprise to meet you (here).' We literally bumped into one another at the market, and she exclaimed, 'Fancy meeting you in a place like this!'

fancy that exclamation, often ironical, indicating surprise or admiration. She says she is going to shoot him. Fancy that! Alternatives are 'fancy!' and 'just fancy!'

FAR. far and away by a decisive margin; easily. His roses were far and away the best in this year's flower show.

far cry from very different from. She lives in a delightful little cottage, but it's a far cry from her once-palatial chateau.

far out eccentric; unusual. The idea may sound a bit far out, but I think it'll work. Similar to **way out**. Along with 'cool', the expression also had a vogue in 1960s American English as an exclamation, meaning 'fantastic'.

FAST. fast track quickest and surest route to a goal. She got an excellent degree, and is hoping that'll be her fast track to a good job.

FAT. fat cat capitalist; conspicuously wealthy person. The fat cats of the city of London seem to have had another good year. Originally American, the term applied especially to wealthy contributors to political campaign funds. There is the assumption that such people usually over-eat and look rather smug (like the cat that got the cream). Similar to **big shot**.

fat chance small likelihood. A fat chance you've got of winning any beauty competitions! Ironic use of 'fat' as an intensifier.

the fat is in the fire the trouble is about to begin. He suddenly discovered that his wife had a lover, and then the fat was in the fire. To develop the pyrotechnical theme, one might add, 'Watch out for the fireworks!'

fat lot not much; very little. She may be rich but her money's done her a fat lot of good. Ironic use of 'fat' as an intensifier.

the fat of the land affluence and prosperity. On

the one hand there was the most ferocious and widespread poverty, and right alongside it were a few lucky people living off the fat of the land. Biblical, from Genesis xlv.18, describing Joseph's lifestyle in Egypt.

FATHER. father and mother of all extreme; ultimate. They threatened us with the father and mother of all battles. The expression is not new, but received a new lease of life during the 1991 war following the Iraqi invasion of Kuwait, and the accompanying apocalyptic propaganda utterances of the Iraqi president, Saddam Hussein. Compare **daddy of them all**.

FEAST. feast or famine extremes of wealth or poverty, availability or dearth, etc. The British housing market is stuck in an endless cycle of stop-go, feast or famine, boom or bust. From the Bible, and the seven years of plenty followed by the seven years of famine, in Genesis xli.

FEATHER. feather in one's cap public recognition of one's achievement; achievement of which one can be proud. It was a real feather in the firm's cap when they won the Queen's Award for Export. From chivalry. Knights were allowed to wear the crest (often of feathers) of people they had overcome in combat. A knight with many feathers in his cap was not someone to meddle with.

feather one's (own) nest enrich oneself, often surreptitiously and at the expense of others. There was a public outcry when it was learnt that so many of our parliamentary representatives were busier feathering their own nests than defending the interests of their electors. From ornithology; certain species of birds use feathers, sometimes their own and sometimes those of other birds, to line their nests. Compare **line one's pockets**.

FEATHERS. feathers fly a battle or a verbal slanging match takes place. He doesn't get on with his sister for some reason, and they have only to be together for five minutes before the feathers fly. Sometimes 'sparks fly'. Not metaphorically dissimilar to **set a cat among the pigeons**.

FEEL. feel-good factor something positive that affects the general mood of the community, making people feel secure, happy, optimistic, spiritually contented. The government, which knows the price of everything and the value of very little, complained that the absence of a feel-good factor was hardly their fault. A journalistic term.

feel groggy feel weak, inclined to totter; feel the worse for alcoholic drink. Naturally enough, he felt groggy for several hours after the operation. The reference to drunkenness comes via Admiral Vernon, whose nickname was 'Old Grog' from his cloak made of grogram fabric (a coarse mixture of silk, mohair and wool). In 1740, he introduced into the Royal Navy a daily ration of rum diluted with water. This soon became known as the grog ration.

feel (it) in one's bones have an intuition (that something is going to happen). Some sixth sense was telling him that something was amiss, and he felt it in his bones that he'd better investigate. Probably related to people whose arthritic or rheumatic bones tell them when it's going to rain. Similar to 'something tells me'. Something tells me that all is not well with the project.

feel no pain be drunk. He was lying on the floor feeling no pain, an empty gin bottle by his side. A euphemism based on the anaesthetising power of alcoholic liquor, now only used humorously.

feel the draught/cold be adversely affected financially. Last summer was a dreadful season for the tourist industry, and all the hotels are really feeling the draught. Financial parlance, in which businesses that catch cold or feel the draught are not performing well.

feel the pinch feel poor, or financially challenged. He lost his job last year, and I think he's now beginning to feel the pinch. Probably from getting 'pinched' or arrested for a minor offence: Victorian.

FEET. feet of clay human flaws or weaknesses perceived in a person of high repute. It was a great disappointment to his fans when their hero demonstrated in such a tacky way that he had feet of clay like everyone else. **Biblical, in Daniel ii.42. Compare Achilles' heel**.

FELLOW. fellow traveller political sympathiser (but one who is not a paid-up member of the organisation). I'm sorry that only members of the organisation are welcome to the meeting; there isn't room for all the fellow travellers and hangers-on. **The expression dates from the 1930s, and is a translation of the Russian word** *poputchik*. **At first it was usually applied only to communist sympathisers, but later it also applied to hangers-on in general**.

FEW. few and far between infrequent. We used to see a lot of him, but recently his visits have become few and far between.

FIDDLE. fiddle while Rome burns do nothing to avert a looming disaster, especially by attending to trivial things while a major crisis is unfolding. Millions were dying of starvation, but all that the developed nations could do was to call a meeting of the United Nations and fiddle while Rome burnt. **From an apocryphal story of the Emperor Nero, who in AD64 is said to have set Rome on fire and played music while it burnt**.

FIELD. field day an advantageous situation. It may have been a tough situation for the royal family, but it was a field day for the press corps. **Field days were originally military festivals where there were parades and inspections and other ceremonial excitements**.

FIFTH. fifth column(ist) traitorous organisation; the enemy within the ranks. The military dictatorship dealt in draconian manner with all fifth columnists, critics and other opponents of the regime. **The idiom dates from the Spanish Civil War. In 1936, General Mola laid siege to Madrid with four columns of troops. He claimed they would be able to take the city with the aid of** *la quinta columna* – **the fifth column** – **of sympathisers within the city**.

FIFTY. fifty-fifty even, equal; half and half. His chances of winning the prize are no better than fifty-fifty. **Originally American, from betting, meaning literally 'on a basis of 50 per cent either way'**.

FIGHT. fight one's corner state one's view and vigorously defend it. The proposal wasn't originally very popular, so we really had to fight our corner to get it accepted. **From boxing, where fighters wore colours and defended 'the red corner' or 'the blue corner', etc**.

fight shy of avoid. He leads a very private lifestyle, and fights shy of any contact with the press.

fight tooth and nail fight with utmost vigour, using every weapon at one's disposal. These people will fight tooth and nail for their basic rights. From animal behaviour.

FIGHTING. fighting fit very fit; in the peak of condition. It was nice to see Jason looking fighting fit again after his illness. **The idea was originally of being 'fit for fighting in battle', nowadays usually on the sports field**.

FIGMENT. figment of one's imagination something which is not real; an invention of the mind. Most of his vast wealth and power is nothing more than a figment of his imagination.

FILLER

Conversational fillers are a feature of unrehearsed speech in all languages, so they are frequently highly colloquial and by definition idiomatic. They are believed to contribute to fluency in speakers, who do not – after all – normally speak in perfectly punctuated paragraphs. Rather do they punctuate their speech with expressions such as *sort of, isn't it?, as you might say, how can I put it?* Fillers have as much to do with maintaining communicative bonds as they have to do with exchanging information. Hence the various grunt sounds like *uh, er, um, ah* and words like *y'know, cool, absolutely* among youths.

Common fillers may be conversational courtesies such as **greetings** (*Hi!, Hello!, How do you do?, Feeling OK?, How's it going?*) or **excuses** (*Sorry!, Excuse me!*) or **thanks** (*Thank you, You're welcome, Don't mention it.*) or **farewells** (*Bye!, See you, Cheerio*) or **requests** (*Would you mind..., Could you possibly...*), etc.

Among the commonest fillers are *and (all) that, as it were, after all, by the way/by, don't you know, you see, in fact, at this time, on the whole, for the most part, not in the least, may I just add, mind you, quite frankly, well I ask you, really, as we all know, speaking for myself.* Sometimes they are amplified: *in actual fact, in point of fact, at this precise point in time, speaking purely for myself.*

As semi-redundant expressions as far as meaning is concerned, only a few fillers are listed and glossed in the main dictionary.

The Polish anthropologist Bronislaw Malinowski's term 'phatic communion' (1923) includes fillers and 'idiot salutations', such as exchanges about a person's health or about current weather conditions. These are examples of language used to establish an atmosphere conducive to the communication of the speakers' feelings rather than their ideas.

FILTHY. filthy lucre money; profit. I hate to raise the subject of filthy lucre, but is there to be a fee for this job? 'Lucre' is from a Greek source, and means 'pecuniary advantage', and the addition of 'filthy' is also a translation from Greek, meaning 'dishonourable'. The expression was common in the 17th century, and is used several times in the King James New Testament: 'not greedy of filthy lucre'. See 1 Timothy ii.3

and 8; also Titus i.7. Nowadays, mainly used in a light-hearted manner.

FINAL. final solution extermination; culling. The fishermen came up with a drastic-sounding final solution for the seal populations along the coast. One of the more spine-chilling euphemisms of our time, the original reference was to Hitler's plan for the extermination of the Jews of Europe. The phrase is a translation of German *Endlösung*, and is thought to have been Hitler's own.

FIND. find/get one's bearings establish one's position; sort out what one should be doing. She's only been in the job for a week, but I think she's already begun to find her bearings. Originally nautical, the reference was to the compass bearings which gave a ship at sea its directions. Opposite of **lose one's bearings**.

find one's feet become more confident in a new situation. It's an excellent career opportunity, and I'm sure it won't take you long to find your feet. Compare **know/learn the ropes; wet behind the ears**.

find one's tongue start speaking after a period of silence, usually by overcoming one's shyness. The group was rather large and intimidating, and it took me a while to find my tongue. Opposite of **lose one's tongue**.

FINDERS. finders keepers if you find something, you can keep it. Finding a 50 Euro note in the hedge, I wondered if I should hand it in at the gendarmerie or if it was a case of finders keepers. From the children's rhyme which supposedly authorises this kind of rough justice, 'finders keepers, losers weepers!'

FINE. (go through something) with a fine-tooth comb (hunt or sift through something) with the greatest care and attention; (examine) very closely. After the tragedy, the police went through the house with a fine-tooth comb, looking for clues. Note that it is a fine-tooth comb (a comb with fine teeth capable of locating the smallest particles of dirt, etc.), and not a fine tooth-comb.

A fine-tooth comb is the standard tool used for removing head lice or fleas.

FINGER. finger in every pie a part or role to play in a large number of activities, organisations, etc. She's one of those frightfully busy people who seem to have a finger in every pie. There is often an implication of meddlesomeness in this expression.

FINGERS. (all) fingers and thumbs very clumsy. She asked me to button her coat for her, saying she was all fingers and thumbs with excitement.

fingers crossed plea for one's good luck to hold. The plane should be landing in about five minutes, fingers crossed. From the popular superstition, that by making the sign of the cross with two fingers one can ensure good luck. Similar to **deo volente/d.v.**

fingers on buzzers! get ready. Literally, buzz when one is ready to answer the question or to do something. A catch-phrase from the popular TV quiz programme *University Challenge* (1962–). Compare **on your marks!**

FINISHING. finishing touches final small details of a project. The generals have now sorted out the finishing touches to their campaign.

FIRE. fire away usually an invitation to go ahead and speak, ask questions, etc. 'May I have a word with you please?' 'Go ahead, fire away – what can I do for you?' **Originally from the firing range.**

fire on all cylinders perform or operate with energy and enthusiasm. The home team is always hard to beat, especially if it is really firing on all cylinders. Sometimes, if the performer is half-hearted, one says he is 'only firing on two cylinders'.

FIRST. first and foremost before anything or anyone else. First and foremost, I'd like to acknowledge the loyal backing of my parents in this project. **An alliterative dyad.**

first refusal opportunity to acquire something before it is offered for sale on the wider market. I've promised Jane first refusal if I ever decide to sell that painting.

first thing before attending to anything else. First thing every morning when I start work, I see to the mail.

FISH. fish in troubled waters take advantage of some disturbance. I'd make no reference at all to the rocky state of their marriage – that might be seen by some onlookers as fishing in troubled waters. From angling; sometimes the best fishing can be had when the water is rough.

fish out of water awkward or uncomfortable person. All dressed up in his best suit, white shirt and tie, John felt a real fish out of water throughout the ceremony. Literally, **out of one's element**.

FIT. fit as a fiddle in excellent health; in good form. The vet came and gave the mare an injection, and now she looks as fit as a fiddle again. A standard simile with a long history, the phrase originally meant that the item under consideration was as fit for its purpose as a fiddle was for making music. Also 'fit as a flea' (same meaning). There is something tiresomely indefatigable about fleas.

fit for purpose effective; suitable; does the job properly. The roof blew off in a gale so now they'll have to have an inquiry into why it was so spectacularly unfit for purpose. A term much used by bureaucracy.

fit the bill be exactly suitable for a particular situation. It's a difficult assignment, and I can't for the moment think of anyone who fits the bill for doing it successfully. Originally American, from the design and layout of printed bill posters advertising an event. If the names of certain acts, etc. could be fitted into the design, they would go on the billing.

FIVE. five o'clock shadow hint of beard growth that looks as if it needs shaving. He looked a mess – hair uncombed, clothes creased from sleeping in them and a strong five o'clock shadow. A feature of many dark-haired men of strong beard growth, for whom a morning shave is insufficient to keep their faces free of stubble through the afternoon. By 5 p.m. they are perceived to need their second shave of the day. From American razorblade advertising slogans of the 1930s. Compare the more recent and more positive **designer stubble**.

FLASH. flash in the pan brilliant but abortive outburst or initiative, especially one that is unlikely to be repeated. We won our first game of the season, but I'm afraid that was just a flash in the pan. From 16th-century firearms. The 'pan' of a gun was the part which held the priming powder. Sometimes this went off without igniting the main charge. The resulting anticlimax was called a 'flash in the pan'.

FLAT. flat footed clumsy. The minister's responses under questioning from the Opposition were extremely flat footed and inept.

flat lining neither rising nor falling; making little or no progress or headway. The economy has been flat lining for several years now. Compare **in the doldrums; tread water**.

flat out 1. exhausted; unconscious. He was lying flat out in the corner of the boxing ring. 2. **with every effort; at full speed**. He drove flat out through the night to get to her bedside.

flat spin state of hyper-excitement. She doesn't cope well with too many visitors these days – she goes into a flat spin if more than two or three people arrive at once. From flying; a 2-propellor plane quickly went out of control when it went into a flat spin.

that's flat emphatic statement, meaning 'that is final.' I refuse to lend you the money and that's flat. More emphatic than the philosophical, 'that's that.' Compare **end of story**.

FLAVOUR. flavour of the month something which is temporarily faddish, or in vogue; the current favourite or craze. The new secretary seems to be flavour of the month just now with the boss – she

can't seem to do anything wrong. From American ice-cream marketing strategy in the 1950s. Often sarcastic. Compare **nine days' wonder**.

FLEA. flea in the ear sharp reprimand; rebuke. He asked if he could borrow my car, but I sent him away with a flea in his ear. The image is of a stinging mosquito.

flea-market market for second-hand goods, or a shop selling second-hand goods. We spent a happy afternoon going round the local flea-market looking for bargains. A straight 1920s-ish translation from the Paris Marché aux Puces.

flea-pit cheap cinema or theatre. There was nothing on telly last night, so we went along to the local flea-pit and watched a good western.

FLEET. Fleet Street the newspaper world. She's one of those media stars that only have to put their nose outside their front doors to have half of Fleet Street chasing her for a picture and a story. A synecdoche, or generic expression, dating from the days before new technology when almost all the major English papers were printed there. Compare **Grub Street**.

FLESH. flesh and blood 1. one's blood relations. One is supposed to try to look after one's own flesh and blood. A dyad, similar to **kith and kin**. 2. one's tolerance. In the end, their spiteful comments were more than flesh and blood could bear, so we left.

fleshpots luxurious and sensual delights. He's a very famous electronics engineer, who's been living in the fleshpots of California for the last 20 years. From the biblical exodus of the children of Israel from the fleshpots of Egypt, in Exodus xvi.3. Now often ironical. Sometimes two words.

FLIGHT. flight(s) of fancy pleasant fantasy. He's full of plans for when he wins the football pools and other flights of fancy. Compare **cloud cuckoo land; pipe dream**.

FLIP. flip one's lid/wig lose one's composure; become hyper-enthusiastic, -active, -emotional.

When he saw what I'd done to his precious car, my father just about flipped his lid. Slang term, the idea being of the lid/wig lifting off the top of someone's head to let the heat, anger, etc. out.

FLOG. flog a dead horse waste time pursuing a subject that is already closed; try to achieve something futile or impossible. I think you're flogging a dead horse trying to revive interest in that scheme. The originator of the expression is said to be John Bright (1811–89), the English Liberal reformer. The metaphor is of a jockey flogging a dead horse in a race, thus doing something completely useless – it fails even to move.

FLOOD. flood the market produce too much of something, so that people (the market) fail to buy/consume it quickly enough. The booming economies of the Pacific Rim have flooded the market with cheap freezers. From economics, and the laws of supply and demand.

FLOTSAM. flotsam and jetsam wreckage of odds and ends; bits and pieces. The search-and-rescue teams found flotsam and jetsam scattered across a wide area of moorland. A famous dyad, the precise and original reference was to floating bits and pieces from a ship's wreckage at sea. 'Flotsam' was a term for floating wreckage, while 'jetsam' was the legal term for goods jettisoned overboard to lighten the load on a distressed ship. 'Human flotsam and jetsam' is a term which has been applied to homeless people like refugees, waifs, strays, etc.

FLY. fly a kite test the reaction to an idea. The government flew a kite about a new tax on housing, but the idea was soon dropped in the face of deep public hostility. From the idea of checking to see in what direction the wind is blowing, and hence of establishing which way public opinion is tending.

fly blind 1. fly a plane solely by instruments, as when visibility is poor. The fog was so thick that the pilot had to fly and land the plane blind. 2. do a job without any instructions or training, by simply

following one's common sense. I was left to run the business during the emergency, and I simply had to fly blind. Compare **on a wing and a prayer**.

fly-by-night untrustworthy, irresponsible and usually shady trader, of dubious ethics and often of no fixed abode. Watch him – he's just a bit of a fly by night. She runs a very shaky, fly-by-night publishing business. Can be used as an adjective or as a noun. Also, for the latter, a 'fly-by-nighter'. The expression suggests something/someone who would look suspicious in the light of day.

fly in the face of (something) oppose, contradict or defy (something). His conduct flies in the face of all the accepted norms. Usually followed by a word like 'convention', 'danger', 'providence', 'public opinion', etc. The original image is of a bird or animal attacking someone.

fly in the ointment obstacle; blemish spoiling an otherwise successful activity, etc. It was a lovely picnic, and the only fly in the ointment was the presence of that horrid Mrs Bloggs. Probably biblical: 'Dead flies cause the ointment of the apothecary to send forth a stinking savour.' In Ecclesiastes x.1.

fly off the handle lose one's temper in a fit of rage. I don't know what's wrong with him; he keeps flying off the handle for the smallest reasons. From the axe-head flying off its wooden handle, a potentially dangerous movement: when its owner loses his head he too tends to do something dangerous – or foolish.

FLYING. flying high performing very successfully, and usually prosperously. I have a few shares in that company, and they seem to be flying high just now. Gives the noun **high flyer**, which has a similar sense. A lot of high flyers joined the company through its graduate recruitment programme.

FOB. fob someone/something off pretend something is better than it seems and unload or dump it on someone; try to trick someone. He thinks he's fobbed me off with a couple of rotten tomatoes in the bag – but he'll get them back tomorrow. **A phrasal verb.**

FOLLOW. follow in the footsteps of succeed or train to succeed one's predecessor in a business. Dr Small was a well-loved doctor, and it's good to know that his daughter will be following in his footsteps.

follow one's nose 1. pursue an unplanned itinerary. I followed my nose and took a short walk round the town. **2. go straight ahead.** Follow your nose to the T-junction and then turn right.

follow suit do as someone else has just done. After you've danced to all the female dancers in the circle, you return to your place, and the next male dancer takes centre stage and follows suit. **From card-playing; literally, to play a card from the same suit as that played by the previous player.**

FOOD. food for thought something to think about carefully. I think the headmaster's address gives us all food for thought.

food chain sequence; pecking order. Mr X has slid further down the Tory Party food chain of recent years. **This is an example of inept idiom usage. The writer means 'further down the command structure', but has taken a phrase from animal and plant behaviour. Compare pecking order.**

FOOL. fool's paradise condition of happiness that is unlikely to endure, because it is based on a misunderstanding, etc. That boy is living in a fool's paradise if he thinks he can afford to marry me.

FOOT. foot the bill pay the bill. It was a splendid wedding, but I'm glad I'm not footing that particular bill. **Probably from 'foot up' meaning 'total up' all the items on the bill, and settling the amount written at the foot.**

FOOTLOOSE. footloose and fancy free without emotional or material ties. He used to be footloose and fancy free, but now he's got a wife and kids to look after. **An alliterative phrase. Footloose people have no restrictions on their movements,** and are able to roam the world. If they are also fancy free, they have no bonds of love tying them to another person. Shakespeare uses 'fancy-free' in *A Midsummer Night's Dream* [ii.1.164] in c.1594.

FOR. for a kick-off for a start. You wanted something to do – maybe you could clean those wine glasses for a kick-off. **From the beginning of a game of football, rugby, etc.**

for a song cheaply. It's a magnificent painting, and yet I was able to pick it up for a song. **From the notion of singing for money to buy one's supper, etc.**

for crying out loud! expression of annoyance, frustration, impatience, etc. Will you stop interrupting me, for crying out loud! Oh, for crying out loud, I refuse to listen to any more of this nonsense! **A sort of rhetorical appeal for support – to the heavens or to whoever happens to be within hearing distance. See also good gracious.**

for dear life urgently. At the last moment, rowing for dear life, our boat inched ahead of the others and we won the race. **Literally, as if lives depended on it.**

for good forever; finally. He said he had only lent her the picture, but she says he gave it to her for good. **More fully, 'for good and all'. See also for keeps.**

for it 1. about to receive a punishment. He's for it when his mother sees the mess his clothes are in. 'It' here means something like 'the high jump' (see below) or some other terrifying punishment. 2. in order to escape (in combinations such as 'jump for it', 'run for it', 'swim for it'). When the boat capsized, the passengers were left to swim for it.

for keeps to keep altogether and for good. He lets us borrow the house for holidays, and he says we can have it for keeps when he dies. **See also for good.**

for kicks for fun, and for the thrill. People do the strangest things for kicks. **Originally American; literally, from the momentary jerk reaction to the high-voltage discharge of an electric current, or perhaps to a discharging pistol.**

for nothing free; at no cost. She wanted to get rid of her piano, and offered it to me for nothing. Sometimes amplified: 'free, gratis and for nothing'.

for one's pains in return for one's efforts. He tried hard to help her, but all he got for his pains was a blank stare.

for real true; correct. He claims to have been managing director of the business, but do you think that can be for real? I don't think that woman's for real. An Americanism.

for the birds not believable; credible only to the incredulous. She pretends to be very interested in her clients' welfare, but that's for the birds; she's only interested in their money. There is a disparaging reference here to the size of a bird's brain.

for the high jump about to receive a heavy punishment. The headmaster is to see the culprits at five o'clock, and I fear they're all for the high jump. The original 'high jump' was the removal of the platform supporting the hanging man under the noose.

for the life of one really; under any circumstances. I cannot for the life of me imagine what he's talking about. Used hyperbolically for emphasis, now much trivialised. Originally and more formally, 'Upon my life, I cannot...'

for the record to ensure that the facts are stated/recorded accurately. I think I'd better tell you for the record that my wife has left me.

for two pins for the smallest reason or provocation. For two pins I would cancel the holiday, since no one seems to want to go. Literally, for a very insignificant consideration.

FORCE. force someone's hand compel someone to do something they don't want to do. Most members of the party had no wish to revert to violence, but knew that a faction was plotting to force their hand.

FOREGONE. foregone conclusion something that should almost certainly happen; an outcome that can be predicted with some confidence. The result of the match was something of a foregone conclusion.

FORK. fork something out/up pay. She decided to go to New York, and as usual expected me to fork something up towards her expenses. Usually indicates reluctance. Also 'cough up'.

FORTY. forty winks a short sleep or nap. After supper I decided to take forty winks on the sofa. Compare **not sleep a wink**.

FOUL. foul one's (own) nest harm or act against one's (own) interests. He didn't want to foul his nest by leaving an old wreck of a car outside his front door at a time when he was trying to sell the house. From the proverb 'It's an ill bird that fouls its own nest.'

foul play criminal, irregular or unsporting action; unfair or treacherous conduct. A man is dead in that flat, and the police are presently checking through the house for evidence of any foul play. A sporting expression, the opposite of 'fair play'.

FOUR. four-letter word swear-word; obscene or taboo word. He was warned to clean up his language, and refrain from using four-letter words. From the fact that so many words in this category have only four letters ('shit', 'fuck', etc.). A euphemism for the many people who regard the use of these words in conversation as offensive.

four-square behind something solidly supportive of something. The entire workforce stood four-square behind their convenor's demand. From the idea of any four-square structure being firm and solid, and thus unlikely to be affected by changing conditions. Hence the American idea of a 'square deal', meaning a 'fair deal'.

FOURTH. fourth estate the press. The fourth estate doesn't enjoy a very good reputation these days. From the division of the pre-revolutionary

French parliament into three 'estates' or États – the aristocracy, the church and the common people. The term was also used much more loosely of the English parliament. By the 18th century, the power of the press had started to worry people and the term 'fourth estate' was applied to the press gallery by Edmund Burke (1729–97): 'Yonder sits the fourth estate, more important than them all.' The term had been used earlier, to apply variously to the army and the mob.

FREE. free hand/rein freedom to do whatever one likes. He's been given a free hand to redesign the entire garden. Similar to the French 'carte blanche' (= a blank sheet of paper). Compare **blank cheque**.

FRESH. fresh as a (mountain) daisy very fresh, bright, and/or alert. After a good night's sleep, you'll all be fresh as a mountain daisy. A standard simile.

FRIEND. friend in need friend one can depend upon. Old Mrs Brown has been a real friend in need to me. From the proverb, 'A friend in need is a friend in deed.' Indeed!

FRIENDLY. friendly fire accidental killing or harming of one's military colleagues in the course of war. Sixty Argyll and Sutherland Highlanders were killed by the US Air Force in a serious friendly-fire incident in Korea in 1950. An oxymoron and a euphemism (usually for a cock-up), the phenomenon of friendly fire has been around from earliest times, but the term dates only from the late 1940s. Compare **collateral damage**, of which this term is a precursor.

FROG. frog in one's throat hoarseness; huskiness of speech. His voice sounds most odd this morning – he's got a bad frog in his throat. A metaphor likening a human voice to a frog's croak.

FROM. from hell something or someone really unpleasant, bad, etc. The whole trip was dreadful, especially one internal domestic flight from hell that we'll have to tell you about sometime. Unfortunately, we live next door to the original neighbours from hell.

from here on in from now until the end (of something). He's always been a bit of a nuisance, but he's promised to behave himself impeccably from here on in if we agree not to sack him.

from pillar to post hither and thither; from one place to another, especially when one is being hurried, harried, etc. The press have behaved in their usual appalling way, hounding the family from pillar to post to try to get a story out of them. The term was originally 'from post to pillar' and until the 16th century it referred to repulse and harassment in the context of the game of royal tennis.

from scratch from the beginning. He lost the entire manuscript in the fire, and had to start the writing from scratch again. From the scratch mark once observed for starting a race or a boxing match.

FRONT. front of (the) house activities which involve looking after relations with the public, etc. They run a good little business – she is an excellent cook and he's very good at the front-of-house stuff. From the theatre.

FUCK. (sweet) fuck-all nothing. She was the favourite grandchild and was left the house and estate, while I got sweet fuck-all. Compare also **FA/ Fanny Adams**.

fuck off go away. Why don't you just fuck off and leave him alone? Mainly used as a vulgar imperative. Kindly fuck off! A phrasal verb.

fuck-up disaster; serious blunder. We're getting quite used to Whitehall fuck-ups these days. Also 'cock-up'.

FULL. full-frontal (nudity) (nakedness) in which the front of the body and therefore the sexual organs are plainly visible. My arrival was clearly unexpected, and when I entered the room I was confronted with a full-frontal exhibition that I could have managed without. The term was devised by the Lord Chamberlain's office to describe total nudity on stage and screen (which used to be censored). Now commonplace, this tended in the past to be partially concealed by fig-leaves, seaweed, beach-balls or other coy passing props.

full of beans exuberant; full of life and energy. It was lovely to see her so full of beans after her illness. Perhaps from the notion of energy in jumping beans.

full monty the totality. It's a popular venue for weddings nowadays, because it does the full monty – hiring a minister, booking the registrar, organising invitations and putting on an excellent reception. Compare **whole shooting match** or 'whole shebang'.

full steam ahead go, proceed, etc. as fast as possible. Since the takeover, it's been full steam ahead to streamline and rationalise the two businesses. From the days of steamships, steam trains, etc.

FUNNY. funny business/work nonsense; dishonesty; fooling about. Come on, I want none of your funny business or I'll phone the police. Sometimes **dirty/funny work at the crossroads** (from whence a thief has a range of escape options).

funny farm psychiatric hospital. He tried to commit suicide, and now he's been taken away to the funny farm for his own safety.

funny money unbelievably large sums of money. Some of these directors pay themselves funny money nowadays. A rhyming reduplication.

G

GAIN. gain ground make progress. Some of these strange ideas have been gaining ground recently. From the literal, military sense of conquering territory from an enemy. Opposite of 'lose ground'.

GAME. game plan strategy for achieving an objective. We are meeting tomorrow to discuss the company's game plan for the next three years. The original reference was to American football in the 1930s, and the term acquired its current idiomatic status there in the 1970s.

game that two can play this expression is a way of saying that the victim of a bad act may be in a position to reciprocate it. She's always saying nasty things about me behind my back, which she may soon discover is a game that two can play. Also 'two can play at that game'. Very often a not-too-thinly veiled threat.

GAME'S. the game's a bogey/bogy childish version of **the game's up**, often heard as a street cry in games such as hide-and-seek, meaning 'the game is spoilt.' Come out, come out, wherever you are, the game's a bogey! The 'bogey' is an old reference to the devil, or bogey man.

the game's not worth the candle the return on the project is not worth the investment one has put into it. I used to work seven days a week, but the taxman took such a large slice of my earnings that I decided the game was hardly worth the candle. Originally French: 'Le jeu n'en vaut la chandelle.' The literal reference was to a gambling session, and indicated that the amount of money at stake would not even pay for the candle needed to throw light on the proceedings.

the game's up the plan, etc. has failed; the trick has been exposed. I knew the game was up as soon as I saw the police car at the front door. Compare **(your) number's up**.

GAS. gas guzzler car that consumes large quantities of fuel. It's a comfortable car, but a bit of a gas guzzler for its size. Alliterative term for the massive American automobiles, symbols of conspicuous consumption, popular up to the 1980s.

GARDEN. garden (or **gardening**) **leave** procedure for making someone redundant and forcing them to stay away from work during their period of notice; effectively, a brutal euphemism for instant dismissal. John's on garden leave till the end of the financial year. Since the recession half the workforce has been put on gardening leave. Compare **spend more time with one's family**.

GAY. gay abandon lighthearted recklessness; without thought, concern, consideration, etc. She buys the most amazing amounts of clothing with gay abandon. Often a cliché, the collocation is tautological: 'reckless recklessness'.

GENTLEMAN'S. gentleman's agreement informal spoken agreement, without written legal supporting back-ups, and therefore only binding as a matter of honour. There was apparently some sort of gentleman's agreement that John was to get the cottage on Margaret's death.

GET. get a bloody nose get hurt emotionally, or in one's pride. It was an excellent debate, but the visiting team won the argument fairly and squarely and I'm afraid it was our guys that got a bloody nose – they had so wanted to win. From the boxing ring. Also 'give someone a bloody nose'.

get a grip (of yourself) control your emotions; pull yourself together. The sergeant bellowed at the squad, 'Stand up straight and get a grip of yourselves!'

get a life expression of scorn, ridicule or general criticism, usually when you are implying that someone lacks a sense of proportion or humour. Why don't you just get a life and stop nagging me! Is it not time for you to move on and get a life?

get a load of that/this 1. take a look at something/someone. Come quick and get a load of what's just walked into the front office. **A sexist comment often expressed by males referring to beautiful passing females. See also eye candy. 2. listen to this.** Get a load of this; it says here that the party's been cancelled. **Usually with the sense of 'Can you believe this?'**

get a word in edgeways manage to say something in the course of a conversation monopolised by someone else. As usual, Mrs Brown talked and talked, and nobody else could get a word in edgeways. **Invariably negative. Compare hold the floor; talk the hind legs off a donkey**.

get one's act together get oneself organised. Her boss has given her two weeks to get her act together, or she loses her job. **The original context was theatrical, and referred to actors memorising their lines in order to perform their act. Compare get it together; pull oneself together**.

get away (with you) exclamation of incredulity: meaning, I don't believe what you are telling me. 'I believe you've won the lottery.' 'Oh, get away!' Also 'get on (with you)'.

get away with murder make serious mistakes, commit offences, etc. without being punished or made to suffer for them. It's strange how strict the parents are with the older child, but let the younger one get away with murder. **A hyperbole.**

get away with something scot-free succeed in some action without penalty. Society will break down if hardened criminals are allowed to get away with their crimes scot-free. **A 'scot' was a medieval municipal tax, so the term really means something like 'tax-free'.**

get/put someone's back/dander up aggravate or annoy someone. Try not to argue with John, because he always manages to get your back up. **From animal behaviour. Cats in particular raise their backs as a warning that they've had enough. 'Dander' is a Scots word for 'temper'.**

get carried away become over-eager or over-enthusiastic about something, to the point that one behaves foolishly or on impulse. He got so carried away that he went up and kissed her.

get one's claws into someone/something acquire power, control or influence over someone/something. Since that rich Mrs Brown moved to town, half the unattached men of the neighbourhood have been itching to get their claws into her. **A zoological metaphor.**

get cracking start working hard and in earnest. He had a cup of tea, but he really got cracking afterwards.

get down to brass tacks discuss the essentials, basics, of something. There were a few formal pleasantries of welcome to representatives, and then the meeting got down to the brass tacks of agreeing the agenda. **Probably from rhyming slang ('brass tacks' = 'hard facts').**

get even get one's revenge. He's very unhappy about losing his place in the team, and has threatened to get even with the selectors.

get/have one's fingers burnt suffer through participation in some risky project. He warned me not to buy shares in that company if I didn't want to get my fingers well and truly burnt.

get fresh become too cheeky, insolent or impudently disposed to take liberties. He tried to get fresh with her, and she slapped him in the face. **Originally American.**

get someone's goat annoy or irritate someone. The children spent the whole afternoon fooling about, and their silly conduct eventually got my goat – so I ordered them out of the house. **One theory is that this expression derives from the American custom of keeping a goat as stable companion for a racehorse. The goat acted as a calming influence on the highly strung thoroughbred before a race. Sometimes the goat was stolen by people trying to sabotage the outcome of the race, with the result that the horse's energy was depleted by fits of nervy pre-race tension and irritation.**

get one's head round something try to understand something. I'm afraid his behaviour is inexplicable to me, and I've never been able to get my head round it. Compare **take something in** or **on board**.

get hold of 1. make contact with. Where's the boss? We've been trying to get hold of him for hours. 2. acquire the idea of. He's got hold of the notion that his telephone is being tapped by the security services. From the literal meaning, 'to grasp'.

get in a dig at something/someone make a critical or hurtful remark about something/ someone. Someone eventually managed to get in a dig about the poor catering arrangements.

get in someone's hair annoy someone. Don't let that man in here – he really gets in my hair. Also **get on someone's nerves/wick/tits, get up someone's nose** (similar meanings).

get in on the act insinuate oneself into a project, etc. started by others in order to share any advantage, praise, profit, etc. It's funny, isn't it: no one wanted anything to do with us at the beginning, but now that we're famous everyone wants to get in on the act. From the theatre. Compare **in the limelight; jump on the bandwagon**.

get into shape literally, make oneself fit for something. Next year we're hosting the Olympic Games, so the city's had to get itself into shape to cater effectively for an enormous invasion of tourists, athletes and media folk.

get into the way of become accustomed to. He bought himself a new computer last year, and he's still trying to get into the way of it.

get it 1. understand the meaning of something. It was a lousy joke – in fact, I still don't get it. 2. be punished, scolded, etc. You'll get it if you're not in bed before your parents come home. 3. **get it (on)** have sex. She's been getting it on with her next-door neighbour for years. An American euphemism of the 1960s. The original sense has widened to include success at any pleasurable activity.

get it in the neck receive a scolding or punishment. She'll get it in the neck from her parents when they hear the news.

get it together get organised. Don't you think it's time you started to get it together? 'It' usually refers to 'one's act': see **get one's act together**, from which this expression has been compressed.

get one's knickers in a twist get agitated or flustered. Can you not just relax and calm down – getting your knickers in a twist won't solve the problem. There are many other picturesque and alliterative variations, all referring to undergarments, including 'get one's tights in a tangle', 'get one's combs (= combinations) in a commotion', etc.

get lost/nicked/stuffed go away, usually with the implication 'and stop annoying me'. I told the kids to go and get lost for half an hour.

get no change out of someone get no help or cooperation from someone. He asked John to lend him a hand – but I could have told him he'd get no change out of that oaf.

get one's oats get sexual satisfaction. He'll probably get his oats tonight unless he gets drunk and disgraces himself. From the idea of sowing one's wild oats, especially for pre- or extra-marital sex. Also 'get one's rocks off', 'get one's nuts', both usually applied to predatory or promiscuous men.

get off someone's back stop annoying or criticising someone. The sales manager doesn't like him, so he picks on him all the time and quite simply won't get off his back.

get off easy/light receive only the mildest punishment for something that in the speaker's view merited a stronger response. The judge only sentenced him to a month in prison; when you consider the crime, I think he got off rather too easy.

get off on the right/wrong foot start a relationship well/badly. We got off on the wrong foot when she heard me say something critical about her darling James. Compare **hit it off**.

get off scot-free completely escape punishment. Why should some offenders receive a heavy fine and others get off scot-free? Also 'go scot-free'. In the Middle Ages, a 'scot' was the name of a municipal tax. Another tax was called a 'lot', or allotted portion, and there used to be an idiom 'scot and lot'. If you paid a person off 'scot and lot', you settled all your outstanding debts to him. The nearest extant idiom to 'scot and lot' is probably **lock, stock and barrel**.

get off the ground get organised and running successfully. Today it's a very successful business, but it took its founders years to get it off the ground. From flying.

get on someone's nerves/wick/tits irritate someone. I wish she'd go away – she really gets on my tits. Compare **get under someone's skin**.

get round someone persuade someone to agree to something they originally didn't want to do. She's very good at getting round her father if she really needs something from him.

get one's teeth into something start working on something in earnest; embark keenly on a difficult project. It was a difficult book to write, and he had several false starts before he really managed to get his teeth into it. From animal behaviour; once a carnivore gets its teeth into a prey, it doesn't easily give it up. Also with similar meanings: 'get one's sleeves up', with the idea of physical effort; and **get/take the bit between one's teeth**, an equine metaphor of being unstoppable.

get the (big) bird get a bad reception. The show was pretty dire, and all the critics gave it the bird next morning in the papers. From the theatre and the long-established custom of audiences hissing a poor performance, like geese. Compare **thumbs up/down**.

get/take the bit between one's teeth become enthusiastic about doing a particular job, and keen to complete it satisfactorily. After we scored the first goal, we really got the bit between our teeth and there was no stopping us. An equine metaphor.

get the boot/heave(-ho)/push/chop be dismissed; lose one's job. She seems to have given her old boyfriend the boot. Also 'give someone the boot', literally meaning to kick someone out, usually of a job.

get the hang of something get the idea of how something operates. She's been trying to learn how to use a computer, but she's still not quite got the hang of it.

get the message understand something that has been only hinted. I kept looking at my watch, and she eventually got the message that I had another engagement.

get the picture understand. Slowly I began to get the picture. It took her a while to get the picture, but now everything's clear to her. Compare **put someone in the picture**.

get the sack lose one's job. After the economic downturn, thousands of workers got the sack. Once upon a time, workmen kept the tools of their trade in a sack. When they lost their job, they literally got their sack of tools back. Also 'be given the sack'.

get (hold of) the wrong end of the stick have the wrong idea; misunderstand. He thinks I'm looking for a job and can't seem to understand that he's got the wrong end of the stick.

get through to someone make oneself understood by someone, if necessary by overcoming any communicative obstructions. I don't think I'm quite getting through to you, am I? Compare **speak the same language**.

get to first/second base idioms of American origin which indicate how well someone has 'scored', or how far they have progressed towards sexual intimacy, with someone. I wonder if John got past second base last night? From the baseball field.

get under someone's skin thoroughly irritate or annoy someone. *He has the kind of posh voice that gets right under my skin.* From the idea of grit or another irritant invading one's bodily defences. Compare **get on someone's nerves/wick/tits**.

get-up-and-go initiative; enthusiasm. *What I like about Andrew is his brightness, and the fact that he has such a lot of vim and vigour and get-up-and-go.*

get up on the wrong side of the bed be in a bad or grumpy mood. *Watch the boss this morning – he seems to have got up on the wrong side of the bed!* From a popular saying based on an old superstition traceable back at least to Roman times. The Romans believed it was unlucky to get out of bed on the left side, because it was on that side that evil spirits lived. These would then proceed to plague your day. Compare **bear with a sore head**.

get (right) up someone's nose (thoroughly) annoy someone. *He may be a famous comedian, but his act usually manages to get right up my nose.* An inelegant expression indicative of a verbally bunged-up or semi-articulate speaker.

get up (a good head of) steam start to make good progress at something. *It was a good meeting, and we had really got up steam by the afternoon.* From the age of the steam train and steamship.

GHOST. (not have the) ghost of a chance (not even have) a very slight chance. *He's running in tomorrow's big race, fully aware that he's not got the ghost of a chance of winning.*

GIFT. gift of the gab persuasive abilities. *That man has always had the gift of the gab – he could charm the birds out of the trees.* Often derogatory, warning that the person may be fluent but lack substance, sincerity, etc. Compare **kiss the Blarney Stone**; **talk a good (something)**; **talk the birds off the trees**; **talk the hind legs off a donkey**.

GILD. gild the lily try to improve on something already almost perfect, especially nature's handiwork. *To wear such jewellery with such a classically beautiful costume – I'd say that was gilding the lily somewhat.* Adapted from Shakespeare's 'To gild refined gold, to paint the lily…Is wasteful and ridiculous excess.' *King John* iv.2.

GIVE. give someone/something a bad name give someone/something a poor reputation. *That restaurant has a very bad name for hygiene, especially since the food poisoning outbreak.* A modification of **give a dog a bad name**.

give someone/something a break 1. stop annoying or goading someone. *Eventually he stopped crying and begged his tormentors to give him a break.* Sometimes exclamatory: 'Give us a break, will you!' 2. offer a career opportunity to someone. *It was old Mr Brown who gave him his big break.*

give a dog a bad name (and it will hang him) say bad things about a person (and they will stick, i.e. they will spoil his reputation for a long time). *This is the kind of irresponsible gossipy comment that gives a dog a bad name, and so I propose to sue the newspaper in question for libel.* From old proverbs which articulate the popular view that a person's plight is hopeless if their reputation has been sullied, as in 'Give a dog a bad name and he'll soon be hanged.' A 16th-century variant is, 'He that has an ill name is half hanged.' See also under the entry **good name**.

give a good/poor account of oneself perform well/badly, often in a challenging situation. *I'm afraid he didn't give a very good account of himself in the interview, so they didn't offer him a job.*

give (someone) a hand 1. help someone. *My son asked me to give him a hand with his homework.* 2. applaud someone. *I want you all to give our speaker a big hand.*

give (someone) a piece of one's mind berate or angrily scold (someone). *She swore to give him a piece of her mind if she ever caught up with him.*

give (someone) a run for his/her money seriously challenge someone in a competition, etc. they were expected to win with ease. It was an exciting game, with the challengers giving the favourites a real run for their money. **From betting.**

give a wide berth to avoid; keep away from. He's fallen out with his girlfriend, and has been giving her a wide berth for a couple of weeks. **From navigation: ships in rough seas gave a wide berth to rocks or other hazards, its 'berth' being the ship's manoeuvring space.**

give (someone) an inch (and he/she will take a mile) allow someone a favour and he will ask for lots more. I wouldn't give that man an inch, or he'll never stop pestering you for favours. Usually negative.

give oneself airs give oneself an air of superiority; behave snobbishly, as if one regards everyone else as being inferior. She can give herself all the airs she wants, but the fact remains that she's no different from the rest of us. **Also 'put on airs'.**

give and take compromise; concession. Most successful marriages seem to be based on the mutual trust of the partners and plenty of give and take on both sides.

give as good as one gets perform in argument or in more pugilistic contest as effectively as one's opponent, whether verbally or physically; adequately acquit oneself. We were worried that John would be too young to look after himself in the navy, but he flourished there and it seems he gave as good as he got.

give chapter and verse quote exact sources, sometimes in a legalistic sense. He claimed to know his rights as a customer, and then in a loud and angry voice he proceeded to give chapter and verse to the terrified shopkeeper. **Once a Victorian Sunday School reference to children's ability to quote the catechism and other biblical texts.**

give one's eye/back teeth for something want something so much that one would do almost anything to get it. She admitted that she'd give her eye teeth for a job like that. **The 'eye' teeth**

are the canines, nearest the eyes. The original expression was 'give one's eyes', which is probably too gory for modern sensibilities. Compare the current **to die for**, also **give one's right arm**.

give ground move back; budge. The prime minister adamantly refused to give ground to his critics over the budget deficit. **The language of the battlefield.**

give or take if you add or subtract a small amount. He always gets here about 11 o'clock, give or take half an hour.

give over stop bothering, interrupting. He kept running through the kitchen and banging the door till I had to tell him to give over being a nuisance. **A phrasal verb.**

give one's right arm for something give anything one possesses in order to obtain something one wants very much. I would have given my right arm for an opportunity like that. Compare **give one's eye/back teeth**, also the more topical **to die for**.

give short shrift to resolve a matter quickly, often briskly and without sympathy. They came asking for a pay increase, but I gave them short shrift. From the very short time sometimes given to a prisoner before execution to shrive or repent his soul. Also **make short work of**.

give the benefit of the doubt to someone assume a person's innocence in the absence of conclusive evidence of guilt. She said she'd not been with him that day, and I gave her the benefit of the doubt. **Originally legal.**

give the cold shoulder to someone treat someone with coldness and contempt; ignore someone. After she was released from prison, the villagers gave her the cold shoulder and eventually she had to move away. **Originally a Scottish reference to withdrawal of the most basic and rudimentary form of hospitality.**

give the devil his due admit an opponent's merits, grudgingly or not. He's a very unpopular footballer, but give the devil his due – he had a very good game on Saturday.

give the game/show away let a secret become known, often by accident. Shhh! Don't say another word, or you'll give the whole show away! Compare **let the cat out of the bag.**

give someone the glad eye show one feels attracted to someone. That man seems to fancy the barmaid; he's been giving her the glad eye all evening.

give someone the runaround deliberately try to mislead or confuse someone. The police are getting fed up with him because he keeps giving them the runaround.

give someone the slip escape from someone. He's a wanted man, but he keeps managing to give the police the slip.

give someone the willies/collywobbles make someone feel very nervous and apprehensive. It's always been a spooky place, and it's quite enough to give most people the willies. The 'willies' are thought to be a colloquialism based on willow trees, once a symbol of grief and mourning. The 'collywobbles' variation originally referred to bowel pains, and was a Victorian blending of 'colic' and 'wobble'.

give something up as a bad job abandon a project that one is unlikely to complete successfully. The match was played in appalling weather conditions, and at half-time they decided to give it up as a bad job. Similar to 'fight a losing battle'.

give up the ghost stop trying. She worked extremely hard last year, and passed all her exams; but this year she seems to have given up the ghost. Literally, to die.

give someone what for give someone a severe telling-off. He's been warned that I'll give him what for if he takes the car away again.

GLAD. glad rags one's best clothes. Everyone seemed to be togged out in their glad rags – it looked like someone was having a party. **Originally American, the expression is usually facetious.**

GLASS. glass ceiling hidden or invisible barrier. There are still not very many women who break through the glass ceiling into British boardrooms.

GLIMPSE. glimpse of the obvious insight into something that is very obviously true. He tells me that British people are dreadfully conservative, which has to be today's glimpse of the obvious. **Usually sarcastic, applied to someone who is slow on the uptake, and who is saying something that everybody already knows and understands.**

GLOBAL. global village 1990s term meaning the world community, and referring to our awareness of its smallness in the context both of global communications and of the scale of 'our' galaxy. Broadcasting to the global village is not hard nowadays.

GLOVES. the gloves are/come off the serious argument or battle is about to begin. At first, the warring factions in Bosnia seemed to be sparring and jostling for position; but then the gloves came off and it was open, bloody war. **From the pre-Queensberry Rules boxing ring, where bare knuckles did much worse damage than a gloved fist.**

GLUTTON. a glutton for punishment person who is willing to keep performing some function in the knowledge that it will continue to be thankless and unpleasant. The challenger took a terrible beating in the first three rounds, but he was a real glutton for punishment, and kept coming back for more.

GNOMES. the gnomes of Zurich faceless international Swiss bankers, who have a key role in the world's economy. The United Nations may want to do this and that, but will the gnomes of Zurich let them? **Gnomes guarded the treasures of the earth, especially its precious ores, according to folklore. Swiss banks are said to be notoriously uninterested in the provenance of**

funds, and equally successful in protecting their clients' fiscal anonymity. So the 'gnomes of Zurich' suggests a powerful, rather anonymous influence on the world's politicians.

GO. go against the grain act contrary to a person's wishes or feelings. It went very much against the grain for her to work on such a dishonest project. The metaphor is from woodworking; it is easier to cut with the grain of the wood than against it.

go ape/apeshit lose one's self-control; become uncontrollably upset, angry, etc. When her parents got home and saw the chaos, they went completely ape. From the furious temper tantrums of apes, chimpanzees, etc. Perhaps a development from the earlier 'go nuts', a favourite monkey food. See **go mad/nuclear/nuts/ballistic**, etc. (similar meanings). Compare **have a fit**.

go AWOL absent oneself without authorisation. She's worried about her husband, who went AWOL at Christmas and hasn't been seen since. From the American military, dating to the Civil War (1861–5). AWOL is an acronym meaning 'absent without leave'.

go berserk totally lose one's temper. When she told him that she'd bumped into his car, he went berserk. From Berserker, the nickname of a fierce Norse warrior in Scandinavian mythology; he would work himself into a violent frenzy before battle. Compare **run amok**.

go by the board be lost or abandoned (especially projects, ideas, etc.). They were planning to have a holiday in America, but that idea seems to have gone by the board. From the sea, and the loss of something overboard from a ship.

go by the book do things strictly according to the written rules, etc. The most successful officers are not always those who go by the book 24 hours a day – sometimes you have to use your initiative, or even your imagination.

go cap in hand beg humbly for something. It's hard to say no to a hysterical customer whose house is flooding and who goes cap in hand to your door to see if you'll fix her burst pipe. From the tradition of beggars holding out their cap for money.

go one's dinger go at something vigorously or boisterously. They were an excellent rock band, and they fairly went their dingers at last night's show. A Scots idiom, 'ding' meaning 'push', 'beat', 'strike', etc.

go down like a lead balloon fail dismally. It was a dreadful speech by the prime minister, and went down like a lead balloon.

go dutch expression used when more than one person is going out for a meal, to the cinema, etc. to indicate that each person will pay his/her own way. When the bill for the meal arrived, it was pretty steep; so we all agreed to go dutch. Once a xenophobic English inference that Dutchmen were mean. See **dutch auction**, **dutch courage**, **dutch treat**, etc. for other evidence that the English used to dislike the Dutch.

go easy on someone/something 1. not punish someone too severely. The police decided they'd better go easy on him since he was only 15. 2. not use too much of something. Go easy on the milk, there's not much left.

go for broke risk everything. The man was desperate, and he went for broke when he held up the bank. From the gambling table.

go for someone/something attack someone/something. One minute the dog was playing happily with them, the next minute it went for them like a wild tiger. A phrasal verb.

go great guns progress very well. The car's been going great guns since its last service. American.

go haywire go wrong or out of control; not work properly. The computer seems to have gone haywire, and we'll need to get it serviced. Nineteenth-century American, from the use of baling wire by farmers for makeshift repair work, who would then leave it lying around as a potential hazard.

go in one ear and out the other hear something and then immediately forget it. Most of what I said to him obviously failed to register – it just went in one ear and straight out the other.

go mad/nuclear/nuts/ballistic get furiously angry. He goes mad if you criticise him. A hyperbole. A more recent intensifier by analogy is 'go nuclear'. When asked to explain the sleaze allegations the prime minister went nuclear and started attacking the press and the opposition. Other variants: 'go off at the deep end', 'go through the roof'. Compare **have a fit**.

go native live according to one's host culture rather than one's native culture. He's lived in France so long that he went native years ago – so don't be surprised when he kisses you on both cheeks. The expression is redolent of the colonial era, and was once highly critical of colonial officers, etc. who identified too closely with the native African or Asian culture of the colony.

go off half-cock fail to function with complete success. The festival was badly organised and funded, so it went off half-cock: it needed much better planning. From 18th-century firearms.

go overboard for show excessive enthusiasm for. She wore a nice outfit, but I wouldn't have gone overboard for her friend's costume. Literally, one wouldn't jump in the sea to rescue it.

go round (and round) in circles work at something but keep failing to make progress with it. Colleagues have been trying for weeks to sort out the problem, but they just keep going round and round in circles getting nowhere.

go steady have a regular, exclusive, long-term relationship. John and Jane have been going steady since they were in sixth form at school.

go straight lead a law-abiding existence, generally after a period in jail. He doesn't find it too easy to go straight, and is very tempted to go back to his old ways. From the biblical idea of keeping to the straight and narrow path leading to personal salvation.

go swimmingly work splendidly; be smoothly run and successful. Everything went swimmingly until the car accelerated on the main road – and then it just seemed to fall to pieces. A 17th-century expression.

go the extra mile make an extra-special effort, usually to oblige, appease or placate someone. If it will make her any happier, I'll be delighted to go the extra mile – just for her.

go the whole hog do something thoroughly and completely. They went out to a concert last night, and then they decided they'd go the whole hog and dine out as well. From the idea of spending a whole shilling, or 'hog', as it was called in the 17th century. Compare **in for a penny**.

go through hell have a particularly difficult or unpleasant time. She said little, but her face said it all – it was the face of a person who has gone through hell.

go through with something finish something; bring something to a conclusion, especially if it is difficult. It was a very risky course of treatment, and there was no guarantee of success, but she decided to go through with it anyway.

go to earth hide. Fed up with the endless attention of the press, the princess decided to go to earth for a while. From the name of a fox's den, a hole in the ground called an 'earth', where it hides when threatened.

go to glory die. At the end of the movie, the hero went to glory in a blaze of gun smoke and there wasn't a dry eye in the cinema. One of a large number of euphemisms for dying, including 'go to one's long home', 'go to one's just reward', 'go to join/meet one's maker', etc.

go too far provoke someone. Don't annoy me by going too far! You've gone quite far enough!

go/come to pieces break up, or down. He just seemed to go to pieces after the death of his wife.

go to pigs and whistles be ruined or in a mess. It used to be a magnificent house, but it's a mess these days, because sadly the present owners have let it go to pigs and whistles. An uncommon idiom nowadays, a 'pig' is an old name for an earthenware pot, while a 'whistle' is a musical pipe; together, as a dyad, they have a poetic connotation of trivial 'bits and pieces'.

go to pot deteriorate to the point of worthlessness. It used to be such a lovely garden, but I'm afraid we've let it go to pot in our old age. See also **go to wrack and ruin** and **go to the dogs**.

go to seed become unfit and run-down. He used to play international rugby, but he's gone to seed a bit since those days. From gardening, and leaving plants to seed themselves rather than cultivate them.

go to the dogs become ruined, often through excess or by neglect. He used to be such a smart and dapper little man, but he went to the dogs after his wife's death. The term can be used of an institution as well as a person, and was well known to Charles Dickens, as in 'He has gone to the demnition bow-wows.' In *Nicholas Nickleby*, ch 64. Compare **go to pot; road to ruin/perdition**.

go to the wall become financially ruined. Business is a jungle in which the least effective always go to the wall. An old idiom, which may date to the days when rampart walls surrounded towns, castles, etc. to defend them from attack. Defending soldiers who went to the wall often went to their deaths trying to protect the citadel. We might call them 'cannon fodder' or 'expendable squaddies'.

go to town do something enthusiastically and without restraint, usually also lavishly and without sparing any expense. The Browns have gone to town on the decoration of their new house. The original US expression literally referred to an expensive shopping spree in the nearest town.

go to work on start working on. I asked him to cut the grass, and he went to work on it right away.

go to wrack and ruin become damaged or ruined beyond repair. It had been a magnificent example of baroque architecture, but it went to wrack and ruin at the beginning of the 20th century. A dyad, with 'wrack' an otherwise obsolete spelling of 'wreck'. Now sometimes spelt 'rack'. See also **go to pot**.

go west become lost, disappear. When I accidentally broke a teacup, she merely sighed and said quietly, 'Ah well, that's another piece of my wedding china gone west!' During the First World War, the expression was also a popular RAF euphemism, meaning 'to die'. That could be an echo of the old pan-Celtic myths of dead people going into Avalon and Tir nan Og, or other legendary islands of the blest in the western ocean.

go with the flow do the easiest thing. Just relax and go with the flow – don't keep trying to fight the problem. Opposite of **kick against the pricks**.

GOD. God and Mammon the forces of selflessness and the forces of greed. People have to choose between God and Mammon from time to time. From the Bible: 'You cannot serve God and Mammon.' Matthew vi.24. Like black and white, or good and evil, the two are often loosely cited as opposites. Strictly speaking, 'Mammon' means the idolisation of wealth, or worldly gains. Nowadays many speakers wrongly regard Mammon as synonymous with the devil.

god-forsaken dismal; desolate. You don't expect me to spend a week in this god-forsaken place, do you? Literally, a place which god has deserted.

god squad the forces of organised religion. He used to be such a sociable, happy person, but then he got in with the god squad at university and he seems to have changed for the worse. Often used ironically, with particular reference to the Christian proselytising tendencies.

GOD'S. (think oneself) God's gift to someone/ something have an extremely conceited idea of one's worth to someone/something. Watch that man – he think's he's God's gift to women! **A term of disparagement.**

God's own country one's own homeland. Welcome to God's own country, and we hope you will enjoy your stay among us. The original reference to God's country was by US Union troops fighting in the American Deep South. Nowadays the term is often used ironically.

GOLD. gold-digger person with a reputation for seeking a partner in marriage on the basis of the partner's wealth. He tends to have a weakness for rich widows, so he's maybe something of a gold-digger.

GOLDEN. golden handshake redundancy payment terminating a person's employment. He lost his job at 53, but received a very generous golden handshake. **Also, by extension, 'golden hello', an incentive to join a company, a sort of 'welcome aboard'. A 'golden parachute', when leaving, may be construed as giving the lucky recipient a soft landing.**

golden opportunity very favourable chance or prospect. He met his boss socially at the weekend, and it seemed like a golden opportunity to ask for a promotion.

golden rule most important rule. If you want to make a good speech, the golden rule is to keep it short. The original golden rule was 'Do unto others as you would have them do unto you.'

GONE. gone for a Burton lost; missing; killed. He spent over £100 at the betting shop last night – another week's pay gone for a Burton! **Probably from an RAF expression in use in the Second World War; planes and airmen failing to return from air-raids over Germany were euphemistically said to have 'gone for a Burton'. It is unclear who or what the original Burton was, though candidates include Burton ale, and – more plausibly – Montague Burton the tailor and seller of ready-made suits. In the latter instance, the wordplay would have been on wooden suits, i.e. coffins.**

GOOD. good as gold very good indeed; angelically well behaved. That child has been as good as gold all weekend. **The standard simile for children's good behaviour. Another standard benchmark of goodness: 'good as new', meaning almost perfectly repaired.** The surgeon has fixed her shattered leg so well that it's as good as new again.

good/bad egg reliable/unreliable person; worthy/worthless person. There was only one bad egg at the party – that notorious troublemaker Jones. **The expression nicely conveys the idea that a person's exterior – like an egg's – can be deceptive.**

good gracious! or **goodness gracious (me)!** or **good God!** apart from the reference to God (taboo for many), these are polite and old-fashioned exclamations of surprise. The car came round the corner so fast that I shouted to my wife, 'Good God, jump for it or he'll hit you!' Compare **goodness knows** and **by jove!** Also **for crying out loud**.

good innings a long and useful life. As John said last week, at 95 he knew very well that he'd had a good innings. From cricket, an innings is the period a team has for batting at the wicket.

good name reputation. He has a very good name in his own field, which is photography. Originally the term meant one's honour. See for example Shakespeare's *Othello* iii.3: 'Good name in man or woman, dear my lord,/Is the immediate jewel of their souls . . . /He that filches from me my good name/Robs me of that which not enriches him/And makes me poor indeed.' Compare **give a dog a bad name**.

good riddance (to bad rubbish) exclamation to show that one is pleased to be rid of something or someone considered worthless. It was a silly sort of job and he didn't enjoy doing it. When it was finished, he exclaimed with feeling, 'Good riddance to that!'

good samaritan person who helps other people, especially if they are in distress. When my car broke down on the motorway, I was lucky enough to get help from a passing good samaritan who stopped his car, reversed up to me, and asked if there was anything he could do to help. The biblical parable of the Good Samaritan, who didn't pass by on the other side but who stopped to help the wounded man, is in Luke x.30–35.

(jolly) good show! exclamation meaning 'That's good!' or 'How nice!' or 'Well done!' You've made a very fine drawing – good show! Old fashioned.

GOODS. goods and chattels one's personal belongings and property. The refugees were a pitiful sight – the luckiest ones had an ox and cart loaded with all their goods and chattels. A dyad, perhaps legal in origin, and probably dating to Anglo-Norman times, when dyads were popular because they often fused a native Anglo-Saxon component with an Anglo-Norman one; this was one way to ensure understanding in a bilingual society. 'Chattels' derives from the same source as 'cattle' (both words are from Latin 'capitale'), and originally meant only one's moveable belongings, including livestock. Compare **bags and baggage**.

GOODNESS. goodness knows I don't know. Goodness knows how much money he earns. A euphemism for 'God knows'. See also **good gracious!** and **by jove!**

GORDON. Gordon Bennett! a watered-down exclamation, used as an alternative to the blasphemous 'Oh God!' or 'gor blimey!' (an erosion of 'God blind me!'). Oh help, Gordon Bennett, what have I done! It was easy enough to replace God with Gordon, and then to add a famous surname. James Gordon Bennett II (1841–1918) was the kenspeckle, socially conspicuous editor-in-chief of the *New York Herald*.

GOSPEL. gospel truth completely and verifiably true. I told her it was the gospel truth I'd never seen her boyfriend. Also **'as gospel'**, meaning true. Don't take everything you read in the newspapers as gospel. The gospel is the Christian revelation, therefore the New Testament of the Bible.

GRASP. grasp the nettle/thistle boldly tackle a difficult problem or assignment. It was a difficult issue, but in the end there was nothing for it but to grasp the nettle and try to sort matters out. From the popular belief that a grasped nettle didn't give a sting, unlike one that was merely touched. 'If you gently touch a nettle it'll sting you for your pains;/Grasp it like a lad of mettle, it as soft as silk remains.' From a poem by Aaron Hill, 1743. Compare **bite the bullet; take the bull by the horns**.

GRASS. grass roots the ordinary folk in an organisation, not their leadership. The parliamentary party may have wanted one thing, the grass roots wanted something else. Originally American, early 20th century. Similar to **rank and file; man in the street**.

grass widow woman whose husband or partner is absent from her. There are several grass widows in our village, with husbands working in the Arabian peninsula or in Europe. The term was well known in British India in the 19th century, where women were often parted from their soldier husbands for long periods and stayed at hill-stations (where grass grew) during the hot season. Variations include 'golf widow' (one whose husband spends a lot of time on the golf course).

GRAVE. someone's just walked on/over my grave shiver involuntarily, usually for an unspecifiable reason. No, I don't feel cold and I didn't get a fright – someone just walked on my grave, that's all! This remark is based on an old belief, that one sometimes shivers with some superstitious presentiment of one's mortality.

GRAVY. the gravy train sinecure position(s), where one is well placed to obtain perks and other advantages. I want you to be quite clear about one thing: a job in local government is not a gravy train to foreign travel at the ratepayers' expense, contrary to popular opinion. 1920s American, 'gravy' is a slang term for easy gain.

GREAT. great Scott! exclamation, probably first adopted as a substitute for the more blasphemous 'Great God!' Great Scott, is that the time? I have to go. **The term is American in origin, and popular from the time of the Mexican War (1847), whose hero was US General Winfield Scott.** Alternatives include 'great grief!', 'great Jehoshafat' and 'great Caesar!'

great unwashed the poor masses of the populace; the proletariat. He had to spend the night in a cell at the police station, but it won't do him any harm to live among the great unwashed from time to time. **The term comes from Edmund Burke (1729–97) and became rare, sounding as it did far too patronising and snobbish for the political correctness of the 1990s.**

Great War the First World War, also called 'the war to end wars'. Both his grandfathers were killed in the Great War. **With hindsight we know that the only great thing about it was the gigantic number of its casualties.**

GREEK. Greek gift dangerous gift. One has to beware of Greek gifts. **The Trojan horse was apparently a Greek gift, but in reality it was a trick leading to the overthrow of Troy.**

(it's all) Greek to me I don't understand it; it's lost on me. He's a student of chemical engineering, and doing all sorts of interesting things with plastics – but it's all Greek to me! **An English chauvinist taunt which is usually a reference to an entire subject area rather than to particular words or sentences; compare double Dutch.**

GREEN. green as grass very naive. I was as green as grass when I started that job. **The standard simile for innocence and inexperience. From vegetation: it is the young and tender shoots that have this colour.**

green belt farm- or parkland around a conurbation which may not be built on. They are trying to get permission to build the new city hospital on green-belt land.

green-eyed monster jealousy. He decided against attending the party, thinking that his ex-wife would be there with her new man, and fearing a public attack of the green-eyed monster. **From Shakespeare's** *Othello*, **where Iago says: 'O, beware my lord of jealousy;/It is the green-ey'd monster, which doth mock/That meat it feeds on.'** *The Merchant of Venice* also has a reference to 'green-ey'd jealousy'. We commonly talk about people being 'green with envy'.

green fingers knack of being a good gardener. She keeps a beautiful garden – like the rest of her family, she seems to have green fingers.

green light the go-ahead to proceed. At last the school has received the green light to hire an extra maths teacher. **From traffic signals; opposite of red light.**

green stuff money; payment. I did a small job for them last year but I'm still waiting to see their green stuff. **Originally American slang, where all US banknotes are green ('greenbacks').**

green welly brigade upper-middle-class Britons of the hunting, shooting and fishing persuasion, whose country 'uniform' is a wax jacket and pair of green wellington boots (wellies). It used to be a very nice country pub, but then it was discovered by the green welly brigade. **Often used pejoratively. Compare Sloane Ranger, to which this social grouping relates quite frightfully well (as they'd say).**

GREY. grey area topic or area of discussion where the categories are not very clear. There's no well articulated demarcation line between our promotion and our publicity departments, so there are one or two grey areas of the business where people aren't sure who does what.

grey eminence influential person in the background to the decision takers. Nobody knew the name of the chief secretary to the Treasury, but he was the real grey eminence behind most of the government's financial policy. **From 17th-century France; the original Éminence Grise was Père Joseph, the adviser to Cardinal Richelieu who governed France in the name of King Louis XIII.**

Joseph wore the grey habit of the Capuchin friars. See also **power behind the throne**, although strictly speaking Père Joseph was the power behind the power behind the throne.

GRIM. grim reaper death. He runs the biggest funeral parlour in town, and the grim reaper ensures a steady trade for him. A poetic Victorian euphemism, personifying death as a farmer with a scythe garnering souls in the same way as the farmer garners corn.

GRIN. grin and bear it put up with something as cheerfully and stoically as one can, without voicing recriminations or complaints. He lost all his savings in the stock market crash, but quickly realised that there was nothing for it but to grin and bear it.

grin from ear to ear grin very broadly and look very pleased or happy. It was a very happy group photo, with everyone grinning from ear to ear at the camera.

grin like a Cheshire cat smile broadly, or in a foolish or uncontrolled way. There I stood, dressed up like a Christmas tree and grinning like a Cheshire cat. A standard simile. The most famous appearance of the Cheshire cat occurs in Lewis Carroll's *Alice's Adventures in Wonderland* (1865), in the following lines: 'How cheerfully he seems to grin,/How neatly spreads his claws,/And welcomes little fishes in/With gently smiling jaws!' Lewis Carroll's beast had the ability to vanish at will, its grin being the last thing to disappear. Although the Cheshire cat has been around much longer than Lewis Carroll, its origins are unexplained. Some claim that Cheshire cheeses used to be stamped with a grinning cat.

GRIST. grist to the mill something that makes life/business/one's job, etc. worthwhile or profitable. Never turn away a job, however small. Remember it's all grist to the mill. 'Grist' was corn for grinding, thus work to keep the mill busy and the miller in funds.

GRIT. grit one's teeth persevere with doing something which one doesn't want to do, and even though one knows it is going to be difficult. After a long and tiring flight nobody felt much like playing a football match, but we just had to grit our teeth and get on with it.

GROW. grow on someone begin to like something one originally didn't like. When I first saw it, I thought it was a horrible picture – but I must admit that it's grown on me over the years and now I think of it almost as an old friend.

grow out of something stop doing something as one gets older. She used to get a terribly red face when she was embarrassed, but eventually she grew out of that problem.

grow up! an exhortation to behave oneself. It's all very well to go off in a sulk and bang the door, but it's time he grew up and got used to criticism. A phrasal verb. Also **act one's age**.

GRUB. Grub Street hack writing; inferior and frequently plagiarised texts of poor literary merit. He's written one or two rather turgid Grub Street novels. From the name of an 18th-century London street inhabited by many 'Grub Street hacks', in the words of Dr Samuel Johnson. A synecdoche, still deprecatory. Compare **Fleet Street**.

GUM. gum up the works cause machinery or a work routine to break down. If you impose any more rules and regulations on the system, you'll completely and utterly gum up the works and it will come grinding to a halt.

GUTTER. gutter press newspapers which deal in scandal and gossip. It was an article unworthy even of the gutter press on a bad day. See also **yellow press**.

GYPPY. gyppy tummy attack of diarrhoea. He was off work for a couple of days after a bout of gyppy tummy. A colonial euphemistic expression, similar to 'Delhi belly', with 'gyppy' a familiar and assonant version of 'Egyptian', punning with colloquial 'gyp' (= pain). Also **Montezuma's revenge**.

H

HACK. hack it do it; succeed; survive. He'd been ill for years, and eventually he just couldn't hack it any more. The original sense was of chopping one's way through some obstacle.

HAIR. hair of the dog (that bit you) an alcoholic drink (taken to help cure a hangover). He went down to the pub, saying that the only thing to sort out his sore head was a hair of the dog. There was a traditional belief that a bite from a rabid dog could be cured by putting a hair from the same dog's coat on the wound.

(make one's) hair stand on end (make one) feel terrified. Some of his stories about the war would make your hair stand on end.

HALCYON. halcyon days peaceful and stress-free times. Those annual holidays in Brittany were halcyon days for all of us. From Greek mythology. The goddess Halcyone and her husband were turned into kingfishers which, according to contemporary belief, built their nests in the sea. The gods ensured that there would be no storms at sea while the birds were nesting. According to legend, kingfishers bred on the seven days preceding and following the winter solstice, and these were the original halcyon days when the gods promised fair weather.

HALE. hale and hearty fit and well; healthy. My Uncle John was hale and hearty right into his 90s. An alliterative dyad.

HALF. half a mind/notion (to do/say something) inclined (to do/say something critical). He's been late for work all week, and I've half a mind to give him the sack.

half an ear a modicum of attention, but not usually enough to hear all the details of what is being discussed, said, etc. He cooked himself a meal while listening with half an ear to the nine o'clock news.

half-assed/-hearted ineffectual and unenthusiastic. The minister gave his usual half-assed speech to an almost empty House of Commons. Originally perhaps a deformation of 'haphazard'.

half-baked stupid; badly thought out. I wish you'd stop coming up with these half-baked ideas.

half seas over drunk. It was obvious to everyone, as soon as he entered the room, that the man was half seas over. The original term was nautical, and meant literally 'halfway across the sea'. By 1700, it also meant halfway between drunkenness and sobriety. Today, it means wholly drunk. Also 'half cut', perhaps from the notion of being partially detached or cut off from one's wits.

HALFWAY. halfway house midpoint between two points of view. The government's latest measures satisfied neither side of the argument, precisely because they were nothing more than a halfway house. From the days when travelling across country was more difficult than it is today. There were many inns or staging posts with this name, situated between two towns and therefore a convenient meeting place.

HALT. halt and (the) blind physically – or often, nowadays, economically – handicapped people. Some people persist in the view that a civilised society has to try to look after its halt and blind. A Biblical dyad from the Gospel of Luke, xiv.21.

HAM. ham actor awkward and unrehearsed actor, often enthusiastic in spite of his natural limitations. He was a real ham actor, but we all enjoyed his energetic performance. Clumsiness is also conveyed by terms like **ham-fisted** and **ham-handed**. Enthusiasm is also a factor in an expression like **ham it up**.

ham-fisted/-handed clumsy. He's too ham-fisted even to be capable of changing a light bulb or fixing a fuse. The literal idea is of ham-sized fists too big to do delicate work.

ham it up respond to attention by elaborate overacting. Pay no attention to his antics, or he'll start hamming it up to the point of complete farce. A phrasal verb, a variant of **play to the gallery**.

HAMMER. hammer and tongs with great force and gusto. They've been fighting hammer and tongs with each other for years – I'm told it's a sign of a happy marriage! A dyad from the blacksmith's forge: these tools made a loud noise when he was working.

hammer away at something/someone continue working persistently on a problem/person until one gets the required result or response. He's been hammering away for weeks at getting a full confession from the prisoner.

hammer something home emphasise a point hard enough to ensure that one's audience fully understands it. It takes a general election every five years to hammer home to the government of the day the fact of its unpopularity.

HAND. hand something down pass something from one generation to another. These baptismal robes have now been handed down over eight generations.

hand in glove (with) in close alliance (with). The Conservative Party has been said to work hand in glove with big business. There is usually a secretive resonance to this idiom, in other words the cooperating parties refrain from publicising their links.

hand in the till stealing money. His career was ruined when his employer discovered him with his hand in the till. A popular euphemism.

hand someone something on a plate give something to someone too easily, and without making him/her work for it. He was one of those insufferable aristocrats who was handed everything on a plate at birth. See also **born with a silver spoon in one's mouth**.

hand it to someone admit one's admiration of someone. I have to hand it to you – you've won the prize that nobody thought you had a chance of winning.

hand over fist fast, and in big quantities. The business is highly profitable, and the company seems to make money hand over fist. The term usually applies to moneymaking, but the original metaphor is of pulling in a big catch of fish with both hands.

hand to mouth subsisting with hardly enough food or money to live on. They live from hand to mouth through the winter, doing little work until the farmers are ready in the spring to hire their labour again.

HANDLE. handle to one's name/jug peerage or other aristocratic title. He's not just plain Mr Brown – he's an earl or something, with a very fancy handle to his jug.

handle with kid gloves treat gently and with care. Many of these children have been utterly traumatised by the war, and need to be handled with kid gloves. The 'kid' is a baby goat, with a very soft hide which produced the softest and most delicate of leather gloves.

HAND'S. hand's turn small amount of work. She stayed for a month and never did so much as a hand's turn about the house. Usually negative, and deprecative of a person's laziness. A Scots expression.

HANDS. hands down easily; decisively. They won the match hands down – the score was 48 to nil. It is said that the expression originally referred to a jockey's handling of a horse's reins. He lets his hands down when he is sure his horse is coasting to victory.

(have one's) hands full (be) busy. I'm afraid I can't take on the job just now because I have my hands full with all sorts of other work.

hands off do not touch. Hands off those sweets! A common imperative for small children.

(have one's) hands tied (be) prevented from acting. I would love to recommend you for the job, but my hands are tied.

HANG. hang by a thread be in a precarious state; be in doubt or danger. For three days, her life hung by a thread, and then she started to recover. Probably from the Greek legend of the **sword of Damocles**.

hang fire postpone a decision. The government have decided to hang fire on their privatisation policy till after the next election. The original term referred to firearms. Riflemen were sometimes ordered to hold their fire, or hang fire, until some development could be followed up off the field of battle. A gun was also said to be hanging fire if it failed to go off properly, and needed further priming.

hang one's head (in shame) show contrition or remorse for one's behaviour. He needs to hang his head in shame for such loutish and drunken antics.

hang in there(, baby) stick with something and don't give up. You'll just have to hang in there, baby, till the rescue team gets to you. American exhortation of the 1960s, still heard but now usually ironic.

hang loose stay relaxed. They told her to hang loose and enjoy her evening. American 1960s idiom of beatniks and flower folk, used to describe a desirable state of detachment and spiritual liberation. See also **keep (one's) cool; let it all hang out**.

hang/stick one on someone punch or hit someone. The fleeing prisoner couldn't resist hanging one on the warder's nose.

hang up one's boots retire. He'd been working for over 40 years, and decided that the time had come for him to hang up his boots. From football, and hanging up one's boots after a game. Compare **call it a day**.

hang up one's hat move in with someone, especially a husband with a wife or vice versa. He spends a lot of time with my sister, and I think he's more or less hung up his hat at her place now.

HANGDOG. hangdog look sneaking, shame-faced or guilty-looking expression. The prisoner looked a bit smarter this morning, with less of the hangdog look about him. A 'hangdog' in the 17th century was a villainous person 'fit to be hanged like a dog'. There is also no doubt that a dog which has disobeyed its owner can often convey a thoroughly guilty-looking expression.

HANKY. hanky-panky slang term for some kind of underhand double-dealing or deception. I suspected them of getting up to some kind of hanky-panky in my absence. Like many terms formed by reduplication the word is often humorous, and sometimes serves as a kind of euphemism for sexual misconduct.

HAPPILY. happily ever after in the end, everything was resolved satisfactorily. Many people like a novel where the villains are punished and the heroes and heroines live happily ever after.

HAPPY. happy as a sandboy very happy. They've been playing in the garden for hours, happy as a sandboy. Other standard similes are 'happy as a lark', 'happy as Larry', 'happy as the day is long' and 'happy as a pig in muck'. The Victorian sandboy hawked sand for sale as an alternative for sawdust on kitchen floors, etc.

happy-go-lucky unworrying. From childhood, she's been a very carefree, happy-go-lucky sort of person and nothing ever seems to distress her.

happy hunting ground heaven; paradise. He recalled Paris as a happy hunting ground for his various youthful amorous adventures. Originally a translation from the North American Indian name for heaven.

happy medium position which avoids extremes. He can't seem to find the happy medium between having far too much work to do one week, and having nothing at all to do the following week. Opposite of 'a hunger and a burst'.

HARD. hard act to follow standard or level that will be hard to attain, let alone exceed. The first speaker of the evening was to be the Lord Chancellor, so I knew I had a hard act to follow. From the stage.

hard-and-fast (rules) 1. fixed and not to be changed; strict. There are several hard-and-fast rules which every car driver must observe. Originally a nautical dyad, used to describe a ship which had run aground and could not be moved. 2. definite. It's impossible to get hard-and-fast information out of the Ruritanian Government about its intentions.

hard as nails very hard; unfeeling; pitiless. There's no point appealing to her 'feminine' sentiments; she's as hard as nails and there isn't a feminine sentiment in her body. A standard simile. There used also to be 'right as nails', meaning absolutely right, but this simile has become obsolete.

hard bitten tough, determined to get what one wants. She was seen as a hard-bitten old tyrant who gave the country the smack of firm government.

hard boiled cynical. I don't like to see youngsters with such a hard-boiled view of life. American, perhaps devised as an alternative to 'sunny side up'.

hard core 1. kernel grouping of committed or stubborn people. There is a hard core of English MPs who are totally opposed to the European Union. In this sense, a journalistic idiom which most frequently refers to political or religious groupings. 2. sheer and utter. The police seized a quantity of magazines described by a spokesperson as hard-core pornography. A journalistic cliché, sometimes confusingly abbreviated to 'hard porn'.

hard done by unfairly treated. Although he has inherited great wealth and influence, he still manages to give the impression of someone who has been hard done by in life.

hard left/right socialist/conservative of extreme views and beliefs. The hard left are not going to accept the view of the party leadership, but do they ever?

hard lines/luck common expression of sympathy, meaning 'bad luck!' The closure of the factory was very hard lines on the workforce in the village. Often an interjection or exclamation. 'I've broken my arm.' 'Oh, hard lines!'

hard nut (to crack) person or problem that is difficult to deal with. I've always avoided discussing the subject, since it's such a hard nut to crack.

hard-on male erection of the penis. Just thinking about Marilyn Monroe or Brigitte Bardot used to give him an instant hard-on.

hard/hot on someone's/something's heels close behind someone/something. We had the sales conference one weekend, and then hard on its heels came the big trade fair.

hard pressed/put to it under pressure. He'll be very hard pressed to come up with the money by next week.

hard put (to it) finding it difficult (to do something). A lot of voters are hard put to it to tell you the name of their MP.

hard sell aggressive selling technique pioneered by the Americans. There's no point trying your hard sell on me – I'm not buying your lousy product!

(a drop of the) hard stuff (some) whisky or other strong liquor. Come in out of that rain and have a glass of the hard stuff to warm you up. Informal and usually jocular.

hard up impoverished. You must expect to be hard up if you lose your job. Originally nautical, the expression meant 'aground' – now perhaps in the present idiom 'waiting for one's boat to come in' (or one's luck to change for the better).

HARK. hark back (to) refer back to something said/done earlier. I wish you'd stop harking back to my accident. Originally from hunting; hunting dogs would hark back in order to pick up a lost scent or trail.

HARM. harm a hair on someone's head cause the smallest hurt to someone. If he so much as harms a hair on that child's head, I'll personally beat him up. Most commonly used either in the negative, or as the alliterative run-up to a threat.

HARP. harp on (about something) talk too much (about something). Our teachers used to harp on and on about reading all the questions before we tackled the exam. From music; the original idiom was 'harp on one string about something', thus talk monotonously about it.

HAT. hat trick a three-in-a-row success. The Conservatives won the last two elections, and will be going for the hat trick this time round. Originally from cricket, and the taking of three wickets with three successive balls. This achievement used to win the player a new hat.

HATCHET. hatchet job attempt critically to demolish or discredit someone in print. Did you read the latest hatchet job on the prime minister in this morning's paper? The term is as common in journalism as the practice, but it started life in the gang warfare of the American underworld where it meant literal assassination rather than character assassination. Also 'hatchet man', being the person delegated to do the hatchet job.

HATE. hate someone's guts thoroughly dislike someone. All the home team are supposed to hate the guts of the opposing team, but they don't really – after all, it's only a game.

HATS. hats off to (someone) all praise and respect to (someone). Hats off to Miss Craig for organising such a popular event.

HAUL. haul ass get something started; move into action. Come on, you guys, time to haul ass and get this show on the road. An American slang expression. Also 'get your ass in(to) gear'.

haul someone over the coals reprimand someone severely. After poor results, the firm's annual meeting took the form of shareholders hauling the directors over the coals for their feeble performance. In the 16th century, heretics were tried by the church by hauling them across a tray of hot coals. If they died, they were guilty as charged; if they survived this agony, they were innocent.

HAVE. have a ball have a good time. It was a wonderful holiday – we all had a ball.

have a bash/crack try; make an attempt. I don't expect it'll be easy, but I've decided to have a bash at climbing Mont Blanc.

have a bellyful/basinful have more than one can tolerate (of something). It was a dreadful job, and I hated it, and eventually I had a basinful of it and quit.

have a bone to pick (with someone) be cross with someone, and have some argument to settle or agree. Tell Jones I've a couple of bones to pick with him if you see him. From dog behaviour, literally something to engross one as a bone engrosses a dog. The metaphor implies that the argument may have festered for some time before there has been an opportunity to articulate it.

have a finger in every pie be involved in most enterprises. She's one of those frightfully busy people who like to have a finger in every pie.

have a fit 1. lose consciousness, sometimes while making sudden uncontrolled movements of the body. It's not easy to know exactly what to do when you see a stranger having a fit in the street. 2. become infuriated. She just about had a fit when she saw the state of her car. Compare **throw a wobbly, go ape/apeshit, go mad/nuts/nuclear/ballistic**.

have a go (at) 1. attempt. I've never ridden a horse before, but I'll have a go at it. Compare **have a bash/crack**. 2. attack; criticise. Our local councillor is extremely unpopular and the newspapers are always having a go at him.

have a hand in be one of those involved in achieving or doing (something). It came as a big surprise to discover that my best friend had had a hand in a robbery. The reference is often to something disreputable.

have (got) a head for be proficient or competent at. Shut your eyes and don't look down if you haven't (got) a head for heights. If you haven't a head for figures, hire an accountant.

have a heart be reasonable; show some sympathy. Hey, steady! Go easy – have a heart, you'll have to try and show me how to do it.

have a knack of be able to do something cleverly, adroitly, effectively, etc. He has a knack of making himself sound terribly important.

have a lot on one's plate have many urgent demands for one's attention. She looks very preoccupied just now, but I know she has a lot on her plate these days.

have a nerve be bold and presumptuous, or rude and disrespectful. He's got quite a nerve expecting me to make his meals for him. Compare **brass neck**.

have a screw loose be less than entirely sane. You need to watch Mr Jones – most people think he has a screw loose at the very least, and he certainly tends to do some odd things. Compare **lose one's marbles; not all there; tuppence off the shilling**.

have a soft spot for someone/something be very fond of someone/something. I must admit I've always had a soft spot for redheads/toffees, etc. Literally, a weak spot in one's defences.

have a thing about have a strong opinion, obsession, etc. about – either for or against. Don't mention the prime minister in Sheila's company – she has a thing about that man. Compare **bee in one's bonnet**.

have an ear for something be adept in some auditory skill such as languages, music, etc. He had a good ear for languages at school so I'm not surprised that he's now a fluent speaker of Arabic.

have an edge on be a little better than. Both candidates for the job were excellent, but I think the first one has a slight edge on the second. Also **a cut above**.

have an eye for be a good judge of. She has a very good eye for antique furniture.

have/keep an eye on watch carefully. I'm not at all happy about his behaviour, and I've had an eye on him for several weeks.

have one's ass in a sling be in trouble. I'm gonna have my ass in a sling if I fail to win that game. 1960s American.

have something at one's fingertips be entirely proficient or knowledgeable about something. Ask her anything about Wagner's music – she has his whole repertoire at her fingertips.

have been around 1. have existed. Surely everybody's seen people using a car phone – they've been around for years. 2. have acquired a lot of worldly experience. There's no need to conceal things from Mr Brown – he's been around and seen most things.

have someone by the short and curlies have someone in one's power, or in such a position that he can only do as one wishes. The Opposition have today shown the Government that they have them by the short and curlies. Impolite, the reference is to pubic hair.

have done with have finished with. You're welcome to use our old pram – I think we've done with it now.

have something down to a fine art know the best way of doing, presenting, etc. something. Their food hall has ready meals for one person down to a fine art.

have someone's ear have influence on someone, so that they listen to what you say. For many years, it is rumoured that he had the prime minister's ear and was able to give some sound advice.

have eyes only for only want to see/have the company of. It was rather obvious that he had eyes only for one person at the whole event.

have one's hands full have many responsibilities. I regret that I cannot take on that job just now – I already have my hands full with other work.

have had one's chips have had all one's chances; be close to defeat, death, etc. He asked for one more chance to resit the exam, but the professor told him he'd had his chips. **From gambling.** A player who has unsuccessfully played all his chips (or tokens) has lost all his money, and is therefore not going to get another chance. An intensified version of **have had it**.

have had it have failed, lost the battle, etc; be dead, ruined, etc. I'm sorry, but next time I'm afraid you've well and truly had it. See also **have had one's chips**.

have one's head in the clouds be daydreaming or impractical; be out of touch with reality. He's the sort of person who has his head in the clouds most of the time, so it's very important to him to have a highly practical colleague. Opposite of **keep one's feet on the ground**.

have one's head screwed on (the right way) be sensible or shrewd in one's conduct or judgment. You can rely on George not to cause trouble; he's always had his head screwed on.

have it coming to one deserve whatever punishment or misfortune is about to happen. I felt no sympathy for him when he was arrested – he's had it coming to him for years.

have it in for (someone) be hostile to someone, and want to cause them problems. For some unknown reason she seems to have it in for him, and she always tries to embarrass him in public.

have it in one have the courage or the skill (to do something). She's organised the entire event herself – I didn't think she had it in her to tackle something like that!

have it off/away have sex. He's not around much these days – he's much too busy having it off with his new girlfriend.

have it out argue about a problem, in order to resolve it. He asked me to come and see him, saying it was time we had it out about who did what.

have one's moments have a few good, happy, successful, etc. times especially during a dull or unsuccessful period. I asked her how that exam had gone, and she replied rather drily that it had had its moments.

have no truck with not deal with; refuse to be involved with or do business with. I advise you have no truck with the mafia – they're just too dangerous. 'Truck' means 'traffic', 'trade' or 'dealings'.

have nothing on 1. bear no comparison with. The team's rather scrappy display last week had nothing on yesterday's outstanding performance. 2. See **have something(/nothing) on someone**.

have someone's number make an impartial appraisal of someone's strengths and weaknesses. He seems to believe he's the best player the club has ever produced; but we have his number and know him for a very erratic performer.

have someone on try to convince someone of something which isn't true. I don't believe you – you're having me on with such a daft story. Compare **pull someone's leg**.

have something(/nothing) on someone have (no) evidence to damage a person's reputation, etc. I told him he had nothing on me that could possibly connect me to the robbery.

have other fish to fry have other business to attend to. He said rather mysteriously that he couldn't come to the party, having other – unspecified – fish to fry that evening.

have the cheek to be bold or brazen enough to. She's not a good worker, and she had the cheek to ask me for more money. Compare **brass neck**.

have the courage of your convictions be brave enough to act according to the dictates of one's beliefs. A lot of people claim to despise bullying, but you don't often meet people who actually have the courage of their convictions and apprehend the bully.

have the face to be bold and unembarrassed enough to. A lot of politicians seem to have the face to say one thing today and the opposite tomorrow. Compare **two-faced**.

have the heart to be willing (to do something). I hadn't the heart to tell her what had happened. Usually negative.

have the nerve to dare to. He crashed my car yesterday, and yet he had the nerve to ask to borrow it again today!

have the whip hand be in control or at an advantage (over someone). If you're the boss, you usually have the whip hand over your workers. **The** original reference was to driving a horse-drawn coach. A more recent idiom with a similar drift is 'be in the driver's seat'.

have what it takes have the necessary skills or qualities (to do something successfully). He wants to go to university, but I don't think he's got what it takes.

have words quarrel; argue. I heard the neighbours having words again last night – they aren't getting on very well just now. **An old-fashioned understatement.**

HAVES. haves and have-nots wealthy and poor people. Some economists still describe society in terms of a battle between the haves and the have-nots.

HEAD. head and shoulders above much superior to, physically, intellectually or spiritually. Shakespeare stands head and shoulders above every other English dramatist.

head/ride for a fall be on course to receive an unpleasant surprise. He's the sort of cocksure youngster who's heading for a fall sooner or later.

head of steam momentum. The campaigners against corporal punishment in schools have now built up such a head of steam that their cause appears unstoppable. **From steam engines.**

head over heels/ears (in love) deeply and completely (in love). At first we thought it was a simple infatuation, but it turns out that the pair of them are head over heels in love with each other.

head start advantage. A university degree used to give you a head start in the jobs market. **A racing term.**

head to head direct and without intermediaries; in confrontational fashion. The parties have been arguing head to head for most of the week.

HEART. heart and soul very much; fervently; with complete devotion. He's worked heart and soul for that business for years. **A dyad.**

(one's) heart bleeds for someone be very sorry for someone's misfortunes. Our hearts bleed for all those thousands of refugees evicted from their homes. **A hyperbole, probably influenced by the Christian metaphor of the heart of Jesus bleeding for the sins of the world.**

(one's) heart goes out to someone one feels pity and sympathy for someone. Our hearts go out to all those sailing on the high seas tonight.

(one's) heart is in one's boots (one is) in a state of depression or distress. When he heard the news his heart was in his boots.

(one's) heart is in one's mouth (one is) in a state of great alarm. My heart was in my mouth when I realised the plane was falling. **The image is of the heart jumping into the mouth with shock, apprehension, anxiety, etc.**

(one's) heart is in the right place (one is) well meaning and generous, even if one appears indifferent. I'm sure his heart may be in the right place, but I still don't quite trust him.

(one's) heart is not in something (one is) doing something reluctantly and without enthusiasm. His heart hasn't been in his work since he heard the news.

(one's) heart misses a beat (one) is affected by some deep emotion. When I suddenly met my old schoolfriend last week after 30 years, it was just so wonderful that I really felt my heart miss a beat.

heart of gold kindhearted and generous to others. He's very gruff and abrupt, but don't be put off by that – he's also got a heart of gold and will do anything to help you. Opposite of **heart of stone**.

(one's) heart of hearts one's deepest and often unspoken intuitions, hopes, fears, etc. I knew in my heart of hearts that I was unlikely to get the job.

heart of stone/flint very hard hearted and unsympathetic. There's no point asking the boss for more money; that man has a heart of stone. Opposite of **heart of gold**.

(one's) heart sinks (one) becomes anxious or pessimistic. My heart sank when I heard the radio report of the school party lost on the mountain.

heart-to-heart (talk) frank and intimate, sometimes critical but ultimately friendly talk. I decided it was time for a heart-to-heart with my son.

HEATH. Heath Robinson ingenious but amateurish, makeshift contraption. Belching black smoke and emitting strange noises, he drove up to the golf club in an incredible-looking, Heath Robinson creation. William Heath Robinson (1872–1944) was a humorous illustrator and *Punch* cartoonist of some of the amazing inventions of the machine age. Some of his more memorable absurdities include machines for raising one's hat in polite greeting, for shuffling a deck of cards or for recovering a collar stud which has slipped down one's back.

HEAVE. heave in sight/into view come into one's line of vision. We'd been stranded on the mountain for several hours before the rescue party hove in sight. The past tense is 'hove'. Originally nautical.

HEAVEN. heaven forfend/forbid please avert something, or let something not happen. Heaven forfend that such a tragedy ever befall you. Also an old-fashioned exclamation, a variant of 'God forbid'. 'Have you ever been to Blackpool?' 'Oh no, heaven forbid!'

heaven knows one doesn't know, and probably nobody else under heaven does. Heaven knows what he was talking about.

heaven sent very welcome, timely and acceptable. The offer of the use of their flat in New York seemed heaven sent, and I took it at once. An old-fashioned hyperbole.

HEAVY. heavy going something which makes a negative impact on one, or on which one makes slow or little progress. We went to the opera last night, but found the music very heavy going. From horse-racing, and the state of the turf when water-logged.

heavy handed excessively severe; unfair. Like most dictators, he is very heavy handed with matters involving civil liberties.

heavy heart feeling of sadness. I speak to you today with a heavy heart.

HECK. heck of a lot an awful lot. He's lost a heck of a lot of money in the stockmarket crash. 'Heck' is an intensifier, a Victorian euphemism for 'hell'.

HEDGE. hedge one's bets bet on more than one option in order to minimise the risk of loss. They're not politicians for nothing: in the party leadership election there was much hedging of bets among MPs until the outcome was clear.

hedge fund a high-risk and volatile investment strategy beloved by speculators until the 2008 credit crunch, when the bottom fell out of them. Sick hedge funds were a key feature of the recent Wall Street collapse. Usually exempt from regulation, they were often located offshore. Compare **short selling**.

HELL. hell bent on something doggedly, or 'fiendishly' determined to do something, however dreadful, and 'to hell with the consequences'. The government seems to be hell bent on alienating its dwindling electoral support.

hell for leather very fast or hard. The robbers drove hell for leather to the airport, in a bid to get out of the country before the alarm was raised. **The original reference was to riding a horse, and may be a corruption of 'all of a lather'.**

hell raiser wild or rowdy person. He had a reputation as a real hell raiser in his young days.

HELP. helpline telephone information and advice service. When the snow blocked our route we were lucky enough to have a note of the mountain rescue helpline, so we rang them up.

help oneself to something 1. take, without waiting to be invited. Please help yourself to some more roast beef. **2. steal.** When I got home this morning, I saw that the car was gone. Someone had helped himself to it during the night. **A euphemism.**

HEN. hen party/night all-female gathering. There was a hen party in full swing at the pub last night – forty women all laughing their heads off! **The term refers to the female equivalent of the all-male 'stag night' before a wedding.**

HER. (at) Her Majesty's pleasure prison. You get locked up at Her Majesty's pleasure for that sort of criminal act. **If you are awaiting trial, the expression is 'pending Her Majesty's pleasure'.**

HEY. hey presto! a cry of jugglers and conjurors to demand audience attention and then applause. Look inside the hat: there's nothing there. But wait a minute – hey presto! – where did the white rabbit appear from? **'Presto' means 'immediately' and gave rise to another stage cry: 'Presto, be gone!' Compare bob's your uncle!**

HIDDEN. hidden agenda the true and underlying rather than the declared or apparent aims, objectives, etc. The government likes to talk about giving parents more choice in the education of their children; the hidden agenda is much simpler – it is the privatisation of our schools. **Sometimes referred to as the 'subtext', or 'reading between the lines'.**

HIDE. hide one's light (under a bushel) be modest; refrain from drawing attention to one's merits and abilities. He's quite a shy person, and

tends to hide his light a bit. **From the Bible: 'Neither do men light a candle, and put it under a bushel, but on a candlestick.' Matthew v.15.**

hide or/nor hair sign of the presence of (someone/something). We looked for him everywhere, but couldn't find hide nor hair of him. **A dyad, usually negative.**

HIGH. high and dry stranded; abandoned. He said he'd pick me up at the station, but he failed to appear and left me high and dry – so I phoned for a taxi. **A dyad from nautical English, the term originally referred to a ship grounded on the shore by an outgoing tide. Now it often refers to people or to views overtaken by the current of events.**

high and low everywhere. I hunted high and low for that dog, but I couldn't find it.

high and mighty with illusions of self-importance or social superiority. She's one of those high and mighty people who treat the rest of us as if we were dirt. **A dyad, invariably derogatory.**

high as a kite drunk; over-excited; on drugs. When I looked into the room to see what all the noise and shrieking was about, it was clear that everyone in there was as high as a kite.

high days and holidays special occasions. He looks very smart in his suit and tie, but it's a pity he only wears them on high days and holidays. **A dyad from the medieval Christian church. High Mass was celebrated on days of high celebration, and the original holy days were also religious festivals. Nowadays there is no real religious resonance to the idiom. It is thought that a high day was once a 'heyday'.**

high falutin' pretentious; sounding pompous or bombastic; up-market. She's a very nice person even if she's got rather a high falutin' accent. **1840s American, perhaps a conflation of 'high' and 'fluting'. The Scottish poet Norman MacCaig once described himself as determinedly 'low falutin'', but that was with the privilege of poets,**

since these two words do not normally collocate.

high flyer person who is obviously going to do well at something. As soon as we met the new manager, we could all see that we were dealing with a real high flyer.

(on one's) high horse in self-righteous and superior mode. It's impossible to argue with him when he gets on his high horse. In medieval times, a high horse on the field of battle was usually genuine evidence of the rider's superior rank and status.

high jinks high-spirited pranks and frolics of people at play. You have to expect high jinks when the Joneses throw a party. The Scots word 'jink' means to trick someone or give them the slip.

high time past the time (for something to happen or be done). It's high time these children were in their beds and fast asleep.

HIT. hit and run (accident) (accident) caused by a driver hitting someone and not stopping to help them. There are more and more hit-and-run drivers on the roads nowadays. A late 20th-century dyad.

hit it off be good friends. They're always fighting – they can't seem to hit it off very well these days. It was love at first sight; they hit it off from day one.

hit list list of people targeted for attention, originally by gangsters or hoodlums planning to 'hit' or kill them. He's been told the local tax inspector has his name on a hit list of people suspected of tax evasion. A modern version of **blacklist**.

hit-man/-squad professional killer or thug, or team of killers/thugs. They were a notorious hit-squad, and the New York police had been chasing them for years. From the American underworld.

hit someone for six shock someone. The sudden news of her death hit us all for six. Originally from cricket, the metaphor describes an event giving someone as big a mental blow as a batsman hitting a cricket ball over the boundary of the field for six runs.

hit or/and miss random, unplanned; careless. They have a very hit-or-miss approach to running a business. A hit-and-miss development is often a completely unpredictable affair.

hit the bottle habitually drink excessive amounts of alcohol. He's had a lot of worries at work, and seems to be hitting the bottle quite badly. A popular euphemism.

hit the ceiling/fan/roof be very angry. My father hit the fan when he heard how much money I had spent. Also 'go through the roof', see **go mad**.

hit the ground running get off to a good start. The new administration seemed to know exactly where it was going, and it certainly hit the ground running. The idea is of showing energy, enthusiasm and purpose. To indicate the reverse one might say 'hit the ground strolling'.

hit the hay/sack go to bed/sleep. At about two in the morning, he decided it was time to hit the sack. Nineteenth century, probably American, from people sleeping rough (vagrants, cowboys, hoboes, etc.).

hit/win the jackpot win great success or fame, or a lot of money. It was not a particularly good novel, but it won the jackpot for its author – the Man Booker Prize and various other awards, plus lots of notoriety because of its subject matter. The original reference was to the pot of money accumulated in the course of a game of poker; this jackpot could not be won until someone started the betting with a minimum of a pair of jacks.

hit the nail on the head be exactly right or accurate (usually in a statement); state the plain truth of something; hit the target. To describe the government as being economical with the truth these days is, alas, to hit the nail on the head. A metaphor from carpentry, and hitting the nail 'true'.

hit the road(, Jack) go, travel, depart. I've enjoyed my visit very much, but I'm afraid it's time to hit the road now. One of the catch phrases of the US Beat generation, because there is a popular hit song with this title and chorus line. 'The road' in American culture was often a reference to the railroad; writers like Jack London and later Jack Kerouac wrote about the migratory labour force of tramps or hoboes hitting the road in search of the next job.

HITCH. hitch one's wagon (to a star) try to improve oneself; be ambitious. Many men used to hitch their wagon to the star of a good education, and see how far in life that would take them. Originally American, from Ralph Waldo Emerson, 'Now that is the wisdom of a man…to hitch his wagon to a star', in *Society and Solitude*, 1870. The idiom is now looser, and one can hitch one's wagon to something or someone else, meaning try to link one's fortunes to those of an already successful person or entity. The French have now firmly hitched their wagon to the powerful German economy.

HIVE. hive of industry hectically busy place. Those workshops are a veritable hive of industry for the whole of the west of Scotland. Usually a cliché. Abraham Cowley and other writers have compared cities and other frantically busy places to hives of bees, wasps or other insects.

hive something off 1. delegate something. I don't have time to do this job by the deadline, so I'll have to hive it off on someone else. 2. dispose of; sell off. They've started hiving off all their subsidiary businesses, and will be concentrating in future on their core activities. A phrasal verb.

HOB. hob-nob with someone associate on terms of familiarity with someone of high social status. She loves going to Ascot and hob-nobbing with the royals and the aristocracy. The 16th-century dyad was 'habbing and nabbing', or getting and losing, having and not having. By 1600, 'hob and nob' described two or more people drinking socially together on terms of good fellowship, perhaps toasting each other with 'hob' and 'nob'. Compare **rub shoulders with someone**.

HOBSON'S. Hobson's choice the option of taking what is offered or nothing, in other words, no choice. I'm afraid supper tonight is a case of Hobson's choice – fish and chips, or chips and fish. The originator of the term was Thomas Hobson (c. 1544–1631), a rich Cambridge carrier who let no customer pick and choose among the horses from his stable – customers had to take the horse nearest the stable door, or none at all. This was not cussedness on Hobson's part; he merely insisted on working all his horses by strict rotation, so that none of his beasts were over-ridden.

HOCUS. hocus pocus trickery; something done to confuse one. I think there's been a bit of hocus pocus by the company's accountants with the figures. The term is from mock Latin, and dates from the 17th century. It may be based on the words of consecration of the host in the Latin Mass: 'Hoc est corpore meum' ('This is My body'). An alternative explanation is that it derives from a completely meaningless send-up of this formula, which went 'hax pax max Deus adimax', and was invented by 16th-century student layabouts. The word 'hoax' derives from 'hocus'. A later reduplicative expression with a similar drift is **jiggery pokery**.

HOG. hog-tied helpless. There sat the car, hog-tied and immobile in the middle of the desert with no fuel in the tank. An Americanism. When pigs, or hogs, are hobbled, all four legs are tied and they are incapable of much movement.

HOI. hoi polloi the masses; the rabble. As a child I'd never even heard of asparagus or okra or pawpaw, but nowadays the hoi polloi buy them all once a week at the supermarket. Usually compared disapprovingly with the rich or more discriminating classes. From Greek. Compare **rag-tag and bobtail**.

HOIST. hoist on one's own petard caught in one's own trap. It is not uncommon for present-day terrorists to be killed in action, hoist on their own assassins' petard. Shakespeare uses the idiom in *Hamlet* iii.4: 'For tis the sport to have the engineer/Hoist with his own petard.' A 'petard' was an explosive, so the image is of the engineer blown up with his own bomb. 'Hoist' or 'hoised' in Shakespeare's time was the past tense of the verb 'to hoise' or 'heeze' (= lift). A hundred years later, 'hoist' was the invariable usage and the hoising of sails, etc. had become an obsolete term. See also **(score) an own goal**.

HOLD. hold a brief for support. I hold no brief for behaviour of that sort. I don't hold much brief nowadays for the royal family. From legal briefs or mandates.

hold a pistol to someone's head force someone to do something by the use of threats, etc. You can hardly expect to hold a pistol to her head with an old story like that.

hold something against someone dislike a person for some known failing or weakness. I'm not going to hold a silly episode like that against him.

hold one's breath wait for something to happen. I'm hoping they'll give me a job with them, but I'm not holding my breath, i.e. I'm not sitting around doing nothing but am continuing busy with some other work. I'm trying to get this car to start, but don't hold your breath. Usually negative.

hold forth state one's views in a loud, dogmatic or opinionated way. I can't stand listening to a Conservative prime minister holding forth on the dangers of Socialism, or vice versa.

hold good apply; be true. You are welcome to your view, but are you sure it holds good in the present case? Also 'holds true' (same sense).

hold someone's hand give someone moral support in a time of difficulty. He's quite capable of accounting for himself, and I'm sure he doesn't need anyone to hold his hand for him.

hold one's horses wait a minute; be patient. Don't be in such a rush – just hold your horses for five minutes. From the days of horse-drawn transport. Also 'hold on' and 'hang on', two phrasal verbs with a similar meaning. Compare **hold it**.

hold it wait a minute. Hold it, hold it! You're talking rubbish and I'd like to reply to some of your comments. Compare **hold one's horses**.

hold on like grim death hold tight to something in difficult circumstances. He'd never waterski-ed before so he hung on to the tow-ropes like grim death.

hold out on someone withhold information or money from someone. He told me he'd lost the key to the safe, but I don't believe him – I think he's holding out on us for some reason.

hold one's own stand successfully against competition from others in a conflict, argument, etc. His speech was a hard act to follow, but I believe you held your own and maybe even spoke better. Also 'hold one's ground'. Compare **keep one's end up**.

hold the floor be in the speaking position in a meeting, etc. I don't much like getting stuck with Uncle Jim – he always holds the floor for hours and won't let anyone else get a word in edgeways. From British parliamentary procedure. In the House of Commons, an MP has or holds the floor when s/he is standing up and speaking with the authorisation of the Speaker, and should not be interrupted till s/he sits down. Compare **get a word in edgeways**.

hold the fort look after something while its owner, or one's boss, is away. I've got to hold the fort this week while my sales director is away at Frankfurt. The original expression was presumably military, an exhortation to soldiers to defend a position against attack. The words were later also popularised in a Victorian hymn: 'Hold the fort for I am coming, Jesus signals still.'

hold the purse strings control the amounts of money spent, and when it is spent. Her grandmother obviously controls the purse strings in that household. In traditional societies, a person was delegated or employed to control a community's expenditure. Highland clan chieftains, for example, had 'pursers' ('sporran-keepers' in their case) up to the 18th century.

hold one's tongue refrain from speech; keep quiet. If you can't hold your tongue for five minutes, I'm going to send you to the headmistress. Kindly hold your tongue till the bell goes, all of you! The latter is a common imperative to chattering children.

hold water be accurate or convincing; bear critical scrutiny. I don't think his comments about the robbery hold water.

HOLE. hole and corner secretive; suggestive of dishonesty; probably disreputable. They've been conducting a hole-and-corner love affair for years, as if they stand much chance of hoodwinking their partners over something like that. **Also hole-in-corner** same meaning. It was a rather hush-hush, hole-in-corner business, and I wanted no part in it.

hole in the wall cash dispenser. He had to get some money from the hole in the wall.

HOLED. holed below the waterline damaged beyond repair. I thought we'd abandoned that idea because John's impeccable logic holed it well below the waterline. From shipping and naval warfare.

HOLIER. holier than thou sanctimonious and self-righteous. She's one of those holier-than-thou folk who enjoys disapproving of her weaker brothers and sisters. From the Bible: 'Come not near to me, for I am holier than thou.' Isaiah lxv.5.

HOLLOW. hollow legs big appetite for food or drink. Most boys of 13 or 14 seem to have hollow legs – they eat vast amounts of food and still seem to be hungry all the time.

HOLY. holy of holies very special place that only certain people may enter. When he was summoned to the board room – the holy of holies –

he immediately suspected the directors had decided to give him the sack. This expression is now used facetiously, but the original reference was to a very holy place; it was the Hebrew name of the inner sanctuary of the Temple at Jerusalem, where the Ark of the Covenant was kept, and which could only be entered by the chief priest.

holy terror badly behaved child. I'm afraid that child will have to be sent home; he's been a holy terror all morning and is disrupting the rest of the class.

Holy Willie religious hypocrite. I didn't want to go to church with a bunch of Holy Willies. The term is from a poem called 'Holy Willie's Prayer' by Robert Burns (1759–96).

HOME. home-alone kid usually a description of an unsupervised youngster left at home to fend for her/himself without adult supervision. Yesterday I read a story about another of those poor home-alone kids whose parents went off on holiday to the Costa Brava. Compare **latchkey child**.

home and dry obtained or safely at home, with a mission or objective accomplished. I believe the contract for the job is now home and dry in the managing director's safe. Probably from cross-country running, or steeplechasing. There are various elaborations: 'home and dried (with the blanket on)', or 'home and fried'.

Home Counties suburban counties – Middlesex, Surrey, Kent, Essex, Hertfordshire and Buckinghamshire – around London from which daily commuters converge on the capital. He spoke with the sort of plummy Home Counties accent which the BBC seem to like.

home from home place where one feels as happy, comfortable, at ease, etc. as one feels in one's own home. We stayed at a lovely hotel in the hills – a veritable home from home, with a delightful host family.

home in on something arrive at a target or conclusion. It's been a long discussion, but I think at last we're beginning to home in on the crux of the problem. Originally from weaponry; electronic and computer-driven modern weapons can home in on their targets with pinpoint accuracy.

home, James(, and don't spare the horses) let's now go straight home. Thank you for a delightful evening, but unfortunately I have to go to work in the morning, so I'm afraid it's time for home, James. Like so many horse-related idioms, this expression is Victorian. It conveys the culture of a wealthy man about town getting into his coach and thus addressing his coachman. Nowadays the term is usually jocular, and the two parts of the expression are often heard separately.

home straight final and usually easy stages of something. It's been a long and difficult project, but I think we're in the home straight at last. From horse racing; the home straight was the final section of the course which led from the final bend to the finishing line.

home truths plain and unvarnished statements criticising a person in a direct way. I decided it was time he heard a few home truths about his general boorishness. Probably based on the idea that such truths are mainly spoken by members of one's family in the privacy of the home.

HONEST. honest broker neutral mediator or intermediary between two antagonists. In the recent war, neither NATO nor the UN was seen as an honest broker acceptable to all sides.

honest injun to speak the truth (used to emphasise that the speaker is not lying). I promise you, every word is true – honest injun! An Americanism, usually humorous, from the speech of Huckleberry Finn and Tom Sawyer. In Mark Twain's lexicon, the term was meant as a humorous frontiersman's oxymoron.

honest-to-goodness/-God 1. genuine. It was an honest-to-goodness attempt to cook a very special dinner, but it wasn't too successful. 2. an exclamation, meaning 'honestly'! Honest-to-God, I never even saw your wallet!

HOOF. hoof it walk. When the car broke down, I just had to hoof it.

HOOK. hook, line and sinker totally; entirely. He told her a rather suspicious story of being in the house by invitation of her brother, and she seemed to swallow it hook, line and sinker. A fishing idiom originally, which refers to a big fish swallowing the baited hook, and then the entire line and sinker (lead weight).

HOORAY. Hooray Henry hearty, affluent upper-class male of a sort most commonly encountered in London and the **Home Counties**, and frequently viewed as offensive elsewhere in the British Isles. His flashy dress, and even flashier car, his loud voice and appalling manners proclaimed him without a doubt to be a typical Hooray Henry. A 1980s expression.

HOP. hop it go away. He was being a nuisance and I told him to hop it. Also an exclamation.

hop/jump to it shift; do something immediately. You'd better hop to it if you want the work completed on time. Similar: 'get moving'.

HORIZONTALLY. horizontally challenged fat. Being horizontally challenged, her sister tries to compensate by wearing flowing robes. A euphemism of the 1990s which nicely oozes political correctitude. See also **challenged**.

HORNETS'. hornets' nest particularly difficult or troublesome issue and the angry reactions to it. His question about the drains had clearly stirred up a hornets' nest at the town hall. The term refers to a particularly challenging problem for gardeners and others: how to dispose of a hornets' nest without getting stung for one's pains.

HORNS. horns of a dilemma quandary; state of indecision when confronted with two equally unattractive options. He was stuck on the horns of the same old dilemma. Compare **in a cleft stick**.

HORSE. horse of another/a different colour quite a different matter. They've been living together for years; now he wants to marry her, but that's a horse of another colour. Probably after Shakespeare: 'My purpose is indeed a horse of that colour…' in *Twelfth Night* ii.3. By analogy, 'bird of a different feather' is sometimes heard. Compare **dark horse**.

horse sense basic common sense, of a sort found more commonly in horses than in certain people. Don't worry about her – she's got all the horse sense she needs, and will cope fine.

HORSES. horses for courses different people are better than others in different contexts or at certain tasks. His experience of championship golf is limited, but his experience of that kind of golf-course is unparalleled – that's why he was selected for the championship, on the grounds of horses for courses. Originally a Victorian observation among the upper, or horse-racing, classes that some horses performed better on certain racecourses, or under certain conditions, than others. By extension, the term then applied to other categories and people.

HOT. hot air worthless verbosity; blether; bluster; false claims or promises. He threatens to do this and he threatens to do that – and it's all a lot of hot air.

hot and bothered angry or agitated. Relax – there's no point getting all hot and bothered about missing a train; you can always get the next one. A popular dyad.

hot desking shared office desk delegated to one's use when no one else is using it. Sometimes I have to work from our Glasgow office, which has lots of hot desking facilities. This practice is suited to workers who only need office space in order to plug in their laptops. By extension, 'hot bedding' facilities are sometimes available to people working shifts in isolated locations.

hot line direct telephone. Come quick, your boss is on the hot line from Paris. From the days of the Cold War, when the US president and the Soviet leader had direct contact in order to ensure avoidance of nuclear and other crises.

hot on something/someone very keen on. She's been hot on him for years.

hot potato controversial topic that is difficult to handle. The party decided to drop the matter of private healthcare from their forthcoming conference agenda, on the grounds that it was a bit of a hot potato. The metaphor is of putting a hot potato into someone's hands. A similar idiom is to say that something is 'too hot to handle'.

hot seat difficult position. It's one of those popular TV chat programmes where the host puts a politician in the hot seat and asks him all sorts of very difficult questions – literally makes him sweat. Originally a colloquial reference to the electric chair, on which American criminals are executed.

hot stuff 1. very good or skilled. She's really hot stuff on the saxophone. 2. sexually passionate. The girls tell me he's very hot stuff.

hot under the collar agitated, angry or embarrassed. Some of the accusations obviously made him very hot under the collar.

hot water trouble. He's going to get us all in hot water if he doesn't watch his spending.

HOTBED. hotbed of something place where something proliferates. According to the police, that club is a hotbed of drugs, vice and violence. Once upon a time the London School of Economics was a hotbed of radicalism. From gardening: a 'hotbed' is a forcing bed for young seedlings.

HOW. how about? informal or colloquial question form meaning 1. 'how would you like to…?' How about going to Paris for the weekend? 2. 'what do you think?' I'm not very fond of shellfish. How about you?

how are they hanging? how are you? How they hanging, my old partner? American slang expression of male greeting, 'they' referring to the testicles.

how come? for what reason? How come I got a pay rise and you didn't?

how the other half lives the lifestyle of people from a different social class to the speaker. It won't do you any harm to come and slum it with me for a weekend and see how the other half lives. From the title of a classic American social commentary (1890) on the living conditions of poor New Yorkers, by Jacob Riis.

HUE. hue and cry loud clamour, outcry. Every time the government raises taxes there's a great hue and cry from the voters. A dyad from an Anglo-Norman medieval cry calling for the pursuit and apprehension of a criminal by members of the public.

HUM. hum and haw noise indicating uncertainty, indecision, embarrassment, etc. Ask a politician a direct question and you get nothing but humming and hawing. Sometimes written phonetically as 'um and ah'. Compare **beat about the bush; chop and change**.

HUNG. hung up on something/someone obsessed. He's completely hung up on political correctness.

HUSH. hush-hush very secret. I'm not quite sure what he does for a living – it's slightly hush-hush, I gather. Originally a military reduplication, dating from the First World War. Compare **on the (strict) q.t.**

hush money bribe given to persuade people to keep something quiet. Some of these enormous redundancy payments are nothing more than hush money, paid out to keep the recipients quiet about their erstwhile employers.

hush something up suppress or cover something up, so that it does not become public. For some reason, the police hushed up the whole matter.

HYPED. hyped up 1. hyperactive, overstimulated. He was in a very excited, manic, hyped-up state: perhaps it was his medication? **2. overstated.** The brochure described the resort in the most hyped-up and exaggerated terms.

HYPERBOLE

Hyperbole is overstatement or exaggeration, used for emphasis and effect. It is a feature of many idiomatic expressions: *old as the hills, spread like wildfire, a whale of a time, a flood of tears, loads of money, waiting for ages* and *frozen to death* (two examples often found together if the speakers are at a bus stop!), *make a mountain out of a molehill, tear someone to shreds*, etc. Other examples include: *work one's fingers to the bone* (= work very hard); *eat someone out of house and home* (= eat huge amounts); *worship the ground someone treads on* (= revere someone); *laugh one's head off* (= laugh outrageously).

Hyperbole is common in journalism, and in comic or burlesque writing, for example in much of the fiction of Charles Dickens and in the 'tall tales' of the American frontier in the mid-19th century.

I

ICING. icing on the cake something that makes a good thing even better. Most people are quite happy to have a job – so I'd say that to actually enjoy your job is icing on the cake.

IDLE. idle rich people who are rich enough not to have to work. The holiday was wonderful, and we especially enjoyed sitting in a café overlooking the yacht marina and watching the idle rich at play. A socialist term from the 1880s.

IF. if push comes to shove if things get difficult. Don't worry about a bed for the night – if push comes to shove, you can always use our sofa. Also 'if the worst comes to the worst', or 'if it comes to the bit/push' (similar meanings). In American English, the 'bit' was of course a coin (worth one-eighth of a dollar).

if the mountain won't come to Muhammad (, Muhammad will go to the mountain) if a person won't come to see you, you will have to go and see them, etc. He says he can't make the time to come and see me until after Christmas, so if the mountain won't come to Muhammad I'll just have to go and see him. A saying, or part of one.

if the shoe/cap fits(, wear it) if you feel that an accusation, etc. applies to you, you should take careful notice of it. Last week her teacher told them that half the class wasn't working hard enough to pass the exam; ever since then, Jane's been working like a Trojan – well, if the cap fits... A saying, or part of one, with the option of a dunce's cap or Cinderella's shoe for props.

ILL. ill-gotten gains money or goods got in a dishonest way. Some of the bank robbers escaped to Brazil, where they are living a life of luxury on their ill-gotten gains.

it's an ill wind (that blows nobody good) nothing is so utterly bad that it doesn't bring some compensations. He missed his flight, but on the later one he met a very interesting person who offered him a good job – so it's an ill wind... A saying, or part of one, from the same stable as **every cloud has a silver lining**.

IN. in a bind in a difficult situation. His business is in a bind right now, with too many bad debtors preventing him paying off his own bills.

in a certain condition pregnant. She takes a rest most afternoons at present, being in a certain condition. An old-fashioned and rather Victorian euphemism, with the variant 'in an interesting condition'. Now humorous.

in a cleft stick in a dilemma; in a situation where none of the options is attractive. Whether to take the train without him, or wait for him and miss the train – I was in a cleft stick. Eighteenth century, from the trapping of snakes and vermin by means of a cleft or forked stick. The original dilemma, having trapped the thing, was what to do next! You couldn't leave it alone or it would escape, and you generally lacked an easy means of killing it. Compare **on the horns of a dilemma**.

in a cold sweat in a panic. He was in a cold sweat in case he would lose his footing and fall.

in a corner in a situation which is difficult to escape from, or to deal with. The business has been in a corner since the banks refused to lend us any more money. Often a 'tight corner'.

in a different league very superior. John is quite a good trumpeter, but James's playing is in a different league. From American league sports. Compare **something else (again)**.

in a flash very quickly; with a sudden blinding realisation. He thought over the night of the crime for several weeks, and then one morning the explanation came to him in a flash of inspiration. Also 'in a trice' or **in a twinkling**.

in a flat spin in a state of over-excitement and downright hypertension. By the time the bell rang for the fourth time that morning, our host was in a flat spin.

in a fog unable to understand. He read the poem three times, and was still in a fog as to its author's meaning.

in a groove/rut stuck in a (usually) boring routine. He decided he was in a bit of a rut and needed a change – so he's going to take a holiday. The 'groove' reference is from the days of gramophone records, when the needle used to sometimes get stuck. Compare **one-track mind**.

in a hole/spot in some difficulty. James is in a bit of a hole just now, and wants me to help him. The context is frequently financial.

in/into a lather emotional, excited and often upset. She's worked herself into a complete lather about the sale of the house. From animal behaviour: dogs and horses froth at the mouth and sweat copiously after strenuous exercise or when in a state of panic.

in a nutshell briefly and succinctly; without all the details. I can't wait to hear the speech so I hope you'll tell me in a nutshell what it's about.

in a state of nature naked. We stumbled on a nudist beach full of people running about in a state of nature. A euphemism from Victorian days when the mention of nudity was almost as shocking as nudity itself.

in a twinkling in a short space of time. It all happened in a twinkling: one minute he was rowing the boat, the next he'd capsized. Also 'in the twinkling or blink of an eye', **in a flash** and 'in a trice'.

in a way from one point of view. He failed his exams and left college, which was a pity – although, in a way, it might help him to decide what he's going to do with his life.

in a word briefly. In a word, he's been forced to resign.

in advance 1. early or beforehand. We had to book our tickets several weeks in advance. 2. very highly developed, often in the pioneering of something. Their design studio has all the latest equipment, and is well in advance of most design offices I've seen. Compare **at the cutting/ leading edge**.

in at the kill/death present at the climax to something. It was a dreadful day when the management was sacked, but fortunately I wasn't in at the kill – I was at a meeting in London. From the hunting field.

in bad odour unpopular. Kenny's in bad odour with the fans at the moment, having let in all those goals on Saturday.

in black and white formally, on paper and in writing. He's often said he'd give me a job, but there was never anything in black and white from him.

in someone's black/bad books unpopular with someone. I've been in Mrs Brown's black books since I bumped into her car. See also **black-list**.

in one's blood part of one's genetic inheritance. He always claimed horses were in his blood, and that his ancestors had been gypsies.

in cahoots in secret or disreputable partnership; in league. It has now been proved that several cabinet ministers were in cahoots with big business. Originally North American, the expression may derive from French 'cahute' (= cabin), where generations of frontiersmen once had to live in enforced intimacy and had lots of time to cook up acts of dishonesty.

in clover contented; affluent. His long-lost uncle has left him a fortune and a French chateau, so I imagine he'll be in clover for the rest of his days. From the observation that cattle and sheep like to eat clover above all other forage. Compare **on (to) a good thing**.

in cold blood deliberately and without pity or other emotion. It is hard to believe that someone could perpetrate such a thuggish act in cold blood.

in one's cups drunk. She's in her cups and talking nonsense.

in deep water in difficulty. Blackmail is a nasty crime, and people who commit it soon find themselves in deep water.

in durance vile in foul imprisonment. The fairy princess was held in durance vile by the wicked stepmother. A 16th-century phrase, now only heard for humorous or literary effect.

in one's element doing something one enjoys or is good at. He's in his element pottering and grubbing about in his garden. Opposite of **fish out of water; out of one's element**.

in fine summarising something as accurately as possible. Everything about the visit was delightful: in fine, we had a wonderful holiday. Literally, 'in the end' (French *enfin*), or 'to sum up' or 'finally'.

in fine fettle in good condition or spirits. The village band was in fine fettle and we enjoyed their playing.

in for a penny(, in for a pound) a saying. The implication is that after a person has spent time or money on something, s/he discovers and accepts the need to spend a lot more. When the job was half done we discovered that the window frames were so rotten they'd need replacing. 'Ah well,' I sighed. 'In for a penny – let's get on with it!' Compare **go the whole hog; point of no return; throw caution to the wind; throw good money after bad**.

in for it about to be punished or experience some trouble. He was ordered to return to his regiment by today, and he knows he's in for it if he fails to turn up. You are 'in for' something if you anticipate the experience, e.g. 'We've organised lots of appointments for our visiting sales team, so they're in for a busy weekend.'

in freefall collapsing. During the latter part of 2008, the world's stock markets were in freefall. From sky-diving.

in full cry in hot and furious pursuit. He fled up the street in an unmarked car with three police vehicles in full cry right at his tail. From fox hunting.

in God's/heaven's name invocation, an expression of intense surprise, annoyance, anger, etc. The expression was once extremely solemn, but is now often used trivially. What in God's name do you think you're playing at, Madam? The Bible reminds us of the original sense: 'God hath also exalted him, and given him a name which is above every other name; That at the name of Jesus every knee shall bow…' Philippians ii.5. Something of the original solemnity is caught in Oliver Cromwell's 1653 blunt message to the Rump Parliament: 'You have sat too long here…Depart, I say, and let us have done with you. In the name of God, go!' See also **in the name of**.

in hand 1. under control or discipline. The riots went on for two days, but the army has now got the situation in hand. Opposite of **out of hand**. 2. being processed at the time of speaking. There is a large backlog of orders for the new car, but I can confirm that your own order is in hand. 3. in one's possession; available. I'll check the warehouse to see if any copies of the book are still in hand.

in harness at work. My father didn't much enjoy retirement at first, and kept saying he wished he was back in harness. From farm horses or oxen.

in high dudgeon indicating feelings of ill humour and resentment. Banging the door behind him, he left the house in high dudgeon. 'Dudgeon' is anger or resentment, but the word is now confined to this idiomatic collocation.

in hock in debt; pawned. She's up to her ears in hock. From the medieval Hock-day or hocking festival, originally connected with the harvest but latterly a sort of general spring-cleaning opportunity when all sorts of unwanted things were offered for sale.

in hot water in trouble. He's in hot water with the taxman for not returning his income tax form in good time.

in limbo forgotten, neglected, in abeyance. The plans for the new office are in limbo now that the company has run out of funds. **In the Catholic Church, Limbo was a place on the borders of Hell and was the destination of unbaptised infants and of the just people who had the misfortune to die before the birth of Christ.**

in mothballs not in active use, service, etc. The old power station has been in mothballs since the opening of the new one 10 years ago. **Originally naval, from the end of the Second World War, the term referred to warships put into a form of protective storage in order to prevent deterioration of their fabric during peacetime.**

in name only in appearance but not in practice. He is headmaster in name only, since most of the management of the school is done by his deputy.

in no time (at all) very quickly. She dialled 999 and the ambulance was there in no time.

in no uncertain terms emphatically and clearly. She told him in no uncertain terms that if he bothered her again she'd call the police. **Also 'in words of one syllable'. Compare lay into someone; spell something out.**

in on the ground floor admitted to a project from the outset, often before it becomes public knowledge. It was an interesting project in its early stages, and I was in on the ground floor way back in the 1980s. **The idea comes from the building trade, and from leasing someone office space in a new high-rise property when only the ground floor had been built.**

in person oneself, not represented by someone else. She received a letter of thanks from the French president in person.

in pocket having made money on a financial transaction. It wasn't a difficult job, but she seems to have come out of it with several thousand pounds in pocket. **Also 'to the good'. Opposite of out of pocket** or 'to the bad'.

in someone's pocket/pay under someone's influence or control. Many people dislike the links between the trade unions and the Labour Party,

because they'd prefer not to see the party in the union's pocket.

in one's right mind sane, sensible. I don't think anyone in their right mind would go there for a holiday.

in stitches pain in one's side caused by excessive laughter. They were very funny, and had the whole audience in stitches.

in stook/schtuk in trouble or difficulty, often financial. He's been living very quietly since his business got in schtuk. **From Yiddish. Similar to in the soup.**

in strength in large numbers. Welsh rugby fans had been arriving in strength all week for the big game.

in the air in people's minds; pending; under consideration or discussion. Some of these ideas have been in the air quite a lot recently. **The reference is to the intellectual atmosphere.**

in the bag certain to be achieved or obtained. He entered the room smiling, and waved his papers in the air. 'The contract's in the bag,' he cried triumphantly. **From the game bag, and the slain game secured within it.**

in the black in profit. The firm had heavy losses for three years, but now it's back in the black again.

in the black books in disgrace. He's in the black books again for falling asleep in his maths class. **Black books and black lists existed in medieval times, and were kept to record misdemeanours, bankruptcies, and other disgraces. King Charles II is said to have kept one, using it methodically after the Restoration in 1660 to settle old scores. See also blacklist.**

in the buff nude. Although it was a cold morning, he had to submit to a thorough medical examination in the buff. **Originally from the buff, or light-coloured, leather skin of the buffalo.**

in the can completed. It turned out to be a very successful interview, even if it took us several weeks to get it all in the can. **From filming and photography.**

in the clear 1. free of blame or danger. If he can satisfactorily explain where he's been then naturally he'll be in the clear. 2. ahead of competitors. There were several applications for the job, but I'm sure Jenny will be in the clear for it.

in the dark in ignorance. I'm completely in the dark about his plans.

in the doghouse in disgrace. The Australians are in the doghouse with the cricketing authorities for refusing to send a team to Sri Lanka.

in the doldrums inactive; very quiet or dull; in a low or undynamic state. The financial markets have been in the doldrums for several months, pending the outcome of the world trade negotiations. From sailing: a boat was in the doldrums when it was becalmed and there was no wind. Ships' crews were sometimes psychologically affected by this condition. The Doldrums is the name given to the area of the ocean near the equator where the tradewinds tend to neutralise each other. Compare **flat lining**.

in the driver's seat in control. My grandmother's been in the driver's seat in my family for as long as I can remember.

in the extreme an intensifier, usually meaning 'very'. Climbing along that ridge in a howling gale was dangerous in the extreme. Shakespeare used the expression 'Perplex'd in the extreme' in *Othello* v.2.

in the family way pregnant. I saw Jane this morning and I noticed that she's in the family way again.

in the firing line in a vulnerable position, and likely to be the target for criticism, hostility, etc. The company management took a silly decision, and they are now quite rightly in the firing line of their angry shareholders.

in the flesh in person. He'd seen her in films many times, but he never expected to meet such a famous actress in the flesh.

in/on the front line in a position of key importance. The police are in the front line of the war against crime. Originally military, from the battlefield.

in the heat of the moment impulsively, impetuously, unthinkingly. It was all said in the heat of the moment – now he wishes it unsaid.

in the know party to confidential information. Only one or two of his closest friends have been kept in the know about his plans.

in the land of the living alive. She hadn't seen him for years, and was actually a little surprised to find him still in the land of the living. The term is used in the Old Testament: 'Let us cut him off from the land of the living, that his name may be no more remembered.' Jeremiah xi.19.

in the lap of luxury in complete comfort. He's been staying at Claridge's in the lap of luxury.

in the lap of the gods depending on luck or fate; in a situation beyond one's control. He's done his best, written a good exam paper and is happy with his interview for the job – but whether or not he will be appointed is now in the lap of the gods.

in the last resort finally. He agreed to sell his shares in the business, but only in the last resort, i.e. only if there was no alternative. Originally legal.

in the limelight in a conspicuous position; at the centre of attention. The surest way for a British politician these days to get into the limelight seems to be to get caught in an act of sexual or financial irregularity. It is also possible to 'steal (or grab) the limelight', meaning to upstage a rival and steal public attention from them. Limelight was a glaringly white light yielded when heating lime in an oxyhydrogen flame. The process was discovered in 1826 by Thomas Drummond, a Scots military engineer and surveyor, who used limelight in measuring distances when making maps. The invention was soon adapted for use in lighthouses, and later in film projection and the theatre, where it became a precursor of the spotlight. Compare **get in on the act**.

in the line of duty in the course of one's regular work. Policemen tend to encounter a certain amount of violence in the line of duty.

in the long run eventually; over a long period. Their policy was fine for a year or two, but in the long run it proved disastrous.

in the loop in receipt of shared information. I'm afraid John wasn't in the loop regarding the office closure – sorry about that. Compare **in touch; keep someone posted**.

in the melting pot undecided. The overall strategy is still in the melting pot, and is unlikely to be announced for several weeks. Literally, decisions, etc. have not yet been finalised, because different ideas, etc. are still being mixed together. A melting pot was a crucible in which substances were melted and mixed together. The term was also used by historians in the 19th century to describe US society, as a place where many races and cultures were mixing together.

in the name of invocation expressing surprise, annoyance, etc. What in the name of all that's holy is he playing at now? Compare the stronger **in God's/heaven's name**. From the church service: 'In the name of the Father…' The expression may be variously adjusted, originally to avoid blasphemy. I beg you to have mercy, in the name of decency. What in the name of fortune do you want? Nowadays a phrase personally favoured by the speaker is often substituted. In the name of the wee man is common among Scots, being the idiom of several generations of *Sunday Post* comic-strip characters. Also heard: 'in the name of Rupert Murdoch/the Chancellor of the Duchy of Lancaster/the Archbishop of Westminster'. In other words, *you* name it!

in the nature of in a form resembling. His rather disparaging remarks came somewhat in the nature of a snub.

in the offing imminent. A cease-fire has been announced, and we are hopeful that an end to hostilities is in the offing. The 'offing' was originally

a spatial and not a temporal concept; it was the area of sea within one's naked vision. Compare **in the wind**.

in the pink in very good health. You're certainly looking in the pink after your holiday. The 'pink' of something meant its essence or perfection, as in 'the pink of courtesy' in Shakespeare, *Romeo and Juliet* ii.4, and 'the pink of perfection' in Goldsmith, *She Stoops to Conquer.*

in the pipeline forthcoming or planned; not yet ready. We've got all sorts of plans in the pipeline for next year. From the oil industry.

in the public eye conspicuous or prominent in public life; newsworthy. He's much less in the public eye nowadays, since retiring from Parliament.

in the raw 1. naked. Having no swimming gear, they decided to swim in the raw. 2. brutal; uncivilised; not prettified. His memoir is a description of prison life in the raw.

in the red in debt. I can't repay you for another couple of weeks because I'm in the red this month. From accountancy, where red ink was used for debiting a ledger, and black for crediting it.

in the running with a good chance of winning or obtaining something. He's only 32 but he's in the running for another promotion.

in the same boat sharing the same problems, circumstances, etc. I can't feel too sorry for Mrs Brown, since we're all very much in the same boat.

in the soup in trouble or difficulty. We'll be really in the soup if the car breaks down. Originally American, the idiom is now old fashioned and overtaken by 'in the shit' (same meaning). If you cause me any more trouble, you'll really be in the shit. The modern expression is offensive to many, with the offending noun often substituted, and so we hear 'in deep doo-doo', 'in the brown stuff' and other euphemisms. Similar to **in stook/schtuk**.

in the swim following the trend or current of opinion, popularity or fashion. Our neighbours like to keep in the swim, and they're forever getting their house redecorated in the latest styles.

in the teeth of against. He walked out of the tent and into the teeth of the gale. The act finally passed through parliament in the teeth of the fiercest opposition.

in the throes of in the middle of something difficult, unpleasant, etc. The company is in the throes of a major downsizing exercise. 'Throes' are spasms, convulsions, even mental anguish, often collocating with 'death' and (natal) 'labour'.

in the wake of following after. In the wake of last night's vote of no confidence, the government is likely to call a general election. A nautical metaphor originally.

in the wind likely to happen, but not yet officially announced. Reports of an uprising in Bolivia have been in the wind over the past few weeks. Compare **in the offing**.

in top gear performing well. Miss Berganza's singing career has been in top gear for the last three years. From driving.

in touch in contact. Please keep in touch while you're travelling. Compare **in the loop; keep someone posted**.

in two minds unable to come to a decision. She was in two minds whether or not to go to New York. Compare **think twice**.

in two ticks/shakes (of a lamb's tail) quickly; immediately. The doctor will be here in two shakes. Once 'in two twos' (or 2 x 2).

in vain without success; ineffectually. We tried in vain to discover what the problem was.

in view of on account of; in consideration of. The concert was cancelled in view of the conductor's death.

in with the bricks expression used to indicate – sometimes respectfully, sometimes contemptuously – a person's long service in an organisation. John can tell you anything about this company – he's in with the bricks in this place. Compare **part of the furniture**.

in your face too direct or socially relentless. I'm sorry, she's far too in your face for my liking: I hide if I see her approaching! See also **come on strong**.

INDIAN. Indian summer period of dry and sunny autumn weather, often accompanied by heat-haze. Hotels in the north of Scotland were busy right through October this year, because of the Indian summer conditions. In the 18th century, the term referred exclusively to the North American climate where the feature was common and for which it was originally coined. Its transfer to the British climate, where it is infrequent, and elsewhere is more recent.

INDUSTRIAL. industrial action strike; work stoppage invariably organised by a trade union. According to the press, there is likely to be industrial action at the factory before Christmas. According to many, this was the archetypal oxymoron of the 1970s, since the workforce was organised into compulsory inaction.

INS. ins and outs small details. I don't know all the ins and outs of the affair, only that we've lost a lot of money.

INSIDE. inside lane/track most favoured position. Office opinion has it that Mrs Worthington is on the inside track for promotion. From the athletics field, where carefully staggered starts mean that the inside track is no longer the favourite position.

INTO. into effect into operation. The new taxes come into effect on 5 April next year.

into line into agreement, so that everyone or everything follows the same plan. The new leadership has had a hard job bringing all the delegates into line on certain controversial subjects. Compare **sing from the same hymnsheet**.

into the bargain also; as well. He's a brilliant linguist and a champion footballer into the bargain. Compare **to boot**.

into the open into public knowledge. Slowly, with great reluctance, the government was forced to bring the whole squalid affair out into the open. Literally, 'into the open air' from some dark place of concealment. Compare **off one's chest; out of the closet**.

into thin air without trace. She walked out on him two years ago and has just disappeared into thin air.

IRON. Iron Curtain the line on the map which separated the capitalist and communist blocs in Europe between the 1950s and the 1990s. He worked behind the Iron Curtain for many years, only returning to the West in 1989. Winston Churchill popularised the expression in a prophetic 1946 speech. Other political uses of 'iron': the Iron Chancellor (Otto von Bismark) and the Iron Lady (Margaret Thatcher).

iron hand/fist in a velvet glove firm and merciless person with a suave and courteous manner. He handled the affair with icy politeness, but it was clear that there was an iron fist in his velvet glove and that he was going to see that she did exactly as he wished.

IRONS. irons in the fire projects in hand; assignments to attend to. I don't know how she copes – she always seems to have so many different irons in the fire at one time. Probably an expression from the industrious blacksmith's forge, rather like **strike while the iron is hot**. Another school of thought suggests that the term originated in an equally busy laundry, where the laundress often had to keep several irons heating at once.

ITCHY/ITCHING. itchy feet urge to travel; **wanderlust**. Even in her late 80s my mother had itchy feet and wanted to visit the Taj Mahal and the Grand Canyon.

itchy/itching palm mercenary and grasping tendencies. He has an itching palm, and he'll be asking you for money before he even starts the job for you. From Shakespeare: 'You yourself are much condemned to have an itching palm.' *Julius Caesar* iv.3. According to an old superstition, an itching palm meant that one was about to receive money.

IVORY. ivory tower 1. sheltered place, away from the hustle and bustle of everyday life; place to hide away from 'real life'. During term time, he teaches in one of the toughest schools in London, but in the holidays he retreats to his ivory tower in Brittany. Originally a French critical reference to the romantic poets, the idiom is now deployed most frequently against the academic community. 2. often used adjectivally: 'an ivory-tower existence', meaning not of the real world. Economists and politicians tend to have the most ivory-tower views of the business world.

J

JAM. jam tomorrow the promise of something at a future date, which one is unlikely to receive. Politicians seeking re-election are very prone to offer jam tomorrow. From a quotation of Lewis Carroll's Red Queen, in *Through the Looking Glass* (1872): 'The rule is jam tomorrow, and jam yesterday, but never jam today.' Compare **pie in the sky**.

JANUS. Janus-faced hypocritical. The Tory Party collapsed in 1995 because of its Janus-faced attitude to the European Union. From classical mythology: Janus was the Roman god of gates and doors, the keeper of the gate. He was able to look outside and inside the gate at the same time. Because of this knack, his name became linked with the idea of hypocrisy, widely described as an ability to face in two directions at once. See also **two-faced**. Also sometimes 'double-faced' (same meaning).

JAW. jaw drop show one's amazement. He thought his wife was in Australia, so his jaw dropped a mile when she walked through the door and into the room.

JEKYLL. Jekyll and Hyde person with two sides to his character, one of which may be nasty. I wouldn't trust a Jekyll and Hyde chap like that to look after children. From the novel (1888) by Robert Louis Stevenson in which the main character was able to change himself chemically from a good (Mr Hyde) to a wicked (Dr Jekyll) person.

JET. jet lag tiredness caused by air travel across different time zones. The main conference speaker was either suffering a bad bout of jet lag, or else he had had too much to drink.

jet set international high society; cosmopolitan people who are rich and successful and who travel regularly and widely, often by jet plane. I've not seen much of her since she became famous and joined the jet set. A 1960s phrase spawned by jet flight.

JEWEL. jewel in the crown the best part of something. The management are very proud of the refurbished Ritz Hotel; they see it as the jewel in the crown of their various London hotels. The original reference was to India, described as the jewel in the imperial crown of Queen Victoria.

JIGGERY. jiggery pokery dishonesty; mischief; humbug. He didn't bet on the outcome of the race, suspecting some kind of jiggery pokery among the jockeys. A Victorian reduplication, originally Scots or Ulster Scots 'jowkery-pawkery' (1782) meaning deceitfulness and evasion.

JOB. job lot mixed collection of goods offered for sale, often at knock-down prices because the seller simply wants rid of them. Sometimes you can pick up something interesting in a job lot at the local sale room.

JOB'S. Job's comforter person who tries to comfort someone but says something which instead makes the person feel worse. When she told me I was looking dreadful, I asked her what kind of Job's comforter she was. From the Book of Job xvi.2.

JOBS. jobs for the boys positions or work kept for certain lucky individuals, usually through nepotism, connections, etc. Three members of the local council are to stand trial for various illegal, jobs-for-the-boys deals. 'Jobs for the girls' tends nowadays to mean work earmarked for women. See **positive discrimination**.

JOCKEY. jockey for position try to manoeuvre oneself into the best strategic position. With the prime minister's resignation, the rest of the cabinet are frantically jockeying for the top position. From horse racing.

JOE. Joe Public typical member of the general public. It was an interesting concert, but not the sort of programme calculated to appeal to Joe Public. American. Compare **man in the street**.

JOIN. join forces unite; merge. From today, our two companies are joining forces: together, they will represent a significant slice of the UK life insurance business. **From military tactics: armies join forces to fight a common foe.**

JOINED. joined-up thinking logical and coherently sequenced argument. We need to achieve more joined-up thinking between government agencies. Compare **right hand doesn't know what the left hand's doing** (its opposite) and the **big idea/picture**.

JOKING. joking aside/apart to speak seriously. I told him, all joking apart, that it was important for him to heed the doctor's advice.

JUMP. jump down someone's throat speak angrily and aggressively to someone. He jumped down my throat when I had the temerity to suggest that he'd drunk enough whisky for one evening.

jump on the bandwagon do something because it is fashionable or profitable. We used to have a profitable business selling sandwiches to the visitors to the castle; but now everybody has jumped on that particular bandwagon, and there's no profit to be made any more. **Originally American: a bandwagon is an ornately decorated truck or wagon used by musicians in a political parade, etc. trying to drum up support for a party or a programme. The term was extended to include all those who then flock to support that party.** Also 'climb/get on the bandwagon'. Compare **flavour of the month; get in on the act**.

jump ship escape. 'I thought Bloggs was going to come with us and lend a hand.' 'Well yes, that was the idea but he seems to have jumped ship.' **Originally maritime, from the days when the press gang virtually kidnapped reluctant seamen.**

jump/kick start force something to go or perform. The chancellor explained to his audience that he had no simple formula which could be guaranteed to jump start the economy. **A motoring term which entered the wider metaphorical lexicon in the early 1980s.**

jump the gun be over-hasty in starting something.

He decided to jump the gun and apply for the job before it was advertised in the press. **From athletics: if a runner begins racing before the firing pistol has gone off, he or she is said to be guilty of jumping the gun.**

jump the queue move in front of other people in a queue instead of waiting one's turn. He tried to jump the queue because he was in a hurry.

jump through hoops/a hoop do things (which are sometimes inconvenient) to please someone else. Eventually she got fed up jumping through hoops to suit the whim of the managing director, so she took another job. **From the circus, with the implication that one is having to perform at the command of some unthinking ringmaster.**

jump to conclusions form an opinion about something before studying all the evidence. Just because she had been seen in the same man's company five or six times, her father jumped to conclusions about their friendship. **Also frequently** 'jump to the wrong conclusions'. Compare **bark up the wrong tree**.

JUNK. junk food(s) snack-type packaged foods that are often of low nutritional value. Lots of children nowadays don't know what good cooking is – they prefer junk foods and ready meals to a healthy cooked diet. **An Americanism from the 1970s.**

JURY. the jury is still out no decision or conclusion has been reached. The match should start at 2 p.m. but the jury is out on that until after an inspection of the pitch at 1.30. **From the law courts.**

JUST. just about almost. The fire was just about out when suddenly there was a massive explosion.

just around the corner about to happen. It's nice to see the snowdrops and crocuses again, and to know that spring must be just around the corner. **From the words of a popular song.**

just now 1. at this precise time. I'm afraid he can't see you just now – he's with another client. **2.** a moment ago. Where have my spectacles got to? They were on the table just now.

just the job/ticket/thing! 1. exclamations meaning, 'that's exactly what is needed!' I've brought you a mug of soup – just the ticket for a cold day like today. **Slightly old fashioned. The 'ticket' idiom may derive from the little books of tickets, or programmes, which were distributed to the poor for food, clothes, etc. in the early 19th century to ensure that they didn't all die of starvation, hypothermia, etc. Similar to just what the doctor ordered**. 2. the precise thing that one needs. She bought a huge yellow hat, saying it was just the thing for the wedding.

just what the doctor ordered what one needs to make one feel better. He had a good night's sleep and a hearty breakfast – just what the doctor ordered for a man who had spent 18 hours marooned on a life-raft.

K

KANGAROO. kangaroo court unofficial court which has no genuine legal authority, and where the principles of justice are disregarded or perverted. Because of the nature of his crime, the prisoner had to be protected from kangaroo courts set up by his fellow inmates. **Perhaps from the animal's occasional vicious streak, because such peremptory attempts at justice ignored the niceties of due process. The term was used in Texas in 1849, which is surprising – given that kangaroos didn't come from the Americas.**

KEEN. keen as mustard very eager, bright, well motivated. John Smith is one of our new trainees, and he's as keen as mustard. A standard simile, from the keen taste of mustard on the tongue. Also 'keen/sharp as a razor', similar sense.

KEEP. keep a low profile cultivate or maintain a self-effacing posture; avoid the limelight. Jones keeps far too low a profile for an effective promotions manager. **Also used adjectivally.** He has a very low-profile approach to his job as a sort of government spy.

keep a straight face try to look serious, even when one wants to laugh. She looked so ridiculous that it was hard for the rest of us to keep a straight face.

keep an eye on watch; look after. We offered to keep an eye on their goldfish for them while the neighbours were away on holiday.

keep at something work at something until it is finished. I admire your willingness to keep at the job.

keep someone/something at arm's length avoid contact with someone/something. Mrs Bloggs is not my favourite person, so I tend to keep her at arm's length.

keep someone/something at bay keep someone/something at a safe distance. She's been dosing herself with various antihistamines to try to keep her hay-fever at bay. **From hunting: hounds** 'bay' at a cornered stag, while the stag will hold the dogs 'at bay' when it turns to face them. The word is from Old French *abayer* (= to bark; modern French *aboyer*).

keep body and soul together earn enough money to feed and keep oneself sheltered; stay alive. Lots of people don't like their work, but they do it in order to keep body and soul together.

keep company 1. stay with someone to help them not feel lonely. She said she was feeling a bit lonely, so I decided to keep her company for an hour or so, and try to cheer her up. 2. **be the girlfriend or boyfriend of someone.** I'm told she's been keeping company with the man in the corner house. **Rather old fashioned.**

keep one's cool refrain from getting too excited or agitated. You'll manage fine so long as you keep your cool. **Opposite of 'lose one's cool'; see also hang loose.** American teenage jargon of the 1950s.

keep something dark keep something secret. For several years she managed to keep the identity of her partner dark.

keep dick watch out; keep a look-out. He escaped by the back door while I was keeping dick at the front. A 'dick' in American English was a private detective, or private eye.

keep one's ear to the ground find out about what is being said and done. The company has good advisers in that market – agents who are paid to keep their ears to the ground for them and report any developments that could affect their business.

keep one's end up sustain one's position or part in an argument, business, performance, etc. He's outclassed by all his colleagues and has great difficulty keeping his end up at meetings. **In the sense of holding to one's end, or aim, or objective. Compare hold one's own.**

keep one's eye on the ball concentrate on the priorities confronting one; avoid digressing or allowing one's concentration to wander. He had a lot of work to get through earlier in the year, but he kept his eye on the ball and got on with it. **From football and golf.**

keep one's eyes peeled/skinned be on the alert; watch carefully. The look-out guards had to keep their eyes peeled for enemy movements. Originally American, presumably with the sense of peeling any coverings or blinkers away from one's line of vision.

keep one's feet retain one's balance. When the plane veered suddenly to the right, a couple of stewards fell over, but I managed to keep my feet.

keep one's feet on the ground be realistic; refrain from getting carried away. After several years of managing the nation's affairs and dealing with the world's leaders, the prime minister still manages to keep his feet planted firmly on the ground. **Opposite of have one's head in the clouds.**

keep one's fingers crossed wish for good luck. I'm not a very good sailor, but I'm keeping my fingers crossed for a calm sea. **This probably originated with people making the sign of the cross to ward off evil spirits; still a popular superstition.**

keep one's finger on the pulse know exactly what is happening in a society, organisation, etc. A foreign correspondent has to keep his finger on the pulse of the country in which he is based.

keep one's hair on not lose one's temper, or get unduly indignant. We had to tell her to keep her hair on and stop shouting and yelling.

keep one's hand in retain one's skill at; remain well practised at. He still enjoys playing the piano after supper, so he's managed to keep his hand in quite nicely over the years.

keep one's head remain calm; refrain from panicking. He survived his ordeal because he kept his head and didn't allow himself to get too frightened. The idiom inspired the beginning of Rudyard Kipling's great poem 'If – ': 'If you can keep your head when all about you/Are losing theirs and blaming it on you…' (1910). This was voted the most popular English poem in 1995. Also 'keep a cool/level head', **keep one's cool**. Opposite of **lose one's head**.

keep one's head above water remain solvent or self-sufficient, often by dint of struggle. He seems to have a lot of trouble keeping his head above water. From swimming; you drowned, or went into debt, when your head sank below the level of the water. Compare **out of one's depth**.

keep one's head down 1. try not to be noticed. I didn't want to speak to the boss, so I just kept my head down till he'd left the building. 2. **concentrate on one's work; work hard.** The exam is next week, so I've got to keep my head down for the next few days.

keep oneself/someone/something in check 1. keep oneself/someone under control or restrained, especially emotions. The children have to be kept very much in check on visits to the swimming pool. 2. prevent something from progressing or advancing. The rebel army has been kept in check now for several months. **From the chess board.**

keep one's mouth/trap shut be silent; say nothing. They threatened me with all sorts of violence if I didn't keep my mouth shut.

keep one's nose clean avoid trouble. He's been out of jail for six months and seems to have kept his nose clean thus far. **Sometimes used as a jocular form of farewell valediction, with or without amplifications, as in: 'Keep your nose clean and wear a deodorant!' Compare play one's cards right/well.**

keep one's nose out of something mind one's own business. The matter has nothing to do with you, so I'd ask you just to keep your nose well out of it.

keep one's nose to the grindstone work hard and continuously. Sarah has worked very hard all summer for her finals – she's given up on her social life, and is concentrating on keeping her nose to the grindstone. He's not a popular teacher, because he really keeps his pupils' noses to the grindstone. There is sometimes a hint of meanness here, as in most things which were once to do with millers in popular mythology, especially if someone else's nose is being kept to the grindstone. There is also the element of grinding people down and oppressing them.

keep on one's toes maintain oneself in a state of alertness. When the visiting side scored the first goal, we all got a fright – but that was enough to keep us on our toes for the rest of the match.

keep one's pecker/chin up keep one's appetite, or courage, or spirits buoyant; don't get down-hearted. He was looking a bit depressed, and I told him to keep his pecker up. A 'pecker' is of course a bird's beak. Usually a valedictory exhortation.

keep someone posted let someone know about any news or developments. I know I'm going to be in Australia and he's in Britain, but we're going to keep each other posted regularly by e-mail. Compare **in the loop**.

keep one's powder dry stay calm and alert and ready for action. Let them make all the accusations they wish to make; I shall keep my powder dry until the trial, but then I will give everyone a surprise. Perhaps based on a quotation from Oliver Cromwell during his Irish campaign in 1649: 'Put your trust in God, my boys, and keep your powder dry.' The 'powder' in question was gunpowder, useless if it got wet.

keep one's shirt/hair on refrain from getting over-excited, carried away, etc. Nobody says you stole anything – so just keep your shirt on for a minute.

keep one's/a weather-eye open watch out for; be alert for. Istanbul is a fascinating place, but you need to keep your weather-eye open for pickpockets. Originally nautical: someone in a ship's crew was always on the look-out for stormy weather.

keep out of someone's hair/road refrain from annoying or provoking someone, sometimes most effectively done by staying out of their way. She managed to keep the children out of his hair yesterday, but only at the expense of doing no work of her own.

keep one's own counsel not share one's views, plans, etc. with others; be reticent about one's intentions. He's a person who keeps his own counsel, so you never know exactly what he's going to say. See also **zip one's lips**.

keep tabs on know what is happening, or what someone is doing. After complaints from neighbours, the police have been keeping tabs on a house in Castle Street. Originally American and singular: a 'tab' means a check or tally.

keep the ball rolling keep things moving; maintain the tempo of a conversation, etc. She's one of those taciturn types who have difficulty keeping the ball rolling in a social gathering. From football: the idea was as much to keep the ball in play as anything else. The idiom was taken as his successful US presidential campaign slogan in 1840 by William Henry Harrison.

keep the wolf from the door get enough food or income to keep oneself fed and sheltered. I'm doing a little job for the neighbours just now; they've promised me £100 for my pains, so that'll keep the wolf from the door for a day or two. The wolf was a popular metaphor for hunger from as long ago as the 15th century. We still say of hungry people that they wolf their food. Compare **live from hand to mouth**.

keep track (of something/someone) follow the development or progress (of something/ someone). She finds it very difficult to keep track of her bank balance.

keep something under one's hat keep secret or confidential. She told me about the divorce last week, but asked me to keep it under my hat for a month or two. Compare **under wraps**.

keep up appearances make one's circumstances appear as affluent as possible, and imply that all is well financially. He's one of those people who find it very important to keep up appearances – so he likes to be seen in expensive clothes and driving an expensive car which he can't really afford.

keep up with the Joneses maintain one's social position vis à vis one's neighbours, etc. After he lost his job, they found it increasingly hard to keep up with the Joneses. One of the tenets of consumerism. From a US comic strip called 'Keeping up with the Joneses', begun in 1911 by I Bacheller, which was syndicated in the New York *Globe* and a number of other newspapers and ran from 1913 to 1941. It was all about people living beyond their means and trying to keep up with their better-off neighbours. In the 1960s, when Princess Margaret was married to Antony Armstrong-Jones, one occasionally heard as a British variant: 'Keeping up with the Armstrong-Joneses', but this has now more or less disappeared. (Note the spelling of Joneses – one Jones, two Joneses; no apostrophes are required.)

keep/have one's wits about one be alert; know exactly what one is doing/saying, etc. She won the debate by keeping her wits about her, and pouncing on all the flaws in her opponent's argument.

keep one's word respect one's promise. If she said she'd take him to the most expensive restaurant in Paris, she will do so: she always keeps her word. Opposite of **break one's word**.

KEYED. keyed up tense and excited. She's all keyed up about flying to America – it's her first flight. From music, a phrasal verb meaning an instrument 'keyed to a higher pitch'.

KIBOSH. put the kibosh on something veto or spoil something, or finish it off. The planned open-air firework display depends on decent weather; if it rains, that will put the kibosh on our plans. Thought to be from Yiddish.

KICK. kick against the pricks resist the irresistible. It took him a long time to learn that there are things in life that you just have to accept, and that there's little point in kicking against the pricks. A quotation from the Book of Acts ix.5, where Jesus says to Saul, who is resisting him: 'I am Jesus whom thou persecutest: it is hard for thee to kick against the pricks.' The phrase originally referred to oxen that kicked against the pricks of a sharp goad, used to drive them forward. Samuel Beckett played on this idiom with his piece *More Pricks than Kicks* (1970). Opposite of **go with the flow**.

kick ass assert oneself in aggressive fashion. The managing director visits the factory once a month, and spends most of the first morning kicking ass and making his presence felt. American, 'ass' meaning arse or backside.

kick/cool one's heels wait for something to happen, in a state of enforced idleness. The Red Cross team were stranded in Chad for several weeks, which they spent kicking their heels and waiting to get their visas sorted out.

kick in the teeth/pants discouragement, especially when one is looking for support; setback. The renewal of fighting in Afghanistan is a serious kick in the teeth for the United Nations.

kick/push (something) into the long grass put something outside the parameters for discussion; remove something from the agenda. Obviously no one wanted to talk about X, and several times the subject was kicked into the long grass. Also 'kick something into touch', from rugby, meaning put the ball beyond play. Compare **off limits**.

kick oneself be very annoyed with oneself. He kicked himself when he discovered he'd forgotten to post the letter.

kick over the traces reject the constraints which formerly bound one. After their final exams, several students seemed to feel the need to kick over the traces and behave rather irresponsibly for a few weeks. The 'traces' are the ropes which connect a horse or ox to its harness; when the animal kicks them over, it gets out of its driver's control.

kick the bucket die. It was one of those depressing old folks' homes where people sat around all day waiting to kick the bucket. A euphemism: there are two main theories behind this colloquial expression. One is that when a hapless victim was to be hanged, or committed suicide, he often stood on a bucket until the noose was secured around his neck. When all was ready, the bucket was kicked away. See also **ready for the drop/off**. The other theory is that the term derives from the slaughtering of pigs and other livestock. The animal was suspended from a bucket yoke or frame, and twitched and kicked against it in its death throes.

kick up a fuss express anger in a noisy or public manner. The diners kicked up a great fuss when the waiter told them that there was no more smoked salmon.

kick someone upstairs appear to promote someone, actually to a position with a fancy or honorific rank but without much power. Old Jones didn't want to retire at 65, so the company kicked him upstairs to the specially created post of Group Chairman. Most frequently used with reference to the 'elevation' of a member of the UK House of Commons to the House of Lords, or 'Upper House' of the British Parliament.

KIDS'. kids' stuff very easy; something requiring no great skill, knowledge, etc. The hours are long, but the work itself is kids' stuff. American: literally, something that even a small kid or child could do.

KILL. kill or cure drastic action that will ruin or resolve everything. His position wasn't very strong, and he decided to put himself up for re-election in a kill or cure gesture. An alliterative dyad, from popular fears of strong and potentially fatal medicines.

kill the fatted calf prepare particularly lavish hospitality in order to honour or welcome a long-absent visitor. When we visited our American cousins for the first time, the hospitality was amazing – they really killed the fatted calf for us. From the parable of the prodigal son, in Luke xv.27: 'Thy brother is come; and thy father hath killed the fatted calf, because he hath received him safe and sound.'

kill the goose that lays the golden eggs destroy a source of income or profit. It is impossible for a good business not to supply goods to customers it doesn't approve of – that would be killing the geese that lay the golden eggs. From a fable by Aesop: the owner of the mythical bird kills it by trying to get at all the golden eggs which he thinks are inside it.

kill time wait for something to happen, while doing nothing useful – usually with feelings of impatience as a result of forced inactivity. Having missed the 10 o'clock train I had to kill time until noon waiting for the next one. Another phrase for time wasting in this manner is 'clock watching'. Compare **twiddle one's thumbs**.

kill two birds with one stone achieve two aims or objectives with one effort, outlay, etc. I had to go to New York for a meeting with my agent, and decided to kill two birds with one stone and go and see my sister while I was there anyway.

kill someone with kindness spoil or over-indulge someone. His doting mother killed that child with kindness long ago, so he's never learnt self-discipline or passed his exams. Shakespeare described the marital strategy of killing a wife with kindness in *The Taming of the Shrew* (1592).

KISS. kiss of death unwelcome support from an unpopular source. A recommendation from her was the kiss of death to his ambitions – she being a very unpopular politician. The original kiss of death was given in Matthew xxvi.48 by Judas Iscariot to Jesus Christ; this was the betrayal which signalled Christ's identity to the chief priests and elders, who immediately arrested him.

kiss of life mouth-to-mouth artificial respiration. Having pulled the half-drowned child from the river, I then had to spend several minutes trying to revive him and giving him the kiss of life.

kiss the Blarney Stone talk very convincingly, persuasively, fluently, etc. – sometimes glibly. That man could sell snow to the Eskimos; he could talk for England; he must have kissed the Blarney Stone. The stone in question is located at Blarney Castle, near Cork in Ireland. Its magic powers were thought to reward anyone who kissed it with the **gift of the gab**. Compare **talk the birds off the trees**.

KIT. kit and caboodle all one's property and possessions. We lost our entire kit and caboodle in the hurricanes. An American alliterative dyad, 'caboodle' was from a Dutch word meaning household effects. Compare **lock, stock and barrel; whole shooting match**.

KITH. kith and kin kinsfolk; family connections. The Golden Wedding photograph provides a good summary of their kith and kin in 1965: the entire extended family was there for that big event. An alliterative dyad, similar to flesh and blood; although the word 'kith' means one's friends and neighbours, with 'kin' meaning one's family, the contemporary resonance of this expression embraces only one's relatives.

KNEE. knee-high to a grasshopper very small. That boy's been mad about cars ever since he was knee-high to a grasshopper. Originally American.

KNOCK. knock something back drink something quickly. It took him very little time to knock back a couple of pints of beer.

knock someone back cost someone. His latest lawsuit knocked him back about £25,000.

knock someone cold punch someone unconscious. The champion knocked the challenger cold in the fifth round of the fight.

knock someone for six completely flummox or surprise someone. The news of the factory's closure has knocked everyone for six. A cricketing idiom: a batsman scores six runs if he hits the ball over the boundary before it comes to earth.

knock someone/something into a cocked hat ruin or damage someone/something; decisively outperform someone/something. Her performance was outstanding, and knocked the rest of the cast into a cocked hat. The expression is American, and is thought to have referred originally to the three-cornered hat (or tricorne) hat worn by the military in the 18th century. Alternatively, it may have referred to the skittle game which was played with three pins set up in triangular position. Similar to **knock spots off**.

knock it off stop doing something. Why don't you two knock it off and stop all this arguing and snarling? Compare **wrap it up**.

knock someone sideways overwhelm someone usually by bad news. His wife's death completely knocked him sideways. Compare **bowl someone over**.

knock spots off do something much better than others; decisively defeat. He may only be 13 years old, but his violin playing knocked spots off all the adult competitors. His batting was phenomenal, knocking spots off some lethal West Indian bowling. American in origin, the reference is perhaps to spots on a marksman's shooting target. Similar to **knock into a cocked hat**.

KNOTTY. knotty problem something that is hard to resolve or unravel. The knotty problem for Eliza every morning was the dreadful dilemma of what to wear. 'Knotty' means wood that is full of knots, hence difficult or awkward to cut true.

KNOW. know a thing or two be knowledgeable. Having worked in the police for a few years, he knows a thing or two about corruption in local government. A meiosis, or understatement (i.e. he knows a lot).

know all the answers be shrewd and knowledgeable, and able to answer all one's questions. Speak to Stephanie if you have any problems; she knows all the answers. Also 'know all the angles' (similar), meaning all the approaches to a problem, etc.

(not) know one's arse from one's elbow (not) be competent or capable or very intelligent. Some of these First World War generals and admirals genuinely didn't know their arse from their elbow – they should never have been put in charge of anybody. Usually in the negative. Sometimes 'not know one's arse from a hole in the ground', or – aiming at assonance – 'not know one's arse from parsley'.

know something backwards/inside out have learnt something perfectly by memory, or off by heart. I have heard that pop song so often that I know it backwards.

know one's onions/stuff be expert. Your car has broken down? Take it to MacAndrew – he is an excellent mechanic who really knows his onions.

know/learn the ropes be/become well informed. It was a good office to train in, but it took me several months to get to know the ropes. Of nautical origin, from the days of tall ships and their complicated rigging. Also 'know the form', meaning be well informed socially. She moved around in high society, and wanted me to get to know the form.

know the score be clear about the real facts of a situation, however unpalatable they may be. I was too young and naive in those days to know the score, so I was easily duped. Also 'know how things stand', 'know what's what', 'know one's way around'.

know where one stands know one's financial or social or other status. Now that the doctor has diagnosed the condition, I know where I stand.

know which side one's bread is buttered (on) know what is to one's advantage. He's far too clever to antagonise his employer because he well knows which side his bread is buttered on.

KNUCKLE. knuckle down (to) start something in earnest, especially involving hard work. There's an exam at the end of this term, so you're all going to have to knuckle down for a few weeks and get some revision done. In the 18th century, literally to get down on your hands and knees, with your knuckles on the ground to play a competitive game of marbles, etc. Compare **pull one's finger out**.

knuckle sandwich punch. He told me to watch it or he'd give my face a knuckle sandwich. An inelegant variation.

knuckle under give in; submit. We had a bit of an argument about what to do, but in the end I knuckled under and agreed to John's plan.

L

LABOUR. labour of love something one does for pleasure rather than for profit. Writing this book has been a labour of love for me, since I don't really expect to make much money from it.

LADY. lady killer man who is very attractive to women and successfully practises the art of seducing them. He used to be a bit of a lady killer in his youth, and most young women still notice the twinkle in his eye.

LAGER. lager lout young thug or layabout, often potentially dangerous because half-drunk. We were warned not to go near the sea front, where a crowd of lager louts were running riot. This alliterative term was coined in the 1980s to describe young hooligans attending football matches and behaving in gratuitously antisocial fashion.

LAME. lame duck an ineffectual person whose powers are handicapped or waning; an unproductive or disabled business enterprise. After the fiasco of the cabinet revolt, a lame-duck government blundered on for a few more months before finally calling the general election which the country had been demanding for months. The original context was financial, and the term referred to 18th-century defaulters or debtors on the London Stock Exchange. Commonly used from the mid-19th century in a political context as an adjective denoting a weak or ailing presidency, premiership, etc. as in 'a lame-duck administration'.

LAND. land/fall on one's feet have good luck in a difficult situation. You have to admire James: he always manages to land on his feet, whatever happens to him.

land of nod asleep, or in the land of sleep. Most nights the children are in the land of nod before I can finish their bedtime story. A pun, 'nod' means sleep, but is also a biblical reference, from Genesis iv.16: 'And Cain dwelt in the land of Nod, on the east of Eden.'

land someone with something give someone an unpleasant or unwelcome assignment. I'm afraid you've been landed with the job of cleaning out the stable.

LAP. (born/cradled in) the lap of luxury (born/brought up in) affluent style. When he goes off on overseas business trips his employers insist that he stay in the lap of luxury at first-class hotels. Compare **born with a silver spoon in one's mouth**.

(in) the lap of providence/the gods (in) the unknown future, whose outcomes are decided by fate – divine or otherwise. Work hard for your exams, read the paper very carefully and then do your best, leaving the outcome where it belongs – in the lap of the gods. The 'lap' is where a small child sits to be comforted by an adult. If something 'falls into your lap', it comes within your reach or power. The phrase was first used in Homer's *Iliad*, in which the gods were ultimately on the side of Achilles.

LASH. lash out on something spend money lavishly; treat oneself to something. Last year we lashed out on a world cruise. A phrasal verb.

LAST. last-ditch effort final and often desperate attempt at something (before giving up). In the final minutes of the match, our side made one supreme last-ditch effort to score a goal. From the field of battle, and fighting desperately in the last ditch or final defensive earthwork.

last laugh the final benefit/advantage of the joke. Our opponents ridiculed us when they saw our team, thinking they'd beat us easily; but we had the last laugh, because small as we were, we were fitter than they were and we won the match decisively. The sense is of the 'laugh' being initially against one, but eventually in one's favour.

last legs tottering; exhausted. Running a marathon race in such heat was unwise: several of the competitors were on their last legs when they reached the finish.

last straw the final insult or episode which guarantees retaliation, etc. They have stayed uninvited in my house for a week, conducting themselves abominably; now they have crashed my car. That is the last straw, and they must leave immediately. **From the proverb 'It is the last straw which breaks the camel's back.'**

last word 1. something that is very elegant and modern. Her car is the last word in style and dash. 2. final remark or decision. John is one of those people who always has to have the last word in an argument.

LATCHKEY. latchkey child neglected child. She belongs to the generation of latchkey children who lacked maternal affection. **Literally, a small child who is given a housekey to use when s/he gets home from school to an empty house because the parents are at work. See also home-alone kid.**

LATE. late in the day when a project, etc. is at an advanced stage, especially when it is too late to make adjustments to plans. The judge's verdict will be published tomorrow, so I imagine it's too late in the day for you to try to affect his verdict now.

late in the field late applicant for a job. Everyone assumed initially that the leadership contest was between the prime minister and his challenger John Redwood; Mr Heseltine may have been late in the field, but he soon overtook the other contestants. **From medieval battle tactics: a good commander would have reinforcements holding back until the ideal juncture for entering the fray.**

LAUGH. laugh on the wrong/other side of one's face/mouth change one's mood from happiness and confidence to sadness and depression. She may be pleased and delighted with her silly trick right now, but I've just reported her to the head teacher, so we'll soon have her laughing on the other side of her face. **Compare change one's tune.**

laugh something/someone out of court derisively ridicule something/someone, and thereby dismiss it from serious consideration. He comes up with some odd ideas at council meetings, but most of them are laughed out of court without much ceremony. **Originally legal.**

laugh up one's sleeve be amused and try not to show it. When one's superiors conduct themselves inappropriately, there's not much we can do except laugh at them up our sleeve.

LAUGHING. (no) laughing matter (not) something to laugh about. It was hardly a laughing matter when she fell off the ladder – she broke her collarbone. **Usually negative.**

LAUNCH. launch a probe start an investigation. The press have decided to launch another probe into the royal family's expenditure. **One of the more over-used journalistic clichés. Originally of course it was ships which were launched, and then any new product from toothpaste to the latest bodice-ripping novels. A 'probe' started life as an investigative surgical instrument. The words came together in the tabloid press in the 1970s, and have alas never looked back. Compare unveil an initiative.**

LAW. law of averages the (unscientific) idea that results are bound to change. The last three weekends have been very wet; by the law of averages, we should get some sunshine next weekend.

law of the jungle law which states that might is right and that the fittest will survive, the articulation of a viewpoint which ignores all ethical considerations. After the civilian government in Ruritania collapsed, society ran according to the law of the jungle. **From the title of a poem by Rudyard Kipling in *The Second Jungle Book* (1895), beginning, 'Now this is the Law of the Jungle – as old and as true as the sky;/And the Wolf that shall keep it may prosper, but the Wolf that shall break it must die.'**

law to/unto oneself a self-willed and maverick person who does things in his/her own often unpredictable or unconventional way; a person who is, or thinks s/he is, in some way above the law. He has never been very successful in the party, being too much of a law to himself to be able to stick to the party line. Since becoming managing director of the business, she's been very much of a law to herself. **Once upon a time, following the King James Bible, we said 'a law unto oneself'. Compare loose cannon**.

LAY. lay a finger/hand on touch or harm. Let him so much as lay a finger on my kids and I'll call the police.

lay something at someone's door blame something on someone. I know her house has been burgled, but she can't be trying to lay the blame for that at my door, can she?

lay one's cards on the table disclose one's resources or a confidence, often with the notion of confessing one's weaknesses or problems. Last night John came to see me and told me all about his bankruptcy: he laid his cards on the table with remarkable candour, and I agreed to help him. **From card games. Compare show one's hand**.

lay down the law issue orders; make dogmatic utterances in discussion or argument. My father still treats me as if I were a child: he thinks he can lay down the law and tell me what I can and can't do.

lay hands on touch; obtain. I'll send you a copy of the book when I can find it – right now I'm very busy and I don't think I could lay hands on it without much hunting around.

lay into someone be very angry with someone, and tell them so. When the waitress spilt the soup, the head waiter laid into her for her carelessness – in front of all the customers. **Also tear strips off someone. Compare in no uncertain terms**.

lay it on the line speak frankly and forcefully, in order to make one's position plain. I want to lay it on the line that I strongly disapprove of these developments. **Originally American. Compare on record**.

lay/pile it on thick or **with a trowel** be excessively unctuous or flattering to/about someone; overdo or overstate something. A few kind words about your predecessor might be appropriate; but remember he's a modest soul, and will be listening to your speech, so there's no need for you to lay it on with a trowel – that will only make him squirm in his seat. **Shakespeare used this figure of speech in** *As You Like It* **i.2, and Disraeli is attributed with the remark: 'Everybody likes flattery: and when you come to royalty you should lay it on with a trowel.' Compare overegg the pudding**.

lay someone off make a worker redundant. When the mine closed, they laid off over a hundred people.

lay/hang one on someone punch someone. He told me to belt up or he'd lay one on me. **Literally, lay a punch**.

lay to rest bury. She was laid to rest alongside her parents, in the village churchyard. **A euphemism**.

LEAD. lead someone a dog's life give someone a bad time; cause someone distress and unhappiness (by treating them as if they were a dog). She's been so much happier and more confident since her divorce; her ex-husband used to lead her a dog's life.

lead someone a merry dance seriously inconvenience someone by making them perform difficult tasks, often needlessly. The old lady is a bit of a tyrant, and she sometimes leads her family a merry dance.

lead someone by the nose make someone do whatever one wants; easily persuade a gullible person; make someone follow your point of view or accept your argument. The poor man is besotted with this woman, who simply leads him by the nose from one expensive jaunt to another. **From farming: a wild bull can be led tamely by the ring in its nose. Also 'lead someone on' (similar sense)**. At last he's beginning to realise that she's been leading him on.

lead the way 1. go first. They didn't know the area, so I led the way. 2. pioneer. Our company has led the way in medical nanotechnology.

lead someone up the garden path mislead, hoodwink or deliberately deceive someone. The management promised him all sorts of things if he came to work for them, but unfortunately they were leading him up the garden path.

LEADING. (at the) leading/cutting edge (at the) forefront or outer limit. Our company is at the leading edge of developments in the electronics industry. In the sense of pioneering on the frontiers of knowledge, and leading/pushing the limits ever outwards. Compare **blaze a trail**.

leading light prominent member of a group, performance, etc. She's always been a leading light in the drama club. From navigation and lighthouses, harbour lights, etc.

leading question question asked in such a way as to elicit the desired answer. 'You'll not be wanting any supper?' she asked – which was a bit of a leading question. A legal term. Compare **loaded question**.

LEAK. leak air talk nonsense. Don't listen to a word he says – he's just leaking air. American; probably from the same source that gave us 'airhead' for a fool or empty-headed person.

LEAN. lean on someone apply pressure on someone (to do something). He's not been helpful in the past, but maybe we should lean on him a little and try to get him to change his mind.

LEAP. leap in the dark a venture whose consequences are unforeseen – and, often, hazardous; an impulsive action of uncertain outcome. She admitted that marrying him on such slight acquaintance was a bit of a leap in the dark, but added that most marriages were exactly that. In 1679, the dying words of the English philosopher Thomas Hobbes are said to have been, 'Now I am about to take my last voyage, a great leap in the dark.' Nowadays the reference is much more all-embracing.

LEAVE. leave someone hanging in the air leave someone waiting, or something incomplete or unfinished – often a conversation. Tell us what happened – don't leave us hanging in the air.

leave someone holding the baby leave someone to arrange something, etc. and fail to assist them. I didn't have time to organise the party myself, so I'm afraid John was left holding that particular baby. Usually passive. The original expression referred to an abandoned mother.

leave someone in the lurch leave someone without assistance, often discomfited and abandoned. Only a truly heartless person could have walked out and left his family in the lurch like that. From French lourche, a board game like backgammon. A player was in a hopeless situation if he was left 'in the lurch', and set to lose the game (French demeurer lourche). The phrase has lost its echo of the card table.

leave one's mark make a significant impact. It is surprising how few politicians actually leave their mark on our society.

leave no stone unturned make an exhaustive search, sparing no effort. He promised to leave no stone unturned in his efforts to relocate the stolen funds. A proverbial expression dating from Euripides' 'move every stone', which was the literal instruction of the Delphic oracle to Polycrates when he was seeking the treasure of the defeated Persians. The expression has become clichéd, and even been turned into a pun 'To leave no turn unstoned' – used to describe the critical ploys of our more destructive theatre reviewers.

LEEWAY. leeway to make up work, etc. yet to be done. We have a lot of leeway to make up if we are to finish this job on time. From sailing: 'leeway' is the opposite of 'headway', and originally meant 'the leeward drift of a ship from her course'. Then, figuratively and more generally, the sense of the word widened to mean 'room for manoeuvre'.

LEFT. left-handed compliment praise which is ambiguous or questionable. She told me I wasn't much good as a cook, but that I did bake the best pancakes she'd tasted – which seemed like a left-handed compliment to me. **From the earlier association of left-handedness with awkwardness and badness (another word for 'left' was 'sinister'). Compare backhanded compliment**.

left, right and centre all over the place; in large amounts. You'll never make a profit if you give away so many complimentary copies of your book left, right and centre. **The original reference was political: to the French Chamber of Deputies, which was laid out in the shape of an amphitheatre. The terminology was transferred by the 1830s from the members' seating arrangements to the opinions they represented. Hence left-wing/right-wing of socialist/ capitalist outlook and views.** There was vocal left-wing opposition to the proposals. **The 'left' refers to the radical and the 'right' the conservative or reactionary extremes of the political spectrum.**

LEGEND. legend in one's own lunchtime famous in one's lifetime. Sociable, gregarious and popular people, especially if they are suspected of having large business expense accounts for entertaining, are sometimes eulogised as being legends in their own lunchtimes. **The point of this idiom is perhaps that most legendary people acquire their status long after their death. Compare out to lunch**.

LEND. lend a hand help. I won't be at home next weekend, because I'll be lending John a hand to move house.

lend an ear listen; pay attention. They tell me he beats his wife, but I refuse to lend an ear to gossip like that. **The most famous use of the term is in** *Julius Caesar* iii.2: 'Friends, Romans, countrymen, lend me your ears.'

lend one's name to something openly back something; publicly support a cause, movement, etc. of which one approves. I refuse to lend my name to such a childish political objective.

LET. let bygones be bygones a saying, meaning 'Let us forgive and forget old (= bygone) arguments, insults', etc. Compare **bury the hatchet**.

let oneself go 1. act in an unrestrained and uninhibited way. After a time the music got really wild and noisy, and little groups in the crowd began to let themselves go. 2. lose interest in one's appearance. He's let himself go a bit since losing his job.

let oneself/someone in for (something) expose oneself to (something disagreeable). It was advertised as the holiday of a lifetime, but little did I know what I was letting myself in for.

let it all hang out exclamation inviting people to relax and abandon their inhibitions. The therapist said it was good for people to let it all hang out from time to time. **Originally American (1960s). Similar expressions are 'do one's own thing', 'let one's hair down', 'make oneself at home'. Compare hang loose**.

let off steam work off excessive energies and emotions. When the exams were over, the students held a huge party to let off steam. **From the age of the steam train: steam was let off from the engine to reduce pressure.**

let something pass fail/omit to question something. His comments were singularly misinformed, but I let them pass on the grounds that we had more important matters to resolve.

let something ride or **stick to the wall** not discuss something; do nothing about something. We had a hefty agenda to get through, so we had to let his invitation to lunch ride. We let his suggestion stick to the wall and passed on to the next item on the agenda.

let sleeping dogs lie refrain from disturbing people or from debating topics not currently causing one any trouble. It may be that he used to live with Miss Bloggs; but I don't think you ought to refer to that topic in front of his wife – it's better to let sleeping dogs of that sort lie. **A saying.**

let the cat out of the bag inadvertently let a secret become known. Nobody was supposed to know the plan, but unfortunately I seem to have let the cat out of the bag. From a trick commonly practised by medieval market traders: instead of selling customers an edible live animal for the cooking pot, such as a piglet, duck or hare, they sometimes had an inedible cat tied up in a bag ready to pass off on the unsuspecting. Wary customers would always check the contents of any bag sold to them, sometimes letting the cat out. The origins of this phrase are thus similar to **pig in a poke**. Compare **give the game/show away; blow the gaff; put one's foot (right/straight) in/into it; shoot one's mouth off**.

let the side down disappoint one's friends, supporters, etc. by doing something they disapprove of. Her behaviour was appalling and really let the whole side down rather badly.

let things slide allow things to deteriorate from neglect. Sorry about the state of the garden, but I've been so busy I'm afraid I've had to let things slide there this summer. The implication is of a downward progression.

LETTER. letter of the law the literal, precise and perhaps rather pedantic interpretation of legality. According to the exact letter of the law, you are guilty of trespass; but you have done no damage, so we'll try to ensure that the judge lets you off. The letter is the opposite of the spirit, as is made clear in II Corinthians iii.5–6: 'Our sufficiency is of God; Who also hath made us able ministers of the new testament; not of the letter, but of the spirit: for the letter killeth, but the spirit giveth life.'

LET'S. let's face it let us be honest about it. He's not a very good prime minister, but let's face it – who else can you see doing the job? A conversational appeal for frankness.

let's see usually spoken as a preliminary to making a calculation. Let's see now, it's 80 miles to the border, so you can't get there much before nine o'clock.

LEVEL. level headed calm, sensible, balanced and logical. We need to have level-headed folk around us in an emergency like this.

level pegging performing equally well or badly. The final of the Open Golf Championship last year was level pegging right up to the 18th hole, so they went to a sudden-death play-off. Probably from using pegs as a method of scoring.

level playing field context in which neither side is given any unfair advantage. Press comment on the election campaign hardly provided a level playing field for the debate, since nearly all the papers were extremely prejudiced in favour of one party over the other. Another appeal for fair play from the sporting arena.

LICK. lick someone's boots/arse act obsequiously towards someone; ingratiate oneself to gain someone's favours. There's something distinctly disagreeable in seeing one adult licking another's boots, even when the other adult happens to be his boss. Gives nouns such as 'boot-licker', 'arse-licker' and the more euphemistic 'brown-noser'.

lick someone/something into shape train someone to become competent at something; sort something out; make something/someone work well. He's quick and keen to learn so we'll soon have him licked into shape. From the rather quaint and unscientific notion, held by the Greeks and still widespread even in the 16th century, that bears and other mammals gave birth not to cubs but to formless and misshapen lumps of flesh. These were then literally licked into cub-shape.

lick one's wounds recover after a setback or humiliation. She's still licking her wounds after last week's fiasco.

LIE. lie low avoid attention; keep out of the limelight. He was a famous actor, but after the scandal of his arrest he had to lie low for a while.

lie of the land the position regarding particular issues or problems, and especially people's views about them. A good MP will carefully appraise himself of the lie of the land among constituents before giving a policy his unqualified support. **From nautical surveys, meaning the direction and nature of the coastline. Compare take soundings**.

lie through/in one's teeth tell outrageous or flagrant lies. Subsequent events have proved that he was lying through his teeth when he told police he didn't know where his wife was.

LIFE. life and soul of the party a vivaciously entertaining member of a social group. John is never happier than when he's being the life and soul of the party, and entertaining his friends with his endless anecdotes.

life in the fast lane hectic, dangerous and perhaps indulgent lifestyle. If you think of all she did before the ripe old age of 26 when she was imprisoned by her cousin Elizabeth, you have to agree that Mary, Queen of Scots spent her early life very much in the fast lane. **From motorways: an Americanism of the 1970s.**

life of Riley have an easy and luxurious life. She's retired to the South of France where she seems to lead the life of Riley. **It is thought that the original Riley – or Reilly – was an Irish American who made good in the 1880s. A popular song of the period, 'Is that Mr Reilly?', has a hero speculating on what to do with a fortune.**

LIFT. lift the veil on expose. These recent press disclosures about arms to Iraq lift the veil on several murky little secrets.

LIGHT. light at the end of the tunnel the glimmer of a solution towards which one is working. We've had a lot of problems on this job, but we're at last beginning to see a bit of light at the end of the tunnel. **From engineering. Now a cliché popular with journalists – and with politicians who like to tell their benighted electors that they alone can help us towards some ephemeral but well-lit destination.**

light dawns the truth of a situation finally becomes clear. John started to ask where everyone was, and then the light dawned on him – they were prisoners.

light fingered liable to steal. I always feel uncomfortable when he's in my house, because he has a reputation for being light fingered.

LIKE. like a bull at a gate hard and headlong; without restraint. It's supposed to be a part-time job, but he goes at it like a bull at a gate. **A simile of aggression and foolhardiness. The reverse of half-assed/-hearted**.

like a moth to a flame irresistibly. Good living and fast cars drew Alan like a moth to a flame. **A standard simile of attraction.**

like a shot instantly, and – usually – with enthusiasm. When he heard there might be a job at the farm, he was round there like a shot to see if they'd have him.

like billy-o with speed and gusto, force and enthusiasm. He ran like billy-o and just managed to catch his flight. **An old-fashioned intensifier, perhaps from a reference to George Stephenson's famous Rocket, the pioneering steam engine which by 1830 was reaching speeds of 30 m.p.h. and was nicknamed 'Puffing Billy'.**

like clockwork smoothly; without organisational hiccups. It was an exceptionally well-organised conference and everything went like clockwork. **Although clockwork was originally specific to the intricate machinery inside a clock, it later came to apply more generally to machinery of automatic action and unvarying regularity, for example in toys and models.**

like hot cakes selling, etc. very quickly. I tried to buy a copy of the report, but there weren't any left – it had been selling like hot cakes, and now the shops are waiting for the reprint.

like it or lump it whether one likes it or not. Fish is all we have for supper tonight, so you'll have to like it or lump it. **'Lump' meaning to be sulky**

and displeased about something. Also **take it or leave it**. Compare also **put up or shut up; stuff it!**

like nobody's business fast, surprisingly well, etc. He drove that ambulance like nobody's business, and we made it to the hospital just in time. An adverbial intensifier and standard simile.

like pulling teeth very difficult. Trying to get information out of that man is like pulling teeth. A standard simile of difficulty. Another is 'like getting blood out of a stone' (same meaning).

like the clappers very fast, hard, etc. I've been working like the clappers all term, so I should pass the exam. A standard simile, a clapper being the tongue of a bell.

(grow) like Topsy (develop) without attention or encouragement from anyone. Some successful businesses have no strategic business plan, no five-year targets, no apparent corporate vision – they just grow like Topsy. Topsy was the name of a little slave girl, in *Uncle Tom's Cabin* (1852), by Harriet Beecher Stowe. She wasn't born, she 'just growed'. A standard simile for unplanned growth.

like two peas in a pod exactly alike. The twins are like two peas in a pod – even their mother sometimes has trouble distinguishing one from the other. A standard simile of likeness.

LIKES. the likes of people like. Why should I waste good time talking to the likes of you.

LILY. lily livered cowardly. He's a contemptible, lily-livered sniveller. From the medieval idea that a coward's liver was starved of blood – the pallor of a lily renders it rather bloodless in appearance.

LIMIT. (just) the limit tolerable – just and no more. Listen to him boasting again; is he not just the limit?

LINE. line of least resistance easiest (and not necessarily best) route to the solution to a problem, etc. You can trust James to take the line of least resistance when it comes to work.

line one's pockets dishonestly acquire funds or property. Some MPs have been found to have lined their pockets with bribes from supporters, paid to them for asking particular questions in Parliament. Compare **feather one's nest**.

LION'S. (enter/go into) the lion's den (go into) the centre of opposition against one; perform a daunting task requiring much bravery. Playing rugby at Murrayfield is rather like entering the lions' den for an English team. From the Bible story of Daniel and King Darius: 'Then the king commanded, and they brought Daniel, and cast him into the den of lions. Now the king spake and said unto Daniel, Thy God whom thou servest continually, he will deliver thee.' Book of Daniel vi.16. Daniel's bravery, his innocence and his faith in God, gave him safe passage in the lions' den, so impressing the generations that the term has entered the language.

lion's share the bigger part. There are two main partners in the business, but Mr Brown owns the lion's share of the equity. From an Aesop fable, in which the lion demands three-quarters of the food (on the grounds of his kingship of the animals, his strength and his courage) and rather superciliously leaves a quarter to be shared among all the other animals.

LIP. lip service superficial and pretended support for something. Far from going to church, nowadays most people in this country don't even pay lip service to religion. From the days of religious persecution in the 17th century: you could appear to support the established religion by lip movements without actually supporting it in your heart.

LIPS. (one's) lips are sealed refuse to say anything on a specific topic. They told me where they planned to go on honeymoon, but my lips are sealed on that. The expression was much repeated by Stanley Baldwin, the British prime minister who in 1937 with these words tried to deflect press interest in the abdication drama of Edward VIII.

LISTEN. listen to reason be persuaded to do something sensible. I've told him for years not to drink and drive, but will he listen to reason? No, he won't.

LITTLE. little fish in a big pond unimportant person in a large business, organisation, etc. He may be a very important member of the community, but in this office he'll just have to get used to being a little fish in a very big pond. Opposite of the much commoner **big fish in a small pond**.

LIVE. live and let live tolerate the lifestyles and peculiarities of others as you would expect them to tolerate yours. In a closed community such as this, you have to live and let live. A saying. Compare **different strokes for different folks**.

live something down live respectably in order – over a period of time – to permit one's reputation to recover from some scandal or setback. His neighbours wouldn't let him live down his undiplomatic comment.

live from hand to mouth earn a precarious livelihood. He has various part-time jobs and tends to live from hand to mouth. Also 'not know where the next meal is coming from'. Compare **keep the wolf from one's door**.

live in clover live well and luxuriously. I suppose everybody dreams of winning the lottery and living the rest of their lives in clover. Clover is of course a much-sought delicacy for cattle and pigs. An older version was 'live like pigs in clover'.

live in sin live together as husband and wife without undergoing a formal marriage ceremony. His parents never married – they always said they were far too happy living in sin. From the days when the church dictated lifestyles and living in this way constituted a sin.

live it up have fun and enjoy oneself. I work hard 50 weeks a year in order to live it up every August for a fortnight in the sun. An idiom of the 1960s.

live on a shoestring manage one's financial affairs on a very small budget. They were young and in love, and happy to live on a shoestring so long as they were together. Perhaps because shoelaces and shoestrings are inexpensive items.

live on one's nerves live one's life in an atmosphere of tension, enervation, etc. Running a large company is not easy for her, and she lives very much on her nerves.

live up to behave/perform in a way which is worthy of. It was a wonderful car, although it didn't quite live up to its reputation.

live wire very bright and vital person. She's a very quiet woman, so it comes as a bit of a surprise to find that her son is such a live wire. Literally and originally, an electric wire from which one could receive a shock.

LOADED. loaded question question which is framed in such a way as to try to trap someone into a specific response, sometimes saying something s/he'd rather not say. The police asked him lots of loaded questions about the crime and about the accused man. From playing dice: if a die was 'loaded' or 'doctored', it usually meant it would tend to fall the same way up and show the same score. Compare **leading question**.

LOCAL. local colour details that are characteristic of a particular time and especially place. Some pipers and dancers performed for our guests, bringing a spot of local colour to the evening.

LOCK. lock horns fight. The two multinationals have locked horns over drilling rights west of the Shetlands. From the behaviour of bulls, deer and other horned male beasts, which fight with their horns to achieve dominance in the herd and the right to mate with the cows.

lock, stock and barrel utterly and totally. The thieves left nothing – the entire contents of the house were removed lock, stock and barrel. The original reference was to the main parts of a gun; if you took delivery of a gun lock, stock and barrel, you got the complete weapon with no parts missing. Compare **kit and caboodle; whole shooting match**.

lock the stable door after/when the horse has bolted take precautions after the need for them has ceased. Since the great fire at Windsor Castle, most of the remaining royal paintings are insured – which is perhaps a case of locking the stable door when the horse has bolted. A saying. Also 'be wise after the event'.

LONE. lone wolf solitary person. I don't see very much of James, but then he's very much of a lone wolf so I wouldn't expect to have his company all that often. Some wolves hunt in packs, others alone.

LONG. long and the short of something the substance of something; the main aspect; the gist. There were endless problems in the organisation, and the long and the short of it was that they had to cancel their plans for a festival. A similar phrase is 'To cut a long story short…'

long face unhappy expression. It was a sad occasion, so there were several long faces at the ceremony.

long in the tooth old. I used to enjoy mountaineering, but now I'm getting a bit long in the tooth for such exertions. Human and other mammalian teeth get longer with age, as the gums recede. A colloquial and derogatory euphemism.

LOOK. look a gift horse in the mouth criticise or complain about something one has received as a gift. They have presented me with the most horrible-looking tie – I don't like to look a gift horse in the mouth, but I could never bring myself to wear such a thing! Often used as a negative saying: 'Don't look a gift horse…' The standard way of working out a horse's age – and therefore its value – is to open its mouth and examine its teeth.

look after number one look after oneself and one's own selfish needs. A lot of investors lost their savings, but the managing director managed to look after number one and seemed to emerge unscathed from the collapse of the business.

look before you leap think about the implications of your actions before you act. They've offered me a very good job, but I want to look before I leap – so I'm trying to find out a bit more about the company before I accept the position. A saying.

look daggers look in an openly and flagrantly hostile way. I suggested an election, then suddenly – too late – noticed that the chairman was looking daggers at me. The idea conveys the glint of cold steel and dates from a time when daggers were used to settle arguments.

look down (one's nose) at/on despise; treat contemptuously, as one's inferior. She regards herself as an upper-class person, and tends to look down her nose at most of us. Compare **turn up one's nose**.

look someone (straight) in the eye face someone directly, to indicate that one is not intimidated by them. The managing director asked for my resignation, but I looked him straight in the eye and told him he could whistle for it. Less confrontational than 'eyeball someone', see **eyeball to eyeball**.

look to one's laurels defend one's reputation; beware of losing one's preeminence. Our team may have won the championship last year, but they'll certainly need to look to their laurels if they're going to win it again. The ancient Greeks presented a crown of evergreen laurel leaves to victors in battle, in competitive sports, and in poetry. These symbols of pre-eminence then had to be protected against competition.

LOOM. loom large feature prominently, in conversation, etc. The impending general election has been looming large in the newspapers for a few weeks. From sailing: this was the term used for the sudden and potentially dangerous appearance of a shape in the mist, dark, etc.

LOOSE. loose cannon maverick; unreliable member of a team. The idea of collective responsibility in government tries to muzzle any would-be loose cannons before they cause too much damage. Originally American, the term became clichéd in the 1980s. The image is naval: of unsecured cannons sliding across the deck of a pitching ship in a heavy sea, to the serious jeopardy of those they are meant to be defending. Compare **law to/unto oneself; maverick (steer)**.

loose ends small bits and pieces of unfinished business, etc. The negotiations were long and difficult, but agreement in principle was reached at last; all that remains to be done is to sort out a few loose ends.

LORD. lord it over someone assume superiority over others in a pretentious fashion, as if one were their boss. It was not the school's policy to make prefects of the kind of pupils who might lord it over the other pupils.

Lord/Lady Muck socially pretentious people who put on insufferable airs of superiority. Would you take a look at Lady Muck over there in the fancy hat? A term of contempt.

Lord knows who/what/how etc. a mainly light-hearted phrase meaning that one knows nothing about something. It was a very stormy night and Lord knows how they got down that mountain without an accident.

LOSE. lose one's bearings lose one's way or sense of direction. With all the feverish speculation about the party's leadership crisis, we must be careful not to lose our bearings. From navigation and mechanics: a 'bearing' is the direction of an object from a particular quarter of the compass. Opposite of **find one's bearings**.

lose one's bottle lose one's courage. When the gang saw the size of the opposition, they soon lost their bottle and fled. Originally Cockney. Whether the bottle supplied Dutch courage or was used as a weapon is unclear. Gives the phrasal verb **bottle out** of something (same sense).

lose one's (competitive) edge cease to have the advantage (over one's competitors). There were worrying signs in the 1990s that the Japanese economy was losing its competitive edge. Compare **at the cutting/leading edge**.

lose face experience a setback to one's reputation or credibility. No political leader, whether democratically elected or a dictator, likes to lose face too publicly: various face-saving formulas are usually devised in such situations. 'Face' in this sense is a Chinese concept and represents the respect in which one's good name is held.

lose one's grip cease to be as competent, etc. as one once was. He's been headmaster for over 20 years, so it's not really surprising that he's been losing his grip a little – though he remains a formidable figure.

lose one's/the head panic. Just keep calm and try not to lose your head. The head was regarded as the seat of a person's intelligence, since it contained the brain. Opposite of 'keep one's/the head'.

lose heart get discouraged; give up. After the visitors scored their fourth goal, the home side just seemed to lose heart completely. Opposite of **take heart**.

lose one's heart fall in love. She's at that teenage stage of losing her heart to the boy next door, at the back of the class, at the bus stop – all over the place. The heart was seen as the seat of affection and the emotions in general – as opposed to the head, which ruled the intellect. A standard poetic conceit, as in Sir Philip Sidney's 'My true love hath my heart and I have his.'

lose one's marbles lose one's wits or intelligence; become deranged. Most of the residents of that ward have lost their marbles to some degree, so it's quite difficult to have a sensible conversation with them. Probably from the schoolboy game. Compare **have a screw loose; lose the plot**.

lose one's nerve lose one's courage; panic. Mountaineers always say that the best way to avoid losing your nerve is not to look down. Animals lose their nerve at the smell of fire.

lose one's/the rag become enraged; cease to control oneself. I only had to mention his wife and he completely lost the rag and started shouting abuse at me. Also 'lose the place' (same sense). Compare **see red**.

lose one's reason become insane, or appear so. Every so often things get too much for her, and she seems to lose her reason.

lose one's shirt lose all one's possessions, down to the shirt on one's back, usually at gambling. It's not unusual for certain people to spend a night at the gaming tables and lose their shirt there.

lose sight of forget; ignore. A good businessman never loses sight of the fact that he has to make a profit.

lose the hang/knack of forget how to do something well. I used to speak a bit of Spanish, but so long ago that I've probably lost the hang of it.

lose the plot 1. become senile. Poor old Mary's completely lost the plot these days and talks a lot of nonsense. 2. become incoherent with fury. When I asked for a pay rise the boss completely lost the plot and starting throwing things at me. Compare **lose one's marbles**.

lose the thread of cease to follow the gist or sequence of something. It was a long and boring sermon, and I lost the thread of it after about five minutes. From storytelling, which has been likened since at least the 15th century to the spinning out of a length of yarn.

lose one's tongue become speechless, usually with shock or surprise. What's the matter with you, who usually has such a lot to say? Lost your tongue, have you? Opposite of **find one's tongue**.

lose track forget; cease to keep a tally. A prisoner soon loses track of the days he spends in a cell.

LOUNGE. **lounge lizard** 'smooth' or disreputable socialite, a person who spends his time lounging about in dancehalls and cocktail bars. The implication of cold-bloodedness hints at the predatory nature of his motives. I don't much thrive in the raffish company of these gin-drinking lounge lizards. Old-fashioned term from the 1920s, nowadays used humorously. Compare **couch potato**.

LUMP. lump sum single substantial payment. He received a lump sum equivalent to a year's salary when his employer made him redundant.

LUNATIC. lunatic fringe political extremists, around the outer edges of any mainstream movement. Unfortunately a small lunatic fringe of hecklers started yelling and chucking missiles at the foreign secretary when he arrived for the debate. From a quotation of US President Theodore Roosevelt in 1913: 'There is apt to be a lunatic fringe among the votaries of any forward movement.'

M

MAD. mad as a hatter completely silly or insane. He may appear to be as mad as a hatter, but he is in fact a brilliant physicist. A standard simile. The old belief was that hat-makers went mad, and a modern theory suggests that this may have been because they worked with metal alloys containing mercury. Also 'mad as a March hare'. The explanation of this simile is more obvious: hyperactive hares are to be observed during their breeding season (March, in Britain). Compare **daft as a brush**.

MADE. made of money very rich. They say he's made of money and owns half of Scotland. An alliterative metaphor.

MAIN. (eye to the) main chance (alert to the) best and usually most lucrative openings, opportunities, or advantages one is likely to derive from a particular situation. Old Bloggs has always been a man with an eye to the main chance, and you can trust him to profit from the most unlikely situations. Often pejorative, the person accused of having an eye to the main chance is nowadays assumed to be good at looking after his own interests, and therefore selfish by nature. The idiom probably derives from the card table, and the 16th-century game of hazard, where the first throw of the dice is called the 'main' (from French *main* = a hand).

main drag main street of a town. If this is the main drag, I don't think Snuffsville can be much of a place. Rural American. The 'drag' or tail position was at the back of a herd of cattle. The cowboys allotted to this position of bringing up the rear were called 'drag riders' or 'drag drivers'.

MAKE. make a beeline for go directly to. As soon as we heard the news, we made a beeline for the boss's office. From the notion of bees flying straight to the hive.

make/earn a bomb earn a lot of money. He's one of the BBC's top performers, and earns an absolute bomb. Such lucky people of course also tend to 'spend a bomb' on items that **cost a bomb**.

make a clean breast of confess. He decided to make a clean breast of his misdeeds. A metaphor of revelation of the secrets concealed in one's breast.

make a clean sweep win a succession of convincing victories. The Labour Party made a clean sweep in the last local elections. From 'sweeping up all the stakes' (16th century: hence 'sweepstake'), or collecting them wholesale.

make a hash. See **settle someone's hash**.

make a meal of something take more than the usual amount of time and effort to do something. I wouldn't ask him to fix your electricity meter – he makes a complete meal out of jobs like that. Compare **make a song and dance**.

make a mountain out of a molehill exaggerate the importance of some trivial matter. It was only a small graze, but as soon as he saw blood John made a real mountain out of a molehill – you'd have thought he was about to lose an arm. An alliterative metaphor, popular since the 16th century.

make/gain/win a name for oneself distinguish oneself in a particular field; become famous. She has made a name for herself as the leading authority on the archaeology of the Picts.

make a night of it organise or participate in a lavish evening's entertainment. After the graduation ceremonies, his parents decided to make a night of it and take him out for supper and to a show. Also 'make a day of it' (similar sense).

make a pass at someone try to make a sexual conquest of someone. If there's a nice-looking blonde in the room, John is sure to make a pass at her. The term came originally from fencing, and referred to a thrust with a foil – an action that demanded an appropriate reaction. Compare **set one's cap at**.

make a pig of oneself over-eat, sometimes also displaying an absence of table manners. They won't get another invitation to supper here – they made pigs of themselves last time. A metaphor for greed and boorishness.

make a play/pitch for something try to obtain something. When the job of export manager came up, Elizabeth made a strong play for it. From chess.

make a rod (with which) to beat one's back do something that is likely to cause one problems later. People who spoil their children often find they've made a rod to beat their backs with. Also 'a rod for one's own back'.

make a scene quarrel or have a row in public; create a kerfuffle. He made quite a scene after he was sacked, calling his boss all sorts of things.

make a silk purse from a sow's ear make something of high quality out of something inferior. You should have seen this tumbledown heap of bricks before they turned it into a country house – talk about making a silk purse from a sow's ear! From a 17th-century proverb which says you cannot do it: it's human nature to challenge received wisdom.

make a song and dance create a fuss. So the waiter has spilt your coffee, but I don't see why you have to make such a song and dance about it. The philosophical response is to say 'Accidents will happen'. Compare **make a meal of something**.

make a splash attract public attention, often as a result of conspicuous or lavish expenditure. The book made a great splash when it was first published. Presumably because it had a successful 'launch', the metaphor is thus extended.

make an example of punish someone in such a way as to discourage others from making the same mistake/error, etc. After she made an example of the ringleader, Miss Brown discovered there were no more problems in her classroom.

make an honest wo/man of someone marry someone with whom one is cohabiting, often because of a pregnancy. They're very happy living together and so far it's never occurred to John to make an honest woman of his partner. Usually humorous. Compare **pop the question**.

make believe pretence. She was dressed in the deepest mourning black, but it was all make believe – she was secretly quite relieved that her partner was dead. From the Victorian children's game of 'make believe' or 'let's pretend'.

make one's blood boil make one very angry and indignant. It made my blood boil listening to that man being so dishonest.

make (both) ends meet budget successfully in order to make one's income balance one's outgoings. She finds it very hard making both ends meet, now that she has to live on her old-age pension. The idiom normally implies a struggle. The original expression is from accountancy.

make eyes at someone look amorously at someone. They stood there making eyes at each other, oblivious to everyone else in the room. Sometimes, perhaps when the look is particularly pathetic or adolescent, 'sheep's eyes' are specified.

make oneself felt act in a noisy, decisive, forceful, domineering, etc. manner, so that others are forced to take notice. The new boss has been in his post for several years now, but he's not exactly made himself felt. Also 'make one's presence felt'.

make one's flesh creep/crawl make one feel terrified. She had a morbid love of the sort of horror stories that make my flesh creep.

make free with something/someone treat something/someone in careless or cavalier or over-familiar fashion, as if they were one's own property. He's not welcome here – whenever he comes, he makes free with the house and treats us as his servants.

make good prosper; succeed. He left school at 15, and emigrated to Australia where he made good and now owns several newspapers. Originally American.

make one's hackles rise make one extremely angry. *That kind of impertinence makes my hackles rise.* From animal behaviour; the 'hackles' are the hairs on the back of an animal's neck, which stand erect when it is angry.

make one's hair stand on end terrify someone. *Swimming through that underground cave in the dark was enough to make anyone's hair stand on end.* Human hairs stand erect from the body in moments of shock or panic.

make hay (while the sun shines) take advantage of a favourable situation, often to enjoy oneself. *As soon as the Joneses discovered they had won the lottery, they were off on a world cruise; making hay, said Mr Jones, while they were able to.* The complete sentence is an agricultural proverb, which advises us to get the crops in while the weather permits. There are many other proverbs in similar vein: 'Gather ye rosebuds while ye may'; 'Never put off till tomorrow what can be done today'; 'Procrastination is the thief of time', etc.

make heavy weather (of something) have great difficulty doing something, especially something which should be easy to do. *He said he'd be happy to plough the field for me, but he seems to be making heavy weather of it so far.* A nautical idiom originally, referring to a ship which sails with difficulty through a heavy sea. Compare **weather a storm**.

make it succeed. *He decided he'd never make it in Scotland, so he moved to London where his career quickly took off.*

make it/life hot for punish. *The army has a way of making it hot for habitual transgressors.*

make mincemeat of someone critically demolish someone. *He's an excellent lawyer, and he soon made mincemeat of my neighbour's case.* A kitchen metaphor, conveying the idea of grinding something up into small and useless pieces.

make one's mouth water make one want (to eat) something very much. *The wonderful smells emanating from the alleys of the old city were frequently enough to make your mouth water. The offer of a month's paid holiday in Barbados made his mouth water.* From the flow of saliva experienced when we are about to eat something appetising.

make neither head or/nor tail of something fail to understand something; make no sense of something. *It looked like writing in Chinese or Japanese, but I could make neither head or tail of it.*

make no bones about something 1. make no objection to something. *As a courtesy, we notified our neighbours that we planned to hold an all-night party, but no one made any bones about it.* A 'bone' was something contentious for dogs, as in **bone to pick, bone of contention**, etc. Perhaps also from the idea that bones in soup or stew made swallowing difficult. 2. be open and frank about something. *He made no bones about telling her she was fired – simple as that!*

make no mistake (about it) be in no doubt (about something). *Make no mistake, I will go to court on this matter, and I will win my case.* An idiomatic cautionary observation, almost a threat, which may introduce a sentence as well as ending one.

make/gain on the swings what one loses on the roundabouts make things balance, or even out, by recouping in one activity what one may have lost in another. *The firm made big profits on the swings of its export market, and these more than offset their losses on the roundabouts of a deeply depressed domestic market.* The idiom comes from the 19th-century fairground. Popular wisdom sometimes abbreviates the idiom thus: 'You win some, you lose some – it's a case of swings and roundabouts.'

make something pan out make something last as long as possible, especially when it is scarce. *I just hope we can make these meagre rations pan out until we are rescued.* From the days of the American goldrush, and the action of gold panning.

make oneself scarce absent oneself; get out of the way. Candidates were asked to make themselves scarce till about 2 o'clock, when the committee hoped to be able to announce its decision.

make short work/shrift of something/ someone dispose of something/someone quickly. It was a very uneven contest, and the champion made short work of the contender. Also 'make short shrift' (similar sense). A shrift was a penance imposed by a priest after confession, and is from the verb 'shrive' (= confess one's sins). A 'short shrift' was a brief space of time given to a criminal to confess all his sins to a priest prior to his execution.

make the grade be good enough to succeed at something, especially by attaining a certain standard at it. Her rowing times were pretty good, but will they make the grade for the Olympic trials?

make the supreme sacrifice give one's life (usually for a noble cause). We pray for all who have made the supreme sacrifice for their country's sake. A euphemism, often rhetorically deployed for nationalistic or patriotic effect.

make tracks set off. At about 3 a.m. he decided he'd better make tracks for home.

make up one's mind make a decision. After several weeks of uncertainty, he suddenly made up his mind to buy the car.

make up to someone ingratiate oneself into someone's favour by flattery, flirtation or other strategy. It was amusing to watch the younger managers making up to the boss at the board meeting.

make water urinate. In the quiet of the sleeping village, the only sound was of some drunkard making water at the street corner. An old-fashioned euphemism for pissing, a word our grandparents avoided.

make waves cause trouble or dissent. John has not been invited to the meeting, because he's too fond of making waves. A nautical metaphor, of a ship disturbing the surface of the sea.

MAN. man and boy all one's working life. I've worked in that same office man and boy, for 40 years.

Man Friday servant or personal assistant. She acts as a sort of Man Friday to the chief executive. From Daniel Defoe's novel *Robinson Crusoe* (1719), in which this character appears.

a man has to do what a man has to do certain things are unavoidable and have to be done, however difficult. It's a dreadful job, but it's all I can get, and a man has to do what a man has to do. Usually jocular, a sexist refrain of the 1980s. Also 'a man's gotta do what a man's gotta do'. Compare **needs must (when the devil drives)**.

man in the street ordinary or average person. It's all very well for the government to announce the privatisation of this and that, but I wonder what the man in the street makes of their plans. A gender-challenged and clichéd expression nowadays, as is the similar 'Joe Citizen'. An earlier version was 'the man on the Clapham omnibus'.

man/lad of parts man of wide-ranging talents and abilities. He was not only a champion Olympic-standard athlete, he was also a distinguished neurosurgeon – a real man of parts, if you like. An ellipsis has occurred: originally 'man of many parts'.

man of straw 1. man of no real substance, sometimes fraudulent or irresponsible, sometimes just plain weak. Sometimes called a 'placeman'. There are one or two men of straw on the board of directors, but you'll need to seek out the key players if you want to advance your case. 2. imaginary or sham adversary, invented in order to be easily overcome. The team have won most of their matches this season, but next week comes their big test against the Bath team – I think they'll quickly find out that these are not exactly men of straw.

man of means/substance wealthy man. They want him to go and lecture in America, and – since he is not a man of means – they have offered to pay his return air fare and hotel costs. 'Means' means private resources (from French *moyens*).

man of the world sophisticated man; someone who has seen life. There is no need to shield him from the details of the case – he's a man of the world and he knows how people behave.

man to man frankly and openly. They had a long man-to-man talk about their differences.

man upstairs God. I don't think the man upstairs would approve of what you're planning. A humorous slang euphemism, now old-fashioned.

MANNA. manna from heaven something good and unexpected. The term comes from the Bible (Exodus xvi.15), and refers to the food supplied to the Israelites on the flight from Egypt. He had been very depressed, so her surprise visit to him was like manna from heaven, and he was soon laughing and chatting away to her. Compare **bolt from the blue**.

MANY. many happy returns (of the day) may you have a long happy life, i.e. 'May this happy day return for many years.' We all sang 'Happy birthday' and wished her many happy returns. A greeting offered on someone's birthday.

MARK. mark, learn and inwardly digest study something thoroughly, and reflect on it. They will be examined in two plays by Shakespeare, which they need to mark, learn and inwardly digest before the end of term. A quotation from the Anglican Prayer Book: 'Blessed Lord, who hast caused all holy Scriptures to be written for our learning: Grant that we may in such wise hear them, read, mark, learn and inwardly digest them…'

mark my words listen carefully to what I say and remember what I say, because it's likely to come true. Mark my words, that child is going to get into trouble very soon now. Compare **you heard/read it here first**!

mark time make no progress; stand still. Business has been very difficult over the past couple of years, and we feel we've done well to merely mark time. From the military parade ground and the action of moving the feet as in marching, but without actually advancing.

MARKED. marked man person who has been ostracised, earmarked or 'marked' out for punishment, etc. After helping engineer the prime minister's downfall, he was a marked man in the party for the rest of his political life.

MASTER. master of one's brief in professional control of one's assignment, and more than equal to its successful prosecution. He was apprehensive about the exam, but when he read the questions he knew that he was master of his brief and that all would be well. From legal briefs.

MAVERICK. maverick (steer) according to one's point of view, either a person with no firm affiliation; a loner or misfit; or someone who takes an independent stand. There are several cliques in our office, but Jones is in none of them – he's the maverick steer of the outfit. From American cowboy culture, the term originally meant an unbranded bullock; thus one of uncertain ownership. Compare **loose cannon**. The eponymous Samuel Maverick (1803–70) was a Texan rancher on a large scale. Contrary to local practice, he did not brand his cattle and is said to have claimed all the unbranded animals as his own.

MEAL. meal ticket person or organisation depended on to provide continuous support. I don't like to see a spoilt brat like John treat his old parents as a meal ticket. Meal tickets were originally issued by the armed forces or some commercial organisations to provide the recipient with free meals. For some people they evolved into luncheon vouchers.

MEAN. mean business demonstrate serious intentions. As soon as I saw the shotgun I knew these people meant business.

mean well have good intentions. There's no point telling me he's a good chap and means well: what does he actually do when we need him – he runs away!

MEANS. means test assessment of one's financial resources. There is usually a means test before patients are admitted to the hospital, to establish how much they can afford to pay. **A bureaucratic term coined by the Welfare State.**

MEANWHILE. meanwhile, back at the ranch reverting to earlier conversation, or to other matters. OK so the company is safe from bankruptcy for another year, but I have to tell you that meanwhile, back at the ranch, your workforce is talking about going on strike next week. **A popular subtitle movie caption from the days of the silent screen. Another was 'In another part of the wood…'** Compare **trouble at mill**.

MEAT. meat and drink to someone source of enjoyment to someone. He is rather a solitary person, but his wife is completely different: partying and social events are meat and drink to her. **From Shakespeare: 'it is meat and drink to me to see a clown'** (*As You Like It*).

MECCA. the Mecca of… a place that must be visited by all… Wimbledon is the Mecca of tennis players, and St Andrews is the Mecca of golfers. **An eponym from the town of Mecca, in Saudi Arabia, birthplace of Muhammad and an Islamic place of pilgrimage. All Muslims try to visit Mecca at least once during their lifetime.**

MEET. meet and right entirely correct or appropriate. It was John who crashed the car, so it is only meet and right that he should pay the garage bill. **A dyad, from the communion service and elsewhere in the Anglican Book of Common Prayer: 'It is very meet, right and our bounden duty, that we should at all times, and in all places, give thanks unto thee, O Lord, Holy Father, Almighty, Everlasting God…' The adjective 'meet' means fit and proper; it is now archaic and only encountered in fixed phrases such as these.**

meet one's match find oneself opposed by someone who is likely to be better at something than one is; or by something that is likely to

defeat one. He's been renovating the house, but I think he's met his match with that huge roof and will have to call in the professionals.

meet one's Waterloo suffer one's final defeat. The world heavyweight boxing champion surprisingly met his Waterloo last night at the hands of an unknown challenger for the title. **The reference is to Napoleon's final military defeat at the battle of Waterloo, south of Brussels, in 1815.**

MEMORY. (down) memory lane remembrance of one's past life. She loves to take out the old family photograph album, and take us on trips down memory lane.

memory like a sieve/hen poor memory. I have to write everything down or I forget – I've got a memory like a hen nowadays. **The standard similes, the sieve retaining nothing, and the poor hen being afflicted with only a 'bird brain'.**

MEND. mend fences restore good relations. They avoided each other for many years because of some long-forgotten feud, but recently they appear to have mended their fences and to be talking to each other again. **The care and maintenance of fences has always been a benchmark for good neighbourliness among country folk.**

mend one's ways reform oneself. I've told him that he either mends his ways or leaves this house.

MERCURY. mercury soars/drops atmospheric pressure rises/falls. Sometimes, before thunderstorms, the mercury soars suddenly. **From the movement of mercury in the barometer. Less frequently, the reference is to temperature.**

MESS. mess of pottage anything of small value received in return for something more valuable. He used to have a very good job in the City, but he's sold out to become a crofter, and is happy to earn his mess of pottage in some Highland glen. **From the Bible: in Genesis xxv, Esau 'sold his birthright for a mess of pottage.' Now uncommon.**

MIDAS. Midas touch facility for profiting from whatever one does. John has the real Midas touch, and everything he does seems to earn him vast sums of money. **From the Greek legend, of the Phrygian king whose touch turned everything to gold.**

MIDDLE. middle of the road 1. **a position which avoids extremes.** British politics has tended to be conducted between two parties both of which try to occupy the most middle-of-the-road consensual position. 2. **of average academic ability.** He wasn't a brilliant student, or a good sportsman – rather just a middle-of-the-road sort of fellow.

MIGHT. might and main strength and physical effort. It was a battle to the death, and both animals fought with might and main. **A common alliterative dyad, the word 'main' survives only in fixed phrases such as this, and also in the repetitive and archaic 'by main force' (by strong-arm force exerted to the full: from French).**

MILK. milk and water something insipid; rather weak and diluted. It was not the sort of strong performance of Beethoven's Fifth one relishes: rather it was a sort of milk-and-water affair, and I'm afraid I fell asleep by the third movement.

milk of human kindness spontaneous concern of people at the plight of others. The charity organisations are raising enormous amounts merely by tapping in to the milk of human kindness which exists in all of us. **From Shakespeare's** *Macbeth* 1.v.

MILLSTONE. millstone round someone's neck heavy – and usually irksome – burden of responsibility. When she got old, she said she felt she was becoming a millstone round my neck, which was quite untrue.

MIND. the mind boggles an expression meaning that one finds something incomprehensible, hard to imagine, etc. The mind boggles at the cost for the taxpayer of this whole enquiry. **The verb 'boggle' means take fright, and derives from 'bogle', a ghost or frightening spirit.**

mind one's own business not intervene in matters that don't concern one. I've had to ask her more than once to keep her nose out of my life and mind her own business.

mind one's p's and q's be careful and precise in one's utterances; be on one's best behaviour. He's quite a slovenly person, and he's going to have to mind his p's and q's if he wants to work for a fussy person like Mr Brown. **There is much debate about the origin of this expression. One explanation is that the reference is to peas, being small seeds which it is difficult to eat delicately; and to cues, small coins which were only worth half a farthing – so 'mind your cues' may have had a similar drift to 'look after the pennies.' If this explanation is correct, the idiom is an example of zeugma – where two unlinked words are unexpectedly brought together. An alternative gloss is that the term came from a pedagogic admonition, to those children who had difficulty distinguishing between these two alphabetical letters because of their scripted similarity. (But why then did the idiom not emerge as 'mind your b's and d's', two letters which are equally baffling to infants?) Compare pull one's socks up, cross one's t's and dot one's i's.**

mind you please note. It was kind of him to give me a lift – mind you, he's a dreadful driver. **An interjection, a filler and a qualifier.**

MIND'S. mind's eye memory; mental vision. He may have been a badly wounded man lying on a bench outside a hospital, but in his mind's eye he was a happy sunburnt lad playing on some long-ago childhood beach. **A poetic term.**

MIRABILE. *mirabile dictu* marvellous to relate! It rained all week before the garden party, but – *mirabile dictu* – the sun came out on the morning of the party itself. **A classical Latin exclamation.**

MISS. miss the boat/bus lose out on an opportunity. You have to see the world when you're young and fit – if you wait till you're old, you'll often find you've missed the boat because you've become too frail to travel.

MIXED. mixed bag variable and perhaps rather motley collection of things, people, etc. The candidates for the job were a distinctly mixed bag. From game shooting.

MIXTURE. mixture as before same again. 'What'll you have to drink?' 'I'll have the mixture as before, please.' Originally the phrase was used by doctors wishing to repeat a patient's prescription.

MOANING. moaning Millie/Minnie person who is always complaining. The prime minister has warned that he wants to hear no more from the moaning minnies of his own party till well after the general election. The term was originally the nickname for a German *Minenwerfer* or artillery shell, named from its distinctive moaning noise as it hummed over the trenches in the First World War.

MONEY. money for jam/old rope money very easily earned. He's got about 10 of these executive directorships which each earn him about £10,000 a year – money for old rope, if you ask me! Compare **piece of cake**.

money to burn so much money that one can afford to burn or otherwise waste it. I told him that I didn't have money to burn, and that he'd have to find his funds elsewhere. Compare **burn a hole in one's pocket**.

MONKEY. monkey business something illegal or dubious. I think he's involved with some monkey business exporting antiques to America.

MONTEZUMA'S. Montezuma's revenge diarrhoea. We didn't see John for several days, and only learnt later that he had been suffering from a bad attack of Montezuma's revenge. A humorous or facetious slang term, Montezuma was the ruler of the Mexican Aztecs in the 16th century. The condition has given a variety of euphemisms ('Delhi belly', **gyppy tummy**, etc.), mostly linked to those parts of the world where Britons or Americans have experienced a challenge to their digestive capacities.

MONTH. month of Sundays a very long time; not ever. He invited me to join his political party, but I told him I wouldn't do that in a month of Sundays. Similar to 'not anytime soon'.

MOONLIGHT. moonlight flit covert removal of oneself and one's belongings, to avoid paying one's rent or other debts. His debts had reached such a large amount that he decided to do a moonlight flit and 'disappear' to London. Originally the removal would have been effected under cover of darkness. Compare **do a runner; up stakes**.

MOOT. moot point debatable matter; arguable subject; something which is contentious and open to discussion. He told me I was a lousy artist, but I replied that that was at best a moot point, i.e. I didn't agree with him. The 'moot' was the Anglo-Saxon predecessor of the Parliament, a place where people went to moot or discuss matters of general importance to the community.

MORAL. moral support encouragement (as opposed to practical help). She doesn't want your money, or even very much of your time; all she wants is a little bit of moral support.

MORE. more or less approximately; nearly. The party was more or less over when we left.

more power to your elbow an expression of encouragement. He's planning to take an expedition to the Himalayas – more power to his elbow! Originally a translation of an Irish Gaelic exclamation.

MORNING. morning after (the night before) usually a reference to a hangover. His eyes were red, his cheeks unshaven, and his hair dishevelled – he was a typical vision of the morning after!

MOTHER. mother and father of all… greatest and often most calamitous… The rebels promised the mother and father of all battles before they'd surrender. This adjectival expression was much rattled – along with various other sabres – by the Iraqis during the 1991 Gulf War.

MOTHERS'. mothers' ruin gin. I don't think you should have any more mothers' ruin – you've already had three glasses. A rather melodramatic 19th-century nickname, now used facetiously. Originally the term was loaded with social comment, about the effects of the 'demon drink' on the body and on the finances, about the use of gin in back-street abortions and about women's supposed fondness for the beverage.

MOUSE. mouse potato sedentary worker who spends his/her day at a computer screen, manipulating a computer mouse. At five o'clock precisely, a silent army of mouse potatoes filed out of the building. A linguistic novelty of the 1990s, a term of disparagement formed by analogy from **couch potato**.

MOVE. move heaven and earth do everything in one's power; make every effort. He moved heaven and earth to get them to change their mind, and they've just announced a rethink. Also 'move mountains', meaning work very hard to achieve something. A couple of hyperbolic clichés.

move the goalposts change the rules of engagement, after the engagement has begun, in order to unsettle the participants. The government tends to lose credibility every time it moves the goalposts for no good reason. A modern idiom from the football pitch, where of course the goalposts are meant to be fixed in one position. The expression is in danger of becoming an overused journalistic cliché – perhaps a half-articulation of a wistful contemporary desire for a return to fixed rules of conduct.

MOVEABLE. moveable feast informal event with no special time for arriving or departing. It's a bit of a moveable feast, but come for the weekend – a lot will depend on the weather. In the church calendar, a moveable feast day was one like Easter, which (unlike Christmas) didn't have a set date.

MOVERS. movers and shakers the people of power and influence, who make things happen. All the movers and shakers of the art world felt they had to be present at the reception. A current and often ironic dyad from the world of business journalism, perhaps an echo of the 'Ode' (1874) of Arthur O'Shaughnessy: 'We are the music makers,/We are the dreamers of dreams… We are the movers and shakers/Of the world for ever, it seems.'

MOVING. moving swiftly on code for 'let's change the conversation' or 'let's stop this conversation'. Compare **don't (even) go there**.

MUCH. much ado about nothing fuss about a trivial matter; a lot about a little. When Mrs Mackenzie burnt her sausages, the fire alarm went off and within minutes there were fire engines at the door as well as a police car and an ambulance. Nothing had actually ignited, and she said she liked her sausages slightly burnt, so it was a case of much ado about nothing. The idiom was common by the 16th century, and Shakespeare made it the title of one of his comedies. Compare **storm in a teacup**.

much in evidence highly visible. Damage caused by the recent fighting is still much in evidence, with shell-marked buildings, fire damage and boarded-up shops everywhere you look.

much of a muchness very similar in size, quality, importance, etc. It was very hard to choose the winning group because all the submissions seemed very much of a muchness to me.

MUD. (here's) mud in your eye old-fashioned humorous toast uttered when raising a glass. Well, friends, cheers, mud in your eye and good health! Probably from the muddy trenches of the First World War.

MUG. mug shot photograph of someone's head ('mug') and shoulders. The police showed us several mug shots, but we didn't recognise any of them. Police jargon, there is a pun on 'mug' which means a fool as well as a face.

MUG'S. mug's game something that only a mug – or fool – would do. After his prison sentence, he decided to reform, saying that crime was nothing but a mug's game.

MUM'S. Mum's the word expression meaning 'no comment!' or 'my lips are sealed!' Remember that her birthday party is to be a complete surprise, so Mum's the word on that subject. The reference to 'Mum' is not maternal here, but to the onomatopoeic sound one makes to keep someone quiet or when refraining from speech: 'Mmmmmm!'

MUMBO. mumbo jumbo superstitious nonsense incompletely heard or understood. It was all mumbo jumbo to me, and I didn't understand a word. Semi-synonymous terms include gobbledy-gook, gibberish, **codswallop**. The term originally referred to a West African tribal spirit invoked by tribesmen to keep their women in order – not easy in polygamous societies without a little extra-terrestrial assistance.

MUTTON. mutton dressed up as lamb something tricked out to look better than it is – or younger or more beautiful. Would you look at that old dear in the wig and the fancy clothes – she's definitely mutton dressed up as lamb. From the butcher's shop.

MY. my foot! exclamation meaning either 'I don't believe it!' or 'I don't approve!' 'He told me he lived in the Ritz Hotel.' 'My foot he does!' Other common exclamations with 'my' include **my goodness!** and **my word!** which convey mild surprise or horror, now slightly old-fashioned. 'Watch out, somebody's firing a gun!' 'Oh, my goodness! Oh, my word!'

N

N. n ways (of doing something) countless ways, or an unspecified number. There are n ways of getting to London. The phrase is from mathematics, by implication when n = a large number whose value is not stated.

(to) the nth degree as well as possible; to a high standard. He is a highly competent speaker, and organises all his lectures and seminars to the nth degree. From mathematics.

(for) the nth time yet again. For the nth time that morning, she asked me if I knew exactly what I had to do. Often used disparagingly, to imply that someone has low intelligence, poor listening skills, short attention span, etc. From mathematics.

NAIL. nail a lie expose an untruth beyond doubt. He said you'd never succeed as a writer, but you can soon nail that lie if you tell him how much you earned in royalties last year. Probably an ellipsis from one of the many obsolete medieval nailing idioms, such as 'nail something to a barndoor' (= expose or exhibit something after the fashion of dead vermin), or 'nail something to the counter' (= expose false coin used by a dishonest shopkeeper).

nail one's colours/flag to the mast express one's views on a subject without equivocation, and then stick to them. Party politicians tend to nail their colours to the mast and follow the party line right or wrong. Originally a naval idiom. Ships of the line sometimes didn't show their colours if they were travelling in hostile waters. But when battle was joined, they nailed their colours to the mast, to show which side they were on. Contemporary English idiom has much less of a salt-sea tang to it, so a term such as **come out (of the closet)** – albeit far less belligerent – would have more currency nowadays. Compare **stick one's neck out**.

nail someone 1. catch/nab someone in the act of doing something (usually something wrong). The police have nailed Bloggs at last – they caught him raiding a bank at the weekend. Compare **catch someone red-handed**. 2. commit someone to something. He has nailed me to having dinner with him next Thursday. Originally it was objects or notices that were nailed, rather than people – as Martin Luther's nailing of the complaints against the sale of Papal indulgences at the church door at Wittenberg. The expression then widened to embrace human dealings and relationships, especially when one party to the relationship is reluctant.

nail someone down 1. oblige a person to make a clear statement. One person you will never nail down is a politician – their trade is equivocation. 2. oblige a person to keep a promise. He offered to pay me £100 and I intend to nail him down to his promise.

NAKED. naked eye ordinary human vision, unaided by telescopes, microscopes, etc. There are millions of stars up there which aren't visible to the naked eye.

NAME. name-dropping make frequent mention of celebrities and famous people in the course of conversation, usually in order to impress one's listeners. Her conversation was all Lord This and the Duchess of That – a cloying lava-flow of name-dropping and obsequiousness. Also 'to drop names'. Often the sign of a snob.

(one's) name is mud one is very unpopular or has a poor reputation; people have a bad opinion of one. His name has been mud in amateur circles since he turned professional. From British parliamentary practice; originally an exclamation indicating that a disgraced member's name had been made public, and thus 'dragged through the mud.' See also **name names**. There is also a trans-Atlantic school of thought which claims that the origin of the idiom derives from Dr Samuel Mudd, the hapless physician who in 1865 set the broken leg of the notorious John Wilkes Booth. Booth was the assassin of Abraham Lincoln, and broke his leg while making his escape from justice. Such was the public hatred of Booth that the name of anyone linked to the episode became quickly synonymous with 'scoundrel' and 'felon'. Compare **drag someone's name in the mud**.

name names make specific accusations against named individuals. He threatened to name names if their campaign of insinuation and innuendo against him didn't cease. The term derives from 18th-century British parliamentary practice. When an MP was 'named' in the House of Commons by another member or by the Speaker, this indicated that he was being disciplined for some misconduct. The parliamentary anonymity which he otherwise normally enjoyed was temporarily withdrawn. Hence the phrase 'named and shamed'. See also **(one's) name is mud**.

name of the game 1. the main point of something; what it is all about. Winning is the name of the game in any competitive sport. 2. **what something is really, and not what it is apparently, about.** He's taken a long time to learn what the name of the game is, that it's all about getting people to trust him completely. The term seems to have originated in American sports journalism, not reaching Britain till the 1970s. It became a catch-phrase with its adoption as the title of an American TV series. Some dislike the phrase for its American origins, and for the slightly smug and patronising tone that often accompanies its use: 'You wouldn't say that if you knew the name of the game' – or perhaps 'if you knew the time of day' – or even 'if you could distinguish your arse from your elbow.' Readers may like to compare the nuances behind these popular expressions.

name to conjure with a very famous, important or influential name. He studied violin under Yehudi Menuhin – now there's a name to conjure with! From the field of Victorian entertainment: conjurors and magicians were once the point of reference.

NARROW. narrow squeak something narrowly avoided – just and no more. By the narrowest squeak, she managed to rescue the child from the sinking ship. Compare **close shave, by a short head, near miss, near thing**.

NASTY. nasty piece of work person who is ill-natured, dishonest, vicious, etc. Smith's arrest came as no surprise because he is such a nasty piece of work. Compare **bad lot**.

NATURE. nature of the beast essential character of someone or something. Working in a dental surgery is bound to be stressful – but that is the nature of the beast.

NEAR. near as dammit very close. We were as near as dammit to winning the contract. Also: 'as near as makes no difference'. These simile phrases often led to ripostes such as 'near enough is good enough', often used to console the speaker; or 'near enough's not good enough', used critically by the perfectionists or sermonisers in our midst.

near miss narrow escape, when two objects almost collide. Two crowded aircraft had a near miss over Heathrow airport yesterday morning. Compare **narrow squeak**.

near the knuckle/bone almost indecent; in bad taste. Most of his jokes were far too near the knuckle for my liking. The 'knuckle' is a bone in the hand, and 'near/close to the bone' has the same meaning. Also **near the mark**. Compare **close to home; over the top**.

near the mark 1. almost on target, or almost true. When she said that his job was in danger, she was nearer the mark than she guessed – he was to lose it a week later. From archery. 2. verging on the impolite, obscene, objectionable. His jokes were pretty near the mark, and most of the audience was embarrassed by them. Literally, 'close to that benchmark separating good and bad taste'. Also **near the knuckle/bone**.

near thing something which almost fails. We just managed to jump to safety before the roof collapsed, but it was a near thing. Compare **narrow squeak, close shave**.

near/close to one's heart especially dear to someone or valued by them. The social work she does with AIDS victims in Africa has always been close to her heart.

NEAREST. nearest and dearest one's immediate family circle – parents, children, husband, wife, etc. Every weekend, they visit her nearest and dearest and do a bit of housework for the old folk.

NECESSITY. necessity is the mother of invention a proverb, suggesting that one always manages to invent a solution to very difficult problems. Although they didn't speak each other's languages, Robinson Crusoe and Man Friday soon learnt to talk to each other: necessity was the mother of invention when there was no one else to talk to.

necessity knows no law a desperate person cannot be expected to respect the fine detail of the law. He shot the thugs because he knew he was cornered by them and that necessity knew no law: it was their lives or his own. **A saying.**

NECK. neck and neck very close together in a race. According to the opinion polls, the two leading contenders for the nomination were running neck and neck. From horse racing. Sometimes the result was so close that a 'photo finish' was called for in evidence.

neck of the woods district, area, part of the country. It's a long time since I was last in this particular neck of the woods. Eighteenth-century American, from an Algonquian Indian word 'naiack', meaning a point or corner: from the days of the frontier.

NEED. need something like a hole in the head a litotes (a special kind of understatement) meaning the opposite of what it states: i.e., that something is not needed at all. He needs trouble just now like a hole in the head – he's had nothing but trouble all year.

NEEDFUL. the needful cash. I wanted to buy my girlfriend a bunch of flowers, but lacking the needful I picked her some honeysuckle from the hedgerow in the lane. **Old fashioned.**

NEEDLE. needle someone or **give someone (the) needle** annoy someone, try to aggravate them. Leave Stella alone, and stop trying to needle her. The boys were not malicious – they were just giving Jones a bit of needle.

needle in a haystack something very hard to find. We hunted high and low for the necklace on that beach, but in vain – it would have been easier looking for a needle in a haystack.

NEEDS. (one) needs must (when the devil drives) one does something unpleasant if it has to be done, and there is no way to avoid it. I dislike working all night, but there is a deadline of nine o'clock for the project, so needs must! **From the proverb.** Compare **a man has to do what a man has to do**.

NEITHER. neither fish/flesh nor fowl (nor good red herring) neither one thing nor the other. I like music and I like dancing but I can't stand ballet – it's neither fish nor fowl. **In the Middle Ages, the term referred specifically to foodstuffs that were characterised as unsuitable for any class of people, whether monks (for whom fresh fish would be acceptable), ordinary men and women (flesh) or the poorest class (red smoke-dried herring).** Compare **fall between two stools**.

neither here nor there not important. She apologised for bumping into me but I told her it was neither here nor there – the car was undamaged and I was unhurt.

NEST. nest-egg savings, financial reserves against emergencies. He said he always kept a nest-egg aside for a rainy day. **From poultry farming. An ornamental china nest-egg was sometimes placed in a nest to encourage the hen, duck, etc. to lay eggs of its own. Similarly, a sum of money set aside for use in emergencies encourages the saver to add to the sum and see it grow.**

NEVER. never hear the end of something receive constant reminders of something. He nags her all the time now – she'll never be allowed to hear the end of her failure.

never mind 1. don't worry. I've lost my job but never mind – I'll soon find something else. **2. not to mention; far less.** He can hardly boil an egg, never mind make a meal for five people.

never-never land mythical place where everything is perfect. He walks about and talks to the flowers and trees in his own private never-never land. From J M Barrie's *Peter Pan* (1904).

never say die stay optimistic. He says his secret is to keep smiling and never say die. Also **never-say-die** (as adjective) determined. In spite of his injuries, his never-say-die attitude ensured his eventual recovery. Dickens was fond of using the term as a catch-phrase in *The Pickwick Papers* (1836–7) and in *Barnaby Rudge* (1841).

NEW. new blood new personnel in an organisation, bringing new ideas to it. Every so often there's a cabinet reshuffle, and the prime minister tries bringing some new blood into the government. Also 'fresh/young blood'.

new broom (sweeps clean) new boss or person in charge (who often wants to make big changes). After their disastrous results, the company is seeking a new broom to sweep the place clean. A proverb.

new lease of life renewal of energy, enthusiasm, etc. They say he's in love – certainly it's hard otherwise to explain his new lease of life.

new one on someone news, new information. He told me he had given up booze and cigarettes, but it's a new one on me. Compare **news to me**.

(put) new wine in old bottles (offer) new ideas in an old format. You can't put the new wines of openness and glasnost in the old bottles of the authoritarian state.

NEWS. news to me a surprise to me. It was news to me that there was to be an election.

Compare **new one on someone**.

NEXT. next to almost. The taxi got me to the airport in next to no time. The weather conditions were next to impossible for flying.

NIBS. her/his nibs the boss. What does her nibs want now, I wonder? Usually a light-hearted reference to an absent employer, line manager, spouse, etc. Sometimes 'her indoors' when referring humorously to a wife. In the 16th century, 'my nobs' meant 'my darling'. By the 18th century, 'my nabs' was merely 'my friend'.

NIGHT. night of the long knives sudden or unexpected political or business reorganisation, in which leading players lose their jobs. Yesterday's boardroom coup at Longman is only the latest in a sudden flurry of nights of the long knives which is jangling nerves in the City. The original night was probably 'Die Nacht der langen Messer' (29 June 1934), when Hitler and the blackshirted SS liquidated the brownshirted SA. The term was also applied memorably to Harold Macmillan's ruthless cabinet purge of 1962.

night on the tiles late-night session of carousing and enjoying oneself. Next time you have a night on the tiles till 3 a.m., kindly refrain from banging doors and singing drunken songs when you come into the house! From the often **unholy din** made by cats on rooftops at night.

night owl/bird person who works (or, more often, plays) at night and doesn't go to bed till early morning. She's a bit of a night owl because she works in a casino and keeps late hours. The owl's habits are nocturnal. Opposite of **early bird**.

NIGHTMARE. nightmare scenario the worst of all options or situations. For most parents the death of a child is the nightmare scenario: nothing worse can happen. The government tried hard to avert the nightmare scenario of the country degenerating into civil war.

NINE. nine days' wonder something that enjoys success or notoriety for a short period but then disappears from notice. Lots of people try to set up as publishers, but mostly they're a nine days' wonder and cease operations within a year or so. Perhaps from the Catholic Novena festivals, which in the Middle Ages offered nine days of devotional or religious entertainment. Alternatively, there was the old proverb which went, 'A wonder lasts nine days, and then the puppy's eyes are open.' Compare **flavour of the month**.

NINETEEN. nineteen to the dozen talk rapidly and with animation, and at length. It was a very noisy party, with everyone talking nineteen to the dozen.

NIP. nip something in the bud stop something or put an end to it in its early stages; discourage an unhealthy trend before it becomes established. I didn't approve of his insolent attitude to his mother, so I decided to nip it in the bud there and then, rather than stand by and watch it deteriorate into something inevitably worse. A gardening idiom: gardeners nipped buds to prevent the plant from flowering too early in the season.

(something) nips your head (something) bothers, annoys or (at worst) infuriates you. Sorry to nip your head with all these questions. Will you just stop going on about that – you're nipping my head! Compare **drive someone round the bend/twist**.

NIT. nit-picking over-attention to small and unimportant details. He is incapable of being constructive but is very good at nit-picking. Often construed as a sign of a person's negativity.

NITTY-GRITTY. the nitty-gritty the basic facts, essential argument. They met at her lawyer's and quickly got down to the nitty-gritty: what the divorce settlement was going to be.

NO. no call to no reason to. He had no call to conduct himself in that petty fashion, i.e. no one asked him to.

no deal/no dice no, certainly not. He claimed I owed him £10 and demanded it there and then – but I disagreed and told him, 'no dice.'

no end very much, to a great extent. He helped me no end. A litotes.

no end of a lot of, a large number of. She has no end of ideas about improving the house.

no flies (on someone) no lack of cunning or native wit (in someone's makeup). You'll not have to spell things out for John – there are no flies on him and he's probably guessed what's happening long ago. Perhaps from the idea of lethargic farm animals attracting flies in hot weather, unlike their friskier or livelier brethren which run around to evade them.

no go not feasible, useless. I tried all sorts of ploys when looking for a job, but it was no go – there was nothing available. As a negative refrain, the expression is immortalised in Louis MacNeice's poem 'Bagpipe Music' (1938): 'It's no go the Government grants, it's no go the elections,/Sit on your arse for fifty years and hang your hat on a pension.' Compare **nothing doing**.

no-go area a place which is beyond the rule of law, where it is dangerous to go. During the riots, whole neighbourhoods of the city became no-go areas. From the fact that the police, army patrols, etc. cannot go into these areas without provoking riots or civil disorder.

no great shakes unspectacular, not very good. I used to play tennis, but I was no great shakes at the game. 'Shakes' conveys the impression of something extraordinary or exciting, capable of giving a real shock to the system.

no hard feelings no grudges are felt, no resentment is nursed. He apologised for the accident and hoped there would be no hard feelings.

no holds barred without restriction. The election campaign was rather a dirty affair, with no holds barred. From a rough-and-ready form of wrestling, in which the usual rules and restrictions are waived and competitors may use any means – fair or foul – to throw their opponent and pin his shoulders to the floor.

no joke not an appropriate subject for joking about; not easy. It's no joke when people lose their jobs. Compare **no laughing matter**.

no laughing matter not funny, very serious. Such a dreadful accident is no laughing matter. Compare **beyond a joke; no joke**.

no love lost no friendship. They've been neighbours since childhood, but they've always been rivals, with no love lost between them.

no man's land area of uncertainty or sometimes of danger; grey area. After the firm went bust, we were into a no man's land of liquidators, litigators and debt collectors. Originally a reference to the empty ground lying between two opposing armies before a battle.

no matter it makes no difference. He promised to phone me no matter what happened. I haven't heard from him for weeks, but no matter: he'll turn up in his own good time.

no mistake without any doubt. She was in some temper – and no mistake!

no names no pack-drill a catch-phrase deriving from a British army punishment, in which a soldier who was undergoing punishment had to march about carrying a heavy pack on his back. Culprits could only receive this punishment if their identity was obvious. If their identity was uncertain, and the guilty party could not be named, the misdemeanour had to go unpunished. The idiom nowadays merely indicates a refusal to point the finger of blame at a named individual. Certain members of staff have been spreading rumours about the business; no names no pack-drill, but I think you all know who I'm talking about.

no news is good news one hears about bad news as soon as it happens, but good news tends not to be broadcast. She hadn't heard from her sister for weeks, but no news from that quarter

was usually good news, so she wasn't at all worried about her. A saying, from the same stable as 'bad news travels fast'.

no object no problem. They have the best of everything, with money no object, i.e. however much money, etc. is needed for a purchase, etc. that sum will be available.

no oil painting expression used to describe a person lacking physical beauty. She had warned me that her new man was no oil painting, so I was expecting something pretty grotesque. A sort of litotes. See also **not a pretty sight**.

no quick fix no simple solution. There are no quick fixes in the war against crime. A 'fix' in American English is often an improper or illegal solution to a problem.

no relish for not keen on, not enthusiastic about. I'm not going in that water, I've no relish for swimming.

no room to swing a cat very small and usually cluttered place, too crowded for some specified activity. He lives in a tiny bedsitter, and there's no room to swing a cat if we all visit him at once. Perhaps from the practice of tying unwanted cats, kittens, etc. in a sack prior to swinging it into the river and drowning them, or using the sack for archery target practice. Shakespeare refers to the latter activity in *Much Ado About Nothing*.

no skin off my nose not important to me; none of my business. It's no skin off my nose whether she passes or fails the exam. The expression really means, 'It's a matter of indifference to me, and isn't doing me any harm.' Probably from boxing, an American variant is 'no skin off my ass'.

no smoke without fire proverbial saying, meaning there is always some substance to a rumour. Everyone assumes he committed the crime, so it may be true: you have to remember that there's no smoke without fire. Compare **set tongues wagging**.

no sooner said than done something is done as soon as one is asked to do it. He phoned for a taxi and – no sooner said than done – it was at the door in less than two minutes.

no spring chicken not young. He still acts and dresses like a youngster, but he's no spring chicken.

no strings attached no secret conditions or restrictions are linked (to a deal). He liked the car very much, and said he'd buy it there and then, no strings attached. **Late 19th-century American in origin.**

no such thing nothing of the sort; nothing like that. He claims that I promised him a lift home, but I did no such thing. Compare **nothing of the kind/sort**.

no sweat that's no problem; no trouble. I asked to borrow John's car for the afternoon, and he said, 'Take it, no sweat, as long as it's back by five.' **An Americanism, meaning 'It takes a person no effort to agree to something.'**

no way! not possible, under no circumstances. No way is he permitted to do that. **Originally American, this is a more emphatic way of stating 'He is not permitted to do that.'** Compare **not likely!**

no (little/small) wonder it's not surprising. No wonder you got lost – the old map you were using doesn't even show the new motorway.

NOBODY. a nobody person of no importance. She refused to take orders from a nobody like Anthony Prune.

NOBODY'S. nobody's fool intelligent person, who is not easily fooled. He tried to sell her a damaged car, but being nobody's fool she refused to take it. **A litotes.**

NOD. a nod is as good as a wink (to a blind man/horse) proverbial witticism meaning that the slightest hint should be enough to convey one's meaning – even to a blind animal. I have no intention of spelling things out any further – on a topic like this, a nod should be as good as a wink to a blind horse.

nod/drop off begin to fall asleep. She started to nod off long before the end of the sermon. **The image is of a nodding head dropping off in fitful sleep, then lifted again as the person tries to stay awake. A phrasal verb.**

NODDING. nodding acquaintance slight acquaintance. You'll need to translate for him – he has no more than a nodding acquaintance with Spanish. **From nodding/bowing hello.**

NOOK. (every) nook and cranny everywhere; literally, every corner and crack. I need that document badly – and I expect you to find it even if you have to look in every nook and cranny in the building. **A dyad.**

NONE. none other than expression used to introduce someone, often a famous person. Guess who's coming to town this afternoon – none other than the Prince of Wales.

none so blind (as those who will not see) proverb signifying that it's very difficult – if not impossible – to persuade people who wilfully refuse to acknowledge facts. The evidence of the case was conclusive, but still the accused refused to admit the crime – there's none so blind… **Parallel to 'none so deaf (as those who will not hear)'.**

none too not very. I'm none too keen on her current boyfriend.

NORMAL. normal course of events manner or sequence in which things usually happen. I don't discuss such matters with the press in the normal course of events – but matters are rather desperate.

NOSE. nose about investigate. The police have been nosing about the back garden all afternoon. **A phrasal verb.**

nose out 1. bring out nose first. After half an hour's wait, we watched the fox nose its way out of its earth. 2. **discover.** Inspector Poirot always manages to nose out the facts of the case. **A phrasal verb.**

nose to the grindstone work hard. His exams are next month so he's keeping his nose to the grindstone. From the miller who, when grinding his corn into flour, had to keep his nose close to the grindstone in order to ensure that the work was proceeding smoothly.

NOSY. nosy parker inquisitive or nosy person. Try not to tell her too much – she's a real nosy parker. In medieval times, a parker was a park-keeper who looked after his lord's rabbits and other game to protect it from poachers. Such a person needed to be observant and very nosy.

NOT. not a patch on not nearly as good as. The book is wonderful, but I'm afraid the film version isn't a patch on it. Compare **not hold a candle to (someone or something)**.

not a pretty sight something ugly looking or unpleasant. There was a bad smash on the motorway this morning – the mangled wreckage was not a pretty sight. A common litotes. Compare **no oil painting**.

not a (living) soul nobody. I thought I heard a noise and looked all over the house for the source of it – but there wasn't a soul in the building.

not all there lacking in intelligence; mentally disturbed; subnormal. Some of these old folk aren't all there. A euphemism. Similar: 'not the full shilling', 'not the sharpest tool in the box', 'not the brightest light in the harbour', etc. Compare **lose one's marbles; tuppence off the shilling**.

not as black as s/he's painted not as bad as her/his reputation. I rather enjoyed meeting Jones – he certainly didn't give the impression of being half as black as he's painted.

not bat an eye/eyelid/eyelash not show any surprise, offence, etc. Suddenly all the dancers stripped to the skin, but nobody batted an eyelid. Compare **not turn a hair**.

not born yesterday not a completely naive person. He thinks he can fool me, but I wasn't born yesterday and I can see exactly what his little plan is. A litotes, usually for someone who is experienced and streetwise.

not by a long chalk/shot not by any means. He's not rich enough to own a car like that – not by a long shot. Probably 'chalk' was from chalking up scores at darts, skittles, etc. A decisive winner would have had to chalk up a lot of points on the board, and would therefore need a long chalk to write them with.

not/hardly cricket not fair; unsporting. She sold her story of royal romance to the Sunday papers, and a lot of people thought that was not quite cricket. From England's national game, and the atmosphere of fair play in which it is meant to be conducted.

not for the world not for anything, under no circumstances. He offered to buy the house but I told him I wouldn't sell it for the world. Also 'not for all the tea in China' (similar sense).

not frighten the horses refrain from doing anything excessively daring, controversial, etc. It's a very ambitious proposal for our company to consider, so I think we need to talk it over carefully with senior colleagues so as not to frighten the horses. A metaphor stressing gentle progress, so that doubters will not balk at or question one's plans. Compare **bring/get/keep people on side**.

not give a hoot or **two hoots** not care. It gives me no pleasure to observe that so many MPs don't give two hoots about their constituents. Also 'not give a toss', or 'not give a monkey's toss/fuck' (same sense, but coarser).

not half exclamation of emphatic agreement. 'Did you enjoy the show?' 'Not half – it was smashing!' A common meiosis.

not have a bean have no money. He asked if he could borrow a tenner from me, but I'm afraid I hadn't a bean. Money has been described as beans since the early 19th century.

not have/stand a cat in hell's chance have no chance at all of success. With over a hundred applicants for the job, he knew he hadn't a cat in hell's chance of getting it. Also 'not have a snowball's/snowflake's chance in hell'.

not have a clue know nothing about something. I haven't a clue what you're talking about. **Also** 'not have the foggiest/faintest idea' (similar senses).

not have a leg to stand on have no justification or case; be wrong in one's assumptions. His claims are very suspect; in fact, I'd say that most of them cannot be proved and don't have a leg to stand on. In other words, no one would stand up and defend them.

not hold a candle to (something or someone) not measure up; not be as good as. She's a wonderful baker, but her scones don't hold a candle to your mother's. Compare **not a patch on**.

not know someone from Adam/a dish of fish be unable to recognise or identify someone. Jimmy Jones? I don't know him from Adam.

not know one is born be spoilt; lead a carefree existence because others look after one, etc. He's never cooked a meal in his life, nor washed nor ironed his clothes – he doesn't know he's born. Usually an observation, made in the simple present tense.

not know what nerves are be fearless. Like all skydivers, he doesn't seem to know what nerves are – he actually likes falling out of the sky!

not let the grass grow (under one's feet) not hesitate or lose any time (trying to achieve something). I admire her industry – she gets things done, and never lets the grass grow under her feet. A gardening metaphor, advancing the notion that grass only has time to grow under the feet of 'slow coaches'.

not lift a finger refrain from offering help. She wouldn't so much as lift a finger to protect him.

not likely! certainly not! Jim offered to drive us home. 'Not likely!' we cried, 'you're too drunk to stand up!' Compare **not on one's life/nelly (duff); no way!**

not much cop lousy; no good. The present goalie's not much cop and everyone agrees that the team needs a new keeper in the net. **Anything of little value is said to be not much cop.**

not on one's life/nelly (duff)! under no circumstances. Last time he borrowed the car, he crashed it. So he's not getting it again – not on his nelly! The alternative version is from London Cockney rhyming slang: where life = puff (i.e. the breath of life) = 'nelly duff'. Compare **not likely!**

not one's pigeon/province/department not one's area of expertise; not one's affair or responsibility. Asked what he thought of the plans for the new building, Jones had no clear view and said that architecture wasn't really his province. Originally 'not my pigeon' was written 'not my pidgin', being pidgin English for 'not my business'.

not pull one's punches not restrain or rein back one's criticisms. It seemed it was to be a day for not pulling our punches – the choirmaster started off by calling us a bunch of constipated canaries. Also 'pull no punches'. Similar to 'not mince one's words'. Compare **pack a punch**.

not put a foot wrong/out of line make no mistakes; do nothing inappropriate. He made an excellent speech, and never once put a foot wrong, i.e. he said all the right things. Compare **play one's cards right/well; tick (all) the (right) boxes**.

not rocket science fairly simple or obvious. It wasn't rocket science to work out what was likely to happen next. **Normally a negative idiom.**

not sleep a wink not sleep at all. She said she just lay there worrying all night and hadn't slept a wink. See also **forty winks**.

not the only fish in the sea or **not the only pebble on the beach/shore** not the only suitable person. Her boyfriend has ditched her, but she'll get over it – she's beginning to realise that he's not the only fish in the sea. Compare the proverb 'There are just as good fish in the sea as ever came out of it.'

not the sharpest tool in the box or **not the brightest light in the harbour** idioms to indicate that someone has a slight mental defect, is almost 'normal' but not quite. Usually negative, compare **tuppence off the shilling; one sandwich short of a picnic; not all there; lose one's marbles**.

not to be sniffed at not to be rejected without careful thought. It was an excellent job offer, and certainly not to be sniffed at. A metaphor of turning up one's nose.

not to mention/speak of in addition to. He ran up huge gambling debts not to mention all his other financial problems.

not to mince words/matters speak frankly and without sparing the listener's feelings. John said she was being economical with the truth, but I refused to mince matters and told her she was a liar.

not to put too fine a point upon it to speak plainly. Our present government are a feeble bunch of hacks – not to put too fine a point upon it, they are a group of political pygmies. Compare **put it mildly**.

not turn a hair show no surprise, distress, emotion, etc. When the judge pronounced her guilty of all the charges, she didn't so much as turn a hair. The original metaphor implied the turning of a person's hair white with worry, shock, etc. (or gold with grief, as Oscar Wilde joked). Compare **not bat an eye**.

NOTCH. notch something up achieve or gain something. The term originally referred to gunmen, who were said to carve notches on their guns for everyone they killed. Fulham have notched up several very important wins this season.

NOTHING. nothing but only. Promise to tell me the truth and nothing but the truth.

nothing doing! no! I asked him to lend me £5 till Friday. 'Sorry, nothing doing!' he said, 'I'm penniless myself.' Compare **no go**.

nothing for it no alternative. I'd missed the last train home so there was nothing for it but to start walking.

nothing if not very, indubitably. His personality is nothing if not colourful.

nothing in it 1. a story is untrue. He asked if it was true that I'd won the football pools, but I assured him there was nothing in it. 2. competitors in a race, etc. are closely bunched, with no clear leader. There was absolutely nothing in it as the horses approached the final fence.

nothing like as good/bad as not nearly as good/bad as. He was an indifferent golfer, nothing like as good as his father.

nothing more (nor less) than equivalent to. His rendition of Chopin's very difficult Second Piano Concerto was nothing more nor less than brilliant. Same as 'nothing short of'.

nothing of the kind/sort not so. He accuses me of offering to pay £1,000 but I did nothing of the kind. An emphatic contradiction or refutation. Compare **no such thing**.

nothing succeeds like success proverb signifying that success is infectious, and that one success usually leads on to another. She's a woman to watch, because all her productions so far have been highly successful sell-outs at the box office – and nothing succeeds like success.

nothing to write home about 1. routine, mundane, not newsworthy. I've had a pretty busy week, but it's been routine stuff mostly with nothing very special to write home about. similar to 'nothing to speak of/talk about'. 2. unattractive. Your brother may think he's special, but I'd say he was nothing to write home about.

nothing ventured nothing win/gain proverb signifying that if you undertake nothing, you achieve nothing. He has decided to take the risk, since, as he points out, he can afford it – and nothing ventured nothing gained.

NUDGE. nudge, nudge. See **wink, wink, nudge, nudge(, say no more)**.

NULL. null and void legal term, a dyad, meaning 'without effect'. After 20 years the marriage was declared null and void.

NUMBER. (your) number's up you are guilty, you are going to be punished. He evaded justice for many years, but now the police are on to him and his number's nearly up. **From gambling. Compare the game's up**.

number one 1. oneself. His motto was: Always take care of number one. 2. **the boss**. Who is number one in this place? **Sometimes Italian 'numero uno' is preferred. Compare VIP**.

number two second-in-command. He was a capable and supportive number two in the platoon.

NUMBERS. (play) the numbers game figures, numbers, etc. used in a confusing way in support of one's argument. The audience started to lose interest in the argument when the two sides started playing the numbers game with each other. **Compare blind someone with science**.

NURSE. nurse a grudge/grievance keep a grudge/grievance constantly in one's mind, 'cultivating' it and refusing to forget it. Jones has been nursing a grudge against Smith for years, because Smith married Jones's old girlfriend.

NUTS. be nuts/nutty be insane, crazy. You need to keep an eye on him – he's completely nuts.

nuts and bolts basics. He'll need to explain the nuts and bolts of the system.

nuts about/on very keen on, fond of. She's nuts about horses.

NUTTY. nutty as a fruitcake mad, eccentric, extremely foolish. That comic actor plays the part of a dotty professor – nutty as a fruitcake and extremely funny.

O

OBJECT. object lesson demonstration; an event or action which gives a practical lesson in how to do (or not to do) something. Watching John's manic antics at the wheel was an object lesson in how never to drive a car.

ODD. odd bird/fish an eccentric, peculiar or unusual person. Mrs Bloggs is a bit of an odd fish but I can assure you she's quite harmless. Sometimes 'oddball', a 1940s American variant, with similar meaning but nowadays shading towards the idea of a 'misfit'.

odd jobs various chores that need to be done around the house, etc. John does most of the odd jobs at the school – painting doors, clearing drains, mending desks, changing light bulbs and putting in new windowpanes. Such a person is often called an 'odd-job man'.

odd man out 1. person left over in a group made into pairs or sets. We all had to take a partner for some sort of dance, but fortunately – for I hate dancing – I was left over as the odd man out. Although gender-flagged, the term may be applied to men or women. 2. misfit; someone or something that differs from others. Please look at these five objects and tell us which is the odd man out.

ODDS. odds and bobs/sods miscellaneous articles of little value; odd remnants. His living room is a junkshop of odds and bobs – I don't know how he can find anything in such a shambles. A dyad. Compare next entry, also **bits and bobs/pieces**.

odds and ends similar to previous entry, but perhaps slightly less chaotic. This is the drawer in which I keep my odds and ends. A dyad.

(the) odds are that it is likely that, probable that. Don't count on getting the job – the odds are that there'll be hundreds of other applicants and all of them raring to get it just as much as you. From betting figures, where the odds on or against state the likelihood of a horse winning a race, etc.

odds-on the balance of probability is in one's favour. His horse is odds-on favourite to win the steeplechase tomorrow.

OF. of a sort/kind of an inferior or less-than-ideal variety. To protect themselves from the blizzard, they made a shelter of a sort behind a drystone dyke. Also found in plural: 'of sorts'.

of age legally an adult. I need some identification document or other evidence which proves to me that you're of age. In the UK, this is when you are over 18.

of all people/things 1. more than any other person/thing. I expected her of all people to support the project. 2. of all the most unlikely persons/things that you can imagine. No one expected them to start punching one another, of all things.

of all shapes and sizes of many different kinds. Before the bell had stopped ringing, children of all shapes and sizes began piling out of the school gates.

of all time ever, that there has ever been. Many people regard Muhammad Ali as the greatest boxer of all time. An often clichéd hyperbole.

of an age old enough. I explained to John about his parents' marital problems, now that he's of an age to understand these things. Originally 'old enough to vote'. See also **of age**.

of late recently. He's been very touchy of late – something must be troubling him.

of little account/of no consequence insignificant, unimportant. Her views on the matter are of no account – tell her to keep them to herself. He was present at the accident, but his role was of no consequence.

of note of some/any significance; important or famous. We waited around for some time, but nobody of note appeared.

of old/yore 1. in times past, long ago. He enjoys telling the children stories about days of yore. 'Yore' is an Old English word meaning 'long ago', now rather literary, and obsolete outside this idiomatic use. 2. from experience (sometimes bitter). Watch out for her nasty temper – I know it very well of old.

of one/the same mind of unanimous opinion. The board of directors was of one mind on the matter – the chairman had to go.

of one's own accord voluntarily. He didn't have to be asked to resign – he went of his own accord.

of that ilk 1. of that name or place. His full title is Sir Thomas Anstruther of that Ilk. Originally from formal, legal titles in Scotland, 'ilk' means 'same' and derives from the same stem as the word 'like'. 2. of the same sort, class or set. Criminals of that ilk deserve every punishment they get. An extension of sense 1, sometimes 'of that kidney': see **of the same kidney**.

of the deepest hue/dye of the extremest sort. Colonel Apoplexy of Eastbourne is one of the mock titles given to a Conservative of the deepest hue. See also **true blue**.

of the first order/water/magnitude highly important, significant, etc. Fleming's discovery of penicillin was a medical breakthrough of the first magnitude. 'Water' is from a now obsolete trade nomenclature for the grading of diamonds. The three highest grades of diamond were formerly described as 'diamonds of the first, second or third water'.

of the same kidney of similar character. They are men of the same kidney so they enjoy each other's company. Probably from Shakespeare's usage, in The Merry Wives of Windsor iii.5. Compare **birds of a feather; of that ilk; of the same stripe**.

of the same stripe belonging to the same class, type, or outlook. Most of the academic experts and boffins of the same stripe take a dim view of our current economic mess. By inviting comparison with the animal kingdom, the term tends to be slightly pejorative. Compare **birds of a feather; of that ilk; of the same kidney**.

OFF. off and on/on and off occasionally, from time to time, at intervals. He's been going off and on for many years to Jamaica on business. A dyad.

off base incorrect; unfair. Her criticisms of the business were totally off base. American English, from the baseball field. Compare **wide of the mark**.

off by heart by memory. At school we used to learn poetry by Burns and Wordsworth off by heart.

off chance slight possibility (that something might happen). She decided not to come out for lunch with us, on the off chance that her friend Mrs Mack would call during her absence, i.e. there was a slight chance that Mrs Mack might call.

off one's chest public, not secret. I felt much better once all the problems had been fully discussed – they were off my chest then. Compare **into the open**.

off one's chump slightly mad, eccentric. It's hard to know if she's just a bit strange and off her chump, or if she's genuinely insane and needs looking after. Old-fashioned; a 'chump' of wood was a 'chunk' or block of wood. Hence also woodenheads, blockheads, etc.

off colour 1. slightly unwell. She was looking a little off colour, and she certainly didn't play a very good game of tennis. 2. in bad taste; indelicate. He's one of those comedians who specialise in off-colour jokes.

off duty not at work. He works in the fire service and goes off duty at eight o'clock. Originally applied especially to people on shift or uniformed work, like nursing, soldiering, police work, etc. Opposite of **on duty**.

off one's food not hungry, perhaps because unwell or preoccupied. She's been off her food for several days – I wonder what's upsetting her.

off (one's) guard by surprise. Fortunately the German army was caught completely off guard by the Normandy landings – they were expecting the Allied invasion to come much further to the east.

off one's hands not in one's ownership, responsibility, etc. I think she gave me the car just to get it off her hands – it had too many unhappy memories for her.

off one's head/chump/nut/rocker/trolley insane with anger; daft, crazy, foolish. She must have been off her head to offer him a lift in her car. Mr Jones goes off his nut if you kick a football into his precious flowerbeds. Compare **out of one's head/skull/(tiny) mind/bonce/tree; or round the bend/twist**.

off key 1. dissonant, striking the wrong musical note. Her voice was very off key and hard to listen to. 2. inappropriate. The president's speech seemed rather off key, as if it had been prepared for a different audience. Compare **off colour**.

off limits area where one is not permitted to go. Public bars are strictly off limits to pupils in school uniform. Originally an American army term, the British equivalent is **out of bounds**. Compare **kick/push (something) into the long grass**.

off one's own bat by one's own initiative, without encouragement from anyone. He wasn't invited to the party; he just arrived, completely off his own bat. From cricket.

off the back of a lorry something obtained in suspicious circumstances. He can get you lots of cheap electrical goods, but never ask him where they came from – off the back of a lorry, if you ask me. Sometimes the item referred to 'fell off a lorry'. Compare **on the cheap**.

off the beaten track 1. in an isolated location, especially one which receives few visitors; out of the way. There's nothing we enjoy better than a trip to somewhere really off the beaten track. Compare **off the map; back of beyond**. 2. not in the mainstream of things, unusual. His music is way off the beaten track and it has very few admirers. Similar to **way out**.

off the cuff 1. in an unguarded way. He spoke off the cuff and without notes about his experiences

in jail. 2. spontaneous. One off-the-cuff remark at Westminster can set the entire British press in uproar. From a Victorian practice widely adopted by some after-dinner speakers of listing the main points of their speeches on their shirt cuffs, in preference to more obviously reading them from a sheet of paper. It used to be considered very bad form if speakers read their speeches, because audiences believed these would then lack freshness or spontaneity.

off the hook out of difficulties. John wasn't looking forward one bit to meeting Jane at the party, so her illness and subsequent non-appearance let him off the hook. From fishing, a metaphor of the one that got away.

off the map inaccessible; hard to find. I'll have to give you very clear directions for finding our cottage – it's a little bit off the map. Compare **off the beaten track**.

off the pace trailing the leader in a race; not keeping up. Her performance at work has been a little bit off the pace since her illness. Opposite of **up to speed**.

off the rails slightly mad. He went off the rails for a time after his marriage collapsed. A metaphor of losing one's way in life's journey, the original reference would have been to the derailment of a train or tram.

off the record unofficially; confidentially. I've learnt that the company's about to go bust, but that information has to be strictly off the record for the present. She's been told off the record that the job is hers if she applies for it. In other words, no minutes or other official records will be kept of what has been said/transacted, etc. Originally American, from the 1920s.

off the scale immeasurable, very powerful. The sub-sea earthquake that caused the tsunami was completely off the scale.

(throw someone) off the scent (give someone) misleading or confusing information. To keep the paparazzi off the scent, the press secretary decided to feed the entire press corps some misinformation about a forthcoming royal wedding. **From fox hunting, where the hunted fox resorts to various tricks like swimming rivers in order to throw the hounds off his scent.**

off the top of one's head without forethought or planning. The police interrogation was quite unexpected, so he was obliged to answer their questions off the top of his head. **Sometimes 'out of the top of one's head'.**

off the wall zany, eccentric, unusual. She has an interesting if rather off-the-wall brood, which isn't surprising for someone with such an unusual lifestyle. **Originally an American idiomatic phrase which may derive from the unpredictable bounce of an ice-hockey puck.**

OFFER. offer/pay the moon be prepared to pay any price, however high. Nowadays top football clubs offer the moon for top players. **The implication is that the person is desperate to acquire something, and will go to any lengths – even intergalactic – to get it.**

offer sweeteners try to bribe. You're asking a lot of me, and you don't say if you'll be offering any sweeteners for my pains. **Literally, a sugar coating for a bitter pill or thankless job. Compare sugar the pill.**

OIL. oil and water (don't mix) incompatible things/people (can't be made to work well together). They did their best to make a go of the marriage for the sake of the children, but you know the saying about oil and water – in the end they just had to go their separate ways. **The complete sentence is an old saying.**

oil/grease someone's palm bribe. Whether it's fully booked or not I'm sure they'll find a place for you on the flight, especially if you oil their palms with a bottle of whisky or some suitable trinket. **The idea is that money slips more easily off an oiled palm into someone's pocket.**

OLD. old Adam man's human and fallible dimension rather than his divine potential. He lives a quiet, celibate existence, but every so often the old Adam seems to require an airing and off he goes on a bit of a spree somewhere. **A metonym associating the biblical Adam with man's fallen nature.**

old as the hills very old. They may sound like a modern and progressive organisation, but some of their prejudices are as old as the hills. **A standard simile of chronological challenge.**

old bag old woman. Even her son agrees she's nothing more than a grumpy old bag. **Highly uncomplimentary. Also 'old witch, bitch, crone'.**

old boy 1. chap; man. I say, old boy, lend us a fiver won't you! **An affectionate, rather English middle-class term. 2. former pupil of a school, usually a private school.** The old boys had a boozy reunion last weekend and some of them haven't recovered yet. 3. **old-boy network** system whereby people from the same or similar privileged schools/backgrounds do favours for one another. He tried for a job in the diplomatic service, but the old-boy network was against him, **i.e. he didn't have the right contacts to help him find work in that sphere of activity. Compare old-school tie.**

old beyond one's years prematurely knowledgeable. You looked in that child's eyes and knew she had seen so much human suffering and tragedy that she was old beyond her years.

old chestnut tired and much-repeated joke, anecdote, etc. Oh no, John, not that hoary old chestnut again! **Perhaps from the idea that only a freshly roasted chestnut tastes good. A reheated one is as savourless as a reheated joke.**

old flame former girlfriend/boyfriend. On holiday in Brittany with her family, she met an old flame from her college years.

old guard elders of the community; conservative element. The Young Conservatives got very little support from the old guard of their movement. **Compare Young Turk.**

old hand experienced or knowledgeable person. This problem isn't for beginners – leave it to an old hand to sort out the mess.

old hat old ideas re-used; out-of-date knowledge, information, styles, etc. She's very traditional in her approach to her subject, and her ideas – like her style of dress – are extremely old hat. From the idea that hats usually outlive their fashionable status.

old/new school traditional/contemporary formation; old fashioned/up to date. An excellent public speaker with never a sign of notes, he was a politician of the old school. Some people use these terms in a very loose way, to mean 'reactionary' or 'trendy'.

old school tie one's contacts from one's schooldays, especially those who help one in later life. He got on to the committee through some of his old-school-tie buddies. There is usually an implicit criticism of privilege and the unfair use of influence. (An item of male attire, the school tie usually has stripes in the school's colours.) Compare **old-boy network**.

old wives' tale tittle-tattle; account or story that doesn't deserve serious consideration; traditional belief or superstition. He gave me some old wives' tale about how he knew it was going to rain – his arthritic knee told him! Until the mid-20th century in some rural areas, an 'old wife' (Scots 'guidwife') was a midwife, often without medical training. She relied on traditional wisdom (rather than on a professional qualification in gynaecology) when attending births.

OLIVE. olive branch symbolic token of reconciliation or peace. The strike went on for weeks, with neither side disposed to offer an olive branch to the other. From Genesis viii.11, when the dove brought the olive branch to Noah in the Ark. This was interpreted as evidence that God had forgiven mankind for his wickedness, and that the Flood was beginning to recede.

ON. on the back burner in abeyance. I think we can put that idea on the back burner for the moment. A culinary metaphor, literally 'to keep warm or cook very slowly'. Compare **on ice**.

on a firm/sound footing on a fair/sound basis; securely. Now that all the business's former debts have been paid off, we hope it will start to develop on a firmer footing.

on (to) a good thing in an advantageous or profitable position (often used sarcastically). Various acquaintances decided they were on to a good thing when they learnt we had a holiday cottage. Compare **in clover**.

on a hiding to nothing with no chance of success. They may be quite a good rugby team but they're on a hiding to nothing against the All Blacks. Betting parlance: a 'hiding' means a thorough beating or defeat, 'to nothing' means with no betting odds in one's favour.

on a par with level with, similar to. He's a very good middle-distance runner, but hardly on a par with Jones. From 'parity' = equality. Now mainly confined to golf, where 'par' = the number of strokes a good ('scratch') player requires for a hole or for the course. See also **below par; up to par; par for the course**.

on a roll on a series or accumulation of successes. Her athletics career has been on a roll this season: first the British, then the European, and now the Olympic champion. From the jargon of the national lottery: the weekly jackpot is 'rolled over' to the following week when there is no outright winner, thus getting bigger and bigger. Also 'on a winning streak' (similar sense).

on a shoestring with a very small amount of money. For years she ran the business on a shoestring, but now it has started earning and spending serious sums of money.

on a sticky wicket in a difficult situation. He's done his best to satisfy his creditors, but financially he's on a very sticky wicket just now. From cricket, where a sticky or muddy wicket after rain makes batting and bowling difficult.

(keep/have someone) on a (tight) string under one's control. She's like most control freaks: no good at properly delegating responsibility and she has to keep everyone on a tight string and dancing to her tune. From puppetry.

on a wing and a prayer with high hopes, but with nothing to support one but good luck and good judgment. They set off to travel overland to South Africa on a wing and a prayer – with almost no money and driving a very ramshackle old jeep. The phrase is thought by Partridge to have been coined by Royal Air Force flyers at the time of the Battle of Britain (1940). Originally it described a damaged aircraft, and the full expression was 'We got back on a wing and a prayer.' The passage of the expression into civilian life was aided by the American song 'Coming in on a wing and a prayer' (1943), by Harold Adamson. Compare **(by the) seat of the pants; fly blind**.

on account on credit. They paid me £500 on account, to be repaid in six months' time. From business English. Also 'as an advance'.

on someone's/something's account 1. for someone's benefit. Don't go to any trouble on my account please. 2. because of someone/something. She received an invalidity payment on account of her illness.

on all fours on four legs; on hands and knees. Uncle John was never happier than crawling about on all fours with the children.

on an even keel in a steady, upright manner; without extremes of emotional turmoil. He's been through some difficult times lately, but seems to have got his life back on an even keel now. The headmaster was commended for keeping the school on an even keel throughout the present crisis. From nautical English, where the ideal sailing position of a ship was with its keel 'even' (i.e. upright) in the water. It was particularly hard to maintain an even keel in stormy seas.

on and off/off and on from time to time. They've maintained an on-and-off relationship for years.

on and on (and on) interminably, often boringly. Yakkity-yak, yakkity-yak, they talked on and on into the evening. I left them to it.

on approval on loan, prior to buying something. He's got the car on approval for the weekend to see if he likes it. Sometimes abbreviated to 'on appro'.

on someone's back nagging/bossing someone. As soon as he gets home, she's on his back to do this, do that, do the next thing. A horse-racing metaphor.

on balance after due consideration. On balance, I'm afraid I don't feel that the press treated him very fairly.

on one's beam ends without funds, resources; broke; financially challenged or jeopardised. She used to live a very affluent life, but now she looks as if she's on her beam ends. Originally nautical. If a ship was on its beam (ends), it was listing heavily on its side and in danger of capsizing.

on board 1. on a ship. The troops are ordered on board at 15.00 hours. 2. into (someone's) consciousness/awareness. It's been a frightful shock to him, and I don't think he's quite taken the enormity of the news on board yet.

on call 1. term used to describe a doctor/nurse etc. on visits to their patients in their homes. I'm sorry, you can't speak to Dr Morrison just now; he's out on call. 2. available for emergencies. There's always a pool of firemen on call at the station overnight.

on duty doing one's work. He had to leave the party early because he was going on duty from 10 o'clock. Opposite of **off duty**.

on easy street carefree; in comfortable circumstances (old-fashioned). They've been on easy street since they won the national lottery. An Americanism, compare British English **on queer street**.

on edge apprehensive, tense, unable to relax. Everyone's been distinctly on edge since the soldiers moved into town. Compare **on pins and needles; on tenterhooks; walk on eggs/eggshells**.

on end without interruption. It seemed to rain for weeks on end.

on faith without evidence or proof. She told us she hadn't time to explain every little twist and turn of the plot so far; we'd just have to accept her account of events on faith, **i.e. have faith in her veracity**.

on one's feet 1. fit and well. She took several weeks to recover from the operation, but she's on her feet again now. 2. **quickly, fluently.** Most politicians quickly develop the knack of thinking on their feet – nothing seems to catch them out. Compare **roll with the punches**.

on hand available. I'm sorry but there's no one on hand to help right now.

on/off one's hands in/out of one's responsibility. She has too many things on her hands right now to take on any additional assignments.

on/in heat sexually aroused. There's a bitch on heat next door and all the dogs of the neighbourhood are after her.

on one's high horse 1. affecting a superior view, giving oneself airs; behaving pretentiously or arrogantly. It doesn't take much to get her up on her high horse and looking down snootily at common folk like you and me. From the days when one could tell a person's social status by the size and breed of his horse rather than the size and make of his car. See also **give oneself airs**. 2. in angry, belligerent mood. There he goes again, up on his high horse attacking all and sundry.

on ice 1. on an ice surface. We watched a thrilling performance of *Swan Lake* on ice at the Lyceum. 2. for use at a later date; into reserve. With all the financial difficulties in the business, they had to put many of their development plans on ice for an indefinite period. The idea being to preserve something by freezing it until a future date. Compare **on the back burner**.

on in years old(er). She plays less golf now that she's getting on in years. A standard euphemism, a predecessor of 'chronologically challenged'.

on/to one's knees 1. begging/praying for something. The company went on its knees to its creditors, asking for more time to pay its bills. 2. exhausted, in a bad state. The country has been on its knees since the civil war, and the UN is now going in to try and help it back to its feet.

on one's last legs tottering, about to collapse; almost ruined. Some of the marathon runners were on their last legs by the time they reached the finishing line. The corrupt regime is now on its last legs.

online 1. into operation. An extension to his original computer could quickly be brought online. 2. done directly, while connected to a computer storage system. The keyboarders are editing the text online before sending it out to proofreaders. Technical terms, now more commonly written as one word than two.

on me (also **on her/him, etc.**) on my account, meaning 'I'm buying'. The next round of drinks is on me. See also **on the house**.

on one's mettle ready to do one's best/utmost; waiting to be tested. After the captain's pep talk, the whole team were on their mettle and raring to go. The word is originally from 'metal', and referred to the temper of a steel sword-blade. It then came to refer to a person's temper or temperament. Other idiomatic phrases were to 'try a person's mettle' and to 'put someone to his mettle'.

on one's mind preoccupying one's thoughts. He didn't seem able to pay much attention to the conversation, and acted as if there was something else on his mind. See also **on the brain**.

on no account under no circumstances; for no reason. She was clearly instructed that she must on no account open the door till I got back. Used for emphasis.

on occasion(s) sometimes; from time to time. You would see him on occasion sipping his pint of stout at the Brazen Head Inn.

on (the) one hand(…on the other) idiomatic expression used to introduce (and often to complete) contrasting facts, views, etc. She's a funny mixture – on the one hand she's a serious academic, on the other she plays in a rock band. **The expression probably derives from the hand gestures used to convey contrasts.**

on one's own 1. **alone.** She lives on her own in that vast mansion. 2. **without help.** Surely he didn't build the house on his own, did he?

on one's own account for oneself. He joined the army in 1939 not on his own account but because he believed the country needed him there.

on pain of death/deportation/dismissal, etc. under threat of the direst consequences, punishments, etc. He was told on pain of instant dismissal not to mention a single word of their conversation outside that room. Formal.

on paper as written down; in theory. It looks all very well on paper – the property's legally his – but don't look too closely at the bricks and mortar! He may be a millionaire on paper but…**The term often suggests that facts or realities are more important than written formalities or appearances.**

on pins and needles extremely apprehensive, nervous, uneasy. All the way home he was on pins and needles: would the letter be there or would it not? **A dyad to describe the physical sensation of sharp tingling; compare on edge; on tenterhooks; walk on eggs/eggshells.**

on purpose deliberately. He claims he didn't start the fire on purpose.

on queer street in bad/difficult circumstances, especially financial trouble. He failed to declare all his earnings so now he's on queer street with the tax authorities. It is said that 'queer' is a corruption of 'Carey', since the London Bankruptcy Court used to be on Carey Street; alternatively the expression may derive from 'queer straits' or dire circumstances. Compare **on easy street**.

on record a public or official statement that may be verified by documentary reference, records, etc. The prime minister went on record to say that he would not resign. I'm told it's been the wettest July on record.

on reflection after consideration. At first I was keen to travel with them, but now on reflection I have changed my mind. A similar term is 'on second thoughts'.

on schedule up to timetable. You are always advised to check the flight is still on schedule several hours before departure.

on seat present; available in one's place of work. Mr Awolowo is not on seat at the moment; he has travelled to his village. A West African idiom (where people also lie 'on bed(s)' rather than 'in bed(s)', no doubt for climatic reasons).

on one's shoulders as one's responsibility. He looks a worried man – as if he's carrying the sins of the world on his shoulders.

on speaking terms 1. in civil, social contact. I don't know her at all well, but we are neighbours so we've been on speaking terms for some years. 2. often used negatively, to indicate a past quarrel. They may live next door to each other but they haven't been on speaking terms for 20 years.

on spec as a form of speculation/gamble. He knew nothing about the car, but it was going cheap – so he bought it on spec with the idea of running it for the summer and then selling it on.

on strike withholding one's labour; refusing to work. We went on strike last week to express our anger with the feckless management of our business. Originally nautical: in the 17th century, reluctant sailors – many of them press-ganged – would refuse to put to sea, and would 'strike' or lower their ships' sails in a gesture of defiance.

on tenterhooks full of nervous apprehension, with nerves taut. She's hoping to go to university in the autumn, and is waiting on tenterhooks for her exam results. **Tenterhooks** were once used on a sort of rack or frame for stretching woollen cloth; thus **on the rack** has a similar meaning. The tenter was the name of the frame on which the cloth was stretched after milling, so that it would dry evenly and without shrinking. The hooks or nails affixed the cloth to the tenter. So while the cloth was on tenter hooks, it was awaiting completion. Now the term applies to people awaiting the outcome of a situation.

on that account/score for that reason. He's very fond of her, so on that account I've no doubt he'll be more than happy to help her.

on the air/airwaves broadcast. The ceremony was broadcast live yesterday; it was on the air for about five hours.

on the alert into a state of watchfulness. When the lion escaped from its cage, the police and army in the area went on the alert. A major alert is sometimes referred to by the phrase 'on red alert', from the colour-coded sequence of alerts at government buildings: red is the highest state of alertness.

on the ball sharp-witted, bright and alert. His lectures used to be very witty and sharp; he's less on the ball nowadays. American in origin, from good players in ballgames.

on the blink not working; faulty. He wants a lift in your car today because his own is on the blink again. The term probably originated with faulty electric light fittings. An alternative American version from around 1900 is 'on the fritz'.

on the brain obsessively interested in. The man's got women on the brain and talks about nothing else. Compare **on one's mind; one-track mind**.

on the breadline very poor; almost starving. He's not exactly on the breadline, but he's down to one car and one house nowadays, like the rest of us. Originally American, a reference to bread queues, or 'lines', of destitute immigrants waiting to receive free bread, in New York and elsewhere from the 1850s.

on the brew unemployed and collecting unemployment benefit money. He's been on the brew since the coalmine closed. 'Brew' is a phonic corruption of the term 'unemployment bureau', a precursor of the job centre. A regional idiom.

on the button 1. exactly. Meet me at the station please, at 10 on the button. Also **on the dot**. 2. correct. We gave him a forecast which was more or less on the button. Also 'spot on'.

on the cards likely. According to the long-range forecasts, a bad winter is on the cards. From fortune telling, especially with Tarot and other cards. Americans prefer 'in the cards'.

on the carpet/mat in receipt of criticism, reprimand, etc. The strike has been unofficial, so all who took part in it will be on the carpet tomorrow. From the perception that management (unlike the shopfloor) usually have carpets in their offices, on which offending workers have to stand and receive their punishment.

on the cheap without paying a fair price. She loves haggling with traders and trying to get things on the cheap. In this country we tend to do all the important things on the cheap and only to pay through the nose for the trivial stuff. Compare **off the back of a lorry**.

on the contrary term of contradiction, indicating that the situation is the opposite of that stated. He calls me a Presbyterian; on the contrary, not only am I not a Presbyterian, I am not even a Christian.

on the dot to the exact minute. The train arrived at King's Cross on the dot of one o'clock/at one o'clock on the dot. A phrase which makes a specific emphasis.

on the face of it as far as can be superficially deduced; apparently. The defending lawyer is the best in the business, so on the face of it my client's chances of an acquittal are good.

on the fence unwilling/unable to take one point of view or another. Most people take one view or another on the subject of the monarchy, but the Raving Loony party sit on the fence on that subject as on many others. Mostly used in a political context.

on the fiddle cheating someone of money/goods. Some of the defence contracts were so massive that it was a long time before any of the authorities actually noticed that someone was on the fiddle. From accountancy, where fiddling of figures is frowned on. Compare **at it**.

on the game working as a prostitute. That one's got a police record – she's been on the game for years. A euphemism, once 'on the loose'. Compare **on the make**.

on the go active, busy. She's marvellous for an 80-year-old, always involved in various projects and invariably on the go with something or other.

on the grapevine via one's informal or unofficial network of contacts. Did I hear on the grapevine that you were planning to remarry? Telegraph wires were humorously referred to as the grapevine in 19th-century America, so rapid was their spread. See also **bush telegraph**.

(hot) on the heels of right behind, immediately after. It's been a bad year; first the war, and then on the heels of that disaster we've had the cholera outbreak.

on the hoof while standing up. There wasn't time for a proper sit-down meal, but we managed to have a quick sandwich on the hoof between engagements.

on the horns of a dilemma in a quandary, paralysed by indecision; confronted with two equally unattractive options. It is probably Hamlet who best personifies the problem of being on the horns of a dilemma; he couldn't decide whether it was better literally or metaphorically to take arms against a sea of problems. The 'horns' are the two metaphoric alternatives, both of equal sharpness hence unattractiveness.

on the home front 1. in a civil defence context in time of war. Our soldiers on the home front are ready to defend our fatherland whenever an attack comes. 2. at home; in a domestic context. Life on the home front has been good to him recently, even if he's been having a bad time at the office. The idiom has now extended by analogy: 'on the government/opposition/trade union front, on the wages front', etc.

on the hour/half-hour exactly at the time the hour/half-hour starts. There's a train to Glasgow every hour on the half-hour. Compare **on the stroke of; on the dot**.

on the house at no charge; paid for by the house/host. He was so pleased to see me he insisted the drinks were on the house. See also **on me** (etc); 'It's on me' being what the speaker says if s/he is paying.

on the job 1. working. Firemen wear special clothing when they're on the job. 2. engaged in sexual activity. The chambermaid forgot to knock on the door of Room 511 and had the awkward experience of disturbing two of her colleagues on the job. A euphemism, also *in flagrante delicto*.

on the level honest and sincere in all one does; trustworthy. I don't think he'll be trying any tricks on you now; he's been on the level since that police scare last year. From freemasonry, an 18th-century idiom.

on the line at risk; at stake. He feels that his job is on the line unless he can increase the company's sales.

on the loose at liberty; free of constraint. He was 12 years in jail for his crime, but now he's on the loose again and said to be looking for a job.

on the make 1. trying to make money/gain advantage at someone else's expense. He's like all young men on the make – none too scrupulous with other folks' property. 2. trying to make sexual advances. She's quite obviously a woman on the make; she's been eyeing up a couple of the lads all night. Compare **on the game**.

on the map well known. You're going to need to

spend a bit of money promoting the company and its brand names before it has any chance of getting itself on the map.

on the market for sale. Since she was a little girl she always dreamt of living in that house – and now at last it's on the market.

on the mend recuperating; getting better from an illness. He's been ill for months, but now the nurses tell us he's on the mend and that in a few weeks he can go home.

on the move going to another place. It was an exhausting holiday; Paris one day, Rome another, we were forever on the move.

on the nail punctually, without delay, at once. They're very good people to work for because they pay on the nail, just as soon as you've submitted your invoice. There are at least two explanations of this idiom. Firstly, a nail mark on a stone table was where tradesmen once exchanged money for goods and settled their accounts. Such tables can be inspected in the market at Bath and also at Limerick. Secondly, in the 16th century the term referred to the rather oafish practice of drinking one's ale straight off, and then turning up one's cup on one's thumbnail to indicate that the cup's contents had indeed been quaffed. Whether this theatrical gesture indicated approval of the hospitality of one's host, or was an unsubtle request for the same again, is not known.

on the never-never on hire purchase; by instalments. They're paying off their new car on the never-never. The rueful – and often correct – popular perception was that the interest charged on these payments never did get paid off.

on the nod without drawing attention; without debate. No one was very interested in the agenda for the meeting, and most of the items went through on the nod. Originally, and literally, by a nod of the head to signal agreement and without recourse to a formal vote.

on the nose on target. These bombs never miss – every one lands right on the nose.

on the off chance in the slightly forlorn hope. I knew I had no chance of winning the prize for best performer, but I kept going on the off chance that I would be contributing to my team's overall victory.

on the point of about to. He appeared on the point of agreeing to the proposal, but then he changed his mind again.

on the principle that/of guided by the idea that/of. He always wears bright red socks on the principle that at least his ankles will appear jolly.

on the (strict) q.t. on the quiet; secretly. I hate the way they act mysterious and do everything on the q.t. and never tell anyone what's going on. Compare **hush-hush**.

on the rack in a state of acute suspense, or mental distress, about the outcome of something. We've been on the rack ever since our son's arrest. Originally referred to a form of physical torture. See also **on tenterhooks**.

on the radar/map/(same) wavelength registering in someone's consciousness. I don't think opera features on John's radar, he's more of a football man. Opposite of 'off/under the radar'. See also **speak the same language**.

on/off the rails out of/in a mess; in the proper way/mixed up. Their affairs have been in a mess for years, but now they're under new management which seems to have got them back on the rails. After the marriage broke up, he seemed to go off the rails for a while. From railways and tramways.

on the rebound on the way up again, usually after the downer or depression caused by the end of a love affair, etc. She married him on the rebound, very shortly after breaking up with her first boyfriend.

on the rocks 1. broken up, destroyed (from the idea of being shipwrecked). That marriage has been on the rocks for years. 2. liquor drunk with ice cubes or 'rocks' (originally American). They've spent the whole evening drinking Scotch on the rocks.

on the ropes at the point of failure, defeat, etc. The government's educational voucher scheme is on the ropes. From boxing; a boxer on the ropes is almost ready to fall down.

on the run trying to evade justice; fugitive. It was one of those movies about gangsters on the run from the law.

on the same wavelength having a good understanding with another person, usually as a result of shared interests and attitudes. I never found it that easy to get on with her – we just weren't on the same wavelength. From the early days of radio communications, and picking up messages.

on the shelf unattractive in appearance or character to the opposite sex. Liz worried that she was on the shelf and unlikely to marry. Compare **past one's sell-by date**.

on the side 1. something done to supplement one's main job/income. He does a bit of book-keeping on the side to help out one or two neighbours. 2. something done furtively. He goes up to London most weekends to see some woman on the side.

on the sly in a secret or underhand way. She seemed to work very hard for that firm, but all the time she was passing on information on the sly to its fiercest competitor.

on the spot 1. at once. He needed £100 and she gave it to him on the spot. Compare **spot cash; spot check; then and there**. 2. in a difficult/ embarrassing position. Her rather shrill and petulant outburst at the head waiter put us all on the spot; the entire restaurant was looking at us. 3. there; at the scene. There was an ambulance on the spot within five minutes.

on the spur of the moment on impulse; without premeditation. Millie was a great one for doing things on the spur of the moment.

on the stage working as an actor/actress. Don't put your daughter on the stage, Mrs Worthington. A synecdoche.

on the strength of on the basis of; on the argument that. On the strength of one poem published in a school magazine, he decided he would become a writer.

on the stroke of at the moment when the clock strikes. Cinderella left the ball on the stroke of midnight. Compare **on the dot of; on the hour/ half-hour**.

on the stump engaged in electioneering, canvassing, fund-raising, etc. He has just completed a tough three-week itinerary on the stump through the Middle East. In 18th-century, pre-Independence America, the 'stump' was a felled tree-stump used by public orators from which to address crowds. Also 'go on the stump'.

on the threshold at the start. You are leaving school today on the threshold of adult life. Literally, at the entrance or doorway.

on the tip of one's tongue word momentarily forgotten. His name's been on the tip of my tongue all morning, but can I remember it – no, I can't.

on the town having a celebration. Having won their match, most of the boys went out on the town for the evening.

on the understanding on the strictly agreed basis. I'm only going to come for lunch with you on the understanding that you'll let me pay for it.

on the up (and up) 1. in an improving situation. Her career isn't exactly on the up and up; most of her successes are behind her. 2. honest. They have guaranteed that the whole business is now on the up. Compare **above board**.

on the wagon not drinking alcoholic liquor. Give John nothing stronger than a glass of orange juice – remember he's been on the wagon for a while. Literally, on the water wagon – from the days before piped tap water, when water wagons used to ply the streets of towns. The idiom is originally American. See also **sign the pledge**.

on the wane in decline. Her political fortune's been very much on the wane lately. From meteorology, where the stars and planets wax and wane. A similar tidal idiom would be 'on the ebb'.

on the warpath very angry. Keep out of the headmaster's way for a while – he's on the warpath just now. From a North American Indian custom of seeking out the person who has offended one or made one angry.

on the/one's way 1. on a journey. The car was on the way to Birmingham when the accident occurred. 2. in the process of attaining. He's well on the way to the managing directorship of the whole group.

on the whole mainly/mostly; generally speaking. It's been a difficult year, but results have on the whole been better than expected.

on the wrong end of something on the unsuccessful side. The team were very quiet after the match, having found themselves on the wrong end of a 6–0 scoreline.

on thin ice in a weak/vulnerable/uncertain position; about to cause offence. He withdrew the argument when he realised that he was (skating) on thin ice.

on tick on credit, trust. The corner shop sometimes gives her a bag of potatoes on tick and she pays it back at the end of the week. Shopkeepers used to write down the price of items supplied in this way, and ticked them off when payment was finally made. The alternative explanation is that they kept an IOU ticket with the details on that.

on time punctually. I don't think the job is going to be finished on time.

on tiptoe 1. standing on one's raised toes. Even standing on tiptoe, he couldn't reach the top shelf. 2. walking very quietly. I went through the classroom on tiptoe, so as not to disturb the children writing.

on one's tod alone. He was sitting on the bench, all on his tod, watching the world go by. From Cockney rhyming slang: 'on one's Tod Sloan' = alone. Tod Sloan (1874–1933) was an American jockey.

on one's toes alert; paying attention. You have to be on your toes all day if you are teaching a class of 10-year-olds.

on top of 1. in addition to. It was his misfortune to learn that, on top of his child's illness, he had lost his job. 2. equal to; capable of. It's a very hard job, but she's more than on top of it.

on top of the world full of joy/happiness/health. It was a fine sunny day, I was in love for the first time, and I felt on top of the world. A hyperbole.

on trial being tested. The latest model goes on trial at the Farnborough Air Show next month. Originally from the Law Courts.

on one's uppers very poor. He was clearly down on his uppers, and I was happy to cook him supper and lend him a tenner till next week. The 'uppers' are the top part of one's shoes. If your shoes are down to their uppers, the soles have worn off and you are presumed too poor to send them to the cobbler's or to replace them. Compare **well heeled**.

on your bike! go away; contemptuous idiomatic interjection inviting someone to move elsewhere. They were making a bit of a disturbance, so I told them to get on their bikes or I'd phone the police. One implication nowadays is that the person addressed is too poor to possess a car. The expression gained notoriety in 1981 in a period of high unemployment when the UK employment secretary appeared to tell unemployed people to get on their bikes and go looking for work. Similar to **push off!**

on your marks! prepare to begin something or to compete. They told us to get on our marks, and the first person to answer the question correctly would win the competition. From the racing sequence of starters' orders: 'On your marks, get set, go!' Compare **fingers on buzzers** and **up to the mark**.

ONCE. once and for all finally (the idea being that one may then drop the subject); now and from this time onwards. Kindly get it into your head once and for all that I don't enjoy your company. An intensifier, used for emphasis.

once in a blue moon very rarely. I used to visit London regularly, but nowadays I only go there once in a blue moon. From the notion that one seldom if ever sees a blue moon.

once in a lifetime on the rarest and therefore most special occasions, opportunities, etc. He knew it was the sort of wonderful opportunity that only comes once in a lifetime. Also common as an adjective: **once-in-a-lifetime** special. They're offering the winners a once-in-a-lifetime holiday of a cruise round the world.

once in a while occasionally. I don't know her all that well but once in a while we meet for coffee and a chat.

once-over cursory inspection. It seemed like a nice enough apartment, but I only gave it a quick once-over.

once seen/heard (never forgotten) memorable. George met Alice in Florence and it was a once-seen-never-forgotten business; he was to love her for the rest of his life. An often ironical catch-phrase.

once too often once again, and with dangerous results which may one day prove fatal. He drove very recklessly, overtaking on blind bends. Beyond Perth he made to overtake once too often, and crashed the car.

once upon a time once (at the start of a story, especially for children); a long time ago. Once upon a time there were three bears and their names were Daddy Bear, Mummy Bear and Baby Bear. Your grandfather went to that school once upon a time. This phrase is one of the traditional and most popular conventions for signalling the start of a story, and it goes back at least as far as the 16th century.

ONE. one-armed bandit gambling machine, with one arm which is pulled by the player. There was a row of one-armed bandits at the back of the snooker hall.

one eye on keep a part of one's attention on. She was enjoying the book but she kept one eye on the baby while she read.

one fell swoop a single terrible stroke, blow, movement, etc. The entire building seemed to collapse at one fell swoop. The metaphor is of a bird of prey swooping pitilessly and unerringly on its victim. Shakespeare uses the expression in *Macbeth* iv.3, when Macduff laments the murder of his family at Macbeth's hands: 'What! all my pretty chickens and their dam at one fell swoop!'

one fine day once; sometime in the future. He's always spending money at present, but one fine day he'll wake up and discover there's none left.

one foot in the grave feeble, unwell; literally, half dead; about to die. I think he's got one foot in the grave, he looks so pale, drawn and very tired. A cliché, sometimes jocular. The standard simile would be 'like death warmed up'.

one for someone who likes/favours something. I've never been one for lying sunbathing on hot beaches.

one hell of a/helluva exceptional, terrible, dreadful. They had one helluva fight last night. Emphatic Americanism.

one-horse town/operator small-time, provincial in outlook, culturally challenged place/person. Who wants to stay in a one-horse place like that? From the American frontier.

one in the eye (for) a serious setback. Blogg's building plans got one in the eye last night when planning permission was withdrawn.

one-night stand short-lasting sexual liaison. Watch that lad, Maggie, he's had more one-night stands than you can count. A euphemism, the original reference was to a one-night theatrical performance.

one of us originally an imputation of homosexuality, the expression was hijacked in the 1980s by the right wing of Margaret Thatcher's Conservative Party – and thus widened in its frame of reference. I don't think he's one of us – his views are far too wet. Non-initiates of whichever grouping would say 'one of those/them'.

one over the eight drunk. Don't give him any more to drink – he's already had one over the eight. This old-fashioned euphemism seems to suggest that it is safe to drink up to eight pints of beer, or perhaps eight measures of spirits, but that one is drunk and incapable thereafter. Compare **over the limit**.

one sandwich short of a picnic not very bright; or (in PC language) intellectually challenged. I didn't need to speak with him for long to realise he might just be one sandwich short of a picnic. Compare **not all there; not the sharpest tool in the box; tuppence off the shilling**; etc.

one small step for man any scientific or social achievement. The discovery of an antidote to AIDS would certainly be one more small step for man. Sometimes jocular: He decided it was time to take one small step for man and get home for supper. Derived from astronaut Neil Armstrong's famous 1969 quotation when he was the first man to step on the moon: 'One small step for man, one giant leap for mankind.'

one step forward(, two steps back) making questionable progress. Sometimes I wonder if this one-step-forward-two-back business is getting us anywhere. From the title of a book (1904) by Lenin.

one-track mind obsessive or restrictive outlook. The boy's car-mad; he has a one-track mind and can talk about little else. From gramophone records, compare **in a groove/rut**.

one-two 1. double punch. Fortunately he'd not forgotten how to land a good old one-two, and soon his assailant was sprawling on the floor. From boxing. 2. termination of something. The planning department weren't keen on the development and now they've officially given it the one-two. Similar to **thumbs down** or **bum's rush**.

one up (on) advantageous position (over). She loves to be one up on everyone else with the latest gossip. A back formation from the 1960s noun 'one-upmanship'. Compare **score points (on someone)**.

one-upmanship art of keeping one up on or ahead of one's opponents or acquaintances, fairly or unfairly. Bill is quite fond of disparaging his colleagues' efforts – it's all part of his strategy of careful one-upmanship.

one way or another somehow; by one of several possible methods. He decided that one way or another he had to raise the alarm. Compare **by hook or by crook**.

ONE-WORD IDIOM

One-word idioms do not fall within the scope of this book. But it is worth remembering that many words, even the most apparently neutral, carry idiomatic as well as literal meanings. I recall in this context asking a Japanese student of English in Honolulu 'how he was finding Hawaii?' He looked at me in puzzlement, and replied that he had come to Hawaii by plane. He failed to realise that 'find' was being used idiomatically, just as I failed to appreciate that such use of 'find' would 'throw' him (another example!).

Sometimes a word has a particular idiomatic gloss in the context of a specific sub-culture, entering the wider language as *slang*; or has an etymology which has led to an idiomatic usage. A handful of examples follow.

anorak: person with an excessive interest in some derisory activity, like trainspotting.

bling: items used for jazzing up one's outfit – bracelets, necklaces, earrings, trinkets, etc.

bottle: courage.

fleshpots: luxurious and sensual delights. (According to the Bible, located in Egypt.)

game: willing. (As in 'Are you game for taking on this project?' Or 'Are you up for it?')

gay: homosexual.

google: search for something, not necessarily on the Internet. (From the Internet search engine.)

hamstrung: ineffective, crippled, powerless.

into: keen on, knowledgeable about.

the limit: only just tolerable and no more.

metrosexual: straight man who like to express his feminine side, or vice versa for a woman.

OK: very acceptable; politically kosher.

online: electronic.

out: publicly homosexual.

rendition: capture and extradition of suspected terrorists, without due process. (A euphemism, from the US army.)

uptight: 1. anxious, nervous, uneasy. 2. rigidly conventional

wannabe: an aspirant or imitator

whatever: abbreviation of 'whatever you say!' (which means 'I'm not going to argue the toss').

winterval: the festive season. (The word itself was created by/for those politically correct souls who try to avoid the use of the word 'Christmas', bless them.)

With most of the above words, the original meaning has been given an additional idiomatic slant. The only new coinages are

bling, *metrosexual* and *winterval*. Some of the words have entered the spectrum of idiom in the form of buzzwords and now hang about in the hope that people will still use them. Once upon a time, to say that a homosexual person was 'gay' or 'out' was a kind of doublespeak; this is an idiomatic device still much used by officialdom, such as governments and the military establishment.

OPEN. open a Pandora's box expose unexpected difficulties in a subject, which is therefore perhaps best left unbroached. I don't think we'll open that Pandora's box tonight – let's keep it for discussion till next week. Pandora, in Greek mythology, was the first mortal woman. By opening a box which she had been explicitly instructed not to open, she let all human sorrows, ailments and diseases loose in the world. Compare **can of worms**.

open an/the account 1. arrange to borrow/deposit money in a bank, etc. He's opened an account at his local building society and is saving up to buy a house. 2. start proceedings. Illingworth was first in to bat and he opened the account for England very effectively by scoring a century. Compare **open the ball/innings**.

open and above board honest. He's a reformed character nowadays, runs a pub down in Sussex, everything open and above board. 'Above board' was originally a term from the card table or board; honest players kept their hands above this, to indicate that they were not engaged in any below-the-board skulduggery.

open-and-shut case conclusive. I don't see how he can deny the charges; the evidence against him is so conclusive that it's an open-and-shut case. The image is of a police case-book, opened at the start of an investigation and shut at its successful conclusion.

open book topic or person that is transparently

clear, easy to interpret; literally, something anyone can read. Her face is always an open book and on this occasion her embarrassment was more than obvious.

open-collar worker employee who may dress informally at his/her place of work. This is an open-collar workstation. The expression indicates a workplace where no tie is required; for example, the home-based computer screen workstation which makes few sartorial demands. An update of older 'white-collar' (= office management) and 'blue-collar' (= skilled workshop or factory floor) distinctions.

open one's eyes (to) cease to have illusions (about); become aware (of). It was her sudden weight loss which opened our eyes to her illness.

open its doors welcome, admit. The club prided itself on being a socially exclusive organisation which didn't open its doors to any old applicant for membership.

open question question which remains unanswered. For many people, the safety of nuclear energy remains a very open question.

open season 1. the period during which wild game may be killed. The open season for grouse shooting in Scotland starts on 12 August. **2. by extension**, a period during which e.g. political parties come under close scrutiny. After the various recent government scandals, it's open season for press speculation about what will emerge next.

open secret badly kept secret. It's an open secret that the new managing director is a buffoon.

open sesame any irresistible means of opening doors and overcoming opposition. He thought that his friendship with half the government would be an open sesame to getting citizenship in this country. From the story of Ali Baba and the Forty Thieves, in which the command 'open sesame' was the magic phrase for opening the door to the robbers' cave.

open the ball/innings start discussion or other proceedings. She opened the ball rather aggressively by asking if the press were still looking for a scapegoat. **Idioms originally from ballroom dancing and cricket, respectively. Compare open an/the account**.

open the door allow to start. The election of a Labour government in 1945 opened the door to the Welfare State in Britain.

open the envelope see **push the envelope**.

open the floodgates release/unleash a large volume of something. The government of South Africa are afraid to encourage refugees to come to their country, knowing they may well open the floodgates to an unimaginable invasion of desperate men, women and children. **Floodgates are opened to release water from canals, weirs, dams, etc. when there is serious danger of flooding.**

open verdict no decision, one way or another. The evidence for the prosecution was inconclusive, so the jury had to return an open verdict. **From legal procedure.**

OPPOSITE. opposite number person who opposes or marks one in team sports; person of equivalent rank and function in another business establishment, branch, etc. He gets excellent market information from his opposite number in Tokyo.

OR. or else an open-ended threat of unspecific (and therefore dire) consequences sometimes effective with small children. Sit still and keep quiet, or else!

or I'm a Dutchman indication of the speaker's disbelief. These aren't real flowers, are they – they're plastic surely, or I'm a Dutchman. **Also 'or I'll eat my hat'** (similar sense). The implication being that a Dutchman is the very last thing a good xenophobic Englishman would wish to be. Like all the other anti-Dutch idioms, this expression dates from the Anglo-Dutch wars of the 17th century.

or so approximately. They're staying with us for a month or so. I can only give you half an hour or so of my time tomorrow.

ORDER. order of the boot dismissal. He was endlessly late for work, and finally the employer got fed up with his bad time-keeping and gave him the order of the boot. **Literally, to kick someone out of a job.**

order of the day 1. agenda for discussion. All conference delegates received a detailed agenda announcing the order of the day for the various sessions. **Originally from the order-of-the-day papers listing the day's business in the British House of Commons. 2. routine; trend.** Hard work and competitive sport are the order of the day at that school. Cross-dressing and unisex clothes are the order of the day with modern kids and anything else is old hat.

OTHER. other fish to fry other commitments to attend to. They wanted me to help them move house but I had other fish to fry that weekend.

other side the spirit world; the dead. So Mr Valiant-for-Truth passed over into heaven, and the trumpets sounded for him on the other side. **The sentence is a quotation from John Bunyan's** *Pilgrim's Progress* (1678). The expression is now a slightly dated religious euphemism, indicating belief in the existence of some 'other place' to which the soul 'passes over' after death.

other/flip side of the coin contrasting arguments; usually when the bad aspects of something are articulated after the good side has been examined/discussed. Some people say 1980s Britain was an age of strong and dynamic government, but the other side of the coin was that it was also the period when the concept of the United Kingdom started to fall apart.

other things (being) equal provided circumstances remain unaltered. He said he'd love to work for us, other things being equal – I guess he meant not if we asked him to take a big drop in salary.

other woman woman with whom a man has a relationship outside his marriage. She's the typical other woman of the glossy magazines –

glamorous, wealthy and thoroughly shallow.

OUT. out-and-out thorough, complete, unmitigated. She's an out-and-out feminist and a very committed one. His appointment has been an out-and-out disaster for the club. **An intensifier, usually applied to something unpleasant, or of which the speaker disapproves.**

out cold unconscious. One well-placed blow from his stick knocked the intruder out cold.

out from under free of; out of difficulties with something/someone. He never much enjoyed working for Mr Murray and had been struggling to get out from under for a few years.

out in the cold ignored or neglected; out of the conversation/friendship. Two of the sisters get on very well with one another, but the third one was always a bit out in the cold.

out like a light fast asleep. He fell exhausted on to the bed and was out like a light before his head hit the pillow. **A standard simile.**

out of bounds private; not to be visited. The family live on the top floor of the building, which is out of bounds to visitors.

out of character untypical behaviour. He was skipping around the garden singing at the top of his voice, which was quite out of character for a man we all knew as a quiet and retiring person. **Opposite of 'in character'.**

out of circulation not in social contact. They are out of circulation most of the summer, staying at their cottage in the country.

out of commission not in regular use. These aircraft have all been taken out of commission until the problem is sorted out. **Literally, not available to be commissioned for use.**

out of condition unfit, needing fixed. The car's been sitting unused in the garage for over 10 years, so it's a bit out of condition. John got rather out of condition after all those weeks in hospital, so now he's become a keep-fit fanatic.

out of date unfashionable. Classical designs and classical architecture never go out of date, only the so-called modern stuff.

out of one's depth unable to cope with something; in an enterprise that is too hard for one to cope with. He's afraid to put too much of his money into the business, knowing how quickly he could find himself out of his depth financially. **From swimming.** Compare **keep one's head above water**.

out of one's element uncomfortable. He was a wonderful classroom teacher, but he's felt a bit out of his element since becoming a headmaster. **Compare in one's element; like a fish out of water**.

out of hand 1. unruly, uncontrollable. As soon as the teacher's back is turned, that class gets completely out of hand. Opposite of **in hand**. 2. summarily, without consideration. She was dismissed out of hand, because the boss thought she'd been dishonest.

out of one's head/skull/ (tiny)mind/bonce/ tree 1. mad, daft, unwise. You must be out of your skull if you think I've got £1,000 to give you. Compare **off one's head**. 2. an intensifier when used with words like 'fear', 'anxiety', 'worry', etc. He's been out of his mind with worry since hearing about the accident.

out of harm's way in a safe place. Let's put the whisky bottle out of harm's way and into the cupboard before John arrives: he's a dreadful boozer.

out of keeping (with) jarring, ill-matched, inappropriate. Some of his latest statements to the press are out of keeping with his known business policies.

out of line (with) inappropriate or unsuitable (for). Some of his views are way out of line with the policies of his party. **From military formation, and keeping one's place on a parade ground.** Compare **out of step**.

out of order 1. not working. He didn't get in touch with you because his telephone was out of order. 2. **out of sequence**. Because the children didn't know their alphabet most of their letter-cards were out of order. 3. **not allowed in terms of the rules.** His question was ruled out of order by the chairman of the meeting.

out of place 1. untypical. We've been trying to find out if anything out of place occurred between 2 and 5 p.m. yesterday afternoon. 2. **inappropriate, unsuitable.** I felt his comments about religion were out of place in a discussion about local politics. Compare **out of line**.

out of pocket having spent money for which one has not been reimbursed. Although his employers said they'd pay all his expenses, John was considerably out of pocket after the whole episode. Compare **in pocket**.

out of print no longer published. The book went out of print after its first edition sold out.

out of season not the growing season. Raspberries are out of season just now, so they are expensive to buy in the shops.

out of shape unfit. He's very out of shape for a boxing champion. Opposite of 'in good shape'.

out of sight 1. excellent, wonderful. The show was a phenomenal box-office success and its sales record was out of sight. 2. an exclamation, sometimes found in hippy parlance of the 1960s with US spelling 'outasight!' Both uses of this phrase have an outdated resonance.

out of sight, out of mind a person or thing that is no longer visible and is therefore soon forgotten. It was a strange thing to be present at the start of a brand new millennium, and watch the old one slip quietly out of sight and out of mind on the stroke of midnight 1999. **An old saying, still popular.** Compare **out of this world**.

out of sorts not very well. Sheila was feeling rather out of sorts this morning, so she didn't go to work today.

out of spite for malicious reasons. People do the oddest things out of spite, just because they dislike someone.

out of step not fitting in. Everyone else managed to work as a team, but John was always out of step and wanting to do something else. From the military parade ground. Compare **out of line; out of tune**.

out of stock temporarily unavailable, usually from a shop. The book's out of stock just now but we've ordered additional copies from the publisher. Compare **out of print**.

out of the Ark extremely old; antediluvian. You should have seen their car; it was like something straight out of the Ark. From the biblical story of Noah and the Flood, the comment nowadays is usually disparaging.

out of the blue from nowhere. The announcement of a general election was quite unexpected; it came right out of the blue. Literally, from the (blue) sky. When a speaker is waxing really poetic he might say 'out of the wide blue yonder'. A standard simile is 'like a **bolt from the blue'**, to indicate complete surprise. Compare **out of thin air**.

out of the/one's box uncontrollable, hyperactive, insane; drunk or drugged and acting dangerously. Will you look at that car – the driver must be out of his box! That child went completely out of the box this morning and has had to be excluded from school. Could this expression have originated with the Punch-and-Judy show?

(come) out of the closet (go) public about something. It took him many years to come out of the closet and admit his interests in the Saudi Arabian oil industry. Originally a 1960s phrase to indicate that a person made no secret of his/her homosexuality and had declared it publicly. A 'closet queen' is a secret male homosexual. One nowadays hears of all sorts of secretive persons, from 'closet thespians' (people who like to dress up?) to 'closet carnivores' (vegetarians who eat meat in secret?), as well as less secretive ones who are, quite simply, 'out'. Compare **into the open**.

out of the frying pan into the fire from one bad, or dangerous, or difficult situation to another. I enjoy James Bond movies, where the hero is forever jumping with great panache and slicked-back hair out of the frying pan of one horrendous and heart-stopping situation and into the fire of yet another cataclysmic disaster… and so on till a happy ending with the girl of his dreams and still never a hair out of place!

out of the ordinary very special; unusual. She's not bad at the job but she's nothing out of the ordinary and I'm sure we could find someone better. Often used negatively.

out of the question unacceptable, not to be considered. He asked for a pay rise but was told it was out of the question for another six months at least.

out of the running/race no longer a competitor or contender for something. In the later stages of an American election campaign most of the minor contenders drop out of the running on grounds of expense.

out of the woods not yet safe. The business may now be run on a more sensible basis, but it is not yet out of the woods by any means.

out of thin air from nowhere. Magicians in large black capes like to convince their audiences that they can conjure white rabbits out of thin air; they don't like you wondering what the large black capes are for. Sometimes 'out of the ether'. Compare also **out of the blue**.

out of this world wonderful, marvellous, of exceptional quality. The hotel, the climate, the courtesy of the people, the whole atmosphere of the place was out of this world. The original hyperbole was of 1930s US jazz coinage; compare **out of sight; something else (again)**.

out of touch not in regular contact with the latest developments. Since his retirement he's got rather out of touch with trends and fads in the industry. The reverse of **up to speed**.

out of training not fit. She's very out of training for the championships next month.

out of tune 1. not playing properly. His playing of the violin was extremely out of tune and hard on the listener's ears. 2. in contradiction; not in agreement. He's always out of tune with the other members of the committee, and always wants to do things his own way. Compare **out of step**, **sing from the same hymnsheet**.

out of turn impolitely; unexpectedly. She's one of those people who never likes to say anything out of turn. Compare **out of step, out of tune**.

out on a limb holding a view that has no support. He's got some rather odd views about life in general; on the subject of politics he's usually right out on a limb. The metaphor is of an isolated and precariously balanced animal, hanging for safety to a tree branch. Compare **stick one's neck out**.

out on one's ear dismissed abruptly and unceremoniously from one's job. Nowadays you don't get a month's notice to quit, you're at work one day and out on your ear the next.

out to lunch crazy, or out of touch. He lives in his own little world and he's been seriously out to lunch for years. Compare **legend in one's own lunchtime**.

OVER. over a barrel in an uncomfortable/ undignified/helpless position. They think they've got him over a barrel with these compromising photographs, and I'm told they're proposing to blackmail him. A 19th-century American expression, perhaps from the method once followed of emptying a half-drowned person's lungs of water – by draping the hapless victim over a barrel, which was rocked to and fro until all the swallowed water had been brought up. The fluctuations in the cost of fuel oil have refreshed this idiom recently.

over and above besides; in addition. Over and above her injuries, the poor woman was also robbed of her handbag. A **dyad**.

over and done with finished, passed/past. The war over and done with, the country tried to return to normality.

over and over (again) repeatedly. The victim was stabbed over and over and left for dead in an alley.

over someone's head 1. by by-passing reference to one's immediate superiors. The government appealed over the head of Parliament in a referendum to the people. 2. too hard for someone to understand. Most of the conversation was in rapid French and passed straight over Tom's head.

over my dead body phrase indicating extreme hostility of the speaker to some idea/proposal. Many Covenanters signed the document with their own blood, indicating that the king's ideas would be acceptable to them only over their dead bodies.

over the hill getting too old to be fully effective. We decided not to give the job to Jones, who is now getting a bit over the hill for such tough assignments. A euphemistic metaphor, to indicate that a person is now 'past his peak' and is firmly embarked 'on the downward slope' – to extend the mountaineering analogies.

over the hump past the worst or hardest bit of something. Business has been very tough for the past few years, but I think that we're over the hump at last.

over the limit drunk. The barman won't serve us any more – he says we're all over the limit. Compare the very similar **one over the eight**.

over the moon delighted. They've just asked her to join the board of directors of the company, and she's over the moon about it. A 19th-century hyperbolic cliché, perhaps under the influence of the old nursery rhyme in which the cow jumps over the moon. In Victorian picture books, this subject was usually illustrated by a drawing of an inanely happy-looking cow in mid-air.

over/under the odds more (or less) than necessary (or appropriate). He told me he paid £300,000 for that house, which I'd say was well over the odds.

over the top outrageous, out of control; exaggerated; too much. What was the point of going over the top about a few tasteless jokes? **The**

idea is often one of over-reaction, and the term itself was sometimes reduced to an abbreviation during its voguish period of use (the early 1980s). Her outfit was rather OTT for a visit to a primary school. 'Going over the top' started life as a euphemism in the horrendous context of the trenches in the First World War. See also **near the knuckle/bone**.

OVEREGG. overegg the pudding overdo something; exaggerate. A little flattery can be very effective, but Roger tends to overegg the pudding when he's telling people how wonderful they are. A baking idiom; see also **pile/lay it on (thick)**.

OVERPLAY. overplay one's hand behave over-confidently, usually through the mistaken belief that one occupies a stronger position than is actually the case. Margaret was exceedingly cool, knowing that her case was unanswerable, and she had no intention of spoiling things by overplaying her hand. From the card table.

OVERSTEP. overstep the mark behave unacceptably, usually by going too far. Press coverage of the private lives of the royal family frequently oversteps the mark.

OWN. (score) an own goal 1. damage/harm done to oneself. The terrorists failed in most respects – their cause completely forfeited public respect when they scored a spectacular own goal by blowing up two of their own membership. From football, where it is possible to score a goal against one's own side. See also **hoist on one's own petard; shoot oneself in the foot**. 2. (commit) suicide. On entering the cell the rather shaken warder found there had been another own goal there during the night. Police jargon.

Naas Library

Issue Summary

Patron: Koybasi, Arif
Id: B232***
Date: 15/02/2020 16:49

Loaned today

Item: 30028000098793
Title: Stories for children / Oscar Wilde ;
    illustrated by Charles Robinson.
Due back: 07-03-20

Item: A850849
Title: Basic mathematics / Alan Graham.
Due back: 07-03-20

Item: 30028001746085
Title: My first coding book / [Kiki
    Prottsman].
Due back: 07-03-20

Item: A851031
Title: Bloomsbury dictionary of idioms.
Due back: 07-03-20

Thank you for using self
service

P

PACK. pack a punch 1. be capable of delivering a powerful punch. They say that a kangaroo packs quite a hard punch when angry. 2. be very powerful. He drives a Lamborghini, which packs a lot of punch. As a hard-hitting and highly critical report on political corruption it was expected to pack quite a punch. A boxing-ring idiom. Compare **not pull one's punches**.

pack it in give up a job, retire. After his operation, the headmaster decided that he'd be wise to pack it in and enjoy a few years of retirement.

pack of lies lot of lies; one lie after another. The magistrate adjourned the case, saying that he wasn't going to sit there another minute listening to such an outrageous pack of lies. Formed by analogy from a pack of (52 playing) cards. Sometimes 'string/ tissue of lies'.

pack up stop or abandon an activity. When it started to rain the two teams agreed to pack up until the following morning. From First World War army slang, from packing up equipment and transporting it to another part of the battlefront – immortalised in the song 'Pack up your troubles in your old kitbag and smile, smile, smile'.

PACKED. packed like sardines tightly packed, like sardines in a tin. The huge crowd in the hall were soon packed in like sardines, and hundreds of latecomers had to be turned away. A standard simile of crowdedness.

packed out with every available seat or place taken. The show was packed out last night so they're putting on an extra performance today.

PADDLE. paddle one's own canoe act independently and reach one's own decisions unassisted. She's a big girl now and quite old enough to paddle her own canoe in a matter of that sort. Originally from the American frontier, where self-sufficiency was once essential to survival. See also **do one's own thing**.

PAIN. pain in the neck/ass/backside/butt nuisance; annoying person/thing. The idea that I'd have to write her a letter of apology was a complete pain in the neck, but I decided I'd better just get on with it.

PAINT. paint the town red have a celebration; go on a spree. Seeing it was the last day of term, they decided to paint the town red tonight. Nineteenth century American, possibly starting life with a gun-toting cowboy threat to paint the town red with the blood of anyone rash enough to get in the way of macho or drunken revellers enjoying themselves.

PALM. (have someone) in the palm of one's hand (have someone) under one's control. He has his employees in the palm of his hand, so you'll never hear a word of criticism about the business from any of them.

palm something/someone off get rid of something/someone, often on false pretences. She's bought herself a brand-new computer and palmed off her old one on me. She's palmed me off with her old computer. The expression originated in the world of conjuring tricks and 'Watch my hand' and 'Now you see it, now you don't!'

PALMY. palmy days great days. In his palmy days he earned a lot of money from advertising sports equipment. In some parts of the Middle East, it was the habit for servants to keep important people cool by fanning them with palm leaves. There may also be an echo of medieval pilgrims here. If you had made a pilgrimage to Jerusalem, surely the most exciting contemporary experience in a person's life, you used to be entitled to show this by wearing a palm leaf. Compare **salad days**.

PANIC. panic stations state of high anticipation and apprehension. It was panic stations all round when we heard that the queen was entering the building. Probably a not entirely serious back-formation from the military command, **action stations**.

PAPER. paper/gloss over the cracks conceal the problems or arguments rather than resolve them. The press statement did its best to paper over the cracks, but it was pretty obvious that the Cabinet was split on the subject. From the practice when trying to sell a house of wallpapering over any suspicious cracks in the walls.

paper tiger apparently powerful but actually feeble person. Don't worry about John; he may be a director of the business but he's only a paper tiger. From the Chinese. Among various other uncomplimentary epithets ('running dogs', 'foreign lackeys', etc.), Mao Tse-Tung described western politicians as 'paper tigers' in the 1940s.

PAR. par for the course more or less what is expected. Last week the television broke down and then the washing machine – which I'm afraid is about par for the course with us these days. From golf, where 'par' = the number of strokes a good player expects to play to complete a hole or the round. See also **below par; on a par with**.

PART. part and parcel an integral part or component. Drinking wine and smelling garlic is part and parcel of a trip to France. A common dyad, originally a legal term.

part company 1. go in different directions; break up a partnership or other relationship. Many couples nowadays part company after their children have grown up. 2. **disagree.** I agree with him about most things but on the subject of the monarchy we part company.

part of the furniture person who tends to be consistently ignored or undervalued; a supernumerary. She works in the general office where they treat her like part of the furniture, and she's such a self-effacing person that she doesn't even seem to mind. Compare **in with the bricks**.

PARTIAL. partial to fond of. He's quite partial to a large whisky and soda before his evening meal.

PARTING. parting of the ways usually an agreement between two people to disagree. After the chancellor and the prime minister fell out, there was obviously going to be a pretty swift parting of the ways. Literally, a place where one's road branches and different options present themselves. From Ezekiel xxi.21.

parting shot hostile comment made at the moment of departure. His parting shot to his former colleagues was a sarcastic, 'It's been wonderful!' From earlier times, when it was felt to be unsafe to pursue a retreating horseman too closely in case he fired a parting shot back at you over his shoulder.

PARTY. party line official point of view or policy. I was told he would be speaking in a private capacity, and that his views did not therefore represent the party line in any way. Commonest in totalitarian and one-party states.

the party's over the good times have come to an end. We had a wonderful holiday, but now the party's over and it's back to work for another six months or so.

party piece song or recitation or other publicly performed act. She's only seven years old, and now she's going to do her party piece up on the big stage – so give her a big clap.

party pooper spoil sport; person who cannot be relied on to encourage pleasurable social interaction. They refrained from telling John about the planned event, knowing him to be something of a party pooper. Compare **damp squib**.

PASS. pass an opinion offer a critical comment, say what one thinks. I've read your novel but I'm not going to pass an opinion on it.

pass as/for something appear to be something that one isn't. In the old days of apartheid in South Africa, it was a crime for a Coloured person to pass as white.

pass away die. I have the sad duty to tell you that your father passed away yesterday. A euphemism, sometimes 'pass on'.

pass belief/comprehension not be believable. His capacity for drinking gin passes belief; anyone else would have been sozzled two hours ago.

pass muster stand up to critical inspection; meet a required standard. This is very shoddy workmanship and it will have to be redone before it passes muster. From the military parade ground.

pass out 1. faint. The hall was so hot that several members of the audience passed out. 2. graduate from a military college, etc. He won every prize available and passed out top of his year. An Americanism, from the ritual of the 'passing-out parade'.

pass someone over fail to promote someone and promote instead a more junior person. Jones has been passed over several times so it doesn't really distress him any more.

pass something/someone off pretend that something is something else. He passes her off as his wife. The episode was passed off as a bit of joke.

pass the buck not accept responsibility by trying to shift it to another person. The press are trying to find out which member of the government is responsible, but everyone passes the buck on to the next person. When the 'buck-passing' can go no further up the hierarchy, the person at the top of the heap often announces with a tinge of smugness, 'The buck stops here.' The whole concept is based on an old American custom: passing a buckthorn knife, or a dollar coin (also called a 'buck') as a way of keeping track of whose turn it was to deal during a bout of betting.

pass (round) the hat collect money. After the war, the relief agencies had to pass round the hat in order to start funding the reconstruction of the country. A begging metaphor.

pass the time of day exchange social chit-chat with someone. We meet from time to time at the local pub and pass the time of day over a couple of beers.

pass something up not accept. Because of his father's illness he's just had to pass up the opportunity of a good job in Japan.

PAST. past one's best no longer at the peak of one's powers. She tried to make a political comeback last year, but everyone knew she was well past her best by then. Also 'past it'.

past master proven expert. Her shortbread biscuits are the best in the world; she's a past master at baking.

past one's sell-by date no longer in prime condition. Several of the players looked well past their sell-by date and ripe only for imminent retirement. The original reference was to the sell-by date mark carried on consumable goods. Compare **on the shelf; run to seed; shelf life**.

PAT. pat on the back gesture of encouragement. Even the best-motivated people like to get a pat on the back once in a while for a good piece of work.

PATCH. patch (something) up resolve (differences), settle (a quarrel). I wish they'd stop grizzling at each other and patch it up.

PATIENCE. patience is a virtue usually a comment on the need for patience. He was all for charging on with the work head-first, but I told him to take it easy and remember that patience is a virtue. The first line of a popular verse saying. The full quotation is 'Patience is a virtue,/Possess it if you can./It's seldom found in woman/And never found in man.'

patience of Job unusual forbearance or long-suffering. It takes the patience of Job to be a good school-teacher. From the biblical patriarch. Compare entry below.

(try the) patience of a saint (test) a person of great forbearance. That child simply cannot concentrate for more than two minutes, so he would try the patience of a saint. Compare previous entry.

PAVE. pave the way for make it more likely that something will happen. Watt's experiments with the kettle paved the way for the invention of the steam engine. Also 'prepare the ground' (same sense).

PAY. pay a visit visit the lavatory; urinate. He'll be back in two minutes; he's just gone to pay a visit. A euphemism; sometimes 'use the facilities'.

pay attention (to) look and listen carefully to something. Please pay attention to what I'm about to tell you.

pay someone back (in his own coin) treat someone in the same way as they have treated you. There's no taking sides in a civil war – first one side commits atrocities, then the other side pays the first lot back in their own coin. Compare **turn the other cheek**.

pay dirt pay very little. I wouldn't work for a skinflint like that – he pays dirt. An Americanism of the 1880s, from the days of gold prospecting and panning through basins of dirt.

pay dividends bring advantages. He was always very nice to the old lady, a policy which paid surprising dividends for him later on. A metaphor from capital invested in a successful business: a 'dividend' being the name of the payment from one's investment.

pay one's (last) respects visit someone who is unwell (or near death). Since I was visiting the hospital anyway on other business, it cost me nothing to pay my respects to Mrs Brown in Ward 15.

pay the piper (and call the tune) pay the costs incurred (and therefore be in a position to dictate what is to be done). It's not for me to dictate policy in this matter, since I'm not the person who's paying the piper. 'He who pays the piper calls the tune' is a saying from the days when the clan chiefs had a private piper in their entourage who played music to them. See also **call the tune**.

pay through the nose pay too much, pay a lot, pay sweetly. They had to pay through the nose to spend a weekend at Claridges, but they can afford it so why worry. The expression may derive from the nose tax which the Vikings are said to have imposed on the native Irish around Dublin when they colonised that area in the 9th century –

those failing to pay taxes were supposed to have their noses slit. Compare **rip someone off**.

pay one's (own) way pay one's own costs without getting into debt. His proudest boast was that he could pay his own way, and that he would never be a bother to anyone.

PECKING. pecking order place in the hierarchy. They never consult me on matters of policy, but then I'm right at the bottom of their sad little pecking order. The original scientific research into rank in animal behaviour was done in the 1920s with domestic hens. Compare **food chain**.

PEEPING. Peeping Tom man who secretly watches people undress, etc. There was something about his face which had 'Peeping Tom' written all over it – probably his rather bulging staring eyes. According to legend, Lady Godiva rode naked through the streets of Coventry, having persuaded the citizens not to look at her. Only one man broke the promise – Peeping Tom – and he was struck blind for looking at her.

PEG. peg to hang something on topic, etc. which gives one a pretext for expressing critical views, etc. The government is ferociously unpopular and all the recent ministerial scandals have given its many critics several convenient pegs to hang their anger on.

PENNY. the penny drops understand. At first she failed to understand what was going on, but after a few minutes the penny dropped. From the long-gone sound of a penny dropping in a metal slot, e.g. to open a toilet door, tell one's weight on a weighing machine, etc.

penny for them/penny for your thoughts tell me what you're thinking. She had been staring away into the distance for several minutes with a frown on her face, so she jumped when I said to her, 'A penny for them!' Compare **brown study**.

penny wise (and pound foolish) save small amounts of money but be rashly lavish with large amounts. They think nothing of buying a

£30,000 car, and then they 'forget' to pay their road tax! Talk about penny wise! **A saying. Compare the traditional wisdom of 'Look after the pennies and the pounds will look after themselves.'**

PEOPLE. people (who live) in glass-houses (shouldn't throw stones) people shouldn't criticise others for having the same faults as they themselves have. The minister conducted a campaign against unmarried mothers, and then it was discovered that he had two illegitimate children of his own; it was left to the opposition to suggest to him that people in glass-houses were not in an ideal position for throwing stones. **The complete sentence is a proverbial saying. Compare pot calling the kettle black.**

PEP. pep talk talk with people to give them encouragement or raise their morale. At half-time the captain gave his flagging team a very animated pep talk which sent them back for the game's second half with renewed purpose, **i.e. he managed to 'pep them up'.**

PERFORM. perform miracles be very good (at something). Every time he gets the ball at his feet he performs miracles of attacking football. **A favourite journalistic hyperbole.**

PERISH. perish the thought may the thought fail to become fact. Perish the thought of an antisocial man like that ever becoming a neighbour of mine. **An apostrophic figure of speech. Compare don't (even) go there.**

PET. pet aversion/hate something one loves to hate. She's a very good journalist on most subjects, but her pet hate is dogs and their impact on public pavements not to mention her shoes. **An oxymoron. Compare blind spot.**

PHRASAL VERB

Phrasal verbs are often highly idiomatic. They are made up of a simple verb followed by a preposition or an adverb such as *across*, *by*, *of*, *to*, etc. These often combine to give a single meaning not easily guessable from the meaning of the separate components.

Look at these pairs. Note that only the second example in each pair is an idiomatic phrasal verb. The first example is a simple verb plus prepositional phrase.

1. They *ran / up* the street.
2. They *ran up* an enormous bill. [*ran up* = incurred]

1. She *looked / up* the chimney.
2. She *looked up* the dictionary. [*looked up* = consulted]

1. She *came / across* the street to tell us her news.
2. She *came across* an old, locked trunk in her attic. [*came across* = discovered]

1. He *sent* the parcel *up* to me by courier.
2. In their act, they *send up* various prominent politicians. [*send up* = satirise]

Phrasal verbs are a feature of colloquial and spoken English rather than of formal or written language. There are thousands of phrasal verbs in English, and to list them would double the length of this book. The main coverage of phrasal verbs in this dictionary is where they feature as elements in a larger idiom. See for example the entries for *get away with murder, get/ put someone's back/dander up, get on like a house on fire, get up (a good head of) steam, knock it off, lash out on something, rip someone off*, etc.

Recent – and with luck temporary – additions to the lexicon include phrasal verbs like *sex up* (= embellish data), *dumb up* (= confuse with science), *big up* (= enlarge), *fess up* (= admit), *listen up* (= listen very carefully). The 'up' part of these phrases is often superfluous: but 'up' is going through a hyper-productive phase.

PICK. pick a quarrel/fight start a quarrel deliberately. Like many bullies, he enjoys picking quarrels with younger or smaller children.

pick and choose select very carefully. He likes the local shops where he can pick and choose exactly what he wants; he says the supermarket's for people who take what they're given. **A dyad.**

pick someone's brains get useful information from someone. Like all well-informed people, he spends quite a lot of time picking other people's brains. I'd like to pick your brains about Normandy.

pick/knock/poke holes in critically demolish. It is not hard to pick holes in most of her political arguments.

pick on someone 1. choose someone for an unpopular job. Why do you always have to pick on me to wash the dishes? **2. speak angrily or critically to someone; bully someone.** He likes to have someone to pick on when he's in a bad mood.

pick up fag-ends try to eavesdrop on other people's conversations. He managed to pick up a few fag-ends of their discussion, but not enough to get the full picture. **The 'fag-end' was an end section of cloth or yarn, so the term originated in the context of weaving.**

pick up the tab pay the bill. When there's a major famine, as there has been in sub-Saharan Africa, the aid agencies send in what they can straight away, and later on there is time to squabble about who is going to pick up the tab.

pick/take up the threads/pieces return to one's normal routines; restart projects or assignments from where one left off. After the volcano erupted, it took the villagers quite a long time to pick up the threads of their life again. **From sewing.**

pick one's way go carefully. Although badly injured, he managed to pick his way across the minefield to the main road.

pick/choose/weigh one's words speak with care and precision. He usually speaks rather slowly, as if picking his words and trying not to cause any misunderstandings.

PICKLED. pickled/pissed as a newt very drunk. Don't let John near the car – he's pickled as a newt. **Standard similes of inebriation.**

PICTURE. picture of health looking very fit and well. A month ago she was very ill, and yet today she's the picture of health.

PIE. pie eyed blind drunk. Most weekends he seems to get completely pie eyed. **Originally American. Also British English 'plastered' (same sense), which originally meant 'soothed', as with a plaster on a wound.**

pie in the sky hollow promises of something that is unlikely to happen. At election time the air is thick with pie in the sky, which is why nobody believes a word of what the politicians say. **From a poem by the American Labor organiser Joe Hill, in his _Songs of the Workers_ (1911): 'You'll get pie in the sky when you die. (That's a lie.)' Compare jam tomorrow; promise (someone) the earth/moon.**

PIECE. piece of cake very easy task. I wouldn't say building my own house has been exactly a piece of cake, but the job's done now. **Compare money for jam/old rope, cushy number.**

piece of one's mind an angry scolding. He'll get a piece of my mind if he tries that trick again.

PIG. pig in a poke something acquired without inspection and which may therefore be worthless. They took the house for a month without knowing a thing about it, so it was a bit of a pig in a poke for them and I hope they won't regret it. **From agriculture: you would want to inspect a pig, etc. very carefully before buying it, and you'd be very unwilling to buy one wrapped up in a bag or 'poke' in case it only had three legs. Compare sell/buy a pup; let the cat out of the bag.**

pig-in-the-middle person who is caught between two squabbling factions. The blue berets of the United Nations have had to play pig-in-the-middle in a number of serious military crises, from

Bosnia to Zaire. From a game for three children where the child in the middle has to intercept a ball thrown between the two other children.

pig's ear a botch, mess or muddle. I don't know where you found that plumber but he made an absolute pig's ear of our bathroom. From the 16th-century proverb, 'You can't make a silk purse out of a sow's ear'.

PIGS. pigs might fly ironic expression of incredulity, meaning impossible things might happen. I suppose pigs might fly and the next board meeting will be a pleasant and harmonious session, i.e. it's normally an acrimonious affair. Compare **pull the other one**.

PILE. pile/lay it on thick overstate something usually in order to flatter, invoke generosity, etc. He piled it on as thick as he could and told her that she was the greatest prime minister of the 20th century and that her name would be written in all the history books for a hundred years. Sometimes 'pile/lay it on with a trowel'. Compare next entry; also see **overegg the pudding**.

pile/put on the agony invent a good sob-story to make people sorry for one's problems. He's really piling on the agony about his wooden leg, and never having worked in 20 years, and living in one room with a wife and 16 children. Is it possible for one man to have so much grief? Compare previous entry.

PILLAR. pillar of society/state etc. person who helps to support society/state etc. just as a pillar supports a building. The 12 disciples of Jesus were the pillars of the early Christian church. A dehumanising metaphor, in which people are given non-human characteristics. The expression 'pillar of society' is found in Milton's *Paradise Lost* (1667) and is also the title of an Ibsen play (1877).

pillar/tower of strength supportive person. He's been her tower of strength for many years and helped her face all her ordeals.

PIN. pin back one's ears 1. listen carefully. Listen to this, he said, so I pinned back my ears. I just sat there with my ears pinned back and listened to the news. **2. run very fast, usually for the finishing line, goal line, etc.** Guscott managed to catch a very low pass, and then all he had to do was pin back his ears and make for the line.

pin one's hopes/faith on rely on. He's been ill for some time and is pinning his hopes on a successful operation.

pin something on someone prove someone was responsible for something. The police tried to pin the crime on John Brown. The image is of having his criminality firmly appended to his lapel, for all to see.

pin-up girl glamorous-looking young woman, or a picture of one which is sometimes to be seen pinned up on a wall. To say she wasn't exactly a pin-up girl was an understatement – she was downright ugly. Nowadays a politically incorrect term.

you could hear a pin drop it is completely quiet. Not a bird moved, there was not a breath of wind in the trees. So I sat there in solitary silence, and could have heard a pin drop.

PINCH. pinch and scrape economise. By careful pinching and scraping we usually manage to afford a good summer holiday. A dyad. Compare **make (both) ends meet**.

pinch someone's lines/lyrics anticipate someone's jokes, comments, etc. I had planned to tell you the story of our rescue, but I believe John has pinched my lines. Compare **steal someone's thunder, take the words out of someone's mouth**.

PINK. pink pound/dollar/euro/yen a reference to the gay economy. The hotel was gay-friendly, and owed much of its commercial success and profitability to the strength of the pink pound. We had the grey pound/dollar, etc. (for the senior citizenry) as an earlier colour-coded currency reference. The pink triangle was the Nazi symbol for homosexuals and has now been adopted as the international symbol of the gay rights movement.

PINS. pins and needles tingling or prickling feeling in the arms or legs, often following numbness. He lay in the same position for so long that he got pins and needles in his elbow. A dyad.

PIPE. pipe down be quiet. He told the class to pipe down or they'd disturb the children next door. Also 'pipe up', with the opposite sense: two phrasal verbs.

pipe dream an imaginary idea which one cannot carry out. She has a pipe dream of getting her health back and making a visit to America, but I'm afraid it's only that. Originally American, from the hallucinatory visions conjured up when smoking opium. Compare **flight(s) of fancy**.

PIPPED. pipped at the post just beaten and no more, usually in the late or final stages of something. Everyone thought he'd won the presidential election but Mr Truman pipped him at the post at the last minute. The 'post' was the finishing post of a race. Also 'beaten by a short head'. See also **beat someone to the post**.

PLAIN. plain as a pikestaff obvious. His hostility to the proposal was as plain as a pikestaff. The original sense of 'plain' was 'ordinary-looking' though nowadays we tend to give it the other meaning of 'obvious'. A pikestaff was a plain-looking firearm, usually with no scrolling or other ornamentation carved on its shaft. Similar to 'clear as the nose on someone's face'.

plain clothes not in uniform. They don't look like soldiers to me; they're all in plain clothes. Also used adjectivally: **plain-clothes** He's a plain-clothes policeman.

plain Jane unglamorous, or not very good-looking person. She works hard at her job and considers herself to be a bit of a plain Jane.

plain sailing easy; progress without problems. You've climbed the hard bit of the rock-face now, so the rest will be plain sailing. From navigation, when sailing used calculations based on planes (note spelling difference) and the assumption that the earth was flat.

plain speaking expressing the truth without considering whether or not it will hurt someone's feelings, etc. It is sometimes necessary to do some plain speaking if one has any regard for honesty and simple facts. Compare **call a spade a spade; straight answer**. For the reverse of plain speaking, see the boxed article headed **euphemism** (page 72).

PLAY. play along with someone/play ball with someone agree to cooperate with someone. They agreed to play along with his plans so long as he agreed to help them with theirs.

play someone at his/her own game behave towards others in the same unfair way as they have behaved towards you. She made several rather catty and cutting comments, but I refrained from retaliating and playing her at her own game.

play ball cooperate. Remember to play ball with the boss and tell him what a wonderful business he runs. Originally American from the 1900s, the baseball field was the genesis of this term.

play something by ear 1. perform a piece of music from memory and without reference to a musical score. He can't read a word of music, but he'll play you anything by ear. 2. improvise one's reaction or response to events as they develop. I'm unable to develop a game plan for the campaign, since there are so many imponderables – we'll just have to play it by ear. Compare **ad hoc; suck it and see**.

play one's cards right/well act shrewdly; make the most of one's chances of success. It's a difficult situation, but if he plays his cards right he might well emerge as their new boss. Compare **not put a foot wrong/out of line; keep one's nose clean**.

play cat and mouse with someone amuse oneself by teasing or confusing a subordinate or someone otherwise in one's power. Her boss has been playing cat and mouse with her for several weeks now and she's no longer quite sure what he's after.

play devil's advocate test an argument by arguing the opposite point of view. My boss likes to play devil's advocate with all my proposals, just to test their soundness – not a very creative role, I'd have thought. From a medieval Catholic Church procedure when the beatification or canonisation of a saint was in process. The devil's advocate or 'advocatus diaboli' had to oppose the candidacy and to put the devil's point of view against the 'advocatus Dei' or God's advocate.

play something down avoid making a big issue or story about something. Once upon a time the press would play down royal scandals, but not nowadays.

play ducks and drakes squander, or use selfishly to suit oneself. He lost his job for playing ducks and drakes with the company's funds, i.e. he was using it for his own purposes. Perhaps from the idle pastime of 'ducks and drakes', or skiffing flat stones across a surface of water to see how often you can make them skip.

play fair play without cheating or bias. She told me I wasn't playing fair if I expected her to do all the housework.

play fast and loose act irresponsibly and deceitfully, especially in matters of the heart. Don Giovanni was never happier than when he was playing fast and loose with a young lady's feelings. A dyad, perhaps from a 16th-century fairground game called Fast and Loose.

play someone for a sucker assume someone is not very bright, e.g. by cheating them. The villains thought they could play Popeye for a sucker, but they weren't reckoning on our wily friend. A 'sucker' is a person who is easily deceived or cheated. An Americanism.

play for time prevaricate; delay a decision in the hope that conditions will improve. Desperate people always play for time, and the condemned man is always hoping for a reprieve. Probably from cricket, and a defensive game played to save an innings.

play gooseberry act as chaperone to two lovers. The pair of them kindly asked me to share their holiday but I didn't want to play gooseberry. There is an obsolete idiom, 'play old gooseberry' meaning 'to cause havoc', which may once have been connected (spoiling lovers' plans?).

play hard to get flirt; make oneself inaccessible to a person's efforts at friendship perhaps in order to get them to redouble their efforts. She's one of those rather flirtatious people who always seem to be playing hard to get.

play/wreak havoc damage, devastate, cause confusion. The floods played havoc with the harvest last year. 'Havoc' was from a French word meaning 'plunder', and gave the medieval shout 'Cry havoc!' – an invitation to plunder and pillage for the spoils of war. See *Julius Caesar* iii.1: 'Cry, "Havoc!" and let slip the dogs of war.'

play into someone's hands give an advantage to someone, usually by doing something foolish. By riding into the pass he was playing into the hands of his enemies – because they were lying in wait to ambush him there.

play it cool conduct oneself without emotion. Try not to get too worked up and distressed; just play it cool and pretend you've got all the answers.

play politics scheme or try to manoeuvre events, circumstances, etc. to one's advantage. I don't like to see people play politics with the problems of others.

play safe act carefully by avoiding any potentially risky action. The weather conditions were atrocious, so we decided to play safe and postpone the trip for another 24 hours.

play second fiddle/string take a subordinate role. She loves to organise everything, and she's not good at playing second fiddle to someone else.

From music, and the organisation of the orchestra into first and second violins.

play the field choose (especially a partner) from a wide range of options. David never married because he enjoyed playing the field too much.

play the fool act like a fool, behave immaturely. He never seems to tire of playing the fool. The Fool of course had a walk-on part in most early dramas and morality plays. Compare **act the goat**.

play the game act honourably or fairly. Tom is always spreading rumours about Betty and I think that's hardly playing the game, is it? From the concept of fair play on the sports field.

play to one's strengths concentrate one's efforts at doing what one is best at. The best advice in an interview is to play to your strengths and make no reference to the things you're not so good at.

play to the gallery try to gain popularity by monopolising the attention, usually of the least discriminating part of an audience. He may be very good at grabbing attention and playing to the gallery, but he's useless at doing an honest day's work. From theatre, where the cheapest seats used to be in the gallery. Compare **ham it up; sob story/stuff**.

play truant/hookey be absent from school, etc. without leave. In the hottest summer weather, lots of schoolkids play truant for days on end. The American version is 'play hookey', as readers of *Tom Sawyer* (1876) will recall. 'Hookey' meant pinching something by means of a long hook and absconding with it.

play one's trump/best card produce the argument/tactic that achieves victory, wins the debate, etc. Their tactics were impeccable, and they didn't produce their trump card till the last minutes of the game – when it was too late for the opposition to fight back effectively. From playing cards.

play with fire take great and dangerous risks. You are playing with fire if you don't pay your debts to the Mafia. A very old metaphor.

PLAYED. played out out of fashion. Like most TV chat shows that have run for years and years, this one's got a bit played out and needs to be replaced soon. Compare **clapped out**.

PLEASE. please/suit oneself invitation to consider options and do one's own thing, do what one wants to do. Come with us to the party, or stay at home and relax: suit yourself. Also 'do as you like' (similar sense).

PLEASED. pleased as Punch extremely pleased with oneself, often to the point of smugness. The smugness may derive from recollections of Mr Punch in the Punch-and-Judy shows, who is always intensely pleased with himself for no very obvious reason. Who did we meet at the garden party but Lady MacLean, looking as pleased as Punch with herself. A standard simile, as is 'like the cat that got the cream' (same sense). To remove the overtone of smugness, one might say 'pleased as a dog with two tails', which is another standard simile.

PLOT. the plot thickens a facetious exclamation, meaning that things are getting more complicated and interesting. It seemed a straightforward murder case, with the victim's sister the obvious suspect. Suddenly the plot thickened when the identity of the victim's sister became known. A quotation from a 17th-century play. Compare **dirty work (at the crossroads)**.

PLOUGH. plough a lone/lonely furrow work in isolation, without help or support. No, we seldom see James; he ploughs a lone furrow and keeps himself to himself. From farming.

plough something back return something; put something back. Most of the profits are ploughed back into the business. From farming, where spoilt crops were often ploughed back into the field to act as fertiliser.

PLUCK. pluck/screw up one's courage force oneself (usually to do something one fears or shuns doing). He's been secretly in love with her for years, but never managed to screw up his courage and tell her. A recent phrasal verb equivalent would be **psych oneself up**.

PLUM. plum in one's mouth posh or noticeably upper-class accent. Who is it that teaches these folk to talk with a plum in their mouth? From the observation that a sour-tasting plum often purses the eater's lips in a similar way to the lips of a posh speaker.

POCKET. pocket/swallow one's pride behave humbly or with contrition. If you've made a silly mistake, the best thing to do is pocket your pride, admit it openly and apologise.

POETIC. poetic justice appropriate and unexpected punishment for wrongdoing, as if by divine providence. It was poetic justice that the stolen car was hit by a falling tree during the storm, and that the thief ended up in hospital. From the idea that the poet is able to play God and make anything happen in his poetic creations.

POINT. point blank bluntly; frankly. She told him point blank that she couldn't stand the sight of him. The 'blank' (French 'blanc' = white) was the white spot at the centre of an archery target. If you pointed at the blank, you aimed directly at the centre of the target. Compare **come/get to the point**.

(this precise) point/moment in time a waffly way of saying 'now', particularly favoured by people like politicians when they are trying to think what to say and/or being economical with the truth. The government has no plans at this precise point in time to join the European Monetary System.

point of no return critical moment in a process or action, beyond which one can only proceed in a forward direction. Would she risk all and put her savings into the business, or would she draw back and play safe? This was her first big moment of decision, the first real point of no return of her career. The idiom originated about 1940 in the early days of long-distance flying across oceans, etc. The 'point of no return' was the technical term

for the plane's location on the map when it was no longer possible for it to return to take-off point because of lack of fuel. Compare **in for a penny(, in for a pound)**.

point the finger blame or accuse someone. Most economic commentators now point the finger at the government for failing to invest in the country's infrastructure.

POISON. poison-pen letter nasty or threatening (and often anonymous) letter. There's only one thing to do with poison-pen letters – take them to the police. It is the content of the letter which is poisonous.

POISONED. poisoned chalice an apparently attractive option, etc. but one which will lead to an unpleasant outcome. It looked like a good job offer at the time, but it turned out to be a poisoned chalice. From fairy tales, in which the wicked fairy (well disguised) presents the hero/ine with a sumptuous goblet or chalice containing a sleeping potion or worse.

POKE. poke/push/shove one's nose in interfere; pry. I wouldn't say too much about our plans in front of Mrs Bloggs, because she'll immediately want to poke her nose in them. The image is based on an animal like a pig or dog, nosing into something.

POKER. poker face expressionless face, which conceals one's feelings. She just sat there with her straight, unblinking poker face, so you couldn't really say whether she was happy or sad. From the card-game of poker, where one shows no facial expression that could suggest whether one has been dealt a good or a bad hand.

POLE. pole position favourite position in a contest. According to most of the press comment, Mr X is in pole position for the job of foreign secretary. From car racing: the car nearest the starter's flagpole occupies this position.

POLES. be poles apart have very different views on something. You'd never think they both belonged to the same political party – their views on just about everything are poles apart. **The literal reference is to the great distance between the North and South Poles.**

POLITICAL. political correctness acceptability to contemporary orthodox thinking. Complimenting her on her smart outfit, he was rewarded with a withering expression which told him that her sense of political correctness took exception to all such comments. Sometimes 'political correctitude' is found, or adjectival phrases like 'politically kosher'. See also **positive discrimination**.

POOH. **pooh-pooh something** deride or dismiss something from serious consideration. I wouldn't automatically pooh-pooh all his ideas, if I were you. A reduplication. A single 'Pooh!' was an exclamation of impatience or contempt in the 16th century. The 17th-century reduplication started life as a noun for a person addicted to making this kind of utterance, not becoming a verb till the 19th century.

POOR. **poor man's (something)** usually refers to what is perceived to be an inferior version of the real thing. We were eating bread and cheese and enjoying a sort of poor man's beanfeast. Facetious analogy has also given us 'thinking man's (something)' e.g. She was described in the article – rather unfairly – as being the thinking man's strumpet.

poor relation person or thing with less prestige or status than another with which it is being compared. Someone has described the short story as a sort of poor relation of the novel. From the idea of an impoverished family relative.

POP. **pop one's clogs** die. We went round to see the old man last night only to discover that he'd popped his clogs earlier that afternoon. A lighthearted euphemism, implying that after the person's death, his shoes or 'clogs' and other personal effects are pawned ('popped').

pop the question propose marriage. It wasn't till she started seeing someone else that John popped the question and asked her to marry him. Compare **make an honest wo/man (of someone)**.

pop up appear. You never quite know when he's going to pop up – but it's usually when he wants something.

PORT. **port of call** destination. It was his first visit to Cairo, so the Pyramids and the Sphinx and the street markets of Khan el Kalili were among his earliest ports of call. From the days of sailing.

POSITIVE. **positive discrimination** a politically correct contemporary form of favouritism. The Labour Party tried to bar men from contesting certain 'women-only' seats on the grounds of positive gender discrimination in favour of women. A contemporary oxymoron, the term sanctions the use of discrimination to fight discrimination. See also **political correctness**, which tends to be the unsatisfactory court of appeal in setting down what is positive and what is negative discrimination. See also **jobs for the boys**.

POSSESSION. **possession is nine parts/ points/-tenths of the law** what you have you hold; ownership of something is based on possession of it. The hotel management tell me the room has been double booked and that I have to give it up for some army general. But I too booked a room here, and I'm actually in the room, and I'm not budging, because possession is nine parts of the law. A proverb or saying.

POST. **post haste** urgently. He's had to go post haste to Argentina, where their subsidiary company is in difficulties. The term is from the old method of sending post by relay systems of messengers on horseback. These early postmen changed their horses at posthouse inns every 20 miles or so along their route. Arriving in the stable yard, they shouted 'Post haste!' This cry usually guaranteed them prompt attention, and the mail was hastened on its way.

POSTCODE. **postcode lottery** term pointing out that (even in theoretically egalitarian times like ours) one's postal address often dictates the scale or quality of the social benefits one receives. When we moved house, our home and car insurance premiums came down, and our children were in the catchment area for a much better school: that's the post-code lottery for you! As Flaubert would have said, in his *Dictionary of Received Ideas*: 'Tonner contre!' ('Fulminate against!').

POT. pot-boiler popular and commercially successful novel, without literary merit. Every Christmas for years there was a new pot-boiler from Annie S Swan or Barbara Cartland – you had to admire their industry. This compound noun derives from the now obsolete, longer idiom 'keep the pot boiling', or earn one's living.

pot calling the kettle black a saying, that somebody criticises faults or shortcomings in another person of which he is himself guilty. He's one of the most parsimonious and ungenerous people I know; so it was a case of the pot calling the kettle black when he accused John of meanness. Compare **people (who live) in glass-houses (shouldn't throw stones)**.

pot/crock of gold future wealth. I suppose we're all looking for that elusive pot of gold. From the fairy story, which located it at the end of the rainbow.

pot-shot unaimed shot or blow. I took a quick pot-shot at the galloping buffalo – there was no time to take careful aim. The original reference was to shooting something for the cooking pot, rather than to exercise one's skill as a marksman.

POUND. one's pound of flesh one's dues; money or goods owing to one. It was a particularly acrimonious divorce, with both parties insisting on every last shred of their pound of flesh. A cliché now, from Shakespeare's character of Shylock, in *The Merchant of Venice*, who says: 'The pound of flesh which I demand of him…'tis mine, and I will have it.'

POUR. pour/throw cold water on show the problems and disadvantages of something. I don't enjoy throwing cold water on other people's enthusiasms, but somebody has to point out the dangers and limitations of his plan.

pour oil on troubled waters appease or calm a turbulent situation; placate belligerents in an argument. Her presence among us seemed to pour oil on troubled waters, and there was no further friction for the rest of the meeting. The idiom is supposed to derive from the use of oil by the ancient Greeks to calm a stormy sea. See also **troubled waters**.

POWER. power behind the throne source of real authority behind the apparent authority. There's no point talking to the managing director. Believe it or not, his secretary is the real power behind the throne, so it's more important to establish good relations with her. From renaissance times, when the king's advisers behind the throne rather than the king upon it began to devise national policies. Compare **grey eminence**.

power nap a short sleep or snooze, which helps to restore and revitalise one's energy levels, usually taken during the day. Similar to 'cat nap', the Spanish call it a siesta. Jim took a quick power nap before his big meeting with the board of directors. The term was coined by James B Maas, a social psychology professor at Cornell University. Since the coining of 'power nap' we've acquired 'power walk' by analogy – thought by some onlookers to be an activity for people who lack much sense of humour.

(more) power to your elbow wish success to someone in his enterprises. She works hard and deserves her successes, and most people wish power to her elbow. From a Gaelic salutation: jocular.

POWERS. powers that be people in authority. He lost his job after he fell out with the powers that be. Biblical, as in 'The powers that be are ordained of God.' In Romans xiii.1.

PRACTISE. practise what one preaches do what one tells or encourages other people to do. He tried to teach them to know and choose right over wrong, and to practise what he preached. An old admonition.

PREACH. preach to the converted try to persuade someone who already agrees with one. The Tories seem to spend a lot of time discussing their plans with the City, which seems to me very like preaching to the converted. **Usually articulated as a simile for an act of foolishness or at least of time wasting.**

PRESENCE. presence of mind calm alertness, especially in the face of danger. His actions in rescuing the children from the burning building demonstrated great presence of mind.

PRESS. press (the) flesh shake hands formally with lots of people. Before making his speech the prime minister dutifully mingled with the party faithful, pressing flesh up and down the auditorium and accepting their best wishes. Journalese, similar to 'put oneself about'.

press the right buttons be a clever or skilful manipulator in a particular situation and achieve the outcome you want. You're not going to win your case unless you press all the right buttons. Also 'know all the right buttons to press'. Compare **tick all the boxes**.

PRESSED. pressed/pushed for something short of something. I can't speak to you now because I'm so pressed for time, but I'll phone you back this evening.

PRESS-GANGED. press-ganged into (doing something) bullied into doing something against one's wishes. He wasn't much interested in children, but he was press-ganged onto the board of governors of his local primary school. **From the 18th century, when the press gang under the command of a government officer existed to press – or force, usually against their will – men into naval or military service.**

PRETTY. pretty/nice kettle of fish disagreeable or awkward state of affairs; a lovely muddle. Often used as an exclamation, as in 'Here's a pretty kettle of fish you've got us into!', meaning 'Here's a fine mess you've got us into!' This is a pretty kettle of fish: the company bankrupt, the directors sacked and the creditors banging on the door! Apparently from a pastoral

expression used literally to describe an 18th-century picnic. Compare entry below.

pretty/fine pass ironical term, used to refer to an absurd state of affairs. Things have reached a pretty pass when a parent is not supposed to smack a disobedient child. Compare entry above.

pretty penny large amount of money. He must have paid a pretty penny for a house like that! **The word 'penny' is used as a meiosis, or understatement.**

pretty well more or less; nearly. He's pretty well finished the job, and now only has to add a few finishing touches.

PREY. prey on one's mind distress or worry one to the point that it begins to affect one's health. Over the years, the memories of his war crimes began to prey on his guilty mind.

prey to victim of. She was a prey to insomnia. **A metaphor from the world of nature, red in tooth and claw.**

PRICE. price on someone's head wanted by the police. There's been a price on his head since he robbed the bank. **A synecdoche nowadays, in civilised societies, though once upon a time the term was used literally.**

PRICK. prick the bubble deflate the hype. Most people were not surprised to see that the economic downturn had pricked the inflationary property bubble. Journalese.

prick up one's ears become attentive and listen carefully. She soon pricked up her ears when the conversation turned to her ex-husband. **From horses or dogs on the alert.**

PRIDE. (be someone's) pride and joy person or thing someone loves very much. His pride and joy is his rock garden of alpine plants. **In figurative language, a dyad, or double. Compare apple of one's eye.**

pride of place place of honour; central position. His latest acquisition, a small Picasso painting of the 'blue period', has pride of place above the mantelpiece. From medieval falconry, where the 'pride of place' was the high point or zenith from which the falcon swooped or fell on its prey.

PRIME. prime mover instigator; person initiating something. Huge teams of people were involved in the publication of the book, but there is no denying that its first mover was Professor Sinclair. From Latin, 'primum mobile', initial or original source, in medieval philosophy often meaning God.

prime of life height of one's powers. It is one of the tragedies of literature that so many great poets – like Marlowe, Shelley, Keats, Burns – died in the prime of life.

prime the pump help something to function or succeed; encourage the growth of something. The government hope that the chancellor's budget will successfully prime the pump of the nation's long-stagnant economy. From engineering.

PRIVATE. private eye/dick private detective. Philip Marlowe in the Raymond Chandler novels was one of the best-known private dicks. American English, the eye comes from the 19th-century trademark of the Pinkerton Detective Agency.

PRODUCE. produce the goods/goodies do all that is professionally expected of one; achieve the desired results. She's a very popular and professional editor, because whatever the problems, whatever the deadlines, whatever the other hassles and constraints, she always produces the goods. Also deliver the goods.

PROMISE. promise (someone) the earth/ moon make extravagant promises to someone that are unlikely to be kept. They promised him the moon to come and work for them, but needless to say they have been unable to deliver. Often used in the context of politics. Compare **pie in the sky**.

PROOF. proof of the pudding (is in the eating) proverb, meaning that the worth of an item or idea can only be properly confirmed after it has been tested or used. He used to think

he wanted to be a teacher: that was before he got into the classroom. He's less keen on the job nowadays, so the proof of the pudding has been in the eating, as you might say. Compare **put something to the proof/test**.

PROS. pros and cons arguments for and against. Marjorie is thinking of moving to a smaller house, but she may change her mind once she's gone into all the pros and cons of the matter with her lawyer.

PROVERBS AND SAYINGS

A ***proverb*** is a quotation from popular wisdom, unattributable to a particular author or thinker. It expresses an agreed truth in a memorable way. Some proverbs are very old, as we realise from their archaic language: *Judge not, that ye be not judged*. Others are recent, reminding us that they continue to be made: *If it ain't broke don't fix it*. Alliteration (*Punctuality is the politeness of princes*), assonance (*A stitch in time saves nine*) and rhyme (*A friend in need is a friend indeed*) are common devices in proverbs. They have given many idiomatic nuggets to the language, often in the form of parts of proverbs bandied about as allusions and catch-phrases. The following brief list of proverbs is the tip of a huge iceberg, the bracketed sections indicating those parts which are often dropped from speech.

All that glisters (is not gold).
All work and no play (makes Jack a dull boy).
An apple a day (keeps the doctor away).
Ask a silly question (and you'll get a silly answer).
Ask no questions (and you'll hear no lies).
Better safe than sorry.
Better late than never.
A bird in the hand (is worth two in the bush).
Birds of a feather (flock together).

A cat may look at a king.
Curiosity killed the cat.
Cut your coat (according to your cloth).
Don't count your chickens (before they're hatched).
Don't cross your bridges (till you come to them).
Don't spoil the ship (for a halfpennyworth of tar).
The early bird (catches the worm).
Empty vessels (make the most noise).
Finders keepers(, losers weepers).
Fine words butter no parsnips.
A fool and his money are soon parted.
Forewarned is fore-armed.
Give a thief enough rope (and he'll hang himself).
God helps them who help themselves.
Half a loaf is better than no bread.
He who pays the piper (calls the tune).
He who sups with the devil (should use a long spoon).
Honesty is the best policy.
If wishes were horses(, beggars would ride).
If you want a thing well done, do it yourself.
In for a penny(, in for a pound).
It is no use crying over spilt milk.
It will be all the same in a hundred years.
Jack of all trades(, master of none).
Laughter is the best medicine.
Let sleeping dogs lie.
Love laughs at locksmiths.
Love your neighbour but don't pull down the fence.
Make hay (while the sun shines).
Many a mickle (makes a muckle).
Many a true word (is spoken in jest).
Many hands make light work.
Necessity is the mother of invention.
Needs must (when the devil drives).
Never look a gift horse in the mouth.
Nothing succeeds like success.
One good turn deserves another.
One man's meat (is another man's poison).

Spare the rod (and spoil the child).
There's many a slip (twixt cup and lip).
There's no place like home.
There's no fool like an old fool.
Too many cooks (spoil the broth).
A watched kettle/pot (never boils).
When the cat's away(, the mice will play).
Why keep a dog and bark yourself?
You can lead a horse to water(, but you can't make it drink).
You can't get blood out of a stone.
You can't make an omelette without breaking eggs.
You can't teach an old dog (new tricks).
You can't judge a book by its cover.

Many proverb snippets have become cliché expressions in the vast cupboard of the English language.

By comparison with proverbs, **sayings** are usually pithier everyday observations along the lines of *Time flies; Waste not, want not; Moderation in all things; It never rains but it pours; Smile, it might never happen; The proof of the pudding's in the eating*; etc. Some of these are local, as Scots *The nearer the grave, the greedier; The loudest buzzer's maybe not the best bee; Ye've never died a winter yet*; etc.

PSYCH. psych oneself up get oneself worked up into a state of aggression, especially in preparation for a competitive sporting event. The entire team psyched itself up by performing a sort of pre-match Maori war dance. American, from the 1970s. A phrasal verb. Compare **pluck/ screw up one's courage**.

PULL. pull a fast one cheat or trick someone. Don't trust that man with your money – he's a swindler and is forever trying to pull a fast one.

pull one's finger out stop prevaricating, and get down to some hard work; stop being lazy. He's been ordered to pull his finger out, or he'll lose his job. Pedantic dog-Latin alternatives of this expression are 'extract the digit' or 'extractum digitum'. Partridge gives the general gist of this originally RAF slang imperative dating from the 1930s as an instruction to courting couples: 'Get your finger out and get stuck in.' Compare **knuckle down (to); roll one's sleeves up**.

pull in one's horns start to economise, scale down one's financial commitments. He plans to retire next year, and says that'll be the best time to start pulling in his horns. The figurative reference is to snails, many of which retract their 'horns' when threatened or disturbed. Compare **tighten one's belt**.

pull someone's leg tease someone, by misleading them. She told her father that he'd won the football pools, but she was only pulling his leg. Originally a Scots idiom, some authorities suggest that the expression derives from the actions of a condemned man's relatives at his hanging: they had the right to pull his legs, thus hastening his death and shortening his agony. The simpler explanation is that the term refers to the public tripping up of the victim, thus subjecting him to humorous teasing. Compare **have someone on; pull the other one**.

pull out all the stops spare no efforts (to achieve something). They pulled out all the stops to ensure that the wedding was a success. From playing the organ: when all the organ stops are pulled out, the instrument plays thunderously and majestically.

pull something out of the hat achieve success, as if miraculously or by magic. It was a real last-minute, 11th-hour win for Arsenal this time, and they only managed to pull their victory out of the hat in the dying seconds of the game. From the stage magician's sleight of hand, when s/he pulls a white rabbit or other unlikely item from an apparently empty hat.

pull one's socks up improve one's previously unsatisfactory performance, behaviour, etc. If you're going to be working in my department, you'd better pull your socks up, my lad – don't think you can wander in here half-way through the morning and slip out for a two-hour lunch. From the image of a slovenly schoolboy in short trousers with his socks around his ankles: smart kids were supposed to keep their socks tidily pulled up. Compare **mind your p's and q's**.

pull strings use one's personal contacts to help one fulfil one's aims. He tells everyone he got the job on merit, but I don't know if I believe him – would you not pull strings if your father was a duke and your grandfather owned a bank? From puppetry.

pull the other one tell me another unlikely story. He was pulling her leg and telling her the house was on fire. 'Oh yes,' she said, 'And now pull the other one.' From the idiom **pull someone's leg**, i.e. try as a joke to make someone believe something which cannot be true. The full expression is 'Now pull the other one, it's got bells on!' and it conjures up the picture of a jester in cap and bells. Nowadays a more laconic response is preferred, such as **aye right!** or 'yeah right!'

pull the rug/carpet (out) from under suddenly unsettle or upset someone. The case was prepared on the basis of the accused's 'Not Guilty' plea. When he changed his plea to 'Guilty' at the last minute, he pulled the rug from under his defence counsel's argument. Compare **cut the ground from under someone**.

pull the wool over someone('s eyes) deliberately deceive. He thinks he can pull the wool over her eyes by saying that he's working late at the office every night. From the days when the gentry wore wigs made of wool (18th century). These fell rather easily over the wearers' eyes and ears, thus rendering them vulnerable targets of pranks or thievish deceits.

pull through recover; survive. He's been at death's door for weeks, but the doctors now think he's beginning to pull through. A phrasal verb.

pull oneself together compose oneself; regain one's self control. The atrocity distressed even the rescue services, and some of the firemen had to receive a lot of counselling before they could pull themselves together and get on with their lives. Compare **get one's act together**.

pull someone up criticise someone. Most of the pupils dislike Miss Jackson, because she's always pulling them up and ridiculing their work in front of the class.

pull oneself up by the bootstraps improve one's humble circumstances by one's own efforts. There was no privileged education for him, no university training, no place in daddy's business, but he pulled himself up by his bootstraps and now he's prime minister.

pull/bring one up short take one by surprise; cause an unexpected pause in the progress of something. They had a good business in former Yugoslavia, but the civil war there pulled them up short.

pull one's weight do a fair share of work; merit one's place, salary, etc. If we want to win this competition, we're all going to have to pull our weight from now on. **From rowing.**

PURE. pure and simple without embellishment; and nothing else. Bloggs is a liar, pure and simple: there's no other word for him. **A dyad. Similar to 'no more, no less'**

PURPLE. purple passage overwritten piece of text; florid and ornate writing. She was a romantic novelist of the old school – much given to the purple passage in her rather torrid prose. **A short extract affected by the same characteristics might be called a 'purple patch'. From the Roman purple, the royal or imperial colour, the literary expression was used by Horace.**

PUSH. push one's luck ask for too much, take too much of a risk. Most of the workforce get on with the boss quite well, until they push their luck and ask him for a pay rise! Compare **chance one's arm**.

push off! go away (exclamation or statement). 'Go away, get lost, push off!' she yelled. I asked him to push off and leave us alone, but he ignored the request. Similar to **on your bike**.

push-over 1. **very easy job.** I'm afraid this assignment's been no push-over: we've seriously under-estimated the problems involved. 2. **easy person to convince or borrow money from.** When I'm broke, I borrow money from my dad – because my mum's no push-over with money. Compare **soft touch**.

push the boat out celebrate; enjoy oneself. Come on, the exams are finished, so let's push the boat out and have a party. **Possibly from boat-launching ceremonies, a cause for celebration in maritime societies.**

push/open the envelope innovate; take a project, idea, etc. beyond its current boundaries. I don't think we've exploited this idea as thoroughly as we might if we really pushed the envelope. Compare **blue-sky thinking**, another cliché of management-speak.

push up (the) daisies die. No, you can't speak to John Brown: he's been pushing up the daisies for 20 years. **A euphemism for death, the daisy is a flower which often grows in graveyards.**

PUSHED. pushed for short of. He said he was pushed for the price of a meal so I gave him a few pounds. Also **pressed for**.

PUSHING. pushing thirty/forty etc. almost thirty/forty, etc. He's very energetic and youthful looking, so people don't believe it when you tell them he's pushing sixty. **A contemporary alternative is thirtysomething, fortysomething, etc. instead of thirty-plus, forty-plus, etc.**

PUT. put a sock in it stop talking; be quiet. It's very difficult getting an old blether like John to put a sock in it and let someone else say a few words. Literally, to stuff a sock in someone's mouth. Often used as an imperative: 'Oh, go on, put a sock in it!' Compare **shut your trap!** or 'belt up!' (same sense).

put a spin/gloss on something explain something from a biased or semi-dishonest point of view. Spinners may accentuate the positives, downplay or suppress the negatives, or seriously distort them. Many people opposed the Second Iraq War (2003) on the simple grounds that the US and UK governments had put a dishonest spin on the whole affair.

put a spoke in someone's wheel make things difficult for someone; thwart or hinder someone. The house was almost finished when the planning department came along and put a real spoke in their wheel: they were told they hadn't got proper planning permission for the house. Old cartwheels used to be made of solid wood, without any 'spokes' of the sort found in modern bicycles. But there were often several round holes in these solid wheels, through which a bar of wood or spoke could be placed to act as a brake on the cart's movement.

put something across communicate something effectively. He's always been good at putting his case across in clear and simple terms. A phrasal verb.

put one's back into something work very hard at something. By really putting their backs into the work, they had the railway line mended by midnight. Compare **elbow grease**.

put/turn back the clock return to a former era, or method of doing something. The union's view was that the government was trying to put the clock back and ban the workers' right to strike.

put one's best foot forward walk quickly. You'll have to put your best foot forward if you don't want to miss that train. Why not 'better foot'? Invariably singular and ungrammatical – unless the expression was originally applied to four-footed animals like horses, etc.

put something down to attribute something to. His geranium seedlings all died, and he put it down to over-watering. A phrasal verb.

put someone's eye out supplant someone in another person's affections, favour, etc. John was only here three days when it became clear that he'd put Dave's eye out with Susan. A Scots idiom.

put one's feet up relax; take a rest. Excuse me if I put my feet up for half an hour.

put one's finger on something precisely identify something, usually a problem. You put your finger on the problem when you hinted that he was probably a lazy good-for-nothing.

put one's foot down firmly refuse. He asked for £100 but I put my foot down and said that he wouldn't get a penny from me until he'd earned it.

put one's foot (right/straight) in/into it say something tactless. I put my foot in it when I asked him how his wife was: she died yesterday. The figurative reference nowadays is to putting one's foot in dogshit or some other pavement mess. Apparently in the 16th century, the phrase was 'The bishop has set his foot in it', meaning some indiscretion had been committed. Bishops have been unpopular with the populace for a long time, although the current idiom is bereft of episcopal spoor. A very similar expression is **put one's foot/feet in one's mouth** meaning accidentally say something offensive or distressing. Some of our more clownish politicians have a distressing knack of putting their foot in their mouth at the slightest opportunity. Usually used humorously, as befits an act of such challenging physical skill. Compare **let the cat out of the bag; step right into it**.

put someone's gas in a peep shut someone up, often by some form of public humiliation. He was preaching on about honesty, so I put his gas in a peep by politely reminding him how I'd caught him pinching apples from my garden not so long ago. From the bad old days when gas pressure often varied just when one needed it for cooking a meal, and it was suddenly and infuriatingly reduced to a tiny 'peep' by agencies beyond one's control.

put our/your etc. heads together devise a plan by mutual agreement and discussion. I know you've got a problem, but we've been putting our heads together and I think we can suggest a good plan of action for you.

put/set one's (own) house in order organise one's (own) business affairs. He decided it would be a good idea to set his house in order before going into hospital for such a big operation.

put in a good word for support, speak well of. Her father put in a good word for her with his boss, and she was offered a good job.

put in an appearance appear at some event from a sense of duty rather than voluntarily. Every so often he puts in an appearance at church on Sunday.

put (one) in mind of remind. She puts me very much in mind of her mother at that age – she's so like her.

put someone in his/her (proper) place teach someone who has caused offence to behave in a manner more appropriate to his/her position. It's time that little upstart was put in his proper place. Compare **take someone down a peg/notch (or two)**.

put oneself in someone's shoes imagine oneself in the position or situation of another person, often with specific reference to their problems. Try putting yourself in my shoes, and you'll soon discover you've got problems.

put someone in the picture explain the position to someone, so that they understand references in conversation, etc. Has the sales manager put you all in the picture about our plans? Compare **get the picture**.

put someone/something in/into the shade outshine something; make something look inferior by comparison with something else. James was very proud of his BMW, but then John came along in his brand-new silver Rolls Royce and put every other car on the street into the shade.

put it mildly understate; describe something less harshly than might be warranted. The

gentleman in question is known to be rather economical with the truth, to put it mildly. Compare **not to put too fine a point upon it**.

put it to someone propose or suggest something to someone. I put it to you, ladies and gentlemen, that the witness you have just listened to is unreliable. The term is often used by lawyers summing up a case.

put one's neck/ass on the line expose one's money, reputation, etc. to risk, usually in defence of something. He's not my favourite person, and I have no intention of putting my neck on the line for him.

put someone's nose out of joint upset or cause offence to someone. Not only was he dropped from the team – his place was offered to his biggest rival, so that really put his nose out of joint for a while.

put something on 1. dress. Be a good boy and put some clothes on. 2. feign, pretend, simulate something. I assumed from her show of tears that she was upset, but I'm told she was putting it all on for effect. A phrasal verb.

put on a brave face/a bold front pretend to be calm; conceal one's fears. The Tories were all but obliterated in the election, but they put on a brave face and said something about failing to get their message across properly. Also 'put a brave face on it'. Compare **stiff upper lip**.

put on an act behave in a false way in order to try and impress someone. She can put on quite a good act if she thinks it'll help her get her own way. From the stage.

put on one's thinking cap think about a problem very carefully. She wasn't quite sure how to handle the problem, but she said she'd put on her thinking cap and try to come up with a suitable course of action.

put out feelers make discreet inquiries. Before deciding whether to publish the book, the publishers put out feelers to try to get a better idea of exactly who would buy it. Occasionally singular, 'put out a feeler'. The image is of an insect's feelers searching out vibrations from potential foes or victims. Similar in sense to 'sounding someone out', a phrasal verb from the market research department.

put (someone) out of the way kill; eliminate. Philip Marlowe is getting too dangerous; he knows too much about our plans; somebody's going to have to put him out of the way once and for all. A euphemism. Compare **bump someone off**.

put out the flags give a big welcome. She hasn't been home for 20 years, so we'll really have to put out the flags for her. Sometimes 'put out the welcome mat'. See also **red-carpet treatment**.

put someone out to grass pension someone off; make someone retire from paid employment. How can they put a good 40-year-old line manager out to grass? From the former (more gentlemanly) practice of leaving old work-horses to graze undisturbed.

put paid to bring to an end; terminate. His injury last week puts paid to his chances of selection for the Olympic Games. From book-keeping, where clerks used to write the word 'paid' beside an account entry when a bill had been settled – thus putting an end to the debt.

put one's shoulder to the wheel get down to some hard work/graft. He knew that if he put his shoulder to the wheel the house could be finished by Christmas. Compare **roll one's sleeves up**.

put that in your pipe and smoke it! usually used as an impolite sort of exclamation, meaning: So there! Make what you can of that! Tolerate that if you can! Offer me twice the salary and a world cruise, offer me the moon, offer me a peerage, but I'm still not going to work for you ever again – so put that in your pipe and smoke it! According to Partridge, it derives from the once widely held belief that pipe-smoking and meditation go hand-in-hand. Humorous variations include 'Put that in your sock and suspend it!' or the American 'Put that in your

Funk and Wagnalls!' (encyclopaedia), a common aside in *Rowan & Martin's Laugh-In* TV show of the late 1960s.

put the arm on someone try to force someone to do something. The headmaster has been putting the arm on his sixth formers to try and show a bit more leadership and public spirit. Originally American. Compare **twist someone's arm**.

put the boot in attack someone literally or metaphorically. When she started to cry, her boss – a noted bully – started to put the boot in and tell her how useless she was.

put/set the cart before the horse do things in the wrong order or sequence. They had bought their new house before getting cash from the sale of their old one – and then they couldn't sell the old one; perhaps they had set the cart before the horse, but finding credit is a difficult problem for many people nowadays.

put the dampers on something discourage something. The president's assassination is bound to put the dampers on the peace negotiations. Piano dampers are used to soften the sound of the notes, while fire dampers are used to put out fires. Dampness also conveys the idea of idiomatically throwing cold water on something.

put the lid/tin hat on something kill or finish something off; spoil something. I'm afraid their last defeat puts the tin hat on Arsenal's chances of winning the cup. The 'tin hat' metaphor is Victorian, being the nickname given to a shrapnel helmet in the Boer War. The name summed up the average soldier's lack of confidence in the effectiveness of the item.

put the mockers on something wreck or spoil something; prevent something succeeding. The heavy snowfalls have put the mockers on this weekend's football fixtures. Originally Australian, 1960s, the idea being that a mockery has been made of something.

put/set the record straight clarify matters; resolve a misunderstanding. Can you just put the record straight for us and tell us exactly when you last saw this man?

put the wind up frighten. Drive slowly please. When you drive at that speed it really puts the wind up me.

put something/someone through its/their etc. paces make something/someone show all its skills or abilities, perform all the tricks of which it is capable. Today is the dress rehearsal for tomorrow's first night, so we're all to be put through our paces. From horse trials, when the judges test a horse to see how well it has been trained. They assess its movements in all four paces – walking, trotting, cantering and galloping. Compare **show one's paces/mettle**.

put to it obliged to make a difficult choice. I don't really know who is my favourite composer, but if I were put to it, I might say Mozart. A phrasal verb.

put/set to rights put in order. The Chancellor of the Exchequer has one more year in which to put the economy to rights.

put to sea go to sea; sail. The ship put to sea half an hour before the German attack.

put someone/something to shame show someone/thing at a disadvantage. He spoke knowledgeably and humorously about the problems they were facing, putting his tongue-tied fellow committee members to shame.

put something to the proof/test establish whether something is true or not. It's supposed to be a record-breaking plane, but it's not due for testing till next month, when it will be put to the proof. Compare **proof of the pudding (is in the eating)**.

put two and two together reach a conclusion based on the evidence one has. We put two and two together when we saw the curtains drawn: we assumed she was still in bed. Also 'put two and two together and make five' is to reach an incorrect conclusion. All of a sudden he started spending huge sums of money, and I'm sorry to say that we put two and two together and made five: we thought he'd been involved in a robbery, when in fact his grandfather had died and left him a large fortune.

put up or shut up prove your point or be silent; back your assertion with cash or withdraw from negotiation. After many hours of debate, his fellow directors got fed up with his endless criticisms: finally, and in no uncertain terms, they told him to put up or shut up. Originally an American idiom, a parallel but more British variant is **like it or lump it**. A similar catch-phrase is 'put your money where your mouth is'.

put-up job hoax; attempt to cheat someone. The entire televised debate was nothing less than an elaborate put-up job.

put someone up to something persuade someone to do something (sometimes in a less than open way). He's written a letter of complaint to his MP, and he's put me and several other neighbours up to doing the same thing.

put upon imposed upon unreasonably. She's very good to her aged mother, but she tends to let herself get put upon by the old lady.

put words in someone's mouth suggest words for someone; pretend that someone has said something which he has not actually said. The police were accused of putting words into the defendant's mouth; it was the police and not the defendant who said the witness was not reliable.

PYRRHIC. pyrrhic victory victory won at a cost which is so high as to render the victory worthless. They won the war, but at a price which was so high that they were thereafter too poor to enjoy the peace – so it was a pyrrhic victory for them. A reference to the costly victory in battle of Pyrrhus, king of Epirus, over the Romans at Heraclea in 280 BC.

Q

QUALITY. quality time time spent with loved ones; leisure time; private space. He usually left for work at 7 a.m. and wasn't home till 8 p.m., so quality time was confined to the weekends. Also 'me-time' or us-time'.

QUEEN. (and) Queen Anne is dead too your news is stale; we all know this. He was trying to explain that the churches had lost a lot of influence in modern society, when some joker shouted out 'And Queen Anne's dead too!' A rather old-fashioned saying used as a refrain, rather like 'and the band played on', or 'tell us something new' but with a slightly different sense.

QUEENSBERRY. Queensberry Rules the rules of boxing; fair play. These jihadists simply want to kill and maim as many people as they can: they've never heard of the Queensberry Rules. The rules and regulations governing boxing are named after John Sholto Douglas, 8th Marquess of Queensberry (1844–1900), who helped to formulate them.

QUEER. queer fish strange or odd person. Nobody speaks to old Mr Snooks; most of the neighbours regard him as a bit of a queer fish. Sometimes fishermen land unusual fish from the depths.

queer one's pitch make it difficult for someone to do as he wishes or intends. By behaving in such a childish way, the students have queered our pitch for future visits to that hotel. From setting up one's pitch, or pitching one's tent-stall, as a petty trader. This was queered if, for example, the police made the trader move on or if another trader set up in direct competition nearby.

QUICK. quick fix quick boost. I find that a quick fix of Mozart on the car stereo usually brightens up the mornings very satisfactorily. Originally American, referring to a narcotic injection; now used much more widely. See also **shot in the arm**.

quick/first/fast off the mark swift to act. He was pretty quick off the mark once you'd told him there was a police reward of £10,000 for the person who'd witnessed the crime. From athletics races, with reference to someone who is a quick starter, as is the variant 'quick out of/away from the blocks'.

quick on the uptake bright; quick to learn. He's not very quick on the uptake before lunchtime.

quick one a quick alcoholic drink. He usually goes into his local pub for a quick one on the way home from work. A euphemism.

QUID. quid pro quo from Latin, literally 'something for something'; one thing in place of another; generally nowadays, a favour given in return for one received. Last night he drank all our whisky, but we regarded that as a sort of a quid pro quo for his earlier hospitality to us.

QUIDS. quids in in a favourable or strong position, especially one that is likely to result in financial advantage. You'll be quids in – as publisher – if you can persuade the ministry of education to support that textbook. A 'quid' is slang for £1.

QUIT. quit while one is ahead stop doing something while one is still at the peak of one's ability. When John was offered early retirement, he accepted it at once, saying he'd be happy to quit while he was ahead. From betting, and stopping betting when one has made some winnings.

QUITE. quite so perfectly true; I agree. 'I should have brought an umbrella – it's been pouring since we arrived.' 'Quite so,' agreed his drenched wife.

quite something something good, or special. You should try her lamb korma – it's quite something. Compare **something else (again)**.

quite the thing correct; fashionable. My daughter seems to think my hairstyle isn't quite the thing.

QUITS. quits with even with; avenged. He punched me, so I punched him – just to be quits with him. From betting. See also **call it quits**.

QUOTE. quote unquote an expression used in spoken English to signal or stress that the speaker is using someone's exact words. The judge indicated that in his view the defendant had been quote unquote economical with the truth. **The verbal equivalent of inverted commas.** See also **words to that effect**.

R

RACK. rack and ruin disrepair; very neglected condition. It was a very old house, and had been allowed to go to rack and ruin over the years. A dyad, in which 'rack' preserves an old word for 'destruction'. Sometimes spelt 'wrack'.

rack one's brains/memory think very hard. I've been racking my brains to recall the title of the book he asked me to get. 'Rack' here means 'strain' or 'stretch'.

RAG. rag-tag and bobtail the rabble; everybody; people without any social graces. I used to share a flat with George, but I moved out after a while; he used to bring all the rag-tag and bobtail home with him. An old-fashioned expression nowadays, dating from about 1820. Sometimes 'raggle-taggle'. A modern equivalent would be 'riffraff', which is in fact a much older term (15th century). Compare **rank and file; hoi polloi; every Tom, Dick and Harry**.

RAGS. rags-to-riches going from poverty to wealth. Like all the best romances, she was a rags-to-riches bride and he was a handsome prince.

RAIN. rain cats and dogs rain very heavily. There was spectacular thunder and lightning for half an hour before the heavens opened and it proceeded to rain cats and dogs. There are several suggested explanations for this picturesque idiom. One is that the phrase is a corruption of Greek 'catadupe', meaning a cataract or waterfall. Another is that, in medieval times when a town's drainage system was rather primitive, the streets were littered with the corpses of drowned cats and dogs after a heavy rainstorm.

rain or shine whatever the circumstances. I'll be at that wedding rain or shine. A dyad.

RAINY. rainy day time when one is faced with unforeseen expense. He's never been reckless with his money, and always kept something aside for a rainy day. The original reference was to farming, and to the idea that farmers could not work, and therefore earn any money, on rainy days. So money or farm produce was kept aside for this eventuality.

RAISE. raise Cain make a disturbance; cause trouble. After a football match there's usually a lunatic few who like to raise Cain and terrorise the local citizenry. A biblical allusion, to raising up the spirit of Cain, who was quick tempered and killed his brother Abel ; from Genesis iv.2. Also 'raise hell', which has a similar meaning and gives the noun 'hell-raiser'. (Idiom has never yet thrown up a 'Cain-raiser'.)

raise eyebrows shock; draw attention. That sort of behaviour in that sort of place is bound to raise a few eyebrows.

raise one's hat to acknowledge; show admiration for. He works very hard to make a success of his business, and I raise my hat to him for developing such a good commercial product. It was once considered good manners for a gentleman to raise his hat in greeting someone.

raise the bar set a higher standard than before. His performance as Othello raised the bar for a whole generation of performances of the role. From the high jump event in athletics.

raise the roof 1. enthusiastically and tumultuously applaud. The appreciative audience raised the roof after La Stupenda's wonderful performance. 2. **be very angry.** When the headmaster saw the culprits he raised the roof and threatened to expel them from the school. The image in both cases is of the roof rafters being shattered by an outbreak of spontaneous strong feelings, whether delight or fury, and the roof itself being swept off the building in a metaphoric tornado of emotion.

RAKE. rake over the ashes return to a forgotten argument or romance; revert to an unpleasant discussion. She loves raking over the ashes of their old battles. The idea is of trying to rekindle a fire that has almost gone out, and coax a few sparks from it.

rake something up try to create scandal by reminding people of some forgotten event. British newspapers always try to rake something up about a politician's past life. From 'muckraking'. The Muckrakers were a group of early 20th-century reforming writers in the US whose work drew the attention of the general public to corruption in politics and business. They in turn took their name from the original 17th-century 'Man with the Muck-Rake', who appeared in John Bunyan's *Pilgrim's Progress*, as an image for 'greed'.

RALLY. rally round offer help. When Sarah's marriage broke up, her friends all rallied round to give her some moral support.

RAM. ram something down someone's throat try to force a person to listen or subscribe to another person's views. It is supposed to be a feature of a democratic society that governments don't try to ram their line down the electorate's throat.

RANK. rank and file common people (as opposed to the political leadership). The conference erupted when the rank and file voted to rescind the party's long-standing policy on nationalisation. This is a popular journalistic dyad, or double, mostly associated nowadays with references to political parties and conferences. It originally had a military connotation which has now been lost. It may also form an adjective: I'm just a rank-and-file member of this organisation. Compare **grass roots**.

RANT. rant and rave get angry and show one's anger verbally. It's not possible to talk to Brian for more than 10 minutes before he's ranting and raving about one thing or another. An alliterative dyad. Compare **sound and fury**.

RARING. raring to go keen to begin. The cars were all lined up behind the starter's flag, revving their engines and raring to go. The word should actually be 'rearing', and originally referred to horses rearing up in eagerness for a race or a gallop.

RAP. rap on the knuckles reprimand. He got a good rap on the knuckles from his superior for forgetting to keep expense receipts. Originally a form of physical punishment for children.

RAT. rat on someone inform. Someone ratted on me to the police for dropping litter in the street. Compare **spill the beans**.

rat pack media people, especially journalists, photographers, cameramen, etc. The princess emerged from the building followed by her customary jostling rat-pack flotilla. A term of contempt for the contemporary media circus.

rat race the competitive life, the endless effort to get ahead and stay ahead of the pack. John and Sylvia have opted out of the rat race and bought a croft in the Highlands. Alliterative overtones of analogy with the human race, animal behaviourism (conditioning) and competitive running.

rat run secondary road favoured by commuter drivers trying to take short cuts to/from work and to avoid bottlenecks. It's no longer safe for children to play on our street now that it's used by so many cars as a rat run in the rush hour. Another alliterative formation derived from **rat race**.

RAW. raw deal unfair treatment. He got a very raw deal in terms of his father's will: everything was left to his sister, i.e. its terms were painful for him.

READ. read between the lines infer; interpret. On the phone she sounded very positive and reasonably happy, but if you knew Sally you could read between the lines and tell that she was actually very homesick. Compare **spell something out**.

read someone like a book correctly guess what someone is thinking. All you have to do is see the look on his very expressive face, and you can read him like a book. Similar to 'read someone's mind'.

read my lips pay close and careful attention to what I am saying. Read my lips – you are not going to Suzy's party. An emphasiser, popularised by an over-quoted statement made by US President George Bush in 1988: 'Read my lips: No new taxes.' The quote became notorious because the promise was quickly broken.

read the riot act be very angry with someone, and say so vehemently. He really and truly read the riot act at me for kicking my football into his precious tulips. The original reference was parliamentary: to one of the many Riot Acts, for example that of 1715 at the time of the first Jacobite Rebellion, which declared it unlawful for people to disturb the peace through riotous conduct. These acts were read aloud from city market places and other places of public assembly up and down the land.

read the runes interpret a given situation, and decide or forecast what is going to happen. The press have spent the last year reading the runes and trying to guess when the next election's going to take place. 'Runes' were the characters of the oldest European alphabet. Runic script was attributed with magical powers by many people, especially those who couldn't read it.

READY. ready for the drop/off 1. prepared to release something illicitly to someone, especially if it is to be done covertly. He said they wouldn't be ready for the drop until they knew we were ready with the cash. From the RAF, which had to drop supplies, soldiers, etc. by parachute behind enemy lines in the Second World War. 2. prepared for arrest, execution, etc. Such was his power that Al Capone was completely unready for the drop at the time of his arrest in 1931. From the action of hanging a criminal, 'by the neck until he is dead.' American gangsters talk about 'dropping' someone as a euphemism for killing them. Compare **kick the bucket.**

ready to hand available and accessible. She always has a good dictionary ready to hand to help her with her work.

ready to drop exhausted. I've been walking all day, and I'm ready to drop.

REAL. real McCoy the genuine article; not fake. It was the best brandy that money could buy, none of your cooking stuff but the real McCoy! Perhaps a corruption of 'the real MacKay', a

Scotch whisky which was promoted under this name in the 1870s. There was also a US boxing champion in the 1890s, called Kid McCoy, who promoted himself as 'the real McCoy'. Also 'real thing', used more as a slogan, i.e. for Coca-Cola, or as a love lyric: 'It's the real thing this time.'

REAP. reap the whirlwind suffer the results of one's earlier actions; reap what one has sown. He had a pretty dissolute life as a young man, and I'm afraid he's now reaping the whirlwind. A contracted quotation. The full, biblical proverb in Hosea viii.7 is 'They have sown the wind, and they shall reap the whirlwind.'

reap where/what one sows receive one's just reward, i.e. good results from previous good actions, bad from bad. In her old age, her children looked after her very well; but then, she had brought them up well, and was now reaping where she had sown. Also 'reap as one has sown'.

REASON. (have) reason to believe (have) justification for concluding. I have good reason to believe this man stole my car. A formal circumlocution favoured by the police when they have obtained clear evidence of a misdemeanour.

RECEIVED. received wisdom sum of conventional views on a topic, etc. She went on television fully aware that she was disregarding the received wisdom of how the British royal family should behave. Also 'received ideas' (same sense, from French 'idées reçues').

RECHARGE. recharge the/one's batteries take a break or holiday in order to relax and regain one's vim and vigour. Knowing how badly he needed to recharge his batteries, he took an unscheduled week's holiday in the country. From motor car engines.

RED. red alert maximum degree of readiness. There's been a red alert on this building ever since the embassy was bombed last month. Originally a military term.

red-blooded sexually potent. He seems to have the normal red-blooded tendencies of most healthy young adult males.

red card signal that a player has to leave the football pitch for foul play. Jones's playing days are numbered: he has been red carded several times this season. From the soccer pitch.

red-carpet treatment special effort to give someone the very best of one's attention, hospitality, etc. Most airlines nowadays are very good with unaccompanied children, or physically disabled passengers, and they give them red-carpet treatment. A metaphor from the practice of rolling out a red carpet for important people, visiting dignitaries, royalty, etc. to walk on. Compare **put out the flags**.

red-handed in the act of committing an action. He came home unexpectedly, and caught his wife red-handed with the milkman. Originally, the reference was to a violent criminal act, and to blood on the hands.

red herring something that diverts or distracts attention from the main argument. All this talk about renewable energy sources is a bit of a red herring, and I'd like to return to the basic argument of the evening. This colourful phrase is said to derive from the days when herrings were dried, salted and smoked to keep them edible for long periods. When herrings were treated in this way, they generally turned reddish in colour. Additionally, of course, they had a pungent smell. If you dragged a red herring across the fox's trail during a hunt, you diverted the hunters away from the hunted. Compare **start a hare**.

red-hot very keen. She's been a red-hot feminist since her youth.

red-letter day special day; a day to remember. Many people will remember VE Day as a real red-letter day in their lives. From the medieval practice of inscribing or printing saints' days and other specially holy days in red ink in early ecclesiastical calendars. Other days were printed in black. The original listing of red-letter days was approved at the Council of Nicaea in AD 325. Much later, there was also a legal significance to the term and judges of the Queen's Bench division still wear special robes on red-letter days if these fall during a law sitting.

red light warning; notification to stop. The project was given the red light by the government as soon as it became clear that it was going to cost too much money. From traffic lights, opposite of **green light** or 'go-ahead'. Also **red card**.

red-light district area of a town with brothels, night clubs, strip joints, etc. Most visitors to Hamburg like to visit the city's famous red-light area around the Reeperbahn. From the colour of the lights in the windows of many sex establishments.

red rag to a bull something that infuriates and provokes. Please don't talk to her about the National Union of Mineworkers or the European Union – these are two red rags to a bull at the moment. From the idea that something coloured red enrages a bull.

red tape heavy emphasis on official forms and procedures; bureaucratic nonsense. It's very difficult for foreigners in Russia to register for employment in that country; there's far too much red tape to be cut through, so outsiders don't know where to begin. The term is nowadays almost entirely pejorative. It originated in the 18th-century practice of tying official papers and documents with ribbons of red or pink tape.

REDEEMING. redeeming feature compensating factor. The weather was horrible, but the hotel was one redeeming feature – it was splendid.

REDOUND. redound to one's credit/shame reverberate or echo in one's praise/shame. The attempted extermination of the Jews by the Nazis will redound to the perpetual shame of the human race. Rather formal and old fashioned.

REFRESH. refresh someone's memory make someone think again about something. I just want to run through your story once again and see if we can refresh your memory about the actual robbery. An expression often used euphemistically, to indicate that the speaker's object is in fact to make the listener change his mind.

REGULAR. regular as clockwork very regular and predictable. He comes for lunch on Tuesdays and Fridays, regular as clockwork. A standard simile. Compare **rain or shine**.

RE-INVENT. re-invent the wheel reformulate a process, or reconstruct an invention, or reintroduce a former practice, often needlessly or for no very good reason. There was something depressing about the idea of all those computer programmer people re-inventing their own little wheels – what was needed was a universal system for everyone to follow.

RELIEVE. relieve oneself empty one's bladder or bowel; urinate or defecate. Excuse me for a minute while I relieve myself. A euphemism.

relieve someone of something take something from someone; often used euphemistically to mean 'steal'. That little ragamuffin has relieved me of my wallet.

REMOVE. remove the scales from someone's eyes undeceive or disabuse someone. Press coverage of parliamentary scandals and corruption have removed the scales from the eyes of the electorate. A biblical reference, to the scales of his blindness falling from the eyes of St Paul at the time of his conversion; in Acts ix.18.

RESIGN. resign oneself to submit to or get used to something unpleasant. After his accident, he had to resign himself to a wheelchair.

REST. rest assured be sure or confident. Please rest assured that we will do all we can to help you.

rest on one's laurels/oars be content with one's achievements, and no longer seek to improve on them; cease to strive, or to be actively ambitious. He had a brilliant academic career until he was appointed professor, but ever since then he's been resting on his laurels. The first

reference is Classical, to the victor's prize of a crown of laurels; the second is from rowing.

RETRACE. retrace one's (foot)steps 1. find one's way back from. They were lost in the forest, and couldn't retrace their steps to safety. A favourite strategy of fairy tales. 2. remember. I want you to retrace your steps through the events of that fateful afternoon exactly as you recall them.

RETURN. return the compliment 1. compliment someone who has paid you a compliment. She told me I was looking younger than ever, and I was happy to return the compliment. 2. behave to others in the same way as they have behaved to you. They're always inviting us for supper, and it's about time we returned the compliment.

return to the fold return to an organisation, system, outlook, etc. one adhered to previously. For many years he avoided the church, but recently he seems to have returned to the fold. The reference is biblical, to the sheep which was lost.

REVEAL. reveal/show one's true colours show one's true nature. She lost her temper and then she began to show her true colours – not a very pleasant sight either. Also 'appear in one's true colours'. Not the same as **true to one's colours**.

RHYME. rhyme or reason good cause or sense, often negative with 'without'. I'm sorry – I can't get rhyme or reason out of him. His behaviour throughout the episode was without rhyme or reason – no one can understand it. A popular alliterative dyad, 'rhyme' is probably thrown in for good measure. Sometimes, in printed versification, an unreasonable statement or observation was justified on the grounds that at least it rhymed. The sense of the idiom denies even that flimsy justification.

RIDE. ride roughshod over tyrannise; behave arrogantly or harshly towards somebody; show a total lack of consideration for someone's feelings. He's a complete tyrant at home – rides roughshod over his wife and children – thinks his family have no rights at all. A roughshod horse was one which had nailheads projecting from its horseshoes.

These projections were useful and prevented the horse from slipping on wet cobblestones or icy ground; but they were also dangerous.

ride something out survive something difficult. The business has been through tough times, but it has managed to ride out all its crises so far. Originally referred to ships riding out a storm at sea.

RIDING. riding/heading for a fall about to experience a setback. His arrogance has antagonised most of his colleagues, and he looks as if he may be riding for a fall. From the biblical expression 'Pride before a fall.' Actually: 'Pride goeth before destruction; and a haughty spirit before a fall.' Proverbs xvi.18.

riding high (in the charts) having lots of success (in the bestseller lists and popularity ratings). Her last film was a box-office sellout, and she's been riding high since then.

RIGHT. right and left or **right, left and centre** indiscriminately; in all directions. It's just been learnt that he's been swindling his customers right and left for years, the rotter!

right as rain very fit and well. Jones was at the party last night, looking right as rain. The sense of this standard simile is 'as right and natural' as rain. Compare **fit as a fiddle**.

right away at once; immediately. I'll phone the doctor right away. Originally an Americanism, this expression was deplored as bad English by Charles Dickens in his *American Notes* (1842).

right hand doesn't know what the left hand's doing idiom which usually indicates an incompetent individual or organisation. The Tory Party is said to want to bring government closer to the people and to cut down on Whitehall bureaucracy, but at the same time it refuses devolution to the regions: one can only conclude that the right hand doesn't know what the left hand is doing. Compare **joined-up thinking**.

right-hand man trusted helper. Jeeves was Bertie Wooster's right-hand man. The right-hand side was regarded traditionally as the place of

greatest honour: Jesus sat at the right hand of God the Father.

right of way 1. path across private property which anyone may use. The path was clearly shown as a right of way on my map, so I wasn't worried about meeting an angry farmer. 2. right of one car, ship, etc. to cross before another one; the privilege of precedence. Cars approaching a roundabout on your left don't have right of way in Britain.

right off immediately. She asked the children what a crannog was, and John was able to tell her right off. Sometimes 'right off the bat' (from baseball). Right off the bat you could see that the storm damage was substantial.

right under one's nose close beside one. He couldn't find his pencil, even though it was sitting there on the desk right under his nose.

right up one's street/alley of special interest to one. They were talking about model railways, a subject which was right up my street.

right you are certainly. 'Come and see me tomorrow please.' 'Right you are, what time?' A conversational gambit expressing agreement.

RING. ring a bell remind one of something. She was talking about some man called Fred Archer – not a name that rang bells for me. This idiom may be singular or plural. It may derive from the bell which rings in a shooting gallery when someone hits the jackpot or bull's-eye. Or it may refer more simply to the church bell, reminding the faithful to attend church service.

ring hollow sound suspicious or untrue. His story rang hollow in several of its details. See also **ring true/false**.

ring of truth a convincing account; something that sounds authentic. His story had the ring of truth about it – I failed to detect any false notes. Also **ring true**.

ring off end a telephone conversation. It was a very quick call, and she rang off before I could tell her my news. **Other phrasal verbs of telephonic reference are 'ring up' (for making a call) and 'ring out' (when no one answers).** I rang up the station to ask the times of the trains. But no one answered and the phone finally rang out.

ring the changes vary the routine; alter the way something is organised in order to vary or improve it. Her sitting-room is different every time you visit her; she's always ringing the changes by moving the furniture around, or painting the walls or window frames. **The idiom comes from the art of bell-ringing, or change-ringing. The more bells there are in the carillon, the greater the range of possible changes.**

ring true/false sound or appear authentic/ suspect. The police officer says he doesn't know if your alibi quite rings true – are you sure you're not concealing something from him? **From the days when coins were dropped to test whether they were made of pure metal (they rang true) or whether they were counterfeit (they made a dull sound). Compare strike the right note; ring hollow; ring of truth**.

RIP. rip someone off cheat or take advantage (of someone). The voters have turned against the government because they feel it has been ripping them off. **Also 'rip-off artist' cheat; fraudster.** He's a rip-off artist who sells damaged cars to little old ladies. **A 1960s American black argot coinage which soon entered the wider hippy culture.**

RISE. rise from the ranks progress from lower to higher ranks, originally from the rank of an ordinary soldier to an officer. He rose very rapidly from the ranks of parliamentary obscurity to be prime minister.

rise to the bait be provoked into anger or be duped into doing something, as a fish often is by a clever fisherman's bait. It is very easy to annoy the boss – just tell him how well his competitors are doing, and he'll rise to the bait every time.

rise to the occasion be able to do what is required of one in an emergency. He didn't expect to have to make the main speech at the wedding, but he rose to the occasion with verve and wit.

rise with the lark get up very early. Many farmers rise with the lark, to make the most of all the daylight hours. **Compare early bird**.

RISK. risk/chance one's neck incur genuine and serious risks. By going back to rescue his climbing partner, John was risking his own neck. **Nowadays mainly found as a hyperbole, the original expression dates from the times when execution by beheading was common.**

ROAD. road hog driver who shows selfish disregard for other road users. In normal life he may have been a caring and courteous person, but behind the wheel of a car he was transformed into the worst kind of road hog you can imagine. **An Americanism dating from the 1880s, the term originally referred to discourteous bicyclists. It draws of course on the legendary greediness and bad manners of the pig.**

road to recovery getting better from illness. He was in hospital for weeks, but he's now started down the long road to recovery, and is making good progress.

road to ruin/perdition often a cliché, meaning the downward path of sin and folly. He has had poor health since he became an alcoholic and started down the road to ruin. **From an old proverb: 'The road to ruin is in good repair: its travellers keep it so and pay the expense of it.' Compare go to the dogs**.

ROB. rob Peter to pay Paul use money borrowed from one person or source to pay another. The Chancellor likes to rob Peter and pay Paul by knocking a few pennies off the tax on whisky and adding them on to tobacco. **The reference is to the two apostles Peter and Paul, who share the same saints' day (June 29). In English folklore, it is Robin Hood who is remembered for robbing Peter (the rich) to pay Paul (the poor).**

ROCK. rock bottom the lowest possible level. She's been depressed for a while, but she hit rock bottom when she learnt of her husband's death.

Share prices reached rock bottom last week, and have now started to rise again. **From a geological concept, meaning the lowest stratum in a section of the earth's crust.**

rock the boat cause problems; put things out of balance; destabilise a stable environment. The company have asked their workforce not to rock the boat and draw attention to the factory's ventilation problems.

ROLL. roll with the punches be flexible; react and adjust to problems as they happen. Don't try to fight this situation – just roll with the punches. **From boxing, where a fighter has to jink and duck to avoid taking the full force of a blow. Compare on one's feet; roll one's sleeves up**.

roll one's sleeves up do some hard work. There was no alternative: we all had to roll our sleeves up and get pushing, hard, until we got that car back on the road. **Compare put one's shoulder to the wheel**.

roll (something) out implement (something) on a wider scale than hitherto. Results of the project in pilot schools have been so successful that it is to be rolled out nationally next session. **A voguish phrasal verb of the new millennium, particularly favoured by government agencies. Similar to cascade down**.

ROLLING. rolling forecast extrapolation of the anticipated income and expenditure of a business. We have been asked to supply a three-year rolling forecast of our departmental projections.

rolling in it/money very rich. He bought the company for his son, and is about to buy another one for his daughter – but that's not a problem for someone who's rolling in it, like he is.

rolling stone person who moves about, never settling in one place for long. He told me that he wasn't going to be a rolling stone all his life, and that one day he'd settle down and marry a good woman. **An expression from the proverb: 'A rolling stone gathers no moss.'**

ROOT. root and branch thoroughly, entirely. The house had woodworm, but we thought we had destroyed that problem root and branch when we brought in the experts and had all the wood treated and fumigated. **An adverbial dyad. There were Root and Branch Bills of the English Parliament in the 17th century legislating for the thorough and utter eradication of episcopacy. The biblical expression is found in Malachi iv.1: 'The day cometh that shall burn as an oven; and all the proud, yea, and all that do wickedly, shall be stubble; and the day that cometh shall burn them up, saith the Lord of hosts, that it shall leave them neither root nor branch.'**

root for someone cheer someone; give someone moral support. We told her to be patient, and that she was looking wonderful, and that we were all rooting for her. **An Americanism which has taken hold in UK English.**

root hog or die fend for oneself or perish. Marooned as he was on a desert island, it was a case of root hog or die – so he got rooting. **A slightly bewildering Americanism probably referring to the rooting practices and strong survival skills of hogs, and dating to the early 19th century. Used by Davy Crockett.**

ROUGH. rough and ready 1. simple; in basic fashion. He did the job in a rather rough and ready way last month, and will finish it off properly next week. **Compare rule of thumb**. 2. coarse; unrefined. He was just a rough and ready soldier but he'd been trained to fight. **An alliterative dyad. Compare (by the) seat of the pants**.

rough and tumble rigours and challenges. Lots of kids are spoilt at home by their mums and dads, and are quite unready for the rough and tumble of living on their own. **A dyad.**

rough diamond person who is basically good but whose manners are unpolished. Her boyfriend may be a bit of a rough diamond, but we're all quite fond of him. **Americans prefer 'diamond in the rough'.**

rough it live in uncomfortable or primitive conditions, especially outdoors. He became a hermit, roughing it in a cave along the shore all summer, sleeping in farmers' barns in winter.

rough something out explain essentials, sometimes by making a rough outline sketch of something. I roughed out the idea for the benefit of the newcomers to the meeting. From drawing.

rough passage difficult progress. That bill had a particularly rough passage through the House of Commons. A nautical idiom.

ROUND. round figures/numbers the nearest number ending in zero. Tell me the approximate price; the nearest round numbers will do.

round something off complete something in a satisfactory or pleasurable way. We rounded off an excellent dinner with coffee and liqueurs.

round on someone verbally attack someone. Halfway through the meeting, she rounded on me for spending all that money. A phrasal verb, from animal behaviour.

round robin letter of complaint signed by a number of people, sometimes in a circular form so that there is no obvious ringleader. The chairman received a round robin from his fellow committee members, objecting to his foreign trips. Nicholas Ridley, bishop of London, refers to the term in the 16th century as a blasphemous name for the communion sacrament.

round the bend/twist crazy; insane. She's almost round the bend with worry. That noise is just about driving me round the bend. Compare **out of one's head**.

round the clock all day and all night. The mountain rescue teams have been working round the clock rescuing survivors. The victim has been getting round-the-clock protection from the police.

round trip return journey to and from. The round trip to New York only cost her £150.

RUB. rub along with someone have good and harmonious relations with someone. John seems to rub along with Jenny quite well. Opposite of **rub someone up the wrong way**.

rub one's hands anticipate or savour success; sometimes applied to another's misfortune (the Germans call it *Schadenfreude*). She showed herself to be quite nasty, and kept rubbing her hands with glee at his embarrassment.

rub someone's nose in it keep reminding someone in an unkind way of something that is probably best forgotten. Don't keep talking about that holiday. We all know it was a disaster, and there's no need to rub my nose in it. A metaphor from training cats and dogs the hard way, 'it' being something unfragrant.

rub of the green sporting good luck. It was a tough match, but Martina seemed to have the rub of the green, and so she won her game. From golf, where the term meant accidental interference with the course of the ball's run. Originally this could have been helpful or unhelpful to one's lie. The expression is also the title of a funny story by P G Wodehouse.

rub off on someone pass on to someone via close contact or heredity. Her father's musical skills have rubbed off on her and she's become a famous violinist.

rub salt in the wound add to someone's feelings of distress, shame, embarrassment, etc. She missed the party, and her friends unintentionally rubbed salt in the wound by telling her how wonderful it had been. Salt was once used for antiseptic purposes, and was very painful on open sores.

rub shoulders with someone be in social contact with someone. There she was, a youngster from the slums, rubbing shoulders with the Duke of This and the Duchess of That. Compare **hob-nob with someone**.

rub someone up the wrong way antagonise someone. I don't know how it happened, but I seem to have rubbed her up the wrong way, and now she refuses to speak to me. The reference is to an animal's fur. Opposite of **rub along with someone**.

RUFFLE. ruffle someone's feathers annoy someone. It was clear that the speech had ruffled quite a few feathers in the hall.

RULE. rule of thumb rough calculation or estimate, lacking the benefit of more careful or scientific measurement. Most of his work is rule-of-thumb stuff, but he generally gets very accurate results. In Roman times, workmen used their thumbs and feet to measure length. Twelve thumbs (in French, or 'inches' in English) measured one foot, a standard measure for many centuries. Compare **rough and ready; (by the) seat of the pants**.

rule something/one out of court prevent usually a person from being considered for a job or assignment because of some formal disqualification. I was almost given the job, but was ruled out of court at the last minute because I didn't have a university degree. Not from tennis courts but from courts of law, meaning 'inadmissible'.

rule the roost dominate a group; lord it over others. You don't have to stay there long to realise that it's Granny who rules the roost in that household. From the farmyard, where the cockerel usually displays his dominance over the hens.

rule with a rod of iron keep very strict control. Our Latin teacher was a tyrant who ruled us all with a rod of iron. Used in the King James Bible: 'And he shall rule them with a rod of iron.' Revelation ii.27.

RUMBLE. rumble someone find out someone's real intentions, when these have been deliberately concealed. It took us quite a long time to rumble him – he fooled us for years.

RUN. run along! go away! Run along and play in the garden.

run amok/amuck run into a wild frenzy; be completely out of control and looking for blood. When the police arrived, they were confronted with a gang of football hooligans running amuck in the

town's square. From the Malay word for a drug-induced frenzy, in English from 1663. Compare **go berserk**.

run away with the idea draw the conclusion. He seems to have run away with the idea that the world owes him a decent living.

run something by one (again) remind one, refresh one's memory. I'm afraid I've forgotten exactly what happened. Could you please run the whole thing by me again? A phrasal verb, from the cinema.

run counter to contradict. I didn't like working for that company; its ethics ran counter to most of my own.

run for it try to escape. When no one was looking, the captives made a run for it.

run for one's life try to escape to safety. When the volcano erupted, everyone in the village ran for their lives.

(something) runs in the family (some condition, etc. is) hereditary in the family. Most of them are very artistic; in fact, painting seems to run in that family.

run into debt become indebted. He was very careless with money, and soon ran into huge debts.

run something into the ground use something until it becomes useless – literally, until it falls in pieces to the ground. He's been driving an old tractor for years, and says he's not going to get a new one until he's run the old one into the ground.

run of good/bad luck sequence of good or bad luck over a period of time. He's had such a run of bad luck over the past few months that he's become genuinely apprehensive about what's going to happen to him next.

run-of-the-mill average; ordinary; unspectacular. When he came to work for us, most colleagues were very impressed; now, they can see he is just a good, run-of-the-mill worker.

run out of something have nothing left of something. The bank has run out of money.

run something past someone study someone's reaction to an idea, proposal, etc. Let's run that idea past the management committee and see what they have to say. **Probably from film technology: running a section of film past an editor, observer, etc. to check all the details.**

run rings/circles round someone be much better than someone. The Russian chess champion ran rings round his opponent. **From athletics, where a fast runner may bypass a slower one and perhaps win the race.**

run riot behave in wild or riotous fashion. The football fans ran riot through the town, smashing shop windows and terrorising the local people.

run/go round in circles (getting nowhere) appear to be very busy, without actually achieving anything. He's been running round in circles all week trying to organise a reception for his clients – and he's getting nowhere.

run short of something not have enough of something. We seem to be running short of milk – would you please buy me a pint?

run the gauntlet endure/provoke attack from all sides. The prime minister ran the gauntlet of opposition taunts and jeers for her mishandling of the Westland affair. **From a rather savage military practice, of punishing offenders by making them run between two lines of tormentors who try to whip or lash them as they run by. The practice was said to have originated in Sweden, and was in use as a form of discipline in the army of king Gustavus Adolphus during the Thirty Years War (1618–48).**

run the show be in charge. Who's running this show anyway?

run to (something) 1. afford. I'm sorry, but we can't run to a family holiday this year – the budget won't permit it. 2. **include or contain.** It was a nice flat, and the front room even ran to a view across the bay.

run to earth catch or locate someone/something after long search. It's always very satisfying when you can identify a quotation and run it to earth. **From the hunting field: chasing a fox to its earth.**

run to seed become unfit. When I saw Jones last week, I must say he looked as if he'd run to seed a little. **From gardening. Compare past one's sell-by date**.

run wild move about in an uncontrolled way. I took a class of children to the swimming pool, and some of them tried to run wild.

RUNNER. runner up a competitor who takes second place. She was runner up in last year's flower show with her gigantic chrysanthemums. **Originally from dog racing.**

RUNNING. running battle ongoing dispute. There's been a running battle in the press for years between supporters and opponents of nuclear power.

running dog lackey; puppet. People of the world, unite to defeat the US aggressors and all their running dogs! **The phrase was pejorative, a translation of a Chinese idiom much favoured by Chairman Mao in his propaganda wars against the US. Compare paper tiger**.

RUSH. rush one's fences act hurriedly, without thinking carefully. He presented his argument coolly and carefully, without rushing his fences. **From show-jumping.**

rush hour period when traffic is busiest with people getting to and from their places of work. I try not to drive during the rush hour.

rush of blood (to the head) expression meaning that one suddenly does something uncharacteristic, impulsive, daring, foolish, etc. I think he must have had a serious rush of blood to the head when he said he'd take us all out for supper to the Café Royal, i.e. this was not something he usually did.

RUSHED. rushed off one's feet very busy. The New Year sales are the busiest time for our shops, and the assistants are rushed off their feet for a week. **A hyperbolic term.**

RUSSIAN. Russian roulette a reference to a dangerous and potentially lethal activity. There were no fire escapes in the building, and the owners were accused of playing Russian roulette with the inmates' lives. Popular among imperial Russian army officers, the game of Russian roulette involved putting a bullet in a six-cylinder revolver, spinning the chamber, and then firing the gun at one's head – thus accepting a one-in-six chance of killing oneself.

S

SABRE. sabre rattling uttering loud and reckless (but often empty) threats. Nobody pays the slightest attention to all the sabre rattling which emanates from the Ruritanian Ministry of Information. Originally military, the 18th-century reference was to cavalry soldiers armed with sabres. The scary rattling sound of sabres being drawn was often more than enough to quell a disturbance or riot, without the soldiers having to use them.

SACRED. sacred cow something that people do not like to question; a taboo subject. One of today's sacred cows is political correctness – no one likes to be too critical of it. From the Hindu belief in the sacredness of cattle.

SACRIFICIAL. sacrificial lamb scapegoat, often submissive and unprotesting. With the gentlemen of the press shouting for blood, the prime minister thought nothing of throwing a couple of sacrificial lambs to the wolves in the hope of temporarily slaking their fury. In the metaphor of all the European languages, the original sacrificial lamb was Jesus Christ, the 'lamb' of God, who was sacrificed for human sinners. See for example the opening words of the 16th-century Henry Constable's poem 'To the Blessed Sacrament': 'When thee, O holy sacrificial lamb,/ In severed signs I white and liquid see:'

SAFE. safe and sound unharmed and undamaged. In spite of all their adventures, they got back to harbour safe and sound. A dyad, occasionally 'safe and sure'.

safe as houses very safe. We bought shares in that company because we believed it to be as safe as houses. Other common or standard similes are 'safe as the bank of England', 'safe as the rock of Gibraltar'.

safe bet fair assumption; reasonable guess; opinion or view that is likely to prove correct. It's been raining for weeks, so it's a pretty safe bet that it'll rain again tomorrow.

SAIL. sail close to the wind stay only just inside the rules or the law; engage in activities that may not be illegal, but which are definitely shady. They run some sort of scrap-metal business which is said to sail rather close to the wind and supply arms to some of the world's more murderous military regimes. The originally nautical idiom implied the real dangers inherent in this kind of sailing.

SALAD. salad days one's inexperienced and callow but happy youth. She sighed when she recalled all the exciting times of her salad days half a century ago. A quotation from Shakespeare's *Antony and Cleopatra*: 'My salad days,/When I was green in judgment.' Compare **palmy days**.

SALT. salt of the earth people who are good, generous, humane; people who give life its savour and thereby preserve our civilisation. Some of these old crofters are the salt of the earth: they have almost nothing, but they will happily share the little they have with you. The origin of this idiom is biblical, from Christ's words in the Sermon on the Mount, in Matthew v.12–13, to the people who were persecuted because of their loyalty to His cause: 'Rejoice, and be exceeding glad, for great is your reward in heaven…Ye are the salt of the earth.'

SAME. same here conversational gambit, meaning 'I agree'. 'I never eat shellfish,' said John. 'Same here,' Sally agreed, 'I think they're very over-rated.'

same old story usual refrain, excuse or comment. I complained about the confusion to the bank manager, but he gave me the same old story about the computer breaking down and being short-staffed. That's all he can ever think to say.

SANDS. sands (of time) are running out time is running out. He knows how ill he is, and that the sands are running out for him. A metaphor from the hour-glass.

SAUCE. (what is) sauce for the goose (is sauce for the gander) what is good enough for one person should be good enough for another.

He went to South Africa to watch the World Cup last year, so this year it's my turn for a foreign trip – after all, if it's sauce for the goose it's sauce for the gander.

SAVE. save one's bacon/skin save oneself from danger, embarrassment, etc.; avoid injury. His book sold very well and earned him a decent income – it saved his bacon in more ways than one. Perhaps from the medieval idea that if one was able to keep a well-stocked store of smoked or salted bacon through the winter months, one would be safe from starvation.

save one's breath abandon a conversation because it serves no useful purpose. I tried to tell him about the dangers of such a voyage but I might as well have saved my breath, because he was determined to make the trip. Compare **talk to a brick wall**.

save one's face keep a good reputation; avoid public disgrace. He managed to save his face and come to some arrangement with the shop from which he had allegedly stolen the book. Originally Chinese, opposite of **lose face**. Also 'save appearances'.

save one's skin/neck avoid a dangerous or even life-threatening encounter, situation, etc. He was interested only in saving his own skin, and was one of the first people into a lifeboat. The original reference was to execution.

SAVED. saved by the bell reprieved from something dangerous, embarrassing, unpleasant, etc. at the last minute. We've been saved by the bell – tomorrow's meeting has been postponed because of the lawyers' phone call. A sporting idiom from boxing, and the bell rung to signal the end of a round. Familiar also to all school-age children as an expression beloved of teachers when the bell rings at the end of a lesson.

SAVING. saving grace positive feature or quality which redeems a person/thing from obscurity, mediocrity or other disagreeable characteristics. He's a dreadful fellow, and his one and only saving grace is the fact that he lives so far away. The original concept was theological: that a person is saved from damnation by grace.

SAY. I say conversational gambit to signal one's view, or one's intention to initiate a conversation. Sometimes repeated facetiously. I say, I say, I say, look whose car has just driven up!

say a mouthful say more than one realises. When I told him he was a crook, I hardly realised quite what a mouthful I was saying. Only much later did I discover that he was the main drug-dealer in the city.

say one's piece make one's opinion known. He's been worrying about the problem for weeks, but now he's said his piece about it, and we're going to try and help him resolve it. Sometimes 'say one's pennyworth' or the humorous near-obsolete 'add one's groatsworth'.

say the word give the order; tell one what to do. She only has to say the word and I'll marry her.

SCARE. scare stiff terrify. All her life she's been scared stiff of spiders. Other common hyperboles are 'scare to death' and 'scare shitless'.

scare the (living) daylights out of terrify. The spooky darkness, the creaking of the door and the wailing of the cat combined to scare the living daylights out of me. 'Daylights' is a slang term for one's eyes. Verbs like 'beat' and 'knock' are also used in this idiom.

SCHOOL. school of hard knocks tough environment or upbringing. He's one of those folk whose early life was very deprived, so he's grown up in the school of hard knocks. A humorous send-up of the old notion that school was supposed to knock the nonsense out of boys from a privileged background, before they went on to Oxbridge to have it 'all put gently back' (in the words of Max Beerbohm).

SCOOP. scoop the pool win all the prizes. Class prizes for geography, history, French and German – John has more or less scooped the pool this year.

SCORE. score/hit a bull's eye get something exactly right, or on target. The prosecution lawyer knew exactly where the accused's case was weak, and he soon hit the bull's eye and got the accused person to start confessing. **From archery.**

score a hat-trick be phenomenally successful. He's a concert cellist and a distinguished composer; now he will score a hat-trick by conducting his own work. **The expression originally came from the action of taking three wickets with three successive balls in cricket. The bowler used to be entitled to a new hat from his club for achieving this feat. The idiom has now widened to include three related or consecutive successes in any field of endeavour.**

score points (on someone) try to outshine or outperform (someone). Lots of TV news reporters are so unpopular with the viewing public that even politicians know how to score points on them. Compare **one up on** someone.

SCOTCH. scotch a snake temporarily incapacitate an enemy, or alleviate a threat. You may have scotched that particular snake, but I don't think it's gone away for good. **From Shakespeare's** *Macbeth*: 'We have scotch'd the snake, not kill'd it.'

SCRAPE. scrape the barrel use the last or least suitable part of the available resources. I see Bloggs has been brought back into the team, so they're really having to scrape the bottom of the barrel. **The bottom of the barrel contained the dregs, or worst part, of something. If times were good, you didn't use this part, but instead opened a fresh barrel.**

SCRATCH. scratch a living earn a very modest income. He scratches a living by writing poetry. **A** metaphor from subsistence agriculture.

scratch A and find/get B look below the surface veneer and find something different from what appears on the surface. Scratch a suave and urbane English civil servant and you'll often discover a Scotsman on the make. **Commonly used to make a generalisation about something. From the proverb: 'Scratch a Russian and you'll find a Tartar.'**

scratch someone's back (and s/he'll scratch yours) offer help or backing to someone (in the hope that s/he will reciprocate). He did me a considerable favour by giving me that project to complete; I'm more than happy to scratch his back in return.

scratch the surface do something in a superficial way. I'm afraid his analysis of the problem hardly even begins to scratch the surface of it.

SCREAM. scream/yell blue murder scream in great terror and alarm. An old woman ran out of the house screaming blue murder. **The colour blue was once said to be an omen of death, or an indication of the presence of ghosts or the devil, hence expressions like 'blue with fear'.** Compare **blue funk**.

SCREW. screw/pluck up one's courage force oneself to be brave. It took me ages to screw up my courage and ask for a pay increase.

SCRUB. scrub it stop doing it. We were fed up listening to his singing and asked him to give us a break and scrub it for a while. **Perhaps 'scrub' is here derived as a contraction from 'rub', as in 'rub it out' or 'erase it'.**

SEAL. seal/stamp of approval official recognition or ratification. The government seem to have given the project their seal of approval by backing it in such an unambiguous way. **From the old practice of affixing seals to documents which had been officially approved. Seals gave documents legal status and also ensured confidentiality. A more modern version is 'stamp of approval', in an age when seals have become uncommon.**

SEAMY. seamy side of life the worst or roughest side. He worked for a year in a Paris nightclub, and learnt a bit about the seamy side of life. **The 'seamy' side of a garment was the underside, which showed the seams.**

SEARCH. search me I don't know. 'Where are my glasses?' 'Search me, I've not seen them.' **Originally a mock invitation.**

SEAT. (by the) seat of the pants following one's own inspiration and gut instincts. He has always run his business as a seat-of-the-pants operation, rather than in some more conventional textbook fashion. Compare **on a wing and a prayer; rough and ready**.

SECOND. second bite at the cherry second chance to do something. He's very lucky – he gets a second bite at the cherry in October if he fails the exam in June. From the idea that cherries are not often big enough to provide a second bite.

second fiddle inferior part or role. Fred resigned from the job saying he was bored playing second fiddle to an incompetent manager. From the organisation of the orchestra, into first and second violins.

second guess predict, anticipate. It's neither wise nor easy to second guess an unpredictable person like that.

second hand 1. not new. He's a dealer in second-hand cars. 2. derivative, unoriginal. Most of her ideas are second-hand, and she seldom acknowledges her sources.

second nature semi-automatic behaviour; skill or habit that one has learnt. He learnt French in his childhood, so it's really been second nature to him all his life.

second rate mediocre, inferior. It was a dreadful orchestra, and the chorus was pretty second rate too.

second sight clairvoyance. I know one or two people with second sight, and some of them will tell you your fortune for a small fee.

second wind ability to continue with something. I got rather fed up writing my book, and had to put it aside; but now I seem to have found my second wind, and am getting on with it again. From athletics: an athlete in good training can pace himself and get his second wind whereas an unfit one would tire out before reaching that stage.

SEE. see a man about a dog expression used to conceal the exact purpose of one's business. He muttered something about going up to London to see a man about a dog. The term was much used by a character trying to divert attention from a tricky situation in a popular play called *Flying Scud*, by Dion Boucicault, in 1866. Nowadays, the expression is a semi-humorous signal that the speaker doesn't wish to elaborate on a subject; or it is a euphemistic way of saying that one needs to make a trip to the toilet. Nineteenth-century cowboys would use 'see a man about a horse' (same sense).

see daylight see the end or conclusion of a long hard job. After about six weeks' hard slog, we began to see daylight. A metaphor of working through the long hours of darkness in order to complete something. Compare **see the light**.

see eye to eye agree. They are always fighting among themselves, and can never manage to see eye to eye on even the simplest things. From Isaiah lxx.8.

see/think fit decide that it is right, appropriate, convenient, etc. I will help you when and if I see fit to do so, not before.

see how the cards stack up find out what the odds are, for or against. Eventually the prime minister could see how the cards were stacked up against her, so she resigned. From the gaming table.

see how the land lies reconnoitre; check the situation; find out what's happening or how people are thinking. The board of directors are meeting shareholders this afternoon to see how the land lies on the subject of a takeover. Of military origin.

see it/something through continue working with something to its conclusion or completion. He's got a hard job to do, but he's a proud and stubborn man, and he's determined to see the job through.

see no further than one's nose be very short-sighted; be unable to plan ahead; have no vision. Many businessmen can't think beyond next year's company results; they're only interested in the short term and can't see further than their noses. Compare **can't see the wood for the trees**.

see reason accept an argument to be sensible. He can be terribly stubborn and flatly refuse to see reason on certain issues.

see red get very angry; lose one's temper. His colleagues were teasing him, and all of a sudden he saw red and started swearing and cursing at them. The metaphor is of a bull: when it sees a red object, it is said to want to attack that object. See also **red rag to a bull** and compare **lose one's rag**.

see stars be concussed, knocked unconscious. There was a deafeningly loud bang, followed by the noise of crashing masonry, and then suddenly he was seeing stars and lying on the floor.

see the back of someone/something an idiom used mainly with 'pleased/glad/relieved', and also more rarely with 'sorry': glad etc. that something/someone has gone away. It was a long and very severe winter and we were all glad to see the back of it.

see the finger/hand of God in something attribute something to fate or to divine intervention. I decided there was no point seeing the hand of God in my rescue, but nor was there any denying the fact that I'd been monumentally lucky.

see the light 1. understand, realise. It took George a long time to see the light and realise that he was going to have to work a lot harder. The original metaphor was religious, and the light was the Christian, 'inner' light or dawning. Compare **see daylight**. 2. become public. His paintings didn't see the light till 200 years after his death.

see which way the cat jumps/wind blows try to anticipate the way in which majority opinion is going to go, in order to incline that way oneself. Like the Vicar of Bray, the Earl of Mar had such a reputation as a trimmer that they called him 'Bobbing John'; these were two historical figures who liked to see which way the cat would jump

before making their own positions known. From the traditional wisdom that cats were known for their nimbleness and were seldom wrongfooted. Same connotation: 'see which way the wind blows' and 'sit on the fence'. Compare **catch someone on the hop; show one's hand; straw(s) in the wind**.

see with one's own eyes witness directly for oneself. He wasn't interested in what other people thought about the events; he had seen them with his own eyes and needed no further insight. The opposite of second- or third-hand information. A version of **seeing is believing**.

SEED. seed corn resources for the future. Today's schoolkids are the seed corn for the future of the country. An agricultural metaphor. A farmer's seed corn is grain kept for planting next year's crop rather than for immediate sale or consumption.

SEEING. seeing is believing unless one sees something oneself, one does not believe it. I'd never have guessed I'd get to the Pyramids this year, but seeing is believing, and here I am. A saying.

SELL. sell/buy a pup sell/buy something completely worthless. I was sold a real pup when I bought this car – it's always got something wrong with it. Compare **pig in a poke**.

sell someone/something down the river betray someone/something. One or two of my colleagues voiced the opinion that it was a worthless plan, which rather sold it down the river. American, from the early 19th century. Runaway slaves escaping to the North were sometimes sold back down the Mississippi river to the Southern slave states.

sell like hot cakes sell very fast. That book sold like hot cakes, and had to be reprinted several times on publication. From baking: a fresh batch always smells good, and accordingly sells fastest.

sell someone short give someone less than the proper amount. It wasn't till I got home that I realised they'd sold me short.

sell oneself short be modest about someone's achievements. He doesn't project himself very well, and tends to sell himself short.

sell one's soul/granny be entirely motivated by financial considerations. He'd think nothing of selling his granny if he thought it would get him a pay increase.

sell the pass accept the loss of a strategic advantage. There is likely to be a stiff argument from both sides of the debate, and we are not going to sell the pass until we have to. Originally Irish, with the connotation of giving information to the English authorities.

SEND. send someone about his business summarily dismiss someone with whom one is displeased. He's a hopeless van driver, and has just had his fourth driving accident, so we've had to send him about his business.

send someone away with a flea in his ear dismiss someone with a stinging or mortifying reproof. She arrived late for the interview, and they sent her away with a flea in her ear about punctuality.

send packing dismiss; send away. I told him his behaviour was quite unacceptable, and sent him packing. From an old use of 'pack', as in 'pack someone off', meaning 'leave in a hurry, with one's belongings'.

send to Coventry refuse to speak to someone. We decided that the only way to register our disgust at his conduct was to send him to Coventry. The story goes that, during the English Civil War, the townspeople of Coventry were Royalists but the town's garrison was Roundhead. The townsfolk refused to speak to the soldiers, and thus the latter disliked being billeted there.

SEPARATE. separate/sort out the sheep from the goats separate/distinguish the good candidates from the bad, strong from weak, etc. There's nothing like a really tough exam paper for separating the sheep from the goats. From the biblical idea that sheep are helpless creatures in

need of a shepherd to guide and protect them, whereas goats are lascivious and wicked. See for example Matthew xxv.32. Also 'separate the wheat from the chaff', another biblical idiom with a similar drift, the wheat representing good grain, whereas the chaff are the worthless husks.

SERVE. serve hand and foot attend to someone's every need. Her father told her that she was a spoilt brat, and that his job in life was not to serve her hand and foot and dance to her every call.

serve its turn prove its usefulness. I wanted to throw the old desk out, but my wife didn't agree, saying: 'You never know when it might serve its turn.'

serve one right usually an exclamation, indicating that one deserves any punishment one gets.'He was arrested for dangerous driving.' 'Serves him right, he shouldn't be allowed near a car.'

SET. set a cat among the pigeons cause a commotion, uproar, kerfuffle, etc. Don't mention his ex-mistress if you don't want to set a cat among the pigeons. Often followed by seeing **feathers fly**. If it is only a mild commotion, people sometimes fine-tune the metaphor and refer to a 'flutter in the dovecotes'.

set someone at rest allay someone's fears; calm someone. She's been worrying about her pension, but we've set her at rest on that score.

set by the ears cause surprise or aggravation between people. The argument about the boundary wall between their gardens has rather set them by the ears, and now they seem to be avoiding each other.

set one's cap at try to gain someone's love. It's fairly obvious from the way he talks to her at every opportunity that he's set his cap at her. Also **make a play for**. From the days when ladies would wear a fancy headpiece to attract a gentleman's attention.

set one's face against oppose; be determined to resist. She's completely set her face against a foreign holiday. From the Bible, as in Leviticus xx.3: 'I will set my face against that man.'

set one's heart on be very keen on. I've set my heart on going to Australia to visit my son this summer.

set in concrete/tablets of stone fixed and not negotiable. The prime minister's refusal to set in concrete the government's policy on the euro has been seen as a sign of weakness. A 'tablet of stone' is another name for a gravestone, which once engraved stays engraved. Thus is its message rather final, and not easily 'tweaked'.

set someone's teeth on edge make an unpleasant impression; annoy. The pettiness of the argument so set my teeth on edge that I had to leave the room. From the often subconscious practice of grinding one's teeth to prevent one crying out in pain, disgust, etc.

set/start the ball rolling get something started, especially a conversation or a social event. Everyone stood around shyly for a few minutes, but Mr Grant set the ball rolling with a question about our hostess's wonderful garden. Compare **break the ice**.

set/put the seal on ensure; guarantee. Their dismal defeat on Saturday sets the seal on Arsenal's relegation next season. The 'seal' of an important official used to be his mark of official ratification and a guarantee of a document's legitimacy.

set the Thames/heather on fire make a strong impression; do something so wonderful and exciting that people can think and talk of little else. He's quite a good sprinter, but I don't think he's ever going to set the heather on fire and break the world record. The Tiber, Rhine, Liffey, Clyde, Hudson and other rivers are pressed into service, as appropriate.

set tongues wagging cause people to gossip. There's nothing like a little local scandal to set tongues wagging. Compare **no smoke without fire**.

set to with a will work or eat vigorously. As soon as the meal arrived, the starving men set to with a will.

SETTLE. settle someone's hash threaten to subdue or otherwise punish someone. Let him

kick his ball into my garden one more time and I'll settle his hash for him. A 'hash' was a mess (from French 'hachée') and by 'settling' it one sorted it out. It is also possible to **make a hash** (or mess) of something.

SEVENTH. seventh heaven ecstasy, bliss. It was a very happy occasion, and bride and groom both seemed to be in seventh heaven. From the old Judaic and Islamic belief that there were seven heavens, the seventh being the dwelling place of God and the angels. Not dissimilar to **cloud nine**.

SEW. sew (something) up sort out or organise efficiently; finalise. Don't bother with that – it's all been sewn up long ago. A phrasal verb.

SEX. sex (something) up present something in such a way as to make a compelling argument; exaggerate. The argument for going to war with Iraq was not supported by the bare facts of the case, so it was sexed up. A phrasal verb of 2003, one of the Blair government's contributions to the English language. See **spin doctor; dodgy dossier**.

SHADES. shades of echoes or reminders of. It was a lovely husky voice, with shades of Ella Fitzgerald in it. The metaphor is of a person's shadow.

SHADOW. shadow of doubt the smallest, slightest doubt. He's guilty, beyond a shadow of doubt. Sometimes 'beyond a peradventure' is still heard, meaning 'beyond a perhaps'. Compare **sure as eggs is eggs**.

shadow of one's/its former self 1. person who has been seriously incapacitated through illness. It can be quite hard visiting a parent in her 90s who is a pale shadow of her former self. 2. person/thing who/which is less influential or effective than formerly. He can still beat most youngsters at tennis, even though his game is now only a shadow of its former self. Sometimes 'shadow of its former glory', especially in the context of old buildings, etc. Also see **to a shadow**.

SHAKE shake one's head indicate one's disagreement, disapproval, etc.; express refusal.

I saw him shake his head, and knew that the deal was off. The opposite of 'nodding' one's agreement.

shake in one's shoes be very afraid. He knew I was going to punish him, so I left him shaking in his shoes outside my office for 10 minutes or so. Compare **cool one's heels**.

SHAMBLES. (in a complete/utter) shambles (in a dreadful) mess. I hate visiting that house; everything in it is invariably in a complete shambles. The 'shambles' (a singular noun, but ending with 's') was the medieval abattoir or slaughter house. There are still streets called The Shambles in York, Nottingham and Brighton, where long ago there were rows of butchers' stalls. The overtones of mess and disorder have been retained in the modern idiom, but those of blood and gore have now been lost.

SHANKS'S. (on/by) shanks's pony on/by foot. So your car's broken down, has it? You'll just have to get to work on Shanks's pony. Thought to derive less from an actual Mr Shanks than from a jocular or facetious reference to a person's legs or 'shanks'.

SHARE. share and share alike share equally. There was a small cake between five of us, and we decided to share and share alike.

SHARP. sharp end of something place where things get done, where things happen, etc. It's a good dress shop, though hardly at the sharp end of the contemporary fashion scene. Compare **at the cutting/leading edge**.

sharp practice activities bordering on dishonesty. He is under investigation by his professional organisation for some sort of sharp practice at work. 'Sharp' is from the verb meaning 'swindle', which also gives words like 'cardsharper'.

SHED. shed light on make clear. Some of the new evidence begins to shed light on the problem.

SHELF. shelf life duration of something. He opened a restaurant for a couple of years, but I'm afraid it hasn't had a long shelf life. From the retail trade, and the shelf life of consumable goods marked on their label. The idiom **past one's sell-by date** is from the same stable.

SHELL. shell shocked deeply shocked. When the redundancies were announced, the workforce were so shell shocked that there was a deep silence. Originally, the reference was military: to troops traumatised by the effects of heavy gunfire. Similar to the more recent 'gobsmacked'.

SHILLY. shilly-shally be undecided, irresolute. It's time you stopped all this shilly-shallying and made up your mind. An 18th-century term created from 'Shill I, shall I?' A 'reduplicative' compound in which sounds are contrasted and repeated, the term can be used as a verb, adverb, adjective and noun. Compare **wishy-washy; argy-bargy; dilly-dally; hot and cold**.

SHIPS. ships that pass in the night people who meet once, establish a degree of intimacy and never see each other again. There were many ships that passed in the night that summer because the war had started, and people were thrown out of their normal social routines. The original image was nautical of course, of ships passing one another silently and invisibly at sea – their crews so close, yet so unknown to each other. H W Longfellow is attributed with the creation of the metaphor in *Tales of a Wayside Inn* (1874): 'Ships that pass in the night, and speak each other in passing;/Only a signal shown and a distant voice in the darkness…'

SHIPSHAPE. shipshape (and Bristol fashion) neat and orderly. He keeps a very shipshape little garden, with everything in its place. The term originally referred to a ship's seaworthiness; the additional reference to Bristol is to the 15th and 16th centuries when Bristol was a centre of England's maritime trade.

SHIT. the shit hits the fan a problem becomes really serious, and a difficult situation arises. We all knew there was going to be big trouble, so we planned to be out of the way when the shit hit the fan. An Americanism, offensive to many.

SHOOGLY. shoogly peg insecure or vulnerable position. The prime minister's job has been on a shoogly peg since he devalued the currency. Compare **take someone down a peg/notch (or two)**. A Scots idiom, the image is of an insecure coat peg or hook.

SHOOT. shoot a line boast. He's always shooting some line about his marvellous skills as a womaniser. Also 'shoot one's mouth off', meaning to talk excessively or irresponsibly.

shoot one's bolt 1. have enough, especially of food. I'm sorry, I cannot eat another morsel – I've shot my bolt. From warfare with bows and arrows, via a proverb: 'A fool's bolt is soon shot.' 2. ejaculate semen. Slang term for the male orgasm. Also 'shoot one's load/wad'.

shoot down in flames emphatically reject or criticise something. The idea wasn't at all popular and most committee members lost no time in shooting it down in flames. From aerial combat.

shoot from the hip act without considering the potential results of one's actions on others. You need to watch John: he tends to shoot from the hip. Originally from Hollywood cowboy movies. Such people often **take no prisoners**.

shoot oneself in the foot accidentally harm or damage one's prospects or reputation, often while trying to denigrate or criticise someone else. Every week we have an example of some inept politician shooting himself in the foot, frequently in front of a TV camera. Originally American, where the extensive and powerful gun lobby is quite accident prone. Compare **(score) an own goal; hoist on one's own petard**.

shoot the breeze chat in a relaxed, informal, friendly way. After supper we went out for a pint of beer and shot the breeze for a while. **American in origin**.

shoot the messenger see **don't shoot the messenger**.

SHORT. short and sweet (and to the point) very brief; shorter than anticipated (and well focused). Like all good meetings, it was short and sweet and to the point. Compare **beat about the bush**.

short cut quick way from A to B. It started to rain, so we took the short cut through the woods.

short selling selling an asset or security one doesn't own in the hope of buying it back later at a lower price, thereby making a profit. Short selling and short sellers were blamed for the Wall Street Crash (1929) and their role in the 2008/9 crash is thought to have been equally toxic. A version of fiddling the market, sometimes while Rome burns and sometimes even helping to stoke the fire. Compare **hedge fund**.

SHOT. shot across someone's bows warning. By contacting her solicitor at this early stage, Elizabeth has fired a warning shot across Robert's bows. From naval or gunboat 'diplomacy'.

shot in the arm encouragement; moral support; boost. He's been feeling a bit unloved recently, so your encouragement is a great shot in the arm for him. The original reference was to intravenous injection. See also **quick fix**.

shot/stab in the dark random guess. Her suggestion was a bit of a shot in the dark, but the audience clearly liked it and encouraged her to follow it up. From shooting 'blind', normally in self-defence.

shot through with mixed with. The story was a tragedy, but shot through with lighter moments fortunately. From weaving, and the 'shooting' of different colours into the threads of the warp. We still talk about 'shot silk' in this sense. A phrasal verb.

SHOTGUN. shotgun wedding enforced marriage, necessitated by the pregnancy of the female partner. Being heavily pregnant, she made do with a shotgun wedding at the local registry office. The expression suggests that the bride's family may have forced the ceremony on the groom by threatening to shoot him if he failed to **make an honest woman** of the bride. The idiom is less common now that there is less of a social stigma attached to illegitimacy.

SHOULDER. shoulder to cry on someone to go to for sympathy and moral support when one is feeling upset. I'm not his lover or anything like that, I'm just a handy shoulder for him to cry on from time to time.

shoulder to shoulder together. We stand shoulder to shoulder on that particular question. **Also 'side by side'** (same sense).

SHOW. show a clean pair of heels flee. I wanted a word with him, but he had shown a clean pair of heels by the time I got down to his office, and his secretary said he wouldn't be back till the end of the week. **Also take to one's heels**.

show a leg get up. The party went on till late in the night, so no one managed to show a leg much before lunchtime next day. This was once a call to sailors to get out of their hammocks. There were many variations, such as 'Wakey, wakey, rise and shine;/Show a leg, the weather's fine.' In the 18th century, the cry was to those women on board ship who were sleeping with sailors. The sailors had to get up, but if the women threw a leg over the side of the hammock they were allowed to remain abed.

show one's (true) colours show oneself as one really is, beneath any appearances one puts on. He seemed nice enough, but when I needed help he rather showed his colours by declining to do anything for me. **Originally nautical.**

show one's face be present, especially in semi-hostile company. It's a long time since he's shown his face in this office.

show one's hand allow one's plans to be known. He never discusses his affairs, and his wife says he wouldn't even show his hand to her. **From card playing. Compare lay one's cards on the table; see which way the cat jumps**.

show of hands approximate estimate of the support for an idea, proposal, etc., mainly in a political context. The proposal wasn't put to a formal vote, but a show of hands indicated that it had a lot of support among the audience. **Compare straw poll**.

show one's paces/mettle show one's ability or worth. The demonstrators were in noisy mood, and John was right to anticipate that they'd want to make the management show their paces. 'Paces' refers on the whole to present or future challenges, while 'mettle' is most frequently used about a past achievement. Both words are taken from horse-riding. **Also put someone through their paces**.

show one's teeth show one's authority, sometimes in order to try to intimidate someone. She's a delightful person, but she'll not hesitate to show her teeth if circumstances require. From animal behaviour. A phrasal verb with a similar sense is 'back off'.

show the flag make a dutiful or token appearance at a function. I didn't much want to go to the party, but I knew that I ought to show the flag for an hour or two. Originally a nautical metaphor, from the days when Britain ruled the waves and made up – and waived – the rules of the sea. Ships were supposed to show their flags to identify themselves.

show someone the ropes teach someone how to do something. Using a computer is easy enough, if someone is prepared to show you the ropes. From the navy, where apprentice sailors had to be shown what all the ropes in a ship's rigging were for and how to use them properly.

SHRINKING. shrinking violet timid person. You could hardly describe Mrs Ramsbottom as a shrinking violet – look at that outfit she's wearing. From a small and delicate woodland plant so named because it recoils from the touch.

SHRUG. shrug one's shoulders indicate one's helplessness, indifference to something; decline to express an opinion. Asked what he thought about the new building, John just shrugged his shoulders.

SHUT. shut one's eyes to ignore; pretend not to see something. I said I could happily shut my eyes to his boorishness if only he promised to give up his dishonest ways.

shut up like a clam become quiet or withdrawn, usually because one is worried, upset, etc. As soon as we mentioned the war, the entire group shut up like a clam. A standard simile from the seashore, of withdrawal into one's shell at the threat of danger, embarrassment, etc.

shut up shop retire. He was made redundant at 50, but he said that was far too young for him to shut up shop.

shut your trap/gob/mouth/clanger/cakehole or **shut it!** impolite ways of telling someone to stop speaking. Is there no way we can get that guy to shut his trap? Similar idioms include **belt up!; shut up!; put a sock in it!; hold your tongue!**

SICK. sick as a parrot thoroughly ill, depressed, dejected. He was as sick as a parrot when he realised he'd lost his winning lottery ticket. A standard simile, as are 'sick as a pig/dog'. In the 18th century, parrots brought back to Britain as pets often moped and pined for their native warm climate. Nor would the long sea voyage to Europe have done much for their health.

sick of the sight/sound of thoroughly weary or fed up with looking at/listening to. I wish he'd go away – I'm sick of the sight of him. Similar idioms include 'sick to death of', 'sick to the back teeth of', 'sick and tired of'.

SIGHT. a (damn) sight better than much better than. I hope Jones can do the job – he's a damn sight better at it than the other man. A common intensifier, also 'a damn sight cheaper/faster/colder', etc.

sight for sore eyes a beautiful or welcome sight, something or someone that is a pleasure to look at. There he was in his uniform, neat and smart and scrubbed, looking like a sight for sore eyes. Sometimes used ironically to express the opposite.

sight unseen without examining something. He seemed so desperate to live on the island that when we put our house on the market he bought it sight unseen.

SIGN. sign on the dotted line formally endorse something; agree to do something; commit oneself to something. I usually vote for them as the least of several evils, but they've actually never got me to sign on the dotted line or join their party. From legal documents, signed before witnesses along a dotted line.

sign the pledge promise not to drink alcohol. He used to drink far too much, but I gather he has more or less signed the pledge now. The temperance movement in the 19th century encouraged people to sign a public declaration to totally abstain from drinking alcoholic liquor. Such a ceremony was often regarded as evidence that the signer had become a 'reformed' character. See also **on the wagon**.

SILENCE. silence means/gives/conveys consent unless one speaks against something, people may think one agrees with it. He said nothing, and thinking that silence meant consent, I assumed he was happy about the proposal. From a Latin maxim, 'Qui tacet consentire videtur' (= 'He who is silent seems to consent').

SILENT. silent majority the mass of people, who don't have strong views, and who are not heard speaking in public as often as those who do have strong views. It takes a general election in this country for the silent majority to express a political view. Opposite of 'the chattering classes'.

SILLY. silly season high summer. The silly season this year seems to be dominated by discussions about the existence of the Loch Ness Monster. The term refers to the period when the British Parliament is not in session. Parliament's endlessly inventive silliness provides the press throughout the year with an abundance of ready-made trivia with which to fill the newspapers. In August and September, when Parliament is in abeyance, the press corps have to invent their own silly stories for the entertainment of their readers.

SILVER. silver lining compensating factor; the good side of a problem or misfortune. *The election result was a disaster, with one silver lining – the party had won control in Birmingham.* From the proverb: 'Every cloud has a silver lining.'

SIMILE

Simile is defined as a figure of speech which expresses a likeness between two entities, in English usually by means of the words *like* or *as*. The term comes from the Latin word *similis* (= like). Many similes are frequently used catch-phrases, which provide a rich source of more or less idiomatic English.

If we say that we are working *as hard as the Olympic rowing squad to win gold*, or that we are straining *like a rugby pack to win the ball*, we are creating similes. But we are not using idioms. If we say we slept *like a plank*, or *like a corpse*, to indicate that we slept soundly, we are again making similes – slightly clumsy ones. In order to make the statement idiomatic, we have to say we slept *like a log*. This is an established or 'standard simile'.

There are two main ways in which similes become idiomatic. Firstly there are the **standard similes** of the 'slept like a log' sort. These used to be conveniently listed, sometimes at enormous length, in old grammar books and primary school language books. There is a multitude of these semi-fixed expressions of likeness in English, some of them very colourful. A small selection follows.

With 'like'

go at something + *like a bull at a gate* (aggressively and carelessly)

enter a room + *like a bull in a china shop* (roughly and clumsily)

grin + *like a Cheshire cat* (broadly and inanely)

feel + *like a fish out of water* (out of one's element)

have an expression + *like the cat that got the cream* (look smug or slightly guilty)

run + *like the clappers* (fast)

behave + *like a lamb* (obediently and submissively)

respond + *like a red rag to a bull* (as if provoked)

packed + *like sardines* (very tightly)

go away + *like a thief in the night* (stealthily)

get on with someone + *like a house on fire* (very well)

criticism + *like water off a duck's back* (without impact or effect)

stranded + *like a beached whale* (very helpless)

mope about + *like a fart in a trance/ colander* (behave dreamily or ineffectively)

stand out + *like a whore at a christening* (look very out of place)

With 'as' (adjectival phrase)

as bold as brass (brazen, insolent)

as bright as a button (very clever and quick witted)

as cool as a cucumber (laid back, unperturbed)

as daft as a brush (crazy)

as dull as dishwater/ditchwater (utterly uninteresting)

as fit as a fiddle (very well and healthy)

as like as two peas in a pod (almost identical)

as nutty as a fruitcake (crazy)

as plain as a pikestaff (obvious)

as proud as a peacock (openly vain)

as right as rain (in good health)

as sober as a judge (very serious and sober)

as sound as a bell (in good condition, uncracked)
as thick as two short planks (dim, unintelligent)
as thick as thieves (conspiring, in cahoots)

Whether these similes are described as idioms or are accused of being clichés depends on who is using them and in what context. But all users of English should be encouraged to recognise them as part of the warp and woof of English, using them when appropriate and avoiding them – *like the plague* (to use an idiomatic simile!) – when inappropriate.

Often one adjective collocates with several others, as in: *as sure as death, as sure as eggs is eggs, as sure as I'm standing here, as sure as God made little green apples* – all of which are standard similes indicating shades of predictability and inevitability.

Many other standard similes are listed alphabetically in the main dictionary, under their adjective.

The second source of idiomatic similes in the language is the *quotation*. For example, if we say:

My love is like a red, red rose, or
The Assyrian came down like a wolf on the fold, or
I wandered lonely as a cloud.

we are making similes which are idioms. They are idiomatic simply because they are much quoted lines from Burns, Byron and Wordsworth respectively. As often as not, we use them without realising we are quoting, so deeply and widely have they percolated into and through the language.

SING. sing a different song/tune change one's opinion. His business partners used to think the world of him, but they're singing a different tune now that he's walked out on them.

sing from the same hymnsheet have views, opinions, etc. that harmonise with those of others. There used to be a lot of squabbling in our office, but nowadays most of us are singing from the same hymnsheet. Similar to 'pull in the same direction'. Compare **into line; out of tune**.

sing someone's praises praise someone loudly. Since England won the Grand Slam, all the sportswriters have been loud in singing their praises.

SINK. sink or swim succeed or fail; survive or perish. You can't be forever taking children's decisions for them; sooner or later they have to be left to sink or swim on their own.

SIT. sit on the fence prevaricate, especially in politics; decline to support someone. He decided to sit on the fence rather than come down on one side or the other. Similar to 'facing both ways'.

sit tight wait; do nothing. There was not much I could do, so I just sat tight and waited for the rain to stop.

sit up and take notice suddenly pay attention to something, or become properly aware of it. No one paid him the slightest attention till he won the lottery; then, all of a sudden, everyone was sitting up and taking notice of his every move.

SITTING. sitting duck easy target. We'll need to find some cover from the enemy; we're sitting ducks if they catch us here. From hunting, where a 'sitting' or stationary target is much easier to hit than a flying or running one.

sitting pretty in comfortable material circumstances. He's sitting pretty now that he's won the lottery. An Americanism from about 1910.

SIX. six of one and half a dozen of the other nothing to choose between two alternatives. They asked me if I'd rather go by train or by bus, but I said it was six of one and half a dozen of the other as far as I was concerned. Also 'six and two threes'. Compare **as broad as it's long**.

SIXTY. sixty-four (thousand) dollar question the big question (which wins the big prize, or to which everyone wants to know the answer). When I asked her about her marriage, she smiled at me coyly and said, 'Ah, that's the sixty-four dollar question.' The original $64 context was American radio quiz shows; TV upped the payouts a thousandfold.

SKATE. skate on thin ice risk danger or disaster or argument. Don't talk to him about that subject: he has very strong views on it, and to do so might be skating on very thin ice.

SKELETON. skeleton in the cupboard/closet secret, especially if one is ashamed or embarrassed by it. I suppose there must be a skeleton or two in most families' cupboards. The rather macabre image is of the gruesome discovery of a corpse long after its death. The manner of its death automatically then becomes suspicious.

skeleton staff small number of personnel. On public holidays we keep a skeleton staff on duty to provide essential services.

SKID. skid row dire poverty. It's not a street to walk up at night, being full of drunks and no-goods who are clearly just off skid row. Originally Skid Road. This was a street name in many towns of the American West by the 1880s. Logs were skidded along this route to rivers, railheads, etc. By the 1940s the term had acquired its present meaning, and referred to a neighbourhood inhabited by vagrants, alcoholics, etc. living rough or in cheap flophouses (dosshouses) and saloons.

SKY. sky pilot minister of religion. He was in charge of a mission, and like most sky pilots of the period he was very committed to the welfare of his congregation. The name was used by fishermen, cowboys and others, the former because of their superstition against uttering the word 'minister' or 'priest' on board their ships. The American use of the expression is more ironical.

SLAP. slap and tickle usually a reference to amorous foreplay. He may well have been looking for a bit of slap and tickle, but you can tell him from me he came to the wrong woman. A dyad.

SLEEP. sleep on something ponder a dilemma or think it through carefully, until one can reach a decision. We're sleeping on that particular project for the time being, but we'll be giving it a firm decision quite soon.

sleep rough sleep out of doors, as a vagrant, etc. Lots of youngsters run away from home after a quarrel with their parents, and end up sleeping rough in London.

sleep tight sleep well, used as an exclamatory comment. When the children went to bed, they used to say: 'Good night, sleep tight, don't let the bugs bite!'

SLEIGHT. sleight of hand clever knack; manual skill or adroitness; dexterity at deception. He produced the rabbit from the hat with a flourish, by a very slick piece of sleight of hand. They made the sales figures look semi-respectable, by some discreet sleight of hand in the presentation of their accounts. The word 'sleight' with this sense is now rarely found outside this expression; it is related to 'sly', as 'height' is to 'high'.

SLICE. slice/piece of the action payoff, share of the profits; proportion of the excitement. Before agreeing to help the gang, he insisted on being assured that he could expect to receive a sizeable slice of all the action. The term has moved from the underworld to the business community.

SLIP. slip one's mind forget. He was supposed to be at my office at four o'clock, but our meeting seems to have slipped his mind.

slip of the tongue small verbal error, often made unintentionally. I was so impressed by her charms that I accidentally called her Mrs Darling – a small freudian slip of the tongue perhaps.

slip through one's fingers miss an opportunity to do something pleasant, profitable, etc. Don't let this wonderful chance slip through your fingers – grab it while you can!

slip through the net escape. She's been trying to get him to come to her parties for years, but he always slips through the net with stories of prior engagements. From fishing.

SLIPPERY. slippery customer elusive or evasive person. I wouldn't trust that slippery customer too far.

slippery slope dangerous policy, which is to be avoided. For some people, the eurocurrency is a slippery slope to a united Europe. Frequently a political/journalistic cliché dragged out in an effort to frighten voters, etc., usually in the absence of an unemotive argument, against something suspect on the grounds that it might lead to something else even worse.

SLOANE. Sloane Ranger generic term of the 1980s for a young, loud, posh-sounding Briton who affected a certain style of dress and life. The bar was very noisy, full of Sloane Rangers braying excitedly at one another. Sloane Square was a 'good' address in central London favoured by the breed; the term also plays on the famous cowboy character of the 1950s, the Lone Ranger.

SLOW. slow boat to China person who is very slow. Come on James, haven't you finished your work yet? You are a slow boat to China today, aren't you? From the days of sailing ships and steamships. Presumably the slow boat to China must have seemed to take for ever to get there. Also 'slow coach' (similar sense).

slow on the uptake slow to understand. You may need to tell him what he's got to do more than once; he's a bit slow on the uptake these days.

SMALL. small talk light conversation; social chit-chat. We sat in the waiting room exchanging village gossip and small talk for half an hour.

small time minor, petty. Last summer the neighbourhood was terrorised by a gang of small-

time crooks and thugs. Opposite of **big time**.

SMART. smart Alec disparaging term for a person who tries to show off his wit, etc. often at the expense of someone else. I dislike these smart Alecs who poke fun at the more serious students. Compare **too clever by half**.

smart money is on something/someone something/someone is likely to succeed. Most of the smart money is now on Chelsea winning the Premier League. From big-time betting, especially by the **smart set**.

smart set affluent people dedicated to doing fashionable things and being seen at fashionable venues. Last week I mingled with the smart set at Henley and next week I'm going to observe their antics again at Ascot. American, from the 1920s.

SMASH. smash hit musical 'hit' recording which has 'smashed' or beaten previous ratings for popularity. He remembered the song well, as a smash hit of his teenage years. American teenage lingo of the 1950s.

SMELL. smell a rat be suspicious of something. There's something not quite right about his story – I smell a rat. From the days when its horrible smell led one to the offending corpse – under a floorboard or behind a cupboard.

SMELLING. smelling of roses untainted by scandal; innocent. In spite of several police investigations into his past, John still managed to emerge smelling of roses. Compare **clean as a whistle**.

SMOKE. smoke screen camouflage, used to conceal one's behaviour, etc. Behind that smiling smoke-screen of neighbourliness, Jones was plotting his wicked deeds. Originally military, from First World War.

SMOKING. smoking gun(s) evidence of skulduggery or criminality. The Financial Services Authority investigated the collapse in HBOS share values, but found no smoking guns. From the notion that gunsmoke tends to indicate the direction of a shot.

SMOOTH. smooth operator suave and sophisticated person. Like him or hate him, you have to admit that old Bloggs is a pretty smooth operator. One precursor of this idiom was perhaps 'cool customer'.

smooth someone's path make it easy for someone to achieve something. Mrs Macdonald was a useful neighbour who could, if she chose, smooth one's path to social acceptability in the village.

SNAKE. snake in the grass person who successfully conceals his evil or untrustworthy intentions; hidden enemy. We treated that man like one of the family, but he was nothing more than a snake in the grass and quite happy to betray our interests.

SNAP. snap decision decision taken quickly, without thought of all the possible consequences. She's gone to America for a holiday – one of her famous last-minute snap decisions. Now a popular journalese word, 'snap' here means speedy or fast, an American usage from about 1870. The word is also found in expressions like 'snap election', 'snap vote', etc.

SO. so and so 1. unpleasant person. That shopkeeper is a real so and so, and I never buy anything from him. Originally a circumlocution favoured by a speaker wishing to avoid the use of swear-words. 2. an indefinite location, person, number, etc. We went to number so-and-so at such-and-such a street, but he wasn't at home. This usage is older than sense 1.

so far until now. The story so far is not very encouraging. In broadcasting, previous episodes of a story are sometimes summarised as 'the story so far' as a preface to the newest chapter as it goes on-air.

so much for used to indicate how little value should be placed on someone's views, opinions, etc. The doctor assured her she was fine and the next day she was dead – so much for medical opinion.

so-so coping even if not flourishing; in moderate circumstances, not too well, prosperous, etc. Asked how he felt, he shrugged and replied, 'Oh, just so-so, but I can't complain.' The comment 'mustn't grumble' carries a similar drift; both are examples of understatement.

so there! childish retort, trying to terminate a conversation and stressing that one is going to do something despite instructions to the contrary. I'm *not* going to bed, and I *am* going to watch the late programme – so there! Meaning, 'There's no point arguing about this any further!'

so to speak an expression of qualification, meaning 'as one might say'. I'm afraid your husband is not terribly well, so to speak – in fact, he's drunk. Also 'in a manner of speaking'.

so what? rhetorical question, meaning 'what is the relevance of that?' So she doesn't approve of cigarettes. So what? I'll smoke in my own house if I wish to.

SOAP. soap (opera) radio or TV series about family life, often sentimental and melodramatic. She likes to eat at six sitting in front of her favourite TV soap. The term – like many of the most successful soap opera series – originated in the US in the late 1930s, and derives from the fact that many of the early versions were sponsored by big US soap manufacturers.

SOB. sob story/stuff story which aims to appeal to a person's sentiments. He told a wonderfully convincing sob story about how he'd just got the sack from his job, and how he had an invalid wife and ten starving children to feed – so, of course, I just had to lend him some money. Compare **play to the gallery**.

SOBER. sober as a judge (on circuit) totally sober and serious. It was too soon after the funeral for him to enjoy himself, and he just sat there sober as a judge. The comparison is with a judge in the course of onerous legal duties. You could also say 'He sat there like an old sobersides', with a similar sense.

sober fact/truth, etc. plain and unadorned truth. She asked me what I thought of her novel, and the sober truth was that I thought it unutterably dull.

SOCK. sock it to me(, baby) catch-phrase exclamation popularised by *Rowan & Martin's Laugh-In* TV show in the late 1960s. The original phrase meant 'tell me bluntly', but latterly and by dint of much suggestive repetition, it sometimes (though not invariably) acquired a sexual connotation. Muttering provocatively under his breath to the oncoming bowler, the opening batsman seemed to be saying, 'OK baby, sock it to me for all you're worth!'

SODA. soda fountain soft drinks counter or dispenser, usually in a drugstore or pharmacy. They used to stop off at the soda fountain and grab a milk shake. The expression is not used outside American culture.

SOFT. soft in the head insane, mentally deranged; weak-headed. When I asked her to marry me, she looked at me as if I'd gone completely soft in the head. Also 'soft-headed'.

soft job easy job. Lots of people think of teaching as a nice soft job, but that's because they don't know much about the contemporary classroom.

soft on someone sentimentally attached to someone; keen on someone romantically. Half the boys in Mrs Mitchell's class of 11 year olds are completely soft on her. Also 'to have a soft spot for someone'.

soft option the easiest available course, particularly when it is not the best course of action to follow. He thought about the various alternatives, but unfortunately there didn't seem to be a single soft option among them. Typical John – go for the soft option every time.

soft pedal refrain from emphasising. When they discovered how unpopular the idea was, they soft pedalled very hard to diminish its prominence in their political manifesto. From piano playing – the soft pedal muffles the sound of the notes.

soft soap flatter; ingratiate. He's very good at soft soaping important customers. There's no point trying the soft-soap line on me. A more hygienic version of **butter someone up**.

soft touch easy person to borrow from. My nephew always comes to me when he needs some money, because he knows from experience that I'm a bit of a soft touch. Literally, a person whose sentiments are easily 'touched' by a good **sob story**. Compare **push-over**.

SOMETHING. something else (again) something or someone special or extraordinary; something so good that it is incomparable. Her soups are always excellent, but her desserts are something else again. An Americanism. Compare **out of this world; in a different league; different ball-game/ball park; quite something**.

something has to go/give the pressure or strain is becoming intolerable or irresistible, and is consequently about to cause a rupture, breakdown, etc. They were a jetsetting family of hardplaying workaholics, and it was impossible to keep up with any of them, so I wasn't surprised to discover the parents were to divorce – something just had to give.

something like 1. approximately. There were something like 50 people at the party. 2. similar to. She wore a dress something like yours.

SONG. song and dance fuss. They made an unholy song and dance about trespassers on their land. A 'song-and-dance routine' is a vaudeville act.

SOONER. sooner/rather you (etc.) than me idiomatic expression of relief, indicating that I'm glad that you and not I have to (do something). She's off to India for a holiday. 'Sooner her than me,' I said. 'I can't cope with heat and spicy food.'

SORT. sort someone out punish or reprove someone. I'll soon sort him out if he tries to get cheeky.

SOUND. sound and fury noisy bluster, often without much substance. He got very worked up, and vented much sound and fury about the dreadful state of modern society. **A dyad, from Macbeth's observation that life 'is a tale/Told by an idiot, full of sound and fury,/Signifying nothing.'** The *Sound and the Fury* (1929) was also the title of one of the major novels of William Faulkner. Compare **rant and rave**.

SOUR. sour grapes feeling of comfort derived from despising something one wants but can't have. He says my new computer is a waste of money, but I think that's just sour grapes, and that he'd rather like to have one himself. **From Aesop's fable of the fox and the grapes. The fox longs for the juicy grapes above his head, but cannot reach them. So he declares them sour, in a moment of piqued self-delusion.**

SOW. sow the dragon's teeth inadvertently do something that may cause subsequent dissention. Many believe that it was Mrs Thatcher's administrations that sowed the dragon's teeth from which our society later suffered grievously. **From the Greek myth of Cadmus, who planted dragon's teeth from which armed men arose. Cadmus was afraid of the armed men and threw stones at them. Thinking one of their own number had thrown the stones, the armed men fought among themselves and all but five of them were killed.**

sow/plant the seeds anticipate certain developments by the performance of certain actions; start a process which causes a certain problem to arise. By making an unwise comment like that, he sowed the seeds of his later dismissal.

sow one's wild oats commit youthful excesses and follies; conduct oneself in a wild or dissipated manner. She seems to be sowing her wild oats and enjoying herself, but maybe she'll settle down when she's older. **The image is agricultural, of a young and foolish person sowing wild oats, which yield no food crop, instead of following the more sensible course of his elders, and sowing the cultivated variety which does.**

SPACED. spaced out 1. dazed or stupefied, as if by drugs. He's looking a bit spaced out this morning. Late 1960s, from the American drug culture. 2. weird; fantastical. The kids were watching some spaced-out SF fantasy DVD.

SPANNER. spanner in the works impediment or obstacle to the smooth or mechanical running of an operation. Her sudden decision to resign really constitutes something of a spanner in the works.

SPARKS. sparks fly people argue loudly and vocally. I knew the sparks would fly when she saw the mess. **A violent metaphor from the blacksmith's forge: of the hammer banging on the anvil, accompanied by the flying sparks of hot metal.**

SPARROW. sparrow fart very early in the morning, when the birds wake. We had to get up at sparrow fart to meet Auntie Joan off the eight o'clock boat. Jocular slang.

SPEAK. speak for itself require no comment or explanation, being self-explanatory. His action speaks for itself: it is the action of a good person.

speak one's mind say exactly what one thinks. I regard it as a serious matter, and I will speak my mind on the subject at the next council meeting. Literally, say what is in one's mind.

speak/talk of the devil! exclamation used when a person about whom one has been speaking suddenly appears. I was telling the guests about Lady Macbeth's lovely party, when Lady Macbeth herself came into the room. Speak of the devil! **Based on an old superstition: people were once afraid to say the name of the devil in case the utterance of the name would make him appear. Instead they talked about 'him who must not be named', etc.**

speak the same language communicate effectively. He and I never quite manage to speak the same language about anything. Compare **on the same wavelength; get through to someone**.

speak volumes be highly expressive or significant; be full of unspoken meaning. The expression on her face spoke volumes, and I knew she was about to cry. **Metaphorically with all the**

eloquence of several volumes or books.

speak with (a) forked tongue attempt deceit; tell untruths. His comments are usually unreliable – you'll find out that he speaks with forked tongue when it suits him. Said to be a metaphor of North American Indian origin. Compare **double talk**.

to speak of worthy of mention (usually in the negative). He got a couple of bruised ribs in the accident, but nothing else to speak of.

SPECIAL. special needs the requirements of people with particular mental or physical disabilities. She attends a special-needs school at the other side of town. A (currently) politically correct nomenclature found mainly as a noun or adjective phrase in fields such as education or health.

SPELL. spell something out give a detailed and literal explanation/description of something. He's always cracking silly jokes, most of which I fail to understand, so I usually have to ask him to spell them out. Compare **in no uncertain terms; read between the lines**.

SPEND. spend a penny urinate. Please excuse me for a minute – I've just got to spend a penny. A euphemism, from the days when one put a penny in the slot to gain admission to a public toilet.

spend money like water spend a lot of money freely and indiscriminately. Some of the tourists to this country will spend money like water – but only so long as we provide them with suitable baubles to spend it on. A standard simile, as is 'spend money like it's going out of fashion' (same sense), literally as if it might be about to be withdrawn from circulation.

spend more time with one's family 1. enjoy quality time at home. 2. another brutal euphemism for losing one's job. He lost his parliamentary seat at the last election when the voters decided he should be spending more time with his family. In other words, they didn't want him any more.

SPICK. spick and span neat and clean; fresh and unworn; brand-new. Here she is, all spick and

span in a bright new summer dress. A dyad, preserving an otherwise obsolete word; a 'span' was a newly chipped piece of wood and the word 'span-new' used to mean 'newly cut'. Compare **apple-pie order**.

SPIKE. spike someone's guns silence someone; spoil someone's plans. The government will do anything to spike the opposition's guns – even to the point of pinching some of their policies. A spike used to be driven into an enemy's captured cannon to render it unserviceable.

SPILL. spill the beans tell a secret. We've been trying to get her to spill the beans about the project for weeks, but she won't tell us a thing. It is said by some that this idiom came about as a result of the secret method the Greeks once used for voting to elect members to their closed societies. If they approved a candidate, they dropped a white bean into a jar. If they disapproved, they dropped a black. Only the head of the society was allowed to count the beans after the members had voted. If the beans were inadvertently spilt, the delicate secret of the applicant's popularity became known to the membership at large. Compare **rat on someone**.

SPIN. spin a yarn fabricate a story of uncertain veracity. I don't know what to think of her comments – she's always spinning some yarn or other. Originally a nautical term, meaning 'to tell a long and often fantastic story for amusement'. Telling a story was thus compared to spinning out a long hank of woollen yarn for making ropes.

spin doctor media term, meaning a public relations adviser. The spin doctors of New Labour seem to be winning the current propaganda battle. Originally a US term coined on the baseball field around 1980. It derived from the spin that a baseball pitcher was able to give the ball in order to make it gyrate or wobble in flight. Doctoring the spin means the pitcher successfully disguises his intention to deceive the batter. By analogy, in 1990s mediaspeak, the spin doctor's job was to take the politicians' plans and dress them up in the most attractive packaging, in the hope of deceiving the electorate into believing that the 'message' is an acceptable one. Compare **damage limitation; dodgy dossier; sex (something) up**.

SPIRIT. one's/the spirit is willing (but the flesh is weak) one has good intentions (but lacks the strength to implement them). When asked if she'd like to go to the party, she thought for a moment then shook her head, saying that although the spirit was willing she wanted to get a decent night's sleep. From Christ's agony and prayer in the Garden of Gethsemane the night before his crucifixion. In Matthew xxvi.41.

SPIRITS. one's spirits sink/rise one becomes distressed/cheerful. As the train drew closer to his destination, his spirits began to sink; he was not looking forward to this visit one bit.

SPIRITUAL. spiritual home place where one feels the greatest sense of fulfilment, inner peace, etc. They've gone to their cottage in Brittany; it is a sort of spiritual home for them.

SPIT. spit and polish thorough cleaning and polishing. The guests lined up to be presented to Her Majesty, each in a best outfit which had clearly received a special spit and polish for the occasion. A dyad, the original connotation was military uniforms. Compare **elbow grease**.

SPITTING. spitting image the exact likeness. Wait till you see him – he's the spitting image of his father. The idiom, the title of a satirical TV chat show in the 1980s, is a modification of the dyad 'spit and image', or 'the very/dead spit': He's the dead spit of his father, where 'spit' means 'likeness'. Compare **to the life**.

SPLICE. splice the mainbrace take an alcoholic drink to refresh oneself. It was a very hot afternoon, and halfway through the job they decided to splice the mainbrace at the local pub for an hour or so. The term is now usually heard jocularly. From the navy, where the original nautical slang meant 'to serve out rum rations'

after physical work or after battle. The mainbrace was the principal strap or rope connecting the mainsail to the ship. You spliced it when you formed a knot in it. Compare **sun is over the yardarm**.

SPLIT. split hairs argue about niceties. What's the point splitting hairs when they can't even agree about a basic problem like that?

split second the shortest possible flash or instant of time. He looked away from the steering wheel for a split second, and that's when the accident happened.

SPOIL. spoil sport person who takes pleasure from spoiling someone else's fun; a whinger. Children at play-groups learn to take turns, to share toys and not to be a spoil sport.

spoil the ship (for a ha'penny worth of tar) spoil a major undertaking (by shoddy or pennypinching work on an important part of it). They did all that interior renovation to the house, but I'm afraid they'll find they've spoilt the ship by not getting the roof properly seen to. Originally a shepherd's idiom, the 'ship' was actually a 'sheep': tar was used to disinfect its skin and keep it healthy. Compare **tarred with the same brush**.

SPOILING. spoiling for a fight in belligerent mood, and looking for a pretext to fight. Keep clear of Ron if the team lose their match – he'll be spoiling for a fight. From an old verb, meaning to strip people forcefully of their goods and keep the 'spoils'.

SPOT. spot cash cash given on the spot, or at once. There's a man at the door offering spot cash for any old iron. See also **on the spot**.

spot check random and unannounced check. The police seem to be making a spot check on every 10th car or so. See also **on the spot**.

SPRAT. sprat to catch a mackerel small bait to catch a big prize. He invested a small sprat in the business, in the hope of catching a decent-sized mackerel once the profits started to come through. A fishing metaphor.

SPREAD. spread one's wings do something more ambitious than one has previously attempted. The business has had another good year, and it is our plan to spread our wings overseas next year with a major export drive. **A metaphor of young birds learning to fly.**

SQUARE. square meal good, substantial meal. All he needed was a bath and a good square meal. From the idea of 'square' meaning fair, solid and substantial.

(back to/at) square one (back) where one started. We seemed to be making reasonable progress with our offer for the house, but now the seller has decided he doesn't want to move after all, so we seem to be right back at square one again. From the days of radio, when for the benefit of listeners commentators referred to the football pitch in terms of squares, with 'square one' representing the goalkeeper's territory. If you passed the ball back to the goalkeeper, you passed it back to square one and lost any territorial advantage your team had previously gained in attack.

square peg (in a round hole) person unsuited to his position. I don't think she's ever been entirely happy here, and so she's always been a bit of a square peg. Sometimes also expressed as a 'round peg in a square hole'.

square the circle perform a difficult or nearly impossible task. He has the unenviable task of squaring the circle between organising a cost-effective conference and giving delegates a memorable and enjoyable experience. Originally from mathematics.

SQUEAKY. squeaky clean completely free of any trace of moral taint. Governments are not expected to be squeaky clean all the time, but it is unwise for them to sink too deep into a pit of sleaze. Literally, so clean that one squeaks.

STAB. stab in the back treacherous and hurtful betrayal. Parents often feel they've had something of a stab in the back when their children let them down badly.

STAGE. stage whisper loud or theatrical whisper, especially one which is meant to be overheard. I don't know who he's trying to kid with that stage whisper of his – presumably he wants it to be audible at the back of the room. From the theatre.

STAKE. stake a/one's claim make a claim. If she wants any of the furniture, she'll have to come and stake her claim. From land claims, when the claimed ground was staked out with pegs. Compare **up stakes**.

stake-out surveillance of a person or area. There was a big police stake-out in downtown Buffalo last night. Originally a US police term.

STALKING. stalking horse decoy; an underhand means of making an attack. The Tories all hate the leader, but how do they try to get rid of him? By asking some parliamentary wimp to stand as a stalking horse against the leader this autumn; if a big enough number of malcontents back the stalking horse, it will then be time for one of the cabinet's heavyweights to stand for election. In the Middle Ages, a horse was used to help huntsmen stalk wild game and get close to it. They approached from behind the stalking horse, which was trained to move gently. Compare **dark horse**.

STAMPING. stamping ground favoured place where one spends much time. On Saturday nights his favourite stamping ground is a pub called the Blue Blanket.

STAND. stand corrected admit one's error. He corrected me by saying he'd been away for six months, not a year. 'I stand corrected,' I said, 'I thought it had been a year.'

stand fast/firm maintain one's position; not change one's opinion, etc. He decided to stand fast by his earlier statement. Also 'stand one's ground', 'stand pat'.

stand not upon the order of one's going depart without ceremony, usually quickly. The situation got more and more volatile, so standing not upon the order of my going, I got the hell out of it.

Often misquoted as 'stand not upon the manner...' From Lady Macbeth's command in Shakespeare's play: 'Stand not upon the order of your going, but go at once.'

stand on ceremony be formal and rather rigidly polite. He told me to relax, make myself at home and not to stand on ceremony. Usually negative.

stand on one's dignity insist on the respect one feels due in one's position. We all felt a bit uncomfortable when the archbishop started to stand on his dignity – not easy with somebody dressed up in a daft outfit like that, either!

stand on one's own two feet act independently. Sooner or later, he's got to stand on his own two feet and make his own decisions.

stand or fall survive or not survive. The government will stand or fall by the prime minister's decision.

stand the pace be able to resist tension, exhaustion, competition, etc. All this hard work and fast living puts heavy pressures on people, and a lot of them can't stand the pace. Also the more specific **stand the heat** be able to resist hostile criticism. From the proverb, 'If you can't stand the heat, get out of the kitchen.' Also 'stand the strain' meaning cope physically. He couldn't stand the strain of sharing a cell with two other convicts. Compare **stay the course**.

STANDING. standing start stationary position. From a standing start turning over £16,000 three years ago, their business is now budgeted to turn over half a million pounds this year. From the lexicon of pseudo-technical hyperbole of the American car industry of the 1950s. As in: The new model Ferrari hits 60 m.p.h. from a standing start in 4.7 seconds.

STANDS. it stands to reason the conclusion is obvious. It stands to reason that you won't be a concert pianist if you don't practise. Similar to 'it is staring you in the face'.

STAR. one's star has set one's reputation is in fixed decline. Mr Brown's star will probably be seen

to have set after his amazing drunken outburst on television last week. An astrological metaphor; one's 'stars' govern one's fate. Opposite of 'one's star is in the ascendant'.

star studded featuring a cast which includes a large number of famous film stars. It was a glittering star-studded show. Usually a cliché.

START. start a hare introduce a diversion into discussion, etc. A classic tactic of this government is to start a hare going as soon as they get into the slightest difficulties. From the dog-track, where an artificial hare is released for the greyhounds to chase. Compare **red herring**.

start from scratch start from the very beginning. His computer has broken down and he's lost a lot of files for his book; so he's going to have to start from scratch and write it all again. The 'scratch mark' used to indicate the starting point for races; later, it meant the starting point in the handicap race of a competitor who receives no odds or other advantages. Old idioms from this expression include **up to scratch** and the obsolete 'toe the scratch'. Nowadays we get a 'scratch golfer', one who 'plays off scratch', i.e. no handicap.

start the rot begin process of deterioration or decline. You will find that the resignation of Sir Geoffrey started the rot – afterwards the government just unravelled. Also 'the rot set in'.

STARTER. starter for ten something to get you started, or to set the ball rolling. The first question is usually just an easy one, a starter for ten. Catch-phrase from the long-running TV quiz-show University Challenge (1962–).

STATE. state of the art up to date; at the current level/stage of development. We are planning to install a state-of-the-art online information system accessible to all library members.

STAY. stay put remain in one place. I'm not taking a holiday this year; I'm just going to stay put in the comfort of my own home and have a rest.

stay the course complete a project, assignment, etc. He's not looked too good since his illness, and I don't think he's going to be able to stay the course in that particularly arduous foreign posting. From horse-racing. Compare **stand the pace**.

STEAL. steal a march obtain an advantage over a rival or opponent. By winning the contract to supply medicines to such a large hospital, we have stolen a temporary march over our main business competitors. From the Middle Ages, when armies tried to move troops by night, without the enemy's knowledge, and thus gaining the element of surprise.

steal someone's clothes adopt someone's policies or ideas as one's own. It is a measure of the Tories' failure that they're afraid Labour have stolen their clothes.

steal the show win all the critical acclaim, applause, etc. Film stars hate working with children, because they know that it is generally the children who steal the show, and completely upstage them.

steal someone's thunder spoil a person's plans to do something by doing it oneself. I believe Mr Jones is going to tell you the story of our escape, so I will refrain from stealing his thunder and talk to you now about our capture. Compare **beat someone to it; pinch someone's lines/lyrics**.

STEER. steer clear of keep away from; avoid. Steer clear of fatty foods and too much starch in your diet. From navigation, and avoiding rocks, reefs, etc.

STEM. stem the flow/tide of something 1. check or stop something. The coming of the oil industry has temporarily stemmed the flow of school-leavers to the mainland in search of jobs. 2. **make progress against something.** It is hardly reasonable to expect that one speech will stem the tide of popular hostility to the new tax.

STEP. step by step gradually. His recovery has been slow, but he's making progress step by step.

step in the direction of move that will help to achieve a desired aim. I don't think anyone will try to argue that this very indecisive election result is a step in the direction of good government. Also 'step in the right direction'.

step into someone's shoes inherit or acquire someone's job, position, responsibilities, etc. He may not be able to do the job, but there are lots of good people waiting to step into his shoes.

step out of line do something unacceptable. The company was god, employees knew the rules, and no one was allowed to step out of line for a minute. From the military parade ground.

step right into it unintentionally say or do something distressing or embarrassing. It wasn't till after the party that I realised I'd stepped right into it when I asked about Timothy. The unspoken metaphorical reference is to that omnipresent pollutant of British pavements – dogshit. Similar to **put one's foot in it**.

step up to the plate/mark rise to the occasion; be equal to the challenge. Amazingly, at the time of the accident, there was no one in that large audience able or willing to step up to the mark and treat the wounded. American, from the baseball field, the original reference was to the player approaching the home plate to take a turn at batting.

STERNER. sterner stuff worthier, or of more resilient substance. All the other guests went home by taxi, but John was made of sterner stuff – he went home on foot. 'Stuff' was a woollen fabric. The softer weaves tore, but the stronger (= sterner) ones did not. The idiom is probably much influenced by Shakespeare's *Julius Caesar*, and Mark Antony's speech at Caesar's funeral: 'Did this in Caesar seem ambitious?/When that the poor have cried, Caesar hath wept;/Ambition should be made of sterner stuff.'

STEW. stew in one's own juice live with the results of problems one has created; suffer as a result of one's own errors or foolishness. It was originally James who caused the problems, so I think we'll have to leave him to stew in his own juice, especially now that we have serious problems of our own to resolve. From the kitchen recipe book.

STEWED. stewed to the gills drunk. He came home stewed to the gills on Friday night. Probably an elaboration of standard similes such as 'drunk as a newt/fish'. 'Stewed' may once have been a pun, a medieval stew being a fishpond in which live fish were kept until they were required at the table.

STICK. stick in one's craw/gizzard/gullet be hard to accept. It sticks in my craw to have to take orders from a buffoon like that. The image is from the farmyard. Hens and turkeys appear to have physiological difficulty in swallowing things. Compare **come the raw prawn**.

stick-in-the-mud unprogressive person; dull or unadventurous person who doesn't mind spoiling things for others. John is too much of a stick-in-the-mud for parties; his sister's much better fun. The term was once used as a contemptuous alternative for 'what's-his-name'.

stick one's neck out risk displeasing or upsetting others by identifying oneself with a particular point of view. She asked what I thought of the prime minister, but I declined to stick my neck out on a controversial matter like that. Compare **brass neck; out on a limb; nail one's colours to the mast**.

stick one's oar in make one's opinion known, especially if it has not been sought. Maggie isn't the sort of person who can listen to a conversation for very long without sticking her oar in. A rowing metaphor.

stick to one's guns maintain one's point of view; refuse to abandon one's position. I see no reason for changing my mind about capital punishment now; I've always been in favour of it, old fashioned or not, and I'm sticking to my guns on that topic. From warfare: brave soldiers or sailors stuck with their guns under fire from the enemy. Similar to **stick with it**.

stick to one's last remain faithful to one's trade or training or expertise. A lot of people have tried to diversify, and failed; but John has stuck to his last, and his business has survived and flourished. A shoemaker's 'last' was the wooden model of the foot on which he made his shoe. And as the Victorian academic Benjamin Jowett remarked: 'Great evil may arise from a cobbler leaving his last and turning into a legislator.'

stick with it be persistent. John's not the sort of person to give up at the first sight of trouble – he'll stick with it till the job's done. Similar to **stick to one's guns**.

STIFF. stiff upper lip calmness; refusal to show emotions, especially of love, pain and sorrow. Come, come, old boy, let's keep a stiff upper lip and hide our feelings at a time like this – we have to pretend that we're jolly well enjoying ourselves. For its critics, the stiff upper lip is an over-valued British characteristic shading too easily into hypocrisy and downright inhibition.

STINKING. stinking rich, etc. intensifier, meaning extremely rich, etc. Anyone with a car like that is making a fashion statement which says only one thing: I am stinking rich.

STIR. stir up a hornets' nest cause great and ongoing controversy. His views on God stirred up a real hornets' nest. The metaphor is of starting something which cannot easily be quelled, hornets being notoriously vicious when disturbed.

STITCH. stitch in time (saves nine) preventive action (can often save expense, effort, etc.). The windows probably don't need painting for another year or so, but I'm doing them now because I know that a stitch in time often saves quite a bit of expense later on. From the proverb.

stitch someone up frame someone on false evidence, or otherwise silence them. He used to be very outspoken and critical, but the management seem to have stitched him up somehow or other. A phrasal verb from police jargon, giving the noun 'stitch-up'. The entire case was a stitch-up from start to finish.

STONE. stone dead completely dead. It was too late to do anything when the ambulance arrived – he was stone dead. From the simile 'as dead as a stone'. A 17th-century saying was, 'Stone-dead hath no fellow.' Also 'stone deaf', 'stone cold', 'stone blind' and so on, meaning 'deaf as a stone, 'cold as a stone', 'blind as a stone'.

STONE'S. stone's throw from not far from. He lives only a stone's throw from the railway station.

STOP. stop at nothing be very dangerous, not prepared to be halted by anyone or anything. Do not approach this man; he's armed and violent and he'll stop at nothing.

stop the rot prevent further deterioration. The business was unsound for many years, and went through several receiverships, but the current owners seem to have stopped the rot and got things going properly at last.

STORM. storm in a teacup big fuss about a trivial matter; or, as Shakespeare put it: **much ado about nothing**. We caused a fearful storm in a teacup by putting our washing out to dry on a Sunday – we were told we mustn't do that sort of thing in the Outer Hebrides. Probably after Cicero: Fluctus excitare in simpulo, 'to stir up waves in a ladle'.

STRAIGHT. straight and narrow the virtuous path; the honest, celibate and sober way of life. He's a rather weak man, and since his imprisonment he's found it very hard to get back on to the straight and narrow. From the biblical 'Straight is the way and narrow the gate which leadeth unto eternal life: and few there be that find it.' In Matthew vii.14.

straight answer direct and unadorned response. When she asked if I'd enjoyed the book, I gave her a straight answer and said I thought it was lousy. Compare **plain speaking**. The opposite of euphemism, see also **call a spade a spade**.

straight away at once. When news of the shooting came through, the emergency services were on the spot straight away.

straight from the horse's mouth on the best authority, i.e. the word of the person most concerned with the subject under discussion. I didn't know what to think about the various rumours, but then I got the full story straight from the horse's mouth. From the humorous idea that the best tip on a horserace comes from the mouths of the participating animals.

straight from the shoulder directly, bluntly, without prevarication. I gave it to him straight from the shoulder – warning him to keep off my land or I'd call the police. From boxing. Compare **beat about the bush**.

straight out of Central Casting stereotypical person, whether hero or villain. If you were looking for a quintessential spy, you couldn't get a better one straight out of Central Casting. From the Hollywood movie industry, which set up a facility with this title in 1926.

STRAIN. strain at a gnat (and swallow a camel) argue about all sorts of trivialities (but fail to question serious matters). There wasn't much point straining at procedural gnats, having swallowed the substantial camel of signing a no-strike agreement. From the King James Bible, in Matthew xxiii.23: 'Woe unto you, scribes and Pharisees, hypocrites!...Ye blind guides, which strain at a gnat, and swallow a camel.' In other translations, they stumble at a straw and scale a mountain. Compare **big idea/picture**.

strain one's eyes try hard to see, usually in fog, gloom, mist, etc. In the half-light, they were all straining their eyes to try to get some idea of what was going on.

STRAIT. strait laced strict and unbending; severe. He was a schoolmaster of the old school – an authoritarian and strait-laced figure. Literally, from a lady's corset tightly laced up. A more modern equivalent might be 'uptight'.

STRANGE. strange bedfellows unlikely partners, friends, etc. They may seem strange bedfellows, but they are an unstoppable business partnership. Probably from Shakespeare's *The*

Tempest ii.2: 'Misery acquaints a man with strange bedfellows.'

strange to say surprisingly. I'd almost forgotten about Norman, but strange to say I saw him at the shops last week.

STRAW. straw(s) in the wind omens and assessments of how a situation is likely to develop. Daily we see new straws in the wind indicating the depth of the recession. A journalistic cliché describing an atmospheric indicator. Compare **see which way the cat jumps/wind blows**.

straw man not a serious adversary; someone who is easily led or overcome by opposition, etc. He treats his fellow directors as the bunch of straw men they probably are.

straw poll rough test of opinion, as opposed to a proper, democratically conducted election. An American practice, first conducted in 1824 by reporters in Wilmington, Delaware. Citizens were questioned by the press about their presidential preferences. We took an informal straw poll around the office to gauge opinion about the ban on smoking. Compare **show of hands**.

straw which breaks the camel's back the crowning and unendurable insult; the final and intolerable burden. It was an uncongenial hotel – surly service, poor food, draughty rooms. When they told me I had to change rooms, I decided that was the straw that broke the camel's back, and walked out. From the proverb, 'It is the last straw which breaks the camel's back.' Compare **last straw; enough is enough**.

STREETS. streets ahead (of) much better (than). This year's candidates are streets ahead of last year's. A spatial metaphor.

STRIKE. strike a balance consider the alternatives, or the range of one's responsibilities, in order to choose an acceptable middle course which adequately accommodates the various sides, points of view, etc. He tries hard to strike a balance between his teaching duties and his domestic

ones. Also 'strike a happy medium'.

strike a chord/note produce a response. The sight of him struck a faint and disagreeable chord from the past in my mind. From music.

strike/hit home expression meaning that a truth is realised, however painful or uncomfortable, although it may not be accepted. You have to visit one of the war zones and see the damage before the full horror of the events begins to strike home to you.

strike lucky/gold be lucky. At last he's struck lucky and won a major competition. He didn't realise till a few months after he opened it that his little corner shop would strike gold for him. Originally from the various 19th-century gold-rushes, where some prospectors were indeed lucky. Also 'strike it rich', 'have a stroke of good luck'.

strike the right/wrong note say the appropriate/inappropriate thing. They were all very distressed and upset, so it was very important that the speaker managed to strike the right note. A musical idiom.

strike while the iron's hot act at the most suitable or appropriate moment. The boss congratulated me on a very good set of results, so I decided to strike while the iron was hot and ask her for a decent payrise. The image comes from the blacksmith's forge, where iron had to be hammered into shape while still hot. Compare **irons in the fire**.

STRONG. strong meat a book, film, etc. that might shock its readers, viewers, etc. because of its strong language, forthright views, etc. The audience found the play to be strong meat, and there was a mass walkout after Act 1. Originally biblical, as in Hebrews v.12: 'Ye are become such as have need of milk, and not of strong meat.'

strong point/suit subject about which one is knowledgeable. Please don't ask me anything about moths – entomology is not my strong point. 'Suit' is from the card table.

STRUCK. struck all of a heap flabbergasted, astounded. When I heard the news, I was struck all of a heap; I couldn't believe my ears. The original meaning was 'paralysed' or 'destroyed'. It may come in part from the biblical story of Lot's wife, who ended up a pillar or heap of salt. Variations include 'struck dumb' (with amazement), giving later 'dumbstruck', 'dumbfounded'. Similar to 'gobsmacked'.

STRUT. strut one's stuff preen oneself; physically flaunt oneself. There she goes again, Old Tightpants, prancing and strutting her stuff across the Golden Sunset Ballroom. Usually ironical, a slang term in which 'stuff' is a euphemism for male genitalia or female curvature.

STUFF. stuff and nonsense rubbish. There was a lot of stuff and nonsense in the story about the royal wedding.

stuff it! coarse all-purpose exclamatory idiom, meaning 'Forget it!' or 'Keep it!' If he didn't like it, I told him he could stuff it. Amplified variously, as 'stuff it up your jumper/arse', etc. The politer version is 'lump it!' (same meaning, see **like it or lump it**).

STUFFED. stuffed shirt pompous and unrelaxed person. He seemed a bit of a stuffed shirt, but he improved a bit once you got to know him.

STUMBLING. stumbling block something that metaphorically blocks one's smooth progress. He is only 24, but he refuses to see his youthfulness as a stumbling block to getting the appointment.

STUNG. stung to the quick deeply offended. She was stung to the quick by his accusation. The 'quick' is the vulnerable skin under the fingernail.

SUBJECT. subject to 1. liable or prone to. He is very subject to hay-fever, poor thing. 2. **conditional upon**. He's very welcome to come to us for the weekend, subject to the approval of his parents.

SUCH. such and such a given (but unnamed) quantity or brand. He always made a point of buying such and such a tobacco and such and such a whisky.

such as it is qualifying phrase, meaning 'considering its limitations' or 'if you could call it that'. They made the best of their shelter, such as it was, for the duration of the storm. Sometimes ironic, as in: He asked to borrow my car, such as it is, i.e. it's falling to bits.

such being the case in these circumstances. He asked me if I was tired, and such being the case, suggested that I lie down for half an hour.

SUCK. suck it and see 1. a derisive retort or invitation. 'Is the soup good?' 'Suck it and see!' 2. try something out to see if it works. They offered me a job which sounds deadly, but I need the money too badly to turn it down, so I've taken it and I'm just going to suck it and see how it progresses. Compare **play something by ear**.

suck up to someone try to please someone by flattering her/him. Because they're all terrified of the new boss, they're all sucking up to her like mad.

SUDDEN. sudden death playoff additional play to find a winner for a drawn game. The teams were very evenly matched, as the 2–2 scoreline indicated before the game went to a sudden death playoff. From sport: in a tied round of golf, an extra hole may be played. In a tied team game like football, a set of five kicks at goal by each team may be agreed to settle the score. Also called a 'tiebreak' in tennis.

SUGAR. sugar daddy rich male benefactor, often a lover. I've lost touch with Gemma since she took up with that sugar daddy of hers. An old-fashioned slang term from the 1920s, now mainly disparaging.

sugar the pill sweeten a bitter assignment; try to make an unpleasant job less so. They want to build a motorway across his fields, and they are trying to sweeten the pill by offering to build him some new barns and underpasses. Compare **offer sweeteners**.

SUIT. suit someone's book/bill agreeable to someone; accord with someone's plans. You'll find that it doesn't always suit his book to work on a Saturday.

SUN. sun is over the yardarm jocular expression meaning it's time for a drink, usually not before it starts getting dark. He opened the drinks cupboard and announced to his guests that the sun was over the yardarm. Originally a naval expression, indicating that a tot of rum would be dispensed. Compare **splice the mainbrace**.

SUNDAY. Sunday best best clothes. They made a handsome group standing there smiling into the camera in their Sunday best. From the days when people kept their best clothes for wearing to church on Sundays. Compare **best bib and tucker**.

SUNNY. sunny side up egg fried on one side only. How do you like your eggs fried – both sides or sunny side up? From the 1920s, and the extensive slang lingo developed in the American catering and fast-food industry.

SURE. sure as eggs is eggs beyond a shadow of doubt. That business is heading for receivership, as sure as eggs is eggs. Probably a corruption of 'as sure as x is x' – a statement of formal logic, favoured by Dickens in *Pickwick Papers* (1836–7) and elsewhere. Compare **shadow of doubt**.

sure enough as expected. The team were expected to lose the game, and sure enough they lost handsomely.

sure thing reliable guess; something worth betting on. They say that he's a sure thing to win the snooker championship.

SWEAR. swear (that) black is white stubbornly argue in one direction against clear evidence pointing in the other; be a flagrant liar; be compulsively argumentative. You only have to say one thing for him to say the opposite; he's one of those annoying folk who enjoys swearing that black is white.

swear blind insist with vehemence. He swore blind that he'd been in bed fast asleep, but I knew he was lying. From the idea that if one insists hard

enough, one's listener may disregard the evidence (of his own eyes, ears, etc.). The American version is 'swear up and down'.

swear like a trooper/fishwife express one's anger by using oaths and blasphemies. She was so incensed with him that she lost control and started swearing like a trooper at him. Standard similes which make reference to two trades once noted for the foulness of their lingo.

SWEAT. sweat blood work very hard. I sweated blood to get that job finished in time for him, and he didn't even say thank you for it. A hyperbole.

sweat it out endure a period of great stress or anxiety. He sweated it out for a couple of nights, waiting for news from the airline.

SWEEP. sweep someone off his/her feet elicit strong feelings of affection, love, etc. in someone. She was strikingly beautiful, so it was no surprise that she swept half the young men in the village off their feet.

sweep the board win every prize. The school tennis team has swept the board again this year. From the card table: you sweep the board if you take all the cards, or pocket all the stakes.

SWEEPING. sweeping statement rash generalisation. John is not a man to measure his words; in fact, he's much given to making the most ridiculous sweeping statements.

SWEET. sweet FA/fuck all/Fanny Adams nothing. When asked what he'd been doing all day, he mumbled, 'Sweet FA.' Fanny Adams was the child victim in a famous Victorian murder case. The nickname was applied sarcastically to the watery stew which was served up to sailors as their meagre rations, and was soon thereafter abbreviated and applied to anything worthless.

sweet nothings pleasantries, often amorous. He spent the afternoon in the garden with her, murmuring sweet nothings in her shell-like ear.

sweet tooth fondness for eating sweet things. He has difficulty dieting because he has such a sweet tooth.

SWING. swing the lead dodge, or attempt to dodge, one's share of work; pretend one is unfit to do a certain job. He's not a reliable worker; at the first sign of summer, he'll swing the lead and disappear for weeks. Originally nautical.

swing one's weight add one's support. Once the Liberal Party had swung its weight behind Labour, the combination became electorally irresistible.

SWINGS. swings and roundabouts advantages and disadvantages. Life is full of ups and downs, and swings and roundabouts. Compare the saying: 'What you gain on the swings you lose on the roundabouts.' From the fairground.

SWORD. sword of Damocles threat of impending doom. Many of the young African democracies are very fragile, and the main sword of Damocles that overshadows them is the omnipresent threat of a military coup. From the story of how the Greek tyrant Dionysius of Syracuse (4th century BC) suspended a sword from a single hair above the head of his sycophantic courtier Damocles. He wanted Damocles to understand the insecurity which even powerful dictators are obliged to endure. See also **hang by a thread**.

T

TAKE. take a back seat take a less important position. Now that he's over 60, he's taken a back seat in the business, though he still likes to attend board meetings and come into the office a couple of days a week. From driving.

take a dim view of disapprove of; dislike. Like many elderly people, he takes a pretty dim view of modern society.

take a hint understand and do something that has been suggested or implied, but not openly stated. I wish some people could take a hint and leave me alone.

take a jaundiced view of be pessimistically critical of and unconvinced by. The electorate tends to take a rather jaundiced view of a politician's promises – they know most of them are worthless. From the illness called jaundice, which makes the skin and eyes of sufferers yellowish. Hence the idea that one's outlook or vision becomes tinged, or prejudiced.

take a leaf out of someone's book follow an example set by another person; imitate another person. He needs to take a leaf out of his sister's book, and work a bit harder. The original idea was that a person wrote the rules governing his life in his own copybook, and the person invited to take a page from that book was expected to copy out these rules for his own improvement. Compare **blot one's copybook; turn over a new leaf**.

take a loan/lend of someone make a fool of or take liberties with someone. Somebody shouted fire, but it was a false alarm – some joker had been taking a loan of us. A Scots idiom, meaning take a loan of someone's wits. Compare **take a rise out of**.

take a/the long view look far ahead; show vision. Nowadays short-termism reigns, and nobody bothers to take the long view.

take a notion want (to do something). She took a notion to go out to the cinema last night.

take a pew sit down. The doctor told me to come in and take a pew, and that he'd see me in 10 minutes. Informal; a 'pew' is a church seat, often hard and uncomfortable.

take a raincheck postpone something, or keep it pending. I'm sorry that I can't come to your dinner-party this weekend, but perhaps you'll let me take a raincheck and come to the next one. Originally (1880s) the phrase was American, and referred specifically to a ticket for re-admission to an outdoor sporting event postponed by rain. If it was produced at a later date, it guaranteed the holder free admission to the postponed function. The reference has now widened to include any deferred social or informal get-together.

take a rise out of tease; try to annoy. I wish they'd leave me alone for a while, and stop trying to take a rise out of me all the time. There may be a piscatorial image here, of trying to get the victim to rise to the proffered bait. Compare **take a loan/lend of someone**.

take a running jump idiom used by an angry speaker to tell someone to go away. I was fed up with his smart comments and eventually told him to take a running jump. Similar to **drop dead**. Compare **tell someone where to get off**.

take a shine to become fond of. He's a shy lad, but he seems to have taken quite a shine to the old couple who have moved in next door.

take account of pay attention to. Take no account of John if he starts to snore.

take an oath swear a binding promise. He took an oath not to rest till the killers were brought to justice. A metaphor from the court of law, where oath-taking is done with one's hand on the Bible, as a signal of one's truthfulness before God.

take someone as one finds her/him etc. a way of welcoming unexpected guests and at the same time indicating that one is not properly prepared for entertaining them as well as one would have wished to. Well, now you're here, please do sit down and have a cup of tea. You'll just need to take us as you find us, as the saying goes.

take someone at his/her word act on what someone has said. She told me to eat as much as I wanted, so I took her at her word. I just hope I've not been too greedy.

take someone's breath away astonish or astound someone. His behaviour was outrageous, and completely took my breath away.

take by storm make a powerful impression on. The Beatles took the pop world by storm in the 1960s. Originally military, the term meant the taking of a castle, etc. by violent attack. Often used, especially in journalese, in the battle of the sexes.

take by surprise 1. come on (people) unexpectedly. She jumped out from behind the bush and took us all by surprise. 2. be against predictions or expectations. When the favourite horse fell at the first fence, everyone was taken by surprise.

take care of look after; attend to the needs of. I told her to take care of herself till I saw her again.

take charge (of) assume responsibility for, or control of. The army have taken charge of security during the visit.

take one's courage in both hands summon up one's courage to take a risk. The fire was getting closer; finally, taking his courage in both hands, he jumped from the window. This is a concretive metaphor, where an abstraction (courage) is made concrete, and portable – with effort. Compare **put someone in his/her proper place**.

take someone down a peg/notch (or two) deflate someone's feelings of self-importance or pride, especially when these are unjustified. He's been taking on too much responsibility lately, and his boss has had to take him down a peg or two for his own good. Flags used to be raised or lowered on ships by a system of pegs. A flag flying high carried more weight than one on a lower peg. Slightly

gentler and less deflationary than **put someone's gas in a peep**. Compare **shoogly peg**.

take effect come into operation; become effective. The whisky took effect very quickly on his empty stomach, and he was soon slurring his speech. The new tax takes effect from midnight.

take exception indicate one's dislike, usually by complaining or objecting. I have to say that I took exception to all those slanderous comments.

take one's eye off the ball fail to concentrate; lose one's focus. To succeed as a stockbroker you must never take your eye off the ball.

take someone/something for granted 1. believe to be true, without actually so verifying. There was a 'Do Not Disturb' sign on the door, so I took it for granted he was resting. 2. **fail to appreciate** or realise the values or characteristics, usually of a person. He'd been living with her for years, and clearly he took her for granted: he ignored her.

take someone for a ride dupe someone. He asked us for a guarantee of £1,000 each in advance, and then took us for a ride by disappearing with all our money.

take French leave go away without notice or permission. They had the bad habit of taking French leave from hotels, leaving their bills unpaid. The original reference may have been military: the English thought French soldiers were cowardly, and tended to leave the battlefield without awaiting orders from their officers. The French were not slow to return the compliment (hence their 'filer à l'anglaise', which has the same meaning). Another view is that the original reference was more purely social: based on the English observation that French guests had the habit of leaving a function without bidding formal farewell to their hosts.

take heart be encouraged; gain confidence. She took heart from Andrew's success in the exam – thinking that if he could do it, so could she. Opposite of **lose heart**.

take something in comprehend something. The news of the disaster was so awful that for a while we had great difficulty taking it in – it was unbelievable. A phrasal verb. Also 'take something on board' (same sense). He seems to have taken our criticism on board and improved his manners.

take something in good part accept something with a good humour. The headmaster seemed to enjoy the satire as much as everybody else, and took his teasing in good part.

take someone/something in hand bring someone/something into one's control. He's started to get a bit too cheeky, so I'm going to have to take him in hand this summer.

take something in one's stride accept something (often unpleasant) without worrying about it too much. He still seems the same happy-go-lucky little boy, so I guess he's managed to take the death of his mother in his stride.

take something into account remember to include something in one's calculations. She doesn't seem to have taken the cost of the trip into account.

take issue with argue against; disagree about. When I took issue with the speaker about his comments on the miners, many people started to boo me.

take it 1. assume. I take it the argument is now settled? 2. tolerate punishment, criticism, etc. He's a typical bully – he loves to dish it out, but he can't take it.

take it as read take it for granted; assume it is done. She asked for fresh asparagus, so you may take it as read that she got fresh asparagus. Legal English.

take it easy relax, refrain from exertion. If you'll just take it easy for a minute, I'll try to explain what happened.

take it into one's head suddenly decide to do something, often without obvious logicality. He's just taken it into his fat head to buy a dog.

take it on the chin accept something bravely, without trying to fuss unduly or to make excuses for it. So, you've failed your exams! I suggest you take that little setback on the chin, work harder and try again. From boxing. Compare **take one's medicine**.

take it or leave it 1. make up your mind if you want something or not. The price is £100 – take it or leave it. Can be hyphenated and used as an adjective phrase: This is the holiday of a lifetime – a take-it-or-leave-it offer of a week in Mauritius. 2. be able to accept or refuse something. I'm sorry there's no sugar for your coffee. That's all right – I can take it or leave it. Also **like it or lump it**.

take it out of one exhaust one. All that walking around these archaeological sites takes it out of one. 'It' being one's strength and stamina. A phrasal verb.

take it out on someone vent one's anger on someone. He's been in a lousy temper for several days, with no one to take it out on. A phrasal verb.

take it upon oneself assume responsibility for an action, often without due consideration. She seems to have taken it upon herself to lend John my car.

take kindly to approve of; favour. He doesn't take very kindly to people kicking footballs into his flowerbeds. Mainly used in negative senses.

take leave of one's senses act in an apparently insane or unintelligent way. Surely he's not going to jump out the window – has he completely taken leave of his senses?

take liberties with go beyond accepted limits, e.g. of behaviour, scholarship, etc. I think my editor has taken major liberties with my book, i.e. he's changed bits of the text without asking my permission to do so.

take one's life in one's hands risk death. He hated being driven by Maria, and thought that he was taking his life in his hands every time he got into her car.

take something lying down accept without protest. He's in for a big surprise if he thinks I'm the sort of person who'll take his insults lying down.

take one's medicine accept one's punishment, especially if it is well deserved. He's been found guilty of theft, so now he's going to have to take his medicine. In less gender-challenging times, one was often exhorted to take one's medicine 'like a man'. Compare **take it on the chin**.

take one's name in vain use someone's name disrespectfully. 'I do believe I heard you taking my name in vain,' said John as he ambled towards us. Often used jocularly nowadays. Biblical, from Exodus xx.7: 'Thou shalt not take the name of the Lord thy God in vain.' Compare **(someone's) ears are burning**.

take no prisoners ignore the other party's feelings in a confrontation. He had a stand-up shouting match with his boss, and neither side took any prisoners – much to the amusement of their colleagues in the open-plan office. Compare **shoot from the hip**.

take something on board understand and remember something; get one's mind round something. The news has been dreadful; we've not really had time to take it properly on board yet. Originally nautical, a metaphor of one's intellectual cargo. Compare **get one's head round something**.

take pot luck 1. eat what the host happens to be eating. She often comes in around supper time and takes pot luck with us. Originally referred to an unexpected guest eating whatever happened to be in the host's cooking pot that day. 2. accept whatever happens to be available. I asked her to bring me a book from the library – anything at all, as I was quite happy to take pot luck.

take root become established. Funny ideas take root in your mind. From gardening.

take shape assume a specific form. The outlines of a plan of attack began to take shape in the captain's mind.

take sides support one person, argument, etc. rather than another. As chairman, I try not to take sides in a debate.

take soundings discreetly sample people's view of something, or assess their likely reception of an idea or proposal. Before declaring the election, you may be sure that the government took extensive soundings about the likely public response to the announcement. Originally nautical: meaning 'check the depth' of the water one is sailing in, by dropping a measured line with a lead weight on the end. Compare **lie of the land**.

take steps take action to make something happen. I want to know what steps can be taken to prevent flooding in the future.

take stock 1. list all the stock in a business, shop, etc. Our accountants try to make us take stock every three months. From which, 'stock-taking'. We are closed this afternoon for our annual stock-taking. 2. consider a situation carefully, in order to decide a course of action. I think we need to take stock of what we are trying to achieve.

take/have/get the bit between one's teeth become determined or eager to do something, spurning any restraint. Once she takes the bit between her teeth, there's no stopping her until the job is done. From horse-riding: the bit is a metal bar which fits across the horse's mouth, and is attached to the reins. The rider pulls on the reins in order to control the horse. Should the bit fall between the horse's teeth, the horse cannot feel it and becomes difficult to restrain or control.

take the bread out of someone's mouth remove someone's livelihood or means of support. By doing that work, you are taking the bread out of the mouths of your fellow workers.

take the bull by the horns deal decisively with a difficult problem. I needed the money urgently, so I took the bull by the horns and asked John to lend me £100. From farming: it is said that the best way to deal with an angry bull is to take it by the horns and show it that you are the boss – a theory that most people would be very reluctant to test. Compare **grasp the nettle/thistle**.

take the cake/biscuit 1. deserve the prize; be outstanding. There were some splendid exhibits, but Sally Parker's has to take the cake. **2. be outrageous.** His last remark takes the biscuit for sheer impudence. This second sense is now commoner than sense 1, of which it is a refinement.

take the edge off blunt the effect of; reduce the impact of. Don't eat a snack now or you'll take the edge off your appetite for dinner.

take the floor 1. stand up and get ready to perform, dance, etc. Take the floor, ladies and gentlemen, for a slow waltz. **2. get up to make a speech.** Mr Wilson took the floor to outline the government's Open University policy.

take the gilt off the gingerbread diminish or spoil the attractiveness of something. The company car is an attractive feature of the pay package, although the taxman will do his best to take the gilt off the gingerbread. From baking: gingerbread cakes often used to have ornate shapes which were then gilded with multi-coloured icing. The finished result was attractive, but when the icing was removed the cake looked very plain.

take/plead the fifth say nothing; keep silent. Asked what he thought of the painting, he took the fifth and said 'No comment!' An Americanism. Literally, the reference is to someone exercising his constitutional right to keep silence according to the Fifth Amendment of the US Constitution. Ratified in 1791, this gave citizens the right not to testify at law as a witness against themselves.

take the huff become sulky, peevish, grumpy, etc. He's very sensitive, and inclined to take the huff for the slightest thing. Cockney rhyming slang sometimes has 'take a cream puff'.

take the law into one's own hands administer justice oneself, instead of waiting for the proper authorities to do so. He's convinced that Bloggs is the killer of his daughter, and my great fear now is that he'll try to take the law into his own hands.

take the liberty of presume (to do something) without awaiting someone else's permission. I took the liberty of borrowing your car in order to get the injured man to hospital – I hope you don't mind.

take the measure of someone/something make an accurate assessment, usually of a person's qualities. It's very hard to take the measure of such an intensely private person.

take the mickey/piss tease; send up. I don't like that man – he's always taking the mickey out of people. 'Mickey' is from Cockney rhyming slang: 'take the Mickey Bliss' = piss. The phrase was itself sent up in the pseudo-formal or pedantic variants 'extract the Michael/urine'.

take the occasion to use the opportunity to. I want to take this occasion to remind you of how much we all owe to Mr Churchill.

take ownership (of something) assume responsibility (for something). The boss has asked Tom and his team to take ownership of the new project. Management-speak.

take the plunge finally take a big or even momentous decision, about which one may have been prevaricating. They lived together happily for many years, when all of a sudden John took the plunge and asked Suzy to marry him. From diving, which is preceded by the taking of a deep breath. So too in this metaphor.

take the rap take the punishment. It was a major robbery, and the police are anxious to get someone to take the rap. A former punishment favoured by schools would have been a rap over the knuckles.

take the rough with the smooth accept or tolerate the bad times as calmly and philosophically as one accepts the good times. Most jobs have their boring parts as well as their exciting parts, but people just have to learn to take the rough with the smooth.

take the wind out of someone's sails nonplus or confuse someone; render someone temporarily speechless. He used to boast rather a lot about his skill as a squash player, so it took the wind out of his sails when you beat him so decisively. From the days of sailing ships becalmed at sea.

take the words out of someone's mouth anticipate what someone is going to say by saying it oneself. I was about to say what a happy occasion it was, but you have taken the words out of my mouth. Compare **pinch someone's lines/lyrics**.

take one's time not hurry; proceed without haste. There's no need to rush – just take your time and watch the traffic.

take something to heart be affected or influenced by something (usually advice or criticism), often to the point that one decides to act or think differently in future. The judge found him guilty of dangerous driving, and he took the judgment very much to heart; he's afraid to get into the car now.

take to one's heels flee. He smelt the smoke, then all at once he saw the flames and took to his heels. Also **show a clean pair of heels**. Compare **turn tail**.

take someone to task criticise someone for something wrong or badly done. The painter left a terrible mess in the garden, for which I had to take him to task.

take someone to the cleaners cheat or strip someone of all his money, assets, etc. usually in gambling or business. In the privatisation of public utilities, it is found time and again that it is none other than poor old Joe Taxpayer who is taken to the cleaners. Generally found in the passive.

take umbrage take offence. I'm afraid I take umbrage from the fact that you have been telling all these stories about me. From Latin 'umbra', a shadow. If you take umbrage at someone or something, you feel overshadowed or inhibited by them.

take something with a pinch/grain of salt accept a statement with some reservations. She has told me several blatant lies in the past, so nowadays I tend to take what she tells me with a grain of salt. From a very old Latin idiomatic phrase 'cum grano salis'.

TAKEN. taken aback astonished; disconcerted by a sudden disclosure or other check. We were all quite taken aback when John suddenly announced that he was emigrating to America. Originally nautical: a sudden shift in the wind could catch the front of a ship and drive it astern.

taken short experience the sudden (and usually inconvenient) need to urinate or defecate. The children were all sent to the toilet while I was filling the car with petrol, because I didn't want anyone taken short on the motorway.

TAKING. taking one thing with another averaging out the good and bad features of something. It had been a dreadful experience, but we survived it; and taking one thing with another, we had to conclude that we'd been very lucky.

TALK. talk the birds off the trees persuade people to do something against their instincts or better judgment. He can talk the birds off the trees if he wants something badly enough. Compare **talk the hind legs off a donkey; gift of the gab; kiss the Blarney Stone**.

talk a good (something) said of a boastful or over-talkative but unconvincing person. He talks a very good round of golf but he is in fact a lousy player. Compare **gift of the gab**.

talk double Dutch talk incomprehensibly, or in a manner inaccessible to the listener. It was a very boring lecture for me – the lecturer seemed to be talking double Dutch most of the time. Dutch is a language that sounds very difficult to English speakers, and during the 17th century the English held the Dutch in such contempt that they regarded their language as little more than gibberish! (See next entry.)

talk gibberish talk incomprehensibly; talk nonsense. *They were talking some foreign gibberish from which I could only pick out a few words of sense.* 'Gibberish' is perhaps formed from 'gibber' and 'jabber', and reduplicative 'jibber-jabber' (meaning rapid and unintelligible speech), by analogy with Spanish, Turkish, Swedish, etc.

talk shop discuss business affairs, often in an inappropriate social context. *I decided to leave the party early, knowing they'd do nothing but talk shop for the rest of the evening.*

talk the hind legs off a donkey talk excessively and endlessly. *I got stuck with Mrs Potter at the party, and she'd talk the hind legs off a donkey: she just goes on and on for ever.* The idea is probably of even that most patient-natured of animals, the donkey, losing its patience. See also **get a word in edgeways; talk the birds off the trees**.

talk through one's hat talk ignorant nonsense; express opinions about something without any real knowledge of it. *Why don't you shut up instead of talking through your hat about a subject you know nothing about?*

talk till one is blue/black in the face talk endlessly but ineffectually or to little avail. *She can tell me her story till she's blue in the face, but it won't get her very far.* The image is of a person wasting his/her last gasp – either dying or at least with a badly bruised physiognomy.

talk to a brick wall try unsuccessfully to communicate with someone. *I told him to put his coat on before he went out in the rain, but I might as well have been talking to a brick wall,* i.e. the request was ignored. A standard metaphor of communicative failure, as is the simile 'like talking to a brick wall'. Compare **save one's breath**.

talk turkey talk frankly and seriously, especially about important business. *I left the pair of them to talk turkey about the job which was on offer.* The idiom is American and dates from about 1830; the original reference was to the US Thanksgiving dinner, which still features turkey on the menu and once also featured a thought-provoking address to diners.

talk oneself out of a job prevaricate negatively about something one is being offered. *His comments were along the lines of how difficult the assignment was going to be, and how expensive, and how long it would take – in effect, he talked himself out of the job, and we hired someone else.* Compare **write oneself out of the script**.

TALL. tall order request or order which is difficult to fulfil. *I know it's a bit of a tall order, but could you finish the job by Monday?*

tall story/tale story which is full of exaggeration, and difficult to believe. *He keeps the kids entertained for hours with tall stories about his life in the African bush.* A popular genre in American literature from around the 1840s.

TARRED. tarred with the same brush possessing the same features, usually faults. *I distrust all politicians – as far as I can see they're all tarred with exactly the same brush.* Originally from farming: shepherds mark all the sheep in their flock with the same paint or tar to distinguish their sheep from those belonging to other farmers. Not quite the same as **touch of the tarbrush**. See also **spoil the ship (for a ha'penny worth of tar)**.

TASTE. taste/dose of one's own medicine receive the same treatment as one has given to other people, especially if it was unjust. *When the government in a democratic society persists in treating the electorate as an ass, sooner or later the electorate will give the government a taste of its own medicine and vote it into oblivion.*

TEACH. teach/give someone a lesson punish someone by giving him an experience he will remember. *I caught them breaking windows and decided it was time to teach them a lesson they wouldn't forget in a hurry. So I called the police.*

teach one's grandmother to suck eggs try to give advice to someone who doesn't need it, being far more knowledgeable about the subject than the speaker. Some bosses seem to think they have to tell you what to do all the time, forgetting that much of the time they're trying to teach their grandmother to suck eggs. A proverbial usage from the days when many of the older generation were toothless, and didn't require advice about sucking food from younger people who still had their own teeth.

TEAR (noun). **tear bucket** person given to much weeping. I told her to stop crying, blow her nose like a big girl and stop being a silly tear bucket. Originally from the name of a character in a Hollywood melodrama – a 'weepie' or 'tear jerker' movie – who cries a lot.

TEAR (verb). **tear one's hair out** be overcome with anxiety. It was a dreadful accident, and the next-of-kin are tearing their hair out waiting for information about their loved ones.

tear strips/a strip off someone rebuke someone severely. She tore a strip off those boys when they broke her window. From physical flogging of someone's bare back, which was wont to tear strips of skin off the victim. Compare **dressing down; lay into someone**.

TELL. tell someone apart make a visual distinction between. The twins were identical, and always wore the same clothes, and even their class teacher could never tell them apart.

tell it like it is tell a story, etc. in plain and unadorned language, without euphemism. Some of you may find some of the language distressing, but you have asked me to tell it like it is, and that is exactly what I propose to do.

tell it not in Gath keep something quiet. Tell it not in Gath but the rumour is that she committed suicide. A quotation from the Bible, in 2 Samuel i.19-20: 'How are the mighty fallen! Tell it not in Gath, publish it not in the streets of Askelon, lest the daughters of the Philistines rejoice...'

tell it/that to the marines a colloquial expression used to signify disbelief. When they told me I'd won the football pools, I said they could tell that one to the marines! The idiom could have originated from the incredulity of landlubbers when bombarded by mariners with stories of fabulous distant lands, amazing beasts, unbelievable wealth and so on; or more prosaically – and more probably – from the landsman's view that the marines were not very intelligent. Compare **aye right!**

tell someone where to get off tell someone that he has gone beyond the limits of acceptable behaviour, etc. He tries to treat me as one of his underlings, so every now and again I have to tell him where to get off. Compare **take a running jump**.

TEMPT. tempt fate/providence do something risky. It was tempting fate to go out without a coat, and sure enough the heavens opened. In more superstitious times, it was felt to be unwise and dangerous to do anything that might tempt one's fate, and people went to great lengths to avoid this.

THANK. thank one's lucky stars be grateful. There was a bad smash on the M8 last night – when I saw the wreckage and ambulances and police cars I thanked my lucky stars I'd not been there at the time. From astrology: the idea being that stars in a certain configuration were lucky or unlucky for one.

THAT'LL. that'll be the day! a way of expressing disbelief: meaning, the day when that happens I'll be very surprised. He tells me he's going to get fit and stop drinking beer and smoking cigars, but that'll be the day! See also **get away!** and **aye right!**

THAT'S. that's flat emphatic statement, meaning 'That is final.' I refuse to lend you any more money and that's flat.

that's that there's nothing more to be said or done on a given subject. He's lost his job and that's that. He's just going to have to go out and look for something else. Slightly milder than **that's flat**.

that's the way the cookie crumbles that's how things turn out. He wasn't expecting to lose his job, but that's the way the cookie crumbles these days for so many folk. **An Americanism. Also 'that's how the cookie crumbles'.**

that's torn it that has spoilt our plans, etc. I'm told Mrs Thatcher has resigned. That's torn it for the Tories then, who's going to run the show for them now? **Also 'that's done it'. And compare been and gone and done it**.

THEN. then and there at that time and in that place. I told him how much I liked his dog, and he gave it to me then and there saying I'd be able to offer it a better home than he could. **Compare on the spot; without further ado**.

THEIRS. theirs (ours, yours, etc.) not to reason why their job is merely to obey orders, not to inquire why something has to be done. We were ordered to jump in the river and – ours not to reason why – we did just that. **A quotation from Tennyson's poem 'The Charge of the Light Brigade' (1854): 'Theirs not to make reply./Theirs not to reason why./Theirs but to do and die…'**

THEREBY. thereby hangs a tale there is an interesting or surprising story connected with this subject. I'm told Mr Bloggs has resigned from Parliament, and thereby hangs a tale or two, I have little doubt. **Frequently used by Shakespeare. ('And so from hour to hour, we ripe and ripe,/ And then from hour to hour, we rot and rot:/And thereby hangs a tale.' As You Like It, 1599.) A conversation marker which often alerts the listener to an oncoming anecdote.**

THERE'S. there's life in the old dog yet! humorous comment that though a person may be old or feeble-looking, his physical or mental abilities are still active. He spent half the evening on the dance-floor with his partner, so there's obviously life in the old dog yet!

there's nothing in it 1. the competitors in a race, etc. are equal and there is no obvious winner. There was nothing at all in it as the three leading horses galloped for the finishing line. 2. **it's not true**. I heard that the business was about to collapse, but I hoped there was nothing in it, **i.e. no truth in the rumour.**

there's nothing to it 1. it is easy to do something; no advanced skills are required. He's going to teach me to drive – there's nothing to it, he says. 2. **it's not serious; there is no substance to the problem, story, etc.** They had a little argument last night, but there was nothing to it and they're good friends again.

THICK. thick as thieves very friendly; in cahoots. They went to school together in the 1970s and they're still as thick as thieves. **A standard simile.**

thick as two short planks unintelligent. He's supposed to be a brilliant barrister, but I know that he's as thick as two short planks. **A standard simile of stupidity or intellectual challenge. Compare not all there.**

thick/thin on the ground plentiful/rare. Decent job opportunities have never been very thick on the ground in this area of high unemployment. Good writing is very thin on the ground nowadays – there's just not much of it about.

THIN. thin end of the wedge insignificant-looking beginning of a more serious problem. I used to do small voluntary chores for her, but that turned out to be the thin end of the wedge – now I look after her day and night. **From quarrying, etc: the wedge is a tool the thin end of which is hammered into a rock to force an opening in it.**

THINK. think (the) better of reconsider; change one's mind about. He said he was going to leave all his money to a cat-and-dog home, but he must have thought the better of it before making his final will.

think highly of admire. The supporters think highly of their team's new goalkeeper. **Opposite of think little of.**

think little of 1. not worry about. He thinks little of getting up every morning at five o'clock, **i.e. it's no problem to him. Also 'think nothing of'.** 2. **have a poor opinion of**. I'm afraid I think very little of someone who conducts himself in such a way. Opposite of **think highly of**.

think no end of like very much. He'd do anything for his children and obviously thinks no end of them.

think on one's feet think quickly. She's a bit too slow on the uptake to make a good teacher – you have to be able to think on your feet in a job like that.

think outside the box think laterally or unconventionally; look at the broader context of a problem, challenge, etc. He likes routines and has a very blinkered outlook: so he's not much good at thinking outside the box. A form of management-speak, probably from puzzle games.

think twice reconsider; have second thoughts. The political problems in that part of the world make you think twice about going there for a holiday. Compare **in two minds**.

THIRD. third degree torture or severe bullying, often applied in order to force the victim to confess to or disclose something. From the noise in the cellar, I knew they were giving John the third degree.

third party person other than the two principals in an argument, etc. It was a reasonably amicable divorce, with no third party involved. A legal term.

third rate of inferior or poor quality. It was a lousy third-rate performance.

third world originally the bloc of states which were aligned neither to the Capitalist, 'developed' states nor to the Communist bloc. He worked in the third world for many years. The term later became synonymous with the under-developed states of the world.

THOSE. those and such as those certain select and superior individuals. I believe there's a big party at the Castle tonight, but it's only for those and such as those – not for the likes of you and me! The opposite of **all and sundry**.

THREE. the three Rs the basic school subjects (reading, writing, and 'rithmetic). Modern education is often accused of forgetting the three Rs in favour of gender issues, multiculturalism and ecology. The term is attributed to Sir William Curtis (1752–1829), onetime Lord Mayor of London, who once proposed a toast to 'the three Rs' at a public dinner.

THREESCORE. threescore (years) and ten term sometimes used to describe man's 'allotted span' of time on earth. Medical science nowadays ensures that more and more people live well beyond their threescore and ten. Biblical, from Psalms xc.10: 'The days of our years are threescore years and ten.'

THROUGH. through and through thoroughly; utterly. He's an old-fashioned gentleman, through and through. Compare **to the fingertips**.

through the mill through difficult times. I was looking forward to seeing him again, though I knew he'd been through the mill somewhat since our last meeting.

through thick and thin despite whatever hardships, difficulties, etc. He was a faithful friend, and stuck by me through thick and thin. A dyad of opposites, apparently the original reference was to 'thicket and thin wood', or to plentiful and sparse vegetation.

through with finished with. He's a bit depressed this morning because last night his girlfriend told him she was through with him. Originally American.

THROW. throw a party give a party. Once in a while we throw a party for all our friends in order to return their hospitality. Probably by extension from 'throwing open one's doors' to give hospitality, etc.

throw a spanner in the works spoil a process, plan, etc. I hate to throw a spanner in the works, but have you considered what we should do if we run out of funds? The image is of a metal tool such as a spanner being thrown deliberately into a delicate piece of machinery and jamming it.

throw a wobbly become distressed, incensed, mentally unstable; show symptoms of shock.

From time to time our maths teacher gets really upset when someone is fooling about in class, and then she throws a complete wobbly. An Americanism, compare **have a fit**.

throw caution to the wind(s) behave recklessly or dangerously. He's a headstrong sort of man, so I expect he'll throw caution to the winds and try to attack the enemy. Compare **in for a penny**.

throw down the glove/gauntlet issue a challenge. The Leader of the Opposition has thrown down the glove and rightly challenged the Prime Minister to an immediate election. From the medieval etiquette of duelling, when a glove was literally flung down. 'Gauntlet' is from Old French, and means a little glove. To signal your acceptance of the challenge, the gauntlet was picked up. Originally the slight could be personal, involving a knight's honour, or a knight could fight on behalf of his lady. The idiom nowadays has an old-fashioned literary resonance of the age of chivalry.

throw good money after bad spend more money in order to try and recoup funds already spent. We'd spent thousands renovating the house before we learnt that the local authority planned to build a motorway through the grounds. We had to decide whether to challenge the authorities, or whether that would just be a matter of throwing good money after bad. Compare **in for a penny**.

throw in one's hand give up. He's very unhappy at work these days, and it wouldn't surprise me at all if he threw in his hand. From cards. Also 'jack it in' (same sense).

throw in one's lot with ally oneself to. After Bonnie Prince Charlie took Edinburgh, many Scots threw in their lot with his Jacobites.

throw in the towel/sponge give up; admit defeat. Their business has never really got established, and last year's season was a disaster. I think they'll throw in the towel this year unless they get a really good summer. From boxing: in the 18th century, prize-fighters would signal to their corner when they had had enough, and their team would throw the towel or sponge into the ring as a request for the fight to be stopped.

throw light on clarify, usually a problem, etc. This exhibition throws some fascinating light on the artistic abilities of our prehistoric ancestors.

throw someone off the scent divert or mislead someone. The robbers were extremely clever, and laid various false trails. These successfully threw the police right off the scent for several days. From the hunting field.

throw something/someone out of gear disrupt the smooth running of something. We had some surprise visitors last weekend, and though we enjoyed their company very much they have succeeded in throwing our entire week completely out of gear. From car driving.

throw the baby out with the bathwater destroy or dispose of the essentials as well as the trivia, incidentals, etc. The English view of the French Revolution tends to be that it was too extreme, and that they threw the baby out with the bathwater in a mad rush to get away from the monarchy. From a folk saying that one should avoid doing this.

throw the book at furiously accuse a person of various crimes, faults, etc. He threw the book at me when he learnt I'd crashed his car. The metaphor is of a book containing a list of all one's crimes being hurled at one's head.

throw up one's hands/arms often **in horror, surprise, despair, etc.** get a fright; show one's shock, horror, etc. e.g. by raising the hands. He threw up his hands when we jumped out on him from behind that tree.

throw one's weight about be bossy and domineering. Who does he think he is coming in here and throwing his weight about as if he's royalty?

THUMB. thumb a lift hold out one's thumb in order to try to stop a car for the purpose of obtaining a free ride; hitch-hike. I left him off at a roundabout outside town, which was as good a place as any for hitch-hikers thumbing a lift.

thumb one's nose at a sign of scorn or derision made by putting one's thumb to the nose and waving the fingers at the object of one's mockery. Since leaving school he has tended to thumb his nose at any form of authority. Compare **cock a snook**.

THUMBS. thumbs up/down indication of approval/disapproval of something. Today's by-election results are yet another clear thumbs down for an unpopular government. The action of showing a raised thumb or a lowered one is thought to date back at least as far as Roman times. Compare **get the (big) bird**.

TICK. tick (all) the (right) boxes meet (all) the criteria, expectations, etc. It wasn't a speech to which I could respond positively; it ticked none of my boxes. From multiple-choice questions and 'objective' testing. Compare **not put a foot wrong/out of line; press the right buttons**.

TICKLE. tickle/take someone's fancy feel attracted to someone or something. There was a splendid landscape painting in the window which instantly took his fancy, so he went into the shop and asked the price of it. One's fancy is one's taste or critical judgment.

tickle the ivories play the piano. She went into the living room and tickled the ivories quietly for half an hour. 'Ivories' is slang for the notes on the keyboard, in this jocular circumlocution or inelegant variation.

TICKLED. tickled pink/to death highly amused or delighted. She was tickled to death to meet her old friend after all these years. The suffusion of pinkness implies laughter and good humour.

TIE. tie someone down commit someone (to do something). I'll try and look in on Sunday afternoon, but don't tie me down to giving you a precise time.

tie someone's hands prevent someone (from doing something). I'm afraid I can't help you; my hands are tied by the terms of my contract.

tie the knot get married. They decided to tie the knot before John left for his regiment overseas. Tying

the knot is a symbolic gesture in many cultures; after it is tied, the unity of the marriage partnership is publicly recognised and should not be broken.

tie someone up in knots cause someone confusion and uncertainty. The witness was obviously unreliable, and the defence lawyer soon had her completely tied up in knots of her own making.

TIED. tied to one's mother's apron (strings) dominated by one's mother. It was a bit degrading to see this otherwise intelligent man of 51 so firmly tied to his mother's apron.

TIGHT. tight wad mean or miserly person. Don't expect that old tight wad to buy you a cup of coffee. An Americanism, the reference to a 'wad' of notes indicates there is no shortage of wealth in the person so accused, merely a reluctance to peel off a few notes and share it around.

TIGHTEN. tighten one's belt economise. Most people expect to have to tighten their belt when they lose their jobs. A dietary metaphor, of eating less and therefore of losing weight.

TILL. till/to kingdom come 1. for ever; for a long time. I could have waited there till kingdom come as far as that doctor was concerned. A popular exaggeration of impatient people. 2. to heaven. They were shot at point blank range and went straight to kingdom come. These are references to the second coming of Christ, which people still tend to assume is a long way off, and to God's kingdom. The phrase is influenced by the wording of the Lord's Prayer: 'Thy Kingdom come.'

till the cows come home for a long time. She's a wonderful cellist, and I could have listened to her playing Elgar till the cows come home. From farming: left to themselves cows take a very long time to return to the barn for milking.

TILT. tilt at windmills attack imagined but fanciful enemies. He was a lovable old soul, rather inclined to tilt at windmills, but otherwise quite harmless. From the Spanish story of *Don Quixote de la Mancha* (1605), by Miguel Cervantes. The possibly shortsighted Don, his head full of fanciful ideas, attacked the sails of a windmill, thinking himself under attack by giants. He got his lance entangled in the moving sails, and these pulled him from his horse.

tilt the scales/balance give the advantage (to one side over another). The intervention of the headmaster tilted the scales in favour of the children who had been bullied. From the scales of justice, which are supposed to be evenly balanced.

TIME. time and a half the normal hourly rate of pay plus 50 per cent. You'll be paid at time and a half if you agree to work on Saturday nights. A rate of pay sometimes offered to induce people to work anti-social hours, e.g. at weekends or at night, for overtime, etc.

time is ripe it is the right time. After his illness, he decided the time was ripe for him to give up playing rugby and take up a gentler form of exercise. From farming and gardening.

time of life 1. age. I explained that I couldn't climb ladders at my time of life – I'm 86, after all. 2. a euphemism for the menopause. She's been getting a lot of headaches and dizziness, but the doctor tells us that these are not uncommon symptoms of the time of life.

time of one's life very enjoyable time. It was a lovely party and we all had the time of our life.

time on one's hands time to spare if one is not busy. He's very active in the scouts and he has a morning paper round before school, so he hasn't got much spare time on his hands.

TIMES. times without number frequently. That bus is late times without number.

TIP. tip of the iceberg small proportion of the total amount; small part of the whole subject, problem, etc. Jane's accident is a tragic one, but the real shame is that she's only the tip of the iceberg – a tiny statistic in a huge annual loss of life.

tip someone the wink/nod give someone a surreptitious hint or warning. A friend tipped him the wink that the police were looking for him, so he left town.

TIRED. tired and emotional drunk. You just have to leave George alone for a while when he gets tired and emotional like that. A journalistic euphemism of the 1970s coined to describe the frequent condition of a certain British cabinet minister. See also **half-seas over; pickled/pissed as a newt; pie eyed**.

TIT. tit for tat one blow or stroke or insult in retaliation for another. It had all the hallmarks of a petty feud, each party giving tit for tat. The original usage assumed the physical contact involved in – at the least – an exchange of taps. Similar to Latin 'quid pro quo'.

TO. to a band playing with gusto and enthusiasm. She loves ice cream and tells me she could eat it to a band playing, i.e. she could never get too much of it. Originally American; compare **to beat the band**.

to a man unanimously. Members voted to a man in favour of the amendment. Politically incorrect.

to a nail to perfection, to a nicety. The three bridesmaids were decked out to a nail, and they looked quite exquisite. An old-fashioned idiom, from Latin 'ad unguem'.

to a shadow thin and weary looking. She's worn away to a shadow since I last saw her. Also **shadow of one's former self**.

to and fro back and forth between two places. The ferry goes to and fro between the mainland and the island six days a week.

-to-be prospective. I was introduced to his wife-to-be at last night's party.

to beat the band with intense conviction or adeptness. They've been arguing and yelling to beat the band in that office for several hours. Originally American, a variant of **to a band playing**.

to boot into the bargain; as well. Not only is she a brilliant nuclear physicist, she's also a very competent pianist to boot. A frozen idiom, now often used for humorous effect. 'Boot' is an old noun meaning advantage or profit, as in 'Apply thy days to better boot' (Edmund Spenser), i.e. make better use of your time. Compare **into the bargain**.

to cap it all in addition to everything else. First you borrow my car without asking, then you crash it, and now – to cap it all – you claim you 'forgot' to tell me about it. Usually an indication of hurt, injury, etc. Compare **add insult to injury**.

to coin a phrase as one might say; to repeat an expression, quotation, etc. I have to say that we were not amused, to coin a phrase. Usually a less than entirely serious marker drawing attention to something one has said, or to the fact that one is referring to a well-used quotation, cliché, etc. Originally American.

to death an intensifier used with certain adjectives such as 'bored', 'scared', 'worried', etc. and indicative of extreme boredom, fear, worry. He's scared to death nowadays to go out in the dark.

to-do argument; noise. There was quite a to-do in the street last night – did you hear it?

to someone's face directly, to a person in their presence. She seems to say a lot about me behind my back, but she never says much to my face.

to goodness an emphatic term, meaning 'very much'. I wish to goodness someone would tell her to shut up.

to hand within one's reach; in stock; in one's possession. I'll send you a copy of the report as soon as we have one to hand – right now it's still at the printers.

to one's name belonging to one. He's got hardly a penny to his name.

to the fingertips thoroughly; entirely. She's a professional politician to the fingertips. Compare **through and through**.

to the letter exactly. I followed your instructions precisely and to the letter.

to the life an exact likeness. It was a splendid portrait, and it was Mrs Siddons to the life. From the life class, in art. Also 'to a T'. Compare **spitting image**.

to the manner born with spontaneous or natural assurance. He'd never acted in his life, but he took the part and performed it as if to the manner born. From *Hamlet*: 'I am native here/And to the manner born...'

to the marrow/core utterly. I'm sorry to say it but that boy's idle to the marrow. Literally, to the marrow of his bones. Compare **bone idle**.

TOE. toe the line obey orders; conform; submit to authority. She tried to make her children toe the line, but they didn't listen to her. His boss has told him to toe the line or look for another job. From athletics, where runners have to keep their toe behind the starting line. Originally, 'toe the mark' or 'toe the scratch'.

TONGUE. (with) tongue in cheek insincerely or jokingly. He made a rather tongue-in-cheek comment about being pleased to see us, but I knew well that he was not.

tongue tied speechless with shyness, nervousness, etc. Asked to say a few words, the poor man suddenly became totally tongue tied with confusion.

TOO. too bad that's a pity. 'He seems to have broken his leg.' 'Oh, too bad,' I said. A conversational commiseration.

too big for one's boots conceited; bumptious. I'm afraid that young man has got far too big for his boots if he thinks he can go around giving us orders to do this and that.

too clever by half far too clever. That young man is just too clever by half, and one of these days he is going to come a cropper. The phrase is used sarcastically to describe a person who imagines himself smarter than he is, and whose conceit will be his undoing. Sometimes 'too clever for one's own good'. Compare **smart Aleck**.

too close to call too hard to predict the outcome of something with any degree of certainty. All the commentators are agreed on one thing at least: that the outcome of the election is now far too close to call comfortably. From athletics before the days of the photo finish, now a journalistic cliché.

too many cooks (spoil the broth) too many people (are trying to help). There was a huge crowd at the scene of the accident, and on the grounds of too many cooks and so on, I decided that the rescue operation was unlikely to require my help as well as everyone else's. From the proverb.

TOOTH. tooth and nail fiercely, with all one's strength. The committee swore to oppose tooth and nail the building of the bypass. Originally 'with tooth and nail', meaning with the use of one's teeth and nails as weapons.

TOP. top dog the dominant or leading member of a group. Now he's top dog in this office, I expect there'll be a few changes. From animals fighting, where the winner emerges on top; or from animal behaviour more generally, where there is usually a dominant male leader of the pack. Sometimes 'alpha male'.

top drawer the best available. She seems to have had a top-drawer schooling. From the domestic strategy of keeping one's best or most precious possessions in the top drawer, out of the reach of small children. Compare **bee's knees**.

top of the range the best and most expensive version of something. It's supposed to be a very classy shop specialising in top-of-the-range Scandinavian furniture. The 'range' was initially 1950s US motor marketing jargon for the various amplifications available on the basic car model, with the top-range model having the most lavish accessories.

top of the tree/ladder pinnacle of a career. She was quite young when she reached the top of the ladder in her profession.

TOPSY. topsy-turvy turned upside down; disorderly. The entire street was topsy-turvy with roofing and cars and telegraph poles and other bits and pieces – all this as a result of one little whirlwind. A reduplication.

TOUCH. touch and go of uncertain outcome. She's had a very serious illness, and her survival is still touch and go. Perhaps nautical: if a boat had the misfortune to scrape rocks, the big question was whether it would sink or whether it would be able to go on.

touch base make or renew contact; check in with someone. I'd been wanting to see Michael for some time, so it was a pleasure to touch base with him yesterday. Originally from the American baseball field.

touch of the tarbrush person who may have some black African ancestry in his racial makeup. People like Hitler and the South African apartheid regimes were very active in hunting out that touch of the tarbrush in people's ancestry. Originally an American expression from the Pre-Emancipation period, the term is now offensive. See also **tarred with the same brush**.

touch wood term used when speaker wants to have good luck, or to avoid bad luck. There's been a bad epidemic of flu in the school, but touch wood I've avoided it so far. The expression is often accompanied by the speaker touching a wooden object. The origin of the expression may be pagan (touching the good spirit of the trees) or Christian (touching the wooden cross of Christ). The US variant is 'knock on wood'.

TOUGH. tough as nails very tough and strong. Don't worry about John – he's as tough as nails. A standard simile, as is 'tough as an old boot' when referring to meat, etc. I can't manage that steak – it's tough as old boots.

tough cookie courageous person. Most people who knew her agreed that my grandmother was a pretty tough cookie. An Americanism, where a 'cookie' is a biscuit, thus a metaphor of a person who declines to crumble under pressure.

tough nut person or problem that is difficult to deal with. The problem of global warming is a very tough nut to crack, and no easy solutions are in sight. Literally, 'hard to crack' or resolve. Compare **hard nut (to crack)**.

TOWER. tower/pillar of strength dependable person who always gives strong support when it is needed. She was his tower of strength when he lost his job. A standard metaphor, found in Shakespeare's *Richard III* and in Tennyson's 'Ode to the Duke of Wellington' (1852), now often a cliché.

TOXIC. toxic waste waste products that cannot be safely disposed of, often nuclear. Most parties with strong 'green' credentials are strongly opposed to nuclear power stations because of their toxic waste. 'Toxic' has become a very productive adjective of the early 21st century: as well as toxic effluent, we now have toxic loans, toxic debts, toxic banks, toxic shares, etc. – in other words, a toxic legacy. (But we need to remember the real meaning of 'toxic assets', which is simply 'bad debts' by any other name.)

TOY. toy boy male lover. Jane's latest toy boy is from Brazil, and I'm told he's very good looking. Usually a term of disparagement, the man in question is usually regarded as a juvenile sex object or fashion accessory. A rhyming reduplication; compare **fancy man**.

TRACK. track record reputation of a person or organisation, based on their previous successes and failures. He's been hired to do the job because he's got a good track record of achieving prompt results. A metaphor from the athletics running track.

TREAD. tread water not make much progress; perform unsatisfactorily. The firm's business in Japan has been sluggish for many years, and now they're beginning to tread water in their home markets as well. Swimmers tread water to maintain themselves in one position by moving the feet as if treading up stairs, as in the dog paddle. Compare **flat lining**.

TRIAL. trial and error method of trying something out, solving a problem, etc. by making many attempts and learning as one progresses from any mistakes one makes along the way. By trial and error he has taught himself how to use a computer.

TRICK. trick(s) of the trade skill(s) learnt as part of one's job. I found teaching very difficult for a year or two, but slowly I began to acquire a few of the tricks of the trade.

TRIM. trim one's sails curtail one's activities; adapt according to prevailing circumstances. Politicians tend to promise the earth before they are elected, and then spend their political career trimming their sails before the wind of budgetary constraints. Originally nautical: sailors trimmed or adjusted the boat's sails in accordance with the direction and force of the wind.

TRIP. trip the light fantastic dance. It was a really good band, and all the wedding guests tripped the light fantastic till the early hours of the morning. Now a humorous literary cliché. From John Milton's poem *L'Allegro* (1632): 'Come, and trip it as ye go/On the light fantastic toe.'

TROUBLE. trouble at mill problems or difficulties, usually at a place of work. We had a good meeting but someone interrupted us towards the end, and Mr Bloggs had to rush off and attend to some trouble or other at mill. A mock-serious euphemism often pronounced 'trooble', to mimic a Yorkshire or Lancashire accent (where there used to be lots of industrial mills). An American alternative might be **meanwhile, back at the ranch**.

trouble brewing trouble likely to occur. I knew from the expression on his face that there was trouble brewing. Originally from the concocting of beer.

TROUBLED. troubled waters confused or dangerous situation. A number of people have been fishing in the troubled waters of Middle East politics. See also **pour oil on troubled waters**.

TRUE. true blue staunch or loyal to one's principles; very Conservative (in British politics and society). He appealed to all true-blue members of the club to refrain from speaking to the press about their problems. In the 17th century, the True Party was the nickname for the Protestant or Whig following, later associated with the colour blue. See also **of the deepest hue/dye**.

true to one's colours loyal to one's cause or point of view. I've been true to my colours throughout this debate, and I'm not going to change them now just because they're not supported by the majority of my audience. A naval metaphor: one's colours were one's flag. Not the same as **reveal/show one's true colours**.

true to form in the expected/predictable way. He had a notorious temper, and true to form he lost it again at yesterday's meeting. From betting, the implication being that it would be safe to bet on him losing his temper, etc.

TRY. try conclusions with engage in a trial of strength or skill with; enter a power struggle with. I hope the various factions are not about to try conclusions with one another on the battlefield. Originally meant 'to experiment'. A similar more recent expression is 'to mix it with someone'.

try one's hand at attempt to do something for the first time; test one's ability at something. He's never been on a pair of skis in his life, but now that he's in Switzerland he's decided to try his hand at it. Note that the idiom is no longer confined to an activity demanding the use of one's hands.

TUPPENCE. tuppence off the shilling not entirely intelligent; mentally retarded. He may be a lovely kid, and very sweet natured, but he's tuppence off the shilling and he's going to need a lot of looking after. Also 'not the full shilling'. From pre-decimal British currency, where a full shilling comprised 12 pence. Compare **have a screw loose; not all there; not the sharpest tool in the box**.

TURN. turn a blind eye choose not to see. I've decided to turn a blind eye to your conduct last night,

but don't let it happen again! The most famous historical episode involving the turning of a blind eye occurred when Lord Nelson put the telescope to his blind eye before his victorious sea battle at Copenhagen and announced, 'I see no signal' (to withdraw from engaging the enemy).

turn a deaf ear choose not to hear; refuse to listen. A government that consistently turns a deaf ear to the clearly articulated demands of its electors must sooner or later expect to hear a very loud protest indeed. The expression was already old when Jonathan Swift used it in 1724.

turn one's back on choose not to speak to; have no further contact with. Now that he's an important man he seems to have turned his back on his childhood friends.

turn one's hand to be capable of. She turns her hand to most things – painting, car maintenance, baking…

turn one's head give someone an inflated sense of his own importance. Marrying into the royal family seems to have turned her pretty little head.

turn in one's grave hypothetically cause serious distress, rage, disappointment, etc. to the supposed views or tastes of a person now dead. If Mozart could hear some of the latest musical hits, I'm sure he'd be turning in his grave.

turn of events change of circumstances, usually unexpected. Last week saw a very strange turn of events in the world of horticulture.

turn of phrase particular way of expressing something. We listened to that tape many times, trying to solve the problem: every turn of phrase uttered by the suspect was analysed and discussed.

turn of the tide time when circumstances change. It's hard to date precisely or to a single event the turn of the tide in our favour. Supremely, a Churchillian phrase descriptive of a crucial stage in the Second World War. The original phrase refers to the time when the sea tide changes, from coming in to going out, or vice versa. See also **turn the tables; turn the tide**.

turn on one's heel angrily turn away. She turned on her heel and left the room, angrily slamming the front door behind her. There is surely a hint of flouncing in this expression, more appropriate to the stage or the TV screen than to real life.

turn over a new leaf make a fresh start; reform one's conduct. Since his marriage he's turned over a new leaf and has become a respectable member of the community. The metaphorical idea was that you could turn to a clean page unsullied by graffiti in the book of your life. Compare **take a leaf out of someone's book**.

turn one's stomach make one feel sick. It turned my stomach every time they showed pictures of the refugee camp.

turn tail turn back and flee. When General Cope was defeated at Prestonpans, he turned tail and made for Berwick. The original term was from falconry. Compare **take to one's heels**.

turn the corner begin to improve. The pundits agree that it'll be a year or two yet before the economy finally starts to turn the corner.

turn the other cheek decline to be provoked; be patient or forgiving when unkindly treated. In the end I got fed up turning the other cheek, so I thumped him. From the Bible: 'Unto him that smite thee on the one cheek, offer also the other.' In Luke vi.29, but see also Matthew v.39. Opposite of **pay someone back in his own coin**.

turn the tables reverse the position and gain the advantage. We lost the opening game, but we managed to turn the tables in the second round. From the idea of players reversing their position at a board game, and thus reversing their fortunes.

turn the tide change the circumstances in which one finds oneself, either to one's advantage or disadvantage. We were winning the game convincingly at half time, but Logan's injury

seemed to turn the tide against us, and then everything started to go wrong. See also **turn of the tide**.

turn something to (good) account gain useful advantage from something. He claimed to have turned his illness to good account, since that was what prompted him to work in his garden.

turn turtle turn upside down; capsize. The bus turned turtle in the crash, and there were several wounded passengers. The original idea was of catching turtles by turning them on their backs so that they couldn't then get away.

turn-up for the books chance improvement in circumstances, affairs, etc. Often used pejoratively. They told me that our boat had been disqualified from the race, which was a fine turn-up for the books, I must say! From the chance turning up of a winning card or dice. 'The books' is a reference to a bookmaker's betting book.

turn up one's nose scorn, despise. He turns up his nose at holidays in the Highlands – it's always Jamaica or Mauritius or somewhere exotic for him. Compare the very similar **look down one's nose**, which has a similar meaning.

turn up the heat apply increased pressure on someone to do something. The Tories should start turning up the heat on the Labour Party if they want to win the next election. A cooking idiom snaffled into political journalese.

turn up trumps achieve an unexpected success or triumph. For once the weather turned up trumps and we had a glorious sunny weekend. From card games, where the trump card is the most valuable one to hold. From French 'triomphe' meaning triumph.

TWICE. twice round the houses all over the place. I'll chase him twice round the houses if he tries that trick again. A mildly humorous threat.

TWIDDLE. twiddle one's thumbs waste time doing nothing useful. I'm not going to sit around here all day twiddling my thumbs – give me some work to do! See also **kill time**.

TWIST. twist someone's arm try to persuade someone to do something against his will. They keep twisting my arm to revise my plans, but so far I have managed to resist them. **Sometimes humorous.** 'Have some chocolate cake.' 'Oh no, I shouldn't really, but – well, twist my arm! Please!' Compare **put the arm on someone**.

twist someone round one's little finger know how to manipulate someone to one's advantage. She's never short of money, because she twists her father round her little finger and gets anything she asks for from him.

TWO. two/ten a penny very common. Cars like that old Morris used to be two a penny – everybody had one. The combined impact of inflation, hyperbole and decimalisation make 'ten a penny' the commoner idiom today, though 'two a penny' is the older expression. The American equivalent is 'a dime a dozen'.

two bites at the cherry two chances at something. He failed the exam last summer, but fortunately he gets two bites at the cherry and will do the resit in September. Also a **second bite at the cherry**. There is an element of good fortune in these expressions, from the idea/saying that we don't often get two bites at a cherry – because it isn't usually big enough.

two-faced insincere; saying one thing and meaning another. It's impossible to believe a word she says, she's such a two-faced person. Also 'double-faced', **Janus-faced**. John Bunyan created Mr Facing-Both-Ways to represent Hypocrisy in his allegory of *The Pilgrim's Progress* (1678). Compare **double talk; have the face to**.

two of a kind two people of the same trade, outlook, character. I wouldn't trust old Jones – he's like his friend Pritchard – they're two of a kind. Compare **birds of a feather**.

two strings to one's bow two skills to one's credit. He has two very useful strings to his bow: he's an excellent after-dinner speaker and he's also a very competent opera singer. Also 'a second string to one's bow', 'several strings to one's bow'.

two-time someone cheat or deceive someone, especially in matters of sexual fidelity. She's been two-timing her husband for many years.

U

U. U/non-U correct/incorrect social usage. He spoke with a particularly non-U sort of antipodean accent. The coinage of this deeply English style of social categorisation is attributed to Nancy Mitford (1904–73), 'U' referring to upper-class, 'non-U' to non-upper class behaviour, language, etc. These terms and the mindset which coined them are now dated, and not to be taken too seriously.

U-turn 1. complete turnaround of a car, etc. on a road, in order to face in the opposite direction. Suddenly the road stopped, so we did a U-turn and came back. 2. complete change of policy. The prime minister warned colleagues in government that there would be no U-turns in their European policies. Journalese.

UGLY. ugly customer dangerous or potentially violent person. This man is an extremely ugly customer, and the police have warned the public not to tackle him.

ugly duckling young person who lacks photogenic features. Poor little John Brown is a bit of an ugly duckling, especially when compared with his beautiful sister. The origin of the phrase is a classic children's story by Hans Christian Andersen. The story is of the duck which hatches a brood of ducklings, one of which – the ugly one – later turns out to be a swan. Thus the hatchling which was at first despised for its ugliness grows into a bird of unsurpassed beauty.

UGANDAN. Ugandan affairs/discussions sexual intimacy. She hadn't seen him for many years, but remembered with somewhat wistful affection her Ugandan discussions with him during their student days. A euphemism once dear to the hearts of readers of the satirical magazine *Private Eye* in the 1970s and 80s; now out of vogue.

UNCLE. Uncle Sam personification for the US, especially the US government. In the First World War it was 1917 before Uncle Sam sent in the troops. The term is probably a humorous extension of the initials US, and is similar to the British equivalent John Bull, or the French Marianne.

Uncle Tom old-fashioned person who is happy to be told what to say and how to vote, etc. He's a bit of an Uncle Tom and not the sort of person to stand for election to the local council. Not politically correct in our more aggressive times. From the eponymous hero of *Uncle Tom's Cabin* (1852), by Harriet Beecher Stowe.

Uncle Tom Cobley and all everybody. Yes, we're giving a party, and everybody's invited – Uncle Tom Cobley and all! From the chorus of a popular Edwardian song, similar to 'the world and his wife', 'every Tom, Dick and Harry', etc.

UNCO. unco guid literally, the 'extremely good' – being the self-righteously pious or moral set in society. He liked to keep up appearances, knowing that there was a strong streak of the unco guid in this rural community and not wishing to antagonise them. A Scots expression, 'unco' is probably best glossed here as 'ultra' or 'exceedingly'; 'guid' is merely the Scots spelling of 'good'. A satirical poem by Robert Burns, 'Address to the Unco Guid, or Rigidly Righteous' (1787), popularised the expression.

UNCROWNED. uncrowned king/queen of unofficial champion of. Ladies and gentlemen, please give a warm welcome to the uncrowned king of rhythm and blues music.

UNDER. under a cloud in disgrace. There was some trouble at their hotel, and the team had to leave the competition under a bit of a cloud.

under age below the legal age. It's against the law for shopkeepers to sell cigarettes to under-age customers.

under one's belt forming part of one's experience. Now that he's got a few championship matches under his belt, he's becoming quite a powerful player.

under one's breath in a whisper; quietly. We could hear him muttering and cursing under his breath.

under cover of under the protection of. We managed to shelter from the storm for a while, under cover of the sea wall.

under fire 1. with guns, etc. being fired at one. The defending troops came under heavy fire from the enemy artillery. **2. under heavy criticism.** The government are under heavy opposition fire for not properly resisting the latest EU fishing directive.

under one's hat secret; confidential. I'll tell you a secret if you can promise to keep it under your hat for a few days. Compare **under wraps**.

under one's nose in full view; right beside one. I couldn't find my pencil for fully 10 minutes and all the time it was sitting on the table right there under my nose.

under one's own steam by one's own efforts; without assistance from anybody. I asked him if he'd like a lift to town, but he said he'd manage under his own steam. By the early 19th century, the word 'steam' had become a synonym for energy and physical 'go'.

under/on pain of at the risk of incurring – usually followed by some specific or dire punishment. Pupils are forbidden, under pain of instant expulsion, to go into such a place wearing school uniform. Often facetious.

under par below one's average ability or condition; not up to the usual standard. He's been feeling a bit under par this week, so I suggested he go home and take a couple of days off. 'Par' is an abbreviation of 'parity', and the abbreviated term was first used in commerce ('at par' = at face value) and later also in sports like golf ('par' = the number of strokes a scratch player should take to a hole or round a course). Opposite of **up to par**. Compare **below par; on a par with; par for the course**.

under protest while protesting or objecting. The demonstrators were removed from the site under protest.

under the auspices of with the backing, support, patronage of. He works for a voluntary writers' organisation which is under the auspices of the Arts Council. 'Auspices' means 'favourable guidance', and is from Latin 'auspex', a soothsayer, a person who looked for favourable signs by studying the behaviour of birds.

under the/these circumstances in this particular situation. The storm is obviously going to get worse, not better; there is really only one thing to do under the circumstances, and that is to call the picnic off.

under the counter surreptitious and or unofficial, usually because illegal. I'm told they have some kind of under-the-counter business selling antiques to America. The Americans prefer 'under the table'. A similar sense is conveyed by 'in a brown envelope'.

under the hammer about to be sold at auction. His priceless collection of Impressionist paintings goes under the hammer next week and is expected to fetch a million. The hammer is the tool of the auctioneer's trade, and it is banged on the table to indicate when the highest bid has been accepted and a sale has been made.

under the influence drunk. Don't let her near the car if she's under the influence. Literally, under the intoxicating influence of alcohol.

under the sun anywhere in the world. He was a wanted criminal, and as such there was nowhere for him to hide under the sun.

under the thumb of subservient to; controlled by. It soon became clear that Mr Bloggs was completely under the thumb of his wife.

under the weather not very well. Sorry I couldn't come to the party, but I was feeling a bit under the weather yesterday.

under way 1. embarked on a journey. We spent the night at a campsite, and got under way again at seven next morning. The original context was nautical. 2. in course of completion. The construction work is well under way, and is due to be finished by July next year.

under one's wing into one's care. He's been suffering badly from culture shock and homesickness, so we've taken him under our wing for a few months to help him to settle down in this country.

under wraps shrouded in secrecy. They've been keeping the project strictly under wraps in order to be able to launch it without too many competitors. American, from the 1940s war effort. Compare **under one's hat**; see also **keep something under one's hat**.

UNHOLY. unholy din horrible noise or disturbance. That was an unholy din in the square last night when the victorious supporters' buses got back to town. Compare **night on the tiles**.

UNITED. united front a 'face' or appearance of unity, alliance, etc. When questioned, the family put on a united front and refused to discuss the affair. Often political, where a 'front' is the title of an umbrella organisation of like-minded parties with similar objectives, i.e. the United Liberation Front. In current political parlance, these are also sometimes referred to as 'open affiliations' or 'rainbow alliances/coalitions'. Compare **broad church**.

UNKNOWN. unknown quantity someone/ something that one has no intimate knowledge of, which is therefore unpredictable. I suppose we should have been ready for punctures and mechanical problems when driving a vehicle that was a completely unknown quantity. From mathematics, referring to a number not yet specified.

UNVEIL. unveil an initiative introduce a proposal, for discussion, assessment, etc. The prime minister has called a press conference to unveil his latest initiative. Journalese of purest vintage. Compare **launch a probe**.

UNWRITTEN. unwritten law long-established custom or convention. There is an unwritten law in this house that the first person up in the morning puts the kettle on and goes out to buy a litre of milk.

UP. up a gum tree trapped in a situation from which it is almost impossible to escape; in serious difficulty. The shareholders are up a gum tree – they are responsible for the company's debts, and sooner or later they'll have to pay them. From hunting in the Australian outback: hunted wallabies, etc. tended to run up a eucalyptus (gum) tree with the idea of escaping from their human foes. It was in fact comparatively easy then to shake them out of the trees. Compare **up the creek**, **bark up the wrong tree**.

up against it in a difficult position. He's been rather up against it since his wife's death and the collapse of his business. 'It' being the fates. Compare **back(s) to the wall**.

up and coming promising; likely to be popular and successful, etc. He's an up-and-coming businessman with a bright future. A dyad.

up and doing busy. She cannot relax for five minutes, but always has to be up and doing.

up and down the country/land in a variety of places in different parts of a particular country. They have branch offices up and down the country.

up and running operational. Is the new regional arts project up and running yet, or is it still at the discussion stage? A contemporary and often clichéd dyad.

up for grabs available; easily obtainable; on the market. The whole business is supposed to be up for grabs, but who would be daft enough to buy it?

up front open and honest. I'm quite happy to be up front with you and tell you the whole story. Originally American.

up hill and down dale 1. everywhere. The police have been hunting for him up hill and down dale. 2. vigorously. They cursed me up hill and down dale for my pains.

up in arms ready to take offence and action. The whole office is up in arms at the news. Originally military.

up in the air unresolved, undecided. Can we leave these matters up in the air until we reconvene our meeting in the morning?

up-market posh; exclusive. She has a very up-market and sophisticated air about her. A marketing idiom, now ubiquitous. Opposite of 'down-market'.

up one's sleeve held secretly in reserve, to be used to one's advantage if necessary. It's wise to have something up your sleeve when dealing with a slippery customer like that. Sometimes 'to keep some ammunition up one's sleeve'.

up stakes leave; move away. He appears to have upped stakes and quit the course last night. Originally referred in the US to the formal abandonment of a territorial claim, and the physical removal of the stakes demarcating the land. See **stake a claim**. Compare also **moonlight flit**.

up the ante raise the stakes. It used to cost £1,000 to join the club, but this year they're talking about upping the ante in order to ensure their so-called exclusivity. From betting.

up the creek (without a paddle) in a difficult situation. There I was, miles from home and the car completely written off – right up the creek, as you might say. Also 'up shit creek' and **up a gum tree**.

up the pole completely wrong or wrong-headed. His views about politics are truly up the pole.

up the spout 1. spoilt. The car was completely up the spout after the crash. 2. pregnant. Mrs Bloggs looks as if she might be up the spout again. Slang idioms, as also are 'up the stick/duff', etc. and 'in the pudding club'.

up to a point to some extent; partly but not entirely. I agree with him up to a point, but there are several details on which I disagree.

up to high doh/ninety very tense; ready to snap or lose one's composure. They were fully half an hour late getting to the church, by which time the bride's mother was up to high doh. 'High doh' is a musical reference from tonic sol-fa, while 'ninety' is a reference to fast driving.

up to it capable of something. It's a long walk, and I don't think he'll be up to it.

up to par similar meaning to **up to scratch**, with golf rather than boxing providing the image. The concert had to be postponed, because the lead singer had a bad dose of flu and just wasn't feeling up to par. Opposite of **under par**. See also **on a par with**.

up to scratch up to the required standard. It was a wonderful concert, even if the tenor soloist wasn't quite up to scratch. In ancient times, boxers and wrestlers started a bout with their foot on a scratch marked on the earth. Every so often, the contestants were allowed a break to draw breath. Then after a count of eight they had to return to the scratch and do battle again. Contestants who were unable to get back to the scratch had lost their bout. Compare **start from scratch**.

up to speed familiar with or knowledgeable about something; well versed. He took the file home for the weekend and promised to be up to speed with the entire affair by Monday morning. Compare **off the pace; out of touch**.

up to the hilt completely and utterly. Their farm has been mortgaged and re-mortgaged up to the hilt. When a swordsman plunged his weapon 'up to the hilt' into someone's body, only the handle or hilt remained visible.

up to the mark similar meaning and etymology as **up to scratch**. The mark was the scratch mark. Compare **on your marks!**

up to the minute topical; trendy. His speech was peppered with all sorts of up-to-the-minute references to current events. Take a look at the hat she's wearing: not exactly up to the minute!

up to the neck/ears/eyeballs 1. very heavily involved or implicated in something illegal or criminal. He protests his innocence, but the police have evidence to prove that he's been up to the neck in drug trafficking for years. **2. very busy.** He's up to the eyeballs in preparing his accounts this weekend, trying to get everything ready for the tax inspectors. Also 'up to one's neck/eyes', etc. Compare **(in) deep water**.

up yours! impolite exclamation of contempt or defiance telling someone to be quiet or go away. 'I wish to complain about your impertinent behaviour.' 'Oh, up yours!' he said, offering me two raised fingers. Similar usages include **drop dead!**, 'get stuffed/knotted!', 'two fingers!'

UP-FRONT. up-front 1. in advance or at the time of purchase. I asked if the shop would accept a down payment, but they said everything had to be paid up-front. Compare **down-payment. 2. honest.** He promised he was being completely up-front and on the level. Compare **on the level**.

UPHILL. uphill struggle task, etc. which is hard to achieve satisfactorily. Growing trees in such an exposed and windy position is a bit of an uphill struggle.

UPPER. upper crust people who belong or think they belong in the top layers of society; the aristocracy. How are you enjoying living among the upper crust? Also used as an adjective.

upper hand control, exercised by the person 'on top'. I expect there will be big changes in the company now that Jones has the upper hand in the board room. See also **whip hand**.

UPS. ups and downs good times and bad times. We all have our ups and downs in life.

UPSET. upset the apple-cart spoil or disrupt a plan or arrangement; disprove a theory. We planned to have the party in the garden, but the bad weather has upset that particular apple-cart. According to Partridge and Grose, the apple-cart originally referred to the human body, but today's expression is simply a description of a market stall upended in some forgotten commotion and a morning's trading lost.

UPSIDE. upside down in confusion and disarray. The whole office had been ransacked, and the thieves had left everything upside down. Literally, the phrase describes something which has been placed with its 'up' side facing down.

UPWARDLY. upwardly mobile ambitiously striving to enhance one's career or social prospects. He's one of those bright, upwardly mobile city slickers with a BMW. Suitably, a catch-phrase of Thatcherism redolent of the commercial rat race of the 1980s: a less common expression – and phenomenon – since the 2008 credit crunch.

USE. use one's loaf/head think intelligently. I wish you'd use your loaf from time to time. 'Loaf' is from Cockney rhyming slang ('loaf of bread' = head).

USED. used to 1. verb phrase meaning 'at some time in the past'. I used to live in Paris. **2. accustomed to.** He could never get used to eating British food.

V

VALUE. value judgment subjective assessment. He got a bad mark for his essay, on the grounds that it was full of value judgments rather than the objective criteria he'd been asked to use. From ethics and logic.

VEIL. (this) veil of tears the world. The child was profoundly handicapped, and lived only three years among us in this veil of tears. A poetic and euphemistic term for 'the world, the flesh and the devil', favoured by medieval evangelists and theologians.

VEILED. veiled threat/sneer, etc. a not openly declared threat, sneer, etc. but one which is partially concealed as if by a veil. I felt very uncomfortable listening to the thinly veiled threats of the terrorists.

VENT. vent one's spleen air, articulate or give voice to one's anger. He was a frustrated old guy who just had to vent his spleen on the first person who came along. The spleen is an abdominal organ which was regarded as the source of a person's melancholy or mirth, and gave the adjective 'splenetic', meaning irritable or irascible.

VERY. very thing something very suitable. Tell him to sit here for a minute, I've got the very thing for his headache.

very well formula expression, meaning 'yes' or 'I agree'. 'Please, Mum, may I go in the water?' 'Very well, but don't go in too deep.'

VICE. vice versa expression meaning 'the reverse is also true' or 'contrariwise'. He always looks after our house when we're away on holiday, and vice versa, i.e. we look after his house. Latin, but dating in English only from around 1600.

VICIOUS. vicious circle situation that can only repeat itself; which cannot progress because marred or rendered void by an inherent defect. They won't give me a job until I get some experience, but I can't get any experience until

somebody will give me a job – it's a real vicious circle. From logic, where arguing in a circle was a fallacious way of reaching a conclusion. Compare **Catch-22 situation**.

VILLAIN. villain of the piece bad person; the person who causes all the problems, grief, etc. In this instance the banks are the villains of the piece for calling in their loans. From drama and melodrama, which unlike real life is full of goodies and baddies.

VIM. vim and vigour energy and 'go'. They were young, keen and full of vim and vigour. A dyad and a tautology, 'vim' being the Latin word (accusative of *vis*) for vigour.

VIP very important person. There's some VIP from the Foreign Office in the building, hence the heightened security presence. In some African states, the president or military dictator has felt the need to create a more exclusive category, usually confined to himself, of 'VVIP' (very, very important person). Compare **number one**.

VITAL. vital statistics body measurements. If you go in that room and undress, a nurse will take a note of your vital statistics. Often applied in particular (and sometimes humorously) by the politically incorrect to the bust, waist and hip measurements of women.

VOICE. voice in the matter chance to make one's views heard. The decision had been taken before our views were requested, so we had no real voice in the matter.

VOTE. vote with one's feet show one's dislike of a place, etc. by leaving it. The entire countryside is deserted, because there is no work for young people there and they find it dull, so they vote with their feet at the earliest opportunity – usually as soon as they leave school – and move to the nearest town.

W

WAIT. **wait in dead men's shoes** await a very rare opportunity to do/acquire, etc. something which only occurs if a previous office-holder/recipient, etc. retires or dies. A job in that company only occurs once in a blue moon, so it's like waiting in dead men's shoes for a vacancy to come up.

wait on someone hand and foot do all one can to look after someone. Since her stroke, she's needed someone to wait on her hand and foot.

WAITING. **waiting for Godot** waiting aimlessly for something to happen. He's been standing around idly all morning waiting for Godot. From the title of the play (1952) by Samuel Beckett, in which nothing happens and the two tramps Vladimir and Estragon are waiting for something to turn up.

waiting game delaying tactics. The government likes to play the waiting game in foreign crises like this one, and see how things develop rather than draw up some sort of plan.

WALL. **wall-to-wall** non-stop; with no space in between. It's been wall-to-wall meetings for the entire week, and I'm ready for a quiet weekend. A transposition of a spatial to a temporal term, which originally and specifically referred to carpeting and other floor coverings. Wall-to-wall carpeting means that there is no space between the carpets and the walls; in other words, fitted carpets – once upon a time regarded as the height of affluence.

WALK. **walk of life** job; career; line of business. People from every walk of life attended the memorial service.

walk/tread on air be ecstatically happy. When she heard the good news, she felt as if she was walking on air for the rest of the day.

walk on eggs/eggshells act very carefully, especially to avoid upsetting someone. She was extremely temperamental, and not at all easy to live

with, with the result that for much of the time you were walking on eggshells in order to keep her calm.

walk-over overwhelming victory. With a score of 89 points to nil, the game was a rather obvious walk-over.

walk (all) over someone treat someone with contempt. The boss likes to walk all over his staff, so no one is very fond of him.

WALKING. **walking wounded** 1. injured people capable of moving about unaided in spite of their injuries. All the walking wounded were quickly evacuated from the war zone. An alliterative phrase now broadened to: 2. people exhibiting metaphorical battlescars. The three million unemployed people in this country are the walking wounded of the current recession.

WAR. **war hawk** person with a militaristic outlook or belligerent leanings. Jones used to be a professional soldier, and he remains a bit of a war hawk in many of his views. Hawks have symbolised belligerence for a long time, but this phrase is thought to have been coined in 1798 by Thomas Jefferson, 3rd US President (1801–09).

war of nerves psychological conflict, in which one party tries to unnerve the other. The boy was nothing more than a bully, who kept up a despicable little war of nerves against all the more timid children in his class. Examples of wars of nerves include the 'Phoney War', from the beginning of Second World War (before hostilities really got started); and more recently, the 'Cold War' (the propaganda war between the Superpowers).

war of words verbal contest; argument. A prolonged war of words ensued between the pro- and the anti-European factions of the Tory party.

WARM. **warm the cockles of one's heart** make one rejoice or feel warmly disposed towards someone/something. The story of her kindness and unselfishness warmed the cockles of readers' hearts. A rather sentimental and gooey cliché in our hard-boiled age, and as such open to ridicule; as in 'warm the hartles of one's cock'. Originally tautological, meaning 'the heart of one's heart', since the zoological name for a cockle is Cardium, from the Greek word meaning heart. This partly explains the expression, as does the ancient rudimentary anatomical observation that the heart resembles a scallop or cockleshell in appearance.

WARP. warp and woof fabric; basic elements. Democracy and a respect for human rights and dignities are the warp and the woof of a free society. A dyad from cloth weaving: the horizontal threads are the 'woof' (or sometimes 'weft') and the vertical are the 'warp'.

WARTS. warts and all including all blemishes and faults; with all something's limitations; unidealised. The British system of two-party democracy was exported warts and all to former British colonies in Africa. From the story that Oliver Cromwell, his face badly disfigured by warts, instructed his portraitist Sir Peter Lely to paint him in this way, and not to idealise his appearance.

WASH. wash one's dirty linen in public discuss publicly matters that one should keep private. He decided not to contest the divorce case, as that would only have led to a lot of unseemly washing of dirty linen in public.

wash one's hands of disclaim any responsibility for something, especially something over which one previously had some responsibility. I told them that, if they took the car out after drinking so much beer, I would have to wash my hands of such irresponsible and potentially lethal behaviour. From the biblical story in Matthew xxvii.24 of Pontius Pilate, who washed his hands of responsibility for the crucifixion of Christ. 'He took water, and washed his hands before the multitude, saying, "I am not responsible for the death of this just person, this is your doing".'

wash its face make a small profit; not make a loss. It may be a non-profit-making organisation, but it still has to try to wash its face. A business idiom.

WASTE. waste one's breath talk to no avail; offer advice which is not heeded. I see no point in prolonging this discussion – I'm obviously wasting my breath on you. Compare **bang one's head against a brick wall**.

waste of space useless and lazy person. He is a complete oaf and a waste of space, who doesn't know the meaning of a day's work. A derisive epithet.

WATCH. watch it warning to someone to be careful. He was throwing stones in the street, so I went out and told him I'd phone the police if he didn't watch it.

watch someone like a hawk keep a close and very careful watch on someone. Watch that man like a hawk – he's armed and dangerous. A standard simile of watchfulness.

WATCHED. a watched pot/kettle (never boils) time passes particularly slowly (if one is waiting for something to happen). I never wait for the postman to arrive, because you know the saying about a watched pot: it's better to keep busy. A saying.

WATER. water off a duck's back something that has no effect or result. She nags him all the time, but it's like water off a duck's back – he pays no attention to her. This simile refers to the fact that water drops run off a duck's oily feathers without wetting them.

water under the bridge events and experiences of one's past life. Nothing can be done about your childhood disappointments now – you're a mature adult and that's all water under the bridge. A variation of the metaphoric theme of life as a river. Americans prefer 'water over the dam'.

WATERING. watering hole bar; public drinking place. By the end of Prohibition in the US, Detroit alone had no fewer than 20,000 illicit watering holes. From the name given to drinking-water sources for wild animals.

WATERTIGHT. watertight argument/alibi, etc. totally convincing argument, case, etc. It seems he has a watertight alibi for his movements yesterday afternoon. **Literally, a case that was so well constructed that holes could not be picked in it, nor water leak through it. The reverse of won't wash**.

WAY. way of all flesh euphemism for one's decline and ultimate death. I'm afraid to go back to the haunts of my childhood – I'd probably meet very old friends going the way of all flesh. **An adaptation of the biblical, 'This day I am going the way of all the earth', in Joshua xxiii.14. The title of a novel by Samuel Butler (1903).**

way of the world the selfish style of average humanity. The board of directors has once again, as is the way of the world, awarded itself a massive pay rise and simultaneously made half the workforce redundant.

way out odd; eccentric; fashionably different. He used to write a rather way-out weekly column in the newspaper. **Similar to far out; off the beaten track.** Now an old-fashioned expression, redolent of the 1960s.

WAYS. ways and means methods of achieving something, especially raising money. We are inquiring into the various ways and means of reducing the costs of this assignment. **A dyad.**

WEAR. wear one's heart on one's sleeve make a public display of one's emotions; show one's feelings. He was devastated by her death, but he didn't really show it – not being someone to wear his heart on his sleeve. **Possibly from Shakespeare's Othello: 'But I will wear my heart upon my sleeve/For daws (jackdaws) to peck at.'**

wear sackcloth and ashes be penitent, humble, or apologetic. It's nice to see a pompous old fart like that having to wear sackcloth and ashes once in a while. **The image is biblical, an allusion to the Hebrew custom of wearing sackcloth and marking one's face with ash. These were outward signs of humility for sins or crimes. Some Christians still mark their faces with ash on Ash Wednesday, the first day of Lent, for similar reasons.**

wear the trousers be in charge. It's not hard to see who wears the trousers in that house. **Based on the now-quaint assumption that trouser-wearing men rule the domestic household. Presumably such a provocatively gender-specific idiom would be politically incorrect nowadays had it not been reprieved by the cross-dressing tendency.**

wear thin become ineffective or unconvincing. After a long wait in the queue, his patience began to wear thin and he went away. **Literally, from the wearing thin of cloth, etc. from much use.**

wear well show few signs of ageing. Considering they were built 5,000 years ago, the Pyramids have worn very well.

WEATHER. weather a storm survive difficult or hostile conditions. If the prime minister is to weather this storm, he's going to need the backing of his whole ministerial cabinet. **Originally a nautical idiom, the opposite of make heavy weather.**

weather window 1. short interval of good weather during a long inclement period. The mountain rescue team have waited six hours in the hope of a weather window to permit a search for the missing climbers. 2. general opportunity. Warned in good time of the pending takeover of the company, he realised he had a weather window in which to organise a potentially profitable investment.

WEE. a wee/little bird told me I have learnt from an unspecified source. I think they're living abroad now – a wee bird told me they'd bought a cottage in France. **The expression is old. 'I heard the little bird say so,' wrote Jonathan Swift to Stella, in 1711.**

wee/little folk fairies. Lots of country people still believe in the wee folk, even if they won't readily admit it. **From Celtic folklore.**

wee small hours very early morning. The worst thing about having a milk round is getting up in the wee small hours every day.

WEIGH. weigh one's words choose one's language with great care; speak in a measured

way. The defence lawyer spoke slowly and carefully, weighing his words one by one.

WELL. well away very drunk. He was obviously well away when he emerged staggering from the pub. Also 'away with the fairies', 'well oiled'.

well founded true. At first we thought it was a rumour, but it turned out to be well founded, i.e. its foundation was based on facts.

well heeled rich. One didn't just go to the opera to hear good music – the well heeled of the city went there to be seen in the interval in all their finery. From the observation that rich people often wore good shoes. Poor people by contrast were often 'down at heel'. Compare **on one's uppers**.

well hung 1. hung so that the blood has drained out of butcher meat, game, etc. They presented us with a brace of well-hung pheasants, which we roasted for supper. 2. sexually well-endowed man or woman. Rumoured to be a rather well-hung kid, he suddenly found himself in great demand with certain girls. Also 'well equipped'.

well to do in favourable circumstances; rich. It's a very exclusive golf club for the well to do of the neighbourhood. A transposition of 'doing well in the world', used from about 1820. Similar to the older 'well off'.

WET. wet behind the ears naive; inexperienced. The new apprentice is still a bit wet behind the ears, and will need to be looked after for a few weeks. From the agricultural observation that calves, foals, lambs, etc. are born wet behind the ears. Compare **find one's feet; know/learn the ropes**.

wet blanket person who spoils other people's fun. He had a bad headache so he left the party early, not wanting to be a wet blanket on such a happy occasion. Literally, a wet blanket is an effective way of putting out a fire; thus, by extension, of dousing enjoyment, etc. in an otherwise upbeat gathering.

wet one's whistle have a drink, usually alcoholic. After work, they usually go into the pub for a while to wet their whistle. Also Scots 'damp one's thrapple' or throat (same sense).

WHALE. a whale of a time/holiday etc. a very good time/holiday, etc. They love visiting their granny, who always lays on a whale of a party for them. An intensifier, originally American and meaning 'something of impressive size or scale'.

WHAT. what a nerve/cheek what a piece of insolence. They've invited themselves to stay for the weekend – what a nerve some people have! Often a straightforward exclamation. Compare **brass neck**.

what for 1. why?, for what purpose? 'Can you lend me £5 please?' 'What for?' 2. a severe telling-off. That child is going to get what for if he doesn't behave himself.

what have you things of that sort. She's keen on horse riding and shooting and what have you. Also 'what not' (same sense).

what is sauce for the goose (is sauce for the gander) what is good enough for one person (is good enough for another). Why can't he take a turn at sleeping in the tent? What is sauce for his sister is also sauce for him. The full sentence is a saying. Also 'if it's sauce for the goose…'

(does exactly) what it says on the tin (makes) an honest statement; (is) exactly as described. The Erotic Art Museum does exactly what is says on the tin: presents erotic art. British English, the expression originated (1994) as a slogan in a still-running TV advertising series for Ronseal woodstain and wood dye. Similar to **what you see is what you get**.

what on earth? intensifier of 'what?' What on earth do you think you're up to? Also 'what the hell?', 'what the dickens?', 'what in God's name?', 'what in the world?' (same sense).

what the dickens/devil/deuce? intensifiers of 'what?' What the deuce does she want now? I wonder what the dickens he's up to? 'Deuce' and 'dickens' are devil-substitute words, 'devil' being a word it was once believed prudent to avoid uttering. 'Deuce' means bad luck or the spirit of mischief, and 'dickens' is a colloquial corruption of 'devilkin' or little devil. See also **dickens of a; speak of the devil**.

what the hell? angry (or occasionally resigned) way of asking 'what?' I'd like to know what the hell you're doing in my garden? More aggressive than **what on earth?** or **what the dickens?** Sometimes used as a standalone exclamation. Compare **whatever!**

what with because of. She was terribly distressed what with one thing and another.

what you see is what you get no tricks or mirrors. A catch-phrase dating from the late 1960s and *Rowan & Martin's Laugh-In*, it was used to excuse eccentric behaviour by one of the characters. It was later recycled as the acronym WYSIWYG to describe the accurate replication of print and online information. The phrase is still much used, and is self-explanatory. Similar to **(does exactly) what it says on the tin**.

WHATEVER. whatever! A one-word slogan of indifferentism, with the sense 'anything for a quiet life!' 'Do you mind turning off your radio? There are people trying to sleep.' 'Oh, whatever!' What people say nowadays when told something they don't particularly want to hear but can't be bothered challenging.

whatever turns you on an idiomatic refrain, generally in use as a put-down cliché, with a meaning which often combines 'Do it if you must, but don't expect me to join you' with 'I always knew you were unusual/lacking in good taste (etc.), and this proves it.' 'She's asked us to take tea with her at Fortnum & Mason's this afternoon.' 'Whatever turns the pair of you on, but tell her I'll stick to my pint of beer, thanks.' '**Turn on**' is a phrasal verb which means stimulate or excite, and comes from the 1960s drug scene.

WHAT'S. what's biting someone what is bothering or annoying someone. She doesn't look at all happy; I wonder what's biting her now? The original reference was to midges, mosquitoes, lice, etc.

what's in a name catch-phrase, implying that some hair-splitting or trivial argument is threatened. I called it a lie and she called it a terminological inexactitude – but let's not be petty, what's in a name! Probably influenced by Shakespeare's *Romeo and Juliet*: 'What's in a name? That which we call rose/By any other name would smell as sweet.'

what's the damage question which asks how much something costs, i.e. how much it is going to damage one's funds. I'm buying this meal, so I'll just go and find out what's the damage. Compare **on the house**.

what's the (big) idea? what do you think you are doing? Excuse me, but that is my car you're getting into – what's the big idea?

what's the matter? what is wrong? She's been crying – what's the matter with her?

what's the odds? what is the point of even talking about that? i.e. it's not important; what difference does it make? So the car's had another bash – what's the odds, it's only an old banger. In the same way, you can say 'it makes no odds.' Do you want beer or lager? It makes no odds, I'll have either. Compare **whatever!**

what's up? 1. what's happening? What's up? Why all the noise? 2. what's wrong? What's up with him, standing there with a face like thunder? Compare **what's the matter?**

what's what how things are done properly. My new boss spent the morning showing me what's what around the office.

WHEELING. wheeling and dealing using entrepreneurial acumen. Before and after dinner there was much financial wheeling and dealing between old friends. A modern American dyad, which gives the noun 'wheeler-dealer'. There is often a hint of dishonesty contained in this expression.

WHEELS. wheels within wheels complicated background factors, motives, plots, etc. I'm afraid the problem is more complex than you realise: there are wheels within wheels. From the Bible, in Ezekiel i.16.

WHEN. when all's said and done after everything has been carefully discussed and considered. We may have lost this match, but when all's said and done we had a good season. Similar to **when push comes to shove** and 'when it comes down to it'.

when it comes to the point/bit/crunch in a critical moment or crucial time, or in a tight corner. It's always the same – he promises help, but as soon as it comes to the point he's too busy or he's going on holiday or something. Compare **when the chips are down**.

when in Rome (do as the Romans do) behave as one's hosts do, especially if one is travelling among strangers. In France I like to drink wine with my dinner – after all, when in Rome! A maxim attributed to the 4th-century St Ambrose, a German-born cleric who studied in Rome.

when push comes to shove when the situation becomes volatile. I don't want your half-hearted support, and then when push comes to shove find that I'm on my own. Probably in the sense 'when the gloves come off' between two adversaries, and they start to push and shove one another about. Similar to **when all's said and done**.

when one's ship comes in when one becomes rich. We'll buy a French chateau when our ship comes in. Medieval ship-owners could become wealthy overnight when they unloaded their cargoes at their home port after long absence, as the stories of *Dick Whittington* and of Shakespeare's *Merchant of Venice* remind us.

when the chips are down when things become critical. He's a very reliable person to have around when the chips are down. From the gaming table; literally, 'when the bet has been placed.'

when the going gets tough (the tough get going) when there is a serious crisis (the genuinely toughest people cope very well). It was surprising how well Winston Churchill managed the war effort; obviously a case of when the going gets tough… The full axiom caught the mood of the 1970s, and was attributed to Joseph P Kennedy (1888–1969), father of US President John F Kennedy; it was subsequently sloganised in song and movie. There is a pun on the final part of the sentence: it could also mean they quit.

WHET. whet one's appetite make one want more of something. His visit to France as a 16-year-old schoolboy simply whetted his appetite to learn French properly. A metaphor from dining; literally, the starter was meant to whet your appetite for the main course.

WHIP. whip hand control. Expect to see changes in the company now that I've got the whip hand. From horse riding and coach driving; the person with the whip controlled the horses. See also **upper hand**.

WHIPPING. whipping boy scapegoat. Most prime ministers are of course great survivors, and they like to offer up the occasional ministerial whipping boy if the press bays too loudly for their blood. A whipping boy was literally a person who was punished for the wrongs of his superior. Royal children in medieval Europe were not punished when they were bad; being divine, they had in their entourage paid whipping boys to take their punishments for them. Compare **fall guy; sacrificial lamb**.

WHISTLE. whistle a different tune act in a different way. Last week he seemed to hate my guts; now that I've won the lottery he's whistling a different tune.

whistle in the dark 1. talk from a position of ignorance. Don't listen to him on the subject of my financial affairs – he's whistling in the dark if he presumes to be speaking for me in such matters. 2. **try**

to keep one's spirits up. Although I knew perfectly well that we were whistling in the dark, I felt quite unafraid of what might be coming.

whistle in/into the wind do or say something useless or pointless. He promised that he'd win his race, but I'm afraid he was whistling in the wind.

whistle-stop tour strictly or tightly scheduled visit. The president made a whistle-stop tour of the war zone to inspect US troops. A 'whistle stop' on the American railroads was a short unscheduled stop of the train in response to a blow of the whistle, either from a wayside country station or from a passenger on the train wishing to alight. The idiom acquired its current meaning during the successful if rather frantic presidential campaign of US President Harry S Truman in 1948.

WHITE. white as a sheet/ghost very pale looking. Although unhurt, they'd all had a fright, and John was looking as white as a sheet. A standard simile to communicate fear, shock, etc. 'White as snow' is the standard simile for purity.

white elephant encumbrance; unwanted object, especially something that was once expensive to acquire. The factory owner discovered rather late in the day that there was no market for his product; so his business is in real danger of becoming a white elephant unless he can diversify into something else. White elephants in Siam were rare and sacred beasts. In the 19th century, the astute king of that country bestowed them as gifts on his rivals, knowing that the cost of their upkeep would be financially ruinous for them and thus render them less of a threat to his own royal power.

white feather sign of cowardice. He was accused of showing the white feather. A white feather in a gamebird's tail was thought to be, like cowardice, a sign of inferior breeding.

white knight person or organisation which comes to the assistance of another. Usually when there is a hostile takeover bid for a company, the business concerned looks around for a white knight

to rescue them. From chess, the expression is now common in business.

white lie untruth told for a semi-justifiable reason, i.e. to be kind to someone. When she asked me if she was going to get better, I told her a white lie and said yes.

white man honourable person. Be a white man and buy me a pint of beer please. No longer a very acceptable term, because it is both sexist and racist.

white man's burden euphemism for imperialism. After the Second World War the European nations slowly relinquished the white man's burden and concentrated their ingenuity on building the new Europe. From the title of a poem by Rudyard Kipling (1899), a paean in support of US military intervention in the Philippine Islands.

WHITED. whited sepulchre hypocrite. I wouldn't be too sure about a whited sepulchre like Mrs Jones. Literally, something which is outwardly presentable but which is rotten within. From Jesus' condemnation of the Pharisees in the Bible, in Matthew xxiii.27: 'Ye are like unto whited sepulchres, which indeed appear beautiful outward, but are full of dead men's bones, and of all uncleanness.'

WHO'S. who's who 1. who these people are. It's an interesting old school photograph, but I'm afraid I don't know who's who in it. 2. who are the important people. It's a book that tells you who's who in all the various walks of life. From the title of the annual reference book of important people in the UK.

WHOLE. whole new ball game a significant change in circumstances; a changed turn of events. After the two banks merged we had a whole new ball game. Sometimes 'ball park' is preferred (same meaning). From baseball.

whole shooting match the whole lot. I could see there were a few interesting things for sale as well as the usual rubbish, so I offered £50 for the whole shooting match. A 'shooting match' was a shooting competition. Sometimes 'the whole shoot' or 'the whole caboodle'. Compare **kit and caboodle; lock, stock and barrel**.

whole foods organically produced foods uncontaminated by chemical preservatives, flavourings, etc. There are several newish whole-food shops in our high street. 'Whole' is used to convey the idea of foodstuffs which are wholesome and undamaged by human interference.

WHYS. whys and wherefores reasons or explanations (for something). I'm sorry but we just haven't time to go into all the whys and wherefores of the management's decision. A dyad.

WIDE. wide of the mark off-target or astray in one's opinions or beliefs. We were asked to guess the right answer, but we were all rather wide of the mark. Compare **bark up the wrong tree; beside the point; off base**.

WILD. wild card unpredictable or unknown factor in an equation. One wild card in the forthcoming general election is likely to be the behaviour of the increasingly megalomniac former prime minister. Originally a playing card with an arbitrarily fixed value, then an unseeded tournament player whose form is not well known. Compare **dark horse**.

wild goose chase futile or hopeless errand. The bandits left a trail of false clues, which sent the sheriff off on a wild goose chase through the mountains. Wild geese (and even the more domestic variety) are notoriously hard to catch, so that popular wisdom took the view that it was futile to hunt them by chasing them.

wild horses wouldn't drag one to or **make one (do something)** nothing would persuade one (to do something). She's been invited to visit Russia, but she says wild horses wouldn't make her go to a cold place like that.

wild man of Borneo savage and uncivilised person. What do you mean coming into this room like the wild man of Borneo? A simile which is usually deployed humorously. The original was a

creation in the 1880s of P T Barnum, the American circus impresario; far from coming from the East Indies, he was apparently a native of Paterson, New Jersey, got up to look the part.

WILLY. willy-nilly forcibly; whether one likes it or not. I may not have wanted it, but I was travelling willy-nilly towards my fate. A contracted form of 'Will I, nill I?' or 'Will I, won't I?' Similar to Latin 'nolens volens'. Compare also **shilly-shally**, a similar reduplicative compound.

WIN. win/lose by a neck win/lose something by a very narrow margin. It was a very close election result, with two recounts – so the candidate only won by the shortest of necks. From horse racing.

win hands down gain a decisive victory. It was not a very even match, and our visitors won hands down. From horse racing; once victory in the race is assured, the leading jockey sometimes relaxes his grip on the reins and lets his hands down, leaving his horse to coast up to the winning post. See also **beat hollow**.

win one's spurs achieve public recognition. As a businessman, he won his spurs by engineering a long-term and very lucrative export order to Saudi Arabia. In the Middle Ages when a man was knighted, he was presented by the king with a pair of spurs as a public token or symbol of this honour.

WIND. wind someone up make someone angry, sometimes deliberately; tease someone. Boys can be very cruel, and they love winding up their weaker brethren, especially if the latter have quick tempers. The image is of a piece of machinery, wound up so tight that it has to go off.

WINDOW. window dressing attempt to make something look better than it really is. It's a very old textbook, but the publishers have done a bit of window dressing on it, resetting it and giving it a bright new cover to make it look like a brand new work.

window shopping looking in shop windows but not buying anything. She used to do a bit of window shopping on her way home from work some evenings.

WINK. wink wink, nudge nudge(, say no more) conversational gambit which hints at something (rather than stating it), usually of a prurient nature. I forgot to knock and went straight into the room, and there they were – the pair of them on the bed, wink wink, nudge nudge… This is a catch-phrase popularised around 1970 by the TV comedy show, *Monty Python's Flying Circus*.

WIPE. wipe the floor with someone completely defeat someone, usually verbally but sometimes physically. At the school meeting after the incident, a couple of parents wiped the floor with the headmaster for his lack of leadership and responsibility.

WISE. (be) wise after the event know with hindsight how one should have acted after the real-life situation has passed. In the fire service we need people who can think fast and act on their feet; there's no point in being wise after the event in this business.

wise guy/ass know-all; smug or insolent person who tends to enjoy making fun at the expense of others. There's usually some wise guy in any group of people, trying for the cheap laughs. Sometimes found as an adjective ('a wise-ass comedian'). Also American 'wiseacre' (from Dutch *wijssegger*, 'wise sayer').

WISHFUL. wishful thinking believe that something very unlikely is going to happen just because one wants it to happen. Of course it's just wishful thinking, but one day I'm going to win the pools. To which people nowadays just say 'I wish!'

WISHY. wishy washy half-hearted; vague. He was one of those dreadful wishy-washy liberals who couldn't wait to surrender to both sides. A reduplication.

WITH. with (a) bad grace ungraciously; unsportingly. It is not uncommon nowadays to see competitors losing a game of tennis with a particularly bad grace – swearing, throwing their rackets around and generally behaving like spoilt brats.

with a bang well; successfully. We always enjoy their parties, because they go with a real bang. The term has a slight whiff of musical notation to it; as in *con brio*, 'in a lively way'.

with a vengeance decisively and thoroughly. Our team may have lost their match last week, but they won with a vengeance today. Literally, 'with a curse calling for revenge'.

with an eye for with good aptitude for. She's a girl with a very good eye for a marketing opportunity.

with an eye to with the aim or intention of. He bought the cottage with an eye to restoring it one day and making it into a retirement home. Also 'with a view to'.

with attitude with self-assurance and/or aggression. The man who accosted me was no ordinary beggar – he was a beggar with attitude.

with bated breath holding back one's breath in anticipation or from apprehension. The audience watched the trapeze artist's antics with bated breath. A fixed phrase; to say 'with breath less than bated' would be a humorous way of describing an underwhelming experience.

with flying colours easily and successfully. I'm glad to say she passed her exams with flying colours. From the navy; 'colours' = signal flags.

with it modern; up-to-date. He didn't even know who the Beatles were, so he wasn't exactly with it, was he? Children used to urge their fuddy-duddy parents to 'get with it'. These vogue idioms of the 1960s today sound a little passé.

with one voice unanimously. We demand the resignation of the prime minister, and we demand it with one voice.

with regard to concerning. He seems a conscientious worker with regard to his appearance, time-keeping, etc.

with one's tail between one's legs in a cowed, abject, or miserable manner. Nobody likes losing a game, but there's no need to crawl off the pitch with long faces and your tail between your legs. From the behaviour of a dog which has been beaten.

with one's tail up eagerly anticipating good things; cockily. In the final round of the boxing match, the defending champion came out for the last time with his tail up and scenting victory. From the behaviour of a dog about to get a walk or a treat.

with the best of them as competently as the best people in that particular field of endeavour. When it came to trading insults, he was up there with the best of them, i.e. he could do it as well as anyone else could.

WITHIN. within a hair's breadth very close to. The two countries came within a hair's breadth of all-out war.

within an inch of very close to. The car was within an inch of disaster when I managed to grab the wheel. A pre-metric expression. Also 'within a whisker' (same sense).

within hailing distance near enough to be accessible. He was looking for the police station, and I told him he was within hailing distance of it. Now spatial, this was originally an auditory metaphor from sailing: a boat was within hailing distance of the shore if you could speak to it audibly through a loud hailer.

within reason within the limits of good sense. He's looking for a summer job, and says he'll try anything within reason.

within striking distance near. The fund-raising campaign is now within striking distance of achieving its target figure. From predatory animal behaviour: lions, etc. will not attempt to attack a beast unless they are within striking distance of it.

WITHOUT. without fail surely and certainly. He promised to deliver the equipment this afternoon without fail.

without further ado with no further fuss. And now, ladies and gentlemen, may I introduce without further ado our star guest of the evening. Compare then and there.

without so much as a 'by your leave' without even saying excuse me, please, may I? etc. What do you mean by barging in here without so much as a 'by your leave'?

without strings with no conditions attached. We made her a good offer without strings, and I hope she'll accept it. Also 'with no strings attached' (same sense).

WOE. woe betide fixed phrase, rather old-fashioned and rhetorical, often used in a threatening context; meaning literally, 'Let sorrow accompany someone if…' I lent him my best crystal whisky glasses, and woe betide him if he breaks a single one of them.

woe is me exclamation meaning 'I am unhappy.' I went for a walk on the hillside without my coat, and woe is me, didn't the rain start to pour down. Usually used facetiously, as a translation from Latin 'O me miserum!'

WOLF. wolf in sheep's clothing dangerous person disguised as a harmless one. You may think he only wants to help you, but I suggest you just remember that he's a wolf in sheep's clothing, in other words don't trust him and watch him very carefully indeed. From one of Aesop's Fables, about the wolf which infiltrated the sheepfold by disguising itself as 'one of us'. It then proceeded to do what hungry wolves do to sheep. See also the biblical, 'Beware of false prophets, which come to you in sheep's clothing, but inwardly they are ravening wolves', at Matthew vii.15. If one wishes to really disparage a person's fecklessness and inability to stand up for himself, one might say he is a 'sheep in sheep's clothing'.

WONDERS. wonders never cease ironic exclamation, indicating amazement that someone has done something. Don't tell me the lazy slob's actually got himself a job – wonders never cease! A variant of 'the age of wonders is not over'.

WON'T. won't wash is not believable. He tried to tell us that he'd never seen her before, but that won't wash – two reliable witnesses independently observed him talking to her at length only last night. **Also 'won't hold water'**, i.e. won't stand up to critical investigation. Compare **watertight argument**.

WORD. word for word verbatim; in the exact words. Try to tell me word for word exactly what he said. From Latin 'verbatim et literatim', meaning 'word for word and letter for letter' – for an accurately copied text.

word in your ear confidential chat, usually in order to communicate an interesting piece of information. Excuse me, Mr Brown, but may I have a quick word in your ear. **Sometimes 'a word in your shell-like (ear)'**.

word on the street gossip. I was told by the police that the word on the street suggests that the fire was deliberate.

word to the wise (is enough) an idiom which used to preface an offer of advice. A word to the wise – don't walk down that street after dark, because it's not safe. The phrase often accompanies a warning. Compare **take a hint**.

WORDS. words fail me exclamation or statement of one's speechless amazement. Words fail me when I try to think of his escapades. A rather ugly current word for speechless amazement is the adjective 'gobsmacked'; older equivalents are 'dumbstruck' or 'thunderstruck'.

words of one syllable the simplest language. Remember you are dealing with people who are not very bright, so you may have to spell everything out to them in words of one syllable.

words to that effect phrase used to indicate that what is said is only an approximation or paraphrase of the actual words used by the original speaker. He advised me to give up football till after the exams and to work much harder at my studies…or words to that effect. Compare **quote unquote**.

WORK. work one's fingers to the bone work very hard. By working her fingers to the bone, she raised a family of three kids single-handed. A Victorian metaphor, often a cliché, probably based on the hard manual work done by fishwives, weavers, seamstresses, etc. Similar to 'work/slog one's guts out'.

work hand in hand work in close cooperation, often with a single aim. The two countries now work hand in hand in several spheres, and have a well coordinated foreign policy. Compare **work hand in glove**.

work hand in glove work closely with, usually dishonestly, secretly or secretively. A lot of drug traffickers work hand in glove with the mafia.

work someone off his feet force someone to work very fast. It was a bank holiday, and a very hot day, so the ice-cream vendor was worked off her feet all day.

work to rule work in a very minimal way, pausing for careful, lengthy and frequent reference to the rule-book, usually as a result of an industrial dispute. The coalminers are working to rule in protest at the decision to close more mines. Something of an oxymoron. The rules in question are the health and safety and other government regulations that are meant to indicate how a particular workforce operates. See **red tape**.

work wonders have a wonderful effect (on one). These new hay fever pills are working wonders for many sufferers. The term was popularised by the alliterative advertising jingle for beer, 'Double Diamond works wonders'. In this idiom 'wonders' mean miracles, as in the words of the church hymn, 'God moves in a mysterious way,/His wonders to perform.'

WORM. the worm turns the meek person will finally react, even if s/he doesn't actually fight back. The worm has turned at last, and she's walked out on her bully of a husband. From the saying, 'Tread on a worm's tail and it will turn.'

WORN. worn to a shadow exhausted and drained of energy. I hardly recognised Mr Brown in the street today; he's worn away to a shadow of his former self.

WORTH. worth one's salt deserving one's position or salary. Give him a job for a week and see if he's worth his salt. The word 'salary' means salt money in Latin.

worth the candle worth doing; worth the effort. He wondered whether to attend the exhibition, but decided in the end that it wasn't worth the candle for him in his present circumstances. Originally and literally, not worth the price of a candle to keep a light burning to permit nightwork to be done. Compare **burn the midnight oil**.

worth someone's while profitable; worth doing. He said that it wasn't very pleasant work, but he'd make it worth my while if I'd take the job on.

WORTHY. worthy of the name that deserves to be called by that name. No scholar worthy of the name would have published such an inaccurate textbook.

WOULDN'T. wouldn't put it past someone (to do something) it wouldn't surprise the speaker if someone (did something bad, awful, outrageous, etc.). The workforce were so angry that I wouldn't have put it past them to set the whole place on fire.

wouldn't say boo to a goose wouldn't express the mildest criticism. She's terribly shy and timid and wouldn't say boo to a goose.

wouldn't touch something with a bargepole avoid contact with something at any price; keep one's distance from something. He's offering me a very good five-year contract in Nigeria, but I wouldn't touch a job like that with a bargepole. In Victorian times, expressions like 'I wouldn't touch it with a pair of tongs' were common; the bargepole is a 20th-century variant.

WRAP. wrap it up bring a discussion, conversation, etc. to a conclusion. Mr Smith's interesting comments on the British economy just about wrap it up for today, and I propose we now adjourn our discussions till next week. Compare **knock it off**.

WRING. wring one's hands be in helpless despair. We had been backing that horse to win the race, so we were all wringing our hands when it fell at the last fence.

WRITE. write oneself out of the script draw hostile or critical attention to oneself. He's been very negative at previous meetings, always wanting to know how much time off he was going to get, so I'd say he's already written himself out of the script as far as I'm concerned. Similar to **talk oneself out of a job**, but with a more modern-sounding Hollywood-type resonance.

WRITING. the writing is on the wall one's doom or downfall is anticipated or forecast. The writing was on the wall for typewriters and secretaries once everyone had their own personal computer. From the Bible: Belshazzar was shown the writing on the wall for being contemptuous of God's power, in Daniel v.

WRITTEN. written all over one's face obvious and visible in a person's facial expression. Extreme moral rectitude was written all over his pinched face and tight little mouth.

Y

YEAR. year in year out continuously; one year after another. He's been working down that coalmine year in year out since he left school at 16. Similar to 'day in day out'.

year round throughout the year. They offer a year-round delivery service.

YELL. yell blue murder shout loud and stridently, usually for help. We could hear her yelling blue murder as we ran upstairs to see if we could help her. 'Blue' emphasises the state of fear, while 'murder' in the 15th century was a common generalised cry of alarm.

YELLOW. yellow bellied cowardly. Like most bullies, he had a yellow-bellied streak when he was confronted by someone tougher than he was. Originally American, perhaps from one of the various yellow-bellied tortoises and frogs which are unable to fight if their bellies are in the air.

yellow press unscrupulously sensational newspapers and their writers. The yellow press always go to town on stories like that. Originally American, said to have originated from a picture in the *New York World* in 1895 of a figure in a rather revealing yellow dress. Not to be confused with the later 'yellow pages', which is a trade advertising telephone directory. Compare **gutter press**.

YEOMAN. yeoman service good and reliable use. This faithful old car of mine has performed yeoman service over the years, and it's never let me down. A yeoman was a servant or assistant to an English official, often an honest and substantial person, but below the rank of a gentleman.

YES. yes-man person who always complies with the demands of others, never protesting or questioning their wishes. The trouble with the prime minister was that she surrounded herself with yes-men, so she never had to argue her case very hard.

YOU. you and what/whose army? facetious riposte when one person threatens another in an unfrightening way. 'I'm going to see that you're properly punished for your impertinence.' 'Oh, yeah, you and what army?' Clearly implies an underwhelming prospect.

you bet your sweet life/bippy indubitably; very true. 'Anyone like a beer?' 'You bet your sweet life we would.' A popular affirmative catch-phrase from *Rowan & Martin's Laugh-In* TV show of the late 1960s.

you can say that again I agree; conversational gambit, indicating one's strong agreement with a foregoing statement. 'She's a very pretty girl.' 'You can say that again.' Compare **and how**.

you don't say 1. conversational expression of mild surprise. 'The police have been watching him for a while.' 'Oh, you don't say, what's he been up to this time?' 2. ironic exclamation indicating absence of surprise. 'The police have been watching him for a while.' 'You don't say!' i.e. I knew that all along.

you heard/read it here first! phrase meaning, 'Remember who told you this, or where you first learnt about it'. The expression contains overtones of self-congratulation: a coded hint of 'Am I not clever?' to be breaking this news. Compare **mark my words**.

you name it expression used humorously or seriously to draw attention to someone's talents, aptitudes, possessions, etc. You name it – she's got two of them. He's very well travelled – you name it, he's been there. From a 1940s American advertising slogan: 'You name it – we have it.'

YOUNG. young man's fancy object of a young man's affections. He's gone off into town, probably chasing some young man's fancy. From the poem 'Locksley Hall' (1842), by Tennyson: 'In the spring a young man's fancy lightly turns to thoughts of love.'

Young Turk reformer or activist in an organisation, usually opposed by the **old guard**.

The young turks in the party have comprehensively out-manoeuvred the old guard on this occasion. **The original Young Turks in the 1890s were formed, with substantial student support, in the last days of the decadent Turkish Empire before the Sultan was deposed and the republic finally declared (1923).**

YOURS. yours truly me. Needless to say, it was yours truly who ended up having to clean out the toilets. **Usually facetious. From the way one signs oneself out in letters.**

YUMMY. yummy mummy glamorous mother who appears mysteriously unaffected by the rigours of child-rearing. Wouldn't it be nice to be an immaculate and gorgeous film-star yummy mummy? **A 21st-century reduplication.**

Z

ZERO. zero hour time fixed for something to happen. We synchronised our watches ready for zero hour the following morning at 04.00 hours. The original context was military.

zero in (on something) come in on the centre or zero of a target. The bombers zeroed in on the enemy rocket-launchers. A phrasal verb, from target-shooting.

zero tolerance refusal to accept certain attitudes or behaviour, including racism, sexism, hooliganism and violence. The campaign was called 'Show Racism the Red Card' and it was a strong argument for zero tolerance.

ZIP. zip one's lip(s) keep quiet. He was threatened with all kinds of awfulness if he didn't zip his lip. A 'zipped-up person' is one who keeps his own counsel. Compare **keep one's own counsel**.

Index of additional key words

The 4,500 idioms in the main dictionary are arranged in alphabetical order under headwords printed in bold capitals. These headwords are based on the first word of the idiom in question. Thus, the entry for **rain cats and dogs** is to be found under the headword **RAIN** in the main dictionary.

In the index, the idiom **rain cats and dogs** is also located in bold type under its two other key words, **cats** and **dogs**. The idioms listed under **dogs** in this index are **go to the dogs**, **let sleeping dogs lie** and **rain cats and dogs**. This informs you that these three idioms have an entry in the main dictionary listed under the first word of the idiom, i.e. under the headwords **GO**, **LET** and **RAIN**, respectively.

Note that plurals and possessives are mainly listed as separate headwords, thus **HORSE**, **HORSE'S** and **HORSES**. This affects alphabetisation and plurals do not automatically follow singulars, i.e. **DOG** and **DOGS** are separated by **DOGHOUSE**; **LIBERTIES** precedes **LIBERTY**, etc.

advance
  in advance
advocate
  devil's advocate
aesthetically
  aesthetically/chronologically/intellectually
    challenged
affairs
  Ugandan affairs
after
  happily ever after
  morning after (the night before)
  wise after the event
affronted
  black affronted
again
  come again?
  you can say that again
against
  go against the grain
  hold something against someone
age
  act one's age
  certain age
  of age
  of an age
agenda
  hidden agenda
agony
  pile/put on the agony
agreement
  gentleman's agreement
ahead
  dead ahead
  full steam ahead
  quit while one is ahead
  streets ahead
air
  castles in Spain/the air
  clear the air
  disappear into thin air
  hot air
  in the air
  into thin air
  leak air

  leave someone hanging in the air
  on the air/airwaves
  out of thin air
  up in the air
  walk/tread on air
airs
  give oneself airs
ale
  Adam's ale
Alec
  smart Alec
alert
  on the alert
  red alert
alibi
  watertight argument/alibi
alike
  share and share alike
all
  be-all and end-all
  daddy of all
  damn all
  don't put all your eggs in one basket
  father and mother of all
  know all the answers
  not all there
  of all people/things
  of all shapes and sizes
  of all time
  on all fours
  once and for all
  struck all of a heap
  tick all the boxes
  way of all flesh
  when all's said and done
  written all over one's face
alley
  right up one's street/alley
all-right
  bit of all-right
along
  play along with someone
  run along
amok/amuck
  run amok/amuck

angel
be an angel

answer
straight answer

answers
know all the answers

ante
up the ante

any
at any rate

apart
come apart at the seams
joking aside/apart
poles apart
tell someone apart

ape/apeshit
go ape/apeshit

appearance
put in an appearance

appearances
keep up appearances

appetite
whet one's appetite

apple
Adam's apple
upset the apple-cart

approval
on approval
seal/stamp of approval

apron
tied to one's mother's apron (strings)

area
grey area

argument
watertight argument/alibi

Ark
out of the Ark

arm
chance one's arm
give one's right arm for something
put the arm on someone
shot in the arm
twist someone's arm

arms
throw up one's hands/arms

up in arms

arm's
keep something/someone at arm's length

army
you and what/whose army?

around
just around the corner

arse
know one's arse from one's elbow
lick someone's boots/arse

art
have something down to a fine art
state of the art

ashes
rake over the ashes
wear sackcloth and ashes

aside
joking apart/aside

aspersions
cast aspersions

ass
haul ass
have one's ass in a sling
kick ass
pain in the neck/ass/backside/butt
put one's neck/ass on the line
wise guy/ass

assured
rest assured

attached
no strings attached

attendance
dance attendance

attention
pay attention (to)

attitude
with attitude

auction
dutch auction

Augean
cleanse the Augean stable

aunt
agony aunt

auspices
under the auspices of

averages
law of averages
aversion
pet aversion/hate
away
do away with someone
far and away
fire away
get away (with you)
get away with murder
get carried away
have it off/away
right away
straight away
well away
AWOL
go AWOL
axe
battle axe

B

baby
leave someone holding the baby
throw the baby out with the bathwater
back
behind someone's back
break the back of something
cover one's back/rear
get/put someone's back/dander up
get off someone's back
give one's eye/back teeth for something
knock someone/something back
meanwhile, back at the ranch
off the back of a lorry
on the back burner
on someone's back
pat on the back
pay someone back in his own coin
put one's back into something
scratch someone's back
see the back of someone
stab in the back

straw which breaks the camel's back
take a back seat
turn one's back on
water off a duck's back
backside
pain in the neck/ass/backside/butt
backwards
bend over backwards
know something backwards/inside-out
bacon
bring home the bacon
save one's bacon/skin
bad
give a dog a bad name
give something up as a bad job
in bad odour
in someone's black/bad books
run of good/bad luck
too bad
with (a) bad grace
bag
let the cat out of the bag
mixed bag
old bag
bait
rise to the bait
balance
strike a balance
tilt the scales/balance
ball
black ball
crystal ball
different ball game/ball park
have a ball
keep the ball rolling
on the ball
open the ball/innings
play ball with someone
set/start the ball rolling
take one's eye off the ball
whole new ball game
ballistic
go mad/nuclear/nuts/ballistic
balloon
go down like a lead balloon

band
> to a band playing
> to beat the band

bandit
> one-armed bandit

bandwagon
> jump on the bandwagon

bang
> come down to earth with a bang
> with a bang

bank
> break the bank

bar
> raise the bar

bargain
> into the bargain

bargepole
> wouldn't touch something with a bargepole

barrel
> over a barrel
> scrape the barrel

base
> get to first/second base
> off base
> touch base

bash
> have a bash/crack

basinful
> have a bellyful/basinful

basket
> don't put all your eggs in one basket

bat
> blind as a bat
> not bat an eye/eyelid/eyelash
> off one's own bat

bated
> with bated breath

bathwater
> throw the baby out with the bathwater

batteries
> recharge the/one's batteries

battle
> running battle

bay
> at bay

beam
> keep someone/something at bay
> broad in the beam
> on one's beam ends

bean
> not have a bean

beans
> full of beans
> spill the beans

bear
> grin and bear it

bearings
> find/get one's bearings
> lose one's bearings

beast
> nature of the beast

beat
> dead beat
> to beat the band

beaten
> off the beaten track

beaver
> eager beaver

bed
> apple-pie bed
> get up on the wrong side of the bed

bedfellows
> strange bedfellows

bedpost
> between you and me (and the bedpost/
>   gatepost)

bee
> busy as a bee

beeline
> make a beeline for

bees
> birds and bees

behind
> four-square behind something
> power behind the throne
> wet behind the ears

belief
> pass belief/comprehension

believe
> make believe

reason to believe
believing
seeing is believing
belfry
bats in the belfry
bell
clear as a bell
ring a bell
saved by the bell
bellied
yellow bellied
bellyful
have a bellyful/basinful
below
holed below the waterline
belt
below the belt
green belt
tighten one's belt
under one's belt
bend
clean round the bend
drive someone round the bend/twist
round the bend/twist
benefit
give someone the benefit of the
    doubt
bent
hell bent on something
berry
brown as a berry
berserk
go berserk
berth
give a wide berth to
best
past one's best
put one's best foot forward
Sunday best
with the best of them
bet
safe bet
you bet your sweet life/bippy
betide
woe betide

bets
hedge one's bets
better
think (the) better of
between
fall between two stools
few and far between
read between the lines
beyond
back of beyond
old beyond one's years
bib
best bib and tucker
big
too big for one's boots
bike
on your bike
bill
fit the bill
suit someone's book/bill
billy-o
like billy-o
bind
double bind
in a bind
bird
early bird
get the (big) bird
night owl/bird
odd bird/fish
wee/little bird told me
birds
for the birds
kill two birds with one stone
talk the birds off the trees
biscuit
take the cake/biscuit
bit
champing/chafing at the bit
do one's bit
take/have/get the bit between one's teeth
when it comes to the point/bit/crunch
bite
bark is worse than one's bite
second bite at the cherry

bites
    two bites at the cherry
biting
    what's biting someone
black
    in black and white
    in someone's black/bad books
    not as black as s/he's painted
    pot calling the kettle black
    swear (that) black is white
    talk till one is blue/black in the face
blank
    draw a blank
    point blank
blanket
    born on the wrong side of the
        blanket
    wet blanket
Blarney Stone
    kiss the Blarney Stone
bleeds
    heart bleeds for someone
blind
    fly blind
    halt and blind
    none so blind (as those who will not see)
    swear blind
    turn a blind eye
blink
    on the blink
block
    chip off the old block
    stumbling block
blood
    bad blood
    draw blood
    flesh and blood
    in cold blood
    make one's blood boil
    new blood
    rush of blood (to the head)
    sweat blood
blooded
    blue blooded
    red blooded

bloody
    get a bloody nose
blow
    body blow
blue
    black and blue
    bolt from the blue
    clear blue water
    once in a blue moon
    out of the blue
    talk till one is blue/black in the
        face
    yell/scream blue murder
bluff
    call someone's bluff
board
    above board
    across the board
    back to the drawing board
    go by the board
    on board
    open and above board
    sweep the board
    take something on board
boat
    be in the same boat
    miss the boat/bus
    push the boat out
    rock the boat
    slow boat to China
boats
    burn one's boats/bridges
bobs
    bits and bobs/pieces
    odds and bobs/sods
bobtail
    rag-tag and bobtail
body
    come into the body of the kirk
    keep body and soul together
    over my dead body
bogey/bogy
    game's a bogey/bogy
boggles
    mind boggles

bold
put on a brave face/bold front
bolt
shoot one's bolt
bomb
cost a bomb
make/earn a bomb
bombshell
drop a bombshell
bonce
out of one's head/skull/(tiny) mind/bonce/
tree
bone
dry as a bone
have a bone to pick
near the knuckle/bone
work one's fingers to the bone
bones
bag of bones
bare bones
feel it in one's bones
make no bones about something
bonnet
bee in one's bonnet
boo
wouldn't say boo to a goose
book
bell, book and candle
bring someone to book
closed book
go by the book
open book
read someone like a book
suit someone's book/bill
take a leaf out of someone's book
throw the book at
books
cook the books
in someone's black/bad books
turn-up for the books
boot
get the boot/heave(-ho)/push/chop
order of the boot
put the boot in
to boot

boots
hang up one's boots
heart is in one's boots
lick someone's boots/arse
too big for one's boots
bootstraps
pull oneself up by the bootstraps
bore
crashing bore
born
not born yesterday
not know one is born
to the manner born
Borneo
wild man of Borneo
both
cut both ways
make both ends meet
bothered
hot and bothered
bottle
hit the bottle
lose one's bottle
bottlewasher
chief cook and bottlewasher
bottom
rock bottom
bound
duty bound
bounds
by leaps and bounds
out of bounds
bow
two strings to one's bow
bows
shot across someone's bows
box
not the sharpest tool in the box
open a Pandora's box
out of the box
think outside the box
boxes
tick all the boxes
boy
blue-eyed boy

man and boy
old boy
toy boy
whipping boy
boys
backroom boys
jobs for the boys
brain
on the brain
brains
pick someone's brains
branch
olive branch
root and branch
brass
get down to brass tacks
brave
put on a brave face/bold front
bread
best thing since sliced bread
cast one's bread upon the waters
know which side one's bread is buttered
(on)
take the bread out of someone's mouth
breadline
on the breadline
breadth
within a hair's breadth
break
give someone a break
breakfast
dog's breakfast/dinner
breath
bated breath
hold one's breath
save one's breath
take one's breath away
under one's breath
waste one's breath
breast
make a clean breast of
breeze
shoot the breeze
brew
on the brew

brick
drop a brick/clanger
talk to a brick wall
bricks
come down on someone like a ton of bricks
in with the bricks
bridge
cross a bridge when one comes to it
water under the bridge
bridges
burn one's boats/bridges
cross a bridge when one comes to it
brief
hold a brief for
master of one's brief
brigade
green welly brigade
bring
pull/bring one up short
broad
as broad as it's long
broke
go for broke
broker
honest broker
broom
new broom (sweeps clean)
brother
big brother
brunt
bear the brunt
brush
broad brush
daft as a brush
tarred with the same brush
bubble
prick the bubble
buck
pass the buck
bucket
drop in the bucket/ocean
kick the bucket
tear bucket
buckets
come down in buckets

buff
   in the buff
bull
   cock and bull story
   like a bull at a gate
   red rag to a bull
   take the bull by the horns
bullet
   bite the bullet
bull's
   score/hit a bull's-eye
burden
   white man's burden
burn
   money to burn
burner
   on the back burner
burning
   (someone's) ears are burning
burns
   fiddle while Rome burns
burnt
   get one's fingers burnt
Burton
   gone for a Burton
bus
   miss the boat/bus
bush
   beat about the bush
business
   do the business
   funny business
   like nobody's business
   mean business
   mind one's own business
   monkey business
   send someone about his
     business
but
   anything but
   nothing but
butt
   pain in the neck/ass/backside/butt
butter
   bread and butter

button
   bright as a button
   on the button
   press the right buttons
buy
   sell/buy a pup
buzzer
   fingers on buzzers!
by
   off by heart
   run something by one (again)
   take by storm
   without so much as a 'by your leave'
bygones
   let bygones be bygones

C

caboodle
   kit and caboodle
cackle
   cut the cackle
cahoots
   in cahoots
Cain
   raise Cain
cake
   icing on the cake
   piece of cake
   take the cake/biscuit
cakehole
   shut your trap/gob/mouth/clanger/
     cakehole
cakes
   sell like hot cakes
calf
   kill the fatted calf
call
   on call
   port of call
   too close to call
camel
   strain at a gnat (and swallow a camel)

camel's
straw which breaks the camel's back
can
carry the can
in the can
candle
bell, book and candle
burn the candle at both ends
game's not worth the candle
not hold a candle to (something/someone)
candy
eye candy
cannon
loose cannon
canny
ca' canny
canoe
paddle one's own canoe
cap
feather in one's cap
go cap in hand
if the shoe/cap fits
put on one's thinking cap
set one's cap at someone
to cap it all
card
play one's trump/best card
red card
wild card
cards
lay one's cards on the table
on the cards
play one's cards right/well
see how the cards stack up
care
devil may care
take care of
carpet
on the carpet/mat
pull the rug/carpet (out) from under
red-carpet treatment
carried
get carried away
cart
upset the apple-cart

case
basket case
open and shut case
cash
spot cash
cast
die is cast
cat
bell the cat
fat cat
grin like a Cheshire cat
let the cat out of the bag
no room to swing a cat
not have a cat in hell's chance
play cat and mouse with
    someone
cats
rain cats and dogs
caution
throw caution to the winds
cease
wonders never cease
ceiling
glass ceiling
hit the ceiling/fan/roof
Central Casting
straight out of Central Casting
centre
right, left and centre
ceremony
stand on ceremony
cert/certainty
dead cert/certainty
certain
in a certain condition
chafing
champing/chafing at the bit
chain
food chain
chalice
poisoned chalice
chalk
by a long chalk/shot
different as chalk from cheese
not by a long chalk/shot

challenged
   horizontally challenged
chance
   dog's chance
   eye to the main chance
   fat chance
   ghost of a chance
   main chance
   not have a cat in hell's chance
   off chance
   on the off chance
   risk/chance one's neck
change
   chop and change
   get no change out of someone
changes
   ring the changes
chapter
   give chapter and verse
character
   out of character
charge
   take charge of
chase
   cut to the chase
   wild goose chase
chattels
   goods and chattels
cheap
   dirt cheap
   on the cheap
check
   keep oneself in check
   spot check
cheek
   have the cheek to
   tongue in cheek
   turn the other cheek
   what a nerve/cheek
cheese
   big cheese
   different as chalk from
      cheese
cheque
   blank cheque

cherry
   second bite at the cherry
   two bites at the cherry
Cheshire
   grin like a Cheshire cat
chest
   off one's chest
chestnut
   old chestnut
chew
   bite off more than one can chew
chicken
   no spring chicken
chickens
   count one's chickens
chiefs
   all chiefs and no Indians
child
   latchkey child
chin
   keep one's pecker/chin up
   take it on the chin
china
   bull in a china shop
   slow boat to China
chip
   blue-chip
chips
   cash one's chips
   when the chips are down
choice
   Hobson's choice
choose
   pick and choose
   pick/choose/weigh one's words
choosers
   beggars can't be choosers
chop
   get the boot/heave(-ho)/push/chop
chord
   strike a chord/note
chump
   off one's chump
church
   broad church

circle

come/turn full circle

square the circle

vicious circle

circles

go round (and round) in circles

run rings/circles round someone

run/go round in circles (getting nowhere)

circulation

out of circulation

circumstances

under the/these circumstances

claim

stake a/one's claim

clam

shut up like a clam

clanger

drop a brick/clanger

shut your mouth/gob/clanger/cakehole

clappers

like the clappers

claws

get one's claws into someone/something

clay

feet of clay

clean

come clean

keep one's nose clean

make a clean breast of

make a clean sweep of

show a clean pair of heels

squeaky clean

cleaners

take someone to the cleaners

cleansing

ethnic cleansing

clear

coast is clear

in the clear

steer clear of

cleft

in a cleft stick

clever

box clever

too clever by half

clock

against the clock

put/turn back the clock

round the clock

clockwork

like clockwork

regular as clockwork

clogs

pop one's clogs

close

near/close to one's heart

sail close to the wind

too close to call

closet

come out of the closet

skeleton in the cupboard/closet

cloth

cut one's coat according to one's cloth

clothes

plain clothes

steal someone's clothes

clothing

wolf in sheep's clothing

cloud

every cloud has a silver lining

under a cloud

clouds

have one's head in the clouds

clout

carry clout

clover

in clover

clue

not have a clue

coach

drive a coach and horses through
something

coals

carry coals to Newcastle

haul someone over the coals

coat

cut one's coat according to one's
cloth

Cocker

according to Cocker/Hoyle/Gunter

cockles
warm the cockles of one's heart
coffin
drive a nail in the/someone's coffin
coin
pay someone back in his own coin
to coin a phrase
cold
blow hot and cold
bring someone in from the cold
catch a cold
death of cold
feel the draught/cold
give the cold shoulder to someone
in a cold sweat
in cold blood
knock someone cold
out cold
out in the cold
pour/throw cold water on
collar
dog collar
hot under the collar
collywobbles
give someone the willies/
collywobbles
colour
horse of a different colour
local colour
off colour
colours
nail one's colours to the flag/mast
show one's (true) colours
true to one's colours
column
fifth column
comb
fine-tooth comb
come
easy come, easy go
go/come to pieces
comfort
cold comfort
comforter
Job's comforter

comforts
creature comforts
coming
have it coming to one
up and coming
commission
out of commission
company
keep company
part company
compliment
back-handed compliment
left-handed compliment
return the compliment
comprehension
pass belief/comprehension
conclusion
foregone conclusion
conclusions
jump to conclusions
try conclusions with
concrete
set in concrete/tablets of stone
condition
certain condition
out of condition
conjure
name to conjure with
consent
silence means/gives consent
consequence
of no consequence
contention
bone of contention
contrary
on the contrary
converted
preach to the converted
convictions
courage of one's convictions
cook
chief cook and bottlewasher
cookie
that's the way the cookie crumbles
tough cookie

cooks
too many cooks (spoil the broth)

cool
keep one's cool
kick/cool one's heels
play it cool

coot
bald as a coot
drunk as a lord/coot/skunk

cop
not much cop

copybook
blot one's copybook

core
hard core
to the marrow/core

corn
seed corn

corner
fight one's corner
hole and corner
hole in corner
in a corner
just around the corner
turn the corner

corners
cut corners

corrected
stand corrected

correctness
political correctness

counter
bean counter
run counter to
under the counter

country
God's own country
up and down the country/land

courage
dutch courage
have the courage of one's convictions
pluck/screw up one's courage
take one's courage in both hands

course
normal course of events

par for the course
stay the course

courses
horses for courses

court
ball is in your court
kangaroo court
laugh someone/something out of court
rule someone/something out of court

Coventry
send to Coventry

cover
break cover
under cover of

cow
cash cow
sacred cow

cowboy
drugstore cowboy

cows
till the cows come home

crack
have a bash/crack

cracking
get cracking

cracks
paper/gloss over the cracks

cranny
(every) nook and cranny

crap
all that jazz/crap

craw
stick in one's craw/gizzard/gullet

crawl
make one's flesh creep/crawl

credit
redound to one's credit/shame

creek
up the creek (without a paddle)

creep
make one's flesh creep/crawl

cricket
not/hardly cricket

crock
pot/crock of gold

crook
by hook or by crook
cropper
come a cropper
cross
dot the i's and cross the t's
crossed
fingers crossed
crossroads
dirty work (at the crossroads)
crow
as the crow flies
crown
jewel in the crown
crunch
credit crunch
when it comes to the point/bit/crunch
crust
upper crust
cry
far cry from
hue and cry
in full cry
shoulder to cry on
crying
for crying out loud
crystal
clear as a bell/crystal
cuckoo
cloud cuckoo land
cucumber
cool as a cucumber
cuff
off the cuff
cupboard
skeleton in the cupboard/closet
cups
in one's cups
cure
kill or cure
Curtain
Iron Curtain
customer
slippery customer
ugly customer

cut
short cut
cutting
at the cutting/leading edge
cylinders
fire on all cylinders

D

daddy
sugar daddy
daggers
at daggers drawn
look daggers
daisies
push up (the) daisies
daisy
fresh as a daisy
dale
up hill and down dale
damage
collateral damage
what's the damage?
dammit
near as dammit
Damocles
sword of Damocles
dampers
put the dampers on something
dance
lead someone a merry dance
make a song and dance
dancing
all singing all dancing
dander
get/put someone's back/
dander up
dark
in the dark
keep something dark
leap in the dark
shot/stab in the dark
whistle in the dark

date
out of date
past one's sell-by date
dawn
crack of dawn
light dawns
day
all in a day's work
any day
at the end of the day
bad-hair day
call it a day
D-day
every dog has his day
field day
late in the day
many happy returns (of the day)
one fine day
order of the day
pass the time of day
rainy day
that'll be the day
daylight
broad daylight
see daylight
daylights
scare the (living) daylights
out of
days
dog days
early days
halcyon days
palmy days
salad days
dead
catch someone dead
cut someone dead
drop dead
flog a dead horse
over my dead body
Queen Anne is dead too
stone dead
wait in dead men's shoes
deaf
turn a deaf ear

deal
big deal
no deal/dice
raw deal
dealing
wheeling and dealing
dear
for dear life
dearest
nearest and dearest
death
at death's door
bored to death/tears
dice with death
do something to death
hold on like grim death
in at the kill/death
kiss of death
sudden death playoff
tickled pink/to death
to death
debt
run into debt
decision
snap decision
deck
all hands on deck
card short of a deck
decks
clear the decks
deep
in deep water
deepest
of the deepest hue/dye
degree
(to the) nth degree
third degree
deleted
expletive deleted
den
beard the lion in his den
lion's den
department
not one's province/
department

depth
out of one's depth
description
beggar description
desking
hot desking
deuce
what the dickens/devil/deuce?
devil
be a devil
better the devil one knows
between the devil and the deep
blue sea
give the devil his due
speak/talk of the devil
what the dickens/devil/deuce?
devil's
play devil's advocate
diamond
rough diamond
dice
no deal/dice
dick
keep dick
private eye/dick
dickens
what the dickens/devil/deuce?
die
do or die
never say die
root hog or die
different
in a different league
sing a different song
whistle a different tune
dig
get in a dig at someone
digest
mark, learn and inwardly digest
dignity
stand on one's dignity
dilemma
horns of a dilemma
dim
take a dim view

din
unholy din
dinger
go one's dinger
dinner
dog's breakfast/dinner
direction
step in the direction of
dirt
dig the dirt
dish the dirt
pay dirt
dirty
do the dirty on someone
wash one's dirty linen in public
discord
apple of discord
discrimination
positive discrimination
discussions
Ugandan affairs/discussions
disguise
blessing in disguise
distance
within hailing distance
within striking distance
ditch
last ditch effort
ditchwater
dull as ditchwater
dividends
pay dividends
do
a man has to do what a man has to do
well to do
doctor
just what the doctor ordered
spin doctor
dodo
dead as a dodo
dog
black dog
every dog has his day
give a dog a bad name
hair of the dog (that bit one)

lead someone a dog's life
running dog
see a man about a dog
there's life in the old dog yet
top dog

doghouse
in the doghouse

dogs
go to the dogs
let sleeping dogs lie
rain cats and dogs

doh
up to high doh/ninety

doing
up and doing

doldrums
in the doldrums

dollar
almighty dollar
bet one's bottom dollar
sixty-four (thousand) dollar question

done
easier said than done
over and done with

donkey
talk the hind legs off a donkey

don't
and I don't think

doom
crack of doom

door
at death's door
creaking door/gate
darken someone's door
keep the wolf from the door
lay something at someone's door
lock the stable door after the horse has
    bolted
open the door

doornail
dead as a doornail

doors
open its doors

dose
taste/dose of one's own medicine

dossier
dodgy dossier

dot
on the dot

dotted
sign on the dotted line

double
at/on the double
do a double take
talk double Dutch

doubt
beyond a shadow of doubt
give someone the benefit of the doubt

down
cascade down
chips are down
do someone down
dressing down
have something down to a fine art
nail someone down
sell someone/something down the river
thumbs up/down

downs
ups and downs

dozen
baker's dozen
daily dozen
nineteen to the dozen
six of one and half a dozen of the other

drag
main drag

dragon
chase the dragon

dragon's
sow the dragon's teeth

drain
brain drain
down the tube/pan/drain/plughole

drakes
play ducks and drakes

draught
feel the draught/cold

drawer
bottom drawer
top drawer

drawn
    at daggers drawn
dream
    pipe dream
dressing
    window dressing
dried
    cut and dried
drink
    meat and drink to
      someone
driver
    back-seat driver
    in the driver's seat
drop
    at the drop of a hat
    jaw drop
    nod/drop off
    ready for the drop/off
    ready to drop
dropping
    name dropping
drops
    penny drops
    pin drops
drunk
    blind drunk
dry
    bleed someone dry/white
    high and dry
    home and dry
    keep one's powder dry
duck
    can a duck swim?
    dead duck
    lame duck
    sitting duck
duckling
    ugly duckling
duck's
    water off a duck's back
ducks
    play ducks and drakes
dudgeon
    in high dudgeon

due
    give the devil his due
dumps
    down in the dumps
durance
    in durance vile
dust
    bite the dust
dutch
    double dutch
    go dutch
Dutchman
    or I'm a Dutchman
duty
    in the line of duty
    off duty
    on duty
dye
    of the deepest hue/dye

E

ear
    bend someone's ear
    flea in the ear
    go in one ear and out the other
    grin from ear to ear
    half an ear
    have an ear for something
    have someone's ear
    keep one's ear to the ground
    lend an ear
    make a silk purse from a sow's ear
    out on one's ear
    pig's ear
    play something by ear
    send someone away with a flea in his ear
    turn a deaf ear
    word in your ear
earn
    make/earn a bomb
ears
    all ears

pin back one's ears
prick up one's ears
set someone by the ears
up to the neck/ears/eyeballs
wet behind the ears

earth
come down to earth with a bang
down to earth
go to earth
promise the earth/moon
run to earth
salt of the earth
what on earth?

easy
get off easy/light
go easy
on easy street
take it easy

ebb
at a low ebb

economy
black economy

edge
at the cutting/leading edge
cutting edge
have an/the edge on
lose one's (competitive) edge
on edge
set someone's teeth on edge
take the edge off something

effect
into effect
take effect
words to that effect

egg
bad egg
chicken and egg situation
curate's egg
good egg
nest egg

eggs
don't put all your eggs in one basket
kill the goose that lays the golden eggs
sure as eggs is eggs
teach one's grandmother to suck eggs

walk on eggs/eggshells

eight
one over the eight

elbow
bend the elbow
more power to your elbow

element
in one's element
out of one's element

elephant
white elephant

else
or else
something else

eminence
grey eminence

emotional
tired and emotional

end
at a loose end
at/near the end of one's tether
at the end of the day
at one's wits' end
bitter end
dead end
get the wrong end of the stick
hair stands on end
keep one's end up
light at the end of the tunnel
never hear the end of something
no end
no end of
on end
sharp end of something
thin end of the wedge
think no end of

ends
loose ends
make both ends meet
odds and ends
on one's beam ends

energy
bundle of energy/nerves

enough
sure enough

word to the wise (is enough)
envelope
push/open the envelope
equal
other things (being) equal
error
trial and error
estate
fourth estate
even
break even
get even
on an even keel
event
wise after the event
events
normal course of events
turn of events
evidence
much in evidence
example
make an example of
exception
take exception
extra
go the extra mile
extreme
in the extreme
eye
all my eye
apple of one's eye
cast an eye on/at/over
catch someone's eye
dead eye
eagle eye
easy on the eye
give one's eye/back teeth for something
give someone the glad eye
have an eye for
have/keep an eye on
in the public eye
keep an eye on
keep one's eye on the ball
keep one's/a weather eye open
look someone (straight) in the eye

mind's eye
mud in your eye
naked eye
not bat an eye/eyelid/eyelash
one eye on
one in the eye for
private eye/dick
put someone's eye out
score/hit a bull's eye
see eye to eye
take one's eye off the ball
turn a blind eye
with an eye for
with an eye to
eyeballs
up to the neck/ears/eyeballs
eyebrows
raise eyebrows
eyed
pie eyed
eyelid/eyelash
not bat an eye/eyelid/eyelash
eyes
bedroom eyes
clap eyes on
cry one's eyes out
have eyes only for
keep one's eyes peeled
make eyes at someone
open one's eyes to
remove the scales from someone's eyes
see with one's own eyes
shut one's eyes to
sight for sore eyes
strain one's eyes
with one's eyes open

F

FA
sweet FA/Fanny Adams/fuck all
face
arse about face

change the face of something
egg on one's face
fly in the face of something
have the face to
in your face
keep a straight face
let's face it
long face
lose face
on the face of it
poker face
put on a brave face/bold front
save one's face
set one's face against
show one's face
talk till one is blue/black in the face
to someone's face
wash its face
written all over one's face

faced
Janus-faced

fact
sober fact/truth

factor
feel-good factor

fag-ends
pick up fag-ends

fail
without fail
words fail me

faint
damn with faint praise

fair
play fair

fairy
airy fairy

faith
on faith
pin one's hopes/faith on

fall
land/fall on one's feet
riding/heading for a fall
stand or fall

false
ring true/false

family
in the family way
run in the family
spend more time with one's
    family

famine
feast or famine

fan
hit the ceiling/fan/roof
shit hits the fan

fancy
flights of fancy
tickle/take someone's fancy
young man's fancy

far
few and far between
go too far

farm
funny farm

fart
sparrow fart

fashion
after a fashion

fast
life in the fast lane
play fast and loose
pull a fast one
quick/first/fast off the mark
stand fast/firm

fat
chew the rag/fat

fate
tempt fate/providence

favour
curry favour

feast
bean feast
moveable feast

feather
birds of a feather
white feather

feathers
ruffle someone's feathers

feature
redeeming feature

feed
  chicken-feed
feelers
  put out feelers
feelings
  no hard feelings
feet
  cold feet
  drag one's feet
  fall/land on one's feet
  find one's feet
  itchy feet
  keep one's feet
  keep one's feet on the ground
  land/fall on one's feet
  on one's feet
  put one's feet up
  rushed off one's feet
  stand on one's own two feet
  sweep someone off his/her feet
  think on one's feet
  vote with one's feet
  work someone off his feet
fell
  at one fell swoop
felt
  make oneself felt
fence
  on the fence
fences
  mend fences
  rush one's fences
fettle
  in fine fettle
fiddle
  fit as a fiddle
  on the fiddle
  play second fiddle/string
field
  clear of the field
  late in the field
  level playing field
  play the field
fifth
  take/plead the fifth

fight
  pick a quarrel/fight
  spoiling for a fight
figure
  ballpark figure
figures
  round figures/numbers
file
  rank and file
finds
  take someone as one finds them
fine
  cut it fine
  have something down to a fine art
  in fine
  in fine fettle
  one fine day
  pretty/fine pass
finger
  have a finger in every pie
  keep one's finger on the pulse
  lay a finger/hand on
  point the finger
  pull one's finger out
  put one's finger on something
  see the finger/hand of God in something
  twist someone round one's little finger
fingered
  light fingered
fingers
  burn one's fingers
  cross one's fingers
  get one's fingers burnt
  green fingers
  keep one's fingers crossed
  slip through one's fingers
  work one's fingers to the bone
fingertips
  at one's fingertips
  to the fingertips
fire
  add fuel to the flames/fire
  ball of fire
  baptism of fire
  fat is in the fire

friendly fire
hang fire
irons in the fire
no smoke without fire
play with fire
set the Thames/heather on fire
under fire
firing
in the firing line
firm
on a firm/sound footing
stand fast/firm
first
at first glance/sight
cast the first stone
get to first/second base
of the first order/water/magnitude
quick/first/fast off the mark
you heard/read it here first
fish
big fish in a small pond
cold fish
drink like a fish
have other fish to fry
little fish in a big pond
neither fish/flesh nor fowl (nor good red
    herring)
not know someone from Adam/a dish of
    fish
odd bird/fish
other fish to fry
pretty/nice kettle of fish
queer fish
fishwife
swear like a trooper/fishwife
fist
hand over fist
iron hand/fist in a velvet glove
fit
blue fit
fighting fit
have a fit
see/think fit
fits
by fits and starts

fives
bunch of fives
fix
no quick fix
fizz
face like fizz/thunder
flag
nail one's colours/flag to the mast
show the flag
flame
like a moth to a flame
old flame
flames
add fuel to the flames/fire
shoot down in flames
flash
in a flash
flat
in a flat spin
that's flat
flea
send someone away with a flea in his ear
flesh
in the flesh
make one's flesh creep/crawl
spirit is willing (but the flesh is weak)
way of all flesh
flies
as the crow flies
no flies on someone
flint
heart of stone/flint
flit
moonlight flit
floodgates
open the floodgates
floor
hold the floor
take the floor
wipe the floor with someone
flow
go with the flow
stem the flow/tide of something
fluff
bit of fluff

flush
  busted flush
fly
  feathers fly
flyer
  high flyer
flying
  with flying colours
fog
  in a fog
fold
  return to the fold
folk
  wee/little folk
folks
  different strokes for different folks
follower
  camp follower
food
  junk food(s)
  off one's food
  whole food(s)
fool
  nobody's fool
  play the fool
foot
  boot is on the other foot
  get off on the right/wrong foot
  my foot!
  not put a foot wrong
  one foot in the grave
  put one's best foot forward
  put one's foot down
  put one's foot (right/straight) in it
  retrace one's (foot) steps
  serve hand and foot
  shoot oneself in the foot
footed
  flat footed
footing
  on a firm/sound footing
footprint
  carbon footprint
footsteps
  follow in the footsteps of

for
  take for granted
  what for
forbid
  heaven forbid/forfend
force
  drive/force someone to the wall
forces
  join forces
forecast
  rolling forecast
foremost
  first and foremost
forked
  speak with forked tongue
form
  true to form
former
  shadow of its/one's former self
forsaken
  god forsaken
fort
  hold the fort
forth
  and so forth
  hold forth
forward
  put one's best foot forward
founded
  well founded
fountain
  soda fountain
fours
  on all fours
fowl
  neither fish/flesh nor fowl (nor good red
    herring)
free
  make free with something/someone
freefall
  in freefall
French
  take French leave
fresh
  get fresh

Friday
　man Friday
friend
　fair-weather friend
friends
　bosom friends
frighten
　not frighten the horses
fringe
　lunatic fringe
front
　in the front line
　on the home front
　put on a brave face/bold front
　united front
　up front
frontal
　full frontal
fruit
　bear fruit
fruitcake
　nutty as a fruitcake
fry
　have other fish to fry
frying
　out of the frying pan, into the fire
fuck
　sweet FA/Fanny Adams/fuck all
fuel
　add fuel to the flames/fire
full
　come/turn full circle
　hands full
　in full cry
　in full swing
fun
　bundle of nerves/fun
funk
　blue funk
furniture
　part of the furniture
furrow
　plough a lone/lonely furrow
further
　without further ado

fury
　sound and fury
fuse
　blow a fuse/gasket
fuss
　kick up a fuss

G

gab
　blow the gaff/gab
　gift of the gab
gaff
　blow the gaff/gab
gain
　make/gain a name for oneself
　make/gain on the swings what one loses
　　on the roundabouts
　nothing venture nothing win/gain
gains
　ill-gotten gains
gallery
　play to the gallery
game
　ahead of the game
　beat someone at his own game
　fair game
　give the game/show away
　mug's game
　name of the game
　numbers game
　on the game
　play someone at his/her own
　　game
　play the game
　talk a good game
　waiting game
garden
　bear garden
　common or garden
　lead someone up the garden path
gas
　put someone's gas in a peep

gasket
blow a fuse/gasket
gate
creaking door/gate
like a bull at a gate
Gath
tell it not in Gath
gauntlet
run the gauntlet
throw down the glove/gauntlet
gear
in top gear
throw someone/something out of gear
get
bring/get/keep (people) onside
come and get it
come/get to the point
find/get one's bearings
tell someone where to get off
what you see is what you get
ghost
give up the ghost
white as a sheet/ghost
gibberish
talk gibberish
gift
God's gift to someone
Greek gift
look a gift horse in the mouth
gills
stewed to the gills
gilt
take the gilt off the gingerbread
gingerbread
take the gilt off the gingerbread
girl
pin-up girl
give
not give a hoot/two hoots
something has to go/give
teach/give someone a lesson
gizzard
stick in one's craw/gizzard/gullet
glad
give someone the glad eye

glance
at first glance
glass
people (who live) in glass houses (shouldn't throw stones)
glory
go to glory
gloss
paper/gloss over the cracks
put a spin/gloss on something
glove
hand in glove (with)
throw down the glove/gauntlet
gloves
handle with kid gloves
gnat
strain at a gnat (and swallow a camel)
go
all systems go
come/go with the patch/territory
don't (even) go there
easy come, easy go
have a go
let oneself go
no go
no-go area
on the go
raring to go
run/go round in circles (getting nowhere)
something has to go/give
touch and go
goal
own goal
goalposts
move the goalposts
goat
act the goat
get someone's goat
goats
separate/sort out the sheep from the goats
God
act of God
good gracious/God!
honest-to-goodness/-God
see the finger/hand of God in something

Godot

waiting for Godot

gods

in the lap of the gods

going

when the going gets tough (the tough get going)

gold

good as gold

heart of gold

pot/crock of gold

strike lucky/gold

golden

kill the goose that lays the golden eggs

good

as good as

for good

give a good/poor account of oneself

give as good as one gets

hold good

make good

no news is good news

on (to) a good thing

run of good/bad luck

take something in good part

talk a good game

throw good money after bad

goodness

honest-to-goodness/-God

to goodness

goods

all one's worldly goods

deliver the goods

produce the goods/goodies

goose

cook someone's goose

kill the goose that lays the golden eggs

sauce for the goose (is sauce for the gander)

wild goose chase

wouldn't say boo to a goose

gooseberry

play gooseberry

grabs

up for grabs

grace

saving grace

with a bad grace

graces

airs and graces

gracious

good gracious!

grade

make the grade

grain

against the grain

take something with a pinch/grain of salt

grandmother

teach one's grandmother to suck eggs

granny

sell one's soul/granny

granted

take for granted

grapes

sour grapes

grapevine

on the grapevine

grass

green as grass

kick/push something into the long grass

not let the grass grow (under one's feet)

put someone out to grass

snake in the grass

grasshopper

knee-high to a grasshopper

grave

one foot in the grave

turn in one's grave

grease

elbow grease

oil/grease someone's palm

green

rub of the green

grief

come to grief

grievance

nurse a grudge/grievance

grind

axe to grind

grindstone
  keep one's nose to the grindstone
grip
  get a grip
  lose one's grip
groove
  in a groove/rut
ground
  break new ground
  common ground
  cut the ground from under
  gain ground
  get off the ground
  give ground
  happy hunting ground
  hit the ground running
  in on the ground floor
  keep one's ear to the ground
  keep one's feet on the ground
  run something into the ground
  stamping ground
  thick/thin on the ground
grow
  not let the grass grow (under one's
    feet)
grudge
  nurse a grudge/grievance
guard
  off guard
  old guard
guess
  second guess
guid
  unco guid
gullet
  stick in one's craw/gizzard/gullet
gum
  up a gum tree
gun
  jump the gun
  smoking gun(s)
guns
  go great guns
  spike someone's guns
  stick to one's guns

Gunter
  according to Cocker/Hoyle/Gunter
guts
  hate someone's guts
guy
  fall guy
  wise guy/ass
guzzler
  gas guzzler

H

hackles
  make one's hackles rise
hailing
  within hailing distance
hair
  bad-hair day
  get in someone's hair
  harm a hair on someone's head
  hide or hair
  keep one's hair on
  keep out of someone's hair/road
  make one's hair stand on end
  not turn a hair
  tear one's hair out
hair's
  within a hair's breadth
hairs
  by the short hairs
  split hairs
half
  and a half
  better half
  not half
  time and a half
  too clever by half
half-cock
  go off half-cock
hammer
  under the hammer
hand
  bird in the hand

bite the hand that feeds one
cap in hand
dab hand at
eat from someone's had
force someone's hand
free hand/rein
give (someone) a hand
go cap in hand
have a hand in
have the whip hand
hold someone's hand
in hand
iron hand/fist in a velvet glove
keep one's hand in
lay a finger/hand on
lend a hand
live from hand to mouth
old hand
on hand
on (the) one hand(, …on the other)
out of hand
overplay one's hand
(in the) palm of one's hand
ready to hand
right hand doesn't know what the left hand
     is doing
right-hand man
second hand
see the finger/hand of God in
     something
serve hand and foot
show one's hand
sleight of hand
take someone/something in hand
throw in one's hand
to hand
try one's hand at
turn one's hand to
upper hand
wait on someone hand and foot
whip hand
work hand in glove
work hand in hand

handed
red handed

handle
fly off the handle
hands
all hands on deck
be in good hands
change hands
have one's hands full
lay hands on
off one's hands
on one's hands
play into someone's hands
rub one's hands
show of hands
take one's courage in both hands
take one's life in one's hands
take the law into one's own hands
throw up one's hands/arms
tie someone's hands
time on one's hands
wash one's hands of
win hands down
wring one's hands
handshake
golden handshake
handsome
do someone proud/handsome
hang
get the hang of something
lay/hang one on someone
let it all hang out
lose the hang/knack of
peg to hang something on
hanging
how are they hanging?
leave someone hanging in the air
happy
demob happy
many happy returns (of the day)
hard
come down hard on
come on strong/hard
die hard
no hard feelings
play hard to get
school of hard knocks

hardly
not/hardly cricket
hare
start a hare
harm's
out of harm's way
harness
back in harness
in harness
hash
settle someone's hash
haste
post haste
hat
at the drop of a hat
brass hat
eat one's hat
hang up one's hat
knock someone into a cocked hat
old hat
pass (round) the hat
pull something out of the hat
put the lid/tin hat on something
raise one's hat to someone
score a hat trick
talk through one's hat
under one's hat
hatch
down the hatch
hatches
batten down the hatches
hatchet
bury the hatchet
hate
pet aversion/hate
hatter
mad as a hatter
have
keep/have one's wits about one
take/have/get the bit between one's teeth
havoc
play/wreak havoc
hawk
war hawk
watch someone like a hawk

hay
hit the hay/sack
make hay (while the sun shines)
haystack
needle in a haystack
haywire
go haywire
head
above someone's head
bear with a sore head
big head
bite/snap someone's head off
can't make head nor tail of something
get one's head round something
get up (a good head of) steam
harm a hair on someone's head
have a head for
have one's head in the clouds
have one's head screwed on
hang one's head (in shame)
keep one's head
keep one's head above water
keep one's head down
lose one's/the head
make neither head nor tail of something
need something like a hole in the head
(something) nips your head
off one's head/nut/rocker/trolley
off the top of one's head
out of one's head/skull/(tiny) mind
over someone's head
price on someone's head
shake one's head
soft in the head
take it into one's head
turn one's head
use one's loaf/head
heading
riding/heading for a fall
heads
put our heads together
health
clean bill of health
drink to someone's health
picture of health

heap
  struck all of a heap
hear
  never hear the end of something
heard
  once seen/heard (never forgotten)
  you heard/read it here first
heart
  at heart
  break one's heart
  cross one's heart
  eat your heart out
  have the heart to
  heavy heart
  lose one's heart
  near/close to one's heart
  off by heart
  set one's heart on
  take heart
  take something to heart
  warm the cockles of one's heart
  wear one's heart on one's sleeve
hearty
  hale and hearty
heat
  dead heat
  in the heat of the moment
  on/in heat
  stand the pace/heat
  turn up the heat
heather
  set the Thames/heather on fire
heave
  get the boot/heave(-ho)/push/chop
heaven
  manna from heaven
  move heaven and earth
  seventh heaven
heavy
  make heavy weather of
    something
heel
  Achilles' heel
  down at heel
  turn on one's heel

heeled
  well heeled
heels
  cool one's heels
  dig in one's heels
  hard/hot on someone's heels
  kick/cool one's heels
  on the heels of
  show a clean pair of heels
  take to one's heels
hell
  come hell or high water
  from hell
  go through hell
  one hell of a/helluva
  what the hell?
hell's
  all hell's let loose
  not have a cat in hell's chance
hen
  memory like a sieve/hen
here
  from here on in
  neither here nor there
  same here
  you heard/read it here first
herring
  red herring
hiding
  on a hiding to nothing
high
  flying high
  for the high jump
  in high dudgeon
  on one's high horse
  riding high (in the charts)
highly
  think highly of
hill
  over the hill
  up hill and down dale
hills
  old as the hills
hilt
  up to the hilt

hind
   talk the hind legs off a donkey
hindmost
   devil take the hindmost
hint
   drop a hint
   take a hint
hip
   shoot from the hip
hit
   score/hit a bull's eye
   shit hits the fan
   smash hit
   strike/hit home
hock
   in hock
hog
   go the whole hog
   road hog
   root hog or die
hold
   get hold of
   not hold a candle to (something/
      someone)
holding
   leave someone holding the baby
holds
   no holds barred
hole
   ace in the hole
   black hole
   burn a hole in one's pocket
   in a hole/spot
   need something like a hole in the head
   square peg (in a round hole)
   watering hole
holes
   pick/knock/poke holes in
holiday
   busman's holiday
holidays
   high days and holidays
hollow
   beat someone hollow
   ring hollow

home
   bring home the bacon
   bring home to someone
   charity begins at home
   chickens come home to roost
   close to home
   drive something home
   eat someone out of house and home
   hammer something home
   on the home front
   spiritual home
   strike/hit home
   till the cows come home
honest
   make an honest woman of someone
honours
   do the honours
hoof
   on the hoof
hook
   by hook or by crook
   off the hook
hookey
   play truant/hookey
hoops
   jump through hoops/a hoop
hoot
   not give a hoot/two hoots
hop
   catch someone on the hop
hopes
   pin one's hopes/faith on
hornets'
   stir up a hornets' nest
horns
   draw/pull in one's horns
   lock horns
   on the horns of a dilemma
   pull in one's horns
   take the bull by the horns
horse
   back the wrong horse
   dark horse
   flog a dead horse
   high horse

lock the stable door after the horse has
   bolted
look a gift horse in the mouth
on one's high horse
one-horse town/operator
put/set the cart before the horse
stalking horse
horse's
straight from the horse's mouth
horses
change horses
drive a coach and horses through
   something
hold one's horses
not frighten the horses
wild horses wouldn't drag/make one
hot
hard/hot on someone's heels
in hot water
like hot cakes
make it/life hot for someone
red hot
strike while the iron's hot
hour
eleventh hour
on the hour/half-hour
rush hour
zero hour
hours
wee small hours
house
eat someone out of house and
   home
front of house
halfway house
on the house
put one's (own) house in order
houses
safe as houses
twice round the houses
how
and how
any old how
Hoyle
according to Cocker/Hoyle/Gunter

hue
of the deepest hue/dye
huff
take the huff
human
milk of human kindness
humble
eat humble pie
hump
over the hump
hung
well hung
hunting
happy hunting ground
hymnsheet
sing from the same hymnsheet

I

ice
break the ice
cut no ice
on ice
on thin ice
skate on thin ice
iceberg
tip of the iceberg
idea
big idea
run away with the idea
what's the (big) idea?
idle
bone idle
ilk
of that ilk
image
spitting image
imagination
figment of one's imagination
impulse
blind impulse
in
all in

do someone in
have it in for someone
have it in one

inch
give someone an inch (and he/she will take
a mile)
within an inch of

Indians
all chiefs and no Indians

influence
under the influence

initiative
unveil an initiative

injun
honest injun

injury
add insult to injury

innings
good innings

inside-out
know something backwards/inside-out

into
kick/push something into the long
grass

invention
necessity is the mother of invention

inwardly
mark, learn and inwardly digest

iron
rule with a rod of iron
strike while the iron's hot

issue
burning issue/question
take issue with

it
asking for it/trouble
for it
make it
make it/life hot for someone
rolling in it/money
rub someone's nose in it
run for it
shut it
up against it
up to it

watch it
with it

ivories
tickle the ivories

J

jack
every man jack

Jack Robinson
before one can say Jack Robinson

jackpot
hit the jackpot

jam
money for jam/old rope

Jane
plain Jane

jaundiced
take a jaundiced view of

jazz
all that jazz/crap

jib
cut of someone's jib

jinks
high jinks

job
give something up as a bad job
hatchet job
just the job/ticket/thing
on the job
put-up job
soft job
talk oneself out of a job

Job
patience of Job

jobs
odd jobs

joint
put someone's nose out of joint

joke
beyond a joke
crack a joke
no joke

Joneses
keep up with the Joneses
jove
by jove
jowl
cheek by jowl
joy
pride and joy
judge
sober as a judge (on circuit)
judgment
value judgment
jug
handle to one's name/jug
juice
stew in one's own juice
jump
for the high jump
hop/jump to it
take a running jump
jungle
blackboard jungle
concrete jungle
law of the jungle
justice
poetic justice

K

keel
on an even keel
keep
bring/get/keep (people) onside
earn one's keep
keepers
finders keepers
keeping
out of keeping (with)
keeps
for keeps
kettle
pot calling the kettle black
pretty/nice kettle of fish

watched pot/kettle never boils
key
off key
kibosh
put the kibosh on something
kick
for a kick-off
jump/kick start
kicking
alive and kicking
kicks
for kicks
kid
handle with kid gloves
home-alone kid
kidney
of the same kidney
kill
dressed to kill
in at the kill/death
killer
lady killer
kin
kith and kin
kind
of a sort/kind
two of a kind
kindly
take kindly to
kindness
kill someone with kindness
milk of human kindness
king
uncrowned king/queen of
kingdom
till/to kingdom come
kirk
come into the body of the kirk
kite
fly a kite
high as a kite
knack
have the knack of
knees
bee's knees

bring someone to his/her knees
on/to one's knees

knight
white knight

knives
night of the long knives

knock
don't knock it
pick/knock/poke holes in

knocks
school of hard knocks

knot
tie the knot

knots
at a rate of knots
tie someone up in knots

know
in the know
not know someone from Adam/a dish of
fish
not know one is born
not know what nerves are

knows
dear knows
goodness knows

knuckle
near the knuckle/bone

knuckles
rap on the knuckles

L

laced
straight laced

lad
man/lad of parts

ladder
top of the tree/ladder

lag
jet lag

lamb
mutton dressed up as lamb
sacrificial lamb

land
cloud cuckoo land
fall/land on one's feet
fat of the land
in the land of the living
lie of the land
never-never land
no man's land
see how the land lies
up and down the country/land

lane
inside lane/track
life in the fast lane
memory lane

language
bad language
speak the same language

lap
in the lap of luxury
in the lap of the gods

large
at large
by and large
loom large

lark
rise with the lark

last
as a last resort
drink in the last-chance
saloon
famous last words
in the last resort
on one's last legs
stick to one's last

late
of late

lather
in/into a lather

laugh
last laugh

laughing
no laughing matter

laurels
look to one's laurels
rest on one's oars/laurels

law
  lay down the law
  letter of the law
  necessity knows no law
  possession is nine parts/points/-tenths of
    the law
  take the law into one's own hands
  unwritten law
lay
  pile/lay it on thick
lead
  go down like a lead balloon
  swing the lead
leading
  at the cutting/leading edge
leaf
  take a leaf out of someone's book
  turn over a new leaf
league
  in a different league
leap
  look before you leap
leaps
  by leaps and bounds
learn
  know/learn the ropes
  mark, learn and inwardly digest
lease
  new lease of life
leather
  hell for leather
leave
  garden (or gardening) leave
  take French leave
  take it or leave it
  take leave of one's senses
  without so much as a 'by your leave'
left
  hard right/left
  right and left
leg
  cock a leg
  not have a leg to stand on
  pull someone's leg
  show a leg

legs
  hollow legs
  last legs
  talk the hind legs off a donkey
  with one's tail between one's legs
lend
  take a loan/lend of someone
length
  keep someone/something at arm's
    length
less
  more or less
lesson
  object lesson
  teach/give someone a lesson
let
  not let the grass grow (under one's feet)
letter
  dead letter
  poison-pen letter
  red-letter day
  to the letter
level
  on the level
liberties
  take liberties with
liberty
  take the liberty of
licker
  arse licker
lid
  flip one's lid/wig
  put the lid/tin hat on something
lie
  nail a lie
  white lie
lies
  pack of lies
life
  cat-and-dog life
  change of life
  dog's life
  facts of life
  for dear life
  for the life of one

get a life
kiss of life
make it/life hot for
new lease of life
not on one's life/nelly
prime of life
run for one's life
seamy side of life
shelf life
take one's life in one's hands
there's life in the old dog yet
time of life
time of one's life
to the life
walk of life
you bet your sweet life/bippy

lifetime
once in a lifetime

lift
not lift a finger
thumb a lift

light
bring to light
come to light
get off easy/light
green light
hide one's light (under a bushel)
leading light
out like a light
red light
red-light district
see the light
shed light on
trip the light fantastic

like
read someone like a book
sell like hot cakes
shut up like a clam
something like
tell it like it is
watch someone like a hawk

likely
not likely

lily
gild the lily

limb
out on a limb

limbo
in limbo

limelight
in the limelight

limit
over the limit

limitation
damage limitation

limits
off limits

line
bee line
bottom line
cross the line
down the line
draw the line at
drop a line
end of the line/road
hook, line and sinker
hot line
in the firing line
in the front line
in the line of duty
into line
lay it on the line
on line
on the line
out of line (with)
party line
put one's neck/ass on the line
shoot a line
sign on the dotted line
step out of line
toe the line

linen
dirty linen
wash one's dirty linen in
public

lines
along the right lines
hard lines/luck
pinch someone's lines/lyrics
read between the lines

lining
  every cloud has a silver lining
  flat lining
lion
  beard the lion (in his den)
lip
  stiff upper lip
  zip one's lip
lips
  read my lips
list
  black list
  hit list
little
  of little account
  think little of
  wee/little bird told me
  wee/little folk
living
  in the land of the living
  scratch a living
lizard
  lounge lizard
load
  get a load of that/this
loaf
  use one's loaf
loan
  take a loan/lend of
      someone
locker
  Davy Jones's locker
loggerheads
  at loggerheads
lone/lonely
  plough a lone/lonely furrow
long
  as broad as it's long
  by a long chalk/shot
  in the long run
  not by a long chalk/shot
  take a/the long view
look
  dirty look
  hangdog look

loop
  in the loop
loose
  all hell's let loose
  at a loose end
  hang loose
  have a screw loose
  on the loose
  play fast and loose
lord
  drunk as a lord/coot/skunk
lorry
  off the back of a lorry
lose
  win/lose by a neck
loser
  back a winner/loser
loss
  at a loss
  dead loss
lost
  get lost/nicked/stuffed
  no love lost
lot
  bad lot
  fat lot
  have a lot on one's plate
  job lot
  throw in one's lot with
lottery
  postcode lottery
loud
  for crying out loud
lout
  lager lout
love
  cupboard love
  head over heels/ears in love
  labour of love
  no love lost
low
  at a low ebb
  high and low
  keep a low profile
  lie low

luck
> hard lines/luck
> push one's luck
> run of good/bad luck
> take pot luck

lucky
> strike lucky/gold
> thank one's lucky stars

lucre
> filthy lucre

lump
> like it or lump it

lunch
> out to lunch

lunchtime
> legend in one's own lunchtime

lurch
> leave someone in the lurch

luxury
> in the lap of luxury

lying
> take something lying down

lyrics
> pinch someone's lines/lyrics

M

McCoy
> real McCoy

mackerel
> sprat to catch a mackerel

mad
> go mad/nuclear/nuts/ballistic

magnitude
> of the first order/water/
>   magnitude

main
> eye to the main chance
> might and main

mainbrace
> splice the mainbrace

majority
> silent majority

make
> on the make

Mammon
> God and Mammon

man
> anchor-man
> best man
> dead man
> every man jack
> fancy man/woman/piece
> hit man/squad
> marked man
> odd man out
> one small step for man
> right-hand man
> see a man about a dog
> straw man
> to a man
> white man
> wild man of Borneo
> yes-man

manger
> dog in the manger

manner
> to the manner born

man's
> no man's land
> poor man's (something)
> white man's burden
> young man's fancy

map
> off the map
> on the radar/map/wavelength
> on the map

marbles
> lose one's marbles

march
> steal a march

maria
> black maria

marines
> tell that to the marines

mark
> leave one's mark
> near the mark

overstep the mark
quick/first/fast off the mark
step up to the plate/mark
up to the mark
wide of the mark

market
black market
flea market
flood the market
on the market
up-market

marks
on your marks!

marrow
to the marrow/core

mast
nail one's colours/flag to the mast

master
past master

mat
on the carpet/mat

match
whole shooting match

matter
no laughing matter
no matter
voice in the matter
what's the matter?

may
come what may

me
on me

meal
make a meal of something
square meal

means
man of means/substance
ways and means

measure
take the measure of someone

meat
strong meat

medicine
take one's medicine
taste/dose of one's own medicine

medium
happy medium

melt
butter wouldn't melt in someone's
mouth

melting
in the melting pot

memory
refresh someone's memory

mend
on the mend

mention
not to mention/speak of

mercy
angel of mercy

message
get the message

messenger
don't shoot the messenger

mettle
on one's mettle
show one's paces/mettle

mickey
take the mickey/piss

midnight
burn the midnight oil

mighty
high and mighty

mildly
put it mildly

mile
give someone an inch (and he/she will take
a mile)
go the extra mile

milk
cry over spilt milk

mill
grist to the mill
run of the mill
through the mill
trouble at mill

mince
not to mince matters/words

mincemeat
make mincemeat of someone

mind
    bear in mind
    blow one's mind
    bring to mind
    cast one's mind back
    cross one's mind
    give (someone) a piece of one's mind
    half a mind/notion
    in one's right mind
    make up one's mind
    never mind
    of one/the same mind
    on one's mind
    out of one's head/skull/(tiny) mind/bonce/
       tree
    piece of one's mind
    presence of mind
    prey on one's mind
    put (one) in mind of
    slip one's mind
    speak one's mind

minds
    in two minds

Minnie/Millie
    moaning Minnie/Millie

minute
    up to the minute

miracles
    perform miracles

miss
    near miss

misses
    heart misses a beat

mistake
    make no mistake (about it)
    no mistake

mobile
    upwardly mobile

mockers
    put the mockers on something

molehill
    make a mountain out of a
      molehill

moment
    in the heat of the moment

moments
    have one's moments

money
    colour of one's money
    dirty money
    funny money
    give (someone) a run for his/her money
    hush money
    made of money
    rolling in it/money
    smart money
    spend money like water
    throw good money after bad

monkeys
    brass monkeys

monster
    green-eyed monster

month
    flavour of the month

monty
    full monty

moon
    offer/pay the moon
    once in a blue moon
    over the moon
    promise the earth/moon

moth
    like a moth to a flame

mothballs
    in mothballs

mother
    father and mother of all
    necessity is the mother of invention

mother's
    tied to one's mother's apron (strings)

mould
    break the mould

mountain
    if the mountain won't come to
      Muhammad(, Muhammad will go
      to the mountain)
    make a mountain out of a molehill

mouse
    cat and mouse
    play cat and mouse with someone

mouth

born with a silver spoon in one's mouth
butter wouldn't melt in someone's mouth
down in the mouth
hand to mouth
heart is in one's mouth
heart is in the right place
keep one's mouth/trap shut
make one's mouth water
plum in one's mouth
put words in someone's mouth
shut your trap/mouth/gob/clanger/
   cakehole
straight from the horse's mouth
take the bread out of someone's mouth
take the words out of someone's mouth

mouthful

say a mouthful

move

on the move

mover

prime mover

much

so much for

mud

clear as a bell/mud
drag someone's name in/through the mud
(one's) name is mud
stick in the mud

Muhammad

if the mountain won't come to
   Muhammad(, Muhammad will go
   to the mountain)

mummy

yummy mummy

murder

get away with murder
yell/scream blue murder

music

face the music

mustard

cut the mustard
keen as mustard

muster

pass muster

N

nail

drive a nail in the/someone's coffin
fight tooth and nail
hit the nail on the head
on the nail
to a nail
tooth and nail

nails

hard as nails

name

clear one's name
double-barrelled name
drag someone's name in/through the mud
give someone/thing a bad name
give a dog a bad name
good name
handle to one's name/jug
in God's/heaven's name
in name only
in the name of
lend one's name to something
make/gain/win a name for oneself
take someone's name in vain
to one's name
what's in a name?
worthy of the name
you name it

names

call names
name names
no names no pack-drill

nap

power nap

napping

catch someone napping

narrow

straight and narrow

native

go native

nature

call of nature
in a state of nature

in the nature of
second nature
near
at/near the end of one's tether
neck
dead from the neck up
get it in the neck
millstone round someone's neck
pain in the neck/ass/backside/butt
put one's neck/ass on the line
risk/chance one's neck
save one's neck
stick one's neck out
up to the neck/ears/eyeballs
win/lose by a neck
need
crying need
friend in need
special needs
needles
on pins and needles
pins and needles
nelly
not on one's life/nelly
nerve
have a nerve
have the nerve to
lose one's nerve
what a nerve/cheek
nerves
bag of nerves
bundle of nerves
get on someone's nerves/wick/tits
live on one's nerves
not know what nerves are
war of nerves
nest
feather one's (own) nest
foul one's (own) nest
hornets' nest
stir up a hornets' nest
net
slip through the net
nettle
grasp the nettle

network
old-boy network
never
on the never-never
new
brand new
break new ground
old/new school
turn over a new leaf
whole new ball game
Newcastle
carry coals to Newcastle
news
bad news
break the news
no news is good news
newt
pickled/pissed as a newt
nice
pretty/nice kettle of fish
nicked
get lost/nicked/stuffed
night
dead of night
fly-by-night
make a night of it
one-night stand
ships that pass in the night
nine
cloud nine
possession is nine parts/points/-tenths of
     the law
nines
dressed up to the nines
ninety
up to high doh/ninety
no
have no truck with
in no time (at all)
in no uncertain terms
make no bones about something
make no mistake (about it)
of no consequence
on no account
point of no return

nobody's
  like nobody's business
nod
  land of nod
  on the nod
  tip someone the wink/nod
noire
  bête noire
noise
  big noise
non-
  U/non-U
nonsense
  stuff and nonsense
nose
  cut off one's nose to spite one's face
  follow one's nose
  get a bloody nose
  get (right) up someone's nose
  keep one's nose clean
  keep one's nose out of something
  keep one's nose to the grindstone
  lead someone by the nose
  look down (one's nose) at/on
  no skin off my nose
  on the nose
  pay through the nose
  poke/push/shove one's nose in
  put someone's nose out of joint
  right under one's nose
  rub someone's nose in it
  see no further than one's nose
  thumb one's nose at
  turn up one's nose at
  under one's nose
notch
  take someone down a peg/notch
    or two
note
  bum note
  of note
  strike a chord/note
  strike the right note
notes
  compare notes

nothing
  for nothing
  have nothing on
  much ado about nothing
  on a hiding to nothing
  stop at nothing
  there's nothing in it
  there's nothing to it
nothings
  sweet nothings
notice
  sit up and take notice
notion
  half a mind/notion
  take a notion
now
  just now
nuclear
  go mad/nuclear/nuts/ballistic
number
  any number
  back number
  cushy number
  have someone's number
  look after number one
  opposite number
  times without number
numbered
  (someone's) days are numbered
numbers
  round figures/numbers
nudge
  wink wink, nudge nudge(, say no more)
nut
  do one's nut/crust
  hard nut (to crack)
  off one's head/nut/rocker/trolley
  tough nut
nuts
  go mad/nuclear/nuts/ballistic
nutshell
  in a nutshell

O

oar
stick one's oar in
oars
rest on one's laurels/oars
oath
take an oath
oats
get one's oats
sow one's wild oats
object
no object
obvious
glimpse of the obvious
occasion
on occasion
rise to the occasion
take the occasion to
ocean
drop in the bucket/ocean
odds
at odds
over/under the odds
what's the odds?
odour
in bad odour
off
back off
have it off/away
on the off chance
ready for the off
right off
throw someone off the scent
water off a duck's back
offing
in the offing
often
every so often
once too often
oil
burn the midnight oil
no oil painting
pour oil on troubled waters

ointment
fly in the ointment
old
money for jam/old rope
of old/yore
omega
alpha and omega
on
at/on the double
have someone on
have something on someone
moving swiftly on
under/on pain of
whatever turns you on
writing is on the wall
one
back to square one
look after number one
number one
of one/the same mind
with one voice
words of one syllable
onions
know one's onions/stuff
only
in name only
not the only fish in the sea/pebble on the
beach
onside
bring/get/keep (people) onside
open
into the open
keep one's/a weather-eye open
push/open the envelope
with one's eyes open
opener
eye-opener
opera
soap (opera)
operator
smooth operator
opinion
pass an opinion
opportunity
golden opportunity

option
soft option
order
apple-pie order
of the first order/water/magnitude
out of order
pecking order
put/set one's (own) house in order
stand not upon the order of one's
going
tall order
ordinary
out of the ordinary
other
every other
have other fish to fry
how the other half lives
pull the other one
turn the other cheek
out
all out
cut it out
down and out
flat out
have it out
jury is still out
odd man out
put someone out of the way
roll something out
rule someone/something out of court
step out of line
take it out of one
take it out on someone
throw someone/something out of gear
way out
write oneself out of the script
outside
think outside the box
oven
bun in the oven
over
all over bar the shouting
all over someone
bowl someone over
do someone over

give over
once-over
one over the eight
party's over
sun is over the yard arm
overboard
go overboard for
owl
night owl/bird
own
come into one's own
hold one's own
mind one's own business
of one's own accord
off one's own bat
on one's own
on one's own account
under one's own steam
ownership
take ownership (of something)

P

pace
off the pace
stand the pace
paces
put something/someone through its/his
paces
show one's paces/mettle
pack
brat pack
no names no pack-drill
rat pack
packing
send packing
paid
put paid to
pain
feel no pain
on pain of death/deportation/(instant)
dismissal
under/on pain of

pains
  at pains
  for one's pains
painted
  not as black as one is painted
painting
  no oil painting
pair
  show a clean pair of heels
pale
  beyond the pale
palm
  itchy/itching palm
  oil/grease someone's palm
pan
  down the tube/pan/drain/plughole
  make something pan out
  out of the frying pan(, into the
    fire)
Pandora's
  open a Pandora's box
pants
  kick in the teeth/pants
  seat of the pants
paper
  on paper
par
  below par
  on a par with
  up to par
paradise
  fool's paradise
parallel
  draw a parallel
parcel
  part and parcel
parker
  nosy parker
parrot
  sick as a parrot
part
  art and part
  take something in good part
parts
  man of parts

party
  life and soul of the party
  throw a party
pass
  come to pass
  let something pass
  make a pass at someone
  pretty/fine pass
  sell the pass
  ships that pass in the night
passage
  purple passage
  rough passage
past
  run something past someone
patch
  come/go with the patch/territory
  not a patch on
path
  cross someone's path
  lead someone up the garden path
  smooth someone's path
Paul
  rob Peter to pay Paul
paw
  cat's paw
pay
  devil to pay
  in someone's pocket/pay
  offer/pay the moon
  rob Peter to pay Paul
payment
  down payment
pearls
  cast pearls before swine
peas
  like two peas in a pod
pebble
  not the only pebble on the beach
pecker
  keep one's pecker/chin up
pedal
  soft pedal
peeled
  keep one's eyes peeled/skinned

peep
  put someone's gas in a peep
peg
  shoogly peg
  square peg (in a round hole)
  take someone down a notch/peg or two
pegging
  level pegging
pen
  poison-pen letter
penny
  in for a penny(, in for a pound)
  pretty penny
  spend a penny
  two/ten a penny
people
  of all people/things
perdition
  road to ruin/perdition
petard
  hoist on one's own petard
Peter
  rob Peter to pay Paul
pew
  take a pew
phrase
  to coin a phrase
  turn of phrase
pick
  bone to pick
picnic
  one sandwich short of a picnic
picture
  get the picture
  put someone in the picture
pie
  easy as pie
  eat humble pie
  finger in every pie
piece
  conversation piece
  fancy man/woman/piece
  give someone a piece of one's mind
  nasty piece of work
  party piece

  say one's piece
  slice/piece of the action
  villain of the piece
pieces
  bits and bobs/pieces
  go/come to pieces
  pick/take up the threads/pieces
pig
  make a pig of oneself
pigeons
  set a cat among the pigeons
pigs
  go to pigs and whistles
pikestaff
  plain as a pikestaff
pile
  lay/pile it on thick
pill
  bitter pill
  sugar the pill
pillar
  from pillar to post
  tower/pillar of strength
pilot
  drop the pilot
  sky pilot
pinch
  at a pinch
  feel the pinch
  take something with a pinch/grain
    of salt
pink
  in the pink
  tickled pink/to death
pins
  for two pins
  on pins and needles
pipe
  put that in your pipe and smoke it
pipeline
  in the pipeline
piper
  pay the piper (and call the tune)
piss
  take the mickey/piss

pissed
pickled/pissed as a newt
pistol
hold a pistol to someone's head
pit
flea pit
pitch
make a play/pitch for something
queer one's pitch
place
out of place
pride of place
put someone in his/her (proper)
place
plague
avoid something like the plague
plan
game plan
planks
thick as two (short) planks
plant
sow/plant the seeds of something
plate
hand someone something on a plate
have a lot on one's plate
step up to the plate/mark
play
child's play
foul play
game that two can play
make a play/pitch for something
playing
level playing field
playoff
sudden death playoff
plead
take/plead the fifth
pleasure
(at) Her Majesty's pleasure
plot
lose the plot
pledge
sign the pledge
plughole
down the tube/pan/drain/plughole

plunge
take the plunge
pocket
burn a hole in one's pocket
in pocket
in someone's pocket/pay
out of pocket
pockets
line one's pockets
pod
like two peas in a pod
point
at this point in time
beside the point
case in point
come/get to the point
moot point
on the point of
strong point/suit
up to a point
when it comes to the point/bit/crunch
points
brownie points
score points (on someone)
poke
pick/knock/poke holes in
pig in a poke
pole
up the pole
polish
spit and polish
politics
play politics
poll
straw poll
pond
big fish in a small pond
pony
shanks's pony
pool
scoop the pool
pooper
party pooper
poor
give a good/poor account of oneself

port
any port in a storm
position
jockey for position
pole position
post
beat someone to the post
from pillar to post
pipped at the post
posted
keep someone posted
pot
go to pot
in the melting pot
take pot luck
watched pot/kettle never boils
potato
couch potato
hot potato
mouse potato
pots
flesh pots
pottage
mess of pottage
pound
in for a penny(, in for a
pound)
pink pound/dollar/euro/yen
powder
keep one's powder dry
power
corridors of power
more power to your elbow
practice
sharp practice
praise
damn with faint praise
praises
sing someone's praises
prawn
come the raw prawn
prayer
on a wing and a prayer
preach
practise what you preach

premium
at a premium
press
gutter press
yellow press
pressed
hard pressed/put to it
pretty
not a pretty sight
sitting pretty
price
at a price
pricks
kick against the pricks
pride
pocket/swallow one's pride
principle
on the principle of/that
print
out of print
prisoners
take no prisoners
profile
keep a low profile
proof
burden of proof
put something to the proof/test
protest
under protest
proud
do someone proud/handsome
providence
lap of providence/the gods
tempt fate/providence
province
not one's province/department
public
in the public eye
Joe Public
wash one's dirty linen in public
pudding
overegg the pudding
proof of the pudding (is in the eating)
pull
draw/pull in one's horns

not pull one's punches
pulse
keep one's finger on the pulse
pump
prime the pump
punch
pack a punch
pleased as Punch
punches
not pull one's punches
roll with the punches
punishment
glutton for punishment
pup
sell/buy a pup
purple
born to the purple
purpose
fit for purpose
on purpose
purposes
cross purposes
purse
hold the purse strings
make a silk purse from a sow's ear
push
get the boot/heave(-ho)/push/chop
if push comes to shove
kick/push something into the long grass
poke/push/shove one's nose in
pushed
pressed/pushed for something
put
don't put all your eggs in one basket
get/put someone's back/dander up
not put a foot wrong
not to put too fine a point upon it
pile/put on the agony
set/put the seal on
stay put
pyjamas
cat's pyjamas

Q

q.t.
on the q.t.
quantity
unknown quantity·
quarrel
pick a quarrel/fight
queen
uncrowned king/queen of
queer
on queer street
queue
jump the queue
question
beg the question
burning issue/question
leading question
loaded question
open question
out of the question
pop the question
sixty-four (thousand) dollar question
quick
cut to the quick
double quick
no quick fix
quits
call it quits

R

race
out of the running/race
rat race
rack
on the rack
radar
on the radar/map/wavelength
rag
chew the rag/fat
lose one's/the rag

red rag to a bull

rage
  all the rage
rags
  glad rags
rails
  off the rails
  on/off the rails
rain
  right as rain
rainbow
  chase a/the rainbow
raincheck
  take a raincheck
ran
  also ran
ranch
  meanwhile, back at the ranch
range
  top of the range
ranger
  Sloane Ranger
ranks
  break ranks
  close ranks
  rise from the ranks
rap
  take the rap
rat
  smell a rat
rate
  at a rate of knots
  at any rate
  at this/that rate
  second rate
  third rate
rattling
  sabre rattling
rave
  rant and rave
raw
  come the raw prawn
  in the raw
read
  take it as read

you heard/read it here first

ready
  rough and ready
reaper
  grim reaper
reason
  listen to reason
  lose one's reason
  rhyme or reason
  see reason
  stands to reason
  theirs not to reason why
  within reason
rear
  bring up the rear
  cover one's back/rear
rebound
  on the rebound
record
  bear witness/testimony/
    record
  off the record
  on record
  put/set the record straight
  track record
recovery
  road to recovery
red
  in the red
  paint the town red
  see red
redhanded
  catch someone redhanded
reed
  broken reed
reflection
  on reflection
regard
  with regard to
relation
  poor relation
relish
  no relish for
rendition
  extraordinary rendition

republic
banana republic
resistance
line of least resistance
resort
in the last resort
respects
pay one's (last) respects
rest
lay to rest
set someone at rest
retreat
beat a (hasty) retreat
return
point of no return
revenge
Montezuma's revenge
ribbon
blue ribbon/riband
rich
idle rich
stinking rich
riches
rags to riches
riddance
good riddance (to bad rubbish)
ride
head/ride for a fall
let something ride
take someone for a ride
right
along the right lines
aye right!
get off on the right/wrong foot
give one's right arm for
something
hard left/right
meet and right
press the right buttons
serve one right
step right into it
strike the right note
rights
bang to rights
put/set to rights

Riley
life of Riley
ringer
dead ringer for
rings
run rings/circles round someone
riot
read the riot act
run riot
ripe
time is ripe
rise
spirits rise/sink
take a rise out of someone
river
sell someone/something down the river
road
end of the line/road
hit the road(, Jack)
keep out of someone's hair/road
middle of the road
roast
dripping roast
robbery
daylight robbery
robin
round robin
Robinson
Heath Robinson
rocker
off one's head/nut/rocker/trolley
rocket
not rocket science
rocks
on the rocks
rod
make a rod (with which) to beat one's back
rule with a rod of iron
roll
on a roll
Rome
fiddle while Rome burns
when in Rome (do as the Romans do)
roof
hit the ceiling/fan/roof

raise the roof

room
elephant in the room
no room to swing a cat

roost
chickens come home to roost
rule the roost

root
take root

roots
grass roots

rope
money for jam/old rope

ropes
know/learn the ropes
on the ropes
show someone the ropes

roses
bed of roses
smelling of roses

rot
start the rot
stop the rot

rough
bit of rough
cut up rough
sleep rough
take the rough with the smooth

roughshod
ride roughshod over

roulette
Russian roulette

round
bring someone round
drive someone round the bend/twist
get one's head round something
get round someone
go round (and round) in circles
rally round
twist someone round one's little finger
year round

roundabouts
make/gain on the swings what one loses
    on the roundabouts
swings and roundabouts

row
skid row

royal
battle royal

rubber
burn rubber

rubbish
good riddance (to bad rubbish)

Rubicon
cross the Rubicon

rug
pull the rug/carpet (out) from under

ruin
go to wrack and ruin
mother's ruin
road to ruin/perdition

rule
as a rule
work to rule

rules
bend the rules
Queensberry Rules

run
cut and run
dry run
dummy run
give (someone) a run for his/her money
in the long run
on the run
rat run

runaround
give someone the runaround

runes
read the runes

runner
do a runner

running
hit the ground running
in the running
out of the running/race
sands (of time) are running out
take a running jump
up and running

rush
bum's rush

rut
in a groove/rut

S

sack
get the sack
hit the hay/sack
sackcloth
wear sackcloth and ashes
sacrifice
make the supreme sacrifice
safe
play safe
said
easier said than done
sailing
plain sailing
sails
take the wind out of someone's sails
trim one's sails
saint
patience of a saint
Sally
Aunt Sally
saloon
drink in the last-chance saloon
salt
rub salt in the wound
take something with a pinch/grain
     of salt
worth one's salt
samaritan
good samaritan
Sam
Uncle Sam
same
of one/the same mind
of the same kidney
of the same stripe
on the same wavelength
speak the same language
tarred with the same brush

sandboy
happy as a sandboy
sandwich
knuckle sandwich
one sandwich short of a picnic
sardines
packed like sardines
sauce
what is sauce for the goose (is sauce for
     the gander)
say
strange to say
you can say that again
you don't say
scale
off the scale
scales
remove the scales from someone's eyes
tilt the scales/balance
scarce
make oneself scarce
scenario
nightmare scenario
scene
make a scene
scenes
behind the scenes
scent
throw someone off the scent
schedule
on schedule
school
old/new school
old-school tie
science
blind someone with science
not rocket science
score
know the score
on that account/score
scot-free
get away with something scot-free
get off scot-free
Scott
great Scott!

scrape
  pinch and scrape
scratch
  start from scratch
  up to scratch
screen
  smoke screen
screw
  have a screw loose
  pluck/screw up one's courage
script
  write oneself out of the script
sea
  at sea
  between the devil and the deep blue
    sea
  not the only fish in the sea
  put to sea
seal
  set/put the seal on
sealed
  lips are sealed
seams
  burst at the seams
  come apart at the seams
seas
  half seas over
season
  compliments of the season
  open season
  out of season
  silly season
seat
  hot seat
  in the driver's seat
  on seat
  take a back seat
second
  play second fiddle/string
  split second
secret
  open secret
see
  let's see
  what you see is what you get

seed
  go to seed
  run to seed
seeds
  sow/plant the seeds
seen
  once seen/heard(, never forgotten)
seigneur
  droit de seigneur
self
  shadow of its/one's former self
sell
  hard sell
  past one's sell-by date
selling
  short selling
senses
  take leave of one's senses
sepulchre
  whited sepulchre
service
  lip service
  yeoman service
sesame
  open sesame
session
  bull session
set
  dead set
  jet set
  put/set one's (own) house in order
  put/set the cart before the horse
  put/set the record straight
  put/set to rights
  smart set
  star has set
sevens
  at sixes and sevens
sex
  fair sex
shade
  put someone/something in/into the shade
shadow
  five o'clock shadow
  to a shadow

worn to a shadow

shakers
movers and shakers

shakes
no great shakes

shame
hang one's head (in shame)
put to shame
redound to one's credit/shame

shape
get into shape
lick someone/something into shape
out of shape
take shape

shapes
of all shapes and sizes

sharpest
not the sharpest tool in the box

shave
close shave

sheep
black sheep of the family
separate/sort out the sheep from the
    goats

sheep's
wolf in sheep's clothing

sheet
white as a ghost/sheet

shelf
on the shelf

shilling
tuppence off the shilling

shine
rain or shine
take a shine to

ship
jump ship
spoil the ship (for a ha'penny worth of tar)
when one's ship comes in

shirt
keep one's shirt/hair on
lose one's shirt
stuffed shirt

shock
culture shock

shocked
shell shocked

shoe
if the cap/shoe fits

shoestring
live on a shoestring
on a shoestring

shoes
put oneself in someone (else)'s shoes
step into someone's shoes
wait in dead men's shoes

shoot
don't shoot the messenger

shooting
whole shooting match

shop
bull in a china shop
shut up shop
talk shop

shopping
window shopping

short
by the short hairs
card short of a deck
draw the short straw
fall short
give short shrift to
long and the short of something
make short work/shrift of
    something
one sandwich short of a picnic
pull/bring one up short
run short of something
sell someone short
sell oneself short
taken short

shot
big shot
like a shot
mug shot
not by a long chalk/shot
parting shot
pot shot

shots
call the shots

shoulder
chip on one's shoulder
cold shoulder someone
put one's shoulder to the wheel
straight from the shoulder
shoulders
on one's shoulders
rub shoulders with someone
shrug one's shoulders
shouting
all over bar the shouting
shove
poke/push/shove one's nose in
when push comes to shove
show
give the game/show away
good show
reveal/show one's true colours
run the show
steal the show
shows
between shows
shut
open and shut case
shy
fight shy of
side
born on the wrong side of the blanket
let the side down
other side
other/flip side of the coin
seamy side of life
sunny side up
sides
take sides
sieve
memory like a sieve/hen
sight
at first glance/sight
heave into sight/view
lose sight of
not a pretty sight
out of sight
out of sight, out of mind
second sight

sick of the sight/sound of
silk
make a silk purse from a sow's ear
silver
born with a silver spoon in one's mouth
every cloud has a silver lining
simple
pure and simple
sin
live in sin
singing
all singing, all dancing
sink
spirits rise/sink
sinker
hook, line and sinker
situation
Catch-22 situation
chicken and egg situation
six
hit someone for six
knock someone for six
sixes
at sixes and sevens
size
cut someone down to size
sizes
of all shapes and sizes
skin
banana skin
by the skin of one's teeth
get under one's skin
no skin off my nose
save one's bacon/skin
skinned
keep one's eyes peeled/skinned
skittles
beer and skittles
skull
out of one's head/skull/(tiny) mind
skunk
drunk as a lord/coot/skunk
sky
blue-sky thinking
pie in the sky

slate
clean slate
sleep
beauty sleep
not sleep a wink
sleeping
let sleeping dogs lie
sleeve
laughing up one's sleeve
up one's sleeve
wear one's heart on one's sleeve
sleeves
roll one's sleeves up
slide
let things slide
sling
have one's ass in a sling
slip
give someone the slip
Sloane
Sloane Ranger
slope
slippery slope
sly
on the sly
small
one small step for man
wee small hours
smoke
no smoke without fire
smooth
take the rough with the smooth
snake
scotch a snake
snap
bite/snap someone's head off
sneer
veiled threat/sneer
sniffed
not to be sniffed at
snook
cock a snook
so
or so
quite so

soap
soft soap
society
pillar of society/state
sock
put a sock in it
socks
pull one's socks up
sods
odds and bobs/sods
soft
have a soft spot for someone/
something
solution
final solution
some
and then some
song
for a song
make a song and dance
sing a different song/tune
sooner
no sooner said than done
sore
bear with a sore head
sight for sore eyes
sorrows
drown one's sorrows
sort
of a sort/kind
separate/sort out the sheep from the
goats
sorts
out of sorts
soul
body and soul
call one's soul one's own
heart and soul
keep body and soul together
life and soul of the party
not a (living) soul
sell one's soul/granny
sound
on a sound/firm footing
safe and sound

sick of the sight/sound of

soundings
take soundings

soup
in the soup

sow's
make a silk purse from a sow's ear

sows
reap where/what one sows

space
waste of space

spade
call a spade a spade

Spain
castles in Spain/the air

span
spick and span

spanner
throw a spanner in the works

spark
bright spark

speak
as we speak
not to mention/speak of
so to speak

speaking
on speaking terms
plain speaking

spec
on spec

speed
up to speed

spending
deficit spending

spilt
cry over spilt milk

spin
flat spin
put a spin/gloss on something

spite
out of spite

splash
make a splash

spleen
vent one's spleen

spoke
put a spoke in someone's wheel

sponge
throw in the towel/sponge

spoon
born with a silver spoon in one's
mouth

sport
spoil sport

spot
beauty spot
black spot
blind spot
have a soft spot for someone
in a hole/spot
on the spot

spots
knock spots of

spout
up the spout

spring
no spring chicken

spur
on the spur of the moment

spurs
win one's spurs

squad
god squad
hit-man/-squad

square
all square
back to square one
fair and square

squeak
narrow squeak

squib
damp squib

stab
shot/stab in the dark

stable
cleanse the Augean stable
lock the stable door after the horse has
bolted

staff
skeleton staff

stage
  centre stage
  on the stage
stakes
  up stakes
stamp
  seal/stamp of approval
stand
  make one's hair stand on end
  one-night stand
stands
  know where one stands
stars
  see stars
  thank one's lucky stars
start
  head start
  set/start the ball rolling
  standing start
starts
  by fits and starts
state
  pillar of society/state
statement
  sweeping statement
stations
  action stations
  panic stations
statistics
  vital statistics
steady
  go steady
steam
  full steam ahead
  get up (a good head of) steam
  head of steam
  let off steam
  under one's own steam
steer
  bum steer
  maverick steer
step
  one small step for man
  one step forward(, two steps back)
  out of step

steps
  retrace one's (foot) steps
stick
  carry a big stick
  get hold of the wrong end of the stick
  hang/stick one on someone
  let something ride/stick to the wall
sticky
  on a sticky wicket
stiff
  scared stiff
stitches
  in stitches
stock
  out of stock
  take stock
stocking
  blue stocking
stomach
  butterflies in one's stomach
  turn one's stomach
stone
  cast the first stone
  heart of stone/flint
  kill two birds with one stone
  leave no stone unturned
  set in concrete/tablets of
    stone
  rolling stone
stook/schtuk
  in stook/schtuk
stools
  fall between two stools
stops
  pull out all the stops
storm
  any port in a storm
  take by storm
  weather a storm
story
  cock and bull story
  end of story
  same old story
  sob story/stuff
  tall story/tale

straight
  go straight
  home straight
  keep a straight face
strain
  stand the pace/strain
straits
  dire straits
straw
  draw the short straw
  last straw
  man of straw
straws
  clutch at straws
street
  man in the street
  on easy street
  on queer street
  right up one's street/alley
  word on the street
strength
  in strength
  on the strength of
  tower/pillar of strength
strengths
  play to one's strengths
stretch
  at a stretch
stride
  take something in one's stride
strike
  on strike
striking
  within striking distance
string
  on a (tight) string
  play second fiddle/string
strings
  hold the purse strings
  no strings attached
  pull strings
  two strings to one's bow
  without strings
strip(s)
  tear strips/a strip off someone

stripe
  of the same stripe
stroke
  on the stroke of
strokes
  different strokes for different folks
strong
  come on strong/hard
struggle
  uphill struggle
stubble
  designer stubble
study
  brown study
stuff
  green stuff
  hard stuff
  hot stuff
  kids' stuff
  know one's onions/stuff
  sob story/stuff
  sterner stuff
  strut one's stuff
stuffed
  get lost/nicked/stuffed
stump
  on the stump
style
  cramp one's style
substance
  man of means/substance
succeeds
  nothing succeeds like success
suck
  teach one's grandmother to suck
    eggs
sucker
  play someone for a sucker
suit
  birthday suit
  follow suit
  please/suit oneself
  strong point/suit
sum
  lump sum

summer
Indian summer
sun
under the sun
Sundays
month of Sundays
sundry
all and sundry
support
moral support
supreme
make the supreme sacrifice
surface
scratch the surface
surprise
take by surprise
swallow
pocket/swallow one's pride
sweat
in a cold sweat
no sweat
sweep
clean sweep
sweet
short and sweet
you bet your sweet life/
    bippy
sweeteners
offer sweeteners
swiftly
moving swiftly on
swim
can a duck swim?
in the swim
sink or swim
swimmingly
go swimmingly
swine
cast pearls before swine
swing
in full swing
no room to swing a cat
swings
make/gain on the swings what one loses
    on the roundabouts

swoop
one fell swoop
swords
cross swords
syllable
words of one syllable
syne
auld lang syne
systems
all systems go

T

tab
pick up the tab
table
drink someone under the table
tables
turn the tables
tablets
set in concrete/tablets of stone
tabs
keep tabs on
tacks
get down to brass tacks
tail
can't make head nor tail of something
turn tail
with one's tail between one's legs
with one's tail up
take
get/take the bit between one's teeth
pick/take up the threads/pieces
sit up and take notice
tickle/take someone's fancy
tale
old wives' tale
tall tale/story
thereby hangs a tale
talk
double talk
pep talk
small talk

speak/talk of the devil

tape
red tape

tarbrush
touch of the tarbrush

task
take someone to task

tea
cup of tea

teacup
storm in a teacup

tears
bored to death/tears
veil of tears

teeth
armed to the teeth
by the skin of one's teeth
cut one's teeth on
get one's teeth into something
get/take the bit between one's teeth
give one's eye/back teeth for something
grit one's teeth
in the teeth of
kick in the teeth/pants
lie through/in one's teeth
like pulling teeth
set one's teeth on edge
show one's teeth
sow the dragon's teeth
take/have/get the bit between one's teeth

telegraph
bush telegraph

ten
starter for ten
two/ten a penny

tenterhooks
on tenterhooks

terms
contradiction in terms
in no uncertain terms
on speaking terms

territory
come/go with the patch/territory

terror
holy terror

test
acid test
means test
put something to the proof/test

testimony
bear witness/testimony/record

tether
at/near the end of one's tether
end of one's tether

Thames
set the Thames/heather on fire

that
at this/that rate
been there, done that
fancy that

then
and then some

theory
domino theory

there
all there
been there, done that
don't (even) go there
neither here nor there
so there

thick
bit thick
lay/pile it on thick
through thick and thin

thickens
plot thickens

thieves
thick as thieves

thin
disappear into thin air
on thin ice
out of thin air
skate on thin ice
thick/thin on the ground
through thick and thin
wear thin

thing
do one's own thing
done thing
first thing

have a thing about
just the job/ticket/thing
know a thing or two
near thing
no such thing
on (to) a good thing
quite the thing
sure thing
taking one thing with another
very thing
things
all things to all men
of all people/things
other things (being) equal
think
and I don't think
see/think fit
thinking
blue-sky thinking
joined-up thinking
put on one's thinking cap
wishful thinking
this
at this/that rate
Thomas
doubting Thomas
thought
food for thought
perish the thought
thoughts
penny for them/your thoughts
thread
hang by a thread
lose the thread of
threads
pick/take up the threads/pieces
threat
veiled threat/sneer
threshold
on the threshold
throat
frog in one's throat
jump down someone's throat
ram something down someone's
   throat

throes
in the throes of
throne
power behind the throne
through
fall through
get through to someone
see it/something through
slip through one's fingers
slip through the net
throw
pour/throw cold water on
stone's throw from
thrust
cut and thrust
thumb
rule of thumb
under the thumb of
thumbs
fingers and thumbs
twiddle one's thumbs
thumper
bible thumper
thunder
face like fizz/thunder
steal someone's thunder
tick
on tick
ticket
just the job/ticket/thing
meal ticket
tickle
slap and tickle
tide
stem the flow/tide of something
turn of the tide
turn the tide
tie
old-school tie
tied
hands tied
tiger
paper tiger
tight
sit tight

sleep tight

tiles

night on the tiles

till

hand in the till

time

at this point in time

big time

double time

high time

in no time (at all)

kill time

mark time

(for the) nth time

of all time

on time

once upon a time

pass the time of day

play for time

point in time

quality time

sands (of time) are running out

spend more time with one's family

stitch in time (saves nine)

take one's time

whale of a time/holiday

times

behind the times

tin

put the lid/tin hat on something

what it says on the tin

tip

on the tip of one's tongue

tiptoe

on tiptoe

tits

get on someone's nerves/wick/tits

tod

on one's tod

toes

keep on one's toes

on one's toes

together

get it together

keep body and soul together

pull oneself together

put our heads together

put two and two together

tolerance

zero tolerance

Tom

every Tom, Dick and Harry

Peeping Tom

Uncle Tom

Uncle Tom Cobley and all

tomorrow

jam tomorrow

tongs

hammer and tongs

tongue

cat got one's tongue

find one's tongue

hold one's tongue

lose one's tongue

on the tip of one's tongue

slip of the tongue

speak with forked tongue

tongues

set tongues wagging

too

go too far

none too

tool

not the sharpest tool in the box

tools

down tools

tooth

an eye for an eye (and a tooth for a tooth)

fight tooth and nail

long in the tooth

sweet tooth

top

big top

in top gear

off the top of one's head

on top of

on top of the world

over the top

Topsy

like Topsy

torn
  that's torn it
toss
  argue the toss
touch
  common touch
  in touch
  Midas touch
  out of touch
  soft touch
  wouldn't touch something with a bargepole
touches
  finishing touches
tough
  when the going gets tough (the tough get
    going)
tour
  whistle-stop tour
towel
  throw in the towel/sponge
tower
  ivory tower
  pillar/tower of strength
town
  go to town
  on the town
  paint the town red
traces
  kick over the traces
track
  fast track
  keep track (of someone)
  lose track
  off the beaten track
  one-track mind
tracks
  make tracks
trade
  trick(s) of the trade
trail
  blaze a trail
train
  gravy train
training
  out of training

trap
  death trap
  keep one's mouth/trap shut
traveller
  fellow traveller
tread
  walk/tread on air
treat
  dutch treat
treatment
  red-carpet treatment
tree
  bark up the wrong tree
  out of one's head/skull/(tiny) mind/bonce/
    tree
  up a gum tree
trees
  can't see the wood for the trees
  talk the birds off the trees
trial
  on trial
trick
  do the trick
  hat trick
tricks
  bag of tricks
trip
  acid trip
  round trip
trolley
  off one's head/nut/rocker/trolley
trooper
  swear like a trooper/fishwife
trouble
  asking for it/trouble
troubled
  fish in troubled waters
  pour oil on troubled waters
trousers
  wear the trousers
trowel
  lay/pile it on thick/with a
    trowel
truant
  play truant/hookey

truck
    have no truck with
true
    show one's true colours
    ring true/false
truly
    yours truly
trump
    play one's trump/best card
trumpet
    blow one's own trumpet
trumps
    turn up trumps
truth
    economical with the truth
    gospel truth
    ring of truth
    sober fact/truth
truths
    home truths
T-shirt
    been there, done that(, bought the
        T-shirt)
tube
    down the tube/pan/drain/plughole
tucker
    best bib and tucker
tumble
    rough and tumble
tummy
    gyppy tummy
tune
    call the tune
    change one's tune
    out of tune
    sing a different song/tune
    whistle a different tune
tunnel
    light at the end of the tunnel
Turk
    Young Turk
turkey
    talk turkey
turn
    come/turn full circle

    hand's turn
    not turn a hair
    out of turn
    put/turn back the clock
    serve its turn
    U-turn
turns
    worm turns
turtle
    turn turtle
twice
    think twice
twinkling
    in a twinkling
twist
    drive someone round the bend/twist
    get one's knickers in a twist
    round the bend/twist
two
    bob or two
    for two pins
    in two minds
    in two ticks/shakes
    kill two birds with one stone
    like two peas in a pod
    not give a hoot/two hoots
    number two
    one-two
    put two and two together
    stand on one's own two feet

U

umbrage
    take umbrage
uncle
    Bob's your uncle(, Fanny's your aunt)!
    dutch uncle
under
    down under
    knuckle under
    out from under
    right under one's nose

water under the bridge

understanding
on the understanding

unseen
sight unseen

unstuck
come unstuck

unwashed
great unwashed

up
all up with someone
brush up well
do something up
game's up
grow up!
hyped up
on the up (and up)
one up (on)
pull someone up
sew (something) up
sex (something) up
thumbs up/down
what's up?

upon
put upon
take it upon oneself

upper
stiff upper lip

uppers
on one's uppers

upright
bolt upright

upstairs
kick someone upstairs
man upstairs

uptake
quick on the uptake
slow on the uptake

us
one of us

V

vain
in vain
take someone's name in vain

valour
discretion is the better part of valour

value
face value

veil
draw a veil over
lift the veil on

vengeance
with a vengeance

venture
nothing venture nothing win/gain

verdict
open verdict

verse
chapter and verse

vertically
aesthetically/intellectually/vertically
challenged

victory
pyrrhic victory

view
bird's-eye view
heave in sight/into view
in view of
take a dim view of
take a jaundiced view of
take a/the long view

vigour
vim and vigour

vile
in durance vile

village
global village

violet
shrinking violet

virtue
patience is a virtue

visit
pay a visit

woods
neck of the woods
out of the woods
woof
warp and woof
wool
dyed in the wool
pull the wool over someone ('s eyes)
word
break one's word
dirty word
four-letter word
get a word in edgeways
in a word
keep one's word
last word
Mum's the word
put in a good word for
say the word
take someone at his word
words
bandy words with someone
eat one's words
famous last words
have words
mark my words
pick/choose/weigh one's words
put words in someone's mouth
take the words out of someone's mouth
war of words
weigh one's words
work
all in a day's work
dirty work
donkey work
go to work on
make short work/shrift of something
nasty piece of work
worker
open-collar worker
works
gum up the works
spanner in the works
world
all the world and his wife

come down in the world
dead to the world
man of the world
not for the world
out of this world
third world
way of the world
worldly
all one's worldly goods
worlds
best of both worlds
worms
can of worms
worth
game's not worth the candle
wound
rub salt in the wound
wounded
walking wounded
wounds
lick one's wounds
wrack
go to wrack and ruin
wraps
under wraps
wreak
play/wreak havoc
write
nothing to write home about
wrong
back the wrong horse
bark up the wrong tree
born on the wrong side of the blanket
get off on the right/wrong foot
get the wrong end of the stick
get up on the wrong side of the bed
laugh on the wrong/other side of one's
    face/mouth
not put a foot wrong
on the wrong end of something
rub someone up the wrong way

wig
big wig
flip one's wig/lid
wild
run wild
sow one's wild oats
will
set to with a will
Willie
Holy Willie
willies
give someone the willies/collywobbles
willing
spirit is willing (but the flesh is weak)
win
make/gain/win a name for oneself
nothing venture nothing win/gain
wind
break wind
ill wind
in the wind
put the wind up
sail close to the wind
second wind
straw(s) in the wind
take the wind out of someone's
sails
throw caution to the wind(s)
whistle in/into the wind
windmills
tilt at windmills
window
weather window
wine
new wine in old bottles
wing
left/right wing
on a wing and a prayer
under one's wing
wings
clip someone's wings
spread one's wings
wink
a nod is as good as a wink (to a blind man/
horse)

not sleep a wink
tip someone the wink/nod
winks
forty winks
winner
back a winner/loser
wire
live wire
wisdom
received wisdom
wise
penny wise (and pound foolish)
word to the wise (is enough)
within
enemy within
wheels within wheels
without
times without number
witness
bear witness
wits
at one's wits' end
keep/have one's wits about one
wives'
old wives' tale
wobbly
throw a wobbly
wolf
cry wolf
keep the wolf from the door
lone wolf
woman
fallen woman
fancy man/woman/piece
make an honest woman of someone
other woman
wonder
chinless wonder
nine days' wonder
no (little/small) wonder
wonders
work wonders
wood
can't see the wood for the trees
touch wood

see which way the cat jumps
that's the way the cookie crumbles
under way

ways
cut both ways
mend one's ways
n ways of doing something
parting of the ways

wayside
fall by the wayside

weak
spirit is willing (but the flesh is
weak)

weather
keep one's/a weather eye open
make heavy weather of something
under the weather

wedding
shotgun wedding

wedge
thin end of the wedge

weigh
pick/choose/weigh one's words

weight
carry weight
pull one's weight
swing one's weight
throw one's weight about

well
brush up well
mean well
pretty well
very well
wear well

welly
green welly brigade

were
as you were

west
go west

what
give someone what for
have what it takes
just what the doctor ordered
so what

wheel
put a spoke in someone's
wheel
put one's shoulder to the wheel
reinvent the wheel

where
know where one stands
tell someone where to get off

wherefores
whys and wherefores

which
know which side one's bread is
buttered (on)

while
once in a while
strike while the iron is hot

whip
have the whip hand

whirlwind
reap the whirlwind

whisper
stage whisper

whistle
blow the whistle on something
clean as a whistle
wet one's whistle

whistles
go to pigs and whistles

white
black and white
bleed someone dry/white
swear (that) black is white

whole
go the whole hog
on the whole

wick
get on someone's nerves/wick/tits

wicket
on a sticky wicket

wide
give a wide berth to

widow
grass widow

wife
all the world and his wife